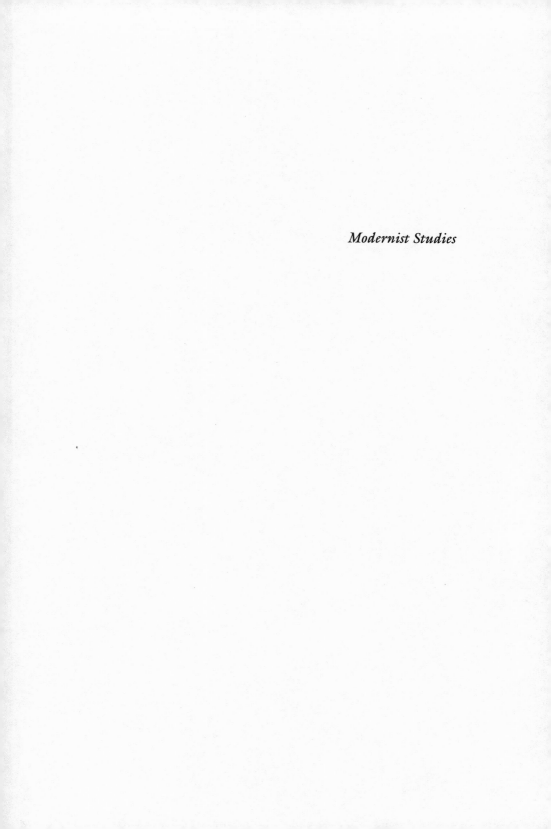

Modernist Studies

NAPOLEON III
and HIS REGIME

NAPOLEON III
and HIS REGIME

An Extravaganza

David Baguley

LOUISIANA STATE UNIVERSITY PRESS   *Baton Rouge*   MM

Copyright © 2000 by Louisiana State University Press
All rights reserved
Manufactured in the United States of America
First printing
09 08 07 06 05 04 03 02 01 00
5 4 3 2 1

Designer: Amanda McDonald Scallan
Typeface: Galliard & Hampton Script
Typesetter: Coghill Composition Co.
Printer and binder: Thomson-Shore, Inc.

Library of Congress Cataloging-in-Publication Data

Baguley, David.
    Napoleon III and his regime : an extravaganza / David Baguley.
        p.   cm.— (Modernist studies)
    Includes bibliographical references and index.
    ISBN 0-8071-2664-1 (cloth : alk. paper)
    1. Napoleon III, Emperor of the French, 1808–1873—In literature.
2. Napoleon III, Emperor of the French, 1808–1873—In
art.   3. France—
History—Second Empire, 1852–1870—Sources.   4. Symbolism in
politics.
    I. Title.   II. Series.

    DC276.5 .B34 2000
    944.07—dc21   00-040573

For Monica

Contents

Acknowledgments xiii
Chronology xv
Prologue 1

chapter 1
Histories I: Coups d'État 8

chapter 2
Histories II: VICTOR HUGO versus louis napoléon 31

chapter 3
Histories III: Op*positions* 48

chapter 4
Histories IV: Uses and Abuses of the Past 69

chapter 5
Biography I: Family Affairs 96

chapter 6
Biography II: A Man of Many Parts 118

chapter 7
Epic Ventures 149

chapter 8
Utopian Vistas 181

chapter 9
Romance 209

chapter 10
Parody, Caricature, Satire 248

chapter 11
Vaudeville 298

chapter 12
Fictions 329

chapter 13
Tragedy 368

Epilogue 391

Bibliography 399
Index 411

Illustrations

FIGURES
following page 136
1 *The Emperor Napoleon III*, portrait by Flandrin
2 *Napoleon III*, portrait by Winterhalter
3 *The Empress Eugénie, Surrounded by Her Palace Ladies*, by Winterhalter
4 *Image d'Épinal* of the imperial family
5 *Allegory to the Glory of Napoleon III*, by Cabasson
6 *Napoleon III, the Empress, and the Prince Imperial Surrounded by
   Their People*, a popular engraving
7 *The Empire Means Peace*
8 *The Emperor at Solferino*, by Meissonier
9 *The Battle of Solferino*, by Janet-Lange
10 Napoleon III as commander in chief of the army in Italy
11 *Napoleon III's Visit to the Slate-Quarry Workers of Angers During the
   Floods of 1856*, by Antigna
12 *The Emperor Visiting the Flood Victims of Tarascon in June 1856*, by
   Bouguereau
13 Empress Eugénie visiting a cholera hospital

following page 288
14 Plan of the building for the Universal Exhibition of 1867
15 *The Empress Eugénie*, portrait by Winterhalter
16 Ratapoil at a Bonapartist military review, drawing by Daumier

17 Napoleon III, "The Vulture"
18 Prince Napoleon, "The Hare"
19 Princess Mathilde, "The Sow"
20 Louis Napoléon leading his troops in the streets of Strasbourg
21 *La danse,* by Carpeaux
22 Hugo striking down Napoleon III
23 The emperor and Marguerite Bellanger
24 Photograph of Napoleon III by Nadar

GENEALOGICAL CHART
The Bonaparte Family (first and second generations) xxiv

Acknowledgments

I wish to thank the Publications Board of the University of Durham for financial support and the following institutions for permission to reproduce illustrations: The British Museum, the Bibliothèque Nationale de France, the Doe Library, the Hôtel de Ville de Tarascon, the Louvre, The Metropolitan Museum of Art, the Musée de l'Armée (Hôtel National des Invalides), the Musée des Beaux-Arts, Angers, the Musée National du Château de Compiègne, the Musée National du Château de Versailles, and the Musée d'Orsay. I should also like to express warm thanks to the editorial and production staff of Louisiana State University Press for their invaluable assistance, and particularly to John Easterly and Eiv Boe for their great courtesy and professionalism. Finally, I wish to express to Monica my deep appreciation for her unfailing encouragement and support.

Chronology

1802   Marriage of Louis Bonaparte and Hortense de Beauharnais, the future emperor's "father" and mother (4 January). Birth of Napoléon Charles, first brother of the future emperor (10 October).

1804   Birth of Napoléon Louis, second brother of the future emperor (11 October).

1806   Louis Bonaparte becomes king of Holland (June).

1807   Death of Napoléon Charles at the age of four (5 May).

1808   Birth of Charles Louis Napoléon, future Napoleon III (20 April).

1810   Louis Bonaparte abdicates from the Dutch throne (1 July).

1811   Birth of Charles Auguste Louis Joseph Demorny (later Morny) (21 October).

1815   Abdication of Napoleon I (22 June), whose son, the king of Rome, later the duke of Reichstadt, is proclaimed "Napoleon II."

1817   Hortense and Louis Napoléon established at Arenenberg (Switzerland) and Augsburg (Bavaria).

1831   Louis Napoléon and his brother, Napoléon Louis, participate in an uprising in Romagna (Papal State). Napoléon Louis dies, probably of measles, at Forli in Italy (17 March). Louis Napoléon and Hortense in Paris (21 March), then exiled to England (10 May), before returning to Arenenberg (end of August).

1832   *Political Reveries*. Death of the duke of Reichstadt ("Napoleon II").

1833   *Political and Military Considerations on Switzerland*.

1834 Captain of artillery, Berne.

1835 *Manuel d'artillerie.*

1836 Abortive Strasbourg coup (30 October). Louis Napoléon deported to America via Rio de Janeiro (21 November).

1837 Arrives in America (30 March). Back in Arenenberg (4 August). Death of his mother, Hortense de Beauharnais (5 October).

1838 Franco-Swiss conflict over the residence of Louis Napoléon. Leaves for London.

1839 *Ideas of Napoleonism.*

1840 Abortive Boulogne coup (6 August). Sentenced to life imprisonment. Confined to the Castle of Ham (until 1846).

1841 *Historical Fragments: 1688 and 1830.*

1842 *Analysis of the Sugar Question.*

1844 *On the Extinction of Pauperism.*

1845 *On the Nicaragua Canal.*

1846 Escape from Ham (25 May). Back in London (27 May). Death of Louis Bonaparte (25 July).

1848 Revolution in Paris (24 February). Special constable in London (April). Official proclamation of the Republic (4 May). Elected to the National Assembly in by-elections (4 June). Resigns (15 June). June Days (23–26 June). Re-elected. Returns to take his seat (24 September). Presidential elections (10–11 December). Inauguration as president of the Second Republic (20 December).

1849 Expedition to Rome (April). Rome falls to French troops (3 July).

1850 Falloux Law on education (15 March). Modifications to electoral law (31 May). Press laws (16 July).

1851 Vote on the revision of the Constitution (19 July). Motion to abrogate electoral law of May 1850 (17 November). Coup d'état (2 December). Resistance in Paris (3–4 December). Death of Baudin (3 December). Shooting on the boulevards (4 December). Resistance in the provinces (5–10 December). Plebiscite on the coup d'état (21–22 December) (Result—Yes: 7,439,216; No: 640,737; Abstentions: 2,171,440).

1852 Installation of Louis Bonaparte as president; *Te deum* in Notre-Dame (1 January). New Constitution signed and published in the *Moniteur* (14–15 January). Confiscation of Orleanist properties (22 January). Legislative elections (29 February–1 March). End of martial law and of the dictatorship (28 March). Tour of central and southern France (14 September–16 October). Bordeaux speech (9 October). Restoration of empire approved by plebiscite (21–22 November) (Result—Yes: 7,824,189; No: 253,145). Second Empire established (2 December). *Senatus-consulte* modifies the Constitution (25 December).

1853 Marriage of Napoleon III to Eugenia de Montijo (29–30 January). *Moniteur* announces amnesty of 4,312 political prisoners (1 February). Haussmann named prefect of the Seine (29 June). Publication of *Châtiments* by Victor Hugo (21 November).

1854 Declaration of war on Russia (27 March). The Garde Impériale re-established (May). Billault replaces Persigny as minister of the interior (19 June). Allied victory at the Alma (20 September). Siege of Sebastopol begins (September). Death of Marshal Saint-Arnaud (29 September). Allied victory at Balaclava (25 October). Morny succeeds Billaut as president of the Corps Législatif (14 November). Franco-Austrian-British treaty of alliance signed (2 December).

1855 Death of Czar Nicholas I (2 March). Play by Dumas *fils*, *Le demi-monde*, Gymnase (29 March). Emperor and empress on a state visit to Britain (15–21 April). Giovanni Pianori's assassination attempt on the emperor (28 April). Drouyn de Lhuys resigns as foreign minister (4 May); replaced by Walewski (8 May). International Exposition in Paris (15 May–15 November). Persigny becomes ambassador to Britain, replacing Walewski (28 May [to 23 March 1858]). Opening of Offenbach's Bouffes-Parisiens (5 July). State visit to France of Queen Victoria and Albert (18–27 August). Paris debut of Hortense Schneider at the Bouffes-Parisiens (31 August). Russians evacuate Sebastopol (9 September). State visit to France of Victor Emmanuel of Sardinia and Cavour (November).

1856 Birth of prince imperial (16 March); all political *condamnés* amnestied on condition of accepting the regime (16 March). Treaty of Paris signed (30 March). Baptism of prince imperial (14 June). Morny named ambassador to Russia (July).

1857 Flaubert prosecuted and acquitted for *Madame Bovary* (January). Legislative elections (21–22 June). Morny returns as president of the Corps Législatif (July). State visit of the emperor and empress to Britain (6–10 August). Baudelaire fined 300 francs for offending public morals with *Les Fleurs du mal* (20 August). The emperor meets Alexander II at Stuttgart and, later, the German princes (26–28 September). Baudelaire's fine reduced to 50 francs after the intervention of the empress (November).

1858 Anglo-French force enters Canton (5 January). Felice Orsini's assassination attempt on the emperor and empress (14 January). General Charles Espinasse replaces Billault as minister of the interior (8 February). General Security Law (27 February). Orsini executed (13 March). Plombières meeting with Cavour (20 July). Queen Victoria's visit to Cherbourg (4–5 August). Franco-Spanish expedition to Cochinchina (September). Offenbach, *Orphée aux enfers,* Bouffes-Parisiens (21 October). Treaty with Piedmont (December).

1859 Marriage of Prince Napoléon and Princess Clotilde in Turin (30 January). French occupy Saigon (16–18 February). Secret Franco-Russian treaty of alliance (3 March). Work begins on the Suez Canal (25 April). France declares war on Austria (3 May). Persigny reappointed ambassador to Britain (9 May [to 24 November 1860]). Napoleon III leaves for Italy; Eugénie as regent (10 May). Battle of Magenta (4 June). Napoleon III and Victor Emmanuel enter Milan (8 June). Battle of Solferino (24 June). Armistice and peace preliminaries of Villafranca (6–12 July). Victory parade in Paris; general amnesty proclaimed (15 August). Billault becomes minister of the interior (1 November). Treaty of Zurich (10 November).

1860 Walewski resigns as foreign minister and is replaced by Thouvenel (5 January). Cobden-Chevalier Treaty of Commerce signed (22 January). Treaty of cession of Nice and Savoy signed (24 March). Anglo-French expedition reaches China (May). Plebiscites and transfer of Nice and Savoy to France (12 and 14 June). Napoleon III meets German princes at Baden (15–17 June). Death of Jérôme Bonaparte (24 June). Syrian expedition (16 August). Napoleon III and Eugénie leave Paris for Algeria (15–22 September). Allies take Peking (12–15 October). Failure of the emperor to secure reform of the French army (October). Garibaldi and Victor Emmanuel enter Naples (7 November). Walewski replaces Fould as minister of state (23 November). Napoleon III publishes liberal decrees (24 November).

1861 William I becomes King of Prussia (2 January). Wagner,

Tannhäuser, Opera (13 March). Ollivier announces willingness to rally to a liberal Empire (14 March). Withdrawal of *Tannhäuser* (25 March). Garnier wins Opera design competition (29 May). Body of Napoleon I placed in completed Invalides crypt (2 April). Death of Cavour (6 June). France recognizes Kingdom of Italy (24 June). Excavations begin for the Opera (27 August). St. Rémy (Morny), *M. Choufleuri restera chez lui le . . .* , Bouffes-Parisiens (14 September). William I at Compiègne (6 October). Anglo-Franco-Spanish convention on Mexican expedition (31 October). Death of Prince Albert (14 December).

1862 Spain and Britain opt out of Mexican intervention (9 April). France declares war on the government of Juárez in Mexico (16 April). French defeated at Puebla, Mexico (5 May). Napoleon III confers the title of duke on Morny (July). Drouyn de Lhuys replaces Thouvenel as foreign minister (15 October).

1863 Polish insurrection begins (22 January). Siege of Puebla, Mexico, begins (10 March). Opening of the Salon des Refusés (15 May). Fall of Puebla (7 May). Legislative elections (31 May–1 June). Renan, *Vie de Jésus* (27 June). Crédit Lyonnais founded (6 July). Bazaine named to command the French forces in Mexico (16 July). Cambodia becomes a French protectorate (11 August). Persigny becomes a duke (9 September). Maximilian agrees to accept the Mexican throne (3 October). Unexpected death of Billault (13 October). New statue of Napoleon I, dressed in the costume of a Roman emperor, is placed on the Vendôme Column (3 November).

1864 Austro-Prussian-Danish war begins (1 February). Archduke Maximilian formally accepts the Mexican throne at Miramar (10 April). Labor reforms: law on "coalitions" legalizes strikes (25 May). King of Spain visits France (16 August). Convention with Italy, providing for withdrawal of French troops from Rome (15 September). Founding of the International Workingmen's Association (First International) (28 September). Encyclical *Quanta Cura* and *Syllabus of Errors* (8 December). Offenbach, *La Belle Hélène,* Variétés (17 December).

1865 Paris bureau of the First International established (January). *Histoire de Jules César,* volume one (9 March). Death of Morny (10 March). Emperor leaves France for Algeria; empress as regent (3

May). Prince Napoleon's controversial Ajaccio speech (15 May).
Emperor returns from Algeria (10 June). Emperor's illness at
Châlons; stone diagnosed (August). Walewski president of the
Corps Législatif (1 September). Paris–Biarritz–Saint-Cloud talks
with Bismarck (2 September, 4–11 October, 3 November). French
evacuation of Rome begins (7 November). Goncourt, *Henriette
Maréchal,* Théâtre Français (5 December).

1866 Duruy's educational reforms, providing primary schools for girls (6
June). Prussia and Italy declare war on Austria (18 June). Austrian
defeat at Sadowa (3 July). Resignation of Drouyn de Lhuys (20
August). Lionel, marquis de Moustier, named foreign minister (1
September). Venetia ceded to Napoleon III, then to Italy (19
October). Offenbach, *La Vie parisienne,* Palais Royal (31
October). Mass arrests of Blanquists, Café de la Renaissance (7
November). Last troops leave Rome (2–13 December). *Histoire de
Jules César,* volume two (December).

1867 Napoleon III publishes reform plans (19 January). Complete
withdrawal of French troops from Mexico (March). Walewski
resigns as president of the Corps Législatif (29 March); Eugène
Schneider succeeds him (2 April). International Exposition in Paris
(1 April–3 November). Offenbach, *La Grande Duchesse de
Gérolstein,* Variétés (12 April). Czar of Russia in Paris (1–11 June).
King of Prussia in Paris (5–14 June). Execution of Maximilian at
Querétaro (19 June). Turkish sultan in Paris (30 June). Napoleon
III meets with Franz Joseph and other German rulers in Salzburg
(8–21 August). Duruy announces introduction of secondary
education for girls (October). Franz Joseph in Paris (23 October–4
November). French Papal troops defeat Garibaldi at Mentana (3
November). Pinard minister of the interior (13 November).

1868 Corps Législatif votes for army reform (14 January). Clash of
students and police over the banning of Hugo's *Ruy Blas* (18
February). Right-wing Bonapartist faction, the "Arcadiens," is
formed (February). Press law passed (9 March). Law on public
meetings passed (25 March). Napoleon III establishes his own
newspaper, *L'Époque,* with Duvernois as editor (April). Jules Ferry,
Comptes fantastiques d'Haussmann (May). *La Lanterne* seized (8
August). Rochefort convicted (14 and 28 August). Equality of
witness in court for worker and employer (18 August). Revolution

in Spain (18 September). Death of Walewski (27 September). Queen Isabella deposed (29 September).

1869 *Journal officiel* replaces *Moniteur* as the official newspaper (1 January). Napoleon III initiates the suppression of the *livret d'ouvriers* (23 March). Legislative elections (23–24 May; 6–7 June). Loire miners' strike (12–24 June). Miners and troops clash at La Ricamarie (15–16 June). Miners' strike at Carmaux (Aveyron) (26 June). Strike of Loire silk workers (July). More reforms announced and the resignation of Rouher (12 July). Unveiling of Carpeaux's Opera sculpture *La danse* (27 July). Napoleon III pardons sixty-two leaders of the Loire miners' strike after their convictions (August). Eugénie and prince imperial in Corsica during the emperor's illness (August). Death of Marshal Niel (13 August). Political offenders granted unconditional amnesty (15 August). Miners' strike at Aubin and clash of troops with miners (7–8 October). Emperor and Ollivier meet secretly at Compiègne (31 October). Suez Canal inaugurated in the presence of the empress (16–18 November).

1870 Ministry of Ollivier (2 January). Haussmann dismissed as prefect of the Seine (5 January). Pierre Bonaparte shoots Victor Noir (10 January). Funeral of Victor Noir (12 January). Pierre Bonaparte's trial (21–27 March). New Constitution adopted by Senate (20 April). Plebiscite on liberal reforms (8 May) (Result—Yes: 7,358,786; No: 1,571,939; Abstentions: 1,894,681). New constitution promulgated (21 May). Ems dispatch published (13 July). France declares war on Prussia (19 July). Eugénie becomes regent (26 July). Napoleon III leaves for the front with the prince imperial (28 July). Napoleon III gives up supreme command to Marshal Bazaine (12 August). French defeat and surrender in decisive battle of Sedan (1 September). Armistice signed; Napoleon III, his generals, and the army of Châlons in captivity (2 September). Flight of Eugénie, fall of the Empire, proclamation of Republic (4 September). Napoleon III imprisoned at Wilhelmshöhe (5 September). Eugénie reaches England (8 September). Siege of Paris begins (19 September).

1871 Armistice (28 January). Paris Commune (18 March to 25 May). Napoleon III released (19 March). Retires to Chislehurst (20 March). Treaty of Frankfurt (20 May).

1873 Death of Napoleon III at Camden Place, Chislehurst (9 January).
1879 Prince imperial killed in Zululand (1 June).
1888 Bodies of Napoleon III and prince imperial moved by the empress to Farnborough Abbey in Hampshire (January).
1920 Death of the empress in Madrid (11 July). Funeral and burial in the crypt with her husband and son in Farnborough (20 July).

NAPOLEON III
and HIS REGIME

THE BONAPARTE FAMILY
(first and second generations)

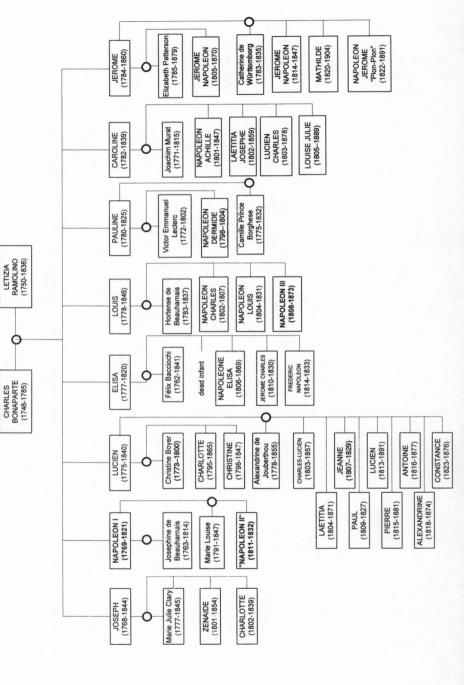

Prologue

The subject of this book, Napoleon III, has significantly come down into history with a title composed of a name of dubious authenticity and a "dynastic numeral" that can be judged more a sign of appropriation than of appropriateness. Problems of entitlement and legitimacy are clearly at the root of his status and reputation. Furthermore, the conflicting attributes that have been suffixed to his name, notably Napoléon le Petit, Napoléon le Grand, Napoléon le bien-intentionné, as if in parodic imitation of a monarchical tradition to which he could hardly claim to belong, point variously to the contrasting interpretations of his failures and achievements, to the complex issue of his motivations, and to the evident gap between his expectations and his accomplishments. Even the legendary inscrutability of the "Sphinx of the Tuileries," as Metternich dubbed him, has been called into question as less a natural disposition than an astute political strategy. As for his practices and plans, they were fraught with the inconsistencies that stemmed from his Bonapartism and from his "Napoleonic Ideas," such as the authoritarian democracy and the program of progressive social and economic reforms that he sought to institute within the anachronistic trappings of an imperial dynasty, or the ever shifting responses of his domestic and foreign policies to changing circumstances and pressures to which his regime was constantly subjected. He was, as Theodore Zeldin characterizes him, "at once conservative and radical, a lover of peace but also a lover of glory, an unbeliever married to a religious wife—a bundle of contradictions, but the very contradictions that were innate in the great majority of his subjects."[1] Paradoxically, his reputation was later tarnished most of all by two of his most popular deeds at the time: his most consequential political feat, the coup d'état of 2 December 1851, and his greatest diplomatic error, the declaration of war on Prussia on 19 July 1870. The one was the founding event of his later Empire, whilst the other was the decisive act that brought about its destruction. But the major blight on his name and fame arose from the wrath and resentment he incurred from France's most eloquent poet, Victor Hugo, who, "with justice in his soul" (as he claimed), inspired by the Muse Indignation (as he believed), poured out his scorn on the "bandit" of the Tuileries, shaping posterity's view of Louis Napoléon for generations to come.

Inevitably this situation has given rise to a long revisionist tradition, which, along with the corrective influence of the work of professional historians modifying the hasty judgments of the time, has sought to reverse the conventional verdicts of history. Few historical figures can have been subjected to such a prolonged process of rehabilitation. "In reality," as James F. McMillan has recently remarked, "a historiography which privileges the 'black legend' is out of date by some forty years." Indeed, some forty years ago, Theodore Zeldin pointedly argued that it was time that the abuse of Napoleon III's enemies "should be appreciated in its true light and not accepted as impartial history merely because they happened to be distinguished men."[2] Yet the need for vindication is still felt, particularly in France, where the persistent effects of a hostile republican orthodoxy and the flagrant vilification of the past still hold sway for many in the present. Symbolically, the remains of Napoleon number three still lie in English exile (in Farnborough, Hampshire), whilst those of his enemy number one occupy the Panthéon.

Two recent books, with significant titles, illustrate this trend, demonstrating also the topicality of their subject and his lasting relevance to contemporary French politics. In his *Louis Napoléon le Grand* (1990), the leading Gaullist politician, Philippe Séguin, a vigorous campaigner for the return of the emperor's remains to France, resolutely defends a man about

---

1. Theodore Zeldin, "The Myth of Napoleon III," *History Today* (February 1958): 105–106.
2. James F. McMillan, *Napoleon III* (London and New York: Longman, 1991), 4; Zeldin, "The Myth of Napoleon III," 105.

whom, he claims, enough ill has been spoken, a man who sought "sincerely, honestly, courageously, to serve France," who accomplished his task with a "personal, moral strength worthy of respect, if not admiration," and who, in many of his ideas, policies, and achievements, anticipated the greatness of General de Gaulle. Alain Minc, in *Louis Napoléon revisité* (1997), is less ardent in his defense of the emperor's reputation, acknowledging the uneasy task of redeeming a regime "forcibly born [*né au forceps*] out of a *pronunciamento*, dying of a military defeat, relentlessly bombarded from Guernsey, . . . difficult to rescue from manicheistic views."[3] But Louis Napoléon is, even in Minc's assessment, superior to the image handed down to posterity. In his political evolution from right to left, in the astuteness and flexibility of his policies, in his economic designs and his pharaonic ambitions, he is to be compared less with the General than with the author of *Le Coup d'État permanent* (1964), François Mitterrand, who, significantly, planned to write a book on Louis Napoléon and the coup d'état, more or less the book that Alain Minc himself claims to have written. Clearly the myth of Napoleon III, however belatedly, is perhaps finally emerging from the shadow of the legend of his illustrious predecessor and out of range of Hugo's poisoned barbs.

The aim of this book is not to enter on one side or the other of the lasting debate about the legitimacy, efficacy, morality, or credibility of Napoleon III, though, inevitably, I shall be dealing with many of the events that brought about such divergent views and many of the texts (and images) through which they have been expressed. Nor do I wish to present another biography of Louis Napoléon or a sequential narrative of the period in question, nor a contribution to the empirical history of an aspect of it on the basis of new archival material. Whilst in no way denying the relevance of known facts and whilst drawing upon a number of strictly documented historical works in this book, I shall be primarily concerned with more "extravagant" texts and images: representations and inventions in a variety of media and forms, pictures, performances, spectacles, rituals, fiction, poems, plays. In using and analyzing such secondary materials, including Louis Napoléon's own writings, this book will not be an attempt to uphold a particular view, but will assume, display, and explore the conflicting visions and interpretations of its central figure. The theme of the

3. Philippe Séguin, *Louis Napoléon le Grand* (Paris: Bernard Grasset, 1990), 19; Alain Minc, *Louis Napoléon revisité* (Paris: Gallimard, 1997), 180.

book is thus the dynamic process, in both its constructive and destructive phases, by which the legend or the myth of Napoleon III was elaborately fabricated and vigorously dismantled. Louis Napoléon's career remarkably illustrates the persuasive and dissuasive power of the name and the image. I would claim that such representations are redundant only in the linguistic sense, repetitive and excessive for effect, for implicit in the process of privileging such images is the view that they were and are by no means gratuitous as history, but have not only contributed to the shaping of contemporary and later views of the events and personalities of the Second Empire, but to the shaping of the events themselves. As Roger L. Williams succinctly remarks: "The key to Louis-Napoleon is this: he was not only the heir but the victim of the Napoleonic legend."[4]

Thus the "extravaganza" of the title of this book refers both to the events of the Second Empire and to their representation in the texts and images that I have chosen to present. Certain specialist historians may also feel that it applies most appropriately to the book itself! The apparently digressive method that I have adopted may seem to require some preliminary justification, not only because it gives undue prominence to "unreliable" texts of a more literary than rigorously documentary kind, but also because the framework of the book itself relates them to a literary system of generic categorization.

It is now commonplace to assert that the discursive aspects of the historian's art, which were once considered ornamental, are fundamental to their practice. Metahistorians have treated historical narratives as verbal artifacts, barely distinguishable from literary narratives, and have employed, most famously in the case of Hayden White's influential *Metahistory*, literary concepts—figural (metaphor, metonym, etc.), modal (diegesis, point of view, etc.), generic (tragedy, epic, etc.)—to categorize and interpret them. There is clearly, for example, a thin epistemological line of distinction between, on the one hand, the historical narrative, with its plot, characters, descriptions, even dialogue, its beginning, middle, and end, and, on the other hand, the fictional narrative that draws upon a rich stock of lived experience and historical fact. Both employ the same discursive strategies, are subject to the same reductive and selective expedients, and are beset by the same constraints, which lead them necessarily—or happily, in

---

4. Roger L. Williams, "A Tragedy of Good Intentions," *History Today* (April 1954): 220.

the case of the partisan historian—to suppress or ignore the full complexity of the Real. If, to make some familiar distinctions in a convenient manner, HISTORY is the sum of all happenings in the past and if History is the totality of writings that attempt to depict IT, histories are the discourses which, partially and selectively, seek to delineate the former and render it intelligible. Any attempt to write History in the sense above is only conceivable, according to Barthes in a famous essay, as an unattainably "zero degree of writing," akin to the mere unstructured presentation of a "series" of notations, as in chronicles or annals. On the other hand, the writer of "histories," to use Barthes's notions again, "assembles not so much facts as signifiers and links them together, that is to say organizes them with a view to establishing a positive sense and *filling the gaps* ['le vide'] *in the series*" (my emphasis).[5] Hence the presence and the separateness, in this book, of a Chronology which presents, selectively and partially of course, a "series" of snippets of History, denoting particulars of HISTORY. As for what follows, almost all the rest is "histories."

A second justification, more particularly for the use of a generic framework in this book, is provided by the example of historians themselves, who, as in Williams's article cited above, frequently employ literary categories not only in their titles but also, more fundamentally, in their interpretations. For example, in one of the periodic skirmishes between postmodernist and empirical historians that appear in the press, Richard J. Evans, in a quite recent attack on the "hyper-relativism" of the former and their discursive constructs, unwittingly perhaps, vindicates, even in the contradiction that his statements contain, this discursive convention as he writes:

> No given set of events is inherently tragic or comic, or whatever, events can only be constructed as such by the historian. . . . The insistence that all history is discourse diverts attention from the real lives and sufferings of people in the past. Auschwitz is not a text. The gas chambers were not a discourse. It trivialises mass murder to see it as a text. Auschwitz was indeed, as Hayden White has recently conceded, inherently a tragedy and cannot be seen as a comedy or a farce. If this is true of Auschwitz, then it must be true at least to some degree of other past events as well. The past does indeed im-

5. Roland Barthes, "Le discours de l'histoire," *Poétique* 49 (1982): 19.

pose its extra-textual reality on historians' interpretations of it, limiting and confining them within a web of facts.[6]

Whether we believe that HISTORY inherently falls into generic patterns or that it is histories that conventionally employ them, their relevance and prevalence are evident. "What a novel my life is," Napoleon I is supposed to have declared, supporting the former view. Chateaubriand, however, though he famously defined the life of his rival and inspiration as a "poem in action," seems to subscribe to the latter view when he observes that, after Napoleon's fall, detached from his age, "his history is finished and his epic begins."[7]

By comparison, the nephew (if indeed he was) and his regime are confined to the lesser genres in the most famous and most quoted (and misquoted) statement of the kind, with which Marx begins *The Eighteenth Brumaire of Louis Bonaparte:* "Hegel remarks somewhere that all facts and personages of great importance in world history occur, as it were, twice. He forgot to add: the first time as tragedy, the second as farce." Marx's comment on the coup d'état is obviously as much a polemical flourish as a historiographic declaration and his use of literary terms a convenient rhetorical device. On the same set of events, whose importance in the historiography of Louis Napoléon's empire, before it became such, is reflected in the extensive treatment at the beginning of this book, Queen Victoria's reference to "the *wonderful* proceedings at Paris, which really seem like a *story* in a book or a play" (her emphasis),[8] may seem too flippant to deserve serious consideration. Yet there is indeed something essentially literary in the course of the Second Empire in general, with its conspiratorial origins, its rising and dramatically falling action, its intrigues, scandals, and its tragic denouement, as if made for writers and artists to find inspiration in its ventures, vices, and vicissitudes. At least one such writer, Émile Zola, believed that historical reality had providentially conformed to his novelistic plans, as he explains in the preface to *Les Rougon-Macquart:* "the fall of the Bonapartes, which I needed as an artist, and which I always fatally

6. Richard J. Evans, "Truth Lost in Vain Views," *The Times Higher Education Supplement,* 12 September 1997, p. 18.

7. Jean-Pierre Rioux, *Les Bonapartes* (Lausanne: Recontre, 1968), 9; François-René, vicomte de Chateaubriand, *Mémoires d'outre-tombe,* Book XXIV, Chapter 8.

8. Quoted in Ivor Guest, *Napoleon III in England* (London: British Technical and General Press, 1952), 102.

predicted as the end of the drama, without daring to hope it to be so close, provided me with the terrible and necessary denouement of my work." Zola went on to write twenty volumes of his (natural and social) history under the Second Empire, from, as he puts it in the same text, "the ambush of the coup d'état to the treason of Sedan." Though far from impartial, the republican novelist's massive achievement has acquired for later historians the status of testimony. Ironically, as we shall see, Zola's fellow novelist, Flaubert, who had a better knowledge of the inner workings of the regime and a more direct acquaintance with its leader, never completed his projected novel on the Second Empire. But he has left, as Maxime Du Camp reports, his own testimonial to the literary potential of the period: "Ah! There are some superb books to be done on that era and perhaps, when all is said and done, the coup d'état and all that followed from it will have no other consequence, in the great scheme of things, than to provide interesting scenarios for some skillful penpushers."[9]

9. Quoted in Marie-Jeanne Durry, *Flaubert et ses projets inédits* (Paris: Nizet, 1950), 255.

chapter 1

Histories I: Coups d'État

Annus mirabilis

It was during the "year of revolutions," 1848, that Louis Napoléon, cautiously and skillfully, and with the immense help of circumstances, could finally maneuver himself into a position of power and set the stage for his access to absolute power three years later. He was living in London when revolution broke out in Paris in the name of the Democratic and Socialist Republic and brought down the July Monarchy, removing from the throne the Orleanist king, Louis-Philippe. The provisional government of moderate republicans and socialists immediately introduced such progressive social and political measures as universal male suffrage, the abolition of the death penalty for political offenses, the abolition of slavery in the colonies, the abrogation of the tax on salt, but it was soon contending with more radical demands and street disturbances. When Louis Napoléon announced his presence in Paris on 28 February, Bonapartist supporters plastered posters throughout the city with his picture under the word "Lui!," perhaps a literary reference to Hugo's poem on the glory of the first Napoleon (in *Les Orientales*) or, more likely, a none-too-subtle pun on the nephew's name. Fearing further commotion, the provisional government asked him to leave the country. After consulting his advisers he complied, arriving back in England just a few hours before the deposed king and queen, who had been in hiding near the Channel for a week. But he would soon be back in France. In the intervening period, in one of the more bizarre twists of his career, at the very time when cries of *"Vive Napoléon!"* could be heard (occasionally) in the left-wing street demonstrations in Paris, back in London Louis, a Bonaparte, was serving a two-month stint as one of the special constables recruited to help the duke of Wellington put down Chartist rebellions!

With calculated caution, he refrained from presenting his candidacy at the first round of elections, which took place on 23 April. The dynasty, however, was well represented: cousins Prince Murat, Pierre Bonaparte, and Prince Napoléon, the sons of Caroline, Lucien, and Jérôme respectively, were elected. In the June elections, Louis Napoléon tested the waters himself, whilst still in London, and was successful in three circumscriptions: Yonne, Charente-Inférieure, and, of course, Corsica, provoking alarm in conservative circles, renewed demonstrations, a rash of new Bonapartist newspapers,[1] and prolonged debate in the Assembly on the validity of his election. When tensions reached a crisis point with rumors of a Bonapartist coup d'état, he prudently resigned his seat. Interestingly, at this stage, he was viewed with suspicion above all as a radical force, garnered support from the extreme left, and was defended in the Assembly by Louis Blanc and Proudhon. Though the Bonapartists were widely blamed for the insurrection of the June Days, which General Cavaignac's troops brutally repressed, Louis Napoléon was to all appearances serenely detached from the action, living it up in fashionable London society, but confident that the disorders could soon be turned to his advantage. Indeed, on 21 September, he was re-elected to the National Assembly. On the 26th he rushed off to Paris to take his seat, having moved into rooms in a hotel on the Place Vendôme that, auspiciously, looked out onto the column bearing his uncle's statue.

Even his inept performance at the rostrum in the Assembly, where eloquence was expected, causing Thiers to dismiss him as a "cretin," was to serve his purposes in the forthcoming presidential elections. Suspicious of

---

1. *Le Petit Caporal, La Redingote grise, Le Napoléonien, Le Napoléon républicain, La Constitution, Journal de la République napoléonienne, L'Aigle républicain.*

Cavaignac's ambitions and convinced that Louis Napoléon could be easily led—by giving him a regular supply of women, according to Thiers—the conservatives rallied to his candidacy. Ironically, in view of later events, even Victor Hugo, a mighty orator in the House, also lent his support. Louis Napoléon now courted the favor of the Party of Order, denied any ambitions, reassured Catholic voters of his good intentions, tapped the popularity of his name. He won a stunning victory in the 12 December elections, securing 5,434,226 votes to Cavaignac's 1,448,107, even though the latter as head of state, in ways that taught valuable lessons to the Bonapartists for future reference, was in a strong position to influence the voters. The revolutionary radical Ledru-Rollin and the moderate republican Lamartine trailed far behind with the other candidates. Louis Napoléon had cut through party and class divisions and secured for himself a massive power base of popular support, which he would never lose even in the year of his downfall as emperor. Extraordinarily, a Bonaparte had become the first democratically elected president of France.

PRINCE-PRESIDENT

At his inauguration on 20 December 1848 Louis Napoléon duly swore allegiance to the new Constitution, which gave him a four-year term of office and extensive powers, such as the right to choose his ministers and to veto legislation passed by the Assembly. But the president was barred from re-election for a second term and could not dissolve the Assembly before the expiry of the three-year term of its deputies. Furthermore, a three-quarters majority was required to change the Constitution, and then only in the last year of the Assembly's tenure. With a fractious parliament and an ambitious leader, the political situation was ripe for strife. With unsuspected guile, the president was able to turn the dissensions to his favor. He chose a right-wing cabinet, with, in influential backroom positions, his own supporters such as Count de Morny, his half-brother, an Orleanist who had rallied to his star and had become, after the faithful Persigny, his chief adviser. Louis Napoléon's term as president can be interpreted prospectively as an apprenticeship to absolute power, as a major stepping-stone of his ascent, as a preparation for the coup d'état and the restoration of the Napoleonic empire. But retrospectively, it was in many respects more a rehearsal for the later role, as the future emperor practiced his politics and policies. Radical and socialist opposition was vigorously repressed, despite or because of its increase in the Assembly.[2] A peaceful radical demonstration was routed by Changarnier's cavalry on 13 June, and disturbances in various provincial towns were violently put down. Newspapers were seized, a new press law introduced, banning the expression of subversive ideas. For months to come, protesters were summarily arrested—it was enough to shout " *Vive la République démocratique et sociale!*" to end up in jail. The press laws of July 1850 further muzzled the opposition. And, earlier that year, on 31 May, the electoral law, which the president agreed not to oppose despite his avowed belief in universal suffrage, disenfranchised almost three million voters, mostly from the left. The Republic, which left-wing opponents of the coup d'état and the Empire would accuse Louis Napoléon of shamelessly violating and for which they fought on barricades, was already a highly repressive regime. There was less of a divide than is usually supposed between the regime over which he presided and the one over which he would rule.

During these months as president of the Republic, Louis Napoléon also rehearsed and perfected the populist politics and public relations skills that he would later put to even better effect as the emperor. He courageously visited hospitals during the cholera epidemic of the summer of 1849. He amnestied rebels of the June Days, even as he had other subversives arrested. He traveled widely throughout the country, adapting his speeches to the prevailing local views, winning over angry crowds in left-wing areas, invoking the glories of France's monarchs in legitimist areas, uttering pieties in Catholic circles. But above all, he developed the common touch, chatting to the workers, visiting a popular theater in Paris, popping in at a popular dance hall in Besançon, dining with two thousand proletarians in the Winter Garden in Lyon. He assiduously attended military parades, distributed chicken and champagne to the troops on maneuvers. He culled favor, not only with the masses, but with influential persons in higher places, aristocrats, diplomats, bureaucrats, including foreign dignitaries, throwing lavish balls at the Élysée Palace in anticipation of the *fête impériale*. Even the major foreign policy initiative of the Republic, the expedition to Rome to discourage Austrian advances from the north and to protect the Pope against the Roman republic, was a preview of the later embroil-

---

2. From 80 to over 200 seats in the general election of 13 May 1849. See Jasper Ridley, *Napoleon III and Eugénie* (London: Constable, 1979), 251.

ment in the Italian campaign of the Empire. There was even a practice run at the seduction of Eugenia de Montijo, as the future emperor's wife suspected at the time, in a private dinner party in the spring of 1849, an attempt that was thwarted by the presence of the president's future mother-in-law, the formidable Maria Manuela.[3]

The president's term of office was due to expire in May 1852. He feigned a lack of interest in holding on to power beyond that date, notably in his address to the Assembly on 12 November 1850. But his actions spoke otherwise. In January 1851 he dismissed the legitimist General Changarnier as commander in chief of the National Guard, a powerful rival, openly contemptuous of Louis Napoléon—to whom he referred as the "melancholy parrot"—and replaced him with General Magnan from his own inner circle of supporters. By now he was in open conflict with the Assembly. He made extravagant demands for extra funds to pay for the style of living to which he was becoming accustomed. In February, the Assembly voted down his request for a further 1,800,000 francs, a sum three times his original annual salary stipulated by the Constitution. It is hard to imagine how, in view of his present actions, his previous writings, and his earlier attempts to seize power in the abortive *coups* in Strasbourg (1836) and Boulogne (1840), there could have been any doubt about the president's intention to prolong his rule or extend his role. But in the uncertain political atmosphere of the time, the imminent power vacuum of 1852 created on both the left and the right a doomsday mentality, with rumors rife of not only a Bonapartist coup d'état, but of a conservative take over, a legitimist overthrow of the Republic, or a socialist revolution. The lack of a viable alternative in such a situation of crisis and uncertainty was almost a *de facto* legitimation of the attempts by the president's supporters to amend the Constitution to allow him to stand for a second term. Two crucial votes in the Assembly in 1851 paved the way for the seemingly inevitable coup d'état. On 19 July the motion to modify the Constitution was in fact carried, but by less than the required 75 percent majority (446 to 278). The recourse to legal means, the degree of support of a hostile Assembly, and the outcome of the vote seemed to provide in a perverse way a legal mandate and a political license to act. A further level of moral justification was provided by the president's motion, presented to the new session of the Assembly on 15 November, to repeal the electoral law of 31

3. *Ibid.*, 246–47.

May 1850 and thereby re-establish universal male suffrage. With dubious logic, he explained his earlier support of the electoral law as a temporary expedient in a time of crisis. Its reversal clearly served his own subversive schemes, for the proposal bitterly cast the left-wing, radical forces of the so-called Mountain against the right-wing, monarchist Party of Order.[4] The motion was defeated by six votes, but Louis Napoléon had further divided, and though he had lost again, he would soon conquer. He had perfected the art of turning defeats into strategic victories.

By then plans for the coup d'état had been carefully laid. Already on 17 November General Magnan's troops were on alert when the Assembly voted on another crucial motion: the attempt by the Party of Order to delegate to three quaestors, elected by the Assembly, the power to call in the army to protect the parliament if under threat. This measure was interpreted by the Bonapartists as a preemptive move to threaten the president. The motion was defeated when the Mountain surprisingly voted with the Élysée supporters. Louis Napoléon called off the coup d'état, but only for a few days. The chosen date was 2 December, anniversary of the emperor's great victory at Austerlitz in 1805 and also of his coronation in 1804. But it was not a question of restoring the Empire immediately. The scenario required a *18 brumaire*.

"RUBICON"

On the eve of 2 December, the plotters, feigning normality, attended the president's ball at the Élysée, all except Morny, who indulged his love of the theater at the Opéra-Comique watching *Bluebeard's Castle* before joining the rest in the president's study. Operation Rubicon, as the president, an admirer of Caesar, or perhaps Mocquard, a disciple of Tacitus, had labeled the secret file of plans and proclamations, got under way after a brief meeting. The grandly named Charlemagne Émile de Maupas, prefect of police since October, went off to order the arrest of some seventy-six deputies, generals, militant republicans, socialist leaders. Saint-Arnaud, now minister of war and commander of the Paris garrisons, went off to supervise the occupation of strategic points in Paris by his regiments. Morny went off for a few hours of gambling at the Jockey Club, then pro-

---

4. *Ibid.*, 294.

ceeded to oust Thorigny as minister of the interior and take over from him. Persigny went off to arrest Dupin, the president of the Assembly, proclaiming that the Assembly had been dissolved, that martial law was in force, and that universal male suffrage had been re-established. Louis Napoléon went off . . . to bed, to read, by some accounts, Victor Hugo's odes, whilst the poet himself, as he claimed, was also in bed with . . . a copy of the Constitution![5]

In the night the troops expelled the deputies in attendance (and still free) from the Palais Bourbon and later arrested some three hundred of them as they congregated in the town hall of the Tenth District. The magistrates were sent packing from the High Court. At ten A.M. on 2 December Louis Napoléon ventured out ceremoniously on horseback in a general's uniform, accompanied by his uncle Jérôme and by his mother's former lover and the father of Morny, Count de Flahaut,[6] along with a number of generals. The family outing was not, however, complete, for the president's cousins, the prince of Canino and Prince Napoléon (Plon-Plon), were fighting on the other side in the action, the latter, dressed as a worker, vainly trying to goad the proletariat to resist. Official and unofficial reports disagree on the warmth of enthusiasm with which the president's parade was met. But it was not warm enough for him to enter the Tuileries Palace or to do other than trot back to the Élysée and lie low for a couple of days more in mysterious circumstances.[7] A strange gap in the "series" at such a crucial time, which would be left for imaginative writers to fill. At one of the two most crucial events in his political life, Louis Napoléon is conspicuous by his absence, and all the more effective for it, just as by contrast at the other event, the Battle of Sedan, he would be rendered totally ineffective by his very presence.

But whatever was going on in the Élysée, there was plenty of recorded action on the streets during the next two days. Though the coup d'état had been directed against a mainly right-wing Assembly, the active opposition, which began in earnest on the 3rd of December, came entirely from

5. See Graham Robb, *Victor Hugo* (London: Picador, 1997), 295.

6. The name often appears as Flahault, but most authoritative sources give Flahaut.

7. Guillemin writes: "It is curious, even, how we lack details of the behavior of the prince from the second onwards, at mid-day. We do not have a single line written by his hand, and those who were in his gang, those who nevertheless did speak and left *Mémoires* (Fleury, Persigny, Maupas, Morny), are totally silent on the facts and acts of the leader." Henri Guillemin, *Le Coup du deux décembre* (Paris: Gallimard, 1951), 377.

the left. The few radical deputies who had not been arrested rallied around such notable figures as Victor Hugo and appealed to the workers to rebel, mainly in the restless district of Saint-Antoine. One of the rare casualties that day was one such deputy, a physician, Victor Baudin, in an incident that would enter republican martyrology some fifteen years later, but which is usually cited to illustrate the reluctance of the people to rally to the defense of the Republic. When one of the workers supposedly taunted him in suspiciously formal language, as it is quoted, referring to the deputy's daily allowance, Baudin is supposed to have mounted the barricade shouting: "You will see a man dies for twenty-five francs"[8] and was promptly shot in an exchange of fire with the advancing columns of troops, either fulfilling his heroic destiny or completing his foolhardy gesture, whichever point of view applies.

On the night of the 3rd, Louis Napoléon, on Morny's advice and against the advice of Maupas, so it seems, withdrew the troops from the streets to allow them to rest in their barracks, either running the risk of or purposely allowing, according to lessons learnt in July 1830 and February 1848, the resistance to regroup and build more barricades, all the better to smash it the next day. The tactic proved to be both highly successful and costly in lives and moral credit. The fiercest fighting took place on the afternoon of Bloody Thursday the 4th, with hundreds of insurgents manning some seventy barricades in the area surrounded by the rue Montmartre, the rue Rambuteau, and the rue du Temple. The bloodiest scene occurred on the crowded boulevard Montmartre, where, by accident or design, a shot was fired on the brigade of General Canrobert, prompting a frenzied riposte in which dozens of bystanders were mowed down. By five P.M. the whole operation was virtually complete as far as the capital was concerned. The estimates of casualties varied wildly at the time,[9] but

8. Variously reported as: "*Croyez-vous que nous allons nous faire tuer pour vous conserver vos vingt-cinq francs?*" or "*Nous n'avons pas envie de nous sacrifier pour les vingt-cinq francs*" or, using the pejorative name for the unpopular deputies, "*A bas les vingt-cinq francs*" (Hugo). According to Dansette, "it is doubtful that the saying was uttered at all." Adrien Dansette, *Louis-Napoléon à la conquête du pouvoir: Le Second Empire,* édition revue, corrigée et augmentée (Paris: Hachette, 1961), 393.

9. *The Times:* 1,200 dead and wounded on 4 December; *Le Moniteur:* 380 dead, including fewer than 50 soldiers; Maupas: 600 dead and wounded; Fleury: 175 dead, 115 wounded; Ambassador Hübner (according to Guillemin): 2,700; Hübner (according to Dansette): 1,700; Viel-Castel: 2,000 "insurgents"; Normanby: 2,000; police report of 15 December: 175 "insurgents" and 26 soldiers killed, 115 and 184 wounded; revised police

modern historians seem to reckon on losses of 400 civilians and 26 or 27 soldiers, with an indeterminate number of summary executions. Whatever the correct figures, the casualties are usually compared to the much heavier losses of earlier and later uprisings, such as the 3,000 civilians and 1,600 soldiers killed in the June Days, if not to exculpate Louis Napoléon but to impose a perspective on the action. Though doubtless only partly responsible for Morny's and Saint-Arnaud's brutal repression, the future emperor would bear the blame, and with an uneasy conscience. In his future wife's metaphor, it was the shirt of Nessus that he would constantly wear, or in his own metaphor, "a ball and chain on one's foot that is dragged along all one's life."[10] In the metaphoric language of his opponents, if 2 December was the transgression, 4 December was the "crime" and the "original sin" of the future regime.

There was also on Louis Napoléon's conscience the matter of the repression of resistance in the provinces between December 4 and 10. Though there was little opposition to the coup d'état in provincial cities, in more rural areas in certain departments in the south and central parts of France large bands of insurgents, sometimes numbering thousands, took up arms (hunting guns, scythes, forks), took over towns, fought against government troops, and were brutally crushed. In the Basses-Alpes, for example, where there were five times as many insurgents as in Paris, the prefect was put to flight and the whole department came under control of the insurrectionists until news that the Paris coup d'état had succeeded caused them to disband. There were massive arrests throughout the country, and martial law was imposed on thirty-two departments until March of 1852.[11]

---

report of 23 (or 25) December: 215 civilians killed, 119 wounded; Kerry: 100–500 civilians killed, 200–250 wounded; Flahaut: 215 civilians killed, 119 wounded. Guillemin estimates, with some reservations: "several hundred" dead (including 1 officer and 25 men) and "several hundred" wounded. The report of the Office of the Prefect of Police of 25 December is reproduced in Kerry as it appeared in the *Morning Post*—see Earl of Kerry, ed., *The Secret of the Coup d'Etat: An Unpublished Correspondence of Prince Louis Napoleon, MM. de Morny, de Flahault, and Others, 1848–1852,* edited and with an introduction by the Earl of Kerry and a study by Philip Guedalla (London: Constable, 1924), 156–57. The argument that the figures of Maupas are likely to be correct, since he was reporting directly to Louis Napoléon, is specious, because the latter's horror of bloodshed was presumably known to his prefect of police, who therefore had good reason to minimize the casualties.

10. See Kerry, ed., *The Secret of the Coup d'Etat,* 9.

11. The usual figures given are 26,000 to 27,000 prisoners, of whom 239 were sent to Devil's Island, 9,500 to Algeria, 1,500 expelled from France, 3,000 imprisoned. Republican

Hardened Bonapartists like Morny and many of their reactionary supporters, whether monarchists or right-wing republicans, justified such repressive measures as the staving off of the threat of the "red peril" or of a new
jacquerie, essential to the survival of civilized society, which the coup
d'état had supposedly saved. Louis Napoléon's personal view of the events
remains largely a mystery.

Whatever pangs of conscience the president felt did not prevent him
from having drawn up in a remarkably short time—by a commission consisting of Flahaut, Persigny, Troplong, Mesnard, and Rouher, who produced the draft—a new Constitution, Bonapartist through and through,
which gave him unfettered powers. He acquired a ten-year term of office
and the power to name his successor. All officials were required to swear
allegiance to the president as well as to the Constitution, despite his own
bad precedent. He alone could appoint and dismiss ministers, call a referendum, conclude treaties, declare wars, initiate laws, propose constitutional changes through the Senate or by plebiscite, nominate members of
the Council of State and the Senate, dissolve the Legislative Assembly.
This body, elected every six years by universal male suffrage, could debate
and vote on laws, which required its approval, but it could not modify
them or question ministers about them. The ministers themselves could
not be deputies. The Senate, composed of eminent persons, would hold
secret sessions and be charged with completing and conserving the Constitution and with the power to veto any laws contrary to the terms of the
Constitution. A Council of State was to prepare laws, but at the president's
prompting, for it had no powers of initiative. In short, a classical Bonapartist arrangement: ostensible republican institutions, token power for the
people, an impotent parliamentary system, and executive power invested
in the president. The new constitution was promulgated on 14 January
1852 after the president had secured massive support in the referendum of
21–22 December. By then a resplendent *Te Deum* on New Year's Day had
also legitimized and now sanctified, in the eyes of some, the new regime,
and Louis Napoléon was already installed in the Tuileries. The dress rehearsal for the Empire had begun in earnest.

refugees, such as Victor Schoelcher and Hippolyte Magen, claimed that there were over
100,000 arrests in the provinces and another 26,000 in Paris. Payne notes that over 9,000
prisoners were quickly released, but a further 19,000 arrests were made in late December
1851 and in January 1852. Howard C. Payne, *The Police State of Louis Napoleon Bonaparte,
1851–1860* (Seattle: University of Washington Press, 1966), 43–44.

S U M M A R Y   V I E W S

This condensed account of the circumstances leading up to the coup d'état and of the event itself, with its own particular omissions and emphases, points to certain significant discontinuities and inconsistencies in the standard historical writings on Louis Napoléon's accession to power. It is typical in scope of the various concise narratives of the event, with their assumption of impartiality, which are to be found in more general histories and from which general readers and students have gained an understanding of this particular episode of French History. Yet as a random sample of such accounts reveals, even at a stage barely removed from the chronicle "series" itself, there are conspicuous and significant differences of emphasis and tone.

In, for example, the most standard of accounts, the Penguin *History of Modern France,* Alfred Cobban adopts a remarkably insouciant attitude to the whole affair, minimizing the import of the repression, noting that "*only* a few hundred were killed," the most "dramatic" episode occurring on the 4th of December, when the soldiers, "in a state of *natural* excitement," fired on passive bystanders (my emphasis). All in all, "*slight* splashes of blood" accompanied the "birth pangs" of the Second Empire. "It was difficult," he argues, "to make a coup d'état without breaking some heads as well as an oath." Indeed, the "feeble resistance in Paris" and the "few minor movements in the provinces" seem to him to have been so insignificant—and clearly only worth a mention—as barely to require repression, except that, the curious argument goes, "unless there were some repression there would hardly have seemed any reason for a coup d'état"! The mystery is that the Second Empire never lived down these trivial events: "Somehow it did not, and even the Emperor never quite put them out of his mind."[12]

John B. Wolf focuses on the fighting in Paris in his brief account, omitting any reference to the reprisals, only mentioning "some scattered opposition" in the provinces, which "a whiff of gun-smoke" put to rights. The coup d'état, he concludes, was "probably a political *necessity*" and in its efficiency "seemed to justify Napoleon's boast that he was the man to end the era of revolutions"—notwithstanding the Commune! In stark con-

---

12. Alfred Cobban, *A History of Modern France,* vol. 2, *From the First Empire to the Second Empire* (Harmondsworth: Penguin, 1961), 158.

trast, Roger Price hardly mentions the "very limited resistance" in Paris and concentrates on the rural uprisings, as does Roger Magraw, who notes that some rebels thought they were revolting to *defend* Louis Napoléon against a royalist coup. Yet the repression, in his somewhat unconventional view, had major political consequences. It showed up the pretense of Louis Bonaparte's populist mask: "The future 'peasant emperor' had come to power by suppressing the largest rural rising in Western Europe in the nineteenth century." Yet, again on the contrary, Robert Gildea, in a chapter on Bonapartism in a recent study, questions other historians' reference to the insurrection in the rural areas of southeast France as signs of popular opposition to the coup d'état. An opposing view is borne out by the support for Louis Napoléon in left-wing areas: "risings in departments such as the Drôme and the Ardèche were *in support* of Louis-Napoleon and against the politicians who were locally trying to frustrate his victory." Indeed, the president's resounding victory in the 20–21 December plebiscite, even allowing for the maneuverings that undoubtedly took place, weighs heavily against any view that the resistance to the coup d'état reflected the will of the nation. Hence the apparent contradiction in Albert Guérard's views on the matter in his *France: A Modern History.* On the one hand, betraying perhaps some native bias, he argues that the events of 4 December transformed what was intended as a "bold appeal to the people" into a "deed of treachery and violence" for which the working classes "never forgave Louis-Napoleon." Yet he must also concede, on the other hand, that the plebiscite was a genuine expression of the opinion of the country: "It was not the use of force that made the *Coup d'Etat* a success: it was the popularity of the President and of his program that made the French condone the fusillade on the Boulevards."[13]

Such brief accounts, though remarkable for their divergences, reveal starkly when taken as a whole, if we can assume that the sample is valid and extensible, the fundamental antinomy of justification/condemnation in which even an apparently objective narrative engages. Furthermore, the so-called massacre on the boulevards and the plebiscite, two apparently

---

13. John B. Wolf, *France, 1814–1919: The Rise of a Liberal-Democratic Society* (New York–Evanston–London: Harper and Row, 1963), 239–40; Roger Magraw, *France 1815–1914: The Bourgeois Century* (New York–Oxford: Oxford University Press, 1986), 154–55; Robert Gildea, *The Past in French History* (New Haven–London: Yale University Press, 1994), 69–70; Albert Guérard, *France: A Modern History,* new ed. (Ann Arbor: University of Michigan Press, 1969), 307–308.

unrelated and contrasting occurrences, reveal an unsuspected equivalency as logical extensions of the essential momentum of the events and the paradoxical equation that they imply. The argument of the perpetrators, supporters and, eventually, acceptors of the coup d'état was one of raison d'état, of *necessity*, of action taken in the particular circumstances to avoid the greater disturbances that supposedly would have arisen if nothing had been done, from the Assembly itself or from the monarchists or from the Mountain or from revolutionary forces in the country, any of which would have caused a civil war. The covert justification was, of course, the advantages of extended powers for Louis Napoléon and his supporters and, despite their immediate show of frustration, for the monarchists the expectation of political gains from an authoritarian regime. The argument of the opponents of the coup d'état was one of principle, of *legality*, as they denounced the violation of the Constitution and condemned Louis Napoléon for breaking the oath which he had sworn to it. The violence of their reaction, however, stemmed to a considerable degree from their resentment at being even further removed from the chance of exercising political power under the new authoritarian regime. The views of both proponents and opponents of the coup d'état are equally suspect, since the one depends on speculation over what might have taken place if it had not occurred, whilst the other, the left-wing view, is based on either the defense of the *status quo* of which the radical republicans were the most vehement critics in any case or on the ideal of a thoroughly democratic or socialist republic which the violated Constitution clearly did not favor. For all the skillful strategy and planning of the perpetrators of the coup d'état, even if a show of force was intended, the "massacre" on the boulevards was the logical outcome of the dynamics of violent action, which takes on a "will" of its own. The orderly deployment of troops on the day, as in a battle, lapsed into the mayhem of slaughter in which responsibility and intentionality dissolve into aleatory impulsiveness. Yet, paradoxically, the gratuitous firing on innocent bystanders served the opposition cause far more than the illegality of the coup d'état itself or the repression of the protesters at the barricades, raising the moral stakes, converting an illegal act into a criminal event. Paradoxically also, the revolt by the deputies of the Mountain and their supporters justified the argument of the Bonapartists that order needed to be established and that "society needed to be saved." In contrast to and, as it turned out, as compensation for the disorder of the violence, the plebiscite was, at least for appearance's sake, an elaborately ordered and orchestrated exercise in democratic choice and deliberation. Whether or not the exchange of ballots for bullets was sufficient atonement is a matter of perception, but the result of the plebiscite totally undermined any claim by the insurgents to represent the will of the nation.

The most notable fuller treatments and discussions of the coup d'état have tended to polarize on these crucial issues. Biographers, betraying, no doubt, their sympathy for the more humane aspects of Louis Napoléon's character and ideas, as well as politicians (leaning to the right), sensitive, no doubt, to the harsh realities of political life, generally support the action as a necessary evil, though acknowledging its illegality. They naturally focus on the immediate circumstances in which it was resolved and emphasize the dangers of alternative scenarios. On the other side, critics of the action, traditionally more numerous in history's own plebiscite on the matter, have tended to be republican historians and writers who consider their pens and ideals to be mightier than the usurper's swords.[14] They, in turn, acknowledge the lack of popular support for the resistance, but focus on the criminality of the event and its bloody consequences, downplaying the extenuating circumstances, as in Hugo's impassioned texts.

One striking exception to the latter tendency, though still in the realm of the summary views, is the series of brief scenes in Flaubert's *L'Éducation sentimentale* in which, at the very end of the novel, the distracted and self-absorbed fictional "hero" wanders into the pages of history to witness the events of 2–4 December, which are presented, of course, in the restricted vision of a novelistic character rather than in the historian's (supposedly) authoritative overview. On the evening of the 3rd, Frédéric Moreau finally shows enough interest in the events to go out onto the streets. Military patrols are dispersing groups of people, but none offers any resistance. When Frédéric asks a worker "Good God! isn't anyone going to fight?" he replies: "We're not so stupid as to get ourselves killed for the sake of the toffs! Let them look after themselves!" And one of the "toffs" (*"bour-*

---

14. As Victor Hugo writes in *The History of a Crime*, with unusual (false) modesty and his usual bombast: "Louis Napoléon has ten thousand cannons, and five hundred thousand soldiers; the writer has his pen and his inkstand. The writer is nothing, he is a grain of dust, he is a shadow, he is an exile without a refuge, he is a vagrant without a passport, but he has by his side and fighting with him two powers, Right, which is invincible, and Truth, which is immortal." Victor Hugo, *The History of a Crime: The Testimony of an Eye-Witness,* trans. T. H. Joyce and Arthur Locker (London: Sampson Low, Marston, Searle and Rivington, 1877–78), 4:190.

geois") looks out of the corner of his eye at the worker, growling "Socialist scum! Perhaps this time we could finish them off for good!" The next day,[15] Frédéric travels to Nogent to seek a chance of happiness with Louise Roque, only to see her coming out of church on the arm of his best friend, the ever resourceful Deslauriers, sporting a prefect's uniform, having rallied to the new regime. Rushing back to Paris in distress, he is just in time to witness the mopping-up operation on the boulevards: "Leaning over their horses' necks, dragoons with drawn swords were galloping along at full speed occupying the whole width of the boulevards; as they rode past, the plumes on their helmets and their large white cloaks billowing behind them stood out against the flare of the gas lamps swirling in the mist. The crowd stood watching in terrified silence."[16] On the steps of the fashionable café Tortoni Frédéric spots the revolutionary Dussardier and watches in horror as a policeman shoots him down when he cries "*Vive la République!*" He then recognizes the policeman, Sénécal, the socialist, who has also gone over to the new regime. Frédéric's political education is now complete.

These brief episodes have more importance within the general framework of the particular novel, as the last throes of the character's political illusions, than they do as a representation of the historical events themselves. But they are a significant form of historical writing. Flaubert did seek to depict the history of the period, with his usual obsessive awareness of the complexity of the task. "What to choose amongst the real facts?" he wrote despairingly to Jules Duplan on 14 March 1868. "I am perplexed; it's so hard." Flaubert's lofty indifference to politics, his aesthetic refusal to express his ideas directly, his scorn for politicians, for political systems and discourses, are legendary. As Jean-Paul Fenaux notes, "Flaubert had understood . . . that one can only write History by not indulging in politics [*en ne faisant pas de politique*]."[17] In Flaubert's version of the episode, though clearly presented in the ironic mode, individual events stand out in stark relief, resisting recuperation into a coherent discourse of

15. In the next episode after the Wednesday, Flaubert writes "*le surlendemain*," which can only be "the day after next" (Thursday) in relation to the coup d'état, which took place on Tuesday, the 2nd of December.

16. Gustave Flaubert, *A Sentimental Education: The Story of a Young Man,* trans. and ed. Douglas Parmée (Oxford–New York: Oxford University Press, 1989), 453–55.

17. Jean-Paul Fenaux, "Roman et histoire: Documents," in *Analyses et réflexions sur Flaubert: "L'Éducation sentimentale": l'histoire* (Paris: Éditions Marketing, 1989), 8.

interpretation. The vision of History that prevails is one of oblique perception, focalized, fragmentary, necessarily incomplete, foregrounding not
resolutions but its inherent unresolvedness. The huge gaps in the novel's
diegesis, the famous blanks in the discourse, the coincidences and the contradictions—a worker refusing to act like a rebellious worker yet perceived
to be one, a republican insurgent shot by a socialist outside a "temple"
of the privileged classes defending the president of a republic ruled by a
Bonapartist conducting a coup d'état led by a group of reactionaries—
resist the foreclosure of interpretation. Flaubert's representation of the
coup d'état is the antithesis of Victor Hugo's, not only because of the lack
of detail in the one and the plethora in the other, not only because of the
relative absence of the author's voice in the one and its overwhelming
presence in the other, but because Flaubert's fractured discourse, haunted
by the fundamental unnarratability and incomprehensibility of history, is
the opposite of Hugo's thundering certainties.

By contrast with these partial portraits of Louis Napoléon the usurper
and the events of the coup d'état, the more substantial historical and literary writings for and against the successful Bonapartist action, of which we
can only analyze a few examples, represent of necessity a retreat from or a
masking of the indeterminacy that Flaubert's text conveys. They do not
necessarily distort the truth, since the truth remains elusive. But to assert
their own validity and impose a coherent view, like Morny's forces in the
field of action, they suppress or ride roughshod over contrapositions. They
are, in Bakhtinian terms, dialogic discourses aspiring to the authority of
monologism.

RAISON D'ÉTAT

One of the most pointed defenses of the coup d'état appears in the correspondence of Charles Auguste Comte de Flahaut de la Billarderie, a man
of impeccable Bonapartist connections. As we have already noted, he had
been the lover of Hortense de Beauharnais, Louis Napoléon's mother, and
had illegitimately fathered by her Auguste de Morny, the future emperor's
half-brother, being himself the illegitimate son by benefit of a clergyman
(at the time), the formidable Talleyrand. His military credentials were no
less impressive: he rode behind Murat when still a boy, rose to the rank of
general at the age of twenty-seven, became Bonaparte's aide-de-camp,

then minister of war during the Hundred Days, accompanied the emperor off the battlefield of Waterloo, and was with him until his final exile.[18] Hence his place of honor in the president's entourage in the less than triumphal ride on 2 December. But Flahaut was also there because he was almost certainly, if only indirectly, party to the coup d'état, as his correspondence reveals. Despite his equally impeccable Orleanist connections, he had rallied like his son to support Louis Napoléon and was staying with Morny at the time of the coup d'état, writing frequently to his wife both as an interested spectator and an aide to Auguste, whose "heroic" actions, along with the "enthusiastic spirit of the army," he extols. "The names of Bonaparte and Napoleon," he gleefully writes on 3 December, "act like magic." His is an upbeat version of events, which he clearly relished. Here is his brief account, written at midnight on the 4th, of what others called a massacre: "Legitimists are found mixed with the *Emeutiers* and shots have been fired from houses of the Boulevard des Italiens, Rue Richelieu, etc. These houses have been broken in by the troops and good execution made. The soldiers are admirable"! He proclaims victory in a telegram later that day. All reference to the brutal repression is conveniently repressed.[19]

Flahaut's reasoned justification for the coup d'état follows immediately, in a long letter of 6 January to his eldest daughter, Lady Emily Shelburne. "It was a tremendous game to play," he writes, "and which necessity alone could justify." He recalls the president's attempts to avoid the action and his own conciliatory role between the president and what he calls the Majority until the quaestors proposal brought matters to a head: "The result would have been civil war between a Presidential and Parliamentary army, the capital and country inundated with blood and the inevitable triumph of the *République démocratique* and *sociale*. It was known also that

18. After Waterloo and a failed attempt to rejoin Queen Hortense in Switzerland, he sought refuge in England, became (ironically) a good friend of Lord William Russell, aide-de-camp of the duke of Wellington, and married in 1817 Margaret Mercer Elphinstone, the daughter of Admiral Lord Keith, after much resistance from her father and from much of the British establishment, for it was Lord Keith who had received Napoleon's surrender and sent him off to St. Helena! Flahaut came to own a castle in Scotland (Tullyallan Castle near Kincardine-on-Forth), became a peer of France under Louis-Philippe, ambassador in Berlin, principal equerry to the duke of Orleans (Louis-Philippe's eldest son), and ambassador in Vienna until 1848.

19. Kerry, ed., *The Secret of the Coup d'Etat,* 122, 124.

on the day that the proposition of the Questeurs was rejected, it had been adopted that the President should be *décrété d'accusation* and sent to Vincennes; and besides that there was a conspiracy in favour of the Prince de Joinville [Louis-Philippe's son], which only wanted an opportunity *pour éclater.*" The theory of the seething plots and the extraordinarily pessimistic prediction on the outcome of civil strife led him to approve "the resolution which has been taken and executed to the satisfaction and joy of all the quiet and honest part of the population." The Panglossian tone of this pragmatist's version of the events slips easily into a convenient relativism as he sermonizes to the English ladies. "For God's sake, my child," he writes, "leave off judging foreign events with English notions." The next day, his wife is urged to read the daughter's letter. "Many energetic measures must be taken," he adds, "and it will be a great pity if the English Government is short-sighted enough to judge of what passes according to English principles and actions. Everything is different—men and things."[20] There is clearly no place for women, especially English women, to meddle in a Frenchman's coup d'état!

Louis Napoléon is noticeably absent as an active figure in this and similar accounts. He only comes to the forefront when Flahaut gives expression to his own and Morny's rapid disaffection with the "leader" of the coup d'état when he confiscated Orleanist properties at the end of January 1852, a measure which prompted Morny to resign. Morny writes to his father on 26 December that the prince "has no real friendship for anyone," that he is "mistrustful and ungrateful, and only likes those who obey him slavishly and flatter him."[21] Louis Napoléon has left no personal account of the adventure, casting a veil of silence over the events and never acknowledging their importance in the various celebrations instituted during the Empire. There does exist, however, a *Récit complet et authentique des événements de Décembre 1851* by Adolphe Granier de Cassagnac, a minor aristocrat, a former Orleanist journalist and a conservative historian, who became a deputy in the Legislative Assembly during the Empire and frequently wrote as a spokesman of the regime.[22] The account is, like Fla-

20. *Ibid.,* 127, 128–29.
21. *Ibid.,* 201–202.
22. The anonymous editor of *The Political and Historical Works of Louis Napoleon Bonaparte* states that the account was commissioned by the president and that Granier de Cassagnac was "a *valet de plume*" in his retinue. He has no doubt that this version of the "atrocities which will remain to history as a monument of disgrace and humiliation to the century in which they occurred" presents the president's own view of the events (332).

haut's, relatively factual and objective until it comes to the events of 3–4 December when, it is claimed, sums of money were paid to the insurgents and handbills inciting people to civil war were seized. On the actions of 4 December, we read this extraordinary statement: "It is melancholy to relate that, notwithstanding the Minister of War's proclamation against the assembling of passengers, or bystanders, several unoffending people fell victims to their curiosity on the boulevards. There, as in the month of February, 1848, the rioters, with diabolical intentions, fired shots close to these groups with the intention of irritating the troops against the inhabitants of the aristocratic parts of the town, and that the populace might appear to be led on by them to retaliate; but, fortunately, the victims were not numerous." By the end of the day of the 6th, all Paris was supposedly rejoicing, the troops were being hailed as heroes, the "evil days were passed." What is more, the report concludes, the "five per cents" have risen by ten francs, an increase of 10 percent, on the markets.[23] What further justification was required!

An abiding theme of the reactionary versions of the events is the accusation of atrocities committed by the Reds in the provinces, who are charged, in Granier de Cassagnac's report, with "imprisoning the authorities," which is hardly surprising, but also with "murdering the soldiers and pillaging the public banks," with destroying property, violating women, even "roasting children alive." Flahaut also, reassured by "rising funds," indulges in extravagant denunciation of the "scoundrels," the "bandits," "the *rogues*" in the provinces: "The papers do not mention the tenth part of the atrocities committed by the insurgents. Schools of young girls violated, women killed after horrid tortures—in short, they are cannibals. . . . This country must be regenerated by an energetic government, for since Napoleon it has been demoralized by weakness."[24] Such charges recall a better-known denunciation of alleged atrocities by the socialists from the pen of a fellow count, Horace de Viel-Castel, a man equally well connected to the Bonapartist traditions, having been a frequent visitor to Malmaison during Louis Napoléon's childhood. His *Mémoires,* which are really a journal, provide insights into the feverish plots and counterplots that preceded the coup d'état and an eyewitness account of the repression,

23. Bernard Adolphe Granier de Cassagnac, *Récit complet et authentique des événements de Décembre 1851* (Paris: Plon, 1851), 377, 380.
24. *Ibid.,* 392; Kerry, ed., *The Secret of the Coup d'Etat,* 139.

about which, given the private nature of the form, he can allow himself to write frankly, as he does of his unmitigated scorn for socialists and Victor Hugo. On 14 December, for example, he writes:

> Socialism is a crime which must be prosecuted just as parricide would be. In eight days, in three or four departments where it could believe itself to have won out for a moment, it has brought about the most monstrous crimes.
>
> Women and young girls have been raped in public, with all the refinements of the vilest forms of lust; some had their throats slit after they had satisfied the depraved desires of the insurgents, transformed into so many *marquis de Sades.*

Socialism, he goes on, is "a scourge that has to be cauterized at all costs"; liberty has become "the right that perverts have acquired to destroy the social state." Louis Napoléon has accomplished "courageously and cleverly the greatest political act of modern times" and is called upon to play the role of "savior of Europe," ready to "march through his century like a bronze figure, inflexible and just, without dangerous pity, with the sword of repression in his hand. This is the price of the salvation of society." To his credit the president and emperor would fail to live up to the count's expectations. Such a naked expression of a right-wing ideology is naturally accompanied by further revelations on the savagery of the insurgents and the cowardice of the bourgeoisie, which had supposedly come to light by 16 December: "At Clamecy, gangs of socialists, who had taken over the town, had dinner served to them and forced thirty-eight of the prettiest and the youngest women and girls of the area to serve them in a state of complete nudity. These wretched victims were raped *coram populo* in the main square. Priests tied to poles were present at these saturnalia; the insurgents took it in turn to rape and every woman became the prey of several of the bandits; in the end, they looked for men with a venereal disease so that they could pass it on to the victims of their brutality." In such a text and its sources, mythical associations between socialism, debauchery, and syphilis run riot in the phantasmal fears of the proponents of a reactionary ideology with as much alacrity as in the more scandalous works of fiction of the time. Tales of sexual excesses are appropriated for political effect, and an illegal act is sanctioned as a moral crusade. Revolutionary opposition becomes a chancre on the body politic, the red peril the symptom of a social infection, the *jacquerie* a *foutoir*. As Alain Minc remarks on

Viel-Castel's version of events: "It is, minus the talent, the exact equivalent, from the winning side, of the horrors imputed by Victor Hugo to the army in *L'Histoire d'un crime*."[25]

L'Histoire d'un crime and *Napoléon le Petit* are clearly the omnipresent "subtexts" or "paratexts," unstated target texts, of much of the later writing in defense of the coup d'état, as is more evidently the case in the titles of books by Éric Leguèbe and Philippe Séguin, *Napoléon III le Grand* and *Louis Napoléon le Grand,* respectively. The former is a remarkable collection of quotations from the works of historians, politicians, memorialists, journalists, that testify in favor of Louis Napoléon, including extracts from Hugo's Bonapartist newspaper of 1848, *L'Événement,* in an attempt to confound the later criticisms. Séguin's book is a more reasoned and far more impressive vindication, in which he initially seeks to demonstrate that the coup d'état, "an illegal act, of course," was inevitably inscribed in the elections of 10 December 1848 and in the crises emanating from—to use a more modern expression—the "cohabitation" of a president and a hostile Assembly with little in common and conflicting views of the future. He argues that the reality of the event is far more complex than history's verdict has led us to believe. He bases his defense of Louis Napoléon on what he considers to be four irrefutable facts (but which invite refutation): (1) the coup d'état was the only possible outcome from a constitutional and political deadlock [*"blocage"*] that only Louis Napoléon sought by legal means to avoid (but he undoubtedly contributed to that deadlock himself); (2) the coup d'état was accomplished in the name of universal suffrage (though Louis Napoléon's support of the principle could be interpreted as a measure to favor the coup); (3) it was ratified by an immense majority of Frenchmen (who, as Hugo points out, had in fact little choice, since there was no alternative to Louis Napoléon to vote for); (4) few perpetrators of a coup d'état have treated their adversaries with such humanity, even "kindness" (a view not likely to be shared by those who were imprisoned, shot, and deported).

Central to Séguin's thesis is the view that Louis Napoléon was a conscientious and compassionate politician compelled by circumstances to act badly and to cause others to do so. The contrary thesis, with its echoes of

25. Horace de Viel-Castel, *Mémoires du comte Horace de Viel Castel sur le règne de Napoléon III, 1851–1864* (Paris: Guy Le Prat, 1979), 111, 112–13; Alain Minc, *Louis Napoléon revisité* (Paris: Gallimard, 1997), 42.

Hugo's overcharged remonstrances, is much easier to confound than his own is to defend, given the lack of evidence about the president's personal motives: "At the very least, whatever judgment is inflicted upon Louis Napoléon's initiative, let us get rid of the legend of a gallant little Republic, humanistic, social and democratic, destroyed by a wicked conspirator; let us finally put to rest the fiction according to which the Republic of February fell beneath the blows of Louis Napoléon."[26] The long demonstration of the parliamentary struggles during the years 1848–1851, however coherently convincing it may seem, requires the reader to believe that Louis Napoléon has no ulterior motives. We are back to the major problem of Napoleon III historiography: sounding out the intentionality of this enigmatic political figure in a world where sincerity is either suspect as a ploy or, if successful, the ultimate ploy. Mythical constructs fill the void left by the lack of testimony. For Séguin, Louis Napoléon was, in the circumstances, a paragon of good intentions; for Hugo, he was Machiavel reincarnate. The sympathetic view naturally deprives the president of any real agency in the coup d'état.

Thus, to take another example, in Fernand Giraudeau's biography, *Napoléon III intime,* after quoted statements by Louis Napoléon on his noble mission, the subject is eclipsed from the scene: "On all sides, the necessity of a violent solution was understood; and, on all sides, preparation was made. A coup d'état became imperative."[27] The impersonal mode and the inanimate subject significantly occult human volition and again abstract the president from the scene of action. For Séguin, however, there is an equally significant substitute agency. "The main architect of the coup d'état, and perhaps its true originator, will be Morny." As for the "massacre," there is almost total dispensation:

> Yet the whole business will take a bad turn. The toll in Paris will be terrible: six hundred dead.
>
> Louis Napoléon has probably nothing to do with it. But his doubts will turn into remorse.[28]

Morny and Saint-Arnaud, then, are blamed for the strategy that led to the bloody event, but Louis Napoléon was to bear the burden of guilt. As for

26. Séguin, *Louis Napoléon le Grand,* 133.
27. Fernand Giraudeau, *Napoléon III intime* (Paris: Paul Ollendorf, 1895), 137.
28. Séguin, *Louis Napoléon le Grand,* 159, 166. The figure is clearly inflated. On the next page, Séguin has 200 soldiers killed. He seems to have counted as the number of dead the usual figure given for the wounded.

the repression in the provinces, a new agency intervenes, France herself, as the coup d'état is presented as merely a pretext for a new White Terror against the Reds (but on whose orders?). "In reality," Séguin claims, "the heart of France [*la France profonde*] turns in hate against a part of itself." And the compassionate Louis Napoléon did his utmost, from March 1852 to the decree of August 1859, to amnesty prisoners and exiles. As for the referendum, Séguin argues, if the coup d'état were a crime, then the majority of the French themselves were the president's accomplices (though, one might object, the plebiscite was not precisely on the coup d'état). Séguin adds with an irony that is directed no doubt at the Hugolians: "We can find all this regrettable, incomprehensible, distressing, deplorable, unbelievable, but there it is: at the time, the electorate did not wish to give the republicans a majority. Tired of the internal divisions, it called for Louis Napoléon."[29]

Séguin ends his chapter "The Author of the Coup d'État" on a rare and typically terse and illusive statement about the events of December 1851 by Louis Napoléon himself, who declared in a speech on hearing the results of the plebiscite: "France has understood that I only abandoned legality to do what was right [*pour rentrer dans le droit*]. More than seven million votes have just absolved me."[30] Taken at face value, the statement is contradictory. If "what was right," as is implied, is a higher form of legitimacy than "legality," there is no need for absolution. Séguin suggests, by way of explanation, as he has consistently attempted to show in his study of the coup d'état "that perhaps the president was less guilty than he believed himself to be."[31] Or perhaps, on the contrary, he was guilty of more than his mere espousal of "what was right" could exempt and required the exoneration of the vote to share the guilt amongst ten million voters. Histories inevitably confront such quandaries of interpretation when they depart from the facts, and when literature leaps in to fill the void. Victor Hugo, indifferent to such fine distinctions, at least in this regard, came rushing in with pen flailing when other means had failed him.

29. *Ibid.,* 168, 176.
30. The prince's speech, as it appears in volume 3 of the *Oeuvres de Napoléon III,* is slightly different and more explicit than Séguin's extract: "*La France a répondu à l'appel loyal que je lui avais fait. Elle a compris que je n'étais sorti de la légalité que pour rentrer dans le droit. Plus de sept millions de suffrages viennent de m'absoudre en justifiant un acte qui n'avait d'autre but que d'épargner à notre patrie, et à l'Europe peut-être, des années de troubles et de malheurs.*" *Oeuvres de Napoléon III* (Paris: Plon, 1856–69), 3:282.
31. Séguin, *Louis Napoléon le Grand,* 178.

chapter 2

Histories II: VICTOR HUGO versus louis napoléon

NAPOLÉON LE PETIT

With all the authority of his position as the leading French writer of his time, Victor Hugo roundly, massively, and magnificently pilloried the deeds of Louis Napoléon and his "bandits" in one of the most sustained polemics of all time, all the more effective in that the victim seemed to have been reduced to silence, though, given his legendary taciturnity and secretiveness, the victim would never in all probability have replied to a lesser work and his silence was perhaps his own most effective and rhetorical response. The official newspapers did report, however, on 23 August 1852, the future emperor's reaction on being presented, at Saint-Cloud, with a copy of *Napoléon le Petit:* "Look, gentlemen, here's *Napoleon the Little,* by Victor Hugo the Great." Hugo, who was furious at his enemy's dry wit, incorporated the anecdote into his poem "L'Homme a ri" (in *Châtiments*), seeking to take his revenge, poetically.

In general, Hugo's excoriation of Louis Napoléon and of those who abetted him in the coup d'état takes on a variety of forms: narratives (first and third person), portraits, dialogues, sketches, documents, lists, essays, and, of course, poems of various types, tones, meters, in which the prose forms and themes recur in verse within the specifically prosodic arrangements. All this in three works: *Napoléon le Petit* (*Napoleon the Little*) (1852), *Histoire d'un crime* (*The History of a Crime*) (1877–78), and *Châtiments* (1853). Most of the substance of these three works was written in a frenzy of indignation during the first two years of the poet's exile, between the date of his arrival in Brussels on 12 December 1851 and October 1853, by which time he was in Jersey.[1] Despite the remoteness of their publication dates, *Napoléon le Petit* and *Histoire d'un crime* are the most closely linked of the texts in their genesis and form and should be treated together as "historical" rather than poetical compositions. The former, a much shorter text, evolved out of the failed attempt by Hugo to obtain a commitment from London publishers to take on a work to be called *Le Crime du Deux-Décembre*, which had grown out of a first project to write what he had called "Faits et gestes du 2 décembre" and which had also grown out of proportion as new documentary evidence accrued to the author in the form of eyewitness accounts from participants in the resistance to the coup d'état. *Histoire d'un crime* remained unpublished until the political crisis of the Third Republic of 1877, when President MacMahon threatened to engineer a monarchist coup d'état, which prompted Hugo to bring out the first volume as a reminder of past offenses, combining material from the period 1852–53 with recent additions. Hence the seemingly ridiculous contrast between the epigraph of the book ("This work is more than opportune; it is imperative. I publish it") and the author's note at the beginning of the first volume: "This work was written twenty-six years ago at Brussels, during the first months of exile."

All three texts deal obsessively with the same themes: the iniquities of the coup d'état, the inadequacies of its main perpetrator, the illegality of the violation of the Constitution, the heinous defilement of the Republic. As their titles suggest, the three works, though they cover the same ground, are generically different, with a marked progression in literariness from text to text. *Napoléon le Petit* is more of a political pamphlet, with its heated tone, its *ad hominem* attacks, its virulent and sarcastic ripostes to recent actions, in short a "cry," as Hugo defined it. *Histoire d'un crime* is

---

1. Hugo claimed to have written *Napoléon le Petit* between 14 June and 12 July 1852. He moved to Jersey on 5 August 1852, then to Guernsey on 31 October 1855.

a more structured work, with historical pretensions, though the bias is evident in the title. "The exile immediately became an historian," as the author claims.[2] The *Châtiments* transpose the same material onto the more elevated plane of poetic expression, refining the polemics and aestheticizing the satire.

Napoléon le Petit, published in Belgium under the imprint of a London publisher, W. Jeffs, on 8 August 1852, was intended for immediate consumption and for immediate political effect, for it appeared in two formats: a normal sized for sales in Belgium and other foreign countries, a much smaller version for smuggling into France, as indeed it was, hidden in baggy pockets, boots, sleeves, false heels, hollow walking-sticks, ladies' corsets, or rolled up loose-leaf in cigars, and even, according to Alexandre Dumas, concealed in plaster-cast busts of Louis Napoléon himself.[3] Hugo's overt aim in castigating the leader of the coup d'état was to shake the French out of the torpor which, "for a nation, is shame." "Yes, men will awaken!" he confidently predicts, then "will the last hour toll!" for France will recoil in horror at his revelations, at "the monstrous crime which had dared to espouse her in the darkness, and of which she has shared the bed."[4] There is little evidence that many of the French were in fact stirred from their beds or lost any sleep because of this work, though it is easy for the modern reader to underestimate the effect of such a text when the issues have been long resolved and the passions long spent. Nevertheless, despite the success of this polemical work in sales and clandestine distribution, it is unlikely to have converted many of the huge numbers who voted for Louis Napoléon in the plebiscite or many of the foreign readers to whom it is also addressed. In general, the more intemperate a polemical work is, the more likely it is to please the converted, and the

2. Victor Hugo, *Histoire d'un crime,* in *Oeuvres complètes: Histoire,* ed. Sheila Gaudon (Paris: Robert Laffont, 1987), vii. Page references for the two texts under discussion are taken from this edition, with the English versions of quotations based on the nineteenth-century translations: *Napoleon the Little* (London: Vizetelly, 1852) and *The History of a Crime* (1877–78).

3. See Robb, *Victor Hugo,* 320–22, who lists the numerous foreign-language editions of Hugo's "best-seller," including two translations issued in Mexico. The first edition published in France (by Hetzel) came out, not surprisingly, in December 1870, a month after the fall of the empire.

4. Hugo, *Napoléon le Petit,* in *Oeuvres complètes: Histoire,* ed. Sheila Gaudon (Paris: Robert Laffont, 1987), 22.

less likely it is to convince the waverers. Hugo's own rhetorical excesses inevitably lead one to suspect that they stem from an almost self-indulgent venting of the spleen from a position of angered and frustrated impotence, or, more intriguingly, from a desire to settle accounts with an enemy who represents more than a political opponent.

Not that, beneath the bombast and bile, Hugo does not make some valid points and create some impressive effects. The work begins with an evocative scene, recreating the ceremony of 20 December 1848, when Citizen Charles Louis Napoléon Bonaparte swore to uphold the Constitution, and contrasts it with the decree of 2 December 1851 that dissolved the Assembly and violated this oath with an act, which, as Hugo claims in a first stretch of logic for rhetorical effect, abolished *all* legality in France and sanctioned theft, swindling, fraud, banditry, murder, since the crime in question "contains within itself all crimes." There is also in Book 1 a potted biography and a satirical portrait of Louis Napoléon which, compared to what follows, are relatively restrained, for the rhythm of this work, and an aspect of its rhetorical effect, is its mounting indignation. He is compared unfavorably with other ambitious conquerors from Nimrod to Napoleon I, but his ambitions, Hugo argues, are paltry by comparison, for the usurper aspires not after a vast empire but only wants horses and girls for his pleasures and to be called "monseigneur." With heavy irony Hugo declares that "the great talent de M. Louis Bonaparte is silence," a trait, no doubt, as infuriating to the voluble poet and orator as his crimes and a source of the writer's antagonism. Irksome too for Hugo is the huge disparity between such an insignificant man and his great success, which is attributed by Hugo to his craftiness and corruptness. Subsequent books denounce the new constitution, the financial dealings of the new regime, the muzzling of the press, the corrupt legal and administrative systems, which serve the ends of this pathetic little man, "who kills, who deports, who banishes, who expels, who proscribes, who despoils; this man with harassed gesture and glassy eye, who walks with a distracted air in the midst of the horrible things which he does, like a sort of sinister somnambulist." He exploits priests and soldiers with his "*jésuitisme*" and his "*caporalisme*"; his socialism is phony and his power is protected and assured by the police. The new police chief, Piétri, even wants to raise a marble statue to the leader—an occasion for Hugo to show off his wit with some Latin puns, likely to baffle far more of his readers than amuse the few with sufficient Latin (or an annotated edition) to understand them: "*Tu es PIE-TRI et super hanc pietram oedificabo effigiem meam.*"[5]

As the text gains pace, the learned, historical, and literary references abound, along with a flow of rhetorical flourishes, particularly after the central parts, which narrate *the* crime itself. All is blamed directly on M. Bonaparte, who periodically appears on the scene to demand that his orders be obeyed. Historical precedents are again invoked to provide a measure of the enormity of Louis Napoléon's crimes: "Crassus had crushed the gladiators; Herod had slaughtered the infants; Charles IX had exterminated the Huguenots; Peter of Russia, the Strelitz; Mehemet Ali, the Mamelukes; Mahmoud, the Janissaries; while Danton had massacred the prisoners. Louis Napoleon had just discovered a new sort of massacre—the massacre of the passers-by." A further blacklist of historical monsters is trotted out to condemn the repression: "if he did not scourge women on the breasts, *testibusque viros,* like Ferdinand of Toledo; if he did not break on the wheel, burn alive, boil alive, skin alive, crucify, impale, and quarter, blame him not, the fault was not his; the age would not allow him. He has done all that was humanly and inhumanly possible. . . . Louis Bonaparte has equalled in cruelty his contemporaries, Haynau, Radetzky, Filangieri, Schwarzenberg, and Ferdinand of Naples; he has even surpassed them."[6]

Such odious comparisons add nothing to the reader's understanding of the events, though a number of sections of the work make telling points: the fear of the "red peril" ["*spectre rouge*"] was totally unfounded, as was the fear of disorder in 1852, when there would have been democratic elections and no revolution; the *jacquerie* of December 1851 was a myth; the tribune, abolished by Louis Napoléon, and parliamentarianism, now destroyed, were the glory of France—surely a dubious claim in view of the Assembly's record; the plebiscite provided no alternative to Louis Napoléon and was invalid as a democratic exercise. But, obsessively, at the end of each section, Hugo comes back to the insults, drawing upon the full repertoire of invective with all its figures, rhetorical, historical, mythical. "Ah! Frenchmen," he urges his compatriots, after invoking the glories of

5. *Ibid.,* 17, 57, 72. The quotation reads (in French) "*Tu es Piétri et sur cette piètre chose je bâtirai mon effigie*"; (in English) "You are Piétri and on this paltry thing I shall build my effigy." See Matthew 16.

6. Hugo, *Napoléon le Petit,* 116, 136.

the uncle, "look at this hog wallowing in his own slime on a lion's skin."
Monsieur Louis Bonaparte, he claims, is "perhaps"—a generous conces-
sion!—the only man in the whole of humanity without any notion of good
and evil. Then he becomes Nero reincarnate: "I cry now, and, doubt it
not, the universal conscience of humanity repeats it with me: Louis Bonaparte has assassinated France! Louis Bonaparte has killed his mother."
God, we are to believe, was marching forward with the century when
Louis Napoléon, "plume on head," stopped him in his tracks. But there
is an obscure light burning in the darkness, that nothing will extinguish.
"The flame will continue to burn upwards, straight and pure, towards
Heaven." The lamp is Conscience. The flame is the flame which "illumes,
in the night of exile, the paper on which the poet writes." There is a
mighty voice in the shadows, the voice of France, the voice of the universal
conscience of humanity, the voice of parliament, which has opened up the
radiant skies of the future, bringing down the blind and fearful despotisms
of the past and ushering in the apocalyptical, "hypertropic" vision of the
poet: "her feet upon the clouds, her bright forehead lost amongst the
stars, a sword gleaming in her hand, her large wings opened in the skies . . .
the Archangel Liberty—the Archangel of the People."[7] Typically, Hugo
himself, antithetically, has taken on the noble, heroic role in the epic, cos-
mic, mythical, but no longer historical, struggle against the mighty tyrant
that Louis Napoléon has become in the poet's imagination.

As if all this is not enough, Hugo extends the allegorization further into
biblical territory, making of Louis Napoléon the crucifier of the French nation, which becomes, of course, "the Christ of peoples." He is, then, the
wretched soldier who plunged his lance into the savior's side and made
him utter "his last cry: *Eli! Eli! Lama Sabachthani*" ("My God! My God!
Why hast thou forsaken me?"). But the logic of this process of mythifica-
tion, which is also a mystification, requires a redemptive turn of events to
match the dramatic turns of phrase:

> All is now finished. The French nation is dead. The great tomb
> is about to open.
> For three days.

As if, in Hugo's vision, which transposes particular historical events into a
vast mythical scenario and by its excesses lays bare the process by which
the literary mind preys upon the turmoil of history to reinvest its fables,

7. *Ibid.*, 146, 182, 188, 155.

the very magnitude of the evil that has been evoked requires the counter-balance of a glorious solution. "The 2nd of December has succeeded," he is amazingly led to write, "because, and I repeat it, in more than one sense, and from more than one point of view, it was good that it should succeed. . . . Louis Bonaparte had committed the crime, and Providence has brought about the event." The rhetoric of imprecation and denunciation gives way to a rhetoric of glorification and exaltation. In yet another fable appropriated for the occasion, Hugo presents Louis Napoléon as "the mute of Providence," by whose services, like the sultan to his viziers, according to the legend, Providence sends the cord with which evil institutions destroy themselves. Then, in Hugo's cosmorama, History intervenes to mock and strike down the clown.[8] Finally, in a long and passionate hosanna to Progress, Hugo proclaims the glorious march of Humanity towards the sovereignty of the citizen, respecting the inviolability of Life, crowning the People and sanctifying Man.

As it turns out, therefore, so it seems, the coup d'état was not such a bad thing after all! Hugo's boundless mythopoeic imagination has turned a rather sordid historical event into a fable of redemption, imposing a grandiose, imaginative order onto the contingencies of political conflict and completely burying the overt political aim of the text with his overindulgence in his visionary providentiality. It is tempting to conclude that, unwittingly, Hugo has undermined the initial purpose and effect of his text with his reassuring conclusion. But there is a logical equivalence in the contradiction, the logic of excess, whereby exorbitant vituperation and inordinate wishful thinking reveal themselves as the two sides of the same outburst of frustration at the impotency of defeat. In the process, the small man who waited fearfully in the Élysée Palace for news of the uncertain outcome of the chain of events that he had set in motion and would respond to Hugo's calumnies with nothing more than a tame witticism, is magnified into a purely mythical figure, a mighty tyrant, the pinnacle of evil, the criminal of criminals. Napoleon the Little has become Napoleon the Enormous.

HISTOIRE D'UN CRIME

Given Hugo's propensity for overstatement and overreaction, it is not surprising perhaps that in such a highly charged polemical work as *Napoléon*

8. *Ibid.*, 237, 206, 214, 216.

le Petit the author should depart from the facts and allow the rhetoric, inspired by what he calls in *Châtiments* the "Muse Indignation," to preclude any serious consideration to a narrative of events. There is, for example, no attempt to describe the circumstances that led to the coup d'état, just a huge leap between the oath-swearing scene of December 1848 and the "crimes" three years later, which would seem to have sprung up by the mere exercise of Louis Napoléon's evil volition. It is, however, somewhat surprising that this should also fundamentally be the case in *Histoire d'un crime,* supposedly a work with a serious historical purpose and based on a mass of testimonial evidence. Once again the crucial period between 1848 and 1851, which Marx, along with other eminent opponents of the imperial regime, would explore in great detail, is largely eclipsed. For reasons which deserve some consideration, however speculative it might be, Hugo chooses to ignore the prehistory of the "crime" and focus on the crucial four days of action, 2–4 December, in a kind of diary of events written in four books with each stage bearing a title indicating the essential phases of the conflict: "The Ambush" ("Le Guet-Apens"), "The Struggle" ("La Lutte"), "The Massacre" ("Le Massacre"), "The Victory" ("La Victoire").

During the three years prior to these events, Hugo underwent a significant political development, which he perhaps did not wish to be recalled. He had been made a peer of France under the July Monarchy, much to the scorn of the republicans. But by the time the new republic was in place, he had abandoned the legitimist cause and had run for election in the new Assembly in June 1848, ironically at the same round of balloting that got Louis Napoléon elected. Whereas the latter resigned his seat and, as we have seen, missed any involvement in the June Days repression, Hugo was very much involved on the side of the government, against the insurgents, in a role that was the total reverse of his part in the latter events as described in *Histoire d'un crime.* By then the son of one of the first emperor's generals and the author of the famous ode "A la Colonne de la Place Vendôme" (1827) had also become an eloquent and ardent supporter of the so-called myth of Napoleon I and gave his endorsement to the nephew's presidential candidacy, founding a Bonapartist newspaper with his sons, *L'Événement.* He was even fascinated, or "hypnotized," as it has been claimed, by Louis Napoléon, bedazzled by his name if not by his person, and temporarily convinced of the sincerity of his ideas on the extinction of poverty. But he became progressively disillusioned by conservative policies on the Roman question, on the issue of relief of the plight of the poor and, more generally, on the president's accommodations with the conservatives, for Hugo was moving to the left and by 1850 was speaking against the president from the Mountain. With his son Charles in prison for an editorial opposed to capital punishment, his attacks became more personal, notably in the famous speech of 17 July 1851, in which he evokes the glories of Charlemagne and Napoleon I all the better to introduce, for the first time, his legendary put-down: "You want to take into your little hands this sceptre of Titans, this sword of giants! What for? What! after Augustus, Augustulus! What! Because we have had Napoleon the Great, must we have Napoleon the Little!"[9]

On the day of the coup d'état Hugo was amongst the group of left-wing deputies who met secretly in the rue Blanche, urging them to take up arms. Less impetuous colleagues, aware of the likely lack of support from the workers, advised caution, and it was decided to resort to propaganda to stir up reaction. Hugo became one of the active leaders of the resistance, rushing around Paris, tearing down government posters, attending impromptu meetings, inspecting barricades, drafting counter-proclamations, and avoiding arrest—for which he had an uncanny knack. On the 3rd he arrived at the barricade of the faubourg Saint-Antoine just in time to see Baudin's body being carried away. The next day he arrived on the boulevards just after the massacre—he seemed also to have a remarkable knack for arriving late for the action!—but did witness the horrific aftermath. When further resistance proved to be futile, he went into hiding with the help of his resourceful mistress, Juliette Drouet. She obtained for him a passport in the name of a worker, Jacques Lanvin, in whose guise Hugo fled to Belgium on the night train to Brussels on the 11th of December.

All this and much more is narrated with remarkable vividness and verve in *Histoire d'un crime,* where Hugo applies all his talent as a skillful and dramatic novelist, combined with a good share of inventiveness, in recreating lived experience, *"choses vues,"* to use one of Hugo's favorite expressions. But the poet is also writing on behalf of a collectivity, giving a voice to other republican participants in the events, who came to visit him in

9. Elliott M. Grant, *Victor Hugo during the Second Republic,* Smith College Studies in Modern Languages, vol. 17 (Northampton, Mass.: Smith College, 1935), 25; Elliott M. Grant, *The Career of Victor Hugo* (Cambridge, Mass.: Harvard University Press, 1946), 157.

exile or sent him documents. Their depositions fill out the poet's own narrative, as the substantial "Cahier complémentaire" reveals.[10] Thus, within the diurnal divisions of the temporal structure of the text, the essential rhythm and tension of this work derive from the centrifugal intervention of different voices, points of view, episodes, directed by the centripetal, overarching narrative viewpoint of Hugo himself, who constantly shifts from being one of many participants in the events to adopting the roles of judge, commentator, historian, narrator, imaginative writer. With its mass of documentary evidence, the work is presented as historical truth, but the guiding inspiration and sometimes heavy hand of the writer are equally in evidence. Like a realist novel, this text invites a dual reading: one in which the inventiveness animates the factual narrative and descriptions or one in which the "*choses vues*" merely serve to authenticate a fundamentally fictional construct.

The narrator/historian, then, has a dual function: participant and spectator, actor and playwright. In the culminating episode, in "The Massacre," the narrator also defines his role in more providential terms:

> I reached the boulevard; the scene was indescribable. I witnessed this crime, this butchery, this tragedy. I saw that rain of blind death, I saw the distracted victims fall around me in crowds. It is for this that I have signed myself in this book AN EYEWITNESS.
>
> Destiny entertains a purpose. It watches mysteriously over the future historian. It allows him to mingle with exterminations and carnage; but it does not permit him to die, because it wishes him to relate them.[11]

Hugo was almost certainly in far less danger than he either thought or wished his readers to think, but he had an acute sense of the dramatic effect. If he could not be a martyr, he could still be a hero.

The narrative of Hugo's own involvement in the action of the coup d'état reads like a Romantic adventure novel or one of his own Romantic plays. All is dramatic gestures, stagy postures, ceremonious phrases. Early on the first morning of the coup d'état, for example, the "intrepid" Colonel Carini arrives at Hugo's home, "one of those Italians who love France as we Frenchmen love Italy." "Every warm-hearted man in this century

---

10. See Hugo, *Histoire d'un crime*, 468–589.
11. *Ibid.*, III, 156–57.

has two fatherlands," Hugo sententiously adds, "the Rome of yesterday and the Paris of to-day." (Ironically, much the same could have been said of Louis Napoléon!) Carini has assessed the situation. "If fighting takes place," he declares, "it will be desperate work." The no less intrepid Hugo replies: "There will be fighting." Then, with a flourish, he adds, "laughing, 'You have proved that colonels write like poets; now it is the turn of the poets to fight like colonels'." The swashbuckling poet enters his wife's bedroom to inform her of the situation; she is peacefully reading the newspaper in bed:

> She turned pale, and said to me, "What are you going to do?"
> "My duty."
> She embraced me, and only said two words:—
> "Do it."

Such is Hugo's charisma that, on the way out in the rue Blanche, four workers are inspired to go off to defend the Republic. He meets Michel de Bourges:

> Michel said to me,—
> "Hugo, what will you do?"
> I answered him,—
> "Everything."

In the streets, a crowd surrounds him, crying " *Vive Victor Hugo!*" He modestly urges them to cry " *Vive la constitution!*" The narrative proceeds with the pace and suspense of a thriller, as if the outcome were still undetermined. It is as if Hugo were writing a historical novel in the manner of Dumas *père*, as, for example, in the scene in which the mysterious Madame K. appears on the boulevard and exchanges a few words with a general. Is this a latter-day Lady de Winter who has wandered into Hugo's text? "She could, according to the side of her beauty which fascinated her victim, inspire either heroism or crime. This strange beauty was compounded of the whiteness of an angel, combined with the look of a spectre."[12] Indeed, in Hugo's narrative, all is heroism or crime.

Other heroic spirits, of course, rise to the occasion, though the poet's verbal effects do not always do justice to their actions. The narrative of the "massacre" itself in particular is framed and presented by such bathetic ef-

12. *Ibid.,* I: 58, 59, 60, 72, 84; III: 137.

fects that it would make a fine anthology piece of fictional writing. The crucial chapter begins:

> Suddenly a window was opened.
> Upon Hell.
> Dante, had he leaned over the summit of the shadow, would have been able to see in Paris the eighth circle of his poem; the funereal Boulevard Montmartre.
> Paris, a prey to Bonaparte; a monstrous spectacle.

Far from narrating the events as the historian he claimed to be, Hugo allows himself to employ a whole battery of poetic figures, including the favorite Hugolian devices of personification, antithesis, and mythical allusion, as if some ancient drama were being played out in the streets of Paris:

> The Fury, Justice, halted petrified before the Fury, Extermination. Against Erinnyes they set up Medusa.
> To put Nemesis to flight, what a terrible triumph! To Louis Bonaparte pertains this glory, which is the summit of his shame.
> Let us narrate it.
> Let us narrate what History had never seen before.
> The assassination of a people by a man.[13]

Hugo's breathless narrative relishes its own grandiloquence with an exorbitant display of self-indulgence beyond the requirements of the exercise. A rather sordid, messy, brutal event, the likes of which history produces with deplorable regularity, is transformed into a Titanic confrontation of epic proportions. Clearly, the discourse is on a far grander plane than the action that it evokes would seem to warrant.

But the type of literary creation that Hugo's account most clearly espouses is the melodrama. The effect of decontextualizing the coup d'état from its political causes and prehistory is not only to present it as an almost spontaneous irruption of evil, but also to abolish the continuity of history, creating the frame for and conditions in which the literary conventions can function. The coup d'état has become exclusively the work of the evil genius, whom Hugo significantly calls a "parodist" after his ridiculous failure in Boulogne and his emulation of the *18 brumaire*, within the standard manicheistic structure of melodrama. In this text narrative history is

13. *Ibid.*, III: 142, 144.

poured into the crucible of the Romantic vision of the dramatic poet, becoming an episode in the universal struggle between evil and virtue, with the bathos of suffering and defeat and the elation and release of its providential ending, in which right prevails after the drama of the unpredictable struggle between the two opposing forces. There is a complete set of the *dramatis personae* of melodrama: the "courageous" and "valiant" workers, victims of the "bandits" and of the evil villain, the diabolized Louis Napoléon, suitably blackened in character, unflatteringly described in the Élysée consulting with his henchmen and cavorting with women—"Treason and debauchery went hand in hand"—with the mysterious Madame K. again making an appearance: a Russian blonde, "absolutely charming and terrifying." Always given to aggrandized effects, Hugo exaggerates the extent of the slaughter, whilst pretending not to do so: "Crime sometimes boasts of its blackness." He quotes as authoritative a witness who claimed to have seen more than 800 corpses on the boulevards. He later writes about mass executions of insurgents after 3 December, for example, 336 shot in one incident on the Champ de Mars with blood running in the gutters for days and wagons full of corpses transported to the Montmartre cemetery dripping blood along the route.[14] The heroes are those who manned the barricades, died like Baudin or were arrested or escaped into exile, with Hugo chief amongst them. The tormented innocent is the Republic herself, defiled by the usurper, but redeemed in the end.

In a final "act" of the volume, entitled "The Fall" ("La Chute"), Hugo describes in lyrical terms his own return from exile across the fields of Sedan, where, with his vivid imagination, he seemed to see "waving over this valley the flashing of the avenging angel's sword," the angel who, in fact, seems to have made extraordinarily frequent apparitions for the benefit of the poet. Inevitably he interprets the defeat of Sedan as the logical outcome of the "monstrous adventure of 2 December," as a "syllogism which is completed; a formidable premeditation of destiny." Like a melodrama Hugo's text combines, conventionally and conveniently, the tension and excitement of a simulated uncertain outcome with the reassurance that all was predetermined by Providence for the good. History has a habit of falling neatly into well-ordered patterns for Hugo. The capitulation at Sedan, which he describes, leaping nineteen years with no concern

14. *Ibid.*, III: 26, 27, 158; IV: 37.

for what happened in between, provides him with the perfect denouement for his historical drama: "That which was knitted together on the 2nd of December, 1851, came apart on the 2nd of September 1870; the carnage on the Boulevard Montmartre and the capitulation of Sedan are, we maintain, the two parts of a syllogism; logic and justice have the same balance; it was Louis Bonaparte's dismal destiny to begin with the black flag of massacre, and to end with the white flag of disgrace."[15]

For a man who had lived through the siege of Paris, had witnessed the Commune, and in 1877 was still involved in the uncertain political life of the Third Republic, there is an extraordinary definitiveness about the conclusion of *Histoire d'un crime,* which has been clearly arranged to balance the abrupt and dramatic *incipit* of the work, like a novel or drama beginning *in medias res* and working through its crises to the euphoric ending. Before embarking upon his rhapsodic eulogy of France and his utopian prediction of harmony amongst the United Peoples of Europe (just as, ironically, Louis Napoléon had done), Hugo meditates upon the lessons of Sedan, which neatly ties up for him the plot of History: "No expiation can be compared with this. The unprecedented drama was in five acts, so fierce that Aeschylus himself would not have dared to dream of them. 'The Ambush!,' 'The Struggle!,' 'The Massacre!,' 'The Victory!,' 'The Fall!' What a plot and what a denouement! A poet who would have predicted it would have seemed a traitor. God alone could permit Himself Sedan."[16] The agitations and uncertainties of history have been neatly packaged into the inherited generic mold of Romantic drama. The characters, larger than life, have been allotted their programmatic roles. The genres are mixed, as befitted the art of a new age; the unities of time and place have been appropriately disregarded, but the unity of action is rigorously applied. Gestures are demonstrative, passions exhilarating, the motivating forces dark and mysterious, the rhetoric overwhelming, and the ideology glaringly transparent. Is it literature posturing as history or Clio cavorting on the stage?

But what is perhaps more remarkable than the literary flourishes of the Olympian genius, even as he purports to write history, or the absolute confidence with which he reduces to the antithetical structures of his art the complexities and indeterminacies of historical events is the less clearly ex-

15. *Ibid.,* IV: 222, 214, 225–26.
16. *Ibid.,* IV: 237.

hibited personal investment of the author himself in the scenarios that he designs and the emphatic manner in which he presents them. Hugo doth protest too much, the reader is inclined to think, not only too much to be convincing but also in excess of the gravity of the events. In the chapter "Page écrite à Bruxelles," he reveals the degree of his revilement felt for Louis Napoléon, as he swears to fight him, defy him, destroy him: "I have only one stone in my sling, but that stone is a good one; that stone is Justice. . . . Let Louis Bonaparte know that an Empire may be taken, but that a Conscience cannot be taken."[17] Such *cris de coeur* reveal not only the depths of his hate for the usurper but also his fascination, even obsession with his opponent, for, by the time he published this text, Napoleon III had been dead for four years, yet he did not see fit to eliminate the threats. On this matter there is a revealing account of one of Hugo's table-tipping seances at Marine House in 1853 on the island of Jersey, when Hugo even calls up the spirit of his enemy whilst he is still alive (but, supposedly, asleep and dreaming at the time). Hugo engages in this extraordinary exchange:

> Who are you?
> Bonaparte.
> The great?
> No.
> The little, then. The one they call Napoleon III?
> Yes.
> Ah! wretch, I've got you. Who sends you?
> My uncle.
> Why?
> To be punished.
> . . . .
> What is your feeling toward me?
> Hatred and respect.[18]

As this anecdote suggests, it is as much the opposition between the two figures that is significant as Hugo's antipathy for the political leader, together with a kind of fraternal enmity under the watchful eye of the Napoleonic father-figure. This equivalence is further illustrated by another

17. *Ibid.,* IV: 191.
18. Quoted by Grant, *The Career of Victor Hugo,* 164.

anecdote, seemingly insignificant, that Hugo slipped into his *Histoire d'un crime*. He tells of a visit received, on 16 November 1851, from Prince Napoléon (Plon-Plon), the second child of Napoleon I's youngest brother, Jérôme. The prince had strong left-wing views, and was, as we have noted, opposed to his cousin's policies and took part in the resistance against the coup d'état. The meeting probably did take place, for, in his biography of Plon-Plon, Holt quotes Jérôme as saying that, before the coup d'état, he had "apprised some of the most eminent republicans of the danger while there was still time for preventing it." In Hugo's account Plon-Plon goes much further, urging Hugo himself to save the Republic, arrest the president, preserve the honor of Napoleon I. What he is proposing is that Hugo himself should lead a coup d'état. With the noblest of tones and the most sonorous of formulas, Hugo refuses, in the name of the law, for nothing could justifying such a crime, he argues. He would prefer exile to a guilty action:

> "Could you bear exile?"
> "I will try."
> "Could you live without Paris?"
> "I shall have the ocean."
> "You would then go by the sea?"
> "I think so."
> "It is sad."
> "It is grand."

Why, Plon-Plon persists, accept exile? What could Hugo value more than his country? "Conscience" is the poet's sententious reply.[19]

Here Hugo himself emerges fully as the antithesis of Louis Napoléon: the Poet opposed to the Prince, the man of noble words to the man of sordid deeds, the Frenchman to the "foreigner," the failed leader to the successful ruler, the eloquent statesman to the silent plotter, the impetuous visionary to the prudent schemer, the great man to the pretender to greatness, a noble conscience to vile opportunism. If we return to the events of June 1848 in the light of this inverse equivalence, a further dimension to the relationship becomes evident. Whatever his protests and indignation in 1851, Hugo played an overzealous part in the repression,

19. Edgar Holt, *Plon-Plon: The Life of Prince Napoleon [1822–1891]* (London: Michael Joseph, 1973), 62; Hugo, *Histoire d'un crime*, IV: 86–87.

storming barricades, directing troops and cannon fire, making arrests of rioters condemned to deportation, preparing the situation for reprisals, for the execution or deportation of thousands of insurgents. As Graham Robb writes: "This means that he was directly responsible for the deaths of untold numbers of workers, whom he himself considered innocent and heroic." It was, as Jean-François Kahn writes, tracing Hugo's "extraordinary metamorphosis" at the time, "the paroxysm of Victor Hugo's battle against Victor Hugo."[20] The struggle clearly persisted. Like a literary *Doppelgänger*, Louis Napoléon came to represent the dark side of Hugo's own self and past, which he, passionately, sought to extirpate, for, no doubt, we most intensely hate in others what we see repressed in ourselves. Perhaps what was stirring Hugo most to such heights and such depths of vituperation was not conscience as much as a bad conscience.

20. Robb, *Victor Hugo*, 275; Jean-François Kahn, *L'Extraordinaire Métamorphose, ou cinq ans de la vie de Victor Hugo, 1847–1851* (Paris: Seuil, 1984), 520.

chapter 3

Histories III: Oppositions

THE RED STAIN

There continued to occur after December 1851, as if the conflict itself naturally generated contrapuntal effects, interesting contrasts between Louis Napoléon and Victor Hugo: the silence of the one and the verbosity of the other, the tacit guilt of the one and the overdetermined blame from the other, the supremacy of the one as emperor and the elevated status of the other as his most prominent opponent, the vilification of the one and the glorification of the other after the fall of the Empire and well beyond. But personal ambitions aside, there were also further significant equivalences. Paradoxically, Hugo, supposedly progressive, acted for the preservation of the *status quo* despite the unpopularity of the Republic with the people, whereas Louis Napoléon acted to abolish a conservative Republic by repressing mainly left-wing elements in the name of democratic reforms. Paradoxically also, despite their fierce antagonism on the day, their long-term goals were not dissimilar, and there was significant common ground in their ideologies: a fervent sense of the mission of France in an ideal of European unity, an avowed commitment to serve the interests of the underprivileged, an idealization of the people, a belief in the need for a strong leader. It would be too neat a formula to claim that one was a republican Bonapartist and the other a Bonapartist republican, but only months before the coup d'état Louis Napoléon was more republican in his views than Hugo, and the latter was far more Bonapartist than Louis Napoléon professed to be. After the repression, Louis Napoléon led a campaign of silence about the events, which, far from being celebrated, were largely concealed or extravagantly legitimized in the elaborate ceremonials of Empire, instituted even before it was officially declared. Victor Hugo led the republican campaign to maintain the focus of attention on the "crime" itself. Two forms of discourse, therefore, perpetuated the struggle after the event. The monolithic Bonapartist discourse of order, stability, and prosperity was short on words and of necessity limited in its range of argument and elaboration but asserted itself by ceremonial displays of power and prestige, which, as we shall see later, were combatted particularly (and appropriately) by parody, satire, and caricature. The writers opposed to the imperial regime, novelists and historians alike, were and have been more resourceful in their use of the many possibilities of historical writing. Hugo's versatility and panache were a source of inspiration, but his manner was clearly too "Hugocentric" to carry total conviction. Interestingly, subsequent writers can be seen to distance themselves from his works.

It would be useful to recall, at this point, the definition that Hayden White gives of the basic modes of historical writing, which vary according to their level of conceptualization. *Chronicle* and *story* are the "primitive" components of the historical account, elements of the "unprocessed historical record" being selected and endowed with characterization and with inaugural, transitional, and terminal motifs to form the story. *Emplotment, formal argument,* and *ideological implication* are the more conceptualized stages at which the history is invested with meaning, explanation, and ideological interpretation.[1] Hugo's works, as we have seen, cover the full range of these modes and go beyond, extending into fiction and pure polemic. The political and historical novelist, though working in a fictional mode, tends to favor the mere emplotment of a story, leaving implicit for aesthetic purposes any interpretive and explanatory elaboration. Such a

1. See Hayden White, *Metahistory: The Historical Imagination in Nineteenth-Century Europe* (Baltimore-London: Johns Hopkins University Press, 1973), 5–29.

position seems deceptively uncommitted, close to "pure" history, but, as the example of Zola (and of Vallès) shows, it is all the more manipulative for adopting the monological strategies of realistic fiction and for suppressing the sort of interpretive argumentation that could lead the reader to adopt a critical approach. The political historian (and literary critic) such as Henri Guillemin works at a more explicit level of conceptualization in presenting an oppositional standpoint, but does so, compared with Hugo, with a more heightened awareness of the alienating dangers of bias, with a more rigorous use of evidence and the more subtle strategy of irony. The political philosopher Marx, with a no less rigorous use of chronicle evidence, works at a higher level of conceptualization in the mode of ideological interpretation.

Like Hugo, the radical novelist and journalist Jules Vallès includes, however briefly, an eyewitness account of the events of the coup d'état in *Le Bachelier,* which is part of his autobiographical trilogy *Jacques Vingtras.*[2] But unlike Hugo, he narrates less an action than a failure to act. The early part of the account is punctuated by the refrain "*on ne se battra pas!*" ("No one will fight!"), as the narrator tries to goad his comrades into action until, on 3 December, as he puts it, the "*redingotes*" ("frock coats") have taken up arms, but not the "*blouses*" ("overalls"). A worker typically responds to his prompting with the words: "Young bourgeois! Was it your father or your uncle who shot us down and deported us in June [1848]?" In this work, Vallès implicitly asserts his independence in relation to Hugo, whom he held in low esteem and called an "empty statue," even in such circumstances, with a text lacking in grandiose effects or rhetorical denunciations, set in stark contrast by its concision to the poet's versions of the same events. The emphasis is on the guilt of the narrator himself and of his associates for their inability to act more than on the guilt of the perpetrators of the "*coup de maillet*" ("mallet blow") of 2 December."[3]

By contrast, Zola had no direct experience of the events of 1851. But as a vigorous opposition journalist in the last years of the Empire—and an even more vigorous opponent after its fall in the wave of denunciation of

2. See Chapter 12, "2 Décembre," in Jules Vallès, *Oeuvres II: 1871–1885,* ed. Roger Bellet (Paris: Gallimard, Bibliothèque de la Pléiade, 1990), 524–30. *Le Bachelier* first appeared in 1881.

3. *Ibid.,* 528–29. See also Jules Vallès, "Un chapitre inédit de l'histoire du deux décembre: À propos du livre de M. Ténot," in *Oeuvres I: 1857–1870,* ed. Roger Bellet (Paris: Gallimard, Bibliothèque de la Pléiade, 1975), 1076. This article was originally printed in *Le Courrier de l'Intérieur* on 8 September 1868.

the emperor and his regime—he took part in the campaign to keep alive the memory of 2 December, or, more precisely, to counteract the phenomenon, which has become familiar to post–World War II generations, of "*oubli*" ("forgetting"), the systematic veil cast over the compromising political deeds of the recent past. In one of his *causeries* for the opposition newspaper *La Tribune* (29 August 1969), the novelist and future author of "J'accuse" pointedly writes: "Does it require ten years, does it require twenty years, for an evil act to become a good one, and from what evidence can we recognize that the guilty man of yesterday is the innocent man of today? The human conscience will have no such compromises, and even if a whole generation were cowardly enough to forget a cursed date, impartial History would be there to protest to posterity: 'On such and such a day, at such and such an hour, justice was violated and France has borne the wounds.' " Far from impartial himself, however, he calls upon the partisans of the Empire, with heavy irony, to continue their whitewash of the regime: "Each generation to come, bringing its own natural sense of eternal justice, will take up the trial and will in turn add its condemnation. Leave us therefore to be indignant in peace, we who will pass on. But you, try rather to efface the bloodstain which sullies page one of the history of the Second Empire. Call in your officials, call in your soldiers, and let them wear down their fingers trying to remove the stain. After you, it will reappear, it will grow, and it will spread over all the other pages."[4] The ineffable bloodstain will be a dominant leitmotif of Zola's texts on the origins of the Empire.

Zola's article was prompted by the publication of Noël Blache's *Histoire de l'insurrection du Var en décembre 1851,* the work of a young lawyer from Toulon dealing with an area in which the repression and reprisals were particularly forceful. The previous year (1868), a more influential example of the genre had appeared, Eugène Ténot's *Paris en décembre 1851: Étude historique sur le coup d'État,* which was heralded, along with the founding of Henri Rochefort's satirical newspaper, *La Lanterne,* as one of the principal events of a movement of "*Réveil*" ("Awakening") to an awareness of the realities of the tainted origins of the Empire.[5] Further-

4. Émile Zola, *Oeuvres complètes,* ed. Henri Mitterand (Paris: Cercle du Livre Précieux, 1967–70), 13:244.
5. See, for example, Vallès, "Un chapitre inédit de l'histoire du deux décembre," 1066–79. On 30 October 1868, Vallès was condemned to two months in prison and fined 2,000 francs for publishing this article on the charge of "*excitation à la haine et au mépris du gouvernement.*"

more, in 1869, Ténot, who was a teacher, journalist, and one of the editors of *Le Siècle,* brought out a new edition of an earlier study, *La Province en décembre 1851: Étude historique sur le coup d'État* (1865). As Stuart L. Campbell writes, "when the gradual liberalization of the press system was crowned by the 1868 press law, republican journalism and history became indistinguishable." Numerous republican journals were founded, launching a "full-scale offensive" against the regime, returning to the themes of Victor Hugo, but in a more moderate tone. Ténot's study of the coup d'état in Paris was a best-seller, running to six editions, according to Campbell, a work that Arthur Ranc acclaimed as more than a book, but a political act in itself. It was particularly influential in raising Baudin to the status of republican martyr and to the erection of a statue to the fallen deputy, rallying republican opposition to the supposedly discredited imperial regime.[6] The earlier novels of Zola's *Rougon-Macquart* series, in particular the first volume, *La Fortune des Rougon,* subtitled at the time of its appearance as *Épisode du Coup d'État en Province décembre 1851,* were very much in the spirit of this movement, and the books by Ténot and Blache were principal sources.

In his article Zola, who was already at the time writing *La Fortune des Rougon,* gives a personal clue as to why he chose a provincial setting rather than Paris for his study of the coup d'état. "This republican voice from the provinces," he writes of Blache's book, "this work by a son of the Var, a work born of the white roads on which rang out cries of 'Long live the Republic! Long live the Constitution!' has deeply touched me, for I was also only a child in 1851 and remember with emotion a visit that I made at that time to the prison in Aix to one of my best childhood friends."[7] In fact, only once does Zola depict any of the events of the coup d'état in Paris in his series, in the first chapter of *Le Ventre de Paris.* Here, very episodically and indirectly, Florent, a mild-mannered idealist who has escaped back to Paris from the penal colony of Cayenne, recalls the circumstances of his arrest: he had found himself on the boulevard Montmartre when the troops opened fire; his hands had been covered in blood from the body of a young woman, who had fallen on top of him; then, wandering in a daze through the streets and eventually helping to build a barricade, he had al-

6. Stuart L. Campbell, *The Second Empire Revisited: A Study in French Historiography* (New Brunswick, N.J.: Rutgers University Press, 1978), 43, 44, 46.
7. Zola, *Oeuvres complètes,* 13: 245. Zola was born on 2 April 1940.

most been shot himself by drunken soldiers and had been condemned on the evidence of his bloodstained hands as a dangerous subversive. He had been transported, six weeks later, to the Gare du Havre, one carnival evening of celebration, seeing, at the very spot where the dead woman had fallen, a coach full of masked women, with naked shoulders, making merry and showing their disgust for the wretched convicts.[8] In a later scene, in the next chapter, where Florent's half-brother, a pork butcher, is shown making black pudding—a variation of the blood symbolism linked to the alimentary theme of the novel which contrasts the well-fed, politically apathetic, dubiously "honest" beneficiaries of the regime (the "Fat") with the emaciated victims of repression (the "Thin")—Florent tells of the inhuman sufferings that he had endured in the penal colony. There is no explicit political commentary in either of these accounts, yet, however fleetingly, Zola effectively conveys and condemns the summary injustices and the excessive indulgences of the new regime. But any criticism of the Bonapartists' political action is overwhelmed by the social satire of bourgeois inaction and by the picturesque depiction of the modern "cathedral," the Halles marketplace where Zola sets his novel, which owes more to *Notre-Dame de Paris* than to *Napoléon le Petit*.

One further reason why Zola chose a provincial setting to show the bloody origins of the Empire was no doubt the wish to avoid more obvious repetitions of a theme monopolized by Hugo as a literary topic, for, after Balzac, the author of *Châtiments* was a major source of that "anxiety of influence" which major writers provoke in their successors and which the latter need to surmount to assert their originality. But there was also the fact that a primary purpose of *La Fortune des Rougon* was to present the provincial origins of the infamous Rougon-Macquart family, whose deeds will provide a unifying scheme to the whole series. Characteristically, the initiatory nature of this first novel is indicated by the prophetic insight of Pascal Rougon, one of Pierre Rougon's sons, who will be, throughout the series and to a considerable degree, the author's surrogate fictional spokesman and visionary, as he recoils in horror at the events that he has witnessed when the troops put down the rebellion: "And for a moment, as by the glow of a lightning flash, he thought he could espy the future of the Rougon-Macquart family, a pack of unbridled, insatiate appetites amidst a blaze of gold and blood."[9] In this novel, Pierre Rougon, the head of the

8. *Ibid.*, 2:573–76.
9. *Ibid.*, 2:332.

powerful legitimate branch of the family, and his wife, appropriately named in the circumstances Félicité Puech, turn the coup d'état to their political advantage with the help of some advance intelligence from another son, Eugène, in Paris and an "ambush" of their own making. The novel unfolds in and around the fictitious town of Plassans, which is based on Aix but set in the Var, where, as Blache confirmed, republican resistance was most vigorous. An element of tragic romance is provided by the fate of two chaste young lovers, the orphan girl Miette, shot carrying the red flag in the confrontation with the troops, and Pierre Rougon's nephew, Silvère Mouret, an idealistic republican who joins the insurrection and is executed in the repression by a vengeful one-eyed policeman.

The novel is remarkable for the implicit associations that it contains beyond the particular context of the local struggle with the insurrection in general, with revolutionary action as a whole, and even with the rebellion in Paris. The political action opens with a stirring evocation of some three thousand insurgents on the march, filling the night air with their impassioned rendering of "La Marseillaise," presented in the transfiguring light of the moon and in the heroic light generated by the narrator's own enthusiasm: "They would doubtless prove blind, intrepid defenders of the Republic. On their shoulders they carried large axes, whose edges, freshly sharpened, glittered in the moonlight." When Miette, dressed in a large purple cloak and a hood like a Phrygian bonnet, joins the ranks of the soldiers of revolution to carry the red flag, the tableau is complete: "At that moment she was the virgin Liberty." She thereby is also yet another avatar of Marianne, the personification of Liberty, of the Republic, and of France, within the remarkably rich literary and iconographic tradition that includes Delacroix's famous painting *Liberty Guiding the People*. The myth of sublimated revolt conventionally personified in the icon of the young woman inevitably invites a fatal, tragic outcome. Even before the soldiers from Marseille have fired a shot in the skirmish at Sainte-Roure, Miette stands to face them and her pelisse "looked like a large red stain—a fresh and bleeding wound." There is too much symbolic blood in the scene for Miette's death to require more than a single drop on the bullet wound beneath her left breast as she lies dead on the flag. Liberty, the Republic, the revolutionary Ideal have been pathetically immolated. As the soldiers, in a mad frenzy of killing that their colonel fails to restrain, shoot and bayonet mercilessly and indiscriminately the routed band of insurgents— "There was a terrible massacre"—and, in their fury, spray with bullets the windows of the Hôtel de la Mule-Blanche where the hostages are being held, killing the tax collector, M. Peirotte, they are repeating by association the untold massacre scene on the boulevards of Paris.[10]

Meanwhile, after the heroics, there is the skulduggery back in Plassans. Pierre Rougon, who will seize the opportunity to replace M. Peirotte in his honorable position, re-enacts the role of a small-town Louis Napoléon. There are delightful burlesque scenes as the cowardly conservative citizens of Plassans, unaware of the outcome of events, hesitate to declare themselves as republicans or Bonapartists. Félicité takes the part of a Morny in springing the trap, bribing Pierre Rougon's half-brother, Antoine Macquart, a turncoat republican. With the opportunist interchangeability that is the recurrent *topos* of political satire, her husband, who is organizing the takeover, simply changes the wording of a republican proclamation that is at hand and has it printed by the local newspaper. Félicité persuades their republican son, Aristide, to write an article in favor of the coup d'état: "The young man made a gesture—the gesture of Caesar crossing the Rubicon." Avoiding Hugo's simplistic oppositions, Zola extends his satire to include republicans in his depiction of the *sauve-qui-peut*, as all sacrifice their principles to save their skins. The National Guard is brought under orders; Commander Roudier, a tin-pot Magnan, has his motley army man the gates of the town. The republicans, assembled by the treacherous Macquart, are massacred in front of the town hall and bodies are left for the citizens of Plassans to appreciate and to encourage them to kiss "the hand that had just rescued them from demagogy." Pointing to a vaster problem of the historical interpretation of events that his own narrative shadows, the narrator ingenuously adds: "The true history of the fusillade was never known," except, of course, by the readers of the novel. Zola's parodic version of the coup d'état is as magnificent in its cynical burlesque effects as Hugo's is in its prodigal bombast. "Thus it was," he concludes on the fortunes of Pierre Rougon, the provincial usurper, "that this grotesque personage, this pale, flabby, tun-bellied citizen, became, in one night, a terrible captain, whom nobody dared to ridicule any more."[11]

10. *Ibid.*, 2:26, 32, 232, 238. For an excellent study of the motif of Marianne and the Phrygian bonnet, which symbolized liberty, since it was placed on the head of freed slaves in Roman times, see Maurice Agulhon, *Marianne au combat: L'imagerie et la symbolique républicaine de 1789 à 1880* (Paris: Flammarion, 1979).

11. Zola, *Oeuvres complètes,* 2:265, 316, 317, 318.

Republican denunciations of the coup d'état invariably end with a cynical description of Bonapartist revelry. The last scene of Zola's novel describes the Rougons celebrating in their "yellow drawing-room," bitterly evoking in a splash of symbolic red stains the bloody origins of their "fortune" and of the "fortune" of the Bonaparte that they represent. There is the improvised pink decoration that, ironically, the veteran of Napoleon I campaigns, Sicardot, pins on Rougon's chest. There is Rougon's blood-stained shoe in the next room and the candle burning "like an open wound" in M. Peirotte's house on the opposite side of the street and the puddle of blood on the tombstone where Silvère met his death. Zola's redundant symbolism provides, more effectively perhaps than a thousand words of overt denunciation, a gloss on the events. Furthermore, a significant passage in the middle of *La Fortune des Rougon,* evoking the moonlit march of the heroic band of insurrectionists through the Provençal countryside, presents a revealing commentary on the generic composition and the historical vision of the novel: "It was like a mighty wave of enthusiasm. The thrill of patriotism, which transported Miette and Silvère, big children that they were, eager for love and liberty, sped, with generous fervor, athwart the sordid intrigues of the Macquarts and the Rougons. At intervals the trumpet-voice of the people rose and drowned the prattle of the yellow drawing-room and the hateful discourses of Uncle Antoine. And vulgar, ignoble farce was turned into a great historical drama."[12] Zola's novel, one of the least known of his works, presents one of the most compelling readings of the coup d'état from an informed, realistic, republican perspective. But it also illustrates a broader truth: that histories are always delicately poised between epic, with its heroes, heroines, and generous enthusiasms, and satire, with its endless, shameful human comedy of roguery.

THE MASK OF PARTIALITY

The political and literary historian Henri Guillemin was renowned for his trenchant manner and his readiness to question commonplace views. Catholic, left-wing, an associate in his early career of both Sartre and Mauriac, Guillemin was an inveterate iconoclast who provoked the most

12. *Ibid.,* 2:176.

extreme reactions to his work. He has been variously called "perhaps the greatest contemporary French historian" by Claude Roy and "a little irritating nobody, a graveyard vampire" ("*suceur de cadavre*") by Bernard Lambert, "a great historian" according to one former president of France (François Mitterrand), a "rummager in garbage cans" ("*fouilleur de poubelles*") according to another (Georges Pompidou).[13] At least, whatever his merits as a historian, he has the rare distinction of being the only one to have turned the coup d'état into a children's story. In this unique and quaint version of events, "Rappelle-toi, petit" ("Remember, Son"),[14] a seventy-five-year-old grandfather narrates to his twelve-year-old grandson in a familiar narrative style his memories of the aftermath of the coup d'état, sixty years ago, in their village near Mâcon, which was Lamartine country as well as Guillemin country. The hero is the village saddler, Goubaux, nicknamed La Fayette, a gentle giant of a man with a blond beard. He is an ardent republican and is the mayor at the time of news of the events in Paris. The wise old narrator interrupts the narrative to sum up for the boy what the coup d'état meant. "It's simple," he declares, "much more simple than piles of very learned books, very proper books will tell you later, with their complicated ideas." In short: "The coup d'état of Louis Bonaparte is just a gentleman with friends, who has decided to make some money. He has a good position; he earns a lot of money, and he wants to earn even more; and his friends will take advantage of the situation. That's all." In the story, the gendarmes come to the village, but Goubaux has organized the local lads to resist and sends the officials packing. On the 4th, a hundred soldiers come, arrest all the men, who will be deported to Africa, and, since Goubaux is away at the time, set a trap. Though the priest tries to warn him from the church tower, he is shot as he enters the village. The villain in the story is the local aristocrat, the comte de Montmain, who has denounced the "reds." He becomes a senator. The story ends: "At Christmas, there was a great ball in the château."

In contrast with this heroic tale and in a more conventional mode,

13. See Patrick Berthier, *Guillemin, légende et vérité* (Lys: Les Éditions d'Utovie, 1982), 9, and Henri Maringue, *Henri Guillemin, le passionné* (Précy-sous-Thil: Les Éditions de l'Armançon, 1994), 8, 86.

14. Written in August 1944, first published in Switzerland, at Porrentruy, in 1945, then reproduced in 1977 in no. 20 of the review *Tripot,* then published as a separate little volume of thirty-two unnumbered pages with numerous illustrations by Bédé in January 1978 by Les Éditions d'Utovie.

though following his own somewhat unconventional brand of history, Guillemin focuses on Louis Napoléon and the coup d'état in his book *Le Coup du 2 décembre* and also in a subsequent article "Louis Napoléon Bonaparte," both of which verge on the satirical and leave no place for the heroic. The book is a sequel to *La Tragédie de Quarante-Huit* (published in 1948) and could well have been titled *La Comédie de Cinquante-et-Un*. Not that the author allows himself liberties with the truth or any imaginative fancies. As he claims in his no-nonsense prologue, "this book is truthful," yet, at the same time, he asserts that it is "not impartial," for he sees no contradiction between truth and bias. "I know of no historian without bias," he explains, "when it comes to events which still continue to concern us." An indefatigable exposer of imposture, Guillemin has no time for neutrality: "For my part, I abhor the deceitful 'objectivities' which hide their hatreds under the mask of detachment." But in order to curb his own "impulses" (*"entraînements"*), he adopts the strategy of preferring to use and to quote evidence presented from writers and political figures who adopt opposing views to his own, thus distancing himself from Victor Hugo and using statements by such participants in the events as Morny, Flahaut, Fleury, Maupas, Granier de Cassagnac, Saint-Arnaud, "those decent folk" (*"ces honnêtes gens"*) as he calls them, with an irony that anticipates his general attitude to their words and deeds. He will be the "historian cum clerk" (*"historien-greffier"*) recording the "succession of spontaneous confessions." His utter scorn for Napoleon I, in his view a cynical adventurer, a bloodthirsty "pillager," a rapacious despot, does not make him any more indulgent to the nephew.[15]

In contrast to Victor Hugo's "history" Guillemin's deals extensively with the period from what he calls with evident irony "the happy victory of June" (1848) to 1 December 1851. Only in the last 100 of 450 pages does he deal directly with the coup d'état itself. The long preliminary study, apart from its historical value, is essential for Guillemin to present Louis Napoléon as the consummate politician, a master of deception and pretense, who not only duped his contemporaries into allowing him to take over the government of the country but masterminded the justification for it. According to Guillemin, he sat on the left-wing benches in

---

15. Guillemin, *Le Coup du 2 décembre*, 9. On his policy of refusing to quote Hugo and other "suspect" enemies of Louis Bonaparte, see *ibid.*, 393. Guillemin's views on Napoleon I are contained in *Napoléon tel quel*.

1848 having secretly assured the right that he was serving their interests. He culled favor in all quarters. He sought to restore universal suffrage to ingratiate himself with the left, whilst he was, in fact, even more popular with the right and more secure in their support even than he believed. He cleverly pretended to be lacking in ambition in 1848, speaking openly of his successor in four years' time. Guillemin wryly adds in his article on Louis Napoléon as if gifted, like a novelist, with insight into the president's mind and inner discourse: "dictating these noble phrases . . . , the 'prince' greatly amused himself inwardly and allowed a subtle smile to spread beneath the hair that covered his mouth. To think that the silly fools would really take him seriously." The Assembly, far from posing a threat as was claimed, would even have agreed to an extension of his mandate, *faute de mieux,* had he persisted. Thus, even on the day of the coup d'état, his duplicity was both effective and evident in his proclamation to the people of France: "My 'duty,' declared Louis Bonaparte, is to 'maintain the Republic' (bravo! say the proletarians) and to 'save the country' (bravo! shout the wealthy). If the latter have every reason to believe that the President will keep his word to them, the former are not aware of the trap that he is setting for them."[16]

Guillemin attributes the president's skilled duplicity to his mother's training in what he calls "multifaceted language." He even argues that the man's somnambulistic manner was put on, "a constructed role [*rôle de composition*], an ingredient of his 'mystery'." His mother had written to him: "Welcome everyone, do not reject anyone, . . . The role of the Bonapartes is to pose as the friends of everybody." Not advice that he would follow, no doubt to his regret, in the case of Victor Hugo! But as Guillemin cynically argues, Louis Napoléon's concern for the poor and his proposals for reform to improve their lives were a mere facade: "With his *Extinction of Pauperism,* 'Prince Louis' gives to his snare the form of a net." The proof lies in the prince-president's repeated demands on the Assembly to fill his purse. Like a relentless satirist, Guillemin endows his victim with an insatiable appetite for lucre, which was, he claims, echoing his children's story, the primary motive for the coup d'état, for not only Louis Napoléon but also in particular Morny, whose mansion was about to be seized, were heavily in debt. Saving society was incidental to saving their

16. Henri Guillemin, "Louis Napoléon Bonaparte," in *Vérités complémentaires* (Paris: Seuil, 1990), 296; Guillemin, *Le Coup du 2 décembre,* 370.

skins. Guillemin sardonically draws up the balance sheet of the spoils of 1851, noting the enormous salaries awarded to ministers, councillors, senators, diplomats, cardinals, archbishops, and bishops, added to the booty of their leader, who, in 1848, was earning a mere 600,000 francs: "Thanks to his initiative, things have taken a more favorable turn and he will, henceforth, be able to live in accordance with his nature. His civil list, including the upkeep of his châteaux, will be 16 million, that is, in round figures, the equivalent of 5 billion in 1951—or 44,000 francs a day in 1851, that is, 13 million a day in 1951." Compared to all this, Guillemin wryly adds: "The average wage of a worker in 1851, when he is not unemployed, is still between 350 and 400 francs a year."[17]

The coup d'état itself was for Guillemin an act of cynical opportunism and show. Even with the police and the army on their side, Louis Bonaparte cowered in his palace and "the members of the gang, despite everything, are vaguely afraid." When the two hundred deputies, mostly members of the Party of Order living in the area, met in the faubourg Saint-Germain in the town hall of the Tenth District, it was only to make token protests. Louis, "the good-natured Tyrant," knew their game: "Just let them have the time to make some grand declarations for the sake of their dignity. Louis Bonaparte is a courteous man." After their feeble protests, they are happily marched off to the safety of prison. The judges of the High Court meet half-heartedly to agree on an adjournment of their meeting before, to their relief, they are sent packing by the police. All this is the stuff of comic opera. But the action in the streets is serious business: "When it comes to a coup d'état, there is no discussion; you strike; you crush." Guillemin has no doubt that the "massacre" was a deliberate, premeditated act of terror, planned by Morny, as a measure *pour encourager les autres*. As for the provincial uprising, he writes: "For anyone who honestly takes the trouble to do some checking and to go back to the sources, what is revealed is the following: the provincial resistance to the coup d'état of 2 December was *not* accompanied by *any looting; not a single* château was burned down; *not a single* woman was raped. There was no 'Jacquerie' *anywhere at all*."[18] There were no saturnalia in Clamecy, notwithstanding Viel-Castel; the 4,000 insurgents even gave a receipt for

17. Guillemin, "Louis Napoléon Bonaparte," 310, 276, 283; Guillemin, *Le Coup du 2 décembre*, 432.
18. Guillemin, *Le Coup du 2 décembre*, 360, 363, 387, 398, 407.

the 5,000 francs that they took and returned 4,760 of the sum three days later, having spent the 240 francs on bread. The "red spectre" was indeed a phantom.

For all his concern for accuracy and for all his maneuvers around his own "impulses" and those of Victor Hugo, Guillemin's own version of the events of December 1851 is to a considerable degree consistent with the poet's satirical presentation, but without any of the heroics. His cynical depiction of political affairs sees only duplicity and rapacity in the words and actions of Louis Napoléon and his accomplices. All was sham and scam. Significantly, he sums up his own version of events in his article on Louis Napoléon by invoking the authority of Hugo's most eminent biographer, André Maurois, "who cannot be considered a man of extremes"—he defensively adds—but who wrote on the reasons for the coup d'état: "Louis-Napoleon wished to remain in power; his gang had decided to give him its backing, but not to defend either his ideas or opinions. The leader and his right-hand men had but one idea: to live it up [*mener grand train*], and to live it up for as long a time as possible."[19] Readers of Guillemin's preface may be excused a little cynicism of their own at such an imposture, which barely dissimulates claims to *the truth* beneath a mask of partiality.

THE RISE OF THE *Lumpenproletariat*

Marx wrote *The Eighteenth Brumaire of Louis Bonaparte* in a flat in Camberwell in the immediate aftermath of the coup d'état between December 1851 and March 1852, publishing it, as he explains in the preface to the second edition (1869), in New York in *Die Revolution,* the short-lived journal of his friend Joseph Weydemeyer, in April 1852 as the whole of the first number. In the same preface, he recommends just two books written in the same period on the same theme as worthy of notice: *Napoléon le Petit* and Proudhon's *Coup d'État* (*The Social Revolution Demonstrated by the Coup d'État of the Second of December*). Even so, Proudhon, he argues, has only succeeded in writing a "historical *apologia*" for the "hero" of the historical development that he has traced, whilst Hugo, from whom Marx

19. André Maurois, *Victor Hugo,* trans. Gerard Hopkins (London: Jonathan Cape, 1956), 316.

must especially distance himself, has failed to notice that his "bitter and witty invective" has only served to elevate Louis Napoléon instead of belittling him, by "ascribing him a personal power of initiative such as would be without parallel in world history." Marx, on the contrary, claims to have demonstrated how "the *class struggle* in France created circumstances and relationships that make it possible for a grotesque mediocrity to play a hero's part."[20] If Marx states in the clearest of terms the "mode of emplotment" and "conceptual framework" in which he interprets this historical event, he reveals also that he was not above a little literary invective himself.

As is well known, Marx introduces his study in generic terms, the whole paragraph of which needs to be quoted: "Hegel remarks somewhere that all facts and personages of great importance in world history occur, as it were, twice. He forgot to add: the first time as tragedy, the second as farce. Caussidière for Danton, Louis Blanc for Robespierre, the *Montagne* of 1848 to 1851 for the *Montagne* of 1793 to 1795, the Nephew for the Uncle. And the same caricature occurs in the circumstances attending the second edition of the eighteenth Brumaire!" The notion of history constantly repeating itself but in a degraded form seems curiously inconsistent with the Marxian view of the progress of history. But as Marx goes on to explain, bourgeois revolutions parade in the costumes of the past and borrow the languages of the past: "the Revolution of 1789 to 1814 draped itself alternatively as the Roman Republic and the Roman Empire"; Cromwell and the English, in a previous century, "borrowed speech, passions and illusions from the Old Testament" for their own revolution. But such a process serves the positive purpose of "glorifying the new struggles, not of parodying the old, . . . of finding once more the spirit of revolution, not of making its ghost walk about." Yet in the most recent instance, according to Marx, the process is curiously inoperative when it comes to "the adventurer, who hides his commonplace repulsive features under the iron death mask of Napoleon," for the nation is plunged back into a "defunct epoch," the past is reinvested in the present, society has fallen back "behind its point of departure," the French have drawn back from the perils of revolution into a nostalgia for the "fleshpots of Egypt," giving rise to the events of 2 December 1851. They have, Marx argues, "not only a cari-

20. Karl Marx, *The Eighteenth Brumaire of Louis Bonaparte* (New York: International Publishers, 1963), 8.

cature of the old Napoleon, they have the old Napoleon himself, caricatured as he must appear in the middle of the nineteenth century."[21] Like a Borgesian Don Quixote, Louis Napoléon is both the real thing and a parody of the original. If Napoleon is one of the "heroes" of the Old French Revolution which set up bourgeois society, Louis Napoléon, the parody of parodies or the false parody, is deprived of such a historical status, even though the tightly argued demonstration that the book contains of the various stages leading to the coup d'état itself does not seem to justify such an exclusion.[22]

Unable to repress his indignation at the recent events, Marx interprets the coup d'état more as farce or satire than as history. Thus, he writes on the events of December: "Bourgeois fanatics for order are shot down on their balconies by mobs of drunken soldiers, their domestic sanctuaries profaned, their houses bombarded for amusement—in the name of property, of the family, of religion and of order. Finally, the scum of bourgeois society forms the *holy phalanx of order* and the hero Crapulinski[23] installs himself in the Tuileries as the '*saviour of society.*' " The problem that Marx sets himself to resolve, since, notwithstanding Hugo's view, the coup d'état did not come out of the blue, is "how a nation of thirty-six millions can be surprised and delivered unresisting into captivity by three *chevaliers d'industrie*" ("high-class swindlers"). The explanation consists of a rigorously argued, remarkably informed narrative analysis of the development of class interests in the parliamentary struggles from February 1848 to December 1851. Marx defines three main periods: 24 February, at the downfall of Louis-Philippe, to 4 May; the period of the founding of the bourgeois republic, from 4 May 1848 to the end of May 1849; the period of the constitutional republic, from the end of May 1849 to 2 December 1851. In the first phase, what Marx calls "the *prologue* to the revolution," the results of the proletarian revolution were commandeered by the older

21. *Ibid.*, 15–18.

22. The idea recurs in a letter to Engels of 14 February 1858 in which Marx writes: "In fact, he is not only Napoleon the Little, in Victor Hugo's sense, that is as the antithesis of Napoleon the Great: he also marvelously personifies the smallness of the great Napoleon." Quoted in Maximilien Rubel, *Karl Marx devant le bonapartisme* (Paris–The Hague: Mouton, 1960), 47). Marx continued to attack Louis Napoléon and his regime during the Empire, notably in articles for the *New York Tribune*.

23. A reference to a character in a Heine poem "Zwei Ritter" ("Two Knights") by association with *crapule* (scum).

powers, reducing it "to a bourgeois scale" and removing the real leaders of the proletarian party with the support of the mass of the nation. Thereupon the bourgeois republic was instituted, crushing the demands of the Paris proletariat in the June Days, serving the interests of the aristocracy of finance, the industrial bourgeoisie, the middle class, the petty bourgeoisie, the army, the *Lumpenproletariat,* intellectuals, clergy, and the rural population. The proletariat was effaced, leaving the bourgeois republic to rule despotically over other classes. The Constituent National Assembly brought about the domination, then the disintegration of the republican faction of the bourgeoisie. Marx brilliantly analyzes the conflicts inherent in the constitution of 1848, which fell down at the drop of a hat, "a three-cornered Napoleonic hat," through the alliance of the factions of the Party of Order, the representatives of the aristocracy of landowners (the Legitimists) and of financiers and industrialists (the Orleanists). In the contradictory allegiances of the third phase, the *mauvaise queue* of the Party of Order, the Bonapartists outmaneuvered the petty-bourgeois democrats and republicans of the Mountain. Bonaparte opposed the parliamentary bourgeoisie, which lost command of the army. The Party of Order disintegrated into separate factions and the bourgeois parliament became alienated from the mass of the bourgeoisie. Marx attributes particular significance to the "Society of December 10," which was founded in September 1849 as a new political organization named after the date of Louis Napoléon's election as president, a vigorous, often too vigorous, support group that he was forced to dissolve a year later. Marx characterizes the variegated cast of the society, with its decadent *roués,* adventurers, vagabonds, jailbirds, swindlers, pickpockets, pimps, brothel keepers, beggars, including, bizarrely, organ-grinders, rag-pickers, knife-grinders, in short the "scum, offal, refuse of all classes," the only class upon which "the real Bonaparte" could "base himself unconditionally," for he was himself an "old crafty *roué* [who] conceived the historical life of the nation and their performances of state as comedy in the most vulgar sense, as a masquerade where the grand costumes, words and postures merely serve to mask the pettiest knavery."[24]

Thus, for all the rigor of his demonstration of the dynamics of the class struggle during this period, Marx does not get away from interpreting Louis Napoléon as a rogue, a knave, a swindler, a "Bohemian," as he calls

24. Marx, *The Eighteenth Brumaire of Louis Bonaparte,* 26, 21, 34, 75–76.

him, a princely member of the *Lumpenproletariat*," who does not belong to the factions engaged in the class struggle through parliament. Indeed, all classes, Marx argues, revealed themselves to be equally ineffective, handing themselves over to the "despotism of an individual." Though one might hesitate to believe that his supporters fell into the categories defined above, Marx is surely correct in emphasizing the president's unrelatedness to an identifiable group united by ideological or class affiliations. He claimed to be the representative of all political shades, but was truly the master of none. Yet Marx, with apparent inconsistency, also argues that Bonaparte *does* represent a class, in fact the most numerous class of French society, the peasants owning very small farms. This group, like their representative, has an ambiguous status, both constituting a class, in that their mode of living and their culture set them "in hostile opposition" to the other classes, and yet not constituting a class, by virtue of their lack of a communal identity and a political organization. The vagabond nephew of the emperor appealed, then, to the "fixed idea" of this most numerous of (non)classes, which, Marx is careful to point out, does not represent the revolutionary peasantry, for it lives in "stupefied seclusion within the old order" and wishes to have its small farms protected and favored by "the ghost of the empire."[25]

Thus, in the "play" of historical forces that Marx depicts, Louis Napoléon has taken on three roles, each corresponding to a particular level or mode of historical writing evident in the *Eighteenth Brumaire*. For Marx the political historian, he is the chief protagonist in the complex scenario of a thoroughly analyzed phase of French history, during which the "upward-striving proletariat" struggled against the ruling bourgeoisie, and has a clearly defined role in the class struggle as the representative of the most numerous class of French society and as the head of the "state machine" which, with his defeat of the bourgeois parliamentary regime at the time of the coup d'état, achieves its independent functioning.[26] But for Marx the political satirist, who cannot, any more than Guillemin, suppress his "impulses," Louis Napoléon has his place as the leader of an even less exalted caste, the rogue and ruffian chief of the *Lumpenproletariat* heavies who abet his criminal intentions, the dregs of bourgeois society who bully their way and his way into power. This class, which is also a nonclass, with-

25. *Ibid.*, 85, 121, 123–25.
26. *Ibid.*, 122.

out revolutionary potential, conveniently affords Louis Napoléon an ambivalent status as both an individual and a group leader, opportunistically seizing power by force of arms, without a constructive historical role. Finally, Marx the literary polemicist in his most flamboyant style presents Louis Napoléon in the most dismissive of terms as a sham, a shadow of an earlier figure, a hollow parody of his uncle, a buffoon, a posturer, an impostor, and, at the same time, a reincarnation, in a degraded, parodic form, of the national hero. Louis Napoléon is at once a setback, a drawback, and a throwback.

The analysis of the coup d'état, which Marx presents in his opening sally in literary, theatrical terms as a farce, is therefore not fully consistent with his full interpretation of it. It is a farce presumably for the complete absence of a heroic dimension. What, then, was the tragedy of which it is a degraded re-enactment? The title, of course, implies that it is the 18 Brumaire. But the overthrow of the Directory on 9–10 November 1799 was hardly more heroic than the later event. There was still a "gang" of conspirators, brothers Lucien and Joseph, Berthier, Réal, Bruix, Talleyrand. There were dubious financial dealings to support Napoleon's bid for power (a two-million-franc loan from the banker Collot to be paid back from the public purse). There was also fear of a left-wing (Jacobin) uprising to prompt Bonaparte to act. The army, likewise, had to be made ready to cooperate. Bonaparte lost his nerve at the crucial moment, gave a rambling speech to the Council of Ancients and had to be hustled out of the Council of Five Hundred, as he was attacked by a number of deputies. His brother Lucien and a squad of grenadiers saved the day for him. Jacobins were condemned to exile in French Guiana. A new constitution gave him unfettered powers as First Consul. Talleyrand made a fortune buying stock on the 17th and selling it on the 19th.[27] As Alain Minc writes, comparing the two events: "Did Louis-Napoléon think of the 18th Brumaire as a counter-example? He learnt the lessons and adopted the opposite course of action to his uncle's, without getting tangled up in legal precautions, without giving his enemies time, without exposing himself: the first Bonaparte is still, in 1799, a political novice; the second an expert."[28] The 18 Brumaire would seem to have been the farce, a parody of 2 December *avant la lettre*.

27. See D. J. Goodspeed, *Bayonets at St. Cloud: The Story of the 18th Brumaire* (Toronto: Macmillan, 1965), 162, 170.
28. Minc, *Louis Napoléon revisité*, 165.

But for Marx, no doubt, it is the course of the revolution in general that can be termed tragic, for, however unheroic bourgeois society is, he argues, "it nevertheless took heroism, sacrifice, terror, civil war and battles of peoples to bring it into being." Following the heroic traditions of the Roman republic, ideals were conceived and art forms elaborated, all the noble self-deceptions that were necessary to conceal "the bourgeois limitations of the content of their struggles and to keep their enthusiasm on the high plane of the great historical tragedy." As Hayden White explains Marx's views, referring in particular to this passage, "The bourgeois revolution of 1789 was Tragic *because* the disparity between ideals and realities was obscured. The revolution of 1848–51 was another matter. It was 'farcical' precisely *because* the ideals were subordinated to realities." But there can be no more than "provisional tragedy" in Marx's scheme—an oxymoron, for tragedy can only be definitive—since the regimes of both Bonapartes represent mere phases in the inexorable advance of the progressive forces of history. Even in the farcical phase, presented in the mode of satire, the heroics are implicit, the epic is tacit. Power may well have devolved to this chief of the Society of December 10, this "adventurer blown in from abroad, raised on the shield by a drunken soldiery, which he has bought with liquor and sausages." But, as Marx makes it clear, the revolution is still taking its course, "journeying through purgatory. It does its work methodically." With the coup d'état, which now acquires a vital transitional significance for Marx, the revolution has completed "one half of its preparatory work," perfecting, then overthrowing parliamentary power, perfecting *executive power* in the second phase, to concentrate "all its forces of destruction against it." When this is done, Marx predicts, with a reference to *Hamlet* (I, 5), "Europe will leap from its seat and exultantly exclaim: Well grubbed, old mole!"[29]

In Marx's study, the conceptualized scheme and the ideological presuppositions abstract the event from its historical particularity, give order and purpose to its indeterminacy and circumstantiality, even sanitize its insalubrities, conferring certainty on its unresolvedness. In a final literary flourish, Marx concludes his study with another prediction, to announce in metaphorical terms the fall of the new Bonaparte regime: "When the imperial mantle finally falls on the shoulders of Louis Bonaparte, the

29. Marx, *The Eighteenth Brumaire of Louis Bonaparte,* 16–17, 123, 121; White, *Metahistory,* 321.

bronze statue of Napoleon will crash from the top of the Vendôme column." The masquerade will be over; the curtain will not fall, but the scenery will come crashing down. What is remarkable about this statement is not that it foretold the end of the Napoleonic era, for it seemed in 1852, and even more so in 1869, that the Empire was unlikely to last significantly longer than previous regimes, but that precisely, on 16 May 1871, during the Commune, which Marx later saw as the "direct antithesis" of the Second Empire, the column in the Place Vendôme, on which Napoleon's statue had stood, was ceremoniously toppled.[30] Ironically, in a sense, the metaphor became fact—though the column and the statue were restored on 30 May 1873 under the Third Republic!—but what Marx took to be the reality of historical development, *pace* a crop of more ruthless dictators and more durable parliamentary regimes, proved to be recalcitrant to his foresight and his system.

30. Marx, *The Eighteenth Brumaire of Louis Bonaparte*, 135; White, *Metahistory*, 326. On 4 November 1863, Napoleon III had had Seurre's statue of the emperor, erected on 28 July 1833, with Napoleon dressed in his frock coat and small hat, replaced by Dumont's reconstruction of the emperor dressed in Roman costume, as he had originally been on the first monument to the soldiers of Austerlitz erected on the same site on 15 August 1810.

chapter 4

Histories IV: Uses and Abuses of the Past

LOUIS NAPOLÉON THE HISTORIAN

Fired by an unshakable belief in her son's destiny and determined to do all that she could to bring it about, Hortense gave Louis Napoléon much practical advice, which reveals her to have been not only more Bonapartist than many of the Bonapartes after Napoleon I's fall, but astutely aware of the realities and illusions of political life, and how best to exploit them. For example, she wrote to her son: "In France it is easy to have the upper hand in discussions when one invokes history: nobody studies it and everybody believes in it. One has every opportunity to arrange it however one wishes. . . . I have told you, survey the horizon. There is not a single comedy or drama that, as it is played out before your eyes, cannot provide you with some motive for intervening like a *deus ex machina* [*dieu de théâtre*]. Be a little everywhere, always prudent, always free, and only show yourself openly at the opportune moment."[1] Such a literary view of history and

---

1. Quoted in P. J. Proudhon, *Napoléon III: Manuscrits inédits, publiés par Clément Rochel* (Paris: Société d'Éditions littéraires et artistiques, 1900), 354, 356.

such worldly-wise advice on the importance of the theatricality of political life would not go unheeded in the young man's later life. Indeed, according to many of Louis Napoléon's detractors, his whole political program was based on pretense, illusion, and posturing. Even his defenders would have to concede that he always seemed to be acting out a part from a script that history had written, but without ever fully identifying with the role. As for history itself, he would be far too busy making it to be able to devote much time to the more difficult task, according to Oscar Wilde, of writing about it. Yet, as is well known, he did produce a lengthy *History of Julius Caesar,* published in two volumes in 1865–66. What is less well known, in addition to his brief account of the Battle of Sedan, which was written soon after the defeat and to which we shall even more briefly consider later, is another historical text, *Historical Fragments—1688 and 1830,* which he composed during the early part of his imprisonment at Ham.[2]

This short study deals with William of Orange's invasion of England during the reign of James II. Louis Napoléon writes that the invader "meditated great things, and resolved on landing and delivering the country from the yoke it laboured under." Louis Napoléon, the erstwhile invader of France, significantly adds: "By those who are ever ready to impute evil motives as the spring of action, this will be attributed to personal ambition." However, the heroic Dutch invader, he claims, acted only from the most laudable of motives: to liberate the English nation from oppression, "establish liberty and maintain order without violence," claim his hereditary rights and his principles, accept only what is sanctioned by "the free vote of the nation, for one cannot force either one's will or one's self on a great people."[3] Any explicit parallel drawn between William's action and those of the July Monarchy in France, which was successfully established after the 1830 revolution, is totally overshadowed by the implicit parallel to be drawn between the enlightened invader of 1688 and the au-

---

2. The preface is dated 10 May 1841. The "Fragmens historiques," according to the anonymous editor of *The Political and Historical Works of Louis Napoleon Bonaparte* (volume 1), were written in response to Guizot's recent *L'Histoire de la Révolution d'Angleterre,* where the parallel between the British revolution of 1688 and the French revolution of 1830 is drawn, Guizot arguing for a moderate or moderating role on the part of the constitutional sovereign. Louis Napoléon, not surprisingly, argues for stronger leadership from monarchs.

3. *The Political and Historical Works of Louis Napoleon Bonaparte* . . . (1852; reprint, New York: Howard Fertig, 1972), 1:404–405.

thor, who had twice sought to invade France and twice failed ingloriously to do so, in a series of events which we should briefly recall.

There was something inherently burlesque about the pretender's attempts to overthrow the government of Louis-Philippe, which was seized upon by the caricaturists of the time. The first fiasco took place in Strasbourg on 30 October 1836. Louis Napoléon had recently teamed up with the self-styled vicomte (then comte) de Persigny, Jean Gilbert Victor Fialin, a fanatical Bonapartist whose father had been killed serving in the Grande Armée and who, according to Persigny himself, was converted from republicanism to the Bonapartist cause at the mere sight of Louis Napoléon in Augsburg in 1831. Persigny would become his main advocate, cheerleader, plotter, his most faithful (humorless and tactless) companion, his impetuous minister of the interior during the Empire. For his loyalty and efforts he would be raised to a dukedom in 1863. In 1836, Louis Napoléon secured the help of Major Denis Parquin, a veteran of Napoleon's campaigns and husband of Hortense's former lady-in-waiting, along with that of Éléonore Gordon, a colorful singer as devoted to the cause as Persigny, being the daughter of an officer in the Napoleon's Guard and despite being the widow of an English officer. The plan was to win over the garrison of Strasbourg, made up auspiciously of the emperor's old regiment, the 4th Artillery, which had welcomed him back from Elba in 1815. They counted on history repeating itself. They had also won over another Bonapartist veteran, Colonel Vaudrey, who, the story goes, was swayed to espouse the cause by Miss Gordon's charms, as well as a certain Lieutenant Laity, who would later be condemned to five years in prison, not for having taken part in this seditious attempt but for having written about it.[4] The plotters secretly met in Freiburg, crossed the Rhine and, fifteen in all, ready to take over the country, spent an anxious night in a little house in Strasbourg, with Louis Napoléon writing out resounding proclamations to the army and to the people of France. The next morning the 4th Artillery Regiment did rally, and a thousand men marched on the city to the accompaniment of shouts of support from the early rising Strasbourgeois. But all went awry when General Voirol, the commanding officer of the 4th

4. In a work which he and Louis Napoléon may well have co-authored, *Relation historique des événements du 30 octobre 1836,* but which, typically, the latter did not sign. See Proudhon, *Napoléon III,* 392–98, and Ridley, *Napoleon III and Eugénie,* 114–15.

Artillery, refused to join forces with Louis Napoléon, who was, ironically, denounced as an impostor. To avoid any bloodshed he tamely surrendered. Three weeks later, on 21 November, he was on a slow warship heading across the Atlantic, having been deported to America. Under government orders, the ship took a detour via Rio de Janeiro, where it remained in the harbor for a month, before dropping him off, after more than four months, in Virginia on 30 March 1837, time for him to rue his failure and, more importantly, to disappear from public attention in France.

Four years later, in 1840, when the second fiasco occurred, Persigny was still attending to his leader's public image. Louis Napoléon was in London, leading a life of abstemious devotion and labor for the cause, according to his Boswell's *Lettres de Londres* (1840).[5] But he was at this time very much a man-about-town according to more impartial biographers, though he did find time to write *Des Idées napoléoniennes* (1839). As he solemnly wrote in the preface to this work, from Carlton Terrace in July 1839: "The Emperor is no more,—but his spirit survives."[6] Yet it was not so much the spirit of Napoleon I that moved him as the decision of Louis-Philippe's government to bring back the emperor's body to France, galvanizing Louis Napoléon and Persigny into action to make another attempt to overthrow the July Monarchy. With Britain finally authorizing the release of the body, Louis-Philippe dispatched his son, the prince de Joinville, to collect it so that it could be laid to rest with elaborate ceremony in the Invalides. Whether seeking to capitalize on the event or outraged by the appropriation of the legend, Louis Napoléon and Persigny chartered a pleasure boat and set out with an "army" of sixty men to invade France again.

It was a ragtag force, much of which had no idea what was happening, composed of Louis Napoléon's servants, some French and foreign supporters, including Persigny and Parquin again, Dr. Conneau, Hortense's doctor, who had sworn to watch over her son, as he did to the bitter end,

---

5. For example, Persigny (perhaps it was) writes: *"Il vivait d'une manière très-convenable à sa situation, s'entourant de savants et de gens distingués, livré à de sérieuses études, allant peu dans le monde, et ne voyant la société qu'autant que cela lui était imposé par sa position."* *Lettres de Londres* (Paris: Levasseur, 1840), 3. The work is attributed to Persigny, who in fact makes an appearance in the last chapter, but it is supposedly written by an old imperial soldier and addressed to his general, who was with the emperor at St. Helena.

6. *The Political and Historical Works of Louis Napoleon Bonaparte*, 1:249.

and none other than General Montholon, who had been beside Napoleon I on St. Helena and who, it has recently been claimed, was a royalist agent responsible for poisoning the deposed emperor. If so, the star of the Boulogne expedition could well have been a double agent, though he did go on to share Louis Napoléon's six-year-long captivity, such was his devotion either to the pretender himself or to his enemies.[7] Horses and ammunition were loaded at London Bridge, along with proclamations and money as means of persuasion. On the quayside at Gravesend, Parquin even bought a tame vulture that was supposed to look like an eagle and added it to the menagerie on board as an appropriate symbol. Dressed in uniforms of the 42nd Regiment, the expeditionary force descended on Boulogne on 6 August, distributing high-sounding proclamations, denouncing Louis-Philippe, and exalting the spirit of the emperor looking down at them from the Column of the Grand Army on the edge of the town.

History did repeat itself this time, but not as the invading force had hoped. The commanding officer of the real 42nd Regiment failed to cooperate, and in the row, Louis Napoléon's gun went off, wounding one of the soldiers of the garrison. As hostilities were about to break out, the prince, anxious again to avoid spilling French blood, withdrew, marched to the Column, ready to die for the cause, but his supporters dragged him away from his heroic last stand into an ignominious retreat to the boat, unaware that it had been boarded by French patrols. With the National Guard firing at him, the service boat capsized and the pretender was humiliatingly fished out of the Channel and arrested. The butt of much ridicule, denounced by the press as a bungler or even as an English agent, he was sentenced to life imprisonment after a lengthy trial. The Chamber of Peers was unmoved by his claim that, because the referendum result of

7. On Montholon's supposed role in Napoleon's death, Colonel John Hughes-Wilson, European coordinator of the International Napoleonic Society, argues that he was the only person in the emperor's entourage with the motives and opportunity to kill the emperor. He had been sacked from a lucrative post after marrying against the emperor's wishes. Forensic tests have shown that Napoleon ingested poison regularly for six months before his death. See *The Sunday Times,* 21 December 1997, p. [1] 8. Ridley notes that the French minister of the interior did have a spy in his household, but dismisses the suggestion of Dansette in his *Histoire du Second Empire* that General Montholon was a spy. Ridley, *Napoleon III and Eugénie,* 129; Adrien Dansette, *Louis-Napoléon à la conquête du pouvoir: Le Second Empire,* édition revue, corrigée et augmentée (Paris: Hachette, 1961), 1:170–74.

1804 was still valid, a Bonaparte was the legitimate ruler of France. On 7 October he was imprisoned in the citadel of Ham in the Somme, eight days before the emperor's body was exhumed at St. Helena. Two months later the uncle was laid to rest in the Invalides, whilst the nephew, buried in his cheerless castle, contemplated the endless days ahead, pondering the lessons of History and of more successful invasions.

Complaining that even as "the Emperor's mortal remains are deified, his nephew is buried alive in a narrow enclosure," Louis Napoléon leaves no doubt in his preface to the *Historical Fragments* that he is far from detached and impartial as a historian. His study will both "repudiate the false accusations" against him, which will be fully contradicted by this present statement of his thoughts and convictions. But since he writes mainly about events that took place over a century and a half earlier with very few references to his own age, the reader is left to draw the analogies with the author's own situation and ideas. The overt purpose of the historical exercise, following the example of Guizot's *L'Histoire de la Révolution d'Angleterre,* is to draw an analogy between the English revolution of 1688 and the French revolution of 1830. But this retrospective lesson in English history quickly becomes a prospective lesson in French history, as he studies the downfall of the Stuarts *after* a monarchist restoration of 1660 and the accession to power of William of Orange in 1688, which, he claims, "procured for England 153 years of prosperity, grandeur, and liberty." What is more, the example of English history will show, he argues, that it is not chance that "rules the fate of nations," but a "general cause which regulates events," called a *"fatality"* when "it is wished to avoid giving the true reason."[8] Words which would have a haunting relevance to the fatalistic historian when he himself would ignore the principles that he outlines emphatically at the end of his study, ironically, as his hope for the future:

> MARCH AT THE HEAD OF THE IDEAS OF YOUR AGE, AND THEN THESE IDEAS WILL FOLLOW AND SUPPORT YOU:
> IF YOU MARCH BEHIND THEM, THEY WILL DRAG YOU ON;
> AND IF YOU MARCH AGAINST THEM, THEY WILL CERTAINLY CAUSE YOUR DOWNFALL.

8. *The Political and Historical Works of Louis Napoleon Bonaparte,* 1:393, 398, 397.

The fall of James II and of the Stuarts was due, Louis Napoléon suggests, to the fact that their beliefs were contrary to the spirit of their country. Indeed, the present policies of the government of France *since* 1830 are based, he claims, upon the system of the Stuarts, suggesting that he has in mind not so much a revolution that has already taken place, but one which will bring an end to the monarchy in France, presumably through the intervention of a new leader of the stature of William of Orange. The failings of the Stuarts are stressed. Despite the promising beginnings of the reign of Charles I and then of Charles II, they abandoned the Protestant cause, espoused absolute power, yielded England's interests to a foreign power, sought to uphold outmoded rights and privileges, and above all were out of tune with their age and society:

> The Stuarts were always in a false position; the official representatives of Protestantism, they were Catholics at the bottom of their hearts.
>
> Forced to represent a system of liberty and toleration, they were by nature absolute; representatives of English interests, they were devoted or sold to France.

By contrast, the prince of Orange, the representative of the Protestant cause and of liberty, came to liberate the English nation, maintain order, assert his hereditary rights, submit his rule to a free vote of the nation, institute a free parliament, "for he did not come as a conqueror, but for the sole object of seconding the wishes of the nation." He combined the independence of a leader with the flexibility of a constitutional monarch. He restored England to its eminence, not only by defeating the French, but by imposing the will of the people of England on their parliament. He was "the founder of a new order of things." The Stuarts had made war "to support their tottering power by a semblance of glory"; William made war to "increase the influence of England." The Stuarts had assembled parliament "to deceive it" and had dissolved it when it was a question of national honor or liberty; William assembled parliament "to convince it" and dismissed it only when it was inspired by "reactionary principles, or sentiments in opposition to the glory of the country." In his final speech to a new parliament in December 1701, William revealed the full depth and patriotism of his policies, appealing for support to be given to the poor, for the development of trade, for an improvement in public morals. He died soon after, in March 1702, but "he must have quitted this world with the intense satisfaction that a great man always feels who has assured the prosperity, the liberty, and the honour of his country."[9]

This apotheosis of William III is very much a convenient version of events to suit the particular historian's own purposes. The opposition between William of Orange and the Stuart kings was not as unambiguous as Louis Napoléon supposes. For example, William had sent over troops to England to help suppress Monmouth's rebellion. He was, after all, the grandson of Charles I and nephew of Charles II of England. He was married to and would reign alongside the daughter of James II, Mary, whom Louis Napoléon barely mentions at all, and was to be succeeded by the last of the Stuarts, Queen Anne. Indeed, contrary to Louis Napoléon's interpretation, James was in fact a staunch defender of the progressive principle of liberty of conscience, whilst William was mainly concerned with avoiding an Anglo-French alliance and bringing England into the war with France, with preventing the overthrow of the Stuart monarchy and the reinstitution of a republic, and with impeding the establishment of a Roman Catholic dynasty when a son was born to James II in June 1688. Thus, though the new monarch from Holland was compelled, much less willingly than his French admirer implies, to accept certain restrictions of power, the so-called Glorious Revolution of 1688 was not particularly glorious and not really a revolution![10]

Louis Napoléon's version of the events, the story of an enlightened, liberal leader, successfully and without bloodshed invading a great nation, restoring it to its past glory on the basis of progressive principles, destroying the corrupt restoration of a reactionary regime, must be interpreted as an example of the practice of history as wish-fulfillment and self-vindication, even as a threat, in the writer's particular case, to the powers that were holding him captive. It was an account of a noble invasion that did not fail, unlike his own attempts; it was a justification of his own motives in acting and of his own sense of grievance; and it was a warning that, in better circumstances, he could fulfill such a heroic role. As he concludes in his preface to this "lesson in history" (signed, with a significant reversal of his

9. *Ibid.*, 1:451, 406, 451, 455, 456, 419.
10. Maurice Ashley pointedly asks: "Was not what happened merely a coup d'état or an enforced change of succession to the throne comparable with Henry IV's overthrow of Richard II or Henry VII's defeat of Richard III?" Maurice Ashley, *The Glorious Revolution of 1688* (London: Panther Books, 1968), 265.

first names, "NAPOLÉON-LOUIS BONAPARTE"), "Supported by an ardent faith, and a pure conscience, I am resigned to my misfortunes, and I derive consolation at the present moment from anticipating the future fate of my enemies, which is written in indelible characters in the history of nations."[11] Louis Napoléon's belief in the recurrence of historical events is hardly surprising for a man in his position. It would drive him on to his bold ventures. But, no doubt, a later comment by a more experienced, more worldly-wise and worldly-weary Napoleon, as his empire approached its downfall, is a more persuasive statement on the same theme. Amongst the "aphorisms" of Napoleon III that the Countess Louise de Mercy-Argenteau noted in her "pretty book," bound in dark red morocco with a silver lock representing two *L*s, is the following assertion: "The lessons of history—how absurd! Two events can no more be alike than two leaves of a tree."[12]

CAESARS

The practice of history writing was far from being a purely scholarly and disinterested activity during the Second Empire. With a strict and watchful censorship imposed on writings about the present, opponents of the regime took to writing about the past as a means of obliquely attacking the regime in the guise of scholarly pursuits. In particular, as Stuart L. Campbell notes, "the liberal elite engaged in scholarship of sublimated politics." Aware of the emperor's admiration for Julius Caesar, historians honored the memory of Tacitus as a code for their objections to the emperor and his regime. "Unable to guide the present, they retreated into the past with the hope of employing it to shape the future. The result was a vast outpouring of historical literature." All opposition opinions were represented. Thiers returned to his history of the first Empire to warn of the dangers of delivering the fate of a country into the hands of one man. Guizot and Rémusat wrote English history to demonstrate the virtues of liberty emerging from aristocratic rule. Distinguished republican historians such as Blanc and Quinet wrote from exile, not to attack directly the origins of

11. *The Political and Historical Works of Louis Napoleon Bonaparte*, 1:394.

12. Comtesse Louise de Mercy-Argenteau, *The Last Love of an Emperor: Reminiscences of the Comtesse Louise de Mercy-Argenteau . . .* , ed. La Comtesse de Montrigand (London: William Heinemann, 1926), 120.

the present regime like Hugo, but to extol France's revolutionary past, whilst others worked from within the system, notably the Blanquists, who founded their own journal, the *Candide*. "To avoid the press law, the journal dealt with historical and religious matters, and its columns were filled with praise for the most radical aspects of the Great Revolution."[13]

Such covert opposition amongst the intellectual elite was most evident in the French Academy, which became extraordinarily politicized during the Second Empire. For virtually the whole period, the Academy systematically sought to thwart the wishes of the emperor by electing opponents of his regime. Eventually the Immortals rallied to the "liberal Empire" in electing the head of the government, Émile Ollivier, to their number in April 1870, but before that, "election of new members to the Académie following the coup d'état on December 2, 1851, was motivated in the majority of cases by a desire to vex the new Caesar."[14] There were factions within the French Academy, with a majority of Orleanists, but almost all parties were united in their determination to outvote official candidates and to elect adversaries of the Empire even if the intellectual achievements of the successful candidates fell below the usual exalted requirements for admission. Indeed a number of Academicians were prosecuted for their political views, and they frequently used their acceptance speech as an occasion for a veiled attack on the Empire. The sense of anti-imperial solidarity was such that, even though the deciding electors of the Academy were anti-clerical, three clergymen were inducted during the Empire. A minor poet but major militant royalist, Victor de Laprade, was elected in 1858; an almost forgotten poet, Auguste Barbier, whom most people at the time thought to be dead, but whose *Iambes* (1832) had attacked Napoleon I, was elected against one of the finest writers of the century, Théophile Gautier, who had the support of the Tuileries and was known to be one of the distinguished habitués of the salon of Mathilde, the emperor's cousin. The emperor, whose stoicism was put to the test, was compelled resignedly to accept the august body's decisions and formally receive the new Academicians. On one such occasion, when the outspoken Orleanist journalist Lucien-Anatole Prévost-Paradol, who had been fined and imprisoned in 1860 for the views expressed in his pamphlet *Les Anciens Partis,* was

13. Campbell, *The Second Empire Revisited,* 32, 43.
14. Robert W. Reichert, "Anti-Bonapartist Elections to the Académie Française during the Second Empire," *Journal of Modern History* 35 (1963): 33.

elected on 7 April 1865 at the tender age of thirty-six and, in his inaugural speech, condemned Julius Caesar as a tyrant, the emperor at least had the wry satisfaction of pointing out to him that some twelve years earlier in his *Essai sur l'histoire universelle,* he had hailed Caesar as a great man![15]

There were, of course, historians writing on the other side in retaliation, notably Troplong, who had been a liberal but had rallied to Louis Napoléon's cause at the time of the coup d'état and was better known as a magistrate and as an expert on Roman and French law. He contributed to the drafting of the 1852 constitution and replaced Jérôme Bonaparte as president of the Senate the same year. In 1855–56 he published a study of the fall of the Roman Republic which presented Caesar in a favorable light and was interpreted as a vindication of the present emperor.[16] Hardly surprisingly, despite his considerable achievements, he was turned down for the Academy, twice, in 1855 and 1866. But the major snub to Napoleon III and his government occurred in 1863. Astonishingly, the previous year, the emperor himself had put forward his own name for membership, commenting with reference, no doubt, to his current project on Caesar: "I am very much interested in all that goes on in the Académie, and I, too, am working to render myself worthy of it." After some maneuvering to avoid the issue, the Academy elected Jules Dufaure, a former minister under Louis-Philippe, who used the occasion of his inaugural speech on 7 April 1864 to present a barely veiled attack on the limits imposed on the freedom of speech under the present regime.[17]

The emperor's researches cannot, therefore, be explained merely as a retreat from the difficulties of coping with the affairs of state of the present into the vicarious satisfactions of triumphs of the past. Nor, however, can his historical project be entirely accounted for within the context of the intellectual disputes, the battle of the history books, during his reign. His decision to write a biography of Julius Caesar stemmed also from a long-standing ambition which may well have dated back to his days as a prisoner in Ham. It was to some degree also, for a man of Louis Napoléon's ambitions, a case of *impérialisme oblige.* As a publisher's note at the beginning

15. See Roger L. Williams, *The Mortal Napoleon III* (Princeton: Princeton University Press, 1971), 30–31. In Book 6, section 6, Prévost-Paradol writes about Caesar's "great genius" and "sublime plans."

16. Raymond Théodore Troplong, *De la chute de la République romaine* (Paris: *Revue contemporaine,* 1855–56).

17. See Reichert, "Anti-Bonapartist Elections," 40–41.

of Volume 2 of his study of Julius Caesar informs us, numerous "Sovereigns and Princes" had "employed themselves" on the same topic, though none had clearly gone to the same lengths as Napoleon III, who, if he did not match the military feats of all of them, certainly outdid them in scholarship. Charles VIII of France greatly admired the *Commentaries*; Emperor Charles V annotated them; his contemporary, the Sultan Soliman II, collected copies of them throughout Europe and had a Turkish translation made; Henry IV of France actually translated the first two books of the *Commentaries*; Louis XIII finished the job by translating the last two books, and the two translations were combined in an edition printed at the Louvre in 1630; Louis XIV only managed to translate the first book; Christina, Queen of Sweden, wrote her *Reflections on the Life and Actions of Caesar*; Louis-Philippe was merely "a great reader" of the *Commentaries,* but did have a map of Caesar's campaigns in Gaul made; and, of course, Napoleon I dictated his *Précis des guerres de César (Outline of the Wars of Caesar)* to Marchand during his ample spare time on St. Helena, a work that was published in Paris in 1836 and provided an inspiration to his nephew.[18]

When he began his task, Louis Napoléon intended to write a short biography, but once started, he became so engrossed in the subject that he mobilized a whole team of experts (archaeologists, cartographers, naval architects, military tacticians, etc.), researchers, historians, writers, to help with the enterprise. With great enthusiasm, he visited a number of Roman and Gallic sites himself. He funded extensive excavations of ancient Roman locations, notably at Puy d'Issole, uncovering the site of Uxellodunum, and near Mount Auxois, the site of the siege of Alesia. He even had catapults built and a Roman war galley constructed, on which, in March 1861, he and the empress took a short ride between two bridges on the Seine. The court entered into the spirit of the occasion, putting on a show at Compiègne in November of 1865, entitled *Les Commentaires de César,* a work which was composed by the marquis de Massa in honor of the august new chronicler, but which seems to have dealt very little with Roman history and more with a more recent theme, the strike of coachmen in Paris that same year. But more serious minds were concerned that the emperor's pastime was causing him to neglect his duties. Viel-Castel

18. *Précis des guerres de César par Napoléon écrit par M. Marchand, à l'île Sainte-Hélène, sous la dictée de l'Empereur, suivi de Plusieurs fragmens inédits* (Paris: Gosselin, 1836).

complains in his diary, on 4 April 1862, about the useless boats and catapults that the emperor is constructing whilst there is a threat of war; he
was being more a Nero than a Caesar. In exasperation, Viel-Castel adds a
year later: "It's all very well to study the life of Caesar, but, for God's sake,
Sire!, study it in the leisure time afforded by a profound and assured
peace" (18 July 1863). Quite possibly it was the very strains of being a
Caesar, or a sense of boredom with the leisure pursuits of court life, that
reawakened his interest in writing and in more scholarly pursuits, even a
sense of nostalgia for his cell in Ham. At this time he significantly buried
the hatchet with Hortense Cornu, his childhood playmate, who had visited him and helped him with his studies in Ham, but had broken off relations with him in her outrage at the coup d'état, and recruited her to help
him with his researches.

Whatever the motives of the emperor in undertaking the task, he was
certainly not inspired, any more than his opponents, by a dispassionate desire to make a lasting contribution to the scholarly field of Roman history,
despite the impression given by his choice of collaborators without regard
to their political opinions. His chief assistant was Alfred Maury, an eminent classical scholar, but an avowed opponent of the imperial regime. Yet
despite his views, Napoleon III respected his learning and achievements so
much that he even appointed him to the ultimate sinecure for a scholar:
librarian of a nonexistent library in the Tuileries! A more cynical view
would see such a move as part of a strategy of recuperation of opposition
intellectuals, many of whom, as we have seen, were working against him.
For Napoleon III writing history was never an innocent pastime.

Another distinguished assistant was Victor Duruy, a former history
teacher at the prestigious Henri IV school in Paris, where he taught two
of the king's sons, and author of a *Histoire des Romains,* the first two volumes of which brought him recognition and promotion as a historian and
teacher. He refrained from publishing until 1872 the third and fourth volumes, which were sympathetic to Caesar, for fear of encouraging a new
Caesar, for he held liberal views and had voted against Louis Napoléon in
the plebiscite. But the emperor managed to engage his services in an advi-
sory capacity and went on to appoint him minister of public instruction in
1863, an enlightened move which led to significant liberal reforms in the
educational system.[19]

19. See Roger L. Williams, *The World of Napoleon III, 1851–1870* (New York: Free
Press, 1965), 187–207. On other collaborators of the emperor on this project, see Melvin

The first volume appeared in 1865, the second, accompanied by a splendid illustrated supplement of thirty-two maps, plans, sketches, in 1866, but the anticipated third volume that the emperor announced was not forthcoming, at least not until Eugène Stoffel, an artillery officer in the imperial army who had done much valuable field work on the emperor's behalf and had been rewarded with an appointment as military attaché in Berlin from 1866 to 1870, went on to produce the missing volume himself as *Histoire de Jules César: Guerre civile.*[20] Stoffel would have a much more vital and much less scholarly mission during the latter years of the Second Empire. He supplied the French government with alarming reports on the state of the Prussian army. He is supposed to have famously remarked: "Prussia is not a country which has an army. Prussia is an army which has a country." His reports were largely ignored, if not by the emperor, certainly by his government, to the immensely costly advantage of the French Caesar's future enemy.[21]

Though the two volumes appeared anonymously, no doubt as an appropriate acknowledgment of the team effort involved in producing them, the preface is, significantly, signed "NAPOLEON." This fact and the preface itself, as much as the contents of the book, have obviously led to the common view that this work is an apologia. Caesar is the prototype of the great leader, who could, with some effort, be presented as an early practitioner of Bonapartist principles, lending by example credibility, authority, legitimation, justification, to the present ruler in France, who was often likened, though usually disparagingly, to Caesar, if not, more complimentarily and in certain respects more appropriately, to Augustus, Caesar's grandnephew, who brought stability to Rome, whose principate was

---

Kranzberg, "An Emperor Writes History: Napoleon III's *Histoire de Jules César,*" in *Teachers of History: Essays in Honor of Laurence Bradford Packard,* ed. H. Stuart Hughes (Ithaca: Cornell University Press, 1954), 87–89.

20. Baron Stoffel, *Histoire de Jules César: Guerre civile* (Paris: Imprimerie Nationale, 1887). Stoffel explains in his preface that his book is based on field work done in 1862–66 and on materials collected on the emperor's instructions whilst he was military attaché in Berlin, along with additional field work done in 1879. The book begins significantly *"César, en passant le Rubicon, avait déclaré la guerre civile. Je prends, à partir de là, le récit des événements."*

21. See S. C. Burchell, *Imperial Masquerade: The Paris of Napoleon III* (New York: Atheneum, 1971), 321, and Chapter 12 of Edward Legge, *The Comedy and Tragedy of the Second Empire* . . . (London–New York: Harper and Brothers, 1911), which includes a number of letters from Piétri to Stoffel.

based on republican constitutional structures, and who famously transformed Rome from "a city of brick to a city of marble." Indeed, it has
been argued that "the entire biography of the Roman leader is a parable
of the Napoleonic ideas."[22]

The preface, undoubtedly all the emperor's own work, is noteworthy
initially and in retrospect suspiciously for its elevated notion of historic
truth, which, the author argues, "ought to be no less sacred than religion," for the lessons of history inspire us with "the love of the beautiful
and the just, and the hatred of whatever presents an obstacle to the progress of humanity." The lives of public men should, furthermore, lead us
to remember "their providential mission." The historian should penetrate
beyond the representation of events to "unfold the secret of the transformation of societies" and to perceive the general cause, the "fatality,"
which "drags with it all the particular accidents" of history.[23] This text, we
see, is already heavily laden with historiographic and ideological assump-
tions: the belief that historic truth can be attained, the conviction that humanity is progressing, that there are definable reasons for change and
general causes embodied in major historical figures, that political history
has more relevance than biography, that Providence guides the course of
history. All this appears to the modern reader, however sincerely it was
meant, as so much rhetoric, as both a distraction from and an abstract justification of the presumed subtext of the work, whose apologetics subsume
the historical text itself if it is to be interpreted as an allegory of the first
and second empires of France. Similarly, the impressive wealth of particular historical detail contained in the two volumes that follow, which in any
case tends to obscure the general themes flaunted here in the preface,
seems to act as a highly elaborate "reality effect," though such a view
clearly does not do justice to the massive scholarly effort that went into
producing the two volumes.

This preface is also remarkable for its exposition of the familiar "great-
man" theory of history. "When extraordinary facts attest an eminent genius," the emperor asks, "what is more contrary to good sense than to
ascribe to him all the passions and sentiments of mediocrity? What more
erroneous than not to recognize the preeminence of those privileged be-

22. Kranzberg, "An Emperor Writes History," 82.

23. Napoleon III, *History of Julius Caesar* (New York: Harper and Brothers, 1865–66),
1:xix, x–xi.

ings who appear in history from time to time like luminous beacons, dissipating the darkness of their epoch, and throwing light into the future?" Thus, when Providence produces such men as Caesar, Charlemagne, and Napoleon, the argument continues, it is to "trace out to peoples the path that they ought to follow. . . . Happy the peoples who comprehend and follow them! woe to those who misunderstand and combat them!" Not surprisingly, the preface ends by invoking the example and the supposedly prophetic words of Napoleon I on St. Helena, or at least of the benign version of the emperor (and of himself) that the new emperor wishes to present to the world, the rampant conqueror having been transformed into a benevolent humanitarian: "How many struggles, how much blood, how many years will it not require to realize the good which I intended for mankind!"[24]

The historical work itself, which is divided into four books, is a massive feat of erudition which extends far beyond a mere biography of Julius Caesar, with the narrative Roman history mediating between the monumental scholarship, much of which is displayed in lengthy footnotes, and the largely implicit articulation of the Napoleonic ideal, which surfaces intermittently in certain discursive passages. Book 1 traces the history of Rome from the establishment of its institutions by the kings up to the birth of Caesar, by which time, the argument goes, the age of stoic virtues had passed and the Republic had lapsed into corruption, dissension, the abuse of personal power, despite the efforts of Caesar's uncle, Marius. The people sought order and repose. Italy "demanded a master" to establish a durable order of things, a man capable of fulfilling such a lofty mission: "That man was Caesar."[25] Any similarity between this situation and France in the middle of the nineteenth century is, no doubt, purely coincidental!

Caesar's exalted origins, supposedly going back to Venus (rather than Mars), are traced at the beginning of Book 2, as is the beneficent influence of a tender and virtuous mother, crucial, according to the son of Hortense, to the formation of the future virtuous leader, who "united to goodness of heart a high intelligence, to an invincible courage an enthralling eloquence, a wonderful memory, an unbounded generosity," as well as the rare quality of "calmness under anger." The enumeration of Caesar's multiple virtues is authenticated in each case by a footnote. He had as well, of

24. *Ibid.,* 1:xii, xiv, xv.
25. *Ibid.,* 1:278, 280.

course, all the physical advantages, was a bold horseman, was "habitually temperate"—no footnote here! He was meticulous in his appearance and habits, despite a tendency to scratch his head with one finger, which seems to have been the only blemish on the personality of a man who "allied the elegance of manner which seduces with the energy of character which commands." The book ends with a glorification of the great man, about to embark on his campaigns in Gaul with "faith in his destiny" and "confidence in his genius," and his biographer setting off in exalted tones into the highly uncertain territory of speculation about the Roman leader's motivation. "Is it truer to say," he asks, "that Caesar, having become proconsul aspired to sovereign power? No; in departing for Gaul, he could no more have thought of reigning over Rome, than could General Buonaparte, starting for Italy in 1796, have dreamed of the Empire."[26] No more, perhaps, but no less!

The two books of Volume 2 are entirely devoted to "The Wars in Gaul," following closely Caesar's own account from the *Commentaries* in Book 3, then going back year by year over the same events and period of time in Book 4 in the light of developments in Rome. In the earlier section, many a picturesque detail of local color enlivens the narrative, which is heavily charged with scholarly minutiae. We learn, for example, of the awesome strength of the Gaulish woman, who would become "especially formidable if, swelling her throat [*sic* for "*gorge*"!] and gnashing her teeth, she agitated her arms, robust and white as snow, ready to act with feet or fists, to give blows as vigorous as if they came from a catapult." Clearly Astérix had less to fear from the Romans! Then there are the cannibal tribes of Britons of the interior of the island, eating the bodies of dead relatives and sharing the women amongst ten or twelve men. Caesar's mission in Gaul is defined benignly, but hardly convincingly, at the beginning of Book 4, as a civilizing task, to protect the people of Gaul "either against their own dissensions, or against the encroachments of their dangerous neighbours." Meanwhile, back in Rome, the intrigues and rivalries of Pompey, Cicero, Cassius, Cato, and the odious Clodius, are described at length. The often beleaguered emperor of the French wryly notes: "We see the game of political see-saw is not new." Indeed, Caesar himself is not beyond reproach, but Napoleon III only ventures to blame him when he can invoke the authority of Napoleon I. But fundamentally, Caesar is the

26. *Ibid.*, 1:287, 289, 290, 463, 462–63.

people's champion, loathed by the aristocracy, who are jealous of his victories and fearful for their own interests. When, in the emperor's narrative, without the consent of the Senate, the aristocracy charge Pompey to raise troops, there are clearly retrospective echoes of the quaestors' affair of November 1851, allowing the narrator to interject with the same logic by which his own action was justified that year: "It is the aristocratic party which places itself above the law, and places right on the side of Caesar." Indeed, the last few pages, as the narrative approaches the moment of Caesar's decision to invade Rome, can be read as an adumbration of the later crisis, at least in the emperor's version: the chief of the popular party feeling "a great cause rise behind him," urging him forward, obliging him to conquer "*in despite of legality,* the imprecations of his adversaries, and the uncertain judgment of posterity"; Roman society "in a state of dissolution," asking for a master; a fractious minority of the Senate "trampling right and justice under foot"; a decisive conflict between the privileged classes and the people. One wonders which political context was uppermost in the emperor's mind when he wrote: "To cling to power when one is no longer able to do good, and when, as a representative of the past, one has, as it were, no partisans but among those who live upon abuses, is a deplorable obstinacy; to abandon it when one is the representative of a new era, and the hope of a better future, is a cowardly act and a crime." The narrative ends on a spectacular note: "An apparition, it is said, strikes the eyes of Caesar: it is a man of tall stature, blowing martial airs on a trumpet, and calling him to the other bank. All hesitation ceases; he hurries onward and crosses the Rubicon, exclaiming, 'The die is cast! Let us go where I am called by the prodigies of the gods and the iniquity of my enemies'."[27] It had been doubtless a ghost of somewhat smaller stature beckoning across the river the present historian, who relives here, vicariously and in the dramatic mode, his own momentous action and, still haunted by its import, still obsessively seeks in history auspices of its vindication.

Why, we are inevitably led to ask, did Napoleon III not finish the project by writing the third volume? Several practical explanations come to mind. Perhaps he was too busy and too preoccupied with immediate problems to go on. In the days of anxiety and decline when the first two volumes appeared, 1865 and 1866, the political climate of the Empire was very different from the apogean days of the regime in 1860 when the em-

27. *Ibid.,* 2:35, 169, 400, 410, 578, 591, 592, 593.

peror had begun the book. The Mexican adventure was going disastrously wrong. Storm clouds were gathering in Europe with the decisive defeat of Austria at the hands of the Prussians. Despite the promise of liberal reforms, opposition to the Empire was growing more vocal within France. There were elaborate preparations to be made for the Universal Exhibition in 1867. Morny had died in 1865. Perhaps the emperor himself was too ill to carry on his researches, especially in the summer of 1866, when stone in the bladder was causing him acute discomfort and forcing him to take the waters at Vichy, then rest. Perhaps he was discouraged and dissuaded from going on by his failure to gain admission to the French Academy and by the prospect of never being able to breach the opposition to his candidacy and to his candidates. Or perhaps he was too preoccupied with other pastimes. Had not Caesar himself given up the writing of *The Civil War* for love of a woman? But Margot-la-Rigoleuse was a far cry from Cleopatra!

Yet certain more intrinsic factors deserve to be considered. There is already in the preface a concern with the theme of the fall of the empire. Napoleon III enjoyed the advantage of the retrospective view over Roman history that the reader of his study enjoys over the French emperor's own regime. Caesar and Napoleon I were weighty sources of inspiration for the latter's nephew, but also, no doubt, sources of considerable anxiety over his own abilities to match their deeds and considerable fear at the prospect of meeting, like them, a lamentable end. The Rubicon, where it was comforting to leave Caesar, remains for the emperor a psychological barrier. To write about the great leader in his potentiality was reassuring and inspiring. To write about him in the full exercise of his powers and in his downfall would have been disturbing. In any case, to pursue the implicit comparison between Caesar and the Bonaparte leaders would be dangerous and as likely to give grist to the mills of the emperor's enemies as to reflect glory upon the present regime. Caesar had, after all, destroyed a republic, provoked a civil war, and created for himself not only a dictatorship but a perpetual dictatorship. Napoleon III, for his part, had not triumphs to celebrate anything like those of Caesar. Nor would he wish to encourage a latter-day Brutus to imagine his mission in life to be to free the land of the tyrant who had put an end to the republican system.

Nevertheless, though incomplete, the emperor's study was well received, translated into several languages, and greeted with enthusiasm, at least by his supporters. Out of the immediate context of its publication, the work has achieved some lasting recognition as a scholarly achievement. One recent Roman historian has called it "one of the most remarkable works of history of the nineteenth century."[28] But the reception of the work during the Second Empire was no more free of political interests than its conception and execution. There were laudatory reviews, a torrent of flattering letters, and a chorus of approval, but also some significant dissenting voices. Typically Sainte-Beuve refused to review a work which did not present the "vices of Caesar," whilst George Sand, dissociating herself from any sympathy for the author or his subject, praised it as a "literary work."[29] In a substantial review of the first volume, which Zola wrote for *L'Écho du Nord* but which was never published, almost certainly because the newspaper would not run the risk of prosecution, the future novelist claims likewise to judge the work by separating the author from the man.

The future naturalist, affecting impartiality, writes: "I absolutely only wish to consider the theoretical question, to judge the historian and not the prince, to study the temperament of a philosopher and not the temperament of a politician." Writing about the emperor's preface, he argues against what he perceives as the author's too systematic, synthetic, speculative form of history in favor of a more realistic, analytical, and what he does not yet call naturalist method: "I am mad about reality, and I demand from any work, even from a historical work, the truth about human passions and thoughts." In this rare example of historical criticism, just as in his better-known art criticism of the period, Zola himself is not above the reproach that he levels at the author of *L'Histoire de Jules César:* "He finds himself in the false position of a man who at times writes his own apologia." But he does make some telling comments on the first volume. He suggests, for instance, that, if four hundred years of Roman history, as the emperor claims, led to Caesar, then they also led to the Empire, Nero, and Caligula. He argues, with more than a hint of criticism of the "prince," that Caesar's reign was retrograde, destroying the Republic, and that the Roman leader was far from being the messiah who regenerated Rome, as he is depicted in this book. For Zola the writer, the scholarship of this work is impressive and its only merit, for the style is far too somber. As for the general theme, for Zola the republican, the emperor's Caesar is far too heroic: "The author has made a delicate choice of fine words favoring Cae-

28. Ramon L. Jiménez, *Caesar against the Celts* (Staplehurst: Spellmount, 1996), 244.
29. See Kranzberg, "An Emperor Writes History," 97–98.

sar; I would like to hear accusations leveled against the great man; only then could we judge in complete equity."[30]

With this in itself sober assessment, understandable in the circumstances, Zola was not, however, finished with the emperor's book. By contrast, in the atmosphere of boundless calumny and blame heaped upon the fallen emperor by the republican press, Zola pulls no punches in a second article on the *Histoire de Jules César,* published in *La Cloche* on 4 September 1872, exactly two years after Sedan. He calls it a "farcical enterprise," with which the emperor "wished to explain and justify the 2nd of December, by narrating the crossing of the Rubicon." Carefully pointing out that no newspaper would publish his own review, Zola mocks the fawning writers, critics, and historians who "groveled before the work and the author" when the first volume appeared and recalls the absolute silence that followed the publication of the second, "one of the most crushing failures of the age." Without any inhibitions now, Zola turns the emperor's allegory against him in derision and aversion: "Whilst Caesar dies stoically under the dagger, he [Napoleon III] would appear smoking the cigarette of defeat and handing over his sword to King William. This providential man, who had begun saving France by killing Frenchmen, was in favor of large-scale, plentiful bloodletting; he accomplished his task leaving the fatherland dying on bloodstained sheets. That was a necessary part of his mission." But Zola's main grievance in this article, in which he wrongly claims that the emperor, with his coffers still full of stolen money, had just bought *"le magnifique domaine de Beaulieu-House"* on the Isle of Wight, is that the author of the *Histoire de Jules César* had left the country owing his publisher, Henri Plon, 332,299 francs and 65 centimes: "This man will thus be odious and grotesque to the bitter end. He bleeds France to death at Sedan, and he runs away, without even paying his printer. The emperor shouts: 'Run for your life!' and the historian is bankrupt. It is not enough for him to leave behind for us ruins and blood, buildings ablaze like torches and dead men demanding vengeance from their graves. He even has to leave creditors behind."[31] Such are the dangers of vanity publishing!

30. Zola, *Oeuvres complètes,* 10:158, 160, 162, 167.
31. *Ibid.,* 14:156, 157, 158, 156. In fact, the ailing emperor was only renting Beaulieu House on holiday with the empress and the prince imperial. See Ridley, *Napoleon III and Eugénie,* 585.

THE TRUE RUBICON

In the earlier of the two articles by Zola presented above, which is free from the polemical excesses of the later one, Zola asks a crucial question, pointedly turning the emperor's study against him: "Did circumstances absolutely require a dictator for life, an emperor? Should not the man of genius who had understood his age have been contented with rebuilding institutions in their pure state, with using his power only to give a new lease on life to the Republic? How great he would have been on the day when, having restored to the nation the strength to govern itself, he handed power back to the country! The master that Italy was then demanding, if indeed it was demanding one, was a friend, a counselor, and not an emperor."[32] Applied to Louis Napoléon in the aftermath of the coup d'état, the question is a valid one. Was it in fact necessary for the president of the Republic, afforded sweeping powers and supreme authority under the new constitution, to reinstate the Empire? Was it indeed inevitable that he would do so?

It is easy to forget that a whole year passed between the coup d'état and the restoration of the Empire. Indeed, this period is frequently glossed over or considered to be merely a *natural* phase of transition, the assumption being that, all along, Louis Napoléon's intention had been to declare himself or have himself declared the new emperor. Thus Giraudeau writes, evoking the act and the public acclaim that led to it: "This consolidation of power conferred on the nephew of Napoleon by popular confidence was so logical, so natural that at the moment when it came about, people were surprised that it had taken so long."[33] But there was nothing in Louis Napoléon's avowed mission, in his proposed reforms for regenerating France in a new age, in his Napoleonic idea(s), that required the re-establishment of the Empire. Of the two foundations of Bonapartism that were held to be in a constant symbiotic relationship—the strong leader in tune with his times and the will of the people—the first could well have been assured by a powerful president. In his "Ideas of Napoleonism," which dates from 1839, the nephew heralds the first emperor as "the Messiah of the new ideas," as the man who contributed more than any other "to accelerate the reign of liberty, by preserving the moral influence of the revolution."

32. Zola, *Oeuvres complètes,* 10:164.
33. Giraudeau, *Napoléon III intime,* 145.

He argues that, in post-Revolutionary France, a "want of fixity and continuity, the greatest defect of democratic republics," necessitated the creation of a hereditary family "to be the conservator of these general interests, but the power of which should be wholly based on the democratic spirit of the nation." But he concedes that "Napoleon may be blamed for having surmounted with a crown his republican laurels." He even suggests that his uncle was reluctant to accept the crown: "Let us, first of all, set forth one fact, namely, that when the French people proclaimed Napoleon, Emperor, France was so weary of disorder and continual change, that everything concurred to invest the chief of the state with the most absolute power. The Emperor, then, had no need to covet it; on the contrary, it was his effort to avoid it."[34] We should be duly skeptical about the democratic ideals of Napoleon I and about his modest reluctance to seek the mantle of emperor, just as we should be suspicious of his nephew's claims about them. But the nephew did have democratic ideals, and there is some evidence to suggest that his characteristic hesitations in the intervening year were not merely about the timing of an inevitable event that would put an end to the Second Republic.

What is clear is that he gave confusing and contradictory signals of his intentions. He used the Tuileries for ceremonial events, but remained resident in the Élysée Palace. He had his effigy placed on the coinage, but retained the symbols and the name of the Republic. The imperial eagle reappeared on the flag, the slogan "Liberty, Equality, Fraternity" was removed from public buildings, but the president declared at the opening of parliament on 29 March 1852: "Let us keep the Republic; it is a threat to no-one and can reassure everyone." Yet despite this, he went to great lengths to revive memories of the first Empire: the Code Civil became again the Code Napoléon; 15 August, the first emperor's birthday, became a national holiday; a generous civil list was drawn up to the benefit of the family. By his entourage and especially Persigny, by the flood of petitions that came in during the summer of 1852, he was being pressed, as before, to act, this time to establish the Empire. But ever the pragmatist, despite his high-sounding ideals, he no doubt wished to test the mood of his own country and the attitudes of other countries to the idea. Declaring "My journey is a consultation [*une interrogation*],"[35] he set off on a tour

34. *The Political and Historical Works of Louis Napoleon Bonaparte,* 1:257, 262, 301.
35. See Pierre de La Gorce, *Histoire du Second Empire* (Paris: Plon, 1905), 1:88, 91.

of the provinces, as in 1849. Persigny, as minister of the interior, made sure through the prefects not only that he was suitably received wherever he went, but that he would be urged to become and hailed as emperor all along the way.

In Lyon, on 20 September, he cautiously declared: "If the modest title of President could make easier the mission that has been entrusted in me, and from which I have not shrunk, I am not the one, out of personal interest, to wish to change this for the title of Emperor." Wherever he went, there were cries of *"Vive l'Empereur!"* and banners ranging from *"Ave, Caesar Imperator"* to *"Quel Bonheur que le 2 décembre!"* ("Happiness is the 2nd of December"). By the time he reached Bordeaux and gave his famous banquet speech on 9 September, he seemed to have made up his mind, proclaiming that France seemed to wish to return to the Empire and carefully adding: "In a spirit of defiance, some people say: The Empire means war. As for me, I say: *The Empire means peace* [*L'Empire, c'est la paix*]. Peace, because, that is what France wishes, and, when France is satisfied, the world is a peaceful place." He enumerated the peaceful conquests of the new Empire, "if the Empire must be established": harmony amongst conflicting parties, religious faith and practices to be restored to the people, roads and railways to be built, ports to be constructed, rivers and canals to be made navigable, as well as, "opposite Marseille, a vast kingdom to be assimilated to France"—presumably also by peaceful means in the usual colonialist manner![36] He did not say why all this could not be accomplished under the Republic. But this part of the speech was mainly intended to reassure the major powers of Europe, who had generally been favorably disposed to the coup d'état as a blow against socialism but were much less likely to approve of the return of the Empire. The British were already extending the breakwater on Alderney to repel a French invasion, just in case.

The president returned to Paris on 16 October in glorious sunshine to a tumultuous reception, also orchestrated by Persigny. Hundreds of banners and triumphal arches welcomed him. Huge cheering crowds saluted him as he rode from the Gare d'Orléans in his lieutenant-general's uniform, like a victorious Roman general, with bands playing "Partant pour la Syrie," to be the new anthem of the Empire, supposedly composed by his mother. At the entrance to the Tuileries an arch awaited him bearing

36. *Ibid.*, 94–99.

the inscription "To Napoleon III, Emperor, Savior of Modern Civilization, Protector of the Sciences, the Arts, Agriculture, Industry and Commerce. From the Grateful Workers." At a gala performance at the Théâtre
Français a few days later, his former mistress, the celebrated actress Rachel,
recited Arsène Houssaye's "Ode to Louis Napoléon" on the theme of
"The Empire Means Peace."[37] If he still had any doubts, how could he
resist such blandishments? The formalities were expedited. On 6 November, the Senate approved the establishment of the Empire by a vote of 86
to 1. His friend Vieillard did him the favor of voting against the decree.
On 1 December the results of the plebiscite were announced, overwhelmingly in favor, and the next day Louis Napoléon signed the statute to become Napoleon III. It was the anniversary of the coronation of Napoleon
I and of Austerlitz and the first anniversary of the coup d'état. The former
to be commemorated, the latter to be eclipsed. As John Bierman notes:
"It was a bitterly cold day and men of the Garde Nationale, on duty outside the Hôtel de Ville where the deed was proclaimed, danced a cancan
to keep themselves warm. It was an extraordinarily appropriate way to
mark the birth of Napoleon's *fête impériale*."[38]

Whether by dint of a cleverly disguised and long-devised plan of campaign or as a result of having carefully pondered upon his options and their
likely consequences or by virtue of following what he conceived to be his
destiny or by submitting to the overwhelming pressures and expectations
placed upon him by the ambitious imperialists who advised and even exploited his name, Louis Napoléon acceded or could not resist the temptation to accede to the imperial crown. Towards the end of October 1848,
when a candidate for the presidency, he had told "a certain personage,"
according to Hugo, in *Histoire d'un crime*: "They think that I wish to re-
vivify Napoleon. There are two men whom a great ambition can take for
its models, Napoleon and Washington. The one is a man of Genius, the
other is a man of Virtue. . . . The Republic being established, I am not a
great man, I shall not copy Napoleon; but I am an honest man; I shall imitate Washington. . . . Between the guilty hero and the good citizen I
choose the good citizen. Such is my ambition."[39] But he had chosen the

37. See Ridley, *Napoleon III and Eugénie*, 318–19.
38. John Bierman, *Napoleon III and His Carnival Empire* (New York: St. Martin's
Press, 1988), 102.
39. Hugo, *The History of a Crime*, 4–6.

way of his uncle. In his *Lettres de Londres,* Persigny had compared Prince Louis to Octavius, yet when they both had come to power, they both chose the way of Caesar. Louis Napoléon had chosen also not to heed the warnings and the appeal of Joseph Proudhon, contained in the anarchist-socialist's *La Révolution sociale démontrée par le coup d'État du 2 décembre* (1852), a rare radical work that was in fact authorized for publication in France, in August of 1852. Despite having been thrown into prison for opposing the president and despite his loathing of the man, Proudhon, temporarily at least, pinned his hopes on Louis Napoléon becoming the leader of the Revolution.[40] In his meandering text, he reluctantly accepts the necessity of the coup d'état, but denounces the signs of the move towards restoring the Empire, the "restoration of emblems, the imitation of prescribed forms, the commemoration of ideas, the imitation of means, the more or less disguised ambition for title." But, he argues, "between Napoleon, Emperor, and Louis-Napoleon, President of the Republic, too many things have happened for the latter to become the continuation, pure and simple, of the former." He advises the president: "Do not try to outsmart the Revolution; do not try to turn it to your personal ends. . . . The Revolution has foreseen everything, conceived of everything; it has set forth the plan of work to be done. Seek and when with an upright mind and docile heart you have found it, give yourself together with your country only to the accomplishment of the Revolution." He has the choice, according to the anarchist Proudhon, between anarchy and Caesarism, between the Social Republic and the Empire. If he chooses the latter, he should give up talking about "represented liberties" and he should know that, when he falls, he will fall, like his uncle, "only by and for the Revolution."[41] But Louis Napoléon, who had inherited from his mother in particular his Bonapartist zeal and from the teachings of Le Bas in particular his republican fervor, chose the way of Hortense rather than that of his revolutionary tutor. Curiously it was left to Plon-Plon, in one of his bids for power, after the fall of the Second Empire and the death of the emperor and of the prince imperial in 1879, to propose the alternative that

40. Proudhon's text is reproduced in English in Halsted (ed.), who writes of Proudhon's views in 1852: "His faith was in the inevitable triumph of the Revolution, despite the machinations of royalists, the weakness of republicans, or the dangerous plans of the Bonapartists." John Halstead, ed., *December 2, 1851: Contemporary Writings on the Coup d'État of Louis Napoléon* (Garden City, N.Y.: Anchor Books, 1972), 221.

41. *Ibid.,* 270, 293, 307.

his cousin had rejected: a marriage of Bonapartism and republicanism, a plebiscitary republic.[42] But by then, of course, it was far too late.

As the length and the contents of this and the preceding chapters have made abundantly clear, it is the coup d'état of 2 December that has been interpreted as the most decisive event in Louis Napoléon's career and has thereby generated substantially far more comment and attention than his elevation to the exalted status of emperor. This is perhaps appropriately so, for with all the intriguing myths and mysteries attached to the episode, the seizure of power was a decisive and pivotal act of *Realpolitik* and an eminently controversial set of events. But the espousal of a *politique réale,* the entry into a politics of illusion to which the new emperor committed himself, with its public displays, fanfares, and fantasies, must also be seen as far more significant a step than a mere matter of course or a decorative supplement of pomp and ceremony to the power previously acquired, as more than the icing on the cake. The renewal of the dynasty brought with it certain obligations, notably the need for an empress, for an heir, for a sumptuous court, for resplendent spectacles, for epic achievements, for monumental accomplishments, for the constant obligation to "match" (in comparison and competition) the feats of the previous Empire. All of this would ultimately bring down the regime, for Louis Napoléon, on the day that he became emperor of the French, entered into the dynamics of dominance and downfall inherent in the dynastic enterprise. It was, then, a crucial move, perhaps his true Rubicon, for, with it, Louis Napoléon crossed the frontier between the already uncertain domain of republican politics into the even more perilous realm of political extravaganza.

42. See Holt, *Plon-Plon,* 262–63.

chapter 5

Biography I: Family Affairs

En famille

In a typical family quarrel in 1851, King Jérôme, Bonaparte's sole surviving brother, envious that a scion of another brother, Louis, should accede to power and convinced, in any case, of the illegitimacy of the upstart, is supposed to have burst out to his nephew: "You have nothing of the Emperor in you." Louis Napoléon is said to have wryly retorted: "Alas! I certainly have something in common with him: his family!" Not that uncle Napoleon was any less tenderly disposed to his family despite all he did to further their advancement, as he is reported to have complained in 1810: "I do not believe that any man in the world is more unfortunate in his family than I am."[1]

Fortunately, by the time the Second Empire was instituted, there were

---

1. Williams, *The Mortal Napoleon III*, 24. See also Giraudeau, who gives somewhat different expressions to the protagonists: "You have nothing of your uncle Napoleon"; "Oh! yes I do; I have his family" ("*Vous n'avez rien de votre oncle Napoléon*"; "*Oh! si; j'en ai la famille!*"). Giraudeau, *Napoléon III intime,* 254–55. On Napoleon's statement, see David Stacton, *The Bonapartes* (New York: Simon and Schuster, 1966), 8.

relatively few truly consequential representatives left of the prolific and prodigal family over which the emperor had ruled so autocratically. Of the emperor's siblings only his youngest brother, Jérôme, was still alive. Many of the next generation had either died or been dispersed throughout Europe and beyond. However, Lucien had left numerous descendants, as had Caroline and her husband, Murat, king of Naples. Élisa had a daughter, Princess Bacciochi. Thus, following his uncle's precedent, when Napoleon III reformulated the imperial family on taking the crown, he perpetuated the distinction between the so-called civil family, excluded from the succession (essentially Lucien's and Caroline's descendants), and the imperial family. However, all the members of the civil family were provided for out of the civil list, which was enormous, amounting to almost three million francs in 1868.[2]

The imperial family now consisted only of King Jérôme and his surviving children by his second wife, Princess Catherine of Württemberg, namely Mathilde and Napoléon, the latter bearing the title Prince Napoléon, but otherwise known as Plon-Plon (from his childhood attempts to pronounce his own name). Jérôme, who had been made president of the Senate under the Republic, and his son were installed in the Palais-Royal, with huge allowances from the state. Relations with the new emperor were strained, but such was the family tradition. Jérôme showed some affection and faithfulness to his nephew, but spent much of his time investigating his paternity to justify the claims of his own descendants. Plon-Plon, who was already next in line until the birth of the imperial prince both demoted and enraged him, was a constant source of embarrassment for the emperor. Apart from his active opposition at the time of the coup d'état, his extravagances, and his hatred of the empress, who had once rebuffed his advances when he courted her as a girl of fifteen, he was appointed minister of Algeria, but never bothered to go there. He took part in the Crimean War, but left early, earning the nickname "Craint-Plomb" for his apparent "fear" of "lead" (bullets). A champagne socialist if ever there was one, his vehement oratory in the Senate attacking the Church, defending Italian unity, advancing radical views for democratic reforms despite

2. For a list, see Le Petit Homme Rouge [Ernest Alfred Vizetelly], *The Court of the Tuileries, 1852–1870: Its Organization, Chief Personages, Splendour, Frivolity, and Downfall* (London: Chatto and Windus, 1907), 213. Chapter 9 of this book, 209–22, contains a wealth of information on the "Imperial Family."

his own privileged way of life, frequently gave offense, particularly to the more conservative elements of the emperor's government and entourage. Yet the emperor was remarkably indulgent with the man whom Edmond About called a "*César déclassé*" ("demoted Caesar"). His cousin had been a childhood playmate in imperial times and a playmate in more manly pursuits in the less responsible days in London in 1846–1847; they were both lovers, for example, of the actress Rachel at that time. What is more, Plon-Plon seemed to hold particular sway over the emperor, who saw in him perhaps a manifestation of his own suppressed reckless self and was fascinated—again in stark contrast to his own appearance and in view of doubts about his own origins—by his cousin's extraordinary resemblance to Napoleon I. It is said that all Plon-Plon had to do to get his way with the emperor was to put his hand inside his jacket and strike a Napoleonic pose!

Mathilde, Plon-Plon's sister, whom Louis Napoléon had once loved and who also became an imperial highness at the proclamation of the Empire, was apparently a more advantageous relative than her brother, becoming the dazzling patron of the arts during the regime, named "Notre-Dame des Arts," thus fulfilling a function for which the emperor himself showed little talent or inclination. She too, then, complemented her cousin, as well as his wife, and her brilliant salon, rue de Courcelles, enlivened by many of the leading artists, writers, thinkers, scientists of the age, Gautier, the Goncourt brothers, Sainte-Beuve, Flaubert, Renan, Taine, Pasteur, contrasted with the stultifying rituals of the official court receptions. This was a cause of rivalry and tension, particularly for the empress, with two cliques forming around the court and the salon and only a few resourceful individuals managing to negotiate a place in both camps. "This very French talent for stubbornly prolonging divisions will bring about seventeen years of disobliging comments, of cutting remarks, of outbursts of anger, of jealousy, of caustic judgments."[3] But Jérôme's other family line, the disinherited Pattersons, that is, the self-styled "Mme. Bonaparte," Elizabeth, and her son, Jerome Napoleon, were also troublesome, coming clamoring from America to France to launch a suit to claim a place in the civil lists. Then, from another branch of the family tree, in the last year of the empire, the reckless adventurer, Prince Pierre-Napoléon, Lucien's third son, caused a major scandal in a dispute with opposition newspapers by shooting a young radical journalist, Victor Noir, on 10

3. Jean Des Cars, *La Princesse Mathilde* (Paris: Perrin, 1988), 259.

January 1870, providing the extreme republican opposition to the regime with a martyr, a "child of the people," and, at the funeral, the drama of a weeping fiancée, invented for the occasion, to embarrass the regime.[4]

In view of such family disunity, it is tempting to suggest that arguably and most significantly the two most energetic, collaborative, and productive members of Napoleon III's extended family during the Empire, Morny and Walewski, were both appropriately illegitimate. This situation was no doubt both a reflection of the decadence of the Bonaparte dynasty and an indication of the nature of the new regime, whose political legitimacy was, of course, not above question. As we have already noted, Charles Auguste Louis Joseph Demorny, as he was registered at birth, becoming the more aristocratic de Morny and usually called Auguste, was of a distinguished illegitimate lineage. He was as consummate a businessman and speculator as he was an accomplished statesman in his various political roles, initially as minister of the interior from December 1851 to January 1852, then as president of the Legislative Assembly from 1854 to 1865 and briefly as ambassador to Russia in 1856–1857. The repeated assurance of the time that "*Morny est dans l'affaire*" ("Morny is involved") was, as his biographers invariably point out, a guarantee of commercial success. He was a liberal like the emperor, but infinitely more pragmatic, and, in many ways, he was a complementary figure to his half-brother, just as he was the opposite, by his wit, subtlety, cynicism, to that other self of the emperor, the dour and intransigent ultra-Bonapartist, Persigny. Louise de Mercy-Argenteau writes: "Morny was the right arm of the Emperor. Napoléon, idealist and theorist, planned; Morny executed."[5] She might have added that, whereas Louis Napoléon wrote a learned "Analysis of the Sugar Question" (1842), Morny actually made a fortune in the sugar industry! He was very much a star of the regime, even coming to represent, in the view of Alphonse Daudet, who was for a short time one of his secretaries and depicted him in his novel on the Second Empire, *Le Nabab*, "the most brilliant incarnation of the Empire." Like the emperor but with greater justification, he lived the drama of his illegitimacy, with its compensatory will to power, success, imperiousness, as if impelled by a deep need constantly to remake himself, to be reborn. He was a man of many

4. See Holt, *Plon-Plon*, 166–67; Roger L. Williams, *Manners and Murders in the World of Louis-Napoléon* (Seattle-London: University of Washington Press, 1975), 131–50.

5. Mercy-Argenteau, *The Last Love of an Emperor*, 14.

parts, a voluptuous dandy, a patron of the arts, an avid racing enthusiast, an amateur playwright. There was much tacit animosity against Morny on the emperor's part, if not for his brilliant present successes, at least for his associations with a troubling past, a constant reminder of his mother's indiscretions and of the least-honorable events of the coup d'état. Morny openly antagonized the emperor by vaunting the arms of their mother on his carriages. But the emperor provided him with a dukedom in 1863— and a new set of arms.

As for Count Alexandre Walewski, one of the illegitimate sons of Napoleon I, born the year before Morny in 1810 of the emperor's Polish mistress, Marie Walewska, though he had been a prominent diplomat under the July Monarchy and Second Republic, he nevertheless did sterling service for the Second Empire as French ambassador to Britain, then as foreign minister and minister of state and of fine arts. He had also been, like Louis Napoléon and Plon-Plon, one of Rachel's lovers. And, in the imperial soap-opera of entanglements, of which the emperor was the central character and his relatives satellite figures, the count's devotion to his cousin or to the Napoleonic tradition or to his own career was such that, as we shall later see in more detail, he diplomatically chose to turn a blind eye to Napoleon III's dalliance with his wife, Countess Marie-Anne Walewska. But he was jealous of Morny and, though reluctant to vaunt his origins, claimed the right to be, as Roger L. Williams puts it, the "precedent bastard."[6] To this effect he remained clean-shaven, like the first emperor, whereas Morny sported an "imperial" moustache like the second. Ironically, and proverbially too, as the wags repeated on the occasion the well-known saying "*Chassez le naturel, il revient au galop*," Walewski replaced Morny as president of the Legislative Assembly when his rival died in 1865!

TOTEM AND CASTE

Thus the remnants of the powerful Bonaparte dynasty were in some respects a heavy burden for the new emperor to bear, on balance more of a liability than an asset. But he was far from unaccustomed already to such family strife. By virtue of his double heritage from the Beauharnais and the

6. Williams, *The World of Napoleon III*, 56.

Bonapartes, grandson of Joséphine and nephew of the emperor, he had been thrust from birth into the midst of the fractious family's dissensions. There was notably the long-standing vendetta of the Bonaparte clan against the Beauharnais ever since Napoleon's marriage to the widow of Alexandre, comte de Beauharnais, whom he would name Joséphine, but who was born Marie Josèphe Rose Tascher de la Pagerie. The emperor's mother, "Madame Mère," who had lived to 1836, had always been particularly resentful of sharing the family spoils with outsiders and had been convinced that the Beauharnais looked down on the Corsican origins and manners of the Bonapartes.[7] The resentment had been aggravated by Napoleon's deep attachment, not only to Joséphine, but to her children, Eugène and Hortense, whom he had adopted as his own, and to her grandsons, to whom, before his divorce from Joséphine and the birth of the "Aiglon" in 1811, he had looked for the continuance of his dynasty.

The Buonaparte tribe, which dubiously claimed long-standing noble Italian ancestry, originated in Tuscany, their forebears having settled in Corsica in the sixteenth century. They moved to mainland France only in 1793, bringing with them their fierce Corsican sense of family loyalty and pride. In fact, they were driven out of Corsica with the French by a nationalist uprising in the wake of the French Revolution. The father of the family, Carlo Buonaparte, who had been a prosperous solicitor in Ajaccio, had fought against the French during the war of independence just after France had acquired the island from Genoa in 1768, the year before Napoleone's birth. But the Buonapartes had rallied to the French side when the nationalist cause was lost and, with Letizia, Carlo's wife, enjoying a particularly close relationship with the new French military governor, the count de Marbeuf, had thrived under French rule, acquired a noble title, and saw their elder sons, Giuseppe and Napoleone, receive scholarships to France. Thus, when the Corsican patriots rebelled against the revolutionary French government, the Buonapartes were now on the enemy's side. Indeed, Napoleone was in charge of the French garrison in Bastia. After a perilous sixty-mile trek on foot from Ajaccio, most of his family joined him there in June 1893. At this time, Napoleone was rising fast up the ranks in the French army, despite an inveterate hatred of the French, which he kept to himself and his family. His father had died in 1785. He was the head of the family, having ousted, in his first significant usurpation, his elder

7. See Susan Normington, *Napoleon's Children* (Dover, N.H.: Alan Sutton, 1993), 1–2.

brother, Giuseppe, to whom the responsibility had naturally fallen by virtue of the rigorously patriarchal Corsican customs, which, henceforth, with typical convenient consistency when it suited his ends, Napoleone would enforce within the family. Curiously leaving behind the youngest children, Maria-Annunziata and Girolamo, the matriarch Letizia, her half-brother, Giuseppe Fesch, daughters Maria-Anna, Maria-Paola, and son Luigi all sailed to France with Napoleone and his troops.

Having abandoned Corsica, but not, by any means, their Corsican sense of honor, pride, ambition, the Buonapartes needed to acquire a French identity and, of course, French names. The girls, who had all been named by Letizia (or Maria-Letizia) after the Virgin Mary like herself—most inappropriately as it turned out, particularly in the case of Maria-Paola—became Élisa (for Maria-Anna) probably on Lucien's advice, Pauline (for Maria-Paola), Caroline (for Maria-Annunziata). "Madame Mère" was a sufficiently French and clannish title for their mother. The brothers became Joseph (for Giuseppe), Lucien (for Lucciano), Louis (for Luigi), and Jérôme (for Girolamo). Napoléon changed the spelling of his name during the first Italian campaign.[8] Like a tribal chief, in conformity, no doubt, with Corsican custom and to a far greater extent than the head of any mainland European family of any class, Napoléon became the undisputed leader of his clan, claiming the right to choose marriage partners for all members of his family, punishing those who defied him and insisting on the prerogative to name their children himself. Indeed, the naming system of the Bonapartes provides a chart and a key to the distribution of power within the family and to its attempts to perpetuate its dynastic privileges.

The Bonaparte tribe practiced a highly selective form of exogamy, what the anthropologist would call "restricted exchange," which is, as Lévi-Strauss observes, "an imitation of endogamy within exogamy itself," open to the outside, but only allowing the incorporation of new groups in such a way that the structure is not disturbed.[9] Thus, not only is the group perpetuated but it also acquires a legitimizing elevated status by marriage exchanges with aristocratic families. Once the elder brother, Joseph, having married modestly but richly into the merchant and banking family of Julie

8. Stacton, *The Bonapartes*, 8.
9. See Claude Lévi-Strauss, *The Savage Mind* (London: Weidenfeld and Nicolson, 1966), 123.

Clary in 1794, had secured the financial viability of the dynasty and once Napoléon had assumed full political powers in the country, the titles were conferred with the conquests, but were also acquired and required in marriage. Thus, to take a significant example, unlike his elder brother, Jérôme received no credit for marrying into the family of the second richest man in America, William Patterson, in 1803. Napoléon, when he heard of the marriage, ordered his brother back to France, without his wife, who was banned from the country. When Jérôme stayed in America, he was excluded from the imperial family and the emperor had his marriage annulled. All was forgiven soon after, when Jérôme was married a second time in 1807, to Catherine of Württemberg, whose father had only just been made king by Napoleon I himself. Jérôme became king of Westphalia, a patchwork kingdom made up of annexed territories.[10] At about the same time, Stéphanie de Beauharnais, Napoleon I's niece by marriage to Joséphine, was to marry Prince Carl of Baden; Eugène, Joséphine's son and viceroy of Italy, unexpectedly received notice from the emperor on 31 December 1805 that he was to marry Augusta of Bavaria, along with a portrait of the young lady concerned on a coffee cup; four days later he received orders to go to Munich immediately for the wedding. For once, the arrangement suited the main parties, who were happily and successfully united; indeed, three of their children were to occupy royal thrones (of Sweden, Portugal, and Brazil), whilst the others would marry a grand duchess, a prince, and a count. Thus the titular names of the extended tribe served not only to ensure the prestige of the dynasty, but acted as "toponyms," stamping its authority on its spatial acquisitions, ensuring its synchronic extensibility, signifying its insatiable voracity for other states, kingdoms, and empires. They are names for public display and affirmation, the very opposite of the intimate, family nicknames that generations of Bonaparte's used: Fifi for Jérôme, the king of Westphalia, and Plon-Plon for his son; Oui-Oui for Louis Napoléon, the future Napoléon III. The first emperor's second wife, Marie-Louise, archduchess of Austria, did not always please him by calling him "Nana" or "Popo," but she did, of course, not only add to the collection of titles but fulfill woman's second and essential dynastic function: to give birth to a son.

10. Joseph became king of Naples, later king of Spain; Murat, Caroline's husband, became grand duke of Berg and Cleves; Pauline, already Princess Borghese from her second marriage, became princess of Guastella; Louis, reluctantly, became king of Holland; and Hortense, even more reluctantly, the queen.

The totem of the Bonaparte tribe was, of course, the eagle, though the emperor did also adopt golden bees as an emblem, a prestigious borrowing from the Merovingian dynasty. Such was the closeness of the identification of the tribal chief with the totem that his son was popularly referred to as the Eaglet ("L'Aiglon"), just as Napoleon III's son, the prince imperial, would later be known as the "New Eaglet." Before the birth of his son in 1811, Napoleon was much preoccupied with the succession, for the tribe adopted a strict rule of primogeniture. This led to a rigorous variation of the use of the patronym, though not indiscriminately, for even amongst the male members of the family, there was a system of inclusion and exclusion according to the will of the chief. At the very time when he became emperor, Napoleon had passed the *"senatus-consulte* du 28 floréal an XII" (i.e., 18 May 1804), which excluded Lucien and Jérôme from the imperial family and thereby from the succession because of their unacceptable marriages. Lucien, who had a propensity for Classical names and liked to call himself Brutus, had incautiously and without Napoleon's knowledge married the illiterate daughter of an innkeeper and fathered two daughters by her. When she had died, he had compounded his disfavor with his autocratic brother, who conveniently ignored the fact that he himself had married a widow, by marrying in 1803 his former mistress, the (probably) widowed Alexandrine Jouberthou, with whom he had nine children.[11] Jérôme, as we have seen, had married Elizabeth Patterson the same year. Thus Joseph and his male descendants, of which there proved to be none, then Louis and his male descendants, were in line to inherit the throne by virtue of this decree, as, indeed, Louis Napoléon eventually did almost fifty years later. There were bitter scenes at the Tuileries when Napoleon's sisters learnt that the wives of Joseph and Louis, Hortense in the latter case, were to be princesses and not they. A few days later, the wrong was redressed to the (now) imperial highnesses, but there was no question of the sisters joining the lineage of inheritance.

A final significant law that the chief imposed on the Bonaparte tribe was that all male children born in the family were to be called Napoléon. This was more than whimsical self-indulgence on the emperor's part. It created a naming system that reinforced the ethos of the tribe, confirmed his own power and status, creating within the family a caste of surrogate selves, of

11. Stacton gives Lucien fourteen children by his two wives, though only nine appear on the standard family trees. Stacton, *The Bonapartes,* 39.

dynasties, in the next generation and, he presumably hoped, beyond. This measure is most obviously an expression of the emperor's egocentrism, for it had the effect of diminishing the status of the family name, Bonaparte, and elevating his own first name to an extended patronymic status, reinforcing the bases on which his usurped power resided—patriarchy emanating from the self—and on which he sought to perpetuate it. But there is clearly also more than a trace of his own difficulties in begetting a male heir with Joséphine, in this overcompensatory strategy to ensure an unlimited supply of male heirs. There is also, no doubt, a vestige of the primitive view that, by imposing the name of an illustrious ancestor on a child, the child becomes a reincarnation of the ancestor.[12] Cruelly, the "Eaglet," named Napoléon François Charles Joseph and proclaimed Napoleon II in the last throes of the Empire, was taken off to Vienna after Napoleon's fall, forbidden to speak French, and renamed Franz Karl Josef; significantly, the "Napoleon" was dropped.

But the emperor had instituted a code of naming that, to a considerable degree, survived him into the next century. In a sense, with the totemic eagle only emerging at the exceptional times of real power, the clan appellation comes to acquire a totemic function. Thus the Bonapartes were not only named, they were caste. The chosen few (males) acquired the magic name, with its burden of privileges and expectations. As Lévi-Strauss observes, "every christian name has a conscious or unconscious cultural connotation which parades the image others form of its bearer, and may have a subtle influence in shaping his personality in a positive or negative way."[13] In the case of Napoleon, which started as a personal name, then became a clan name, then a title, then something akin to what Lévi-Strauss calls a "necronym" after the emperor's death, the influence was far from subtle, as Louis Napoléon's case shows. There is no place in the system for the individual. He is first and foremost *homo napoleoniensis*. He also acquires his own father's name or, in some rare cases, his grandfather's name (Charles), then draws upon the limited stock of male names available in the family, or, in several cases, a prestigious other dynastic name such as François, Frédéric, or even Louis. Thus Élisa's surviving children were called Jérôme Charles, Frédéric Napoléon, and Napoléone Élisa. Caro-

12. See S. Baring-Gould, *Family Names and Their Story* (Baltimore: Genealogical Publishing, 1968), 49.

13. Lévi-Strauss, *The Savage Mind*, 185.

line's children were called Napoléon Achille Charles Louis, Laetitia Josèphe, Lucien Charles Joseph François Napoléon, Louise Julie Caroline, without any trace of her husband's name, Joachim (Murat), but with each male inheriting two or three names from the Bonaparte stock (Napoléon, Charles, Louis, Lucien, Joseph) and with each daughter acquiring a female version of an accepted male name (Josèphe, Louise) plus their mother's or grandmother's name. In Lucien's line, the name Napoleon only crops up after the reconciliation, with the appearance of a fourth son, the later infamous Pierre Napoléon. Generally, bastard sons received titles, but, in a system where links of legitimacy were more binding than blood ties, did not receive the totemic name.[14]

This self-regulating system, which blurs the distinction between family names and given names, creates therefore an intermediate category of dynastic names, sufficiently extensive and flexible to accommodate the issue of a large family, but sufficiently closed as a system to signify and impose the necessary exclusions and inclusions. It is not without its potential for confusion, particularly when the shorter forms of the names are used. Thus, in Jérôme's line, his first son (by Elizabeth Patterson) is Jerome Napoleon and his first son by Catherine of Württemberg is Jérôme Napoléon. Jerome Napoleon's elder son (born in 1830) was called Jerome Napoleon, and *his* elder son (born in 1878) was also called Jerome Napoleon. Shades of Ionesco's parodic dynasty of Bobby Watsons! In another instance, Jérôme's second son, Napoléon Joseph Charles Paul (i.e., Plon-Plon again), provoked Napoleon III's annoyance by signing official papers "Napoléon Bonaparte" and calling himself Prince Napoléon. Significantly, Louis Napoléon wrote to his cousin to make the point emphatically: "Personally, I always call myself 'Louis' to distinguish myself from my relations. I would gladly be called Napoleon-Nebuchadnezzar Bonaparte in order to have a clearly marked personal identity."[15] Supposedly to avoid confusion, Plon-Plon was usually referred to as Prince Jérôme Napoléon!

However, the main point of such replication is that the restrictiveness became all the more acute as the male was, or was perceived to be, close to the throne, and the process all the more rigorously applied as the child was close to the seat of power. Thus, within the extended Bonaparte fam-

14. Though Alexandre Florian Joseph Colonna, Count Walewski, who was "technically legitimate," did receive prestigious names.
15. Quoted in Normington, *Napoleon's Children*, 140.

ily, there emerge two classes of relations denoted by the names of progeny: the broader dynastic usage which links the child metonymically (i.e., contiguously) with the tribe, with the name Napoléon or the name of a brother being the constantly recurrent sign of the patrilineal basis of the system; a more narrowly fixed order, according to which the male child is defined metaphorically (i.e., as a potential substitute) in relation to the emperor himself, with the father's name being used as an attachment to allow for the highly limited range of variations to occur within this rigid, internal system.

If the emperor and Joséphine de Beauharnais pushed the former's brother Louis and the latter's daughter Hortense into marriage in part to reconcile the antagonistic families and in part to provide what are now mockingly referred to as "heirs" and "spares," the future king and queen of Holland singularly failed to live up to the first expectation, but were remarkably successful, in view of their own disunion, in fulfilling the latter. Napoléon Charles was born on 10 October 1802, then Napoléon Louis on 11 October 1804. But the four-year-old Prince Napoléon Charles died of croup on 5 May 1807. As if to compensate for the gap and despite the tortuous emotional, logistical complications that were involved, as we shall see, Charles Louis Napoléon, the future Napoleon III, was born on 20 April 1808, combining the names of his brothers and, with the Charles tending to be dropped, providing the Louis Napoléon to his brother's Napoléon Louis, thus presenting a perfect example of the substitutability required of the Bonaparte naming system in its most intense expression. As if in fatal justification of the practice, Napoléon Louis died on 17 March 1831 in Italy—where the two brothers were fighting with the *carbonari*— almost certainly of measles, though it has often been advanced that he was murdered,[16] and, in July of the following year, the Eaglet died of consumption in Vienna, thus leaving Louis Napoléon as the *de facto* pretender. In fact both his uncle Joseph, the ex–king of Spain, and his father were still alive and ahead of him in the succession. The one was an elderly man who had "only" two daughters and the other an invalid, though the former did move from America to London to involve himself in family for-

---

16. See Ridley, *Napoleon III and Eugénie,* 71–74. According to Guillemin's account, the two brothers were riding towards Forli when, suddenly, "they fall into an ambush in which the older brother dies, struck by a bullet full in the chest." Guillemin, "Louis Napoléon Bonaparte," 272.

tunes and call a meeting of the clan in November 1832, which Louis Napoléon attended in his father's absence.

But there was little appetite for political action amongst the surviving brothers. As the prince complained to his mother: "How would the French remember us when we have tried for fifteen years to have ourselves forgotten! When, for fifteen years, the only motive of all the members of the family has been the fear of being compromised and when they have avoided any opportunity to prove themselves, any means to bring themselves publicly back to the attention of the people."[17] By an amazing series of circumstances, or providentially, as he himself liked to believe, Louis Napoléon was fulfilling Napoleon I's prediction. One day, as he had been about to leave for war and little Oui-Oui, upset at his departure, had wanted to go with him, the emperor had declared: "That boy will have courage and a lofty spirit. . . . Perhaps he is the true hope of my dynasty."[18] The very name Napoléon would become a haunting presence for the future emperor, as he constantly strove to live up to it. The young boy wrote to his mother after the emperor's death in 1821: "When I am bad, if I think of that great man, I seem to feel within me his shadow telling me to make myself worthy of the name of Napoleon." He would later refuse to renounce the name for the right to serve in the French army during the July Monarchy. During his first stay in England, he wrote again to his mother: "You speak to me about my name? Alas! It is an additional burden when one cannot show it off to advantage!"[19] The Strasbourg and the Boulogne coup d'état attempts, when, at the latter, according to Guillemin, he cried: "I am the *son* of Napoleon",[20] were doubtless attempts to do so. As Louis Blanc exclaimed on the occasion of the former, despite its failure: "But what a name he bears!"[21] Failure was for him doubly humiliating, for it tarnished *the* name; success doubly exhilarating for it rekindled the fetishism of the name. Yet the more he sought to assert the name and to realize all the promises that it contained, the more his opponents, mainly his republican adversaries, but also members of his own family, contested his right even to bear it.

17. Séguin, *Louis Napoléon le Grand,* 55.
18. See Normington, *Napoleon's Children,* 39, Proudhon, *Napoléon III,* 332, and *Lettres de Londres,* 46.
19. Giraudeau, *Napoléon III intime,* 43, 46, 48.
20. Guillemin, "Louis Napoléon Bonaparte," 281.
21. Giraudeau, *Napoléon III intime,* 59.

COUNTING THE DAYS

As Philippe Carrard points out, New Historians in their suspicions of the authority of narrative history and of the privileging of political, diplomatic, and military accounts have problematized the notion of the "event." He notes, for example, that, according to Furet, an "obscure birth" can "count as an event as well as a famous battle."[22] The same is undoubtedly true of events shrouded in mystery or events that may never have taken place but were believed to have done so. Far more important than the truth about the circumstances of Louis Napoléon's conception were the widely held suspicions that he was not his father's son, or more important still, his own possible doubts about his origins. If the Second Empire can be interpreted as, to a considerable degree, a lavish attempt to vindicate Louis Napoléon's most far-reaching political act, it can also be seen to fulfill an equivalent prodigious purpose in attempting to dispel any such doubts about the legitimacy of his birthright and to compensate for his mother's suspected prodigality.

By an extraordinary coincidence, unless one believes that family scenarios for mysterious psychological reasons inevitably repeat themselves, the legitimacy of Hortense herself had been questioned by her father. Alexandre, vicomte de Beauharnais, had been betrothed to the sixteen-year-old Marie Josèphe Rose Tascher de la Pagerie, sight unseen, before her arrival from Martinique in October 1779. By the time their second child, Hortense-Eugénie, had been born on 10 April 1783, Alexandre had gone off himself to Martinique with his mistress, Laure de Longpré, and had violently turned against his wife, denying his paternity of Hortense and forcing Marie-Rose into a convent. When the separation had become official in March 1785 and judgment had been passed in the aggrieved wife's favor, in a curious anticipation of Hortense's own fraught relationship with Louis Bonaparte, Marie-Rose had spent no more than ten months in her husband's company. The same Marie-Rose, as is well known, would become as his grandmother the future Napoleon III's most illustrious blood relation upon marrying Napoléon Bonaparte and becoming empress of France. But however short-lived it had been, Louis Napoléon's grandfather, an ardent disciple of Rousseau and the "*philosophes*," had also

22. Philippe Carrard, *Poetics of the New History: French Historical Discourse from Braudel to Chartier* (Baltimore-London: Johns Hopkins University Press, 1992), 35.

had his moment of glory. He had been president of the Constituent Assembly, had made endless speeches advocating liberal reforms, and "at one time . . . was virtually the ruler of France"[23] until he fell out of favor, was imprisoned in Les Carmes, and guillotined four days before Robespierre's fall. Citoyenne Beauharnais, his wife, had been in the same prison and had narrowly escaped the same fate. If Louis Napoléon's Bonapartism was to be bred in the bone, much the same could be said for his liberalism.

Hortense, as we have already noted, grew up with her brother, Eugène, as very much a part of Napoleon I's close family, for the emperor treated them as his own children and adopted them. But mainly at her mother's instigation, so it seems, for Joséphine's fear of repudiation and her desire to consolidate the family links were increasing with her supposed failure to produce an heir, Hortense was called upon to sacrifice her love for her father's former aide-de-camp, Duroc, and marry Bonaparte's favorite brother, Louis. As she later wrote in her memoirs, "I renounced my romantic notions for my mother's happiness." And, as Louis wrote, in his own memoirs, of their marriage on 4 January 1802: "Never was there so gloomy a ceremony, never did man and wife have a stronger presentiment of a forced and ill-assorted marriage."[24] They were only ever to live together, by Louis's calculations, for barely four months, at three periods of time separated by long intervals.[25]

Despite a brilliant military career at an early age beside his brother, Louis was far from an ideal match, being physically repulsive from a skin disease (possibly due to syphilis), with rheumatic disorders, with a twisted spine, with the beginnings of a paralysis of his right hand, and rapidly developing all manner of ailments to compound his misery and to add to his mistrustful, melancholic, morose character. Hortense, by contrast, who was seventeen when they were married, was attractive, lively, charming, sociable, a talented musician and artist. They did not even share artistic tastes, though Louis was a writer, but of largely self-indulgent novels, plays, and poetry. Stacton quotes a sample of his pitiful verse:

> *Victime de ma confiance,*
> *Sous d'injustes noeuds gémissant,*

23. Nina Epton, *Josephine: The Empress and Her Children* (London: Weidenfeld and Nicolson, 1975), 13–17, 27.

24. *Ibid.,* 112–13.

25. Séguin, *Louis Napoléon le Grand,* 23.

Loin des amis de mon enfance,
Je souffre et meurs à chaque instant.

It has been claimed by the Freudian Ernest Jones that Louis was homosexual, with a particular attachment to his powerful brother.[26] It was also claimed by gossips of the Bonaparte court and by more than one member of the Bonaparte family that Napoleon I was Hortense's lover and father of at least one of her children. Since Louis, who claimed to love Hortense, at least in spells, was naturally paranoid, he become even more violently jealous of his wife. He despised his mother-in-law and made a point of dwelling upon her failings to Hortense. Needless to state, the bride and groom's misgivings about their union proved to be totally founded.

As king and queen of Holland, Louis and Hortense spent very little time together in the country, or very little time together at all, with Hortense preferring to stay in Paris. Yet at each brief reconciliation, they seemed extraordinarily able to produce a male heir. Napoléon Charles had been born soon after their marriage, in October 1802. During a first reconciliation a second son, Napoléon Louis, was conceived, born in October 1804. The pope christened the boy whilst he was in Paris for the coronation of Napoleon. Louis's suspicions about the paternity of the child put an end to the reconciliation. When, in May 1807, their elder son died of croup, a second reconciliation supposedly occurred out of their shared sorrow at the loss. The official view is that their third son, the future Napoleon III, born in April 1808, just eleven months after the infant's death, was the compensatory result of this brief reunion. But Louis was even more plagued by doubts on this occasion, and with greater justification, about his own part in the happy event, for the child had been born only eight months and eight days after the first date at which he could have impregnated Hortense. He would continue to complain of the infidelities of his wife and would regularly refer to Louis Napoléon as *her* son. Furthermore, much has been made of a letter that he sent to the emperor in which he wrote: "I shall eagerly conform to Your Majesty's desires on the names to be given to her son." Or there is the even more damning letter to the pope after the older brother had died in 1831: "May God have mercy upon him. As for the other, who usurps my name, you are aware Holy

---

26. Stacton, *The Bonapartes*, 13, 14. His verse reads in English: "Victim of my trust, / Groaning under unjust bonds, / Far from the friends of my childhood, / I suffer and die at each moment."

Father that he, thank heaven, is nothing to me. It is my misfortune to be married to a Messelina who breeds."[27] But at other times he does seem to have acknowledged the boy as his son,[28] and he would later write him firm but affectionate letters. But Louis was not by any means alone in his suspicions. A famous ditty would soon do the rounds:

> *Le roi de Hollande*
> *Fait de la contrebande*
> *Et sa femme*
> *Fait de faux Louis.*[29]

By the time the child was born, the couple was irrevocably separated. When Louis abdicated as king of Holland on 1 July 1810, his strained relations with the emperor worsened; the emperor dispossessed him; Louis refused his offer of a pension, retiring to Austria, thereafter to Italy; the emperor made the separation of his brother and Hortense official at this time, entrusting the children to Hortense. Before the Hundred Days, Louis XVIII, prompted by Czar Alexander, who had a weakness for Hortense, made her the hereditary duchess of Saint-Leu. Even here there was no agreement, for Louis insisted on calling himself the comte de Saint-Leu. After the emperor's fall, there was a bitter custody battle, but in his lonely exile Louis usually claimed only the older boy. He won a legal claim to both boys under the Restoration, but agreed to leave Louis Napoléon with Hortense. She would bring him up and shape his character. Did she ever discuss the truth of his conception with her son? Once again, on such an essential matter, there is a significant gap in the series, for, typically, history can provide no answer. Did the doubts or did the truth bind them closer together, for, as Philippe Séguin argues: "In any case, what complicity between mother and son! A degree of complicity commensurate with the suspicion that surrounded the conduct of the one, the birth of the other, with the trials and hopes that they shared. He adored her. He venerated her. She was everything to him." As for Louis Napoléon's view on the matter, the same biographer writes: "It seems that he scarcely doubted

27. See Ridley, *Napoleon III and Eugénie*, 11; Bierman, *Napoleon III and His Carnival Empire*, 7; Proudhon, *Napoléon III*, 334.

28. See Dansette, *Louis-Napoléon à la conquête du pouvoir*, 26, and Bierman, *Napoleon III and His Carnival Empire*, 7–8.

29. Literally: "The King of Holland / Does some smuggling / And his wife / Makes counterfeit Louis."

his filiation himself. 'I have done my calculations,' he would sometimes affirm."[30] But others, on the basis of the same calculations, came and have come to different conclusions.

WHO DONE IT?

Whether or not it matters if the truth could or should be known, the circumstantial evidence surrounding this (non)event, this "obscure conception," is at least intriguing. "From such stuff, legends are born; from such stuff novels are born."[31]

In June 1807, distraught still at the death of her son the previous month, Hortense left Napoléon Louis with Joséphine and traveled with a small retinue to the Pyrenees for a holiday, arriving at Cauterets on the 18th. Louis joined her on the 28th, but only stayed until 6 July, when he went off for one of his cures at Ussat in the Ariège. During that week, Louis was attentive, but his wife shrank from his attentions and both later declared that they did not have sex at Cauterets. From the 10th to the 19th of July, Hortense went for a trip in the Pyrenees, visiting the waterfall at Gavarnie, high in the mountains, where she was stranded for a night at a small inn on 25 July. Back in Cauterets, she stayed until 10 August, when she unexpectedly expressed the desire to rejoin Louis in Toulouse, where she arrived on 11 or 12 August.[32] After more than three years without sexual relations with each other, they made love several times, so it seems, on the slow, two-week journey back to Paris to attend the wedding of Louis's brother, Jérôme. Just as suddenly the reconciliation broke down. Hortense revealed her pregnancy. Presumably Louis did his "calculations" before departing for Holland, leaving his pregnant wife in Paris, where her doctors advised her to stay away from the chilly climate of the North. The child was born on 20 April 1808, just over eight months after Hortense and Louis had met up in Toulouse. Ladies of the court wrote the day after the confinement that the baby was healthy. But the mother, her doctors,

30. Séguin, *Louis Napoléon le Grand,* 33, 24.

31. Jean-Marie Rouart, *Morny: Un voluptueux au pouvoir* (Paris: Gallimard, 1995), 14.

32. Ridley, *Napoleon III and Eugénie,* 13–14. According to Normington, Louis and Hortense had agreed to meet in Toulouse when he had finished his cure at the spa at Ussat; Hortense wanted to stay on in the mountains, but Louis ordered her to join him in Toulouse. Normington, *Napoleon's Children,* 16.

and her entourage declared that the child was premature, so feeble, according to Hortense's memoirs, that he had to be bathed in wine and wrapped in cotton wool. If indeed the baby had been born prematurely, this does not necessarily mean that the child *was* Louis's, only that it *could* have been his. The fact that the child bore little resemblance to the king of Holland did not help Hortense's case. However, as Dansette points out, several witnesses who knew both King Louis and Louis Napoléon claimed that there were points of resemblance: the upper part of the face, according to Valérie Masuyer; certain gestures, according to Mme. Cornu, Louis Napoléon's childhood companion, whose mother was in Hortense's service; a striking resemblance, according to Alfred Maury, between the "legitimate" son of Louis and his illegitimate son, Félix, the comte de Castelvecchio.[33] It is true that Louis Napoléon, unlike his cousin Plon-Plon, did not look like the emperor. But, then, neither did Louis! There is a remarkable consistency in both the tendency of Louis Napoléon's enemies to see no resemblance and the tendency of his close associates to perceive connections. But the uncharacteristic behavior of Hortense—who, in any case, it was well known, was not faithful to her husband—in renewing sexual relations with a man whom, it was also well known, she found repellent justifies some consideration of the other main candidates:

1. There was Admiral Charles Henri Verhuell, minister of the Dutch navy under King Louis, who could have been in Cauterets despite his duties in Holland and a letter dated 24 July 1807 to that effect. A Verhuell was indeed there, but only on 3 August, for a few days, and it was almost certainly the less charming older brother, Christian-Antoine, the Dutch ambassador to Spain, on his way to Madrid. Yet the local prefect, Boniface de Castellane, in his official report asserts that the admiral himself was in Cauterets. Revealingly, perhaps, four months after the queen's stay in Cauterets, Louis had the admiral posted to St. Petersburg for a mysterious "matter of domestic conduct" (*"raison de conduite domestique"*). Hortense had him posted back to Paris, where he was present for the confinement. It was Verhuell who met the emperor first on his return from Elba to beg him to forgive Hortense for consorting with Louis XVIII. After Louis Napoléon's Boulogne escapade, Verhuell sent a plea on

33. Dansette, *Louis-Napoléon à la conquête du pouvoir*, 25, 33–34.

his behalf to the Chamber of Peers: "Do not condemn him to death. Save his head. It is a father who entreats you."[34] Verhuell had dreamy eyes, slow, deliberate movements, a Nordic goodwill, a taciturn nature, . . .

2. There was Élie Decazes, the future Duke Decazes, then a young widower, who was in Cauterets in July, seeking through the queen a position in the king's service, and still there on the 29th. Tongues wagged, but Louis still gave him a job and, after the Boulogne affair, as a minister under Louis XVIII, he voted in favor of Louis Napoléon's term of imprisonment for life! This was hardly an act of paternal affection or of family solidarity, but in such matters, political considerations often prevailed.

3. There was Charles Adam de Bylandt-Palsterscamp, the queen's equerry, about whom there are some curious inconsistencies in Hortense's memoirs,[35] who, according to police spies, made regular trips to see Hortense between 1821 and 1830 and who made a curious journey, possibly a pilgrimage, to Cauterets in July 1827, exactly twenty years after. . . .

4. There was Count de Villeneuve, the queen's (or the king's) chamberlain, who, according to Boniface de Castellane—who was at Cauterets—ushered him out of the company of Hortense to be alone with her late one evening and kept up links with Hortense in later years.

5. There was Flahaut, who had a large nose like that of Louis Napo-

---

34. See Ferdinand Bac, *Napoléon III inconnu* (Paris: Félix Alean, 1932), 17, 28. According to Bac also, at the time of the coup d'état, there were mysterious searches conducted in the archives of the department in Holland that Ver Huell (as his name is often written) directed in 1807. Furthermore, Ver Huell became a French citizen (*ibid.*, 18–19). See also Dansette, *Louis-Napoléon à la conquête du pouvoir,* 28.

35. This is how the name appears in Hortense's *Mémoires* (see *The Memoirs of Queen Hortense,* ed. Prince Napoleon, foreword and notes by Jean Hanoteau, trans. Arthur K. Griggs and F. Mabel Robinson [London: Thornton Butterworth, 1928]); there are variations, such as Bylandt-Palterslet and Bylandt-Paltercamp, in other works. See also Dansette, *Louis-Napoléon à la conquête du pouvoir,* 28–29, who notes that Hortense makes him older than he was and claims that she sent him away, when in fact he was called away by her husband, in whose service he remained for a number of years. According to Normington (*Napoleon's Children,* 17–18), he was sent back to Holland on about 14 June, so that she would only be left with her closest friends, "a strong indication that she was arranging to meet somebody without her husband's knowledge," possibly Flahaut on a secret trip.

léon, but who categorically declared later in a regal tone, "We were in Prussia at the time." He was, of course, later to be the undisputed lover of Hortense and father of her last son, Morny, as we have seen. Illegitimacy ran in his own family. Not only was his father the apostate statesman Talleyrand, but his grandmother, Adélaïde de Souza, was possibly the illegitimate daughter of Louis XV by Mlle. Irène de Buisson de Longpré, one of the mistresses that the king kept in his high-class brothel in the Parc-aux-Cerfs near Versailles.[36]

6. There were also two outsiders: Boucheporn, another chamberlain, who traveled for ten days with Hortense and her chaperone, Mme. de Broc; and the painter Thiénon, who, with Mme. de Broc again, spent the night at the inn in Gavarnie with the queen.

7. There was last, but not by any means least in importance, if not in probability, Napoleon I himself. According to the Countess Louise de Mercy-Argenteau: "Hortense was one of his weak spots, and from many an incident some people have formed a theory which I share. It's rather difficult to word, considering that Joséphine and Hortense were mother and daughter; but scruples did not exist for the great Napoléon, and there were people found to say that Napoléon I. and Napoléon III. were father and son." She adds that Napoleon III "never spoke about these things."[37] Hardly surprising really! But the emperor was certainly the child's godfather, with his new empress, Marie-Louise, archduchess of Austria, acting, doubtless at Napoleon I's usual tactless insistence, as godmother at the baptism ceremony in the palace at Fontainebleau. Curiously, the ceremony only took place on 5 November 1810, more than two years after the birth. Admiral Verhuell signed the birth certificate in the "father's" absence!

Notwithstanding her husband's suspicions, as one would expect, Hortense seeks to give credence to the official view in her *Memoirs,* where she writes of her reconciliation with her husband after the death of her first son: "Needs must, I was obliged to return to that outer world. My fate decreed it. I accepted that fate, but not without regret, and how far I still was from resignation. My husband insisted upon a reconciliation. I could no longer refuse but shrank from all the difficulties which I had not now

36. Normington, *Napoleon's Children,* 140, 27–28.
37. Mercy-Argenteau, *The Last Love of an Emperor,* 116.

the strength to endure. . . . He longed for it so, and was so happy about it that our reconciliation took place at Toulouse." The editor of the *Memoirs* confidently claims in a footnote that this statement "puts an end to the scandalous stories regarding the birth of Napoleon III."[38] In fact, it made not the slightest difference!

Nevertheless, as Dansette argues, of one thing we can be certain, beyond any reasonable shadow of a doubt: that Louis was the only man that we know about who "shared Hortense's bed" around the time of conception. But just as Napoleon III's supporters can confidently assert, like Frédéric Masson, the Bonaparte family chronicler, that he was "without any possible contradiction—except on the part of a madman—the son of Louis," the enemies of Napoleon III chose to have no doubts at all about the illegitimacy of the emperor, referring to him variously as the "Hollandais" ("Dutchman"), as "Monsieur Verhuell" or "Verhuell-Bonaparte."[39] The truth about his biological legitimacy, like his political legitimacy, still seems to be dependent upon the political views of the commentator. Only a combined Anglo-French operation of exhumation at Farnborough, where Louis-Napoléon is buried, and at Saint-Leu, where King Louis was buried in 1847, to subject their remains to DNA testing would ever solve the mystery. To gain such certain knowledge would not, of course, alter the history. In any case, was Louis Napoléon likely to have been any less determined to live up to the Bonaparte name and legend if he himself had doubts or even proof about his biological right to assume them? They would only have given him, and his mother, more to prove and a greater will to prove it. As Alain Minc writes (about Morny), bastardy can be a distinct advantage: "The bastard is not the legatee of an order that is to be safeguarded, he is the inheritor of a form of rebellion."[40] Louis Napoléon's dilemma was that he had to do both, and more. Whether or not he was conceived a Bonaparte in that mysterious conception, he was certainly born into a Napoleonic destiny, had it very much thrust upon him, and did strenuously all he could to achieve it.

38. Beauharnais, *Memoirs*, 170.
39. Dansette, *Louis-Napoléon à la conquête du pouvoir*, 34–35, 23–24.
40. Minc, *Louis Napoléon revisité*, 14.

chapter 6

Biography II: A Man of Many Parts

THE SPHINX OF THE TUILERIES

There are too many facets to his character to be counted on the fingers of both hands. They are joined up only because History forces us to unify them. This child baptized in the Tuileries, this German schoolboy, this Italian conspirator, this Swiss captain, this American emigrant, this language teacher, this prisoner at Ham, this London adventurer, and this emperor, are *all one*. . . . How can we admit in fact that this collection of such disparate beings could be one and the same person? As we watch his portraits parade by from 1810 to 1870, what powers of imagination are required—what credulity, it is tempting to ask—to accept that there is a single individual under so many disguises![1]

Just as history can only be sure of its "series," biography has only the *curriculum vitae* and is nowadays deemed, in the more modern view, inevitably to impose a deceptive order and consistency, a distorting regularity and

1. Bac, *Napoléon III inconnu,* 280.

a spurious linearity on a welter of circumstances, indeterminacies, complexities, and elusive inner agitations. Perhaps the fault lies less with the genre itself than with its inappropriateness for certain subjects. How could one adequately and convincingly write a biography of a man such as Louis Napoléon, for whom dissimulation was the natural state! Could he have been both the last Romantic leader and the first postmodernist monarch? A plotter without a plot? A mere concatenation of images? A media figure *avant la lettre*? All duty on the outside, all desire within? A fabrication, a role player, an emperor in name and dress, a portrayal behind which lurked the subject which we now know we can never know, a subject whose reality, like all inner selves, no doubt, was transindividual, a collection of shifting identities resisting plausible narrative reconstruction? A man, then, who was always but a shadow of himself! A man about whose self attempts have been made outside the polemical context to define the essential features, but only to agree upon its indefinability. Must we, therefore, content ourselves, without finality, with a few soundings (a topical rather than a chronological approach), some vivid impressions, some well-chosen anecdotes, brief assessments, verbal snapshots, light sketches, along with some revealingly incautious generalities and reductive views to scorn and to reassure us in the certainty of our tentativeness?

Thus each biography or biographical sketch creates its own subject and suppresses others, leaving an apparent multiplicity of versions, amongst which there are many common but also many conflicting or inconsistent traits. Nevertheless, when it comes to Napoleon III, such portraits do tend to belong essentially to one of three types, depending on the (usually political) purpose of the depiction or the (usually unstated) presuppositions of the depictor. There are firstly the unified images, usually drawn for polemical effect: the parodic Napoleon the Pathetic, the undistinguished figure parading as a great leader, or the heroic reincarnation of the legend, the Napoleonic ideal incarnate. Then there is the *homo duplex,* a site of baffling contrasts, the emperor as a bundle of contradictions. "Everything about him," as La Gorce wrote, "provided a contrast. One saw him conduct some intrigues as if he had studied Machiavelli, and then caress humanitarian utopias as if he had wished to copy Don Quixote."[2] Finally the ultimate enigma, whose vacant gaze, taciturn manner, and unpredictable policies betoken a fundamentally unfathomable being. As Viel-Castel ob-

2. See Campbell, *The Second Empire Revisited,* 65.

serves, to the future discomfort of historians: "One should not presume to judge him by his acts alone, for their true meaning often eludes even the most perceptive minds."[3]

If every biography is to some degree a novel, then Napoleon III could well have been the central character, or rather temperament, in a Naturalist novel. His age was a time when the two genres were very closely associated, the age of biography and of physiology, of the physiological biography and physiological novel, of the biographical dictionary, of Sainte-Beuve, Taine, Larousse, of Flaubert, the Goncourt brothers, and the early (hypernaturalist) Zola, even of a latter-day reappropriation of the ancient theory of the four humors. Napoleon I, hardly surprisingly, was declared to be "bilious." But his nephew lived in the age of the first Naturalist novelists, who showed a particular predilection for hysteria, especially in their female characters. Indeed, it was not unknown for a man, "bilious" or not, in the physiological disintegration of his temperament—for the Naturalist novel always dealt with disintegration—to become "hysterical," since the theory did allow, at least when the novelists applied it, for changes in temperament, even changes in dominant gender traits, and on good authority. For example, Dr. Michel Lévy, for a while one of Napoleon III's consultant physicians and president of the Academy of Medicine, hailed the theory of humors or temperaments in his *Traité général d'hygiène* (1851) for displaying a truth that had stood the test of time and had met with universal agreement through the ages.[4] He would probably not have objected to the biographical sketch of Napoleon III, presented with all the authority of the omniscient voice of an unidentified physiologist cited in the following extract from the emperor's entry in the (hostile) *Grand Dictionnaire Universel du XIXe* Siècle of Larousse:[5]

HIS CHARACTER

An anonymous physiologist has just delivered up to public attention a work of a special kind which adds a new, certain, expressive trait to what we had otherwise discovered about him. By means of a series of learned inductions, this master thinker has been able to di-

---

3. Viel-Castel, *Mémoires,* 16 December 1859.

4. See Théodore Zeldin, "Biographie et psychologie sous le Second Empire," *Revue d'Histoire moderne et contemporaine* 21(1974):64–66.

5. *Grand Dictionnaire Universel du XIXe Siècle,* 1874, vol. 11, p. 827.

vine the minutest particularities, both congenital and acquired, about the physical being of Napoleon III.

We shall merely retain from his conclusions one point: the emperor's temperament is lymphatico-nervous. He derives it from his mother.

Thus the nerves and the lymph are mixed in him, as is often the case in women of the Western world in Europe; a fact which illuminates a well-known comment by Mme. Gordon. She was asked, by way of a joke, if she loved Louis-Napoleon: "I love him politically," she replied with a smile. And she added: "To tell you the truth, he seems like a woman to me."

When the nerves dominate, the intelligence is free [*facile*], full of understanding, fertile in plans, with the imagination given to pleasure.

If it is the lymph that dominates, the mind is slow, the senses are dull, and, as has been stated, they have to be goaded [*écorcher*] for them to be stimulated [*chatouiller*].

Let us suppose that these elements are combined: from their fusion is born a new character who has something of the nature of the two principles and modifies the one with the other. Then a man is at once intelligent and dull, rash and calculating, modest and lavish, prompt and tardy, sensual and insensitive, mystical and skeptical, curious and indifferent, changing and tenacious, indiscreet and secretive, credulous and scornful, affable and disdainful, robust and soft, stuttering and verbose, proud and carefree; he can stick with you and abandon you; you have a hold on him and he escapes you; you can drown him and he floats; you can dominate him and he dominates. All in all, a personality that is confusing, without the one idea which brings together all of his divergent properties into a single objective: to live. Add to that the idea of a place, of a rank, of a distinction, whereby life seems to him agreeable and flattering, and you have the complete character.

It is not our fault if the man that we have to describe happens to be so complex. He is and that is how he is! . . . (A. MOREL, *Napoléon III*).

Quod erat demonstrandum!

One of the most penetrating portraits of Louis Napoléon, as subtle as this encyclopedia entry is crude, is provided by Alexis de Tocqueville, who knew him well, presenting a remarkably balanced representation in view of the fact that, as a convinced republican parliamentarian with monarchist leanings, the eminent politician was an opponent of the prince-president, whose coup d'état brought his career to an end and led to his arrest. He had been minister of foreign affairs in 1849 under Louis Napoléon, but had been dismissed as a result of the Roman expedition.[6] He wrote soon after, in his *Recollections,* a portrait which combines a sense of his subject's contradictions and a belief in his ultimate irrationality—a man in tune with the folly of his times:

> As a private individual, Louis Napoleon had some attractive quali-
> ties: a kindly, easy-going temperament; a humane character; a soul
> that was gentle and even rather tender, but without delicacy; great
> confidence in his relations with people; a perfect simplicity; an ele-
> ment of personal modesty mixed with immense pride in his ancestry;
> and a better memory for kindnesses than for resentment. He could
> feel affection, and he aroused it in those who came near him. He
> spoke little and poorly; he had not the art of making others talk and
> establishing intimacy with them, and no facility in expressing him-
> self; he had the habits of a writer and something of an author's
> pride. His power of dissimulation, which, as one would expect from
> a man who has spent his life in conspiracies, was profound, and was
> peculiarly assisted by the immobility of his features and his want of
> expression; his eyes were lustreless and opaque like thick glass port-
> holes that let light through but are not transparent. Careless of dan-
> ger, his courage in moments of crisis was fine and cool, but, as is
> common enough, his plans were very vacillating. He was often no-
> ticed changing course, advancing, hesitating and drawing back,
> which greatly damaged his reputation. For the nation had chosen
> him to dare all and expected audacity, not prudence, from him. He
> was said to have been always much given to physical pleasures and
> not discriminating in his choice of them. This taste for vulgar enjoy-
> ments and comforts increased with the opportunities given by
> power. This was a daily drain on his energy, and it blunted and re-
> duced his very ambition. His mind was incoherent and confused,
> being filled with great thoughts ill-clothed, some of them borrowed

6. See Halsted, ed., *December 2, 1851,* 18–25, from which the quoted passage is taken (23–24).

from Napoleon's example, some from socialist theories, and some from memories of England where he lived for a time—those were different and often contradictory sources. And they were the laborious result of solitary meditations far from men and affairs, for he was by nature a fantastic dreamer. But when forced to come down from these vast, vague regions and confine his attention within the limits of a definite matter, he could take a fair view of it, sometimes with subtlety and compass and occasionally even with a certain depth; but sure he never was, being always ready to put some fantastic idea beside a reasonable one.

One could not be in intimate contact with him for long without noticing a little vein of madness running through his good sense, which constantly brought the escapades of his youth to mind and served to explain them.

But yet, in the actual circumstances, he owed his success and strength more to his madness than to his sense, for the world's stage is a strange place. Sometimes the worst plays are the ones that come off best there. If Louis Napoleon had been a wise man, or a genius if you like, he would never have been President of the Republic.

He trusted his star, firmly believing himself the instrument of destiny and the necessary man.

APPEARANCES

One meter 68 tall in 1840, then curiously 1 meter 66 in 1846, according to official documents of the time.[7] Brown hair, small grey eyes, a large nose, thick lips, a pointed chin, an oval face, a pale complexion, broad shoulders, arched back. Louis Napoléon was not blessed with any of the physical assets that could have made the task easy for his image makers and official portraitists. He was naturally a caricature of his own image. His legs were too short; or, as Queen Victoria put it, there was a "want of proportion about his figure which takes much off from grace."[8] His gait was un-

7. See Hector Fleischmann, *Napoléon III et les femmes* . . . (Paris: Bibliothèque des Curieux, 1913), 8, who quotes from the *Cour des Pairs de France; Attentat du 6 août 1840; Procès-verbal des séances relatives au jugement de cette affaire* (Paris, 1841) and the *Archives communales de Boulogne-sur-mer.*

8. Quoted by Ivor Guest, *Napoleon III in England* (London: British Technical and General Press, 1952), 113.

gainly, Chaplinesque, feet sticking out, head slightly tilted to one side, with stiff and exaggerated movements of his arms when he tried to walk fast. Flaubert did an impressive imitation, much to the amusement of his friends and to the enlightenment of Zola, who was in despair at the difficulties in writing about the emperor and the court at Compiègne for his novel *Son Excellence Eugène Rougon.* As Edmond de Goncourt maliciously describes the scene in the *Journal:* "Half from pity for his ignorance, half from the satisfaction of having two or three visitors who are there learn that he has spent two weeks at Compiègne, Flaubert, in his dressing gown, puts on for Zola a classic impersonation of the Emperor, dragging his feet, one hand behind his stooped back, twirling his moustache, uttering some idiotic phrases of his own invention" (7 March 1875). Though all who met him noted, sometimes with malice, that he bore not the slightest resemblance to Napoleon I, the author of *Lettres de Londres,* presumably the arch-Bonapartist Persigny, saw only heroism in the (future) emperor's bearing, though he does concede that first appearances were deceptive: "One is not long in perceiving that the Napoleonic type is reproduced with astonishing fidelity. . . . There is, in effect, the same raised forehead, broad and straight, the same nose with its fine proportions, and the same grey eyes, though their effect is toned down; there are especially the same lines and the same inclination of the head, so marked with the Napoleonic character that when the prince turns around, it is enough to send a shiver down the spine of a soldier of the Old Guard.[9] Indeed, the emperor's appearance seems to have lain in the political eye of the beholder. Here is a further example, an Orleanist portrait by Charles de Rémusat: "A long face and heavy features, a livid and sickly complexion, a large nose like a parrot's, bad teeth like all the Beauharnais, a lack of expression, lifeless eyes, tiny, the color of his cheeks, with a squint whose only expressiveness is a hint of lubriciousness, and finally a head that is too big for his body, which in itself is too long for his legs, slow and deliberate gestures, a weak gait, as if he has backache, a voice that sounds muffled and nasal, a cold and monotonous way of speaking. Such is the man in his physical appearance, he is most unpleasant to behold."[10] Yet perhaps even Persigny would have agreed with everyone else that the emperor looked at his best on a

9. *Lettres de Londres,* 55.

10. Quoted by Dansette, *Louis Napoléon à la conquête du pouvoir,* 449, from Rémusat's *Mémoires.*

horse. When he mounted a horse, he rose in stature, espoused his public image; Napoléon le Petit became Napoléon le Grand.

Another contemporary observer, Sir William Fraser, is more complimentary about the emperor, though the compliment is hardly flattering: "Speaking with an American of some eminence I described Napoleon III., with hesitation, as having the eyes of that most intelligent of animals, the pig. General R. observed, 'That was the term applied to Washington: the pig-eyed Washington.' After hearing this, I do not hesitate to put it down." They were, it was said, his mother's eyes. They were veiled, dreamy—the famous "*regard éteint.*" According to his aunt Caroline Murat, "his gaze was lost in the unknown, veiled in shadow." "His look of inertness and apparent insensibility," according to M. de la Guéronnière, was "only the mark of an ardent and powerful inner life"; he had "something of Augustus and of Titus under the look of Werther, that type of German dreaminess." The gaze was irresistible to women, it was often claimed, though a vacant look is hardly a seductive feature in a lover. Not so, Ferdinand Bac claims, for the Swiss misses of his youth, troubled by his "*unheimliche Blick,*" by the vagueness of his gaze, by "his habit of never looking the other person straight in the eye, even when their hearts draw close together and their minds are united in the same thought." The man's vacant gaze was not, however, always a liability. It contributed to the emperor's air of inscrutability, which appealed even to Queen Victoria. "He is a most extraordinary, mysterious man," she noted, "whom one feels excessively interested in watching and knowing. There is great dignity and tact in his manner, though none of the former in his *appearance.*" If the gaze added to the emperor's quiet charisma, it contributed also, no doubt, to his fabled somnambulism. "It is not only his look that captivates, that puts people to sleep," writes Bac. "His whole demeanor is under the spell of a strange somnolence." It was as if his gaze were directed inwards rather than to the outside world. His eyes would remain expressionless in conversation and, at times, he would close them completely. Most disconcerting, one imagines, for his enemies, and even more so for his friends![11]

11. Sir William Fraser, *Napoleon III (My Recollections)* 2nd ed. (London: Sampson, Row, Marston, [1896]), 135; Caroline Murat, quoted in Fleischmann, *Napoléon III et les femmes,* 10–11; M. de la Guéronnière, quoted in Bac, *Napoléon III inconnu,* 51; Bac, *ibid.,* 222; Queen Victoria, quoted in Guest, *Napoleon III in England,* 131; Bac, *Napoléon III inconnu,* 221.

The emperor's speech was, by all accounts, no more expressive than his look. In his *Mémoires,* with remarkable understatement, Viel-Castel notes that "the emperor is not communicative," adding that "he can go for whole days, so to speak, without saying a word; his hidden thoughts absorb everything; he seems, like a deity, patient because he believes in his own eternity." Such an inhibited economy with words and his pathetic attempts at public speaking, which provoked such scorn and derision in his parliamentary days, were probably due in part to a sense of embarrassment at his German accent and its comic effect, of which he was doubtless aware even in the politest of company. It was certainly not due to a linguistic insensitivity. He wrote well, enjoyed writing and scholarly pursuits, had a good command of several languages. But it was said that "he knew five languages and could be silent in all of them." He claimed that his words could not keep pace with his ideas. But it is more likely that he preferred to construct a wall of silence between himself and others, at least in public and semi-public places, even when a degree of communication was in order. As Queen Victoria politely put it, on the occasion of the state visit of Napoleon III and Eugénie to England in 1855, "the Emperor is so very quiet, his voice is low and soft, and *il ne fait pas de phrases.*"[12] It was not the taciturnity of the strong and silent man of action. It was seemingly a more deeply rooted inhibition, an unwillingness or an inability to engage with the occasion, with the otherness that is beyond the self. The vacant gaze and the taciturn manner were the ransom of the private being and its integral demands against the public figure and its obligations. A curious visceral rejection of the political in such a prominent politician!

PUBLIC AND PRIVATE SELVES

If, as we have seen, the look of Louis Napoléon was distant, it was also a distancing look. If his general manner appeared somniferous, it betokened a distracted lack of involvement in the moment, as if the prince or the emperor were reluctantly dragging himself to and through his destiny, constantly keeping his political and social dealings at the measureless distance

12. Viel-Castel, *Mémoires,* 16 December 1859; on the emperor's linguistic talents, see Williams, *The Mortal Napoleon III,* 37; Queen Victoria, quoted in Guest, *Napoleon III in England,* 108.

of his absent gaze and demeanor. As we have already noted on the coup d'état, though the monumental event occurred in his name, at his instigation, and to his immense political advantage, he seems to have played no active part in it, withdrawing from the action as if he were an observer rather than a participant in the occasion. On other occasions, he failed to press home what little advantage he had, notably at Strasbourg and Boulogne, by a lack of total commitment to the action when such a commitment was essential to his success. It is as if in all he did Louis Napoléon was going through the motions, diffidently playing a role that was other than himself, disengaged from any total involvement. His imperturbability on the field of battle at Sedan and his stoical acceptance of the fall of his regime would become legendary. Thus, to add (reluctantly) to the fund of denominations, was he then the *distrait* emperor, Napoleon the Reluctant?

This disposition may be ascribed, in pseudo-ethnic terms according to the stereotypes of the age, as has frequently been done, to the predominance of a Nordic, Romantic, wistful temperament, acquired during his early years in more northerly parts or inherited, if not from the Bonapartes with their Corsican or Italian passions or from Josephine's line with its fiery Creole impetuosity, then, no doubt, from an unidentified source. Was he thus a natural Hamlet forced to play the part of a Henry V, or a Werther in the guise of Frederick the Great? Few leaders cast onto the theater of political life to take on a major part could have been less naturally disposed than Louis Napoléon to play a role. He did frequent the theater, particularly during his stay in London in the late forties, but he was more interested in the actresses than the stagecraft. Indeed, as Bac observes, he inherited none of his mother's dramatic sense, none of her ability to throw herself into some melodramatic scene when the occasion demanded it. The Bonapartes, as Talleyrand remarked unflatteringly, "all like to hold the center of the stage [*sont tous des cabotins*]. There is not one of them that escapes this hereditary trait."[13] Except, so it seems, Louis Napoléon, whose performances were rarely more animated than a stubborn silence, a feigned indifference, and whose talent consisted mainly in the art of dissimulation.

Perhaps all this was due to a natural timidity, to the repression of strong emotions and enthusiasms, stemming from, in the formative years, the

13. See Bac, *Napoléon III inconnu*, 83.

kind of combination of circumstances and affective relations in which the psychologist would trace lasting significance: an absent and ineffectual father, an overwhelmingly present superego figure (Napoléon le Grand), a strong-willed mother, with whom he had the deepest of bonds. The empress was led to remark on the profound attachment of her husband for his mother long after her death and even to wonder if she was fully deserving of it. His letters suggest that he craved his father's affection, suffered from the signs of rejection, was deeply touched by the rare shows of fondness and was bemused by his inconsistencies. After a heated scene between his parents during his childhood, he confided about his own father to Ferdinand Bac's father, who was a member of the household: "Even when I am with him and he pays attention to me, I am never quite at ease. I consider him to be more a tutor than a father and it would be impossible for me to show him the displays of affection that I shower on my mother."[14] In compensation no doubt, he would later be the most attentive of fathers himself. His mother, by contrast, gave him without stint not only unqualified affection, but the spur to his ambitions, a belief in his destiny, as well as the Machiavellian advice on how to realize it. But even more significantly perhaps, she provided him with an ideal symbiotic relationship with a person in whom he could freely and openly confide his most intimate thoughts and feelings without fear of retribution, a reciprocal relationship of absolute frankness and expansiveness, a transparency of communication that he would never achieve with any other person and which was the very opposite of his later human relations.[15] The painful, lingering death of his mother, we might be led to suggest, brought about more than a grievous sense of loss, more than an Oedipal disjunction, more than an emotional umbilical severance, but a lasting division between, on the one hand, the

14. *Ibid.,* 76. See also Giraudeau, *Napoléon III intime,* 21–32, on Louis Napoléon's deference to his father.

15. Giraudeau quotes, from letters from Louis Napoléon to his mother dating from January 1832, the following statements: "I see in everything that you tell me the heart of a mother and the concern of a friend. When one is unhappy, one feels a great sense of relief in confiding one's sorrow in someone"; "How happy I am to have a mother as indulgent and tender as you! If only you knew how much you have touched me by looking for a moment into the depths of my heart and excusing its torments!" Giraudeau adds: "From his childhood, by never being rebuffed by his mother, even when he was unreasonable, he acquired the habit of thinking aloud to her and, without any hesitation, and without any reservations, of confiding in her about whatever was preoccupying him, even his fleeting thoughts and emotions." Giraudeau, *Napoléon III intime,* 42.

private, "authentic" self (all internalized narcissism), and, on the other hand, the public figure (all duty and obligation), the artifice, for political purposes, with its taciturn inscrutability protecting the former and marking the vast, unfathomable gap between the two.

Thus, the apparent mysteries and contradictions of the emperor's character could be ascribed to this essential division. The utter separateness and impenetrability of the inner self—his cousin Mathilde once remarked that, had she married him, she would have cracked open his head to see what there was inside—led to an outwardly stoical acceptance of adversity and disaster, along with a cool acknowledgment of that other "impostor," success. As he wrote, banally but significantly, from prison in Ham after his major political setback: "Yet do not think that I am discouraged; no! but there are two beings in me: the political man and the private man."[16] The former was unshakable, the latter suffered (and exalted) in silence. He kept what was essential about himself to himself, at one remove from other people, to be revealed only in the most intimate of circumstances. Thus he moved through the frenzied world of politics with a calm detachment as if separated from all human emotions. Hence the strong element of self-reliance in his character, a reluctance to confide in others, a secretiveness which was often given a political explanation, taken to be the sign of a crafty Machiavellianism, but was more likely than not an inherent incommunicability. He gave the impression that he was enacting his public life, playing the part of somebody else, confiding in no one. The genuine self remained almost totally hidden within the carapace of his impenetrability, all the better to take on the feigned being that his political destiny required.

On the one hand, then, there was in this perpetual exile a profound attachment to his home, even though it was several palaces, and the sincere pain of his separation from his small family, together with an acute sense of the fleeting nature of his domestic happiness. "When I am happy," he wrote to his wife in 1856, "I am afraid!" In this Stendhalian character there was the constant torment of the dictates of duty wrenching him from his search for happiness. "I dare not think," he wrote from Milan in June of the same year about his family, "of the happiness that I shall enjoy to see you both again; today, I must not weaken with such thoughts." This

16. Mathilde, quoted in Williams, *The Mortal Napoleon III,* 14; Louis Napoléon's letter (to la comtesse X), quoted in Giraudeau, *Napoléon III intime,* 101.

soft and tender self was constantly repressed, but it surfaced in the frequently told acts of kindness, of forbearance, and of charity for which he
was responsible. Here too belonged the vigorous enjoyment of the life of
the body in the muscular young man, his pleasure in physical exercise, in
contact with the sensual liberation provided by the sporting feats and
prowess for which he was renowned, in the swimming, the riding, the
fencing of the "wild harum-scarum youth" who galloped about the streets
and roamed the countryside, away from the obligations of public life. As
his health declined in captivity in Ham, he missed above all the release of
this physical activity, was given a horse to ride on the ramparts, but derived
little benefit from the exercise, certainly less than the horse! Thereafter
only his chain smoking, the "eternal" cigarette, would satisfy and denote
his constant need for the gratifications of the body, and, of course, his
often furtive sexual escapades, the minor triumphs of the carnal existence
over the asceticism of ambition. Like Morny, but less overtly, he was a vo-
luptuary, "as if the sexual act indefinitely renewed, repeated with so many
women, only served to explore avidly the enigma of his origins; as if his
insatiable bodily appetite was only a way of rediscovering the gentleness
and the tenderness of an absent mother."[17]

On the other hand, there was the resolute front, the courage, the iron
will, the utter self-control. His mother, aptly summing up the two sides of
his character in a telling expression, used to call him a "gentle stubborn
thing" (*"doux entêté"*). His stoicism in the face of defeat became legendary, but at a much earlier stage, he constantly gave a general impression of
firm resolution, however unpredictable some of his policies and decisions
would be. Thus writes Viel-Castel: "The emperor applies to everything
that he does and thinks an unshakable will-power, he consults nobody and
goes on his way without taking into account the obstacles."[18] Goaded on,
no doubt, by the vicarious ambitiousness of his mother and the towering
example of his uncle—he always carried a letter from them both on his person—and spurred on by his memories of the glory days, such as reviewing
the troops with his brother at the emperor's side, memories that constantly
reminded him of his obligations, he was like a high-born Julien Sorel with

17. The emperor's letters, quoted in Giraudeau, *Napoléon III intime,* 336, 338; his acts
of kindness and sporting feats, see Williams, *The Mortal Napoleon,* 19, 23, 14; Rouart,
Morny, 15.
18. Viel-Castel, *Mémoires,* 19 January 1853.

an ever-present sense of a duty to perform and a mission to fulfill. "Such was Napoleon's destiny," as Stendhal's character muses, watching a sparrow hawk circling above the rock from which he ponders his future, admiring its powerful movements, its strength, and its isolation; "would it one day be his?"[19] But, like Julien's, it was a mission that was never really an integral part of himself. It had to be assumed each day or submitted to with resignation or imposed by others in a perpetual struggle within the self.[20] The stuff of the novelist rather than of the historian.

DANDY

Apart from the six years of captivity in Ham, Louis Napoléon spent most of the period 1839 to 1848 in London. His first stay during this period, from 25 October 1838 until he set sail to conquer France via Boulogne on 5 August 1840, was quite brief, but sufficient for him to make an impact on English society. He was no longer the young prince, an object of curiosity, as he had been during his three-month stay in London with his mother in 1831, or during a six-month stay in 1832–1833 on family business after the death of the duke of Reichstadt. He was the imperial pretender, a man of independent means by virtue of his inheritance from his recently deceased mother and a man-about-town with an impressive train of supporters, warmly applauded, toasted, even lionized wherever he went, as on a trip to industrial sites in the Midlands and the North, enthusiastically received by the mayor of Manchester and vigorously applauded in the Theatre Royal in Birmingham. He was welcomed into exclusive clubs and received in the best society circles. Ivor Guest notes that Disraeli admired Prince Louis for "that calm which is rather unusual with foreigners, and which is always pleasing to an English aristocrat"; and he even approved of his clothes: "his dress was in the best taste, but to a practised eye had something of a foreign cut."[21] Though he did not by any means pass mus-

19. Stendhal, *The Red and the Black,* trans. Catherine Slater (Oxford–New York: Oxford University Press, 1991), 67.

20. Bac claims that the key to the emperor's destiny was that it was entirely *"guided, channeled by the will of others."* It was not a question of an "irresistible atavistic urge to link up with a branch of the genealogical tree and to redress the Eagles of his family." Bac, *Napoléon III inconnu,* 145.

21. Guest, *Napoleon III in England,* 40.

ter in such exacting company, certain gentlemen in particular finding him dull company and not suitably appareled, he did secure the friendship of Count Alfred d'Orsay, the leading dandy of the time.

Louis Napoléon was far too involved in vulgar politics to qualify as a thoroughgoing dandy, but he acquired many of the manners and mannerisms of the dandy during his stay, as illustrations of the time show. He tended to overdress, however, wearing a large diamond eagle on the clasp of his kerchief, and he rode around with eagles painted on his carriage. He frequented all the right places of high society, owned Arab racehorses, hunted, gambled in the casinos, went to Leamington Spa, kept the company of actresses, and almost fought a duel with Count Léon, Napoleon's illegitimate son.[22] After his escape from Ham in 1846, he returned to the fashionable London scene again, picking up where he had left off six years earlier and now taking up with the less than respectable Miss Howard, who had, nevertheless, the double advantage of being very beautiful and very rich.

Whatever his limitations in the part, the role of the dandy very much suited both his character and his present state, giving primacy to appearances as a source of prestige in the temporary frustration of his political ambitions. It provided the advantages of a marked distinction and a reassuring conformity, the satisfactions of narcissism and the protective distancing of impassivity, the posture of complete self-control as an alternative to control over others, the complete separation between the vulnerable inner self and the impenetrable mask. The daily investment of an impeccable attire—as he, no doubt, believed—compensated for his natural imperfections and insecurities, providing a refuge in an elegant appearance for the recent humiliations that life had afforded him. It transformed his natural taciturnity from a failing into an advantage, though he lacked much of the ready, biting wit that should have gone with the role. But he enjoyed the power of his self-created and self-sufficient social self over women, the elegant, aristocratic accoutrements of the horse, and even what Alain Montandon calls "the erotico-nicotinal [*érotico-nicotinique*] pleasure that Wilde also relished."[23] Above all it put into

22. See Ridley, *Napoleon III and Eugénie*, Chapters 10 and 16.

23. Alain Montandon, ed., *L'Honnête Homme et le dandy* (Tübingen: Gunter Narr, 1993), 254. See also the comments by Henriette Levillain and Marie-Christine Natta on the strategies of the dandy and the attraction of military costumes: *ibid.*, 153, 179–93.

effect an essential strategy for his success: to deflect the attention of others from his motives and his means to his displays. In a sense also it was indirectly a signal expression of his socio-political status in a curious state of harmony with his times, for, as Baudelaire claimed: "Dandyism appears especially during transitory periods when democracy is not yet all-powerful, when the aristocracy is only partly threatened with ruin and degradation. In the turmoil of such periods a few men, downgraded [*déclassés*], disgusted, made idle [*désoeuvrés*], but all rich in natural strength, can conceive of the plan to establish a new species of aristocracy."[24] It was also for this particular "*déclassé*," temporarily "*désoeuvré*," a perfect training ground for his later role, with its sense of ritual and ceremony. He would merely need to exchange the dandy's outfit for the military attire, the uniform of the socialite for the emperor's clothes. Another ensemble of signs constructed for external effect but emptied of their referent.

In 1863, Baudelaire defines the true "beauty" of the dandy in words which, with due allowance for some fundamental differences, could well have applied to the leader of his country at an earlier phase of his career, as consisting of "the cold manner which comes from the unshakable resolve to remain unmoved; like a latent fire which comes into being, which could but which refuses to burn forth."[25] Louis Napoléon was no George Brummell, no Count d'Orsay, but temporarily at least, until he could direct the art of cultivating appearances more directly to political ends, his eloquence consisted in the elegance of his attire.

MAN OF DESTINY

Queen Victoria observed just after the state visit of the emperor and empress in 1855 that this "extraordinary man," as she was wont to call the emperor, showed "a great reliance on what he calls his Star, and a belief in omens and incidents as connected with his future destiny, which is almost romantic." She could have little suspected the depth of his belief. Another lady, who knew him much better in later years and who is billed as his "last love," the Countess Louise de Mercy-Argenteau, records in her "reminis-

24. Charles Baudelaire, "Le dandy," in *Oeuvres complètes,* ed. Claude Pichois (Paris: Gallimard, Bibliothèque de la Pléiade, 1976), 2: 711.
25. *Ibid.,* 2:712.

cences" an intimate scene which took place on 26 July 1870, the day before the emperor was due to leave for the front. He revealed not only his foreboding about the outcome of the war, but the conviction that his defeat was predestined. "I know everything that will happen to me, Comtesse," he is supposed to have said, betraying to the lady's surprise a profound belief in prophecies, horoscopes, and astrology. Then he took out of his pocket-book a yellow piece of paper covered in cabalistic signs, his horoscope, which he had found in his mother's papers after her death and which, so he claimed, all that had happened and would happen to him and his Empire was foretold in a mystic code. "So my reign is to finish," he declared, "and the Prussians are to be victorious."[26]

Louis Napoléon inherited, so it seems, not only the predictions but the propensity to believe in them from his mother, who was likewise influenced by her highly superstitious mother, the Empress Joséphine. The Empress Eugénie, for her part, was of a similar mind. Just as in Italy in 1834, a black "somnambulist," put to sleep by "a clever magnetizer," had predicted to Hortense that her son would be the "chief" of a great nation, gypsy fortune-tellers in Carabanchel had prophesied to the young Eugenia that she would marry an emperor and rule over a kingdom. In fact, when the prince was in London as a guest at Lady Blessington's home, a chiromancer appeared at the door, claiming to be a pupil of the same Mlle. Lenormand who had been Joséphine's favorite fortune-teller. Another guest present, none other than Charles Dickens, urged the hostess to admit her and to test her powers. After studying the Frenchman's palm, somewhat predictably, she foretold that he would "reign over a great nation."[27] It is hardly surprising, therefore, that the Scottish medium Daniel Dunglas Home—satirized by Browning as "Sludge"—was such a success in 1857 in the Tuileries and in the imperial summer home in Biarritz, table-turning and table levitating, crystal gazing, making a hand appear under the table, producing mysterious rapping noises, conjuring up spirits, particularly impressing the impressionable Eugénie, that is until he fell out of favor because it was discovered that he had holes cut in his socks to ring bells and knock under the table and because he rashly predicted that the prince im-

26. Queen Victoria quoted in Guest, *Napoleon III in England,* 138; Mercy-Argenteau, *The Last Love of an Emperor,* 166–72.

27. On Joséphine, see Bac, *Napoléon III inconnu,* 49; on Eugénie, see Legge, *The Comedy and Tragedy of the Second Empire,* 10–11, and Ridley, *Napoleon III and Eugénie,* 160; on Louis Napoléon in London, see Guest, *Napoleon III in England,* 65–66.

perial would never reign.[28] At about the same time, of course, Victor Hugo was indulging in furious seances of table-turning at Marine Terrace on Jersey. Needless to say, like his language, his sessions were more lavish than the emperor's.

Louis Napoléon's dabbling with the occult and superstitious beliefs was typically related to and limited to his political destiny, representing no doubt ways of coping with the unbearable responsibilities of his circumstances and passing over to some occult force the burdens of uncertainty. Typically also Victor Hugo's occultism became, in a boundlessly elaborate scheme in which not surprisingly he himself had a central role, the basis for a new vision of the cosmos and the spiritual world, elaborating a new religion which would engulf Christianity just as Christianity had engulfed paganism, a view which Christ himself appeared to endorse on 11 February 1855.[29] But at least according to one prominent English divine, Louis Napoléon was not without his ordained place in a vaster scheme. George Stanley Faber by name, fabler by nature, was a proponent of biblical prophecy and the author of *The Revival of the French Emperorship Anticipated from the Necessity of Prophecy* (1853), a work which ran to a number of editions and which, in the American and Canadian editions, acquired, the better to "announce its peculiar character," a prefix to the original title: *Napoleon III: The Man of Prophecy*. The prophecy, supposedly deriving from historical fact, as the preface claims, and speaking with the voice of History, as the text itself frequently claims, is based on the revelation (from the book of Revelations) to St. John of the Mystery of the Harlot and of the Wild Beast with seven heads from the sea, the latter symbolizing the Secular Roman Empire and its Seven Forms of Polity. According to the Angel's declaration, five of the heads had already fallen: "the One is; the Other hath not yet come; and, when he shall have come, he must remain only a little time. And (relatively to the Wild-Beast that was and is not) he is also an Eighth, and yet he is One of the Seven. And he goeth into destruction."[30]

---

28. See Guest, *Napoléon III in England*, 157; Williams, *The Mortal Napoleon III*, 41–42. According to Le Petit Homme Rouge (Ernest Alfred Vizetelly), he was dismissed from the Villa Eugénie when the empress realized that he was a charlatan because of some ridiculous blunders that he made about "*cosas de España*." Le Petit Homme Rouge, *The Court of the Tuileries*, 266.

29. See Robb, *Victor Hugo*, 331–38.

30. G. S. Faber, *The Revival of the French Emperorship Anticipated from the Necessity of Prophecy* (London: Thomas Bosworth, 1953), 10.

In less allusive terms, it is argued that the Roman emperorship did not become extinct in the fifth century with the deposition of Augustulus, but continued on in the East, with Constantinople as its capital, until its final extinction in 1453. However, the Holy Roman Empire perpetuated the Polity of the Sixth Head until 1806, when the last Roman emperor, Francis, renounced the title and discharged the duties of the imperial throne. "Thus ultimately *fell* the long-lived Basileïs or Emperorship of the Romans. Consequently, *at* or *shortly before* its *Fall,* we may be sure that the Seventh Roman Head or Polity would appear." Indeed, the emperorship of the French became the predicted Seventh Head, which, in fulfillment of the prophecy, was to be "slain by the sword of military violence" but was to undergo a revival from this political death, with the Seventh King reappearing "as a *seemingly* though not *really* Eighth King." Thus the Wild Beast was slain but then "*reëxisted.*" All this, the author claims, he predicted in 1818, then again in the years 1828 and 1844, and it has been confirmed by "the necessity of CHRONOLOGY." Unfortunately for Napoleon III, the necessity of the prophecy demanded that the short-lived, sword-slain and revived Seventh Head "go into destruction," more precisely in the year 1864, in a General War, from which England still had a chance to escape if the country were to give up its expedient policies of Popery and Idolatry and come "with clean hands into the Court of God's Judgment." Events prove, the author claims, "with a force of demonstration little short of mathematical," that Napoleon III's destiny was to complete the prophecy. "Thus speaks History."[31]

Faber died the year after writing this extraordinary work and was thus happily spared the evidence that at least the mathematics of his prophecy proved to be defective. However, the significance of this work lies not in its preposterous assertions but in the example that it provides of the extent to which the figure of Napoleon III was appropriated to fulfill an almost limitless set of roles with which a whole variety of writers, thinkers, theorists, artists, however outlandish, were able to invest him. His destiny was to become a destiny. His seemingly insubstantial public self and private inscrutability clearly abetted the process, making him available for such attributions. He was, in a sense, a floating signifier, his essence bound up in his name, available for any scheme or role, a *buona parte,* more usurped than usurper, more impersonated about than impersonator. A man of many parts and causes, most of which were not his own.

31. *Ibid.,* 33, 35, 40, 46, 54, 15.

1. *The Emperor Napoleon III*, portrait by Hippolyte Flandrin
Courtesy Musée National du Château, Versailles

2. *Napoleon III*, portrait by Franz Xavier Winterhalter
Courtesy Musée National du Château, Versailles

3. *The Empress Eugénie, Surrounded by Her Palace Ladies*, by Franz Xavier Winterhalter
Courtesy *Musée National du Château, Compiègne*

4. *Image d'Épinal* of the imperial family

5. *Allegory to the Glory of Napoleon III*, by A. Cabasson
   Musée National du Château, Compiègne

6. *Napoleon III, the Empress, and the Prince Imperial Surrounded by Their People,*
a popular engraving by Léopold Flameng
Courtesy Bibliothèque Nationale de France, Paris

7. *The Empire Means Peace,* cover illustration for a musical score
Courtesy Bibliothèque Nationale de France, Paris

8. *The Emperor at Solferino,* by Jean-Louis-Ernest Meissonier
Courtesy Musée d'Orsay, Paris, en dépôt au Musée National du Château de Compiègne, 1986

9. *The Battle of Solferino*, by Ange-Louis Janet-Lange
Courtesy *Musée National du Château, Versailles*

10. Napoleon III, commander in chief of the army in Italy, as pictured in *Histoire populaire contemporaine de la France,* one of the officially sanctioned histories of the Empire

11. *Napoleon III's Visit to the Slate-Quarry Workers of Angers During the Floods of 1856,* by J. P. Antigna
Musée des Beaux-Arts, Angers

12. *The Emperor Visiting the Flood Victims of Tarascon in June 1856*, by William Bouguereau

Courtesy Hôtel de Ville de Tarascon

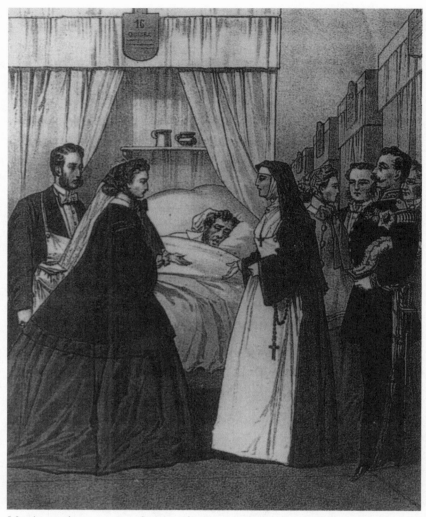

13. A popular engraving showing the Empress Eugénie visiting a cholera hospital
Courtesy Bibliothèque Nationale de France, Paris

chapter 7

Epic Ventures

PUBLIC FIGURE

The private Louis Napoléon, as we have seen, ever privy to himself alone, would hide his sensibilities and contradictions behind a mask of inscrutability. But the effective leader requires, like the heroic literary figure, a singleness of purpose, a stable subject, an instantly recognizable public identity, and an undeviating plot. Thus the emperor needed to construct a public image and, in a manner contrary to his natural tendency to withdraw and obscure, constantly to display it. However fractured and indeterminate the inner self, the public image had to be one and indivisible. He had to become a historical figure, a totalizing subject, abolishing contingencies, both a part of and a representative of a historical totality and continuity. The doubts and hesitations of the existential being had to be entirely suppressed beneath the mask of resolution and assurance.

Louis Napoléon understood well, both before and particularly after he had become the emperor of France, that politics was not a merely a matter of policies but also a figurative art, an invention of symbols, myths, illusions, all the better for being personified in a single individual. He owed his power, prestige, and position to his name and to the myth that it evoked. It was necessary to reactivate that myth, to "repackage" it and to promote it. It was much less a case of "fabricating" a public image, of mythologizing the ruler, than had famously been the case for Louis XIV, constructing images of the king, as Peter Burke has shown, in the likeness of the gods and of heroes of classical mythology or in allegorical association with the sun. There was, it is true, as in the ancien régime, the same emphasis on spectacle, on symbols of centrality and of continuity within a prestigious tradition. There was the same theatricality, a seeking after effect or *éclat*, the same highly elaborate ritualization of significant domestic events such as a wedding or a baptism, and there were the triumphal displays on occasions of military significance. There was, furthermore, the same multiplication of images of the sovereign, surrounded by the symbols of his power and majesty, with equivalent stylization to show the ruler to best effect, abstracting him from the imperfections of his private reality and transposing him into the idealized and ornate modes of representation of his public image. But Louis Napoléon as Pretender and as Emperor knew that his power base was with the people of France. He could not, as earlier rulers had done, enjoy a lofty remoteness from the masses, secure in the conviction that his power derived from God. "The French Revolution marks a watershed," writes Burke, "between old regimes, in which there was no need to persuade the people, and modern states, in which they are the main target of propaganda."[1] Napoleon III and his image makers were obliged to fashion a vision, a *persona*, of the heroic leader, which both evoked the glories of the past and remained in tune with the modern age. Questions of constitutional rights and legalities exercised a fair minority, but the mass of the people responded to images and ceremonies that represented the nation and its heroic aspirations and that appealed to a collective psychology. Schwartzenberg makes the important distinction between personal power and the personalization of power. The former is an institutional reality which may or may not be apparent. The latter concerns the symbolic representation of power, which may or may not reside in the object of representation.

Louis Napoléon sought to marry the two, imposing an image of himself as an inspirational leader, a heroic image of the epic commander of a mod-

1. Peter Burke, *The Fabrication of Louis XIV* (New Haven–London: Yale University Press, 1992), 201.

ern nation. This image, typical of his hybrid allegiances to nationalist, conservative, revolutionary, progressive, military, capitalist values, sought to combine disparate elements into a coherent effigy. As a heroic leader, to take up Max Weber's distinctions,[2] he attempted to conjoin three forms of power: traditional authority, based upon imperial (and, to some degree, royal) customs; constitutional authority, based on an appeal to the voters in his strategic plebiscites; and charismatic authority, which he endeavored to inspire in his staged encounters with the people. This last tendency, as many contemporary politicians show, tends to equate leadership with showmanship, with the theatricality of politics. In the first, the authority is inherited; in the second, it is proven; in the third, it is displayed. On shaky grounds on the first two counts, Louis Napoléon excelled himself on the third, particularly after the coup d'état and the restoration of the Empire, surrounding himself with all the ostentatious trappings of his imperial power, the sumptuous costumes and decors, with their reds, golds, and purples, symbols of strength, wealth, and sovereignty, promoters of the illusion of military invincibility, permanent opulence, and regal entitlement. As the portraits of the emperor and the ceremonials of his regime illustrate, no expense or effort was spared to promote the image of the heroic leader and to provide the most elaborate of stages on which he could strut and play out his Napoleonic destiny. For the new emperor, with his inherently dubious inherited or constitutional powers, to ensure the political survival and justification of his regime, the play, indeed, was the thing.

PICTURE POLITICS

There is, not surprisingly, a marked contrast, particularly as the Empire wore on and as the emperor wore out, between the state portraits of Napoleon III, proud, erect, and resolute, and the usual languid, uninspiring, incongruous figure that he cut even on public occasions, as is attested by those who knew him well and by the few photographs that remain. As Théophile Gautier unkindly remarked of the emperor in uniform, "he looks like a ring-master who has been sacked for getting drunk." Pictures of the emperor tend to hark back to an earlier stage, to representations of

2. See Roger-Gérard Schwartzenberg, *L'État spectacle: Essai sur et contre le Star System en politique* (Paris: Flammarion, 1977), 18.

the more vital pretender or the prince-president. According to Roger L. Williams, "descriptions by eye witnesses of his figure and his movements make us realize that portraits of him painted in the eighteen-fifties or sixties conveyed a flattering image, for his body was ungainly and ill-proportioned, and his swaying gait ungraceful." State portraits traditionally serve to flatter the subject and favor the career of the artist. But their primary purpose is political: to reaffirm the authority of the sitter, to assert the continuity of his or her rule, to create an icon, loaded with the abiding symbols of power reappropriated to stand alongside the appropriate signs of the times. If some degree of resemblance is essential, in the state portrait the semiotic far outweighs the mimetic. The main conformity is not to likeness, but to the conventions of the genre itself, with its assertive postures, its institutionalized pomp, its plush decors, its ermine wraps, its classical columns, its raiments of state and uniforms, its symbols of rule, scepters, swords, orbs, and crowns.[3]

There were numerous busts, medallions, and portraits of Louis Napoléon on display at the Salons or distributed in reproduction widely throughout the country before he became emperor, notably a *Portrait of the Prince President* on horseback by the popular and patriotic Horace Vernet, the principal battle painter of the period, which was shown at the 1850 Salon. There was even on display, at the 1852 Salon, a commemorative medal, by the engraver Oudiné, celebrating the coup d'état, an allegorical representation of Louis Napoléon, guided by Wisdom, slaying the hydra of Anarchy and receiving the civic crown from a grateful nation. Naturally, after the proclamation of the Second Empire, there was an inexhaustible production of such works with their epic themes, particularly during the 1850s. But as far as state portraits are concerned, one of the most widely known and most frequently reproduced is the painting by Hippolyte Flandrin, which was exhibited at the Salon of 1863 (see figure 1). After establishing an early reputation as a religious painter, Flandrin had also become an accomplished portraitist, particularly with feminine subjects, earning many honors and a place in the Institute in 1853. In his portrait of the Emperor, which did not especially please the sitter, the

3. Gautier quoted in Burchell, *Imperial Masquerade*, 37; Williams, *The Mortal Napoleon III*, 17; on state portraits, see Andrew Wilton, *The Swagger Portrait: Grand Manner Portraiture in Britain from Van Dyck to Augustus John, 1630–1930* (London: Tate Gallery, 1992), 22–23.

focus is on the military leader, appearing conventionally in a general's uniform, decorated with the sash of the Légion d'Honneur and the Croix de
Guerre, the left hand fondling in manly fashion the hilt of his sword. The
left hand promises to perform in the present such heroic deeds signified by
the objects on the table on which he has placed his right hand: maps to
guide the conqueror's campaigns, flags, Caesar's *Commentaries,* and a
bust of Napoleon I for inspiration. A martial spirit infuses the picture. The
posture is rigid and resolute, as if the leader were about to spring into action. The more realistic effects, such as the general squatness of the figure
and the creases in the trousers, give him a certain salience that mitigates
against the pose. As does the look, which is (not unrealistically) both distant in the one eye and both direct and intent in the other, suggesting
(charitably perhaps) both the visionary and the man of action, engaging
the spectator confidently to entrust the destiny of his nation to such a valiant leader. The whole person is contained in his role. The contours of the
picture are firm and clear like the emperor's ardent resolve. The light is as
immaculate as his mission, without the slightest shadow of uncertainty.

What this portrait lacks, with its emphasis on the emperor's military
prowess, is provided by the refulgent composition by Franz Xavier Winterhalter (see figure 2), the fashionable portrait painter of European courts,
renowned for the glamor and flair which he bestowed on his high-born
subjects, emphasizing the luxury of their costumes, their wealth and status
more than their individual traits. (In fact, he painted nine portraits of the
empress Eugénie, including the famous composition *The Empress Eugénie
Surrounded by Her Palace Ladies* exhibited at the Salon of 1855, the year
he was a member of the jury—see figure 3.) As Andrew Wilton writes,
Winterhalter "could instinctively endow even the most businesslike of pictures with an impressive panache."[4] Here regal paraphernalia dominate, or
more precisely surround, notably in the form of the ermine cape, the Napoleonic and the militaristic references in the shaded emblems and in the
emperor's dress, the boots, the epaulettes, the white breeches, and the red
sash. The sword is discreetly shrouded at the emperor's side. It is as if the
militaristic Napoleonic image had been stretched, polished, and refined.
But the ornaments, the scepter, the crown, the hand of justice, and the
cloak, refer back to the coronation of the first emperor. The heavy-lidded
gaze and the telltale *impériale* moustache leave no doubt about the iden-

4. Wilton, *The Swagger Portrait,* 22–23.

tity of the subject, but the svelte frame and the remarkably long and elegant legs belie his true physiognomy. One could hazard allegorical interpretations of the grotto-like setting, with its extraordinarily diffused red light, with its blue-sky beyond and the gathering storm clouds, with the hint of a classical cityscape below, to conceive of this remarkably elegant new Caesar, with his aristocratic mien and proud posture, as a fiery maker of war and a serene bringer of peace to the city. But the total effect is to envelop the figure in an ornamental frame of mythical regality, denoting power, prestige, and stateliness, abstracting him from his historical state. It is thus all the more interesting to note that, in view of the image that the regime wished to perpetuate, this picture, with modifications that tone down the lofty nobility of the court painting and include identifiable national tokens, seems to have been recycled and disseminated throughout the country in such productions as the *images d'Épinal* that graced French households and public places. Here, for instance (see figure 4), the Classical background is replaced by a solid column and a view of the flag aloft. The noble attire is less in evidence, but the regal purple backcloth adds majestic dignity to the composition and the laurels of the frame reinforce the militarist and imperialist motifs. The conventionalized postures are even more evident, as is the process of democratization, in the variation which includes the empress and the prince imperial and which blends in typical Bonapartist fashion two contrasting color systems: the gold and purple of majesty with the red, white, and blue of democratic France. The young child, a replica in miniature of his father, dressed in military costume, as indeed he frequently was from a very early age, ensures the continuity of the dynasty, completes the family triangle, and stands beneath the national emblem. The empress, from whom all traces of foreignness have been expunged in the pasty conventionality of the faces, combines the regal elegance that suits her position with a display of the national colors. Indeed, the whole composition is less a portrait of the imperial family than a flag or a badge to be blazoned across the country for the greater glory of the regime.

Such portraits, with their gaze directed at the spectator, give credence to the image of the emperor as a charismatic leader, bodying forth the values of nobility, military prowess, stability, civic and family virtue, national pride, glory, tradition. But they are only one aspect of the visual propaganda by which the emperor and his Empire sought legitimation and permanence, conveying the illusion that the imperial regime was the natural order of things. With their combination of symbolic stylization and stylized representation, their aim was to inspire awe and admiration, and with them adherence to the values, policies, and ideology of the regime. Other examples of Second Empire iconographical propaganda tend more openly to one of these two opposing modes, relying either on the more intellectual appeal of the symbolic in starkly allegorical compositions or portraying the emperor's deeds in specific historical situations. A most remarkable example of the first tendency is Cabasson's *Allégorie à la gloire de Napoléon III* (see figure 5). The artist, a disciple of David and a specialist in religious and historical themes, shows the now familiar figure of the emperor being borne on his exalted mission from war unto peace in a Roman chariot beside a banner-waving version of Marianne, whilst a host of mythical winged figures trumpet his glory from on high and more earthbound figures acclaim his majesty. Less baroque but no less striking is the engraving by Léopold Flameng (see figure 6), the work of the Belgian painter and engraver, who enjoyed a highly successful career in Paris during the Second Empire. His composition shows the familiar figure adopting a messianic pose, his right hand stretched out to receive the adoration of his people of every generation, whilst the empress, in a Madonna-like pose, holds the word and the flesh that proclaim the new age. A shadowy battle scene in the background is a reminder of past glories and, most remarkably, the outline of the figure of the emperor's illustrious uncle provides a halo for his successor. This remarkable conjunction of religious and military imagery is like an altar piece erected to the cult of the new emperor. As in the allegory that adorns a musical score of the time (see figure 7), the recurrent message is that out of the military glories of the past will come a new era of peace, prosperity, industry. Here again, the arms belong to a shadowy past; the symbols of peace and fruitfulness betoken a new future. The martially helmeted figure symbolizing the Empire turns her back on the battles of the past, ushers in a new age, protects the fledgling arts, and dictates the watchword of the new regime: "The Empire Means Peace."

This did not mean, however, that works of a more representational kind, portraying the emperor's specific achievements, were not produced at the time, works which presented the emperor as an inspired military leader. Opportunities were, however, rare, and exploits few, for, before the ill-fated campaign of the Franco-Prussian War, the emperor was only involved in military action and commanding his troops on one occasion, for a two-month period in Italy in the war with Austria in 1859. He was supposedly in the Austrian firing line at Magenta, then again at Solferino, directing operations, though some military witnesses, indifferent to the emperor's heroic image, claimed that his deeds consisted of no more than observing the action and chain-smoking at a safe distance on his horse. Nevertheless, France's leading official painter, Jean-Louis-Ernest Meissonier, in a famous canvas much admired by Gautier (see figure 8), shows him very much in control of operations, at the head of his staff, serenely contemplating the enemy on a promontory, with the battle raging below. Totally dominating the proceedings, he is conspicuously placed at the center of the spacious scene, in splendid isolation despite the crowd of officers attending him and waiting upon his orders. Some Austrians, appropriately, lie dead and in disorder below, and the vast sky above lends grandeur to the august presence of the commander. The artist was unable to resist the temptation of including himself in the company, leaning forward and looking into the distance, dressed partly in civilian and partly in military costume. His painting was shown for the first time at the 1864 Salon, then was prominently displayed, along with portraits by Flandrin and Cabanel, at the 1867 Exposition.

Ange-Louis Janet, known as Janet-Lange, who was a leading history painter of the period, a pupil of Ingres and Vernet and a chronicler in paint of the Crimean, Italian, and Mexican campaigns, devoted a canvas to the same subject, which is not dissimilar in composition to Meissonier's work, though the scene is more animated and the company is shown in the thick of the action (see figure 9). Once again the emperor, receiving news or issuing instructions, a head above the others, cuts a dashing figure, as does his horse. Though there is death and disorder surrounding him, the emperor remains the focus of looks, gestures, and artistic arrangement, despite the distraction of the new casualty in his ranks, all the better to highlight his heroic composure in the face of such danger. His uncle would have been proud, at least of the pictures.

Such heroic images of the emperor, more rapidly produced, indeed mass-produced, were widely diffused in illustrated journals or in officially sanctioned histories of the Empire, notably the *Histoire populaire contemporaine de la France,* where, amongst the hundreds of vignettes in each volume, the debonair commander in chief of the French army in Italy is shown, rather more casually, reflectively, but still authoritatively, sitting on a cannon (see figure 10). But the most significant historical compositions that present a heroic image of the emperor were not by any means re-

stricted to scenes of warfare, not only because circumstances provided limited opportunities, but mainly because, for all the militaristic pageantry of
the regime, martial success was not an essential element of the emperor's
stated aims, ethos, or ideals. Hence the importance of the image of Napoleon III as a humanitarian, as a peacemaker, and as a provider for his
people. The devastating floods in the Rhône and Loire valleys in the summer of 1856, to take a celebrated example, provided him with an occasion
to promote this image. As well as issuing generous relief from his personal
coffers, he visited the stricken regions, and artists unfailingly committed
the event to posterity. There was notably *Napoléon III distribuant des secours aux inondés de Lyon* by Lazerges, as well as Janet-Lange and Antigna's
Napoléon III visitant les ouvriers des ardoisières d'Angers (see figure 11),
in which, rather woodenly, the emperor stands surrounded by a host of
respectful workers and their families arriving in boats by the banks of the
swollen river. Both paintings were shown at the 1857 Salon, as was the
most studied and impressive of such compositions, Bouguereau's *Napoléon III visitant les inondés de Tarascon* (1856) (see figure 12). William
Bouguereau, who received a number of important commissions during the
Second Empire, including the decoration of the Chapel of St. Louis in St.
Clothilde Church and the ceiling of the Grand Théâtre de Bordeaux
(1869), and who became president of the Académie des Beaux-Arts in
1864, was honored for his religious canvases and his monumental decorations. This painting, sponsored by the secretary of state with a handsome
fee of 5,000 gold francs, was commissioned two weeks after the emperor's
visit to Tarascon on 3 June 1856. It is of the same genre and served for
the nephew the same propaganda purpose as Antoine-Jean Gros's better-
known homage to the charity of the uncle, *Les Pestiférés de Jaffa* (*Napoleon
in the Pest House at Jaffa*).[5] In the later work, we see Napoleon III accompanied by Rouher and Generals Niel and Fleury. But the military features
of the scene are totally overwhelmed by the religiosity of the composition,
as the Savior brings succor to his people, with one hand dipping into the
money bag and the other reaching out in a benign gesture to the beautiful
young supplicant girl on her knees, shown in remarkable relief in the full
light. The scene within the scene between the young girl and her benefac-
tor lends an allegorical intensity to the event. The Empire, even in all its
ceremonial dignity, ever brings comfort to its compliant people in their

5. See *William Bouguereau 1825–1905* (Paris: Musée du Petit-Palais, 1984), 49–50.

times of need. Furthermore, the redeemer's act is sanctified by the church, beneath which he dispenses charity and hope even to the most despairing, whilst the victims point, pray, and wave in acclaim of his august presence.

There is at times something absurdly incongruous about such scenes where the stiff and thoroughly conventionalized military presence seems out of place, as in the popular engraving of the empress visiting a cholera hospital shows (see figure 13). The figure on the right verges on the caricatural, like a character from an opéra bouffe. The composition illustrates the degree to which the images of the emperor and of those who were represented in his image became extraordinarily stereotyped, emptied of any natural or particular features, merely creations of a conventionalized form, serving no other purpose than to signify what might be termed (in the manner of Barthes) "Second Empireness" or "Napoleonicity." It is, of course, through such a process of repetition, simplification, and conventionalization that the popular symbols of propaganda are generated, concentrating significance emphatically into stylized forms, establishing a fixity of recognized features that seem to create a semantic coherence, however ambiguous or contradictory the constituent elements might be. Thus the sacred is mixed with the profane, the military with the civil, noble miens and accoutrements with democratic symbols. The leader devoted to peace, order, and harmony amongst the French and the peoples of Europe never abandons the military attire, lest they should forget the source of his power and prestige. The iconography produced to represent Napoleon III mediates all such contradictions, compelling adherence by fostering the illusion of coherence, permanence, and necessity within the appealing harmonies of aesthetic form. The rituals of the Second Empire fulfilled a similar function. In fact, for the purposes of the regime, they were more effective than the higher art, for they allowed for active mass involvement. And in so doing, they also allowed it to indulge to unimaginable lengths in its ultimately fatal taste for extravagance.

RITUAL POLITICS

It is tempting to attribute the indulgence in extraordinarily elaborate and expensive ceremonial, for which the Second Empire is renowned, simply to a taste for ostentation and prodigality amongst its leaders. But as has already been argued, the very act of reinstating the Empire, in this respect as in many others, necessitated extravagant measures and led the regime into the mode of excess. Not only was it necessary for the Second Empire to deny the usurpation of power of the coup d'état by a process of naturalization and legitimization through the implied continuities of rituals and ceremonies and by orchestrating through them the consent of the people, but it was obliged to reinstate much of the ceremonial of the First Empire itself. Yet perhaps even more imperative, if less obvious, was the need to ritualize the epic exploits in order not to have to repeat them in reality. Many of the historical accomplishments of the previous imperial regime were appropriated to accommodate the new ideals and ideology of the new state. Thus, in the most magnificent fashion possible, the sacred and profane rituals, the elaborate ceremonies and the extravagant spectacles of the Second Empire had a threefold function: legitimation—to demonstrate that the regime had the status and prestige of the most glorious reigns of the history of France; restoration—to demonstrate that the new regime was an integral part of the continuity of the Napoleonic dynasty and was inspired by the Napoleonic ideal; commemoration—to celebrate and derive glory from the accomplishments of the First Empire (and to negate its humiliations). To these should be added the ceremonies of democratization by which the emperor sought to show that the Second Empire, as it was claimed of the First, was indeed the successor to the Revolution, investing ultimate power in the people of France. Republican symbols were frequently mixed with the predominantly Napoleonic emblems. Elections and plebiscites, by which the emperor set so much store, were also, in a sense, ritual expressions of the popular will. Particular ceremonies and spectacles could fulfill without apparent contradiction more than one of these functions. All were open to valid political contestation, but the rituals served to suspend all critical reactions and to suppress opposition far more effectively than any rational argumentation or even than any police measures, whether in secret or through a public show of force. As David I. Kertzer writes, "the political leader who wants to create the public impression that he is champion of justice, equity, and the general good is far more likely to achieve a deeper and more lasting impression by staging a dramatic presentation of this image than he is by simply asserting it verbally. His appearance should be replete with appropriate symbols and managed by a team of supporting actors."[6] The rituals and ceremonies of

6. David I. Kertzer, *Ritual, Politics, and Power* (New Haven–London: Yale University Press, 1988), 40. The same commentator notes: "Perhaps the most important ritual of legitimation found in modern nations is the election. Indeed, it is a ritual that has quickly been taken up by countries around the world, nations with very different official ideologies and diverse institutional structures" (49).

the Second Empire were skillfully stage-managed to create such an illusion, that of a just and appropriate order. They served also to construct a prodigious reality, endowed with a coherent meaning and purpose that abolished the disruptions of the past, consecrated the new *status quo,* and created a sense of continuity. They infused in the responsive elements of the population a euphoria of celebration, arousing popular emotions and enthusiasm.

Napoleon Bonaparte, along with several members of his family, had had an unfailing sense of grand spectacles, with themselves at the center, modeled on the ceremonies of great dynasties of the past and mixed with religious overtones and a fair dose of superstition. Typically, Bonaparte, on being elected consul for life on 2 August 1802, had celebrated his birthday on the 15th of that month, which was the day of the Feast of the Assumption of the Virgin Mary, and had had erected above the towers of Notre-Dame a huge illuminated star with, at its center, the sign of the zodiac under which he had been predestined to greatness.[7] The extravagance of his coronation was legendary. All public buildings had been illuminated; the sword of Charlemagne had been brought from Aix-la-Chapelle for the occasion; the pope, of course, had been there; Joséphine had been resplendent in diamonds and a satin dress embroidered with golden bees; twenty squadrons of cavalry had preceded the cortege of eighteen carriages; the emperor's cape had weighed eighty pounds. One of Napoleon I's great ceremonial institutions had been his court, with its grand dignitaries, conceived in the manner of the royal courts of the past and fulfilling a similar political purpose.

Napoleon III fashioned his own court largely on the model of his uncle's, restoring much of the ceremony, with presiding grandees responsible for its organization, the *grand chambellan,* the *grand maréchal du palais,* the *grand écuyer,* the *grand aumônier,* the *grand veneur,* and, most imposingly, the *grand maître des cérémonies.* The empress had her own household of dignitaries, and eventually the prince imperial too. Costumes were lavish in the extreme, especially on state occasions. Relations of the imperial family received pensions and sinecures. Visits of state were, in particular, occasions for extravagant displays at the Tuileries palace, the official residence of the imperial family, for which no expense was spared. At vari-

7. Nina Epton, *Josephine: The Empress and Her Children* (London: Weidenfeld and Nicolson, 1975), 118.

ous times of the year operations would shift to another palace. In May or June the court would usually move to the palace at Saint-Cloud, where a more relaxed atmosphere prevailed in a country setting, then to Fontaine-bleau, where the emperor held court for the cream of French society, who came with all their finery for summer entertainments. After the 15 August celebrations, the calendar dictated a more informal imperial seaside and mountainside holiday at the Villa Eugénie in Biarritz, where the empress felt most at home in proximity to Spain. Then, after another stay at Saint-Cloud, it was off to the château of Compiègne for another season of *séries*, when, laden with mountains of luggage containing the numerous requisite changes of expensive clothes that some could ill afford—Mme. Metter-nich, who could, arrived with twenty-eight cases, not counting her hat-boxes—each week a group of some eighty distinguished guests, visiting foreign dignitaries, diplomats, politicians, high-ranking military men, fi-nanciers, industrialists, scientists, artists, having been made to feel honored at the opportunity to attend, were subjected to a week of programmed ac-tivities: banquets, balls, visits to the medieval castle at Pierrefonds, and the speciality of the Compiègne season, hunting. The hunts, which required their own elaborate costumes in the style of the ancien régime and which Truesdell describes as "butcheries in the best royal tradition"—a typical day would yield for a party of nine 43 deer, 20 hares, 498 rabbits, 316 pheasants, 20 partridges, and a woodcock[8]—were followed by the cere-mony of *la curée* in the torchlit courtyard, the fight for the spoils of the hunt, the offal thrown to the starving dogs, which, for Zola, the author of *La Curée* and *Son Excellence Eugène Rougon,* was a gory allegory of the greed and competitiveness of the Second Empire. Such fierce and frenzied activities, with which *la curée* may be imaginatively linked, took place, of course, beyond the circles of the court. But the hunting itself, like the ceremonies of the court, and the conformist military or civil costumes of the men—the lavish and multifarious costumes of the women confined them to a purely decorous role—were signs of distinction and domination for the new class of rulers of the regime, establishing their dynastic author-ity over property and people, ritually enacting in the artifices of the court their claims to legitimate privilege and distinction with the combination of elegance and ruthlessness that they applied in exercising their dominance in the social and political orders.

8. Martin Truesdell, *Spectacular Politics: Louis-Napoleon Bonaparte and the "Fête Impéri-ale," 1849–1870* (New York–Oxford: Oxford University Press, 1997), 71.

By all accounts, apart from the excitement of the hunt at Compiègne, the distraction of visits from eminent foreigners, and the occasionally more lively entertainments such as the *bals masqués,* in which guests could play roles other than those assigned by the strict protocol of the Tuileries, life in the court circles was excruciatingly tedious, consisting of stiffly ceremonial routines, drab conversation, tiresome evenings enlivened only by a game of charades or a game of lotto at the emperor's suggestion, unless he preferred to play patience by himself or, far worse, unless he insisted on boring all and sundry with dreary readings from some book or other of interest to himself alone.[9] The lunches and dinners in the salon Louis XIV, the long evenings, even the gala events, served no other purpose than to impress, to hold a court for the sake of it, for, significantly, as Truesdell notes, the Court of the Tuileries, unlike the courts of the ancien régime, had very little political power, for the Emperor ruled through his ministers and provincial administrators.[10] Thus the millions of francs spent on the civil list and on the grand receptions for three or four thousand guests were merely a showcase for the regime. It became ceremony for its own sake, pure formality, decorum with little purpose other than its own repeated performance, to be gone through for the sake of appearances, repeated in "series," gratuitously extravagant, a theater of blatant ostentation, showing the regime's dependency on illusion and, towards the end, disguising its precarious hold on real power.

There was nothing at all unusual about many of the public ceremonies involving the emperor and the empress as heads of state. The opening of railway lines, the inauguration of churches, the reception of foreign dignitaries were all part of their responsibilities, though the exhibitions, as we shall later see, had a special significance for the regime. Even the charitable visits which the imperial couple made and to which the empress was particularly devoted, were, of course, expected of the nation's leaders as a sign of their concern for their people. Eugénie in particular, as it befell her woman's role, seems to have derived much of her popularity—or, more accurately, to have detracted much from her unpopularity—by her charitable visits to hospitals, orphanages, schools, hospices, and her sponsorship

9. On life at the court, see Joanna Richardson, *La Vie parisienne* (London: Hamish Hamilton, 1971), Chapter 2, and Maurice Allem, *La Vie quotidienne sous le Second Empire* (Paris: Hachette, 1948), Chapters 2 and 3.
    10. Truesdell, *Spectacular Politics,* 68.

or founding of numerous charitable organizations. Her donation to charity of her dowry from the emperor and of a generous wedding present
from the Paris Council, along with her visits to cholera wards in Paris in
1865 and Amiens in 1866, are cited by Truesdell as examples of her skill
at the "politics of sincerity." But, given Eugénie's background and character, there was as much sincerity as political expediency in such acts. One of
the readers of her household gives a moving testimony to her countless
gestures of humanitarianism for the "immense benefit of the indigent
classes." After a visit to a smallpox ward at the Hôpital Saint Antoine, for
instance, her admirer narrates how the crowds eagerly pressed around her
to kiss her hand and bless her: "When we returned to Saint-Cloud the
Empress had the pleasing satisfaction to find that large pieces had been cut
from her dress, the women having torn off shreds to be preserved as
relics."[11]

But many other examples are presented by Truesdell of what he calls
"spectacular politics" that are more specifically Napoleonic and relate to
the restoration of the Empire and the commemoration of the First Empire, celebrations widely reported and shown in the illustrated press and
described in detail in the official newspaper of the regime, *Le Moniteur
universel*, not, at times, without embellishments. The emperor was naturally central to such displays, posing as the undisputed representative of
both the family dynasty and the people. There was a pervasive militarism
about the regime, which was more ceremonial and symbolic than truly expressive of the political organization and power structures of the state. It
was more to do, as Truesdell notes, with "Louis-Napoleon's claim to his
uncle's heritage and the emotionally resonant place of the military in the
symbolic construction of the French nation in the nineteenth century."
Though he had only received limited military training and seen very little
action, on most public occasions the emperor wore a general's uniform,
assuming a rank that he had not earned militarily. Much was made of the
victories in the Crimean War and in the Italian Campaign, with elaborate
ceremonies to welcome back the troops, whilst the emperor's own departure on the latter campaign was an occasion for unprecedented enthusiasm
and display. At other times military pantomimes enacted great victories
and mock battles became public spectacles. The celebrations of Napoleon

11. Mme. Carette, *My Mistress, the Empress Eugénie; or, Court Life at the Tuileries*, authorized translation (London: Dean and Son, 1889), 335.

I's official birthday, declared a national holiday, were particularly significant, with *Te Deum* masses and troop reviews in the morning, popular entertainments in the afternoon, and fireworks at night, an annual reminder that the earlier regime had been effectively re-established. The celebrations for the imperial marriage and the baptism of the prince imperial were modeled in their pomp and extravagance on the equivalent events, with ceremonies in Notre-Dame, and "vividly re-created the splendor of the Middle Ages and focused the country's attention on the monarchical and hereditary aspects of the new regime."[12] For the religious wedding ceremony, which took place on 30 January 1853, there were representations of statues and frescoes of Charlemagne, Saint Louis, Louis XIV, and Napoleon I, along with eagles, bees, and tricolor banners everywhere. The couple's carriage had been used by Bonaparte and Joséphine. The cathedral was decorated again for the baptismal celebration on 14 June 1856, which was based upon the baptism of the king of Rome and on royal baptisms, with an elaborate procession to the cathedral and an even more elaborate service within. As descriptions of the event show, whether they are faithful to the truth or given to embroidering upon it,[13] and as Zola's evocation of the same event in *Son Excellence Eugène Rougon* also illustrates, there was a fundamental hollow inauthenticity about the occasion. For example, in front of the Hôtel de Ville, false facades were erected and joined by a false triumphal arch. In his novel Zola describes a huge mural painting on a building on the Île Saint-Louis, depicting a frock coat, "emptied of its body," a symbol of Napoleon I. Such details, whether factual or fictional, underline a fundamental feature of Second Empire ritual: the very ambiguity of the status of the regime in relation to its model.

Was it indeed, as was claimed, a reinstatement of the Empire, which such ceremonies served to confirm, or was it a sham of an Empire, not only an imitation, but an imitation of an imitation, as the anachronistic ceremonies, gestures, decorations, symbolism show? David Bell interprets Zola's scene by reference to Deleuze's distinction between the imitation, which acknowledges its status as a copy of a model, and the simulacrum, which usurps the primacy of the original by seeking to replace it. By the

12. Truesdell, *Spectacular Politics,* 137, 59.

13. For example, Truesdell describes the ceremony and studies contemporary descriptions, noting that one illustrated journal shows the three-month-old prince imperial already sitting up and "bearing a marked resemblance to Napoleon I." *Ibid.,* 67.

same token, since the self-coronation of Napoleon I, from which his neph-ew's status and ceremonial derive, was itself of the order of simulacrum, Napoleon III's reign was doubly unfounded, or ungrounded. Thus, in Zola's view according to Bell, "the Empire is a reign of illusion, substitu-tion, appearances, reflections, masks."[14] Such objections, however, are predicated upon the myth of originality, which, in all probability, rigorous research on any reign would easily deconstruct. Rulers imitate rulers be-cause it is politically effective to do so, and Napoleon III was far from orig-inal in relying upon illusion, appearances, masks, and reflections to sustain his power. It is hard to imagine that anyone at the time believed, or be-lieved that Louis Napoléon believed, that he was the reincarnation of Na-poleon I. Indeed, he was ever insistent in pointing out the differences, as, of course, were his enemies in no uncertain terms. The fault was, no doubt, in the excess of the ceremonial, not in its inappropriateness, that is in the inappropriateness of its excess, in the expectations that it aroused, in the immense disparity between what the regime pretended to be and what it could achieve.

Thus, the Second Empire vigorously promoted the cult of Napoleon I and the commemoration of his epic military victories, fully exploiting the association of the nephew with the uncle, erecting statues throughout the country, celebrating the anniversary of his death (5 May), decorating vet-erans of the first emperor's campaigns, naming new thoroughfares or re-naming streets and boulevards by association with past glories or present successes, such as the Boulevard du Prince Eugène or the Boulevard Sébas-topol, outdoing its own extravagances on the annual "*fête nationale*" of 15 August with elaborate decorations and grandiose firework displays. When possible, in these orgies of Bonapartist celebration, in which massive crowds took part, the commemoration of the epic exploits of the past em-peror were linked to supposedly equivalent feats in the present, when, for instance, a Chinese theme was adopted in 1858 and 1861 to acclaim the invasion of China or in 1864 the Place de la Concorde was decked out in Mexican style to celebrate the army's deeds in the New World. Truesdell gives an idea of the lengths to which the regime went to vaunt its tradi-tions and display its emblems: "Eagles, bees, imperial coats of arms, and so forth were always present, and at times they were made the centerpiece

14. David F. Bell, *Models of Power: Politics and Economics in Zola's "Rougon-Macquart"* (Lincoln-London: University of Nebraska Press, 1988), 8.

of the celebration." In 1865, for example, Alphand turned the obelisk into a "needle of fire, on the four faces of which appear[ed] glittering palm leaves supporting the imperial letter and formed from almost 50,000 jets of gas."[15] Thus the epic glories of the past were mobilized to give luster to the present regime with all the showmanship of the future. In the process, the delusion of military invincibility was fostered by such displays. The epic theater was confused with reality—that is, until the Prussian guns in 1870 shattered the illusion.

An epic discourse

From a very early age Louis Napoléon was imbued with the sense that he was born to fulfill an epic mission and predestined to a heroic future, having been nourished by the matriarchal strictures and expectations of Laetitia and Hortense, surrounded by relics of the glorious exploits of his uncle, haunted by the spirits of the heroic past. All this prompted in the susceptible child a nervous anxiety that manifested itself in dreams and nightmares at Arenenberg, nourished, according to Ferdinand Bac, by readings of "exalted literature on the Epic," which, given his sensitive nature, intoxicated him and left a lasting impression. Later on he confided in Hortense Cornu, his childhood friend, a remarkable dream in which he had found himself standing at the top of the Vendôme Column in place of his uncle, and, he significantly added, "as alone" (*"aussi seul"*). Yet at the same time, he felt a strong sense of affinity with the people. His famous claim at Saint-Quentin, "My whole being responds to yours, we have the same instincts and the same interests," was, as several anecdotes suggest, more than a political slogan. This visceral Bonapartism, appropriately, no doubt, before circumstances were to allow Louis Bonaparte to attempt to put it into practice, was first articulated, rationalized, theorized, and rhetoricized, notably in the book that he wrote between his attempts to seize power in Strasbourg and Boulogne, *Des Idées napoléoniennes* (*Ideas of Napoleonism*), published in 1839. The work was composed in a private room at the British Museum library that a friend, Antonio Panizzi, the Keeper of the Printed Books, made available to him. The "ideas" of the book, though it is relatively short, are rather laboriously argued, but they did

15. Truesdell, *Spectacular Politics,* 77.

arouse considerable attention and earned the support of socialists as well as Bonapartists such as his uncle Joseph, not only in France but elsewhere in Europe through several translations. Nevertheless, before the Boulogne coup attempt in 1840, the prince felt obliged to issue shorter and more forceful expositions of his ideas: *L'Idée napoléonienne,* which is presented as a monthly publication, of which only one number appeared, and *L'Avenir des idées impériales,* which was too militant, according to Alain Minc, to be included later in his collected works.[16]

It has often been observed that the emperor remained remarkably faithful to the grand views outlined in these relatively youthful works, and there is evidence that they constituted to a considerable degree guiding principles during his reign. On 24 May 1859, for example, in a briefing to Walewski on the policies of the Second Empire, he wrote: "I go over all this with you, because it is very important that my ministers always be well imbued [with my] basic ideas, and I want you to reread the *Idées napoléoniennes* which I wrote in 1837 [*sic*]. My convictions are unchanged."[17] Such again was the contradictory nature of Louis Napoléon's person that, as a pretender, he managed to be both an opportunist and a visionary, just as, when in power, he became a pragmatist but never lost his idealist vision.

The theory of history which Louis Napoléon expounds in *Ideas of Napoleonism* is resolutely Romantic, Hegelian, dividing the life of nations into two conflicting tendencies, the one divine and leading to perfection, the other mortal and tending to corruption. The great men mark the stages of the progress of humanity: "We advance from Alexander to Caesar, from Caesar to Constantine, from Constantine to Charlemagne, from Charlemagne to Napoleon." The best form of government is one which advances the march of civilization. Napoleon's role was to disperse the chaos brought about by the Revolution in the painful throes of the birth of liberty. "The Emperor may be considered the Messiah of the new ideas." He captured the regenerative genius of the nation, felt as the people felt, and, with his "accurate powers of divination," saw the difficulties of establishing a Republic without firm guarantees of stability. Hence the formula of

16. Bac, *Napoléon III inconnu,* 77, 211. On his affinity with the people, see Giraudeau, *Napoléon III intime,* 156, 186–87; Minc, *Louis Napoléon revisité,* 95.

17. Quoted by Roger L. Williams, *The Mortal Napoleon III,* 21. See also, on the relevance of the writings of Prince Louis Napoléon to the policies of the emperor, William E. Echard, *Napoleon III and the Concert of Europe* (Baton Rouge–London: Louisiana State University Press, 1983), 2.

Napoleonism: "To obviate this want of fixity and continuity, the greatest defect of democratic republics, it became necessary to create an hereditary family, to be the conservator of these general interests, but the power of which should be wholly based on the democratic spirit of the nation." Here boldly stated is the essential axiom of Bonapartism: that the emperor is the expression of the democratic will of the people. Or, as Louis Napoléon also succinctly defines it in *L'idée napoléonienne*: "The Napoleonist idea means, to reconstitute French society, overthrown by fifty years of revolution, to conciliate order and liberty, the rights of the people, and the principles of law."[18]

Conveniently, the doctrine of Napoleonism is both conservative and progressive, both authoritarian and liberal. Louis Napoléon concedes, in the earlier work, that liberty "was not secured by the imperial laws." But, he argues, in a country at war with its neighbors, liberty had to wait. Nevertheless, Napoleon had set about the task of uniting the nation, reorganizing it on principles of equality, order, and justice. But ultimately, what was his aim? "Liberty. Yes, liberty! and the more one studies the history of Napoleon, the more evident is the truth." Any doubts that the reader might have at this point are swept away with a poetic flourish: "For liberty is as a river; in order that it may bring fertility and not devastation, its bed must be hollowed out wide and deep. If in its regular and majestic course it remains within its natural limits, the countries it traverses bless its passage—but if it rushes on like a torrent which has burst its bounds, it is regarded as the most terrible of scourges; it awakens the hatred of all, and one then sees men in their prejudice recoil from liberty because it destroys; as if one should banish fire because it burns, or water because it inundates." Such rhetoric has the advantage both of allegorizing recent French history in the vaguest of terms at the expense of critical judgment and of justifying all manner of abuses of power. In any case, Louis Napoléon argues, even though his premature fall may have prevented the emperor from reaching this ultimate goal, there is the massive accomplishment of the many internal benefits that he brought about, a full catalog of which his nephew provides: the reform of the judicial system, of the financial system, of all levels of administration and government, reforms in agriculture, industry, education, the arts, sciences, and, of course, the army. All is pre-

18. *The Political and Historical Works of Louis Napoleon Bonaparte*, 1:252, 257, 262; 2: 262.

sented with periodic invocation of the mantra that it was always the will of the people: "One may sum up the imperial system by saying that its base is democratic, since all its powers emanate from the people, while its organization is hierarchical, since there are in society various ranks to stimulate all capacities. . . . The government of the Emperor was then, so to speak, a pyramidical Colossus, with broad base and lofty head." The facts themselves constitute the emperor's "eulogium." His glory is "as the sun"; only a "blind man . . . cannot see it."[19] But Louis Napoléon does not point out that most of his uncle's lasting accomplishments of civil rule took place before the proclamation of the hereditary Empire.

Notwithstanding such monumental domestic attainments, it was in the area of foreign policy, his nephew argues, that the emperor truly achieved heroic status, "as one of those extraordinary beings whom Providence creates to be the majestic instruments of its impenetrable designs, and whose mission is so clearly marked out beforehand, that an invincible force seems to compel them to accomplish it." Significantly, in view of his own future role in European affairs, Louis Napoléon plays down the military exploits of his uncle to present him as a master politician, diplomat, peacemaker, thwarted by the ambitions of other nations in his ultimate aim to bring independence to France and to establish European peace! The emperor was not the aggressor. All the wars came from England, which would never listen to propositions of peace. The benefits that Napoleon brought to each country, which despite his peaceful intentions he was obliged to conquer, are outlined: the formation of a great kingdom in Italy, freedom from the terrors of civil war and anarchy in Switzerland, emancipation from the yoke of the Germanic Empire for Southern Germany, and so forth. Once again, in case the reader might be less than convinced of this view of his uncle's military ventures, Louis Napoléon sums up with a majestic simile: "The wars of the Empire were like the overflowings of the Nile: when the waters of the river cover the plains of Egypt, they seem [like] devastation; but scarcely have they subsided, before abundance and fertility arise from their passage!" Once again, the emperor's ultimate intentions were most laudatory: peace throughout Europe and the establishment of a European Confederation. If good fortune had not deserted him, he would have been able to reconstruct Europe, instituting "the uniformity of moneys, weights, and measures, and the uniformity of legislation."

19. *Ibid.*, 1:265, 264–65, 311–12, 317.

In Europe, as in France, liberty would have ensued. In Napoleonic Europe, "each country, circumscribed by its natural limits, united with its neighbour by the relations of mutual interest and friendship, would have enjoyed within itself all the benefits of independence, peace, and liberty. The sovereigns, exempt from fear and suspicion, would have applied themselves solely to the amelioration of their people's condition, and to the diffusion amongst them of all the blessings of civilization!" But the Empire fell before such noble purposes could be achieved, because, the argument goes, the emperor "conquered, so to speak, too promptly," because he was betrayed by his allies, because he sought, "in ten years of Empire, to do the work of several centuries." Yet even though, as Louis Napoléon claims, the "old system" has triumphed, the ideas of Napoleonism "have germinated in all directions." The emperor was all the greater for having founded a system which has survived despite his defeat and which "springs anew from its ashes." His ideas advance "of their own force, though deprived of their author." The system will reconstruct itself, for "sovereigns and people, all will aid to re-establish it, because every man will see in it a guarantee of order, of peace, and of prosperity." In the panegyrical conclusion, the grandeur of the rhetoric is in tune with the resplendence of the achievements that are celebrated. The Napoleonic Idea, Louis Napoléon argues again in a final flourish,

> is not an idea of war, but a social, industrial, commercial, humanitarian idea. If to some men it seems ever surrounded by the thunder of war, the reason simply is, that it was, indeed, too long enveloped in the smoke of cannon and the dust of battles. But now the clouds have dispersed, and men discern, through the effulgent glory of arms, a civil glory, greater and more enduring.
>
> Let the Manes of the Emperor repose then in peace! His memory grows each passing day. Each wave that breaks on the rock of St. Helena, brings with it a breath of Europe, a homage to his memory, a regret to his ashes; and the echo of Longwood repeats over his tomb, "THE FREE NATIONS OF THE EARTH LABOUR EVERYWHERE TO RECONSTRUCT THY WORK!"[20]

Louis Napoléon has thus confirmed his epic vision of history, affirmed the transcendent spirit of the founder of his dynasty, and defined his own heroic mission.

20. *Ibid.,* 1:323, 336, 339–40, 343, 344, 345, 348, 349.

In the field of foreign policy, in particular, with its mixture of wishful thinking and wishful retrospection, with its revisionist view of his uncle's regime, his description of the accomplishments and the aims of the first Empire reads more like a blueprint for the policies (and failures) of the Second than a historical record of past achievements. The main planks of Napoleon III's foreign policy, for all its hesitation and confusion, would be inspired by these views: to revive the prestige and hegemony of France; to negate past humiliations, particularly those of the second Peace of Paris of 1815; to achieve by peaceful means the vast schemes that his forebear had conceived in war, namely, the promotion of independent nationalities; to bring about a peaceful European confederation. William E. Echard concludes his study of Napoleon III's attempts to bring about a "concert of Europe" that was truer and fairer (particularly to France) with the notion that, despite his failure, "surely history would remember him, in light of that tragic century, as the vanquished European."[21] If so, even before embarking upon the heroic enterprise, he had already written the script after the fact for his illustrious uncle, and borrowed it for himself.

EMBROILED IN DIPLOMACY

There has been much debate, giving rise to diametrically opposed interpretations, on the emperor's foreign policy. Such were the complexities and contradictions of his relations with the other European powers that it has even been wondered whether indeed he had a foreign policy at all. Within France, there was much tangible evidence of the success of the domestic policies of his regime that his advocates could cite. But his sallies into the world of international diplomacy have left a confused heritage, open to considerable dispute.

On the positive side, Philippe Séguin presents him as an enlightened leader, only making war to be able to negotiate peace, justly intent on revisions to the 1815 treaties and on substituting a new European order based on legitimate national boundaries, on democratic principles. His rapprochement with Britain, his adoption of a free-trade policy, despite the opposition within his own country, showed a dynamic leadership which would prepare the way for the Entente Cordiale despite Britain's failure to

21. Echard, *Napoleon III and the Concert of Europe*, 308.

live up to the trust. In spite of his initial reluctance and doubts about the validity of the Crimean War, the emperor eventually gained not only a major military victory, the fall of Sebastopol on 8 September 1855, but greatly enhanced prestige for his country as a major power and for himself as a leading statesman in Europe. The war against Austria for "the noble cause of Italy," for all the duplicity and prevarication, secured for France, with the cession of Nice and Savoy, a return to the frontiers of 1813 in the Alps and assured Italy of its very existence, for, without the emperor's initiatives, "she would neither have formed her unity, nor even won her independence."[22] Even the Mexican campaign, generally considered to have been a disastrous error on the emperor's part, had, according to Séguin, considerable merit as an idea, as an exercise in geopolitics, as an attempt to contain American expansion, to open up commercial channels, to extend the "beneficent" influence of France, to create an independent Mexican state. When all went horribly wrong, he made the "wise" decision to withdraw. The failure in Mexico is offset by successes elsewhere, in other distant parts, as the emperor established the basis of a French colonial Empire. The "Emperor of the Arabs" instituted enlightened policies of pacification and development in Algeria, setting the stage for a French protectorate in Tunisia. The benefits of French rule were extended to West Africa, expanding east, culminating in the glorious achievement of Suez, enhanced by gains further afield, in the Far East, with the penetrations into China and the conquest of Indochina and Cambodia, and in the Pacific. Even the defeat of 1870, after which France remained a global power, does not detract, according to Séguin, from the unquestionably positive reckoning of the emperor's achievements:

> Its beneficial presence in the European Balkans, its influence in the Middle East, its presence overseas are, unquestionably, to the credit of the Second Empire: in 1870 France is at the head of a colonial dominion of a million square kilometers and of more than five million people. Without wishing to have recourse to some rather sordid statistics, we have to admit that the mortifications of Sedan are not on the same level as those of Waterloo. Even if Alsace and the Moselle are provisionally amputated from the country, Savoie and the

22. Séguin, *Louis Napoléon le Grand,* 263. McMillan has a significantly more nuanced view: "A new united Italy had come into being, partly because of the policies of Napoleon III, but also, in larger part, in spite of them." McMillan, *Napoleon III,* 93.

comté de Nice have been added to it. Above all, it is felt that the
country is in possession of its means of recovery. It is even tempting
to suggest that the main task is already completed.

The emperor alone, Séguin claims, was truly aware of the "exceptional nature of the destiny of France" and deserves credit for preparing its fulfilment.[23]

Not surprisingly, Alain Minc adopts the opposite view, invoking the authority of Henry Kissinger's condemnation, in his already classical study
Diplomacy, of Napoleon III's disastrous foreign policy, which contributed
to the unification of Germany and to the isolation of France. Kissinger argues that "Napoleon [III] brought about the reverse of what he set out
to accomplish" and, in doing so, threw European diplomacy into a state
of turmoil from which France gained nothing; with the center of gravity
of European policy shifting towards Germany, France, despite all the emperor's efforts, found herself isolated on the Continent.[24] Similarly, according to Minc, the emperor's policies were riddled with contradictions:
between a desire to subvert the European concert and to be recognized as
a major part of it, between his calls for peace and his belligerent initiatives,
between his interventions in favor of Italian unity and his need to preserve
the Austrian Empire as a bulwark against Prussian militancy, between his
deference towards public opinion and his dynastic ambitions, between his
unpredictably prudent and his reckless undertakings. The Crimean War
was a hollow victory with very little achieved, the Italian intervention, despite its gains, only serving to illustrate the fundamental weakness of the
emperor's diplomacy: a pursuit of short-term success with little concern or
understanding of the longer-term consequences. The emperor lost credibility with the other major European powers, particularly in 1863, at the
time of his failure to further the cause of an independent Poland. His
shortsighted policy in not supporting Austria against Prussia and his alienation of Britain by his territorial ambitions with regard to Belgium and
Luxembourg left France totally isolated and easy prey to Bismarck's designs: "By his blunders, Napoleon III contributed to the abandonment of
the only principle, the only guarantee of peace on the European continent,
balance of power (*"l'équilibre"*). His uncle had erred in the same way but,

23. Séguin, *Louis Napoléon le Grand,* 282, 283.
24. Henry Kissinger, *Diplomacy* (New York–London: Simon and Schuster, 1994), 104.

at least, to France's advantage, as a dominant power; as for the nephew, he was an unwitting militant in favor of German domination."[25]

Whatever achievements a willfully positive assessment of the emperor's foreign policy might point up in an attempt to redeem his reputation, it must ultimately be judged a failure, or even, in view of the debacle of the Franco-Prussian War, a disaster. The problem was the enormous gap between his epic ambitions and his limited achievements, between the extravagance of his aspirations and his inability to put them into effect. Critics have emphasized the perplexing inconsistencies of his policies. Thus McMillan writes of the Plombières agreement in 1858 between Napoleon III and Cavour by which the plot to provoke war with Austria was hatched: "Any assessment of Napoleon III which overlooks Plombières (and it is an episode on which his admirers do not always care to dwell) must fail to capture his astonishing amorality and bewildering contradictions. How was he to be the nephew of Napoleon and a defender of the peace? The brother of legitimist monarchs and a friend of revolution? The champion of nationalities and the guardian of treaties? The elected choice of the people and a military conspirator? He himself never resolved these tensions, for, in addition to lacking principles, he also lacked priorities."[26] Such crucial events did serve to highlight the apparently capricious nature of his policies. But rather than substantiating the view of Napoleon III as the inveterate conspirator, as a leader lacking principles and priorities, they show that the principles and priorities which he did sincerely embrace were either inherently contradictory or incompatible with the present circumstances.

Napoleon III did not have the will, the ability, or the means to become a great martial leader. Yet as we have seen, he went to extraordinary lengths to promote the illusion of the military splendor of his reign and did little to temper the craving of his nation for martial glory. When asked in England, as Sir William Fraser recounts, if he anticipated any difficulty in ruling the French, he supposedly replied: "Oh no! Nothing is more easy: *They have to have a war every four years.*" As Viel-Castel notes in his memoirs on the eve of the Italian campaign: "We are a long way from '*The Empire Means Peace*' and from the speeches delivered by the emperor himself in which he publicly declared, before Europe and before his own coun-

25. Minc, *Louis Napoléon revisité*, 199–201, 207.
26. McMillan, *Napoleon III*, 84.

try, his respect for the treaties. . . . If war is declared, the emperor will take command of the army, for he has been consumed with the desire, for a long time, to get his huge battalions on the move. May God protect us from such misfortunes!" Yet to his credit as a moralist—though to his discredit as a military leader—Napoleon III did not have the stomach for war of his uncle, who, it is claimed, could write coldly to Metternich in 1813 that "a man like me has little regard for the deaths of a million men." As Roger L. Williams remarks: "No aspect of the Napoleonic tradition was a greater liability for Napoleon III than that which required him to be a dashing and brilliant commander of armies." Even at the peak of his success as a military commander, the epic script gave way to the reality principle. Sickened by the butchery of Solferino and intimidated by the threat of Prussian troop movements, the reluctant warrior offered the Austrians an armistice and sued for peace, reverting to the usual means by which, throughout his reign, he sought and could only seek to realize the Napoleonic ideal: by diplomacy, not war. But the concert of Europe would not play to the emperor's tune. As he was caught up in the imbroglio of international politics, the other major powers grew ever more distrustful of his proposals to redesign the map of Europe, increasingly impatient at his calls for international congresses and suspicious of his proposals for readjustments which would usually entail some territorial advantage for France. Despite his generous claims, he alienated the other major powers by his "continuous unsettling manoeuvres, pronouncements, and projects which seemed to stem not from evident national requirements but from the Emperor's restless will." Ultimately, he broke the golden rule of the art of diplomacy, which, as Harold Nicolson defines it, "is not concerned with dialectics, propaganda, or invective: its purpose is to create international confidence, not to sow international distrust."[27]

Two other decisive factors in complicating and eventually in undermining the emperor's grand designs in foreign policy were the pressures of public opinion and the dissensions amongst his diplomatic staff and advisers. Even without the dubious advantage of the modern device of the opinion poll and even with the distinct advantage of a muzzled opposition

---

27. Fraser, *Napoleon III,* 179; Viel-Castel, *Mémoires,* 5 February 1859; Geoffrey Ellis, *Napoleon* (London–New York: Longman, 1997), 100; Williams, *The Mortal Napoleon III,* 34; Alan B. Spitzer, "The Good Napoleon III," *French Historical Studies* 2 (1962): 325; Harold Nicolson, *Diplomacy,* 3rd ed. (New York: Oxford University Press, 1964), vii.

press, the emperor, who claimed to be the expression of the will of his people, was ever attentive to the public mood. It was notoriously fickle, demanding to celebrate the triumphs abroad that it had been predisposed to expect, yet reluctant to pay the price. Catholic opinion, in particular, was hostile to the emperor's various progressive initiatives, notably on the Italian question. Here again, the emperor fell victim to the contradictory images that he conveyed. As his hold on the reins of power weakened towards the end of his rule, his decisions were increasingly affected by the pressures of public opinion.[28] Then there was the emperor's need to contend with factions within his inner circle of ministers and advisers. His famous *bon mot* on the divisions within his councils—"What a government is mine! The Empress is a legitimist; Napoléon-Jérôme a republican; Morny an Orleanist; I myself am a socialist. The only Bonapartist is Persigny, and he's mad"—was also true in matters of foreign policy. Morny, for example, was opposed to the emperor's Italian War, as he was to the break with Russia on the issue of Poland, having been ambassador at St. Petersburg in 1856–57 and having come back married to a Russian princess. He also advised a firm stance with regard to Prussia, which the emperor did more to appease than oppose. As for Walewski, who represented the conservative, clerical faction opposed to Napoleon III's liberal measures, he worked to thwart the emperor's policy in the Crimea and, in particular, his attempts to revise the terms of the treaties of 1815. He was curiously at odds with the emperor during most of his time in office as foreign minister—a post from which he resigned seven times—particularly on the question of relations with Austria, which he sought to promote and which the emperor sought to sever behind his minister's back. At the other extreme, Plon-Plon was anti-Russian, enthusiastically pro-Italian, and, as an outspoken representative of the republican, anti-clerical Left, was resolutely opposed to the pro-Austrian, Catholic, royalist policies of the empress and her "clique," who increasingly held sway over the Napoleon III's diplomatic decisions in the declining years of the Empire and of the emperor's powers. Indeed, by 1866, such was the confidence of the empress in her influence that she asked her husband to abdicate in favor of the prince imperial, then ten years old, and commit the government to her as regent. As Nancy Nichols Barker writes of this formidable complication to the direction of the Emperor's policies: "Lack of synthesis was always

28. See Spitzer, "The Good Napoleon III," 326–27.

the Emperor's greatest problem. Not only did the Empress not contribute to its solution, she was herself a major cause of his problem."[29] In diplomatic circles, after September 1870, she took much of the blame for the disastrous end of the regime. Thus neither in love nor war did Napoleon III live up to the imperious example of his uncle, but Eugénie was a more formidable proposition than his aunt Joséphine.

NOT SUCH A GREAT IDEA!

Out of the frustration of his European diplomacy emerged what Eugène Rouher called "the great idea of the regime" ("*la grande pensée du régime*"), the plan to establish imperial rule in Mexico, which became a venture that, in that distant setting, was to epitomize the contradictions and uncertainties, the aspirations and failures of the French regime, a paragon of Second Empire foreign policies, an allegory of the collapse of the epic Napoleonic ideal. All the ingredients were there. A grand conception: the supplanting of an anti-clerical republic, established in 1857 by the legendary Benito Juárez, elected president in 1861, in favor of a Catholic monarchy, to repress radical republicanism, to be part of a vast Latin empire counterbalancing growing Anglo-Saxon, Protestant influence and to act as a bulwark against American expansionism, for the author of the *Ideas of Napoleonism* had long foreseen the emergence of the United States as a dominant world power. A diplomatic maneuver: the choice of Archduke Maximilian, brother of the Austrian emperor Franz Joseph and formerly viceroy of Lombardy-Venetia before the Italian War, to rule Mexico as emperor would compensate for Austria's recent loss of Lombardy and make more palatable the cession of Venetia as part of Napoleon III's Italian policy. Financial speculation: new markets would be created, a huge commercial empire could be opened up, silver deposits exploited, and French investors, linked to a group of international financiers, would profit from the adventure—what is more, *Morny était dans l'affaire*. A religious crusade: stories of religious persecution and of appeals from Catholics and Conservatives in Mexico to the emperor to save the Church provided an occasion to appease the pope and Catholic opinion in France. An epic ad-

29. Nancy Nichols Barker, *Distaff Diplomacy: The Empress Eugénie and the Foreign Policy of the Second Empire* (Austin-London: University of Texas Press, 1967), 207.

venture: to revive French military honor by a more significant achievement than the colonial enterprises; it had been more than the requisite four years since the victory at Sebastopol. As decisive as these factors were, there was a further crucial element: the passionate involvement of the empress in the matter, urged on by, amongst other Mexican Conservatives active in France, the persuasive exile Don José Manuel Hidalgo y Esnaurrizar, who played upon her religious ardor, her hate of American republics, and her sympathy for the Spanish patricians of Mexico; she was tireless in her efforts to see the venture through.[30]

The pretext for the invasion was the small matter of 20 million pesos still owing to the government of France, when Juárez suspended all foreign debts in July 1861. A joint naval force from France, Britain, and Spain was sent in December 1861 to seize the port of Vera Cruz and collect the debts and expenses through customs duties, after the signing of a convention not to acquire territory or interfere in the internal affairs of Mexico. According to Marx, the expedition was "one of the most aberrant enterprises ever consigned to the annals of international History."[31] But Napoleon III had a different view. Seizing upon the opportunity offered by the outbreak of the American Civil War in 1861 to flout the Monroe Doctrine, which discouraged European powers from establishing new colonies or extending their influence on the American continent, the French made their intentions clear in April 1862, setting out to occupy Mexico City. The British and Spanish went home. It took a year for the French to take Puebla, which fell on 7 May 1863, after a chastening defeat in battle and after a long siege during which the defenders repulsed numerous French attacks and bombarded the enemy with newspapers in French and Spanish containing quotations from Hugo's *Napoléon le Petit!* Over another year later, in June 1864, after a costly buildup of troops and a bloody campaign, Maximilian, with his wife, Princess Charlotte of Belgium, entered the capital to great fanfare from the Mexican aristocracy in order to take up the crown.

But in practice the "great idea" went terribly wrong. Opposition to the war in France grew strident. The North won the Civil War and the Ameri-

---

30. See *ibid.*, 86–94, 126–35, who adds on the Mexican adventure: "No other feature of Imperial foreign policy can be identified so exclusively with the Empress" (93).

31. Quoted by Rubel, *Karl Marx devant le bonapartisme*, 108, from *The New York Tribune*, 23 November 1861.

can government recognized Juárez as the president of Mexico. His dogged resistance with help from across the Rio Grande persisted. In the face of American pressure, Napoleon III agreed to withdraw his troops, announcing to the new session of the French parliament in January 1866 that Maximilian's rule was assured. By then even the empress was pressing hard for a disengagement from Mexico—Hidalgo was out of favour. Juárez was systematically reversing all the French military gains of the previous three years since the fall of Puebla. In desperation, Empress Charlotte returned to Europe to beg Napoleon III not to abandon her husband and went mad in the process. The last French troops left Mexico on 16 March 1867. On 15 May Maximilian surrendered to the Juarists at Querétaro. By the cruelest of coincidences, which only the most cynical of epic poets might have imagined, news of Maximilian's execution by firing squad, immortalized in Manet's savage paintings on the theme, arrived in the midst of the most extravagant celebration of France's achievements during the Second Empire, the Great Universal Exhibition. As Paris gaily danced and sang to the airs of Offenbach and crowds marveled at the accomplishments of the regime, on the very day when he had heard the report of the event that sealed the most humiliating defeat of his reign, the emperor, in his general's uniform, listened impassively at the splendid prize giving ceremony to Rossini's hymn of praise to the glorious conqueror.[32]

The general effect of the unheroic Mexican venture was to transpose to another continent the pretensions, the ideological dissensions, the confusion, the crass compromises, the hesitations, that characterized the European policies of the regime. Significantly, such was the failure of the enterprise that it brought about, in the long run, the very opposite effects to those intended, promoting a deeper sense of Mexican nationalism and the entrenchment of the secular, federal republic. It was typical of a general pattern of the imperial regime: much self-interest, vainglorious ambition, and nationalist zeal, promoted as stemming from the most righteous of intentions, coming to grief on the bedrock of political reality. It was typical too in the almost gratuitous extravagance and recklessness of the "idea," revealing a disastrous Eurocentric cultural ignorance about the true conditions and the native aspirations of a land which the emperor seemed to view as an alternative Second Empire across the sea and the empress as an extension of Spain, inhabited by some troublesome bandits. As

32. Ridley, *Napoleon III and Eugénie*, 531–32.

Lecaillon is led to observe on the basis of the venture, Napoleon III, contrary to his stated beliefs, revealed himself as "the man of *the right of established Nations to dispose of peoples.*"[33]

If the Mexican escapade was, in an analogous sense, the emperor's retreat from Moscow, the crushing defeat of France's new ally, Austria, by the Prussians on 3 July 1866 at the Battle of Sadowa ominously prepared the way for his Waterloo. By the following year, when the Mexican calamity had run its full course, the imperial regime, as if following the plot of a well-turned pathetic drama, at the height of its illusory apex, was already entering its cataclysmic phase. The Second Empire witnessed the collapse of the Napoleonic legend and with it the disintegration of the image of its epic leader. Yet as we shall later see, out of the debacle would emerge the rudiments of a tragic figure, who would retrieve, if not the prestige that he craved, at least the deference that is due to fallen heroes.

33. Jean-François Lecaillon, *Napoléon III et le Mexique: Les illusions d'un grand dessin* (Paris: L'Harmattan, 1994), 225.

chapter 8

Utopian Vistas

D REAMER

"A man of action, the nephew of the dictator of Brumaire? What a misconception," mused Émile Zola, ironically and rhetorically, in an interview on Napoleon III published in *Le Gaulois* on 20 August 1895, as the twenty-fifth anniversary of the Battle of Sedan approached. In his general assessment—or reassessment—of the emperor, the author of *La Débâcle* acknowledges that in his own younger days he had been swayed by Victor Hugo's eloquence, had considered *Napoléon le Petit* to be "an absolutely truthful history book," and had learned stanzas of *Châtiments* off by heart to declaim them. But he has come to realize that the Napoleon III of *Châtiments* is a fantasy figure, comic even in its exaggeration, no more than a "Bogeyman in boots and spurs sprung from Victor Hugo's imagination." Particularly as a result of his researches in preparing *La Débâcle*, he has come to a radically different estimation of the fallen emperor: "A dreamer, a humanitarian socialist, a fatalist, a man with his gaze ever fixed on his star and walking towards it like a believer following his faith, and calmly, confidently, being directed by events. . . . Fundamentally a good man, haunted by generous dreams, incapable of a wicked action, very sincere in the unshakable conviction which carries him through the events of his life, the conviction of a man with a predestined role, with an absolutely determined and unshakable mission, the inheritor of the name of Napoleon and of his destiny."[1] Other commentators, notably Maxime Du Camp, the writer, critic, chronicler of his age, drew a similar picture of the more philanthropic side to the emperor: "He was good, kindly to the point of prodigality, imbued with ill-digested socialist notions; like Thomas More, like Campanella, like Cabet, like so many other visionaries, he would have wished to establish a utopian kingdom and to invite humanity to the banquet of universal felicity."[2] Yet such was the complexity of the man, as we have seen, that it was as much a distortion to present him as an outright utopian reformer as it was to condemn him as an unprincipled opportunist. It was probably true, however, that in general his thoughts were nobler than his deeds, or at least than many of the deeds that were perpetrated in his name. They stemmed from the more worthy part of Oui-Oui's double inheritance from his ambitious mother and from Le Bas, his austere, republican tutor, during his formative years (1819–1827). Offsetting his cult of military glory was his belief in universal justice and the emancipation of the people. Despite his efforts, Louis Napoléon never fulfilled to his satisfaction either of these programs. But he did become something of a philosopher king, whose more estimable ideas were not totally without effect and did guide his policies. As Minc neatly, and somewhat grudgingly, sums up this aspect of his being: "A socialist prince, a writer and a pretender, an intellectual politician, Louis Napoléon is not an ordinary personality: neither light-minded, nor superficial, nor unthinking, respectful of the written word, deferential towards intellectual endeavor, he is worth more than most of his fellow creatures, aspiring to power or exercising it."[3]

Predictably, as in so many other areas of the emperor's activities, opinion is sharply divided over the sincerity and effectiveness of his progressive

1. Dorothy E. Speirs and Dolorès A. Signori, eds., *Entretiens avec Zola* (Ottawa: Les Presses de l'Université d'Ottawa, 1990), 154–58.

2. Maxime Du Camp, *Souvenirs d'un demi-siècle*, vol. 1, *Au temps de Louis-Philippe et de Napoléon III, 1830–1870* (Paris: Hachette, 1949), 141. Du Camp adds: "If he had generous ideas—and he surely did—they remained sterile; for he could find nobody in his circle to help him to apply them."

3. Minc, *Louis Napoléon revisité*, 97.

social and political ideas. He was clearly in tune with the democratic ideals of the period, particularly during the July Monarchy (1830–1848) when he elaborated his views, absorbed some of the political idealism and social romanticism that were current at the time, and saw the necessity of combining the nostalgic appeal of the glories of the past with an acknowledgment of the importance, in the present and the future, of social questions. Louis Napoléon's version of Bonapartism, in the jaunty jargon of contemporary politics, astutely hijacked the conservative agenda of the monarchists and the progressive ideals of the republicans, liberals, and democrats, combining them with certain socialist themes and the alluring appeal of his name and its associations into an irresistible formula. In practice, the winning combination disintegrated, particularly under the strains placed upon it by the expectations and ambiguities created by the restoration of the Empire. But enough was achieved for the emperor to have been hailed as an effective progressive reformer, who, despite the difficulties and opposition that he encountered, inspired with his enlightened ideals considerable economic and social improvements, achieved all the more effectively because of the limitations of constitutional and political liberties that his authoritarian regime imposed. His defenders enumerate his accomplishments: an unprecedented economic growth, a spectacular expansion of foreign markets (thanks to enterprising free-trade policies), a phenomenally productive monetary policy, a remarkable level of agricultural and industrial development, an amazing program of public works, a drastic improvement in communications, enlightened educational reforms, and, astonishing to many, the emperor's insistence, eventually, upon the liberalization of his regime. All of which, it is claimed, benefited not only the investors but the people as a whole.

The emperor's detractors concentrate less on his achievements in power, many of which were, in any case, evident in other European countries, than on the political advantages of the ideas that he advocated to obtain power. "Why not the proletarians?" writes Guillemin, as we have seen, in contempt of Prince Louis's populism and his book on the extinction of poverty. "A master stroke if, abandoning for the time being the theme of the grey frock coat and the little hat, he could succeed in concentrating on himself the hopes of the starving!" In his view the emperor's avowed "passion" for the happiness of the working classes and his stated love of the people, even if he sincerely wished to improve their conditions, were but empty words, for he could make no fundamental changes, since, quite simply, his regime was devoted to and depended for its existence upon the success of the ruling classes in making money: "The *raison d'être* of the Empire is to ensure, with its police and its army, the smooth running of the machine to make some rich by the exploitation of the poor."[4]

THE EXTINCTION OF PAUPERISM

The work that is invoked as evidence of Louis Napoléon's social ideals is a pamphlet that he wrote during his imprisonment in the fortress of Ham, where, it is pointed out, he corresponded with George Sand, received Louis Blanc, contributed and subscribed to left-wing journals. This text did most to earn him a reputation as a progressive social theorist, as well as the famous nickname, coined by Sainte-Beuve, of "Saint-Simon on horseback," though there is no convincing evidence of direct influence by the Saint-Simonians on its author.[5] It is, however, typical of the swell of utopian reformism that characterized the years up to 1848, when secular thinkers of all shades of opinion expounded new religious, moral, and social systems in the belief that the force of ideas could regenerate society. It is also typically utopian in its political optimism and in its naive optimism about human nature, in the rationalist model that it seeks to impose upon society, in its disregard of adversarial politics, in its belief that progressive change can be brought about by social organization rather than by political activity, in its trust that power can be replaced by acquiescence, delega-

---

4. Guillemin, "Louis Napoléon Bonaparte," 283, 316. See also Spitzer, "The Good Napoleon III," 319–20.

5. Campbell points out that Louis Napoléon was familiar with Blanc's *L'Organisation du travail* and adds on his links with the Saint-Simonians: "Although few direct ties between the Prince and the sect can be established for the period before 1848, some did exist. On the other hand, there may have been only a common set of attitudes shared by the Prince and the Saint-Simonians of the 1840s. The group's impact upon social romanticism alone would have proven sufficient to have influenced the Prince." Campbell, *The Second Empire Revisited,* 5, 7. On the later period, however, McMillan is more categorical: "The influence of Saint-Simonian doctrine under the Second Empire was largely mythical, invented by propagandists at the time, and subsequently exaggerated by twentieth-century historians. . . . Certainly, former Saint-Simonians such as Michel Chevalier and the Pereire brothers were involved in the economic achievements of the Second Empire, but it is not possible to demonstrate that Napoleon III himself was directly influenced by Saint-Simonian thought." McMillan, *Napoleon III,* 138–39.

tion, and agreement, and that individual interests can be easily sacrificed to the advantage of the collectivity. Paradoxically, as a close examination of the *Extinction of Pauperism* reveals, it is the very status of the working class in Louis Napoléon's utopian scheme that is one of the essential problems. A closer look at the text might also have reassured the extraordinarily hostile editor of the English translation, who, in presenting the work, writes that the author's scheme is "only a modification of the Principles of Socialism or of Communism" and as such "repugnant to all sound principles of political economy, and the dictates of common sense." Indeed, the work is offered as an example of "the frauds, by which unscrupulous persons delude public opinion and achieve a temporary power."[6]

The preface, dated May 1844, claims that the sole purpose of the work is "the welfare of the working classes"; it is the author's hope that, if his ideas are developed and put into practice, they will "tend to the relief of mankind." The treatise argues initially that the wealth of a country depends upon the prosperity of agriculture and industry and, with a decidedly Saint-Simonian analogy, that society is a body of flesh and blood which can only prosper "when all the component parts are in perfect health." The working classes have nothing but "the sinews of their arms." They are "as a tribe of Iliotes in the midst of a tribe of Sybarites." They must be given rights and a future; they must be raised "in their own good opinion by promoting association, education, and good order."[7]

The solution is a three-part plan. Firstly, a law would transfer by right to what the author calls "the workman's association" the 9,190,000 hectares of uncultivated land in France, paying to the owners the revenue that these lands currently generate, allowing for the creation of agricultural colonies "of which the poor workmen should be members, without being personally proprietors." Secondly, the government would invest an advance of 300 million francs over a period of four years, after which the colonies would be self-supporting. Thirdly, the "multitudes" would need to be governed by an organization, "enabled to express their wishes, and disciplined, that they may be directed and enlightened for their own advantage." This would be achieved by the creation of an intermediary class of "men of integrity" ("*prud'hommes*") between the workmen and their employers, elected by all the workmen and distinguished by their probity.

6. *The Political and Historical Works of Louis Napoleon Bonaparte*, 2:94.
7. *Ibid.*, 95, 97, 99, 100.

Each middleman, who would either remain in private industry or be employed in the agricultural colonies, would "guide" ten workmen and receive a salary double the amount paid to his workmen. "These middle men should fill the same part that the non-commissioned officers do in the army."[8] Significantly, the rest of the work focuses almost exclusively on the administration and the benefits of the agricultural colonies.

By virtue of this scheme 25 million workmen would become the owners of a quarter of the arable lands of France, for the ownership of these lands would progressively be transferred to the workmen's association. The industrial unemployed, currently condemned to misery when business is stagnant or when new machinery makes them redundant, would find, along with poor families, refuge and employment in the colonies, where there would be women and children to cooperate on the work of the farms and workmen constantly employed to clear new land and to build establishments for the old and infirm. Reciprocally, private industry, when labor was needed, could draw upon the workforce, but controls would ensure that this would not be to the financial disadvantage of the workers themselves. Indeed, to promote such exchanges, a bonus scheme, regulated according to the good behavior and length of service of the worker, would be introduced, allowing the worker to amass in time enough to "insure his comfort for the remainder of his life, even out of the colony." Such is the enthusiasm of the author for his scheme that we are treated to a familiar simile linking the flow of the Nile with the stream of wealth created by the plan, if properly controlled. This typical rhetorical flourish brings about a more subtle effect, neatly providing the author with a transition from the conditional and the optative to the indicative. Now, we are told, the project *will* be administered by directors, "elected by the workmen and middle-men united" for their expertise in agriculture, and, above them all, a governor for each colony, chosen by the middlemen and directors.[9]

Much detailed attention is given to the administration of the scheme. A committee formed of a third of the directors and two-thirds of the middlemen will submit annual accounts to a general assembly of workmen and to the council-general of the department, who will audit them and have the power to dismiss incompetent middlemen or directors. Every year also,

8. *Ibid.*, 101, 102, 103.
9. *Ibid.*, 106, 107.

the governors will go to Paris to discuss with the minister of the interior the best use to be made of the annual profits. Such rigorous accountability is matched by the regimen of the colonies themselves, where strict discipline will be maintained, where man will be ennobled "by healthy and remunerative labour," and where lodgings, pay, and food will be regulated according to the tariffs of the army, "for military organization is the only one based at once on considerations of the welfare of all its members, and the strictest economy." No Land of Cockaigne, this Napoleonic utopia! The author insists, nevertheless, that, even though, until each colony yields a profit, the workers will live in barracks, only certain organizational principles will be borrowed from the army; the colonies will be regulated by *association* and directed, not by blind obedience to the orders of chiefs, but by the exercise of the general will. Even more detailed attention is paid to calculations of receipts and expenditure, according to the reckoning of such factors as the average productivity of each hectare of land or the annual food consumption of the inhabitants, and to the evidence of "explanatory tables" setting out such particulars as the annual yield of mulberry trees and the value of mules and donkeys![10]

The prince is eloquent on the advantages of his project. The workingmen themselves will eventually alone share all the revenues from their labors. There will be ample scope for expansion; indeed, in a Saint-Simonian flight of fancy, "the association" will extend its operations to Algeria, even to America, and "may one day invade the world"; wherever there will be a hectare of uncultivated land and a poor person to feed, there will be the association, "with its capital, its army of labourers, and its unceasing activity." The project will not only provide for that tenth part of the population in rags and dying from starvation, but give them all that "improves the condition of man—independence, education, and government—and to each the possibility of raising himself by merit." The welfare of the multitude will be assured: "Poverty will no longer be seditious when opulence is no longer oppressive." In conclusion, enlightened governments are enjoined to bring about a time when men may exclaim: "The triumph of Christianity has destroyed slavery—the triumph of the French revolution has put an end to bondage—the triumph of democratic ideas has caused the extinction of pauperism!"[11]

10. *Ibid.*, 108–109, 121–26.
11. *Ibid.*, 111, 119, 120.

Several of the characteristics of the prince's scheme, as indicated above, derive from the utopian impulse, as do a number of its impractical features. It is hardly feasible to imagine the landowners of France consenting to the construction of such colonies on their property with any more grace than the modern dwellers of leafy suburbs welcome housing developments near their properties. It is even more improbable to imagine the working-class population as a whole agreeing to live and work in such dreary places under such austere conditions. Like many a utopian fantasist, Louis Napoléon shows little understanding of the "people" whose interests he seeks to further and with whom he claimed to possess such a bond of sympathy. He paternalistically disposes of their lives at will as pawns in his grandiose plan, drafting them into his army of workers, with a little military discipline to keep them in order, for their own betterment, shifting them and their families from factory to farm according to the needs of the economy. The women, of course, are kept firmly in their place, mere instruments of labor, doubly subservient in a regimented plan which reduces all individuals to the status of units in a scheme, a scheme that only seems to value them for their labor and to offer them the prospect of rising by their toil and obedience to the status of low-level capitalists. Indeed, the whole plan, far from proposing an alternative society to correct the evils of the present arrangement, merely provides a palliative to the capitalist system, solving the embarrassing problem of unemployment and working-class misery, but leaving the social and political structures of the capitalist system intact, even providing industry and the propertied classes with a disposable source of compliant manpower. Democratic institutions only function within the framework of the workers' association, as if it were enough to satisfy within the circumscribed bounds of their organization their desire for democracy, leaving the other classes to determine their own system of government. The prince's scheme, together with its elements of the military organization of the Napoleonic administrative system and of the Chinese commune, is essentially an elaborate workfare program. Like all utopians, Louis Napoléon fashions the world in this text according to his own will, which he identifies with the public good, or at least in part, for with all his good intentions he creates in the language of socialist utopianism the rudiments of a capitalist El Dorado. If more of the workers had read, or been able to read, his views more carefully, doubtless fewer would have so readily voted for him.

PROPAGANDA AND DISPLAY

It was particularly gratifying for the pretender to indulge his utopian fantasies when in opposition, especially from the confines of a prison where his imagination was free to build castles in Spain and utopias in France. Even the empress, in her youth, had been for a short time a fervent disciple of Fourier, roughly at the time when Louis Napoléon was dreaming of improving society.[12] But it was another matter for the president and the emperor to put such fancies into practice when he came to power. Here again, we might suggest that the restitution of the Empire became for the more utopian aspect of Louis Napoléon's aspirations a decided encumbrance. He could well have made far more tangible advances in promoting social justice if he had preserved the Republic and continued as its president with his increased powers after the coup d'état. But given the inevitably anti-democratic leanings of the majority of the likely republican representatives, it would not have been an easy task, even under a republican banner, to institute progressive legislation serving the interests of the working classes. In any case, despite his advocacy of universal suffrage, the emperor was far from convinced of the viability of a republican form of government, as we observe, for example, in one of the aphorisms noted down by the emperor's "last love": "Under a monarchy the Government is responsible for the whole people; under a republic the whole would be responsible for its government. That is why a republic will always be an Utopia."[13] Nevertheless, according to his conception of a democratic Empire, Napoleon III had at least to pretend that the people were ultimately responsible for his own government and that his own government was there to serve their interests. Whatever its vicarious and intoxicating appeal, the pomp and immoderation of the imperial pageantry of the regime did not chime, in the harsh light of day, with the claims to be representing the will of the people and the welfare of the downtrodden. The solution was typical of the regime: to seek to convince by propaganda and public spectacle that the people could only benefit and flourish under the Empire, to make grand gestures in place of fundamental measures of reform, pallia-

12. The empress declared, according to Ollivier's diary: "When I was sixteen, I was a Fourierist." She was born in 1826. See David I. Kulstein, *Napoleon III and the Working Class: A Study of Government Propaganda under the Second Empire* ([Sacramento?]): California State Colleges, 1969), 90.
13. Mercy-Argenteau, *The Last Love of an Emperor*, 125.

tives instead of policies, to promote elaborate projects and exhibits that would mediate between conflicting ideologies and between the opposing needs and demands of different interest groups to demonstrate that the utopian Empire itself had somehow reconciled the glories of the past with the progressive achievements of the future, matching the resplendence of an elite with the supposed well-being of the multitude.

One of the major problems in assessing the achievements of Napoleon III's regime lies in measuring the gap between what it claimed to have achieved and what it did in reality achieve for the people, for, as Kulstein observes in a thorough study of the issue, the "tendency to exaggerate the improvements of the condition of the working class during the Second Empire is due, in part, to Bonapartist propaganda." Napoleon III, drawing upon the experiences of his presidential campaigns, inspired by Persigny, and drawing upon a natural talent for self-promotion, was for his time an expert propagandist. The often elaborate efforts of the imperial regime to influence and annex public opinion were, at critical times, carefully orchestrated, if not always effective, and unprecedented in their scope. What the imperial administration achieved, for instance, was to broaden the range of the officially sanctioned press to reach and seek to influence public opinion in the entire population. Pro-government newspapers such as *Le Constitutionnel, Le Pays,* and *La Patrie,* which had a wider readership than the official *Moniteur,* but followed the party line, ceaselessly lauded the accomplishments of the regime and celebrated the visits made by the emperor and empress to workers' housing projects, factories, workshops. A familiar theme of government newspapers, which devoted more space to such deeds than to any other topic but foreign affairs, was to contrast the real accomplishments of the government with the vain ideals of socialist reformers. "While the opposition protests and promises," *Le Peuple* wrote on 13 April 1869, "the Imperial government acts and achieves results," responding to "utopian dreams" with positive and practical reforms. Placards, another traditional propaganda technique, were also liberally displayed, exhibiting Bonapartist slogans, pictures of the emperor making generous gestures, brief accounts of his munificence to the workers. Pamphlets circulated extensively, outlining the policies and benefits of the regime. No less than 170,000 copies of the *Titres de la dynastie napoléonienne* were distributed by mail.[14] The pamphlets were des-

14. Kulstein, *Napoleon III and the Working Class,* x, 97, 83. See, in general, on this question, Chapters 2 and 3 of Kulstein's book.

tined for peasants as well as industrial workers, as a scene from Zola's *La Terre* shows. One winter's night, Jean Macquart reads to the assembled Fouan family a potted history of the peasantry, *Les Malheurs et le triomphe de Jacques Bonhomme*, "one of the books of Bonapartist propaganda with which the Empire had inundated the countryside." As the title suggests, it narrates the "calvary" of the peasant from ancient times up to the time of the glorious Revolution and the radiant period of the Empire of Napoleon, "child of the Revolution," and the "happy peasants" of the new Empire are enjoined to relish the pleasures of country life for which they are the envy of all the citizens of France.[15] Zola's Naturalist novel, like much of his Naturalist project in general, presents in fictional form the hard and cruel facts that the discourse of the regime (and of the one that followed) sought to euphemize.

There were also, of course, more direct forms of propaganda, unmediated by the written word. Workers' banquets, festivals, meetings of mutual-aid societies, prize-giving ceremonies gave government officials opportunities to praise the emperor and his devotion to the workers' interests. The emperor famously sponsored a delegation of French workers to the London Exposition of 1862 and decorated three of the delegates on their return. But the most spectacular and most widely reported events involving the emperor, and often the empress too, were benevolent ventures which they sponsored, inaugurated, or merely financed to project an image of a caring regime, ever watchful over the welfare of its unfortunate subjects. Thus, amongst the benefits and paternalistic relief measures that the emperor and the empress promoted to improve the lot of the working-class population, defenders of the social policies of the Empire could cite numerous instances to prove the liberality of its leader: tax relief and grants to developers willing to build housing for the workers; the construction of workers' housing developments, called "*cités Napoléon*," in Paris, Marseille, Lyon, Lille, Amiens, and Mulhouse; the provision of soup kitchens ("*fourneaux du Prince Impérial*") in 1867 in the poorer areas of Paris, a home-help service for convalescents in certain districts, and controls on the price of bread on a wider scale; the establishment of the "Société du Prince Impérial" to help provide tools for needy workers; the creation of insurance schemes, retirement plans, and mutual-aid societies for the

15. Émile Zola, *La Terre* [*The Earth*], Part I, Chapter 5 in *Oeuvres complètes,* ed. Henri Mitterand (Paris: Cercle du Livre Précieux, 1967), 5:812–20.

workers, with subsidies from the public purse; even a system of special chaplains who, "without charge," would accompany the coffins of the dead to the common grave in poor districts and utter appropriate prayers; the purchase of the château de Longchêne near Lyon and the property of Lamothe-Sanguin near Orléans by the empress and emperor, respectively, as convalescent homes for workers, along with the one opened in 1857 in Vincennes with much fanfare; the founding of a charitable society for expectant mothers, of the prince imperial orphanage, of a number of nurseries, of schools for poor girls, a school for deaf-mutes, various hospices and hospitals.[16] The claim to be a kind of welfare state *avant la lettre,* providing protection for the worker from cradle to grave, was a recurrent theme of imperial propaganda. In addition, the emperor and his government also introduced, or attempted to introduce, certain measures to improve the political condition of the workers, notably: the establishment of the *"droit de coalition"* in 1864, authorizing the right to strike, followed soon after by the right to hold meetings (*"droit de réunion"*) and an edict tolerating trade unions in 1868; a revision of the Civil Code which established equality of testimony between employers and employees in the courts; an attempt, in 1869, at the emperor's initiative, to have eliminated the *"livret,"* by which employers could control the movement of workers and record any real or imaginary misdemeanors. Even after the fall of the regime, the emperor was busy working out a retirement scheme for the workers.[17]

Public relations, image making, working a crowd with the common touch, even "human interest stories"—anecdotes about how the emperor as a young lad gave his purse to a pauper boy and his clothes to a needy family, anecdotes to which historians subsequently have given the stamp of authenticity—indeed, many of the devices of populist politics, which we often take to be, with more than a hint of disdain, the more vulgar tricks of ambitious modern politicians, were mooted during the Second Empire by Louis Napoléon and his supporters to ingratiate the emperor in particular with his public. The regime went even one stage further in the process

16. See Éric Leguèbe, *Napoléon III le Grand* (Paris: Guy Authier, 1978), 92–111, and Séguin, *Louis Napoléon le Grand,* 312–14. Giraudeau gives a detailed list of the emperor's expenditures that includes a number of these measures. Giraudeau, *Napoléon III intime,* 289–90.

17. Séguin, *Louis Napoléon le Grand,* 314–19.

by appropriating the support of workers themselves to solicit backing for the emperor and his government or to allow direct expression of their grievances all the better to deflate opposition: appeals for the election of official candidates signed by workers, columns in pro-government newspapers (*"chroniques ouvrières"*) in which workers could air their complaints or write letters about their problems, even subsidizing some of the activities of Plon-Plon's Palais-Royal group, a somewhat curious association of craftsmen who campaigned for the empire under the patronage of Prince Napoleon, discussed problems of industrial relations, and sent delegations of some two hundred workers to the London exhibition of 1862. As Kulstein concludes: "Although there was not yet a 'science' of propaganda, the publicists of the Second Empire had already arrived at some of the basic principles of mass indoctrination. They perceived that affirmations were more effective than discussion, that a simple statement or phrase was more convincing than a reasoned argument."[18]

Even more effective were the lavish public displays of the achievements of the regime, what Truesdell calls "spectacles of prosperity" and shows to be another aspect of the "spectacular politics" with which the emperor bedazzled the French nation. Such events were the ritual ceremonies that accompanied inaugurations of statues, of railway lines, lakes, boulevards, or stone-setting and tree-planting occasions, accompanied by the requisite speech proclaiming the benefits that the empire was bringing to the grateful nation. The inauguration of the Boulevard de Sébastopol on 5 April 1858 was a particularly splendid affair, conducted with great theatricality, the streets lavishly decorated with, significantly, alternating tricolor banners and Napoleonic emblems, together with painted allegorical figures of Commerce, Industry, Art, and Science. Even some of the workers who had labored on the project, along with their tools and machines, were put on display. Prosperity was the unfailing leitmotif of such occasions, all the better if it could also be associated, as on this occasion, with military glory.[19]

18. Kulstein, *Napoleon III and the Working Class,* 109, 126–27, 204. On the Palais-Royal group, whose delegates returned with demands for improved working conditions and, in some cases, contributed to the founding of the First International, see Holt, *Plon-Plon,* 194–95.

19. See Truesdell, *Spectacular Politics,* 82, 89–92. The author notes that the first stone of the new Sorbonne was ceremonially placed in 1855, but by 1871 there was still no sign of the second (83)!

But the most significant spectacles were the international exhibitions, over which France openly competed with Britain in their displays of triumphalism. The Second Empire sought to outdo Britain's Great Exhibition of 1851, with London retaliating in 1862 with the British International Exhibition.[20] The 1867 Universal Exposition was to outdo them all. Such showcase events were the most complete examples of single occasions when the regime sought to demonstrate its power, authority, legitimacy, prosperity, perpetuity, centrality, and perfection. Art and industry were the two dominant themes, and representatives of all branches of art were mobilized for the occasion to consecrate the achievements of the modern age with the decorous inventiveness of the past. In the 1855 event, there was much grandiose allegory. For example, Ingres showed his *Apothéose de Napoléon 1er* (*Apotheosis of Napoléon I*), with accompanying gloss: "He is carried on a chariot to the Temple of Glory and Immortality; Fame, the Crown, and Victory guide the horses; France mourns him; Nemesis, Goddess of Retribution, casts down Anarchy."[21] Napoleon III's bust appeared on the ornate facade of the 1855 Exposition building, along with an array of allegorical figures representing the arts, crafts, and sciences. In 1867, however, as Truesdell points out, the significance of the exhibition was represented less by allegory than by the physical arrangement of the Exposition palace itself, formed by a series of seven concentric oval galleries organized around a central garden, allowing the visitors to follow a theme within the gallery or view the products of the exhibiting nations by crossing the galleries within each national segment (see figure 14). The arrangement is spectacularly utopian, reminiscent of the model villages or towns conceived by utopian socialists or geometric conceptions of their predecessors, such as Ledoux's "ideal city," the elliptic Chaux. Here the civilized world is contained in the symmetrical spatial arrangement, with France in the most prominent position, making accessible in real or symbolic form the tangible proof or the mediated evidence of the regime's eminence, power, and achievements. The machinery and artifacts themselves that were on display not only fulfilled an instructive function, but became material symbols of progress, signifying modernity, technical prowess, ad-

20. There had been other exhibitions in the intervening years: Brussels in 1857, Algiers in 1862, Dublin in 1865.
21. See Patricia Mainardi, *Art and Politics of the Second Empire: The Universal Expositions of 1855 and 1867* (New Haven–London: Yale University Press, 1987), 51.

vanced civilization, partaking thus of a whole rhetoric of progress and of power, but also instituting a pragmatics of participation by the spectators. The exhibitions provided for the visitors a sense of fulfillment at several levels: awe at the spectacle of France's accomplishments and of the manifest proof of the nation's economic, technological, and artistic success; pride at being a part of that success and thereby at being complicit in the imperialist, technocratic, capitalist ideology that inspired it; joyful acquiescence to the authorities that made it possible; indulgence in the fetishism of scientific progress and of the commoditization of commerce and industry; the pleasure of witnessing the grand occasion and the added pleasure of witnessing others, especially foreign dignitaries, witnessing the occasion; contentment and reassurance at the sense of order which prevailed and in which France, the Empire, the emperor, were so evidently the focal point in a world of universal harmony. With such a glorious past and such a glorious future on exhibit, the appeal of the present regime could only be compelling. But such success brought with it heady delusions, an extravagant excess of its own, which would necessarily have its price. As Séguin notes of the regime, "taken up entirely with enthusiasm for—and with the delights of—progress, it will fail to give itself the army that it needs."[22] Like any utopia, France, secure in its illusions of grandeur and of lasting prosperity, may have been irresistible in its appeal, but it was still vulnerable to an invasion by the forces of reality.

I D E A L   C I T Y

Despite the emperor's hope of massive popular involvement in the exhibitions—free transport was provided in 1855 and workers themselves were put on display in 1867 demonstrating their skills—there was a disappointing response from the working classes. There was no lack of popular involvement, however, in the rebuilding of Paris, for the working class had no choice but to be involved, either by being employed to bring it about or by being displaced from their homes as a result of its effects, or both. Here again, the spokesmen of the regime claimed that it was the working classes that had most to gain from the vast program of public works, not

22. Tony Bennett, "The Exhibitionary Complex," *New Formations*, no. 4(1988):80, 94–95; Séguin, *Louis Napoléon le Grand*, 333.

only because it provided employment for the workers, but because it also created for them a healthier and more spacious environment, with capacious boulevards and parks, a supply of fresh water, and a new sewerage system. But the remarkable transformation of Paris under the emperor's direction was of wider significance, representing the true "great idea" of the regime and the one which, to a considerable degree, was most spectacularly put into practice and in an impressively short period of time. Already by the summer of 1855, Prince Albert found Paris "signally transfigured" and was prompted to add: "How all this could have been done in so short a time, no one comprehends."[23]

For Napoleon III the program of reconstruction of Paris had one immense and overriding advantage: it allowed him to reconcile his Caesarism and his humanitarianism better than any collection of eloquent speeches or any series of ceremonial events could do. It was, in a sense, his most convincing text. As commentators invariably note when discussing his plans for the city, he had dreamed while a prisoner in the fortress of Ham of becoming a second Augustus, imitating the emperor who had "made Rome into a city of marble," building upon the improvements brought about by the First Empire, but, above all, leaving his own, more permanent legacy. As a Paris guidebook of the 1860s enthused, capturing the spirit of the emperor's enterprise: "The day will come when history will call the capital of France, changed as if by magic in less than a quarter of a century, THE PARIS OF NAPOLEON III as it has called the Eternal City THE ROME OF AUGUSTUS CAESAR."[24] Louis Napoléon had been impressed by New York in a brief stay in that city and even more so by some of the more appealing sites of London, notably Hyde Park, during his much longer stays in the English capital. At the same time, the emperor was aware of the humanitarian advantages of such improvements, recommended by social reformers, notably by the Saint-Simonians during the July Monarchy or in the elaborate plans of Cabet and Fourier to construct ideal communities where all the evils of city life would be eliminated. In the new tree-lined boulevards, broad avenues, parks, and squares, the poor could find relief from the stifling conditions in which they lived and worked, if they cared to frequent the new avenues, whilst members of the upper crust would have more room in which to parade in their elegant car-

23. Truesdell, *Spectacular Politics,* 106–107; Burchell, *Imperial Masquerade,* 82–83.
24. Quoted in Burchell, *Imperial Masquerade,* 82–83.

riages. There is also the widely held view that the emperor's primary motivation in building wide and straight boulevards was to make it more difficult to erect barricades and easier to move his troops along them to crush any insurrections. There is evidence that such strategic advantages were certainly a consideration and were discussed, but that they were in the end incidental to the emperor's plans. He was convinced, in any case, that the improvements to the city and the employment opportunities that his program of public works entailed would solve the very problems which gave rise to insurrection.[25] There were just as impelling health reasons to clean up a city which all too often witnessed cholera outbreaks, as in 1848, when almost twenty thousand Parisians died. But the emperor had yet a grander vision: to transform the squalid maze of narrow streets and insalubrious dwellings of a medieval city into a resplendent modern metropolis, into a thriving commercial center, to make Paris into the capital of Europe. Like many an ambitious ruler before him, he sought to construct a grandiose monument to his rule. Paris was at the heart of the Empire, at the center of his universe. He aspired no less than to construct an urban utopia.

Not only was the emperor himself the guiding spirit of this transformation, he conceived the prototype. He devised a map of Paris on which he had drawn lines to indicate the new streets that were to be built, sketched in four different colors to signify the relative urgency of each undertaking. The emperor presented the map to the man chosen to execute his plan, a career civil servant, Georges Eugène Haussmann, an ardent Bonapartist, who, as the prefect of the Gironde, had organized the triumphal visit of the emperor to Bordeaux in October 1851, when the reinstitution of the Empire was announced. Haussmann was summoned to Paris to continue the task of revamping the city, which had already begun according to the president's and then the emperor's instructions, but required a firm hand to direct the operations. The emperor's map of Paris, variations and copies of which have mostly been lost, would undergo some important modifications, but essentially his was the blueprint for the whole venture. The emperor proposed, Haussmann disposed.

In fact, the rebuilding program became an obsession with the emperor, who kept a map of Paris on the wall in front of his desk in the Tuileries Palace for reference and was reported to have met with Haussmann almost

25. Ridley, *Napoleon III and Eugénie*, 351; David H. Pinkney, *Napoleon III and the Rebuilding of Paris* (Princeton: Princeton University Press, 1958), 35–37.

every day for consultations. The executor of the emperor's civic will shared his passions. Grandson of an imperial general and son of an officer in Napoleon's army, the new prefect of Paris, whose middle name had been inspired by Prince Eugène de Beauharnais (Louis Napoléon's uncle on his mother's side), had the proper Bonapartist credentials to be trusted with the venture, as he was for seventeen years. During this time, he accomplished the transformation of Paris with remarkable energy, resourcefulness, acumen, and authority. His capacity for raising capital for construction from loans, deficit funding, investment banking, credit arrangements, and income from the resale of condemned property was prodigious, or "fantastic," as the republican deputy Jules Ferry wrote in a famous series of articles in *Le Temps,* collected together in a short volume with the punning title *Comptes fantastiques d'Haussmann* (1868).[26] Ferry was not the first to denounce the sharp practices of Haussmann, accused of contracting secret loans through deferred payment contracts and delegation bonds, of spending taxpayers' money without consent, and of covering up his use of public funds.[27] When the matter of the irregularity of his dealings was debated in a hostile Assembly in February 1869, it was clear that Haussmann had to go, but he did not do so until the following year, reluctantly and in style, "through the front door," ceremoniously surrendering his emblems of office. Whether or not he was a crook—real estate was then as now an area in which moral distinctions were often blurred—he had not neglected his personal fortune, retiring a rich man, with a barony, directorships, a villa in Nice, and a mansion in Longchamp. He was, in a sense, another Morny, whose *coup* was to rebuild Paris where his predecessor had conquered it.

Utopias are by nature paternalistic, dictating to the masses a mode of existence for their own benefit prescribed by their inventors. They are also narcissistic, transforming personal dreams, obsessions, and values into social reforms for the supposed betterment of humanity. They are characteristically visions of an ideal city which serves as a model for a totally harmonious society. They ensure not only a stable unity of purposes, func-

26. The reference was to the macabre tales of the German writer E. T. A. Hoffmann, adapted for the Paris stage in 1851 as the *Contes fantastiques d'Hoffmann,* and not, of course, to the *Contes d'Hoffmann* (*The Tales of Hoffmann*), which Offenbach only completed just before his death in October 1880.

27. See Pinkney, *Napoleon III and the Rebuilding of Paris,* Chapter 8, "Money and Politics," for a thorough study of the financial side of the public works projects.

tions, and ordered structures, but also, more significantly, a harmonious dynamic, an uninhibited circulation of energies, tasks, passions, goods, indeed of all that serves to maintain in a permanent state of euphoria, as the conventional analogy significantly suggests, a healthy social body. Louis Napoléon's utopian vision is characteristically divided. On the one hand, a theoretical program devised to solve the misery of the working classes with the pretense that society, even the world, would ultimately benefit from it, but which leaves the rest of society intact and which, in practice, turned out to be little more than a few remedial measures and charitable acts. On the other hand, with the same pretense to the general good, a concrete program of public works, a network of communications extending out to the whole country (mainly through the railway system) and radiating into the splendors of the capital. There an ideal space of decorous facades, monuments, and greenery was created in which an elegant society could freely circulate and display its riches, a sumptuous space in which ceremonies, exhibitions, and parades could take place for the greater glory of the emperor and his extravagant regime and to which an eminent foreign elite could be invited to admire the accomplishments, an uninterrupted vista of grandeur protected from an awareness of the harsh industrial realities that made it possible to construct this imperial utopia.

Building of necessity to a considerable degree on the basis of the existing topography of the city and seeking to link, for easy access of traffic, significant monuments and communications centers that were already in place, the renovation plan was, of course, subject to historical constraints. Nevertheless, a remarkable preoccupation with symmetrical and abstract design went into the process, which can be attributed to some extent to a taste for classical monumentalist architectural traditions, but which also derived from the utopian impetus. "Everything now," writes Rupert Christiansen, "was designed to conform to a logic of urban geometry." Wits of the time speculated that Haussmann even planned to straighten out the river Seine, so inconvenient were its curves. Parisians who did not share the emperor's passion for urban renewal complained that the city was like a permanent building site. The displaced occupants of the demolished dwellings were naturally resentful, unless they could profit from the compensation deals. But the needs and wishes of individuals were remorselessly sacrificed to the juggernaut of progress. The extraordinary spirit of social engineering that prevailed led to a ruthless imposition of a conceptual order onto the contingent, the circumstantial, and the idiosyncratic, leading to "the nineteenth century's most radical experiment in shaping and governing urban society."[28] Both the emperor and Haussmann were keen also to impose a uniform design on the buildings that lined the new avenues. Particular attention in the Second Empire was given to facades.

There were two main axes to the restructuring: the completion of the (roughly) east-west line, with the extension of the rue de Rivoli, linking l'Étoile with the Place du Trône, and the construction of the north-south axis along the boulevard de Strasbourg and the boulevard de Sébastopol to the boulevard Saint-Michel. Then there was the almost regular line of peripheral boulevards, mainly on the right bank, from the boulevard Pereire, west of l'Étoile, around to the boulevard Mazas in the southeast up to the river. Other major roads were built to provide access to the railway stations, to the Place de la Concorde, to the Invalides, whilst an array of boulevards clustered around l'Étoile. Certain romantics and aesthetes deplored the destruction of such a huge part of old Paris, with its labyrinth of small streets, where Balzac found inexhaustible inspiration for his human "comedy" and where Baudelaire perfected the art of *flânerie*. The Goncourt brothers were famously put out, as they wrote as one in their diary on 18 November 1860: "I am a stranger to what is coming, to what is, as I am to these new boulevards with their lack of bends, adventures and sights, unrelenting in their straightness, deprived of the savour of Balzac's world and making one think of some Babylon of the future." But one man's Babylon is another man's utopia. As Christiansen neatly defines the planner's aims: "The absolute priority was moving from A to B with the minimum amount of interference, in the minimum amount of time. Parisians may have sighed nostalgically for twists and turns, corners and dead ends, the ramshackle variety and spontaneity of centuries of organically accreted urban life, but Haussmann knew that their city needed air, light, space and mobility more than it needed romance."[29] Whatever local opposition it encountered, the whole operation was sufficiently successful for several cities in Europe and Latin America to follow the example of Second Empire architecture and urban engineering. In any case, the new thoroughfares were only a part of the achievement. The main market in Paris, Les Halles, was reconstructed of iron and glass, on the model of the Stras-

---

28. Christiansen, *Tales of the New Babylon: Paris, 1869–1875* (London: Sinclair-Stevenson, 1994), 94, 95.
29. *Ibid.*, 101.

bourg Railway shed and the Crystal Palace in London. The emperor's gift of government property to the people of Paris led to the creation of the Bois de Boulogne as an elegant park, with its lakes, promenades, grottoes, restaurants, and cafés, as well as Morny's pet scheme, the racetrack at Longchamp; in fact this showpiece was only one of several parks that were created—notably the Bois de Vincennes, the Parc Monceau, the Parc de Montsouris—to respond ostensibly to the Parisians' need for recreational space, but mainly to conform to the reforming emperor's taste for symmetry and elegance. Amongst the other major projects, the Louvre was completed (after six centuries) and joined with the Tuileries Palace, the Hôtel-Dieu refurbished, and the renovations of Notre-Dame were finished. With his fondness for the more visible and grandiose manifestations of his dynastic aspirations, Napoleon III was less than enthusiastic about Haussmann's plans for radical improvements of the water supply and sewerage systems. But there were significant achievements below ground too. The length of the city's water mains was doubled, as was their capacity. The eighty miles of underground sewers in 1851 had grown to nearly four hundred miles by the end of the regime. For Edwin Chadwick, a distinguished public health crusader from Britain, such sanitary improvements were a major accomplishment of the regime, as he earnestly complimented the, no doubt, bemused emperor on the feat: "Sire, it was said of Augustus that he found Rome brick and left it marble. May it be said of you that you found Paris stinking and left it sweet."[30]

KEEPING UP APPEARANCES

Despite the sweet smell of apparent success of the emperor's rebuilding program, the achievement should not entirely be taken at its face value. The Second Empire certainly did go a long way towards building a utopia, but only for the benefit of the most affluent Imperialists. Indeed, as Pinkney notes, even the building regulations showed little concern for the standards of the dwellings behind the facades; they "were concerned almost exclusively with appearances." There were undeniably huge practical improvements in transport and communications, not to mention the sewers. But the impression left by the public works program was that the embel-

30. Pinkney, *Napoleon III and the Rebuilding of Paris*, 127.

lishment of Paris had been the primary objective. The monumental architectural forms of the past were taken up, but a new, overelaborate, eclectic style was developed. Emphasis was more on decorativeness than on utility. "Haussmann and Napoleon were prone to treat architecture as an artistic overlay that would provide a fitting backdrop for the imperial pageantry."[31]

One project in particular exemplifies this tendency. As the emperor and the empress arrived at the opera in the rue Le Peletier on the evening of 14 January 1858, an assassination attempt on the emperor was made by 4 Italian revolutionaries, killing 8 people and wounding more than 150, but leaving the emperor and empress unscathed. This incident prompted a plan to build a new opera house on a more spacious and less dangerous site. In 1861, work began on the construction of the new building on the boulevard des Capucines, following the plan devised by the young architect Charles Garnier, who had won the commission. Garnier's stunning neo-baroque creation, adorned with statues, busts, columns, and pediments, was meant both to fit into its elegant setting and to outdo it in audacity. If indeed, as we shall later see, the dazzling edifice came to symbolize the style, ornamentation, ostentation, and extravagance of the Second Empire, it did so also at the time in another sense. For six years construction went on hidden from view until in 1867, at the time of the Universal Exposition, Parisians and visitors were given a glimpse at the south front. Only in 1869 were they to see all the facades, but little did they realize that the building was an empty shell.[32]

It was evidently of far more consequence for the remodelers of Paris to make the city attractive than to make it habitable, at least for the majority of its inhabitants. Despite their professed wish to destroy the slums and to improve the living conditions of the poor, the emperor and Haussmann did little to avoid new slum areas appearing in place of the old ones. To make way for the new dwellings for the rich and the middle classes, the poor were pushed out to the peripheral zones between the old *octroi* wall and the fortifications, creating suburban slums like Belleville or Les Batignolles. Behind the elegant frontages of the new Paris, the old Paris continued to fester. The phenomenal migration to the capital from the provinces and, to a lesser degree, from abroad—the population of Paris rose from

31. *Ibid.*, 93, 219.
32. *Ibid.*, 86. The interior was completed in 1874 during the Third Republic.

roughly 1.25 million in 1851 to almost 2 million in 1870—provided the
workforce needed in the boom years, but also added to the population of
beggars, prostitutes, thieves, and paupers, who survived the emperor's best
efforts at improving the conditions of the needy. Far from being extinct
by the end of the Second Empire, the poverty-stricken hordes increased in
number. Over 35,000 beggars and vagrants were taken into custody in
1868 alone.[33] For the workers in employment, conditions were little better, so it seems. There was, and there still is, little agreement over the figures according to which the situation of the working class can be
measured. Defenders of the regime write blithely about the improved
standard of living of the workers during the Second Empire. Thus the author of *Napoleón III le Grand* astutely quotes a report, written in 1875,
on working conditions by a Republican deputy, M. Ducarre, in which it is
claimed that workers' wages rose by 45 percent during the reign of Napoleon III. The author of *Louis Napoléon le Grand* is more measured, noting
that the 45 percent increase served only to compensate for the increase in
prices. Guillemin, by contrast, claims that there was an increase of 30 percent in wages and that it was the cost of living that increased by 45 percent. In his study of daily life under the Second Empire, Maurice Allem
presents more detailed figures, based mainly on household budgets published in the press, with variants for different occupations.[34] Many working-class families could make ends meet, particularly in the provinces. In
Paris especially, very many could not. The budget of a coachman, published even in a pro-government newspaper, *Le Pays*, on 20 June 1865,
shows an annual expenditure of 1,700 francs (64 percent for food, 14 percent for lodgings, 15 percent for other living expenses) set against an income of 1,250 francs. Even a government employee fared no better, as the
very detailed budget of a family with three children shows: expenditures,
including coal at 0.20 francs a day, bread (4 pounds) at 0.75, wine (half a

33. Burchell, *Imperial Masquerade*, 104.
34. Leguèbe, *Napoléon III le Grand*, 92–93; Séguin, *Louis Napoléon le Grand*, 309; Guillemin, "Louis Napoléon Bonaparte," 320. Allem refers in particular to Georges Duveau's
classic study, *La Vie ouvrière en France sous le Second Empire* (Paris, 1946). Duveau notes
that 1,700 francs per annum was the minimum salary with which a household could decently
live in the capital and that very few workers earned as much. He argues that, during the Second Empire, the social classes became more entrenched and that capitalism, especially during
the 1860s, took on "the aspect of a monolith crushing the worker." Allem, *La Vie quotidienne sous le Second Empire* 397, 415–16.

liter, watered down) at 0.40, secondhand clothes at an average of 0.80, rent at 400 francs a month, amounted to 2,609.76 francs per year, to be paid out of a salary of 2,000 francs, minus 100 francs for the retirement fund.[35] There were, then, all shades of indigence which the Second Empire, despite the fine words, did very little to reduce. By comparison, Plon-Plon, supposedly a champion of the working classes, had to manage on an annual allowance of a million francs. Cora Pearl, the courtesan, earned 5,000 francs a night!

Whatever the precise figures, there was no shortage of eyewitness accounts of the atrocious living conditions of the urban poor from sociologists, socialists, philanthropists, artists, and not least of all, writers, who exposed the shame of the regime and dwelt upon the contrast between, in Maxime Du Camp's words, "the permanent spectacle of abject misery adjacent to the most grandiose opulence." Quoting these words, along with other testimonies, Burchell perceptively adds: "The empire fell through its denial of reality—a denial nourished by middle-class hypocrisy and an insolent display of luxury. The immorality of the time is hardly shocking; it is the luxury which offends." But even the lavish luxury was justified and rationalized by the privileged few, or at least by the naive hangers-on who were fed the line, as a boon for the people. Thus one of the private readers of the empress notes that the four grand official balls held between January and Lent, to which four or five thousand people were invited, caused "millions of francs to be circulated in Paris." Likewise, Countess Louise de Mercy-Argenteau, a woman of the older aristocracy, who, nevertheless, appeared in the imperial court and, as she admits, "was fond of being well dressed," for her husband's wealth allowed her to "indulge in every luxury"—he "had taken a very active part in the building of the new *boulevards,* and was increasing a fortune already very considerable"—remarks in her memoirs on the "unimaginable" luxury of Empress Eugénie's underwear. No lady before her time, she claims, "had worn chemises costing from five hundred to a thousand francs." When other women followed suit, some husbands complained, but "the Emperor approved. This luxury, said he, was a source of wealth for the workers"![36]

35. Allem, *La Vie quotidienne sous le Second Empire,* 101–103.

36. Burchell, *Imperial Masquerade,* 115; Carette, *My Mistress, the Empress Eugénie,* 230; Mercy-Argenteau, *The Last Love of the Emperor,* 36, 14.

Perhaps the true scandal of the regime was less the abject poverty that its policies perpetuated and the luxury that they promoted alongside it—a far from unusual state of affairs in the world in any age—than, more specifically, the blatant contrast between the utopian discourse of its leaders and the reality that they publicly denied, even when privately aware of the extent of the destitution in the city. (The emperor received regular reports.) Significantly, it was during the Second Empire that a new literary school emerged, whose program, at least in part, was precisely to expose and denounce, usually implicitly, the contrast between the extravagant luxury of the few and the abject poverty of the many with the techniques of realist fiction. The Goncourt brothers, two aristocratic aesthetes, unlikely social reformers but avid observers of contemporary life in all its aspects, were, before their better-known associate, Zola, the first "Naturalists" to focus upon the true plight of the poorer classes in their literature. At the very end of their novel *Germinie Lacerteux* (1864), having buried their wretched heroine, a pitiful servant, in an anonymous common grave in the cemetery of Montmartre, they (uncharacteristically) break into the narrative to apostrophize Paris with an impassioned plea which reverberates with ironic echoes of the official utopian discourse of the regime:

O Paris! you are the center of the world, you are the great humanitarian city, the great city of charity and brotherhood! You possess gentleness of spirit, age-old generosity in your customs, sights that inspire people to give alms! The poor are your citizens as much as the rich. Your churches speak of Jesus Christ; your laws speak of equality; your newspapers speak of progress; all your governments speak of the people; and this is where you cast off those who die in your service, those who destroy themselves creating your luxury, those who perish from the evil of your industries, those who have sweated away their lives working for you, giving you your comforts, your pleasures, your splendors, those who have made up your vigor, your noise, those who have shackled their existences to the preservation of your status as a capital, those who have been the crowd in your streets and the people on your grand celebrations! Every one of your cemeteries has a corner of shame like this one, hidden behind a stretch of wall, where, hastily, you bury them, throwing a few shovelfuls of earth so begrudgingly that the feet of their coffins can be seen sticking out! It is as though your charity ends with their last breath, and your only gift to them is the bed on which they suffer.

Curiously one of Haussmann's "utopian" schemes, which did not however obtain authorization, was precisely to empty all the cemeteries of the city and to build a huge necropolis thirteen miles away at Méry-sur-Oise.[37] The plan, no doubt, the ultimate utopian dream, was to banish death itself from the great city.

TWO TEXTS

I. Napoleon III to a workers' delegation ("Comité des ouvriers de Paris et de la banlieue"), 7 December, 1852:

Those who work and those who suffer can count on me.[38]

II. "What Poor Young Girls Dream Of" by Émile Zola, in *Le Rappel*, 3 February 1870:

She has been working for twelve hours. She has earned fifteen sous. She is going back in the evening to her sordid abode, walking along sidewalks white with frost, shivering beneath her thin black shawl, lean and furtive, moving with the fearful haste of a poor abandoned beast.

Her stomach is crying out for food, so she buys some cheap leftovers from the pork butcher, carrying them away wrapped in a scrap of newspaper. Then, breathlessly, she climbs the six floors.

Up there the attic room is desolate. A candle end casts some light on this misery. There is no fire. The wind whistles under the door so briskly that the flame of the candle seems to shudder in fear. A bed, a table, a chair. It is so cold that the water in the water jug has frozen.

She makes haste; perhaps she will be able to warm up a bit in bed, under the bundle of her clothes that she piles up each evening at the foot of the bed. She has hurriedly sat at the little table; she has taken

37. Edmond Goncourt and Jules Goncourt, *Germinie Lacerteux,* ed. Nadine Satiat (Paris: Flammarion, 1990), 260–61; Christiansen, *Tales of the New Babylon,* 95.
38. Quoted in Kulstein, *Napoleon III and the Working Class,* 97.

a piece of bread out of a cupboard, she is eating her scraps of meat with the greedy and indifferent look of the starving. When she is thirsty, she has to break the ice in the water jug.

She is a child of eighteen at the most. To keep out the cold a little, she has kept on her shawl and her bonnet. She eats like this in her outdoor clothes, occasionally burying her hands when the wind turns them blue with cold. If she could smile, she would be charming; her delicate lips, her soft grey eyes would have an exquisite gentleness. But suffering has pinched her mouth, and lent a dull harshness to her eyes. She wears the rigid, menacing look of the destitute.

She looks vaguely, vacantly, ahead, her mind a blank, eating like an animal in a hurry to finish feeding. Then her eyes alight upon the scrap of newspaper, stained with grease, that she is using as a plate. She starts to read it, forgets to finish her bread. There has been a ball in the Tuileries, and she discovers that a prodigious amount of wine and fine dishes has been consumed: nine thousand bottles of champagne, three thousand cakes, six hundred kilograms of meat, and so on. She smiles strangely, says to herself that those people must be really fat.

But she is a woman, she pays more attention to the descriptions of the toilettes. She reads:[39]

"Mme. Metternich: white dress, with deep purple waistband. A river of diamonds supported an adorable cluster of pearls and diamonds."

There is a hard look on her face. Why do other women have rivers of diamonds, when she doesn't have a warm dress to put on? She carries on reading:

"The Empress, in a soft green dress, covered in a demi-jupe in foaming white tulle, with silver lamé, trimmed with sable at the bottom and at the corsage. In her hair, clusters of flowers and a simple headband of diamonds. Around her neck, a velvet choker on which is attached an ornamental fret of lovely diamonds."

Always diamonds, and here enough diamonds to make a hundred families rich. The child has stopped reading. She is leaning back in her chair, she is dreaming. Wicked thoughts show in her grey eyes.

---

39. Zola's character is reading from *Le Figaro* of 29 January 1870.

She no longer feels the cold, she has given herself entirely to evil temptation.

And when she comes out of her daydream, she shudders, and, looking around her sordid abode, murmurs:

"Why bother? . . . What's the point in working? I want diamonds."

She will be getting some tomorrow.[40]

40. Translated from Zola, *Oeuvres complètes*, 13:258–59.

chapter 9

Romance

"THEIR EYES MET . . ."

It was a beautiful day in September 1849. Parisians had flocked to Satory near Versailles to see the military parade, the women decked out in the gay colors of their late-summer dresses, the men in their somber black suits. Near to the official enclosure a ravishing young Spanish woman on horseback, her delicate oval face, her bright blue eyes framed by her long auburn hair of a golden hue, held tightly in place by the black bands of her hat gaily decorated with blue ribbons. She had come with her friends, hoping to catch more than a glimpse of the man of the moment, the prince, the conspirator, the gallant escapee from the fortress of Ham, now president of the Republic and a Bonaparte. Her father had fought on the side of his uncle against the British at Trafalgar, where he had been wounded in the arm by a sniper's fire, then against his own countrymen in the defense of Joseph Bonaparte, serving in the French army, wounded in action in the leg and in an accident in the eye. He was with the French army that withdrew from Spain and fought in the last defense of Paris. She had listened, fascinated, to her father's stories. As a twelve-year-old girl in Paris, she had been entranced by Stendhal's accounts of the Napoleonic campaigns when the novelist visited her mother, every Thursday, in the autumn of 1837 and the following year. Even at this tender age, the novelist admired her beauty and, no doubt, her *espagnolisme,* and was more than a little in love with her in his way. He included coded messages to her and to her sister, Paca, in the footnotes of the novel that he was writing, *La Chartreuse de Parme.* She had met Prince Napoléon (Plon-Plon) in Madrid in February 1843 at a lavish carnival ball given by her mother, Maria Manuela, for local grandees, for those who aspired to be grandees, and for distinguished visitors. She had spurned his advances, so the gossips said; she little knew that a higher destiny would bring her back in contact, indeed in conflict, with Jérôme Bonaparte's son. There had been many suitors unable to resist her beauty, but fate, in which she passionately believed, had other designs. Tantalizingly so. She and her mother had eagerly accepted an offer to visit Louis Napoléon in his captivity, but her mother was called to Madrid on urgent business. She had caught sight of him once, according to Madame Carette, "soon after the Strasbourg escapade," when, visiting with her mother and sister the wife of the prefect of police in Paris, she saw him as a prisoner escorted by an officer of the gendarmerie.[1] Here, at least, was a chance to behold him as a free man, in the fullness of his power, the nephew of the great Napoleon.

The trumpets sounded. He appeared. Not, perhaps, at first sight, the most seductive of figures, with his short legs and long nose. But in his general's uniform, "everything about him is *romanesque.* . . . And, straightaway, the young *cavalière* sees a strange charm in that impenetrable look which seems shrouded in a veil of reverie. Suddenly, the President's eyes meet hers."

—Who is that splendid creature over there, on horseback, in that pretty hat with blue ribbons? he whispers to the prefect of police beside him.

—She's an Andalusian, Eugénie de Montijo, comtesse de Teba. She has lost her father, a grandee of Spain, who followed the fortunes of King Joseph.

1. Carette, *My Mistress, the Empress Eugénie,* 194–95. The author gives 1840 as the date of this event and should therefore have written "Boulogne" instead of "Strasbourg."

—Ah! The daughter of a Josefino! the Prince interjects, looking at
her admiringly like some extraordinary being.
—She is twenty-six years old and lives with her mother in an apartment on the place Vendôme.[2]

It would not be long, it could not be long before they would meet again,
for Eugenia was to be seen in society, in the Bois, at formal balls, or at the
theater, in the company of her mother and her mother's faithful companion, Mérimée. At one of Princess Mathilde's receptions their paths crossed
again. She was wearing a pale blue dress, *"largement décolletée,"* showing
her shoulders, her slender waist, and her silky skin. The prince was entranced, demanded that his cousin introduce them. They talked. He revealed that he had noticed her on the day of the parade. She was flattered.
They talked more. That evening, in the carriage home, she confessed how
much she liked the prince. "Hardly surprising!" remarked Mérimée. "He
only had eyes for you."

But true love's course never runs smoothly. Not that the prince lacked
ardor. He arranged an intimate dinner party at Saint-Cloud for the Montijo ladies. Eugenia had to remind him, as he took her arm for a walk in
the park, that her mother should be his escort. Besides, it was well known
that Louis Napoléon had a beautiful mistress. The ladies left for a European tour. Eugenia and the prince exchanged letters. Mérimée polished
the young lady's style. The president's star was on the rise. In the autumn
of 1852 Eugenia was back in Paris. The prince was returning triumphant
from his tour of the provinces, where he had everywhere been greeted with
cries of *"Vive l'Empereur!"* As he rode his chestnut charger through the
streets of Paris on 16 October, he was met by a column of mounted generals. From the apartment of a friend and former suitor, Ferdinand Huddleston, Eugenia was watching. "His horsemanship was superb. . . . It was on
that day that Eugenie decided that he was the man for her and that she
would share her life with him. It was both the figure and the courage
which touched her heart." *Her* equestrian skills were superb too, as she
demonstrated less than a month later, when she was one of the many
guests at a hunting party organized by the prince at Fontainebleau at a
time when he was waiting for the referendum on the reinstatement of the
Empire to take place. Mounted on one of the finest thoroughbreds of the

2. Alain Frerejean, *Napoléon IV: Un destin brisé* (Paris: Albin Michel, 1997), 17–18.

stable, she cut quite a dash, dressed in a tightly buttoned habit, a wide skirt, grey trousers, high-heeled leather boots, and a felt hat, sporting an ostrich feather fastened by a diamond clasp. The handle of her whip was encrusted with pearls. She stole the show, was first to the kill. But was it the prince who was her real quarry? "That evening he sent her a bouquet of flowers. Next day he gave her the horse which she had ridden. He was in love and he made it plain to see." As one of her ladies, Mlle. Bouvet, later wrote: "The great beauty of the young Countess de Teba, and her brilliant and superior spirit, made a deep impression on the Prince-President, and from that time every other female influence was eradicated from his mind, and he grew to love this one woman sincerely and completely."[3] How appropriate that the unofficial anthem for the regime over which the two lovers would preside was to be Hortense's chivalric composition "Partant pour la Syrie."[4]

It was only a matter of time, and a short time too. But time enough for Eugenia to make it clear that she would not agree to be his mistress, time for tongues to wag, for some ladies at the court to show their displeasure at the intruder and for some politicians to express their opposition to the prospect of marriage. Yet the emperor was steadfast in his love. On 12 January 1853, at supper during a ball at the Tuileries, he invited Eugenia and her mother to the table of the imperial family. Three days later he formally requested her hand. The public announcement soon followed in typical style. The emperor called a meeting of the Senate, the Council of State, and the Legislative Body in the Tuileries on 22 January, and made a touching and daring speech, which the *Moniteur* duly printed the next day.

His intended marriage, he declared, would fulfill the wishes of the nation. But the union would not conform to the "policy of the past." Royal

---

3. David Duff, *Eugenie and Napoleon III* (London: Collins, 1978), 85, 86; Carette, *My Mistress, the Empress Eugénie*, 55.

4. Which, for the record, begins:

Le jeune et beau Dunois	On leaving for Syria,
Venait prier Marie	The young and handsome Dunois
Partant pour la Syrie,	Came to pray to the Virgin Mary
De bénir ses exploits:	To bless his exploits:
"Faites, Reine immortelle,"	"Grant, Immortal Queen,"
Lui dit-il en partant,	Said he to her on leaving,
"Que j'aime la plus belle	"That I may love the most beautiful woman
"Et sois le plus vaillant."	And be the most valiant man."

alliances had created a false sense of security, often placing "personal interests before those of the nation." One woman alone brought happiness to the people, "the modest and virtuous wife of General Buonaparte"; she was not of royal blood. He, the new emperor, would only succeed "by always calling to mind his origin, by preserving his character inviolable, and by boldly standing before Europe as a *parvenu*—a glorious title when acquired by the free votes of a great people." Putting aside the precedents set by "crowned heads," his marriage was a purely personal choice, the choice of a woman of noble birth, French in sympathy and education, a woman whose father had shed his blood on behalf of the Empire, a woman who, by her Spanish birth, had no relations in France on whom it would be necessary to confer "honors and dignities." She was endowed with "all the great qualities of the soul" and would be "an ornament to the throne," its fearless supporter in hours of danger, a Catholic whose prayers would be as his own, for the prosperity of France. Her court would be "renowned for its virtues as was that of the Empress Josephine." After the prolonged applause and the cries of *"Vive l'Empereur! Vive l'Impératrice"* had died down, the august speaker broached his eloquent finale:

> Gentlemen, what I wish to state to France is this: I have preferred a woman whom I love and respect to one whose alliances might have had advantages *mêlés de sacrifices*. Although despising the opinion of no one, I yield to my inclination, but not before consulting my reason and convictions.
>
> Thus, by placing independence, the dictates of the heart, and the welfare of family above dynastic prejudices and ambitious aspirations, I shall not be weaker, being more free. (Enthusiastic applause.)
>
> On my way to Notre-Dame I will present the Empress to the people and to the army; the confidence they place in me insures their sympathy for her whom I have chosen; and, Gentlemen, when you have become acquainted with her you will then be convinced that in my choice I have been inspired by Providence. (The Chamber resounded with continued applause.)[5]

Only a week later the civil marriage took place on the evening of 29 January. The great master of ceremonies, the duke de Cambacérès, and the

5. Quoted in Carette, *My Mistress, the Empress Eugénie,* 60–65.

Spanish ambassador escorted the bride from the Élysée to the Tuileries Palace. There, a procession of ministers, diplomats, officers of State and of the Household, marshals, admirals, paid their respects. The emperor wore the order of the Golden Fleece and the collar of the Legion of Honor that had belonged to his uncle. The bride was in a satin dress trimmed with Alençon lace and a double row of pearls around her neck. In the Salon des Maréchaux, the old register of the Imperial House was signed, and the whole company moved into the Salle des Spectacles, where they heard a cantata composed for the occasion by Auber with words by the Provençal writer Méry, who celebrated Spain on having formed the new empress from one of its rays of sunshine.[6] The next day, Sunday, 30 January, the day of the religious ceremony in Notre-Dame, the weather was splendid. Bells rang out all over the city, festooned with banners and pennants, with eagles and bees and *Ls* and *Es* in every street and square all along the processional route. Crowds of Parisians and provincials who had streamed into the capital lined the streets and the troops gleamed in their new uniforms and helmets. The emperor was in his general's uniform. The empress Eugénie, in a white velvet dress, was more radiant than the sun. "She stole the day. Tribute after tribute came from those who saw her pass. No more beautiful picture graced the nineteenth century. Even her dentist, Dr. Evans, accustomed to a more prosaic view, was bowled over as he watched the divinely beautiful bride who sat beside the emperor like a captive fairy queen, her hair trimmed with orange blossom, a diadem on her head."[7] Viollet-le-Duc and Lassus had transformed the cathedral, decorated in a blaze of colors, red velvet drapes fringed with gold palm leaves, ermine-bordered tapestries, friezes of eagles and garlands, the standards of eighty-six departments, the arms of France and Spain, the escutcheons of the Bonapartes and the Montijos on prominent display, and from the summit of the towers, in proud company, four eagles and two tricolor banners. Fifteen thousand candles illuminated the cathedral. As the imperial couple entered, an orchestra of five hundred struck up the march from Meyerbeer's *Le Prophète*. The ceremony was performed by the archbishop of Paris. As the couple left the church, drums and trumpets, bells and salvos of artillery fire filled the air with celebration.

6. See *ibid.,* 66, and Patrick Turnbull, *Eugénie of the French* (London: Michael Joseph, 1974), 79.

7. Quoted in Duff, *Eugenie and Napoleon III,* 101.

Soon their union was blessed with a child, an heir. At 3:15 A.M. on 16 March 1856, the cannon of the Invalides fired their hundred-and-one-gun salute, announcing to the nation that a boy was born. He was christened Napoléon Eugène Louis Jean Joseph. The baptism ceremony of the prince imperial in Notre-Dame on 14 June 1856, with 5,600 guests, was as splendid an occasion as the imperial marriage. Thereafter, according to one account from within the imperial household, "the Emperor never ceased to love the Empress with a warm and sincere affection; and to the end of his life she, with his son, was the only object of his tenderness. At all times he showed himself affectionate and kind, addressing her always in the second person, and calling her by her pet name. His looks, and the charm her beauty exercised over him, together with his familiar and loving manner, betrayed always the lover in the person of the husband."[8]

BEHIND THE SCENES

A touching tale, much of which, however—and not only the clichés—does not stand up to scrutiny. Fuller and more reliable versions of the imperial romance present a somewhat different picture. For instance, even though the Montijos did attend military reviews at the Carrousel, the Champ de Mars, and Satory, the romantic encounter described above on the basis of Frerejean's account almost certainly did not take place in September 1849, if at all. That year Eugenia had left Paris in July with her mother in the company of her suitor at the time, the duke of Osuna, to escape the cholera outbreak in the French capital and was probably in Brussels in September.[9] In any case, by then, she had already met the prince-president for the first time earlier in the year, though there is disagreement amongst biographers about precisely when and about whether this first meeting took place at one of the receptions at the house of Princess Mathilde or at the Élysée Palace.[10] Recent biographers agree that she met him for the first

8. Carette, *My Mistress, the Empress Eugénie,* 67–68.

9. See Le Petit Homme Rouge, *The Court of the Tuileries,* 59; Ridley, *Napoleon III and Eugénie,* 320–21.

10. Ridley, for example, has them introduced at the Élysée and quotes from a letter to Paca, after Princess Mathilde's party, complaining that nobody spoke to her there. Ridley, *Napoleon III and Eugenie,* 246. Martinoir has her meet him at another reception at Mathilde's "a few days" after the unproductive evening. Francine de Martinoir, *Mathilde et Eu-*

time in April at a reception in the Élysée, but that it was a most inauspicious encounter. Eugenia tactlessly mentioned that she had often spoken of him with Éléonore Gordon—whom Louis Napoléon had treated ungratefully and who had recently died. At the unwelcome mention, her embarrassed host "moved on and spoke to her no more. It was a strange way to meet his future wife."[11]

There is little doubt also that, however tender their feelings for each other might have been, the motives of the two lovers were far from disinterested. Though she sincerely admired Louis Napoléon's courage and was grateful for his love, Eugenia was more enthralled by his position and the "divine mission" that it entailed than by the man. In any case, she was possibly still in love with Pepe, the marquis of Alcañices, and sent him a telegram to inform him that the emperor had proposed, but he replied with congratulations rather than, as she may have hoped, with an alternative proposal.[12] Doña Manuela was desperate for her second daughter to marry well and unscrupulous in her attempts to bring about a marriage, with Mérimée's help. Though undoubtedly possessed of a will of her own and quite ready to give up on the whole enterprise to return to Spain, Eugenia doubtless received "coaching" from the two of them. There is the famous scene at Fontainebleau, with its variants, whereby the ardent prince-president is supposed to have enquired how he might best reach her/her heart/her room/her bed; "Through the chapel, Monseigneur," was supposedly her unequivocal reply.[13] Simone André Maurois describes the tension and uncertainty of the tactical council of the three with Doña Manuela's cousin, Ferdinand de Lesseps, in early January 1853, when the

---

génie: Deux cousines pour un Empereur (Paris: Criterion, 1992), 53, 87–88. Kurtz writes: "It has often been said, and the error has given rise to much unintelligent comment, that Eugénie first met her future husband in the house of Princesse Mathilde, Louis Napoleon's cousin and former fiancée. From a letter written by Doña Manuela soon after the event we find that the first meeting took place at the Elysée on the evening of April 12th." Harold Kurtz, *The Empress Eugénie, 1826–1920* (Boston: Houghton-Mifflin, 1964), 29.

11. Duff, *Eugenie and Napoleon III,* 58. See also Ridley, *Napoleon III and Eugénie,* 246–47.

12. Ridley, *Napoleon III and Eugénie,* 327. See also her letter to her sister, Paca, quoted in full in Turnbull, *Eugénie of the French,* 72–73.

13. See Turnbull, *Eugénie of the French,* 60; Simone André Maurois, *Miss Howard and the Emperor,* trans. Humphrey Hare (London: Collins, 1957), 73; Duff, *Eugenie and Napoleon III,* 86; Ridley, *Napoleon III and Eugénie,* 327, who adds: "It is very unlikely that she ever said this to him, but both he and his advisers knew it."

trap had been baited, and quotes the assessment of the outcome by Lord Cowley, the British ambassador: "We are living in a society of adventurers. The great one of all has been captured by an adventuress. . . . In fact, she has played her game with him so well that he can get her in no other way but marriage, and it is to gratify his passions that he marries her."[14] As for the fervent prince, he was initially far more interested in seducing Eugenia than in marrying her. Viel-Castel, whose brother, he claimed, had been Doña Manuela's lover, narrates with great relish some years after the marriage an anecdote gleaned, he also claimed, from a most reliable source: at Compiègne, the future emperor forced his way into her room and "wanted to employ force to overcome the energetic resistance of the heroine"; she fought him off; he was forced to retire; "he judged it necessary to take by a marriage the place that had resisted the assault. The doors were then opened and we had an empress."[15]

But before this could be achieved, there was the not insignificant matter of his relationship with the beautiful Miss Howard, a high-class courtesan, of considerable means and social graces, to whom he had been attached emotionally, domestically, and financially since 1846–47. She had helped finance his political rise to power and he had installed her in a house in the rue du Cirque close to the Élysée Palace. He had found irresistible, as Bierman puts it, "the combination of hauteur and harlotry," and she, no doubt, had aspirations to play the role of a Pompadour.[16] But she was not a suitable match for an emperor. One of the first consequences of his fateful decision to restore the Empire was the no less fateful decision to abandon Miss Howard and find a wife worthy of his exalted position in the eyes of the world. Had he remained as president of the Republic, the relatively discreet relationship with the woman he loved and who was devoted to him could have run its course. She provided a home, satisfied his senses and, in private, was an admirable consort. But protocol dictated that the new Caesar should have a wife above suspicion and of noble rank. Thus he embarked on the extravagant adventure of finding such a woman. His marriage to Eugenia is often considered to have been his most drastic error. But his new status totally transformed his relationship with women, totally changed the rules of the game. He lost the initiative sentimentally,

14. Maurois, *Miss Howard and the Emperor,* 83–85.
15. Viel-Castel, *Mémoires,* 28 June 1860.
16. Bierman, *Napoleon III and His Carnival Empire,* 56.

as he would eventually lose it politically, condemned to live the lie of a harmonious dynastic marriage and to resort to furtive erotic escapades to satisfy his desires. His first deception was with Miss Howard. He tricked her into being away when his marriage was announced, had her house broken into in order to regain possession of his compromising letters, repaid, with a handsome dividend, the money that she had lent him, and made her countess de Beauregard. But far more so than he suspected, he had crossed another Rubicon.

References to Joséphine's virtue were not the only traces of blarney in the emperor's speech announcing his marriage—Bonaparte's wife was not renowned for her chastity. Notwithstanding the lofty sentiments and the disparaging remarks about royal alliances, vigorous efforts had been expended to secure for Napoleon III a truly royal spouse. Far from wishing to break with precedent, he had recently tried and failed to do the opposite. First there was a Swedish princess, belonging to the exiled royal family, Carola av Vasa, a granddaughter of Louis Napoléon's cousin, Stéphanie de Beauharnais, who had married the grand duke of Baden in 1806; he visited her in Baden and returned under the illusion that the marriage had been arranged, but, as a result of diplomatic pressures, Carola was married off to the duke of Saxony. Then he tried, through negotiations by his foreign minister, Drouyn de Lhuys, and Count Walewski, the French ambassador in London, to arrange a marriage with Princess Adelaide of Hohenlohe-Langenburg, daughter of a minor German prince, but, most significantly, niece of Queen Victoria. The union would have had inestimable political advantages. The emperor agreed to postpone a proposal to Eugenia until Adelaide had made her decision, which turned out to be a refusal, coming on January 1, 1853. The sweet young girl of seventeen was willing, in fact "dying to be Empress," but Albert and Victoria, along with Prince Albert's uncle, King Leopold of Belgium, had other ideas and turned down the proposal on her behalf. The new emperor was in fact relieved, for by then he was determined to marry Eugenia. But he still needed to check with Doña Manuela the accuracy of a rumor according to which Eugenia was really the daughter of Lord Clarendon, whom her mother had known intimately in Paris in 1825. Not surprisingly, Doña Manuela dismissed the idea, with a retort worthy of Hortense: "Sire, the dates do not correspond."[17]

17. Duff, *Eugenie and Napoleon III*, 88–96; Ridley, *Napoleon III and Eugénie*, 324–29.

There was fierce opposition to the marriage both from prominent members of the emperor's government and from the imperial family, not out of concern for his personal happiness, but because such a union threatened either their diplomatic aspirations for the regime or their personal ambitions. Persigny, minister of the interior, was against the emperor's choice, because he had grander ambitions for the Empire. Saint-Arnaud argued that the army would be opposed, but there was more at stake in the matter for him than military honor. Drouyn de Lhuys threatened to resign as foreign minister. Speculation on the outcome was so rife at the time that Fould, the minister of the imperial household, astutely gambled on the result and, when the stock exchange panicked and a fall in securities occurred, made himself a bundle, whereas Saint-Arnaud lost his shirt and had to be bailed out by the emperor! But it was the family that was particularly put out by the event. The emperor's uncle, ex-king Jérôme, was so distraught that he had to stay at home for several days, for the marriage would clearly jeopardize his son's chances of succession. As for Plon-Plon himself, he is supposed to have bitterly remarked: "One does not *marry* Mademoiselle de Montijo." As for Plon-Plon's sister, Mathilde, who had previously turned down Louis Napoléon's proposal also in part to protect her brother's interests, she is said to have begged her cousin on her knees to give up the Spanish woman, whom she despised and would continue to do so. But to a considerable degree, the emperor's primary motives for marrying Eugenia were precisely the very same diplomatic and dynastic reasons that prompted the opponents of the union to dissuade him: to defy the monarchical European powers who had excluded him from the matrimonial stakes by creating his own regal consort; to secure the line of succession within his own branch of the family and thwart the hopes of Jérôme.[18]

Nevertheless, whatever the incentives of his family and advisers, the emperor would have done well to have heeded their warnings, for the luster of the marriage was only a matter of public display; the marital relations of the imperial couple, despite their shared devotion to their duties, was by all accounts far from being a palmy affair.[19] After about six months, the

18. Ridley, *Napoleon III and Eugénie*, 329; Duff, *Eugenie and Napoleon III*, 93; Viel-Castel, *Mémoires*, 19 January 1853.

19. Nevertheless, Ridley writes that "in 1856 Louis Napoleon and Eugénie were still a happily married couple," even though "his original passion had cooled," and that at Biarritz in September of that year, observing the way the emperor looked at his wife and fondled her,

emperor's adulteries began. The frustrated husband turned first to Miss Howard again for consolation. Ironically, it was at the camp at Satory that he would meet her, review the troops, then slip into a waiting carriage, Miss Howard's, to change out of his uniform, and off they would go through the streets of Versailles to the Château de Beauregard. Thus already began the battles of the empress to stay the wanderings and curb the desires which she either could not or would not satisfy. She disliked the act of love, so it seems, finding the whole business "disgusting." She held a cynical view on the topic of conjugal relations, as she later revealed in her advice, conveyed via Walewski, to Anna Murat, who, in 1865, was due to marry Lord Granville: "Tell her that after the first night it makes no difference whether the man is handsome or ugly. By the end of the week it's the same old thing." But at least in the early days, she had a powerful hold over her husband because of his desire for an heir. Thus she could bring him to heel by denying him access to her bedroom or threatening to leave him. In September 1853, Miss Howard was banned from Paris and sent for "a long sojourn abroad." He had no choice. Then, following a number of anguishing miscarriages, the heir duly appeared on 16 March 1856 after a particularly long and painful labor, which almost cost the empress her life. There were complications and she was informed in no uncertain terms that another pregnancy would probably be fatal. But she had done her duty and she could now, as an ardent Catholic, with a free conscience, renounce all sexual relations with her husband. As she remarked to Mérimée, with dramatic finality, and mocking the emperor's distorted pronunciation of her name, "there is now no longer any *Ugénie*. There is only the Empress."[20] For the emperor, though the road to Beauregard was still closed, he was now freer to look elsewhere for solace. Eugénie would turn to motherhood, fashion, and foreign affairs to fill the gap.

FLASHBACK I: THE LOVELY SEÑORITA

When she became a serious contender for the position of the emperor's wife, there was much scurrilous gossip about Eugenia's past, and even

---

Dr Barthez "had no doubt that he was still lusting after her." Ridley, *Napoleon III and Eugénie,* 402.

20. Maurois, *Miss Howard and the Emperor,* 112, 113, 127–28; Eugénie's advice to Anna Murat quoted in Williams, *The Mortal Napoleon III,* 53.

more about her mother's. Maria Manuela's colorful life had in fact been a frequent source of scandal in the French press for some twenty-five years. But now scandalous stories, initially confined to the court, circulated about her daughter: not only was she said to be the illegitimate daughter of Lord Clarendon, but she had led a wild and immoral life in Spain; she wore a red wig because she had lost all her hair in a suicide attempt. Such opprobrium, which became associated with the political opposition to the new regime, grew more intense and open at the time of the marriage with the result that the emperor ordered perpetrators and publishers of such libels to be prosecuted. Thereafter most were printed abroad. Ridley, for instance, quotes a clever poem, "La Badinguette," the satirists' new name for Eugénie, a slanderous dialogue between Uncle Jérôme, Badinguet, and la Badinguette on the price of the lady's honor, a work which would cost the anonymous author, if indeed the man concerned was in fact the author, a long sentence in the penal colony in Cayenne when he was caught pinning it to the gate of the Tuileries! Ridley also quotes the following typical verse that did the rounds on the wedding day:

> *Montijo, plus belle que sage,*
> *De l'Empereur comble les voeux,*
> *Ce soir, s'il trouve un pucelage,*
> *C'est que la belle en avait deux.*[21]

But such calumnies were not, by any means, limited to the republican press. King Leopold of the Belgians made a hobby of collecting scandalous stories about Eugénie and of sending them to Queen Victoria. Even Mérimée joined in the spirit of the occasion with a joke that, presumably then, was still fresh: "Whereas Louis Napoleon had become Emperor by election, Eugénie had become Empress by erection."[22]

In fact Eugenia's early years, before she was condemned to the trials of her status as empress of the French, read far more like a Stendhalian romance than a Brantôme tale. She was of irreproachable noble ancestry, the daughter of Don Cipriano Guzmán Palafox y Portocarrero of Teba, Banos,

---

21. Ridley, *Napoleon III and Eugénie,* 341–43. The verse reads: "Montijo, more beautiful than chaste, / Fulfills the emperor's wishes, / If he finds a virginity, tonight / Then the beauty had two of them."

22. *Ibid.,* 343.

and Mora no less,[23] three times a grandee, for he had become count of Montijo, marquis of Ardales, and duke of Penaranda on the death of his brother, Eugenio, in 1834, when, as much to the point, he also inherited a sizable fortune with vast estates, a splendid family home in Madrid, and a country residence just outside the city. Eugenia's mother, Manuela Kirkpatrick, had a Scottish father, William, who was a mere but successful fruit and wine merchant and had been appointed United States consul in Malaga. She was no less proud of her ancestry, for her mother was the daughter of a Belgian baron, Françoise de Grévégnée, whilst the Kirkpatricks, despite a downturn in their fortunes when they had supported Bonny Prince Charlie, were of distinguished Scottish lineage. A branch had been barons of Closeburn, and their early kin could be traced to the slayer of Red Comyn, the enemy of Robert the Bruce, in 1306. What is more, William Kirkpatrick claimed that the family could be traced back to the King of the Fenians, Finn MacLual, who ruled in the second century.[24] The Bonapartes, and even the Beauharnais, were but upstarts by comparison.

As if in foreboding of the turbulence of her later life, Maria Eugenia Ignacia Augustina, who was named after her uncle Don Eugenio, was born on 5 May 1826 in the garden of her mother's house in Granada during an earthquake, at a time when her father was still under house arrest for his involvement in the Liberal revolution of 1820. In the turmoil of the civil war between the Isabelinos and the Carlists, at the age of eight, she was sent with her sister to school in Paris, to the Convent of the Sacré-Coeur, where her Catholic faith deepened, and to the Gymnase Normal, Civil et Orthosomatique, a progressive co-educational school, where she

23. The titles and spellings tend to vary in different biographical sources. Le Petit Homme Rouge (Vizetelly), for example, gives "Don Cipriano Portocarrero, Palafox, Lopez de Zuniga, Rojas y Leiva, Count of Montijo (Conde del Montijo), Duke of Peñaranda, Count of Miranda del Castañar, etc., and grandee of Spain." He notes also that Eugenia's sister, Francisca de Sales, known as Paca, was married in February 1844 to "a lineal descendant of James II. of Great Britain, that is, Don James Stuart FitzJames, Ventimiglia, Alvarez de Toledo, Belmonte y Navarra-Portogallo, eighth Duke of Berwick, fourteenth Duke of Alba, Duke of Leiria, Jerica, Galisteo, Montoro and Huesca, Count-Duke of Olivares, Count of Lemos, senior grandee of Spain, twelve times a first-class grandee, constable of Navarre, etc." Paca's husband is generally referred to as Alba! Vizetelly adds: "In giving the Count de Montijo's name we spared the reader a full enumeration of his titles. It is certain, however, that his two daughters were of high lineage, coming as they did on his side from the ancient houses of Guzman and Palafox." Le Petit Homme Rouge, *The Court of the Tuileries*, 62–63.

24. Turnbull, *Eugénie of the French*, 21, 15–16.

received physical training. She was a spirited child, highly strung and adventurous. During a brief stay at school near Bristol, she tried to stowaway on a ship to India with a newfound Indian friend. She was inordinately fond of her father, who had taught her to ride from a young age, but whose political obligations only allowed him to be with his family intermittently until he died in 1839. For the time being, Maria Manuela stayed in Madrid with her daughters. Paca married their cousin and childhood friend, the duke of Alba, one of the noblest grandees of Spain and one of the richest men in Europe. Eugenia loved him too and may well have tried to commit suicide in her despair. As she wrote to her cousin before the wedding, with remarkable insight and foresight: "I love and hate to excess and I don't know which is better, my love or my hate; passions mingle within me, some terrible, all of them violent; I fight against them but lose the battle and in the end my life will finish, miserably lost in a mire of passions, virtues and follies."[25] She would live on, and long beyond, to experience many such passions, virtues and follies. Her love persisted, but the despair did not endure, for there were too many exciting distractions.

Her mother, anxious to find for her second daughter a suitable match and adept at establishing good relations with the changing governments of the time, embarked upon a dazzling round of extravagant receptions, lavish balls, amateur theatricals, visits to the theater and the opera, of which Eugenia became, no less than in the heady days of the Second Empire ten years later, a central attraction. She went riding alone, galloping through the countryside, her red hair swept in the wind behind her, up into the mountains or to visit a Gypsy encampment, where fortune-tellers told her that she would marry an emperor. She dined with actors and actresses, road bareback through the streets of Madrid smoking a *cigarillo*, went to bullfights dressed in scarlet boots, a dagger in her belt, carrying a whip instead of a fan, was rumored to be the mistress of a leading matador, El Chichanero, stole the heart of the foremost nobleman of Spain, the young duke of Osuna, more important even than the duke of Alba. He gallantly rescued her when her gondola overturned at a garden party at Vista Alegre. At one of the balls to celebrate the marriage of Queen Isabella in the autumn of 1846, she vigorously danced polkas and waltzes to an orchestra conducted by Johann Strauss and won the heart of Dumas *fils*, who was there with his father. She even got involved in political intrigues

25. Dated 16 or 17 May 1843; quoted in Turnbull, *Eugénie of the French*, 26.

in defiance of the brutal rule of the Isabelino general Ramón Narváez, with whom her mother was fortunately on the best of terms; she was said to have tried to stop the execution of Radical revolutionaries, to have smuggled a terrorist out of Madrid, and to have demonstrated her courage to the dictator himself by plunging a dagger into her arm to show that she was not afraid to face cold steel. She narrowly escaped being kidnapped with Alba and Paca by Carlist bandits and, in a castle "somewhere in Spain," toyed with a robber hidden under her bed until the servants arrived to arrest the man. She turned down prominent suitors, fell in love with Pepe, the marquis of Alcañices, but discovered that he had deceived her and really loved her sister, and there was, according to later reports, another—if it was not indeed her first and only—dramatic suicide attempt.[26] For one biographer this episode was a watershed, marking Eugenia's "farewell to love and happiness" and prompting her to "emotional withdrawal from the heartless world of sensual, frivolous men."[27] Whatever the prompting, Maria Manuela's fall in political favor at home being a primary incentive, mother and daughter left Madrid and set off on their travels in late 1848, flitting around Europe, socializing in various capitals, spending winter seasons in Madrid, until circumstances, helped by her mother's determined prompting, led her to the altar of Notre-Dame and to an even more heartless world of sensual, frivolous men and women. Whether or not her meeting with Louis Napoléon ignited a spark of love, with her marriage to the emperor of the French, though she would not lack for admirers, all the romance of her life was truly and definitively extinguished.

FLASHBACK 2: THE GALLANT PRINCE

There is a curious equivalence between the life and the loves of the emperor and the empress before they were married. Both moved in cosmo-

26. For more details on this narrative, see Ridley, *Napoleon III and Eugénie*, 137–72. See also 169–71 for a cautious account of the Alcañices incident. Other biographers, with variations in the spelling of the offending gentleman's name, present a more dramatic version, based on an account by Ethel Smyth, in which Eugenia, on discovering that he had deceived her, took poison, hovered between life and death, and only took the antidote in "a blaze of contempt" when Alcañices came to ask her where she kept his letters; she declared: "Like Achilles's spear, you heal the wounds you made." See Turnbull, *Eugénie of the French*, 30; Kurtz, *The Empress Eugénie*, 26–27; Duff, *Eugenie and Napoleon III*, 71.

27. Kurtz, *The Empress Eugénie*, 28.

politan circles within a context of political turmoil. Both were fiercely independent and adventurous spirits, but earnestly directed by a strong-willed mother to fulfill their destiny. Both were remarkably athletic and made a splash in society, particularly on horseback. Both were less than fortunate in their attachments, though Louis Napoléon, by virtue of his gender and circumstances, had far more opportunities to bestow his affections. Yet, as Williams remarks, "by the standards of his day for a man of his rank, Louis-Napoleon's love affairs before his marriage were moderately respectable."[28] Nevertheless, legends abound, revealing, as well as some remarkable inconsistencies both on points of detail and on whether or not they occurred at all, another side to the idealistic and studious youth. The earlier ones in particular are invariably narrated, with suitable embroidering, in the complicitous, cavalier, nudge-nudge, wink-wink tones of the gay dog's confessions. He certainly got, so it seems, an early start. When he was but "a mere stripling," according to Vizetelly, and staying with his mother in Florence, he was seized with "a desperate attack of calf-love" for a high-ranking Italian lady, Countess Baraglini, otherwise known as the *"anticamera del paradiso,"* and disguised himself as an itinerant flower-boy to gain admittance to her house. But when, *"à la Trovatore,"* he threw himself at her feet, her servants threw him out, and "Prince Precocious was compelled to quit the city."[29] Bac is quite lyrical about the young prince's exploits at Augsburg and Arenenberg, evoking the "quantity" of romantic girls who fell in love with the dashing young cavalier and whose "virgin fancies" (*"imaginations virginales"*) he nourished by his "thousand acts of bravery," leaping hedges, jumping over a cow, courageously saving lives by stopping a runaway cart, "acclaimed as a hero by the frenzied populations." A veritable throng of young blondes, the same author affirms, would flock to him, "with the characteristic attraction that women feel for unhappy heroes. They would sing his mother's romances and would lull themselves with the tunes of the troubadours that filled the air in those innocent times." It was, after all, the height of the Romantic period. But there were far less innocent displays of his "prowess," as fathers complained, according to Bac, at the ravages brought about by the irrepressible Louis, who was accused of renting a bark every night to take

28. Williams, *The Mortal Napoleon III,* 52.
29. Le Petit Homme Rouge, *The Court of the Tuileries,* 181. See also Dansette, *Les Amours de Napoléon III,* 24.

young girls to the middle of the lake, "out of territorial limits, and of bringing them back at dawn in a dishevelled state." At the age of sixteen he was involved with a certain Fraulein Kümich, then with a certain Frau Stahli von Frauenfeld, whilst, thirty years later, a certain Frau Nüssi (or Nussy), formerly Fraulein Laubli, popped up in need of money to go to America, alleging that she was not only the carpenter's daughter from Er-matingen but the emperor's offspring, conceived in 1822 or 1823; but, since he was only fourteen or fifteen at the time, she failed to convince. "Strange young man," Dansette writes, "Don Quixote and Lovelace in turn." As was no doubt the custom at the time, sundry *"demoiselles d'hon-neur"* and *"femmes de chambre"* were tumbled. But more disturbing to modern sensibilities is an incident that occurred during Louis Napoléon's involvement in the Italian insurrection. The tale is couched in pastoral eu-phemism, narrating how the prince's companion, the marquis Zappi, spot-ted a young peasant girl, stopped their carriage, allowing the two to pursue "the nymph of the fields, to fool around with her behind a rock and to kiss her by force."[30]

But it was not all wild oats, for the prince revealed a sentimental dispo-sition, falling in love, even contemplating marriage at an early age. At Are-nenberg, Marie de Bade, who was only fifteen, turned him down. He was forced by his mother to break off a relationship with the widowed Mme. Saunier, who lived with her children and dogs in a nearby château. Mlle. Padoue did not have a sufficient dowry, nor did Louise Chapelain de Séré-ville, the adopted daughter of the neighboring marquis and marquise de Crenay, who, in any case, were legitimists. Even the daughter of Don Pedro, the former emperor of Brazil, Maria da Glória, who had just been placed on the throne of Portugal (as Maria II), was not considered a suit-able match.[31] Hortense was protective of her *"doux entêté"* and had high aspirations for him. Cousin Mathilde, however, though still a giggly girl of fifteen in 1835, was a different matter; she was a Bonaparte. She im-pressed him with her vivacity and her décolleté; he recited Schiller to her; they fell idyllically in love; negotiations on the marriage and the dowry were under way in 1836, with King Louis and King Jérôme, the latter seri-

30. Bac, *Napoléon III inconnu,* 173–75; Dansette (who writes "Kümick"), *Les Amours de Napoléon III,* 22, 23, 26, 29. See also Williams, *The Mortal Napoleon III,* 49.
31. Dansette, *Les Amours de Napoléon III,* 32–38; Fleischmann, *Napoléon III et les femmes,* 27.

ously in debt, haggling furiously. But the attempted Strasbourg coup
d'état put paid to the protracted matter as far as the pretender's disapprov-
ing uncle was concerned, and Mathilde either would not or could not contact him thereafter. By the time Louis Napoléon became a suitable match
again, as president of the Republic, Mathilde was already (unhappily) married and, though separated from her brutish and poxy Russian husband,
Prince Demidov, was in love with the handsome aristocratic sculptor
Count de Nieuwerkerke. The ideal imperial marriage, according to some,
which would have changed the whole course of French history—in many
ways she was to be the opposite as well as the rival of the empress—was
never to be.[32] The failure of the match marked the end of Hortense's attempts to further the dynastic aspirations of the Bonaparte family through
marriage, for by the time such considerations became appropriate again
after the successful coup d'état of 1851, the pretender's mother had died.
A new phase began in which dynastic considerations were temporarily
shelved and in which romance and politics, or, more pertinently, romance
and finance, would be inextricably linked in the fits and starts of his rise to
power.

Whilst Hortense was plotting her son's marriage with Mathilde, Louis
Napoléon was plotting his first coup d'état attempt at Strasbourg with the
help of a picturesque figure, a formidable young woman, Éléonore Gordon (*née* Brault), who had a taste for adventure and sound Bonapartist credentials. She rode, drank, swore, shot and fenced like a man; she was a
professional singer, daughter of an officer in Napoleon I's Guard and the
widow of a Scottish mercenary who fought for the queen of Spain. She
was, in a sense, a cross between a kind of poor-man's Eugénie and a
Dumas character. She was Persigny's mistress and was often said to have
shared her affections with "her Prince," as would Persigny's wife much
later, such was their devotion to the Bonapartist cause. But the received
view, based mainly upon their mutual denials, is that they never became
lovers.[33] In any case, on this particular occasion, as we have seen, she was

---

32. According to Viel-Castel (*Mémoires*, 16 July 1865), Louis Napoléon, in prison in
Ham at the time, had wept bitterly when he had heard of her marriage to Demidov. On the
relations between the two women, see Martinoir, *Mathilde et Eugénie*. As already noted,
Mathilde's salon in the rue de Courcelles became a rival social center to the imperial court.

33. Dansette, in *Les Amours de Napoléon III*, 51, is of the opposite opinion, not surprisingly, given the nature of his book, which errs on the side of a somewhat prurient incaution.
He is convinced that they were lovers, in view of Louis Napoléon's taste for "overwhelming

required to be bait for the amorous Colonel Vaudrey, who was enlisted into the group of conspirators and became her lover. As for Louis Napoléon, by the time he made his next coup d'état attempt, he had secured far more sophisticated and far more gifted support, both physically and financially. During his stay of almost two years in England, from October 1838 to August 1840, the Continental adventure novel of his life turned into an English society novel, with its posturing, prejudices, and pride, and the eager impulsion to gain social and financial advantages. Prince Florestin, as he appears in Disraeli's *Endymion,* moved dandified somewhat on the fringe of the best society, in the fashionable circles to which his friendship with Count d'Orsay and Lady Blessington gave him entry. He "gained a certain notoriety as a remorseless romantic as far as the opposite sex was concerned." There was talk of an engagement to Emily, the daughter of a rich builder, Henry Rowles, but nothing came of the relationship except that she would later lend him money, in 1851, when he was in dire financial difficulties. As Fleischmann confidently asserts, this "fiancée" was not at this time, "in addition to the British mistresses of the Prince," his only matrimonial prospect. There was also a certain Burdett Coutts, granddaughter of a successful banker, who had the estimable advantage of being in a position to inherit 30 millions, but, as it turned out, only if she married an Englishman![34] Louis-Napoléon would have to wait much longer before he hit the jackpot with Miss Howard, after his stay at Ham.

The farce of the Boulogne incident, which ended in humiliation and surrender in the Channel, was appropriately spiced up by local legend with the rumor of a brief fling with a local lass, Mimi-la-Bouchère, who had a weakness for soldiers and worked at the military prison where he was detained for two days.[35] With his imprisonment at Ham, Louis Napoléon's *"roman-feuilleton"* took a new twist to become a domestic drama, a Balzacian scene from provincial life, an *Eugénie Grandet* in reverse, with the dashing man about town as the captive in a real prison, or an inverted fairy tale, with the prince in the castle and the lovely maiden, another Éléonore, providing relief—though she would end up twice pregnant and aban-

women" and her lack of "Platonic intimacy." Her disavowal, which has already been quoted and according to which he impressed her only politically and seemed to her like a woman, is taken to be a typical case of "the impudence of the fair sex when it defends its reputation"!

34. Turnbull, *Eugénie of the French,* 45; Fleischmann, *Napoléon III et les femmes,* 32–36.
35. On this apocryphal incident, see Fleischmann, *Napoléon III et les femmes,* 92–95.

doned, and he would escape without her! Alexandrine Éléonore Vergeot was an attractive, twenty-year-old laundress, known locally as "la belle Sabotière." She was tolerated by the authorities as the prisoner's mistress and companion during what was expected to be his life sentence.[36] According to Fleischmann, who quotes from her birth certificate, her father was in fact a weaver, Antoine-Joseph Vergeot—her mother's name was Marie-Louise-Françoise-Éléonore Camus—and her nickname was probably an invention of the pamphleteers, who claimed that he once seduced and bought off the daughter of a clog maker. She had been unlucky in love with a local painter and decorator and worked as a daily help in the town, doing the ironing for Mme. Renard, the porter's wife at the fortress. She would take the prince his meals. *"Mon Dieu,"* as Fleischmann writes with a certain relish, "many a novel begins this way. . . . Her education having been neglected, Louis-Napoléon applied himself to complete it; he instilled in her the elements of syntax and enjoyed teaching her. He did not stop there, and did better by her, notably two sons." Dansette gives the relationship a somewhat more romantic (pan)gloss, but cannot repress the Voltairian quip: "Alexandrine gave Louis-Napoléon her youth, her gaiety, her devotion, her simple love. Amongst other things, he gave her lessons in spelling and grammar." The ending was far from happy, but by no means tragic, rather a convenient realistic accommodation. Éléonore was married off to Pierre-Jean-François Bure, the prince's foster brother, who became the official father of the two boys. In a handy arrangement, Miss Howard would bring them up. They were both called Louis, of course, and both were made counts in 1870, just in time, before the fall of the Empire.[37]

36. Bierman gives her name as Alexandrine Éléonora Vergeot, her nickname deriving from her talent as a clog dancer. Bierman, *Napoleon III and His Carnival Empire*, 47. Ridley calls her Éléonore Veugeot-Camus, known as Alexandrine by the local people of Ham. Ridley, *Napoleon III and Eugénie*, 176. Turnbull gives the twenty-three-year-old redhead's nickname as "la belle sabatière" and explains that her father was a shoemaker! She was employed, he suggests, as the Prince's valet. Turnbull, *Eugénie of the French*, 51. According to Duff, Alexandrine Eleanora Vergeot was a twenty-year-old ironer, who cared for items of the apparel of the officers of the garrison that needed ironing and lived in the house of one of the gatekeepers; she was, he states, voluptuous, with chestnut hair. Duff, *Eugenie and Napoleon III*, 51.

37. Fleischmann, *Napoléon III et les femmes*, 108; Dansette, *Les Amours de Napoléon III*, 73. On the two sons, see Fleischmann, *Napoléon III et les femmes*, 108–12: Alexandre Louis Eugène (1843–1910) became the Count d'Orx, and Alexandre Louis Ernest (1845–1882) became the Count de Labenne. The older boy was vice-consul in Rosas, then consul in Zan-

Back in London, Louis Napoléon set about "furiously" making up for lost time politically and sentimentally, for, as Fleischmann puts it, "for the high liver that he is, Éléonore Vergeot is meager fare." Among the possible candidates cited are a Creole lady, Favart de Langlade, to whose refuge Morny was to plan an escape if the coup d'état attempt of 1851 had failed; a certain Countess d'Espel, who may not have been a countess at all; a certain Mme C., who may have spied on him for the English.[38] Of more reliable authenticity, due to the illustrious fame of the lady concerned, is a relationship during the summer of 1846 with the tragedienne Rachel, whose repertoire of lovers, including Alexandre Walewski, Napoleon's illegitimate son, by whom she in turn had an illegitimate son in 1844, was as distinguished as her stage roles. Élisa Rachel Félix had risen meteorically from the status of street singer to become the most famous actress in Europe, mainly through her electrifyingly passionate performances as a tragic heroine, notably as Phèdre, which contributed above all to a revival of the popularity of the Classical theater. On 3 January 1858, at the age of thirty-six, she would die from tuberculosis, or as Viel-Castel wickedly claimed— even before she had passed away—with some scabrous anecdotes to support his view, from "debauchery as much as from the fatigues of the theater." Eugénie was one of her admirers. Louis Napoléon assiduously attended the theater in his London days, not so much out of a taste for the plays but more because it was the thing for fashionable gentlemen to do, especially if, like the prince, they enjoyed the company of actresses. He saw Virginie Déjazet, who had visited him in Ham, admired Jenny Lind, was received by Rose Chéri alone in her lodgings, made unsuccessful advances to the calculating Eugénie Doche, but was apparently more successful with her rival, a ballet dancer named Scheffer.[39] But above all, he was "en-

zibar, married well, had three children, and died in his château in Saint-André-de-Seignaux, where he was mayor. The younger son lived in Mexico until April 1870, when he returned to France and tried to gain the favor of his father, signing his letter Louis-Napoléon! Moving in financial circles, he married a banker's daughter in 1879 and had a son who died in 1884, two years after his father.

38. See Fleischmann, *Napoléon III et les femmes,* 120–25. The chronology of these affairs is as vague as their authenticity is uncertain.

39. Viel-Castel, *Mémoires,* 13 August 1857. On these various liaisons, see Ridley, *Napoléon III and Eugénie,* 197–98; Guest, *Napoleon III in England,* 66–67. Dansette adds to the list, after Louis Napoleon's return to France, a mysterious marquise de C.T. and a Miss Plunkett, along with Alice Ozy, whom Victor Hugo had "known," and various actresses from the Comédie Française. Dansette, *Les Amours de Napoléon III,* 100–103. Fleischmann adds fur-

chanted" by Rachel's Phèdre at the St. James's Theatre on 15 June 1846, less than a month after his escape to London, and she became his mistress during the summer. There was in the real-life relationship, however, no tragic, consuming passion, as a famous anecdote, more Feydeau than Racine, shows. Plon-Plon had joined his cousin in England in the fall of 1846. On a train from London to one of the northern engagements of the actress, Prince Louis nodded off, waking to find his mistress in the arms of his cousin; he tactfully closed his eyes again, pretending not to have seen them, and, without a word on the incident, caught an early train back to London alone the next morning. Clearly the importance of Louis Napoléon's relations with Rachel did not live up to what one would expect from the respective celebrity of the lovers themselves.

In complete contrast, Louis Napoléon's liaison with the far less renowned actress Miss Howard has much more than an anecdotal significance. Again, as with Mathilde, there are telling links and contrasts with Eugénie, and not only because Miss Howard too was a redhead. To dismiss her as a glorified harlot and him as an unscrupulous exploiter of her ill-gotten gains is to belittle unjustly their relationship. True, Elizabeth Ann Haryett, a bootmaker's daughter from Brighton, had a scarlet past. She became an accomplished horsewoman in her youth, was a passionate reader of poetry and scandalized her churchgoing parents by announcing that she wanted to be an actress. She ran away from home with a jockey called Jem Mason, acted in various London theaters, but drew more attention to her radiant beauty than to her talent, was won over by a major in the Life Guards, who, though still married, gave her generous terms and, when their illegitimate son was born, a fortune. Major Mountjoy Martyn was by marriage a cousin of Lady Blessington, at one of whose receptions, in June 1846, she was introduced by d'Orsay to Prince Napoléon. Simone André Maurois has made a case for there existing a profound and lasting love between them. "Never was a woman more utterly devoted," she writes of Miss Howard's readiness to follow her Bonaparte and to offer her whole fortune for his cause.[40] She was twenty-three when they met, highly sophisticated by then, in the process of improving her education and ready to provide an elegant and com-

---

ther names, many of which are taken from anti-Bonapartist propaganda. Fleischmann, *Napoléon III et les femmes*, 155–64.

40. Maurois, *Miss Howard and the Emperor*, 37.

fortable home for the refugee and his two illegitimate sons. Before and after the coup d'état, which she largely helped to finance, she was his faithful companion, ran an elegant salon in Paris, and was loved devotedly by the prince-president, as he revealed in an angry letter denouncing the hypocrisy of a snub by an official when Miss Howard had stayed at his house in Tours.[41] Could she not legitimately aspire to a permanent place in his affections? As it turned out, she was destined to be a figure of transition. Their love survived the coup d'état, but, as eventually would be the case with her lover's political career, not the coup de grâce of the restitution of the Empire. As we have seen, never to be a Pompadour, she had to be sacrificed so that Eugénie could be brought to the imperial altar.

What this wealth of anecdotal evidence reveals, with due allowance for some whimsical embroidery from the enthusiasts on the topic, is not only the compulsive eroticism of Louis Napoléon, but also, given his status, the complex and conflicting requirements that he had in his relations with the opposite sex, requirements which only Mathilde and Miss Howard came close to fulfilling: the stimulus of sexual pleasure, combined, if possible, with a sense of adventure, the esteem of social status and accomplishments, the comfort of domestic security, the promise of the realization of dynastic ambitions. His more casual affairs, as with Rachel, gratified the first, and in some cases also the second of these demands. "La Belle Sabotière" took care of the third in the special circumstances in which he found himself with her. Mathilde might have fulfilled all requirements if the timing had not been out of joint. Miss Howard seems admirably to have conformed to the first three specifications. Eugénie seemed to fit the bill to its full extent. When she did not, a fundamental new phase in Louis Napoléon's relations with women set in. The sexual demands became totally dissociated from the other considerations, which in the past had provided something of a check. With the added power, prestige, and opportunities afforded by his eminent position as emperor, the libertine tendencies were, in flagrant contradiction to his public image and moralistic discourse, given free rein in the semi-public confines of the court and in private, to seek and obtain unlimited erotic satisfaction, with, in the view of some, quite ruinous consequences.

41. See Ridley, *Napoleon III and Eugénie,* 258–59.

ON HIS MAJESTY'S SERVICE

One of tragic aspects of the Empire was surely that two such spirited souls as Louis Napoléon and Eugénie should have been condemned by dynastic ambition and political necessity to live out a life of empty sham: for him a series of undignified intrigues, for her the perpetual torment of outrage, suspicion, and shame at his faithlessness. Somewhere between the radiant fantasy of the public spectacle of a perfect family and the scurrilous calumnies of the republican propagandists, hammering relentlessly away in their denunciations of the orgies of the Tuileries and of the sleazy roué that supposedly presided over them, was the day-to-day reality of a marriage fraught with dissension. Eugénie grew ever hardened and watchful at her husband's evident interest in beautiful women, of which there was no lack in the receptions, balls, theaters that they attended. The legendary dull and vacant gaze would light up at the sight of a court beauty. There were frequent violent scenes. "How many times," writes Frerejean, "do the servants and the guests of the Tuileries hear angry outbursts, when, shut up with her husband, she [Eugénie] heaps reproaches on him." He is not the first to suggest that there was more at stake than the aggravation from such painful domestic scenes: "To avoid domestic scenes, the emperor accepts the intrusion of the empress in political life: there is so much for him to be forgiven!"[42] It was now the very antithesis of romance. No more adventure, only intrigues. No more noble sentiments, only jealousy and resentment. No more passion, only obligations. No more obstacles to overcome for the fulfillment of love, only furtive escapades and a bolted marital door. No more prince and ravishing maiden, only the querulous wife and the errant husband of situation comedy, or even of farce.

The emperor's goings-on were pruriently recorded, no doubt, with added spice, not only in republican propaganda printed abroad, but also, and to no less damaging effect on the reputation of both the emperor and the empress, by the gossips of the court, notably Viel-Castel, whose memoirs, according to certain more sympathetic commentators such as Vizetelly, "are studded with scandalous tittle-tattle, resting at times on very slight, and at others on no foundation whatever." But the problem is again one of historical veracity, of the gaps that are even more yawning in matters of the private lives of historical figures. There were no semen-stained

42. Frerejean, *Napoléon IV*, 64–65.

dresses to submit to laboratory analysis and to display before the cameras. The rebuttals themselves are no more reliably grounded than the scandalous revelations, and there is only the evidence of apparent authenticity, a matter of textual analysis, upon which we can rely. To take a prime example, Viel-Castel quotes a recent discussion between Mathilde and the emperor's chamberlain, Chaumont-Quitry, on whether or not Walewski, the foreign minister, was aware that his wife was the current favorite of the emperor. To respond to the doubts of the princess, the chamberlain narrates an incident in which, in the presence of Walewski and himself, Mocquard opened the door of the emperor's bedroom to reveal Marie-Anne Walewska in the sovereign's arms. Mathilde is not convinced that Walewski would be as corrupt as to accept the emperor's recent gift of land worth a hundred thousand francs in exchange for his wife's favors, though she does concede that her cousin is "very imprudent" in such matters and recalls another incident: on a journey to (or from) Compiègne, with Eugénie, Walewski, and Mme. Hamelin, the jolting of the imperial train caused the door to a separate compartment to fly open and reveal the emperor sitting on Marie-Anne's knees, kissing her on the mouth with a hand down her bosom. The revelations continue as Mathilde reports a conversation the previous year at a ball at the Tuileries, at which the emperor seemed particularly anxious, complaining to Chaumont-Quitry that he was being pursued by three women:

> I have, you see, the emperor went on, the blonde on the ground floor that I'm trying to shake off (Mme. de La Bédoyère).
> Then I have the lady on the first floor (the comtesse Castiglione), who is certainly very beautiful, but she is insignificant and insipid, she bores me stiff.
> And then I also have the blonde on the second floor (Mme. Walewska) who is chasing after me and follows me around.
> But the empress? I objected.
> As for the empress, the emperor answered me, I was faithful to her for the first six months of our marriage, but I need my little distractions and I always come back to her with pleasure.

We can be reassuredly skeptical about the exact *discours* of such secondhand reporting, unless we believe that Viel-Castel and Mathilde were endowed with a remarkable memory for diction (or took notes). But, as for the *récit* of the anecdotes, which are frequently reproduced by biographers to illustrate the emperor's profligacy, to dismiss them as fiction would be to strain incredulity. Yet given that this single account forms the basis of so much speculation about the emperor's love life at the time, it certainly requires examination. The emperor's liaison with the countess de Castiglioni was common knowledge, but there was much less testimony to substantiate the same claim for the countess de Walewska. As for the countess de La Bédoyère, the only hard evidence seems to have been that her husband was a well-known *cocu*.[43] It would, however, have required an inventive maliciousness, which Chaumont-Quitry or Mathilde had no particular reason to employ against her cousin—the latter was less well disposed towards the empress—to have entirely concocted the incidents. In any case, the whole conversation as reported shows a preoccupation for the truth in the individuals themselves, which confers an air of authenticity on the scene. This reflective dimension contrasts with the blatant assertions of the opposition propagandists.

It is impossible, of course, and of no particular significance, to have an accurate idea of the number of women with whom the emperor made love. Unlike Don Juan, he did not keep a catalog of his "conquests," nor, like Victor Hugo, a coded record of his copulations, though, as the supposedly virtuous Countess Mercy-Argenteau discovered to her discomfort, the republican "secret police" did keep a "voluminous register" on every Bonapartist, full of "malign calumny and base defamation." When Ollivier let her see a copy, she read, amongst details of Madame de Montijo's gambling house and brothel, of Eugénie's many lovers since her marriage, of the emperor's numerous illegitimate children, the suggestion that the prince imperial was not the son of Badinguette but possibly of Marguerite Bellanger or Mme de X (Marie-Anne Walewska) or "more probably" of Mademoiselle de Caraman-Chimay, the writer by her maiden name![44] Any degree of certainty about the identity of the emperor's mistresses or about the nature of his relationship with them is entirely a function of their visibility at court and their social distinction or the political significance of their husbands, if not of themselves. The four main protagonists have already been mentioned, paragons of dubious virtue and paradigms of the emperor's "distractions."

43. Le Petit Homme Rouge, *The Court of the Tuileries*, 193; Viel-Castel, *Mémoires*, 28 October 1858; on the Countess de La Bédoyère, see Dansette, *Les Amours de Napoléon III*, 198.
44. Mercy-Argenteau, *The Last Love of an Emperor*, 139–40.

The so-called "divine countess," Virginia de Castiglioni, was supposedly sent to Paris by Cavour at the tender age of nineteen to influence the emperor's Italian policies in the direction of unification. If Napoleon III proved to be quite impervious to her political overtures, since she seems to have lacked the wit and astuteness of a diplomat, he was decidedly susceptible to her physical charms, which she displayed quite outrageously, notably at a fancy-dress ball given at the Ministry of Foreign Affairs on 17 February 1857, when she was famously dressed and provocatively décolletée as the Queen of Hearts. She was known not only for her costumes (Roman Lady of the Decadence and Salammbô outfits also caused a stir) and for her stunning beauty (her bosom in particular was remarked upon) but for her lack of social graces and her incorrigible narcissism. She probably became the emperor's mistress early in 1856, during the pregnancy of the empress, whose response was some public barbs and, no doubt, some private remonstrations. He installed her in a mansion in the avenue Montaigne, where he ran some personal risk in visiting her. Indeed, in April 1857, his coach was set upon by three would-be assassins. The affair lasted into the summer until la Castiglione left with her parting present, an emerald worth 1,000,000 francs. There was talk of an illegitimate child, who became a dentist by the name of Dr. Arthur Hugenschmidt, but he proved to be a hoaxer. All through the affair, the count had been totally discreet, boasting one day to Morny: "I am a model husband. I see nothing and hear nothing." "Yes," Morny replied, alluding to the financial advantages of his situation, "*mais vous touchez.*"[45]

Countess Marie-Anne Walewska's husband, as we have already noted, was equally obliging and received from the emperor generous compensation at the end of the affair—large salaries as a privy councillor and as a senator in addition to the land mentioned above—in exchange for "services to the Empire." As most biographers claim, these included his complaisance as far as la Walewska was concerned—Cowley referred to him in a dispatch as a pimp—a claim that is invariably based on Viel-Castel's revelations and, no doubt also, by association with his past as the illegitimate son of the Napoleon I. She was of an aristocratic Florentine family, born Marie-Anne de Ricci, blond, blue-eyed, and much cleverer than the more beautiful Castiglione. Williams, however, makes a strong case against the view that she was in fact the emperor's mistress, a charge which emanated

45. Williams, *The Mortal Napoleon III,* 62–65.

largely from the anti-Walewski faction at court, including Mérimée and Viel-Castel. The empress remained on the very best of terms with the countess, who was a devout Catholic and, at the time, a woman of thirty-four, the mother of three children and pregnant again—a much less attractive proposition for the emperor than many a younger and prettier woman at the court. No doubt too, Louis Napoléon had other reasons than that he was sleeping with his wife to be generous to his foreign minister, who was after all a relative, a direct descendant of Napoleon I, just as he was generous to almost all the members of his family. As for the attitude of the empress, it would be to implicate her in the Machiavellianism that, according to Mérimée, characterized Madame Walewska, to suggest: "Does Eugénie become a friend of the women that the emperor distinguishes in order to maintain, through them, a little influence over him?"[46] The most that can be said with any certainty is that the emperor and Anne-Marie were on very good terms.

No such demureness is required as far as Justine Marie Le Boeuf, otherwise known as Marguerite Bellanger, otherwise known as Margot-la-Rigoleuse, is concerned. She was a former chambermaid from Boulogne, who had run away with a traveling salesman and become a minor actress, then a favorite of the officers of the École Militaire, after a spell as an acrobatic dancer and bareback rider in a circus, where she learned some impressive tricks and contortions. Indeed, it was rumored that part of her appeal to the jaded spirits of the emperor, as well as her blond curls, her sensuality, her youth—she was twenty-five at the time—was her zest, her equestrian skills, of course, and her ability to perform "certain tricks." As Dansette coyly writes: "He is tired of society women, too often dull lovers. Margot is an expert [*une technicienne*] who adds a little spice." By the middle of 1863, when this affair probably began—the origins of the liaison remain obscure—his health had seriously declined. He was frequently in pain from arthritis, hemorrhoids, and especially from a bladder stone, lapsing into spells of torpor, which the empress, never fully aware of the seriousness of his condition and the extent of his physical suffering until his

46. Cowley quoted in Bierman, *Napoleon III and His Carnival Empire*, 189; Williams, *The Mortal Napoleon III*, 66–68; Mérimée on the empress in Dansette, *Les Amours de Napoléon III*, 235. Mérimée, with characteristic wit, is supposed to have said of Marie-Anne Walewska: "I do not know if it is true, as she claims, that her family originates with Machiavelli; what is certain is that *she* is descended from him." Maurois, *Miss Howard and the Emperor*, 130.

death, attributed to his sexual excesses. Margot, no doubt, brought him welcome distraction and stimulation. He bought her a house in Passy and took her on trips. The empress was outraged that he had sunk so low. In an extraordinary show of initiative sometime in 1864, she dragged Amédée Mocquard, the brother of the emperor's former private secretary, who, ironically, had probably introduced him to Marguerite, to confront her at her home. To the astonishment of the witness to the scene, after some initial sallies between the two rivals, which sent Mocquard away in embarrassment, he returned to find them chatting amiably. Eugénie embraced her new friend and, so it seems, tolerated the affair. It is not certain whether Margot joined the emperor on his month-long trip to Algeria in May 1865. As Bierman notes: "Eugénie can hardly have been unaware of the gossip surrounding her husband's overseas trip, but she apparently made no attempt to discourage the journey. Indeed, it was said that she was looking forward to the exercise of power as regent in his absence."[47]

The emperor's so-called "last love," Countess Louise de Mercy-Argenteau, whom we have had frequent occasion to quote, was of a very different social order. She was a tall, statuesque blond woman, the daughter of Prince Alphonse de Caraman-Chimay, thus born Countess de Caraman-Chimay, of Franco-Austrian-Belgian aristocracy. She was widely traveled and was an accomplished miniaturist and musician, with a particular talent for playing Chopin and Liszt. She married Count de Mercy-Argenteau, of equally worthy stock, in 1860. She was therefore part of the older nobility which was legitimist and stayed aloof from the upstart imperial court. But after the scandal of the suicide of her admirer, Count de Stackelberg, she accepted an invitation to take part in a charity bazaar on 18 November 1866 in the Élysée Gardens, where she impressed the em-

47. Dansette, *Les Amours de Napoléon III*, 244; Bierman, *Napoleon III and His Carnival Empire*, 244. It is important to note that Marguerite gave birth to a boy on 24 February 1864 and claimed at first that the emperor was the father. The emperor refused to accept the paternity, though he did make generous provision for the child: a château and an estate near to Compiègne. Marguerite subsequently sent letters at the prompting of the empress to Adrien Devienne, the president of the Cour de Cassation, and to the emperor, stating that the child was not his. On the visit of the empress to Marguerite Bellanger's house noted below, see Le Petit Homme Rouge, *The Court of the Tuileries*, 202–206. There are more details in Dansette, *Napoléon III et les femmes*, 257–90. On the whole affair and, in particular, on the emperor's donation to the child, Dansette writes: "As for me, I admit, I no longer understand anything about it and I suspect that in this vaudeville there are some hidden motives that I just do not understand." Dansette, *Les Amours de Napoléon III*, 286.

peror, and moved henceforth into court circles. As she narrates, with some immodesty, in her "reminiscences," she stole the show in the *tableaux vivants* at Compiègne during the Exhibition, in the presence of King William of Prussia and Count Bismarck, and bowled over the emperor in a scene that she describes as follows:

> "Comtesse, Comtesse, why was such a jewel hidden for so long from us?"
>
> I could see that he was deeply moved. His eyes were shining with an unusual fire. I answered, at once trembling and smiling:
>
> "A jewel, Sire? If there is one, it is at Your Majesty's service."
>
> We talked for a few minutes longer, and when he left me the Emperor kissed my hand before all the Court.
>
> From that moment I was the recognized *amie de l'Empereur* and treated as such—that is to say, courted, petted, fawned upon by everybody.
>
> I tasted all the pleasures of worldly power and glory, and sweet pleasures they were.[48]

Despite the suggestiveness of this scene, she claims that she was never his mistress, though they did meet secretly and regularly, as Persigny contrived in 1869 to sell her husband his house adjoining the Élysée Palace, hoping to use her to influence the emperor's policies. There was conveniently a secret passage between the buildings and an electric warning bell was rigged up to avoid surprise interruptions. They spent many hours together, wrapped in conversation. She showed remarkable devotion and loyalty towards him and his fading star, visiting him even in Wilhelmshöhe when he was a prisoner of the Germans after Sedan. It was a high note on which to end his sentimental adventures.

These fairly well documented liaisons are both interesting and significant not as the most-evident cases of the emperor's consistent marital inconstancy but by virtue of their variety, appealing as they seemingly did to the differing needs that we have defined of a man bound within the constraints of a marriage that was not, for many reasons, unsatisfactory but was decidedly unsatisfying. There is a certain desperation in his willingness to engage upon such semi-public affairs, to run the gauntlet of Eugénie's opprobrium and of the gossip of the court. But there was clearly in him

---

48. Mercy-Argenteau, *The Last Love of an Emperor*, 52.

also an irresistible impulsion to mediate between the demands of his office
and the opportunities that it provided for illicit gratifications, to engage in
a kind of institutionalized adultery, or, more precisely, an adulteration, a
mixture of defiance and compliance that was contained within the strictures of the permissiveness of the court. Virginia provided the combined
excitement of love, politics, adventure, risk, exoticism. Ridley notes his
penchant for foreign women: Swiss misses, Fraulein and Frauen, English
girls and ladies, the vagabond Jewish Rachel, the Austrian-Belgian Louise,
and, of course, the Spanish-Scottish-Belgian Eugenia de Montijo.[49] Marie-
Anne, though not lacking in exotic appeal, provided, by contrast, a means
of keeping his wanderings within the family or the clan, by such an extra-
marital but intradynastic arrangement, an errance that did not stray far,
satisfying a domestic need that Eugénie could not satisfy, with or without
the consent of the offended parties, as if the mistress were the extension of
the wife. Mme. de Persigny, who was born Églé Napoléone Albine Ney,
hence with appropriate background qualifications, and who was also
linked with the emperor—probably, according to Fleischmann, at the time
when her husband became a duke, in September 1863—may have fulfilled
a similar role, though her own entanglements were as notorious as the emperor's.[50] With Margot, his most eccentric liaison, there was also, no
doubt, a certain exotic appeal, a welcome change from all those contessas
—at the time, for such as Louis Napoléon, the popular classes were still an
object of fascination. Hence, she may well have represented for him the
People of France with whom he had, as has been noted, an abstract sense
of identification, along with a sentimental attachment, but of whom he
had very little direct experience. She did, however, provide him, above all,
with unspecified physical diversions, along with the dubious paternalistic
pleasure of giving instruction that he had previously enjoyed with "la Belle

49. Ridley, *Napoleon III and Eugénie,* 493.
50. See Fleischmann, *Napoléon III et les femmes,* 303–12. Such was the intricacy of court
connections that Countess de La Bédoyère, German by birth, whose husband had reputedly
owed his position as a senator to her relations with the emperor—prompting the ditty: *"Ah!
Monsieur le Sénateur / Je suis votre humble serviteur"*—would marry the prince of Moskowa,
Napoléon-Henri-Edgar Ney, and thereby join Mme. de Persigny's family. The senator's
father, Count de La Bédoyère, had been a friend of Hortense and, having been arrested
along with Marshal Ney in 1815, had been executed on the orders of Louis XVIII. See
Fleischmann, *Napoléon III et les femmes,* 303–12, 314–15, and Ridley, *Napoleon III and Eugénie,* 44–45.

Sabotière." As for Louise, she brought the gratification of refined company, of social prestige, for which he always craved but which he could
through her only furtively enjoy. By then, though, as his Empire was col-
lapsing around him, almost all his pleasures were furtive.

DON JUAN?

There were, of course, many other women with whom Napoleon III became involved during the heady days of the *fête impériale,* and the specialist writers on the topic, such as Fleischmann and Dansette, have provided
names, and usually little more.[51] But for our purposes, their identities,
along with those of the nameless others, however many there were, their
looks, their circumstances, the occasions when they did or did not sleep
with the emperor, all lost in the limbo of history, are less important than
the combined effect, the seriality of the affairs and amorous adventures in
which they took part, that bring us out of the uncertainties of history and
back into legend and myth, once again in the mode of excess and extravagance. It was Count Félix Bacciochi, a distant cousin, Napoleon III's social secretary—more commonly known as the provider of his "minor
pleasures" or supervisor of *"le service des femmes"*—whose job it was usually to arrange the trysts, and many a beautiful woman, it was reported,
would ingratiate herself with him for the privilege of enjoying the emper-
or's favor. At other times, there were games amongst the ladies of the
court with the emperor as the prize. Standard representations describe
how his dull gaze would light up, as if in some ocular erection above the
phallic moustache, at the sight of a beautiful woman, in the theater, at a
ball or reception, as in Zola's evocation of the success of the wayward heroine of *La Curée* (*The Kill*) in attracting the sovereign's lustful gaze when
he passes along the line of guests, in the company of an elderly general, at
a ball in the Tuileries:

51. See Dansette, *Les Amours de Napoléon III,* Chapter 29, and Fleischmann, *Napoléon
III et les femmes,* Chapter 5, who list notably la Barruchi; Clara Blum; Mme. de Brimont;
Mme. Korsakoff; Mme. Drouyn de Lhuys, another minister's wife; the singer Caroline Ha-
maekers; Mlle. de M.; Mme. de Malaret; Mlle. Sniell, supposedly English; Mary Craven, another Englishwoman, "large and supple"; an American, "who comes from nobody knows
where"; Mme. Gréville; a certain Mme. de ***; Mme. Kalergi, who was supposedly Gautier's
inspiration for his famous poem "Symphonie en blanc majeur"; Mme. de Cadore; and so on.

They looked at the bowing ladies, and their glances, cast to right and left, glided into the bodices. The general leant on one side, spoke a word to his master, and pressed his arm with the air of a jolly companion. And the Emperor, nerveless and nebulous, duller even than usual, came nearer and nearer with his dragging step.

They were in the middle of the room when Renée felt their glances fixed upon her. . . . The Emperor, half-raising his eyelids, had a red light in the grey hesitation of his bleared eyes. Renée, losing countenance, lowered her head, bowed, saw nothing more save the pattern of the carpet. But she followed their shadows, and understood that they were pausing for a few seconds before her. And she thought she heard the Emperor, that ambiguous dreamer, murmur as he gazed at her, immersed in her muslin skirt striped with velvet:

"Look, general, there's a flower worth picking, a mystic carnation, variegated white and black!"

And the general replied, in a more brutal voice:

"Sire, that carnation would look devilish well in our buttonholes."

As Vizetelly remarks, recalling similar scenes at Compiègne: "The right hand was raised in the familiar fashion to twirl the pointed moustache, the eyes glanced almost stealthily to right and left, momentarily glittering as every now and then they espied some vision of particularly attractive loveliness. Again and again the simile which that spectacle suggested to the mind was that of a Sultan passing his odalisques in review."[52]

The actual intimate encounter, according to existing accounts, was brief and to the point. The Goncourt brothers record in their *Journal*, on the basis of a doctor's testimony, that the chosen woman was brought to the Tuileries in a carriage, undressed, and was led naked by the chamberlain, Bacciochi, into a room where the emperor awaited, with the instruction: "You may kiss His Majesty anywhere, except on the face." Paulette de Lérignan gives a more vivid account of the routine, based on her own experience two years previously, to the marquise de Taisey-Chatenay, who has just found favor with the emperor—neither lady appears in the lists referred to above. She narrates her wait for the emperor's visit in a luxurious

52. Emile Zola, *The Kill*, trans. A. Teixeira de Mattos (London: Granada, 1985), 122–23; Le Petit Homme Rouge, *The Court of the Tuileries,* 208.

bedroom, describes his appearance in the light from the corridor, as he opens the door and enters the room at precisely one-thirty in the morning, not in his ceremonial costume, but almost unrecognizable in a mauve silk outfit. Then the imperial Don Juan stumbles into a chair in the dark, then there follows "a brief period of physical exertion, during which he breathes heavily and the wax on the ends of his mustaches melts, causing them to droop, and finally a hasty withdrawal," from the room; as she wryly remarks, the clock struck two and "it had only taken a half hour to make me an empress." As Camus aptly remarks of the "real" Don Juan: "to anyone who seeks quantity in his joys, the only thing that matters is efficacy." Napoléon III took his women, so it seems, rather as he took his food, quickly, routinely, and without fuss—much to the discomfort of his guests who were obliged to eat at the same pace—with the rapid efficiency of the chain-smoker that he was. "A jaded being," in Guillemin's no less expeditious estimation, "already quite badly jaded, at the age of forty-five. Too many sexual diversions. Always several mistresses at a time and the taste, the passion, for whores. A harem man."[53]

Amongst the many faces of the "Hamlet of History," the "Sphinx of the Tuileries," was Louis-Napoléon, then, also a new "Machiavelli of Love," as the fabled lover has been called, or an inveterate, *natural* Don Juan, as the emperor has sometimes been described?[54] The apparently whimsical notion that he was a kind of late incarnation of Tirso de Molina's baroque hero of *El Burlador de Sevilla y convidado de piedra (The Trickster of Seville and the Stone Guest)*, the dissolute seducer with his ever changing roles and masks, constantly multiplying himself, usurping the place of the husband, fiancé, or lover, to serve his ends, is not entirely fanciful, given the emperor's record of "conquests." Like the mythical figure, he seems to have been driven by an insatiable sexual appetite, which, in the terms of the literary gloss, compelled him beyond the bounds of good and evil—or at least of propriety—such that he embodies an irresistible natural

53. Entry of 15 March 1862, Edmond and Jules de Goncourt, *Journal: Mémoires de la vie littéraire,* ed. Robert Ricatte (Paris: Laffont, 1989), 1:787. For accounts of the emperor's bedroom antics, see Pierre Labracherie, *Napoléon III et son temps* (Geneva: René Julliard, [1967], 59–61, Bierman, *Napoleon III and His Carnival Empire,* 241, Burchell, *Imperial Masquerade,* 71–72; Camus quotation from *The Myth of Sisyphus,* trans. Justin O'Brien (London: 1955), 61; Guillemin, "Louis Napoléon Bonaparte," 310.

54. For example, Maurois dubs him "this xenophile Don Juan." Maurois, *Miss Howard and the Emperor,* 128.

force, an affirmation of pure desire, unchained eroticism, fulfilling the Promethean urge of the third libidinous order, *sentiendi* (sensual pleasure), to go consistently with his impulsions in the other orders of desire: *imperandi* (power) and *sciendi* (knowledge).[55] For the silent and stealthy ravisher the single act must be endlessly repeated; identities, personalities, particularities, circumstances, are irrelevant, as love is reduced to pure pleasure, as the don is reduced to the *juan* (or *juanito*), a popular name for the penis. Not surprisingly, the myth has given rise to psychoanalytical interpretations, in oedipal terms, as an expression of defiance of the patriarchal order, of the Lacanian "name of the father," which imposes through the laws of marriage and sexual restraint an order of culture that, heroically, excessively, and, in the end, tragically, the figure of Don Juan challenges to the limit. The role of the father, so the interpretation goes, is usurped in an infinite possession of the phantasmal mother. For Eugénie, then—if we are to apply this view—her true competitors in love were not fundamentally her husband's numerous women. Whilst she took on the censorious role, the true rival, as she may have consciously or unconsciously suspected, was Hortense. If King Louis, or whoever it might have been, hardly qualified as the threatening "ideal" father, there was, of course, the ever intimidating ghost of the "mimetic" father, to emulate, to defy, generating the anguishing anxiety of influence or mighty precedent that would always hang over his nephew's life, the statue on the top of the Vendôme Column with its awful symbolic presence, *père* become *pierre*. Thus the compulsive conquests of the feminine territory are both in imitation and in defiance of the fearsome model. But in subverting the order of the father, far from subjugating women, as the actions of the mythical figure have been construed, Don Juan is a liberating force, creating temporarily—for only the moment counts—a sexual utopia *à deux*, freeing the woman from the shackles of her social condition and her patriarchal subservience within the economic, marital system. Such *hubris*, of course, necessarily invokes the retribution of the law in the shape of the Commodore.

In a less exegetical mode, we can point to certain fundamental limitations to the analogy between the emperor and the archetypal libertine. To begin with, our own nocturnal seducer was, as we have seen, more often

55. For an excellent interpretation of the myth, see Camille Dumoulié, *Don Juan, ou, l'héroïsme du désir* (Paris: Presses Universitaires de France, 1993).

the pursued than the pursuer. If he freely violated the rules of marriage, it was frequently with the husband's consent. Furthermore, the imperial deceiver was an uncharacteristically scrupulous Don Juan, who always paid his debts and rewarded with jewels and estates those that he may have seemed to have abused. But there are even more fundamental factors to give us pause. Dansette, for instance, hints vaguely that, as the years of the Empire wore on, the emperor was less of a Casanova than is usually thought. Towards 1865, with his health seriously deteriorating, there is, he suggests, what he calls a "a rapid decline in his possibilities." The emperor has become like one of those old seducers, a long way past their best, who cannot see a woman without desiring her, but "by virtue of being artificially provoked, their excitement is prolonged even when it becomes difficult for them to satisfy it"; and for whom, more sinisterly, he suggests, "nature is taking its slow revenge." In a similar vein, but far more clinically, Williams notes disturbing features in the emperor's physical condition, suggesting that what was diagnosed in May 1856 by Dr. Robert Ferguson, brought in from London for consultation, as "nervous exhaustion" would be called in modern times neurasthenia, a neurosis brought about by emotional conflict and causing fatigue, depression, and "a debilitating impact upon sexual appetite and performance." He adds: "The subject will have great difficulty in mobilizing his energies, and he will often be impotent. Men under fifty as Napoleon III was at the time, rarely suffer from impotence for physical reasons; one of the chief psychological reasons is a frigid wife with whom sexual relations are unsatisfactory." Thus, contrary to his reputation and contrary to the prevalent view of his time, which attributed exhaustion and impotence to an excess of sexual activity, the decline in his sexual performance and satisfaction, which the emperor did, in fact, report to Dr. Ferguson, can be attributed to sexual inactivity. Indeed, to develop the point, we now know that, in pre-Viagra days especially, the condition of "erectile dysfunction" was considerably more commonplace than was ever admitted or believed, whether from psychological or physiological causes, or usually a combination of both, and that the incidence of impotence is particularly high in men with medical problems of the kind that plagued the emperor. Rather than fixing the blame on the stress of his political responsibilities or on Eugénie's castratory frigidity— after all the emperor did not lack opportunities for alternative arrangements—we should take into account the generally debilitating effects of the combination of ailments that afflicted him, namely, bladder calculus, kidney disease, arthritis, gout, hemorrhoids, possibly diabetes, and the fact that certain of these conditions are known to cause impotence. What is more, the emperor's sedentary way of life, the evidence of his increasing obesity and premature aging—contrary to the virile official portraits—the heavy smoking were doubtless contributory factors as well as symptoms. Thus it is not unreasonable to suggest that, in all probability, from the time of the conception of the prince imperial (1855) and the Ferguson report (1856), the emperor was progressively afflicted with impotence. By the middle 1860s, we can imagine, with his Empire at the height of its powers, his own, in this regard, had decidedly waned.[56]

Was the revelation of this fact in Margot's house in Passy in 1864 the reason for the extraordinary change of attitude and subsequent tolerance by the empress, safe in the knowledge that her son's position was assured and that the regime was secure? Was the emperor's supposedly platonic relationship with Louise less a matter of virtue than of necessity? In this area, then, as in many others, the nephew failed to live up to the image of his uncle, with his legendary *machismo*. Napoléon le Petit did not, as it were, measure up to Napoléon le Grand. Morny's comment on the gap between his half-brother's compulsive preoccupations and their limited realization takes on a new significance. "The difficulty with the Emperor," he once remarked, "is to remove a fixed idea from his mind and to give him firmness of will."[57] Was the Lothario of the Tuileries, then, like so much in his reign, an illusion, a kind of fictional tumescence? Thus did the lusty prince become a parodic Don Juan, a false *burlador*, an *hombre sin nombre* in name and reputation alone, whose retribution came, not in the dramatic form of the stone Commodore condemning him to eternal damnation, but, as an infinitely more prosaic sarcophagus, as a stone in the bladder.

PLAISIRS D'AMOUR

Enchantingly, in the midst of the disasters of the present, romance returned to the ex-emperor's life when his reign was over. As Flaubert understood best of all, if there is a romance of longing, of promise, and of

56. Dansette, *Les Amours de Napoléon III,* 261–62. On the emperor's medical condition, see Williams, *The Mortal Napoleon III,* Chapter 6 ("The Case Revisited") and, in particular, 190–91.

57. Quoted in Maurois, *Miss Howard and the Emperor,* 79.

aspiration directed to the future, there is a romance of resignation and regret, for romance cannot survive in the reality of the present, only in the
imagination and in texts. Typically, two women were involved. Louise de
Mercy-Argenteau describes in moving terms the scene of her visit to the
captive emperor at Wilhelmshöhe after the defeat of Sedan. As she played
to him on an old spinet the exquisite minuet of Boccherini and "Plaisirs
d'amour" by Padre Martini, the defeated leader closed his eyes and listened entranced by "the sweetness of the tunes." Then, she recounts, "I
came nearer and knelt down beside the couch. And as I was slightly leaning my head on his shoulder he put his arm with infinite gentleness around
my neck. Thus we remained, without uttering a single word, for a long
time."[58] The next morning as she left, Thélin, the emperor's faithful servant, gave her pearls that Hortense had worn.

Thus, after Sedan, there were to be no more adventures. The dynastic
house of cards had collapsed. The beast inside was stilled. But as if in just
compensation, the family affections grew. After his release by the Prussians, the emperor without an Empire was a fugitive again, back in England. Eugénie was restless, railed against their fate, was impatient with
her husband's patience. But redeemed in her eyes by his suffering and by
his courage in defeat, liberated from the pretense, the ostentation, the extravagances, and the temptations of the imperial court, her husband was
free to discover, despite the physical pain of his condition, a peace of mind
and a domestic contentment in his new exile that he had never known before. The emperor and the empress had become, as they had always been
to some degree in the intimacy of their home, even in the heady days of
the Empire, a bourgeois couple. On the emperor's death, in his yellow
leather wallet were found a letter from Hortense, a letter from Eugénie, a
lock of the prince imperial's hair, "testimonials to the three most profound
feelings that he had experienced: his filial love, his conjugal love, his paternal love."[59]

58. Mercy-Argenteau, *The Last Love of an Emperor*, 257–58.
59. On the bourgeois couple, see Bac, *Intimités du Second Empire*, 24; on the emperor's
possessions, Dansette, *Les Amours de Napoléon III*, 280.

chapter 10

Parody, Caricature, Satire

PARODY AND PARADES

Like all parodies themselves, the use of the term in a historical context should, no doubt, in deference to the literary purists, be accompanied by inverted commas, for the term is normally applied in discussions of inter-textuality to imitations of literary works or of comparable artistic creations with a derisive or, more rarely, a deferential aim. However, the notion of parody has been applied with a residual metaphorical sense and a polemical intent to broader, nondiscursive cultural manifestations which imitate previous models, even to those manifold occasions when history is perceived to have basely repeated itself or, as R. Debray nicely puts it, when "Clio stutters."[1] In any case, not to put too fine a point on the issue, imitations of past epochs are not likely to be of their history but of their histories, events, customs, and beliefs, mediated through semiotic systems. Marx, as we have seen, like Nietzsche and Tocqueville, did not hesitate to employ

1. Quoted by M. Vernet, in Groupar, eds. *Le Singe à la porte: Vers une théorie de la parodie* (New York–Berne–Frankfurt am Main: Peter Lang, 1984), ix.

the concept to characterize the tendency of even revolutionary movements in the nineteenth century to reinvest the forms of the past, a tendency which Flaubert "parodied" absurdly in Pellerin's painting in *L'Éducation sentimentale* (*A Sentimental Education*) at the time of the February Revolution of 1848, showing "the Republic, or Progress, or Civilization, in the shape of Jesus Christ driving a train through a virgin forest."[2] As for the requirement of parodic intention, basic reception theory now allows us to assume that, however serious the purpose of an imitative artist or performer might be, in the new context, or according to the different "horizons of expectation" of the receiver, parodic effects may be appropriately perceived. Thus, for all the earnest endeavor that during the Second Empire went into designing the ostentatious imitations of costumes and customs of prestigious previous ages, in the eyes of the opponents of the regime such mimicry became by its very nature the object of ridicule.

In one of the emperor's "aphorisms" recorded for posterity by Louise de Mercy-Argenteau, he supposedly declared: "A king ought to have enough originality never to need to imitate a great reign. In the previously unpublished style of his government lies the genius of a king."[3] Assuming that the lady got it right, there was, here again, another yawning gap between what he preached and what he practiced. We have already noted, as have many other commentators, the contrast between the progressive nature of many of the policies of the Second Empire and the derivative nature of much of its ceremonial, harking back to the First Empire in particular for the purpose of legitimation and popular appeal. What is at issue here is the way in which the anachronistic and thereby parodic imitation of figures and styles of the royal and imperial courts of bygone days in dress, ceremony, and architecture supplied the material for caricature and satire. The process may be summed up schematically in the following way: Historical reality or referent of the past → prestigious image of heroic figure and exploits of the past → ostentatiously parodic imitation in the present for prestige and approbation → debunking by opposition in the present in caricature and satire.

We have already reviewed enough examples of the attempts of Napoleon III to parade as, and thereby be perceived to parody, Napoleon I. A less obvious and, in many ways, more interesting case, which illustrates the

2. Flaubert, *A Sentimental Education*, 325.
3. Mercy-Argenteau, *The Last Love of an Emperor*, 122.

process, is that of the affectations of the empress. Eugénie had an abiding nostalgia for the late eighteenth century and its values, with an obsessive sense of identification with Marie-Antoinette. She collected memorabilia, portraits, had her apartments in the Tuileries decorated with furniture and articles that had belonged to the wife of Louis XVI, stayed in the suite of the executed queen at Saint-Cloud, where she set up a dairy in imitation of the queen. She also had a model built of the Petit Trianon in the park. In her bedroom was a single picture, of Marie-Antoinette. She insisted on visiting the cell in which the queen had been imprisoned and, in 1867, she organized an exhibition at the Trianon dedicated to Marie-Antoinette. The best way to obtain her favor was to pander to this obsession. Viel-Castel sent her a copy of his book on Marie-Antoinette and received an invitation to dinner. More significantly, the image of herself that she con-structed in the official art of the time was frequently a reworking of images of her model. A Winterhalter portrait of her in eighteenth-century dress in 1854 (see figure 15) shows the extent of her identification and the ends to which she would go to adopt, anachronistically, the modes and postures of the woman that she so admired. In another Winterhalter composition, done after the birth of her son, she is portrayed in the manner of Vigée-Lebrun's 1787 portrait of the queen with her children. In a different con-text, she attended a masked ball in 1866 in a costume based on another Vigée-Lebrun composition. Just as the emperor imposed a Napoleonic style with his own uniforms and military postures so that, in a sense, the Napoleonic image was multiplied throughout the realm not only in the visual representations that we have noted but also in the proliferation of an army of clones, Eugénie used her style of dress to an equivalent effect, inspiring by imitations of an imitation a vogue that became *de rigueur* in the court and beyond and that had powerful monarchical connotations, notably the crinoline, which derived from the pannier of eighteenth-century high fashion. As Therese Dolan notes on what the empress called her "political wardrobe": "By manipulating the signs of fashion, she (mis)construed her own image as a female monarch. Eugénie's adaptation of a *style Marie-Antoinette* in dress and decor reflected her effort to link her imperial reign with the court of Louis XVI; she wished to connect her personal image with what she perceived to be the political astuteness and personal courage of the beheaded queen."[4]

4. Therese Dolan, "The Empress's New Clothes: Fashion and Politics in Second Empire France," *Women's Art Journal* 15 (1994): 26.

Such manners were clearly intended as an elaborate political statement. The Second Empire was a marriage of the Napoleonic style, with its associations with the glorious imperial dynasty—and, at least it was argued, with the Revolution—and of the distinction of the ancien regime. It was thus a synthesis of the most resplendent periods in recent French history, but a history that was largely a mythical construct. Yet, more significantly, the historical associations that the empress propagated were not particularly propitious, as the lampooning revealed. The fashion for the crinoline, for example, by the very nature of its hypertrophied form inevitably became a natural object of mockery (we shall return later to explore its full-blown significance). More particularly, Eugénie's fixation with Marie-Antoinette was doubtless rooted in a somewhat superstitious and morbid fascination with her famously humiliating and violent end, which the emperor's wife may have feared to have to repeat. Even this gave rise to humor typical of the time, as the fad for eighteenth-century items of dress set in, including the Marie-Antoinette hat, which prompted a wag from *Punch* to remark: "We presume this is a bonnet to be worn when the lady has entirely lost her head."[5] Marie-Antoinette was also known to have been most unpopular with the people, reviled for her extravagances, and disdained for her foreignness, leading to the obvious charge that "l'Espagnole" was taking on the role of "l'Autrichienne." This was particularly the case when it became evident at the time of the Italian crisis of 1862—she vigorously defended the interests of the pope against the policy of her husband—that Eugénie was having an increasing say in the affairs of state, for Marie-Antoinette was renowned for the political influence that she exercised over her ineffective husband. Thus Viel-Castel reports, without naming the party concerned, threatening murmurings in the court in 1862: "*One* is furious against the Empress, for *one* can only see her political aims in the *matter. One* said to me this morning: 'Marie-Antoinette succumbed beneath the unpopularity of her nickname the *Austrian woman!* . . . the *Spanish woman* had better watch out!' "[6] The same year, in a lighter vein but making the same point, *La Reine Crinoline,* a musical play, was put on, satirizing crinoline power, in which, on an imaginary island, the women are in charge of war, politics, and government whilst the men are occupied with household chores until two shipwrecked art students per-

5. Quoted in Dolan, "The Empress's New Clothes."
6. Viel-Castel, *Mémoires,* 16 October 1862.

suade the men to revert to their proper ways. The same year too, a cartoon in *Punch* showed Napoleon III, in a submissive pose, and Eugénie, *sans crinoline* however, mock-heroically in the guise of Hercules and Omphale.[7]

Both in intention and effect, Eugénie's cult of Marie-Antoinette and her aura may well have acted to countervail the dynastic purposes of such display. Indeed, it is significant that she did not parade in the style of Joséphine or even of the more historically relevant "Austrian woman," Napoleon's second wife, Marie-Louise. It is as if, even as she was seemingly fulfilling the role ascribed to her, she were asserting her independence from the Bonapartist clan and affirming her legitimist sympathies and convictions. Yet the mere differentiation is also important, for the *"grand style"* of the Second Empire was in fact a mixture of "grand styles" of the past, each one derivative of others, and for which, to write again in the manner of Barthes, an *effect* of "grand stylishness" was more portentous than the details. Thus, as well as the Napoleonic displays and celebrations, there were modes of dress and address, elaborate rules of decorum and etiquette, which harked back to earlier ages. As Legge notes, for example, the emperor wore a hunting costume at Fontainebleau which was a remake of a Louis V costume, with a green Napoleonic tunic and a Regency waistcoat. English followers of the hunt, made most welcome by the imperial couple on such occasions, "thought the costume picturesque, but theatrical."[8] The court and dinner guests at the Tuileries, the ancient palace of Catherine de Médicis, modified and used by the kings of France through the ages down to Louis-Philippe, assembled in the "Salon d'Apollon," surrounded by mythological paintings beneath the Chariot of the Sun on the gilt ceiling, crossed the *"salon"* of the First Consul, in which a portrait of General Buonaparte dominated the scene, before entering the *"salon"* of Louis XIV for their (*faste*) food, graced by a monumental bust of the Sun King on the mantelpiece and a statue of Napoleon I in a toga. Dinner was served to the accompaniment of a military band. The protocol was elaborately orchestrated and strictly enforced. Thanks to the revenues from the Civil List of some twenty-five million francs a year, of which six

---

7. See Dolan, "The Empress's New Clothes," 25–26. The play was by Hippolyte Cogniard and Ernest Blum: *La Reine Crinoline, ou le Royaume des femmes; pièce fantastique en cinq actes et six tableaux,* music by M. A.-D. Duvivier (Paris, 1863).

8. Legge, *The Comedy and Tragedy of the Second Empire,* 114–15.

million were allocated for the expenses of the imperial household and twelve million for the improvements and decoration of the imperial palaces, libraries, museums, estates, and forests, the court could move in grand style in the hallowed royal tradition from one splendid monument of the royal past to another, according to the season: to the Renaissance Palace of François I and Henri IV at Fontainebleau, to Charles V's château, reconstructed under Louis XV, at Compiègne, to Marie-Antoinette's royal residence at Saint-Cloud. There was also the Villa Eugénie at Biarritz, but it was built by the emperor himself. The empress was apparently at her happiest there even though Marie-Antoinette had never set foot in the place.

Palaces aside, if there was a familiar uniformity to the less grandiose and more recent buildings along the new boulevards, there was a decided lack of a dominant style in the grander creations of the regime. Richardson notes that the architecture of the new buildings "lacked decision. It seemed to live on eclecticism or on compromise. People wanted to act grandly in accordance with the Emperor's ideas. In general they acted pompously." Churches were in a pseudo-English Gothic style (Sainte-Clotilde), a pseudo-Roman Byzantine style (Saint-Augustin), a pseudo-Renaissance style (La Trinité). What they and the *"hôtels privés"* had in common was not only a taste for pomp and grandeur, but an impulse for replication. Delacroix complained in 1860 that architecture had fallen into a state of degradation, wanting to do something new but only able to copy.[9] The combination of nostalgia for the architectural splendors of the past and of a thrusting industrialized need to construct anew, together with a fondness for superficial grandeur, whatever the style, and the urge to create novelty out of the antiquated, along with the ostentatious "bricolage" that brought it about during the Second Empire, were a "concrete" testimony to both the values and the uncertainties of the age and, in many ways, anticipated modernist trends. Significantly, the two most famous architects of the period were Viollet-le-Duc, famed for his studied archaeological restorations of buildings of the past, and Charles Garnier, whose flamboyant creation, the Opera, when it was finally completed during the Third Republic, would exhibit the eclecticism and taste for opulence of the Imperial Age.

One solution to this uncertain demand for a sanctioned and showy

9. Richardson, *La Vie parisienne*, 222, 225.

originality was to favor a form of extravagant exoticism. In or near to the Champs-Élysées there sprung up the Moorish house of de Lesseps, the Roman Palace of Émile de Girardin, the Gothic castle of the Count de Quinsonas, the pink *hôtel* of the duke of Brunswick, and the fabulous Renaissance *hôtel* of the courtesan Mme. de Païva. But the most striking example of this trend was the brainchild of Plon-Plon, who allowed himself, thanks to his allowance, to combine residence in established stately homes with the creation of a fantasy abode. Not content with dwelling in the Palais-Royal, built for Richelieu and a royal residence of Louis XIV, and at his country quarters, the château de Meudon, just outside Paris, the Renaissance abode of the duchess d'Étampes, whose gardens had later been designed by the royal architect Le Nôtre, he set about having built a reconstructed Roman villa, which became one of the sensations of the Second Empire. The Villa Diomède, or Palais Pompéien, was complete with *atrium* (reception area), *triclinium* (dining room), *peristylium* (inner courtyard), *exedra* (sitting area), *cubiculum* (bedroom), along with some anachronistic features such as a smoking room, windows, and fireplaces. There were clearly limits, even for Plon-Plon, to the Bonapartist mania for imitating authentic noble edifices. There were limits also to his enthusiasm, for he was to sell the house in 1865 to raise money to entertain his new mistress, the English courtesan Cora Pearl, who was a demanding woman. He would, however, be able to entertain her later in a different style in his room at the 1867 Universal Exposition building, which he had decorated like a Turkish drawing room. The Pompeian Palace was opened in March 1858 with a Classical performance of writers and actors from the Comédie-Française. Such was the spirit of emulation, of doing as Pompeii did, the program claimed to represent the reopening of the theater there "which had been closed for repairs for 1800 years."[10] But far from being a serious commitment on the part of the cultivated Prince Napoleon to Classical art, it was but a step away from the kitsch of Caesar's Palace.

Séguin sees a positive value in all this Second Empire display. The court, he argues, was the showcase of France, reflecting the splendor, the power, and the glory of the country. It was a political necessity. "It is a matter of astonishing and impressing, at home and abroad. The concern is to convey two things: the foreigner has to accept as self-evident the dominant role that falls to France; the French who count, the creative, the

10. See *ibid.*, 34, 225; Holt, *Plon-Plon*, 118–19, 217.

imaginative, the inventive ones amongst them, have to be urged to rally round, identifying themselves with the national cause that they have to serve.["][11] All to the good of the glory of France, then! But it was all too much, as the caricaturists and satirists made clear, and all too easy for them to deflate with their contemptuous humor the pretensions of the emperor and his regime. The Second Empire sought to establish its legitimacy not only at the ballot box but by its displays of pomp. It sought to pass off the replica as the original, to create a new essence out of appearances, not, in anticipation of the postmodernist relativization of authoritative models, but to ground its own precarious authority in the prestigious icons of the past. The Second Empire was vulnerable to its critics because, to a considerable degree, it created a world of make-believe and depended for its prestige on a continuous process of replication. There was, just as there would be in future eras, and certainly in our (post)modern times, nothing original in this process, but the Second Empire took it to extremes. It veiled the harsh truths of its real historical initiatives (a coup d'état, industrial exploitation, capitalist speculation, diplomatic wars, colonialist conquests) beneath the fake drapes and the masks of its mimicry. Its detractors, Platonists for the occasion, denounced such appropriations as illusory simulacra and sought to expose the truth.

In general, the nineteenth century, from the fall of the Bourbon monarchy in 1830—the date of the founding of *La Caricature,* soon to be followed, in 1832, by *Le Charivari*—to the Dreyfus affair, was a golden age of caricature and satirical journalism. Despite the regime's attempts to repress and eliminate them, works of visual and verbal satire constitute an important chapter of the history of representations of the Second Empire. The two modes of "caricature" and "satire" are, for our own intents and purposes, virtually indissociable, the former being a visual variant of the latter, though, in practice, it can often be complimentary or merely illustrative, whereas satire is always disparaging. Both rely upon some degree of realistic representation, which is particularly evident in extensive satirical narratives or in caricature, as in Daumier's case, when its satirical incisiveness was blunted by such restraints as government controls. But the realism functions normally as an authenticating device, along with such authoritative discourses as science or history, on which satirists frequently ground their attacks and which serve to render the bias of satire more con-

11. Séguin, *Louis Napoléon le Grand,* 205.

vincing to the reader, since representation persuades far more effectively than argumentation. The humor, of course, in all its shades, fulfills a similar function, adding an affective impact to the criticism. As far as the themes of anti-Bonapartist criticism were concerned, just as Napoleon III drew upon a tradition of imperial pomp, the satirists, in order to deflate it, could draw upon a well-established tradition of caricature directed against Napoleon I, particularly in the foreign press.[12] The topics of satirical opposition to the Second Empire are thus predictable: odious comparisons with Napoleon I, the dubious legitimacy of his birth, the illegality of Louis Napoléon's seizure of power and the violent repression that followed, the extravagances of the court, the supposed depravity of the emperor, and even of the empress, the contrast between his slogans of peace and his warlike adventures, and dishonest financial speculation. The staple of satire is universal and two-fold: political, that is, military, governmental, diplomatic, financial; and moral, usually sexual, with variations and imbrications in the contingent details from age to age. The development of the emperor's career witnessed something of an evolution from the first to the second, from an initial emphasis on political denunciations of his rise to power towards scathing attacks on the moral decadence of his court, with constant shifts between these two zones. The usual procedures of caricature and satire naturally recur: reductiveness, exaggeration, emphasis on bodily functions and on sexual practices, associations with animals and animal behavior, juxtaposition of the pretensions, usually discursive, as in such Napoleonic slogans as "Society Is Saved" or "The Empire Means Peace," and the actions of the targets of the satire. To these various parameters of classification must be added the important factor of location, for the history of satire is linked to the history of press censorship, since much of it could only be published abroad. Its intensity and degree of explicitness depended on such circumstances. Finally, there are the variations due to the prestige, eminence, and talent of its practitioners, ranging from the mass of ephemera of the minor and often anonymous or pseudonymous cartoonists and lampoonists to the usually neglected minor works of major writers famous for more elevated creations, rising to the lofty heights of

12. See, for example, the fascinating and lavishly illustrated collections in John Ashton, *English Caricature and Satire on Napoleon I* (London: Chatto and Windus, 1884), with 115 illustrations, and in A. M. Broadley, *Napoleon in Caricature, 1795–1821* (London-New York: John Lane, 1911), which has sections on caricatures from several countries.

Hugo's *Châtiments*. The latter, it should be stated, were not necessarily more effective than the former.

INTERNAL DISSENT

Though the forces of order sought to keep in check all forms of criticism in the country, we cannot assume that there were not signs of protest even within the innermost circles of the regime. The emperor himself, who, contrary to his usual demeanor, was not without a sense of humor, did not though have the critical distance, the disposition, or the creative talent to indulge, at least publicly, in the ironic pleasures of self-censure, though he was reported to be much amused by the travesties of Offenbach's *La Belle Hélène*. His son, however, did show a penchant and even a certain talent for caricature. In his idle moments, the boy made sketches of soldiers and, on one occasion, when told by a tactful courtier that he took after both his father and his mother in appearance, drew his own caricature: "on one side, the dull look, twisting distractedly the end of an imaginary moustache; on the other, the smiling, animated face of his mother." But, presumably, there was no hint of mockery. Morny, however, who had a lively and caustic wit as well as literary ambitions with several comedies to his pseudonym (Saint-Rémy), did write a short satirical play for the court, *La Corde sensible, ou les dadas favoris,* in which he mocked his half-brother's current hobbyhorse, his meticulous preoccupation with the trivialities of Roman history, and, then, after singing her praises, the empress's propensity for cluttering up rooms, as well as his own taste for horse racing and vaudeville. It was all genteel fun. But there were limits as severe to the regime's tolerance of mockery of the emperor's attempts to write history as of his efforts to conduct it, as a provincial schoolteacher, Louis-Auguste Rogeard, discovered. He wrote for *La Rive Gauche,* a republican weekly, under the pseudonym of Labienus, a heavily ironic sketch of life in Rome in the thirty-eighth year of the reign of Augustus, a time of brutal repression of republicans, of censorship, and of the persecution of the historian Labienus, a man with "fantastic ideas and incredible manias, and especially an odd taste, strange and inexplicable: . . . he loved liberty!" Amongst his swingeing "strictures" to Gallio (Junius Gallion) about Augustus, who has just written his memoirs, he declares: "When a man is guilty enough to make himself king, and fool enough to make himself God, I think he cannot have all the qualities requisite for writing history."[13] Rogeard's version of this segment of Roman history, and, by clear implication, of the recent history of France, patently did not accord with the emperor's view of the earlier age, or of his own. The new Labienus was compelled to escape to Brussels to avoid a five-year prison sentence. Clearly any telling criticism or satire emanating from the inner circles had to appear either heavily disguised or not at all.

An intriguingly possible (though unlikely) example of the first tendency is provided by Prosper Mérimée's *Épisode de l'histoire de Russie: Les faux Démétrius,* which was published in December 1852, very soon after the establishment of the Empire. Now Mérimée, whose efforts as a matrimonial agent for Eugenia soon after are well known, was to become a valued friend of the emperor and empress, a member of their court, a senator (from 1853), and a supporter of the regime. Yet this work, it has been claimed, attests to a far more critical attitude to the Empire, at least at the time of its initiation. It is a historical chronicle, narrating how an impostor from Poland or Lithuania posed as the son of Ivan the Terrible and seized power. Scott E. Carpenter, who has recently studied the text, points out that there are striking analogies with the situation of the new pretender, then emperor of France. Dimitri played upon his supposed regal past, displaying noble emblems, ingratiating himself with the family of the former czar, spoke Russian with a Polish accent, and, abandoning the title of czar, declared himself emperor. The text, which, if Mérimée had the contemporary situation in mind at all, would be more a critical historical allegory than a work of satire, is remarkable for two reasons. Firstly, despite the similarities between the Russian impostor and the widespread view of Louis Napoléon himself as such a fraud, the seditious implications of the text seem to have gone unnoticed when the work appeared.[14] Secondly, as

13. Frerejean, *Napoléon IV,* 68; Rouart, *Morny,* 230–31; M. A. Rogeard, *The Strictures of Labienus: The Historical Critic in the Time of Augustus,* trans. Dr. W. E. Guthrie (Philadelphia: T. B. Pugh, 1865), 13, 12. This pamphlet was widely disseminated, with editions published in Paris, Brussels, London, New York, and Munich, in 1865. A definitive edition appeared in Brussels in 1866. A further edition was issued in Paris-Brussels in 1870.

14. Not surprisingly perhaps, depending on one's own reading of the work, there is no mention of possible links with the current political situation in the standard biography of Mérimée by A. W. Raitt, who interprets the text as a product of the French author's interest in Russian history. See his *Prosper Mérimée* (London: Eyre and Spottiswoode, 1970), 285–88. In all probability, since Mérimée had no particular reason to attack Louis Napoléon, the work is merely a historical narrative of a particularly turbulent period of Russian history

Carpenter points out, if indeed it can be interpreted as an oppositional text, we need to ask if it is even possible in this way "to write oppositionally *from the center?*" As we have seen, Louis Napoléon himself had been and would be not averse to presenting propaganda in the fairly subtle guise of historical writing. Indeed, there is a huge difference between the license for criticism possible in late 1852, by which time Louis Napoléon had a firm grip on the reins of power, and the same man's situation as it was lampooned in the blatant caricatures of the pretender in the French satirical press of 1848. Furthermore, we cannot assume that there were not divisions within the "center" and that there was unanimous support of the legitimacy of the emperor's right to his position even amongst his supporters, particularly at a time when there was no guarantee, indeed there were serious doubts, that the Empire would survive. Mérimée's narrative, like similar works, was no doubt less anomalous within the imperial corridors of power than it may seem to the modern reader. As in any other age, court circles, salons, and rival gatherings were a hotbed of criticism, gossip, and mockery about the figures of authority of the time. There were, however, limits. Typically, Alexandre Dumas, with his irrepressible irreverence and lack of social graces, went too far at a dinner engagement in Mathilde's house in 1853, wishing to entertain the company with some verses stemming from the republican exiles in Brussels. As Viel-Castel reports, he began with a vulgar jingle about Monsieur Troplong and his success in a *"concours,"* then trotted out a series of impious ditties about such dignitaries as the emperor, the empress, and the bishop of Paris, before he realized from the stony silence in the room that his bravura performance was not having the desired effect. But Viel-Castel cannot resist reproducing a stanza on the emperor:

> *Dans leurs fastes impériales*
> *L'oncle et le neveu sont égaux:*
> *L'oncle prenait des capitales,*
> *Le neveu prend nos capitaux.*

The anecdote serves to illustrate, as does perhaps Mérimée's text, in a remarkable way, that, in Carpenter's words, "the efficacy of acts of opposi-

---

which appealed to the Russophile Mérimée, as did similar periods in inspiring him to write other texts. Scott Carpenter takes up his interpretation of Mérimée's text again in " 'Les Faux Démétrius': Les ratés de l'histoire," in *Prosper Mérimée, écrivain, archéologue, historien,* ed. Antonia Fonyi (Geneva: Droz, 1999), 63–73.

tional speech are thus seen to rely heavily on circumstances," as they rely also, we might add, on the reader's interpretation.[15]

Our second case in point—satire that was not published—belongs to Count Horace de Viel-Castel, who was a poet, a novelist, a critic, and a historian, but who is far better known, as our frequent references to his major work have shown, as a memorialist, or more accurately as a diarist, of the reign of Napoleon III. Though he was in better odor in Mathilde's court than at the Tuileries, that is until her lover, Count de Nieuwerkerke, director general of the imperial museums and his superior, fired him from the staff of the Louvre in 1863, he remained an ardent Bonapartist and was very much a part of the establishment. But with his acid pen, his misanthropic spirit, and his taste for court gossip, "Fiel-castel" was no less critical of the emperor at times and of those around him at every opportunity. Historians writing on the Second Empire are frequently concerned about the reliability of his memoirs.[16] Yet Viel-Castel was in fact an avowed satirist, using an apparently objective, historically accurate mode in which to vent his spleen and rail against the vices and follies of his age. For example, in an outburst against Mérimée's pride at his membership of nine committees, he writes on 16 April 1851: "In this century, there is a lack of a satirist with a whip. Let's get on with the job, whip, whip!!" He will do so relentlessly, acting as the self-appointed private satirist of the court in lieu of the emperor himself, whom he blamed for being too indulgent with those around him. He could only do so because, like the Goncourt brothers, he was not really writing his memoirs, but a diary. Now the diary is not a genre of objective history but, however much directed it might be to observation of the behavior of others, it remains essentially a repository of personal impressions and obsessions, ideas and sensations, tastes and distastes, grudges and complaints, which readily and uninhibitedly admits a satirical perspective and which is not subject to the censure of others, since the diary has, initially at least, no other reader than the diarist. Viel-Castel's "memoirs" were only published more than a decade after the end

15. Scott D. Carpenter, "Of False Napoleons, and Other Political Prostheses: Writing Oppositionally from the Second Empire," *Nineteenth-Century French Studies* 25 (1997): 303, 316; Viel-Castel, *Mémoires,* 6 June 1853. The ditty reads: "In their imperial splendors / The uncle and the nephew are equal: / The uncle took capitals / The nephew takes capital."

16. For example, Williams, in his annotated bibliography to *The Mortal Napoleon III,* writes: "The assistant superintendent of the Louvre, an outstanding busybody and gossip. Opinion differs on his reliability. Handle with care" (207).

of the Empire and after the author's own death. He was thus able to rail freely and with complete frankness against the society that he deplored.

THE MUZZLED MUSE

For most of its span of eighteen years, the Second Empire was not a period to be amused from within its borders by derisive attacks on its policies and customs, any more than it tolerated more serious opposition to its policies or subversive political action. Before he came to power, Louis Napoléon, who cut a rather pathetic figure, was, as we have noted, fair game for the humorists. Though the surveillance and censorship that earned the regime the reputation of being a police state was not as original or as effective as the label implies, there was not only a strict control of what was published but even control of private correspondence by the infamous and mysterious *cabinet noir.* As Payne notes: "Certainly no invention of Louis Napoléon's era, the clandestine opening, reading, and forwarding of private mail undoubtedly continued throughout the Second Empire. Surveillance of the mails actually was of two kinds: that done legally and openly by competent authorities following specified procedures; and that of the true *cabinet noir,* done illicitly behind closed doors by the secret police."[17] Press censorship also took on two forms: the official activities of the VIe Chambre Correctionnelle of the district court of the Seine, on whose benches many a distinguished journalist and writer, including the authors of *Madame Bovary* and *Les Fleurs du mal,* would sit; and the self-imposed censorship which the newspapers and printers, who were also liable, forced upon journalists for fear of suppression, as well as the self-restraint of the journalists and caricaturists themselves, who depended on the good will of the authorities and the newspaper owners to make a living.

Though active opposition could be effectively suppressed, as a sometime journalist himself, if only on the strength of a few articles in the provincial press, the emperor had a strong appreciation of the power of images

17. Payne, *The Police State of Louis Napoleon Bonaparte,* 270. The actual "*cabinet noir,*" as Payne explains, was variously located in the prefecture of police, the ministry of the interior, the Tuileries, the telegraph headquarters, and in the Paris post offices, and the practice was almost certainly limited to the affairs of a relatively small number of "notables" (270–71). See also *Les Papiers secrets du Second Empire* (Brussels: Office de Publicité, 1870–71), Nos. 4–5, 1871.

and words in the newspapers. In fact, in 1868–69, Rochefort would gleefully quote for satirical effect extracts from the emperor's forceful articles
published over forty years earlier in *Le Progrès du Pas-de-Calais*. The press
laws of February 1852 required government authorization for the publication of a newspaper, which had to be renewed if the owner or director
changed. Every daily newspaper had to pay a security deposit and a tax of
six centimes a number, measures that were aimed particularly at the political press, as was a system of warnings, fines, and threats of suspension.
Only official accounts of government debates were allowed to be published. Even after 1860, government censors edited such accounts when
they were allowed to appear. And even after the so-called liberal measures
of the press laws instituted in July 1868, which abolished the requirement
of government authorization for the founding of a newspaper, the deposit
and the tax were maintained and the censors were still actively engaged,
scrutinizing pictures, captions, and articles, finding (and sometimes overlooking) grounds for banning the newspaper.

Paradoxically, however, despite the fetters, the Second Empire was a
period of dramatic expansion of the fourth estate, as a result of technical
innovations, an expansion of the middle-class reading public, an increase
in advertising, improved distribution via the new railway system, and large-
scale investment in journalism by prosperous bankers of the time. The repression of dissident opinion was not by any means absolute, even during
the early years of the Empire. Alongside the austere official newspapers, *Le
Moniteur*, *Le Constitutionnel* and *Le Pays*, subsidized by the government
and therefore "servile, exclamatory, fetichistic," there were the cautious
opposition dailies, *La Presse*, *Le Siècle*, and *Le Journal des Débats*, as well as
newspapers following a strongly clerical or monarchist line, and thereby
frequently critical of government policies, such as the *Journal des Villes et
Campagnes*, a Catholic publication with a circulation of 3,500 in 1866,
and the monarchist *Gazette de France*, which ran to 6,000 during the sixties. But significantly, the tolerance extended much further to the right
than to the left. Liberal dailies and weeklies, during this period, usually had
a brief lifespan and had to present themselves as literary journals. Lack of
political engagement was not only prudent but profitable. The largely apolitical *Le Figaro*, which was launched in 1854 by Henri de Villemessant as
a literary weekly, only became a daily in 1866, but it almost immediately
achieved a circulation of 55,000. Its popularity was unsurpassed except by
Le Petit Journal, which was instituted in 1863 by Moïse Millaud and

which both confirmed and exploited to the full the trend towards the mass-circulation and politically noncommittal daily, for by the end of 1869 it was running to almost half a million copies. Even so, during this time, the satirical press was not entirely unrepresented. *Le Charivari*, with cartoons by Cham and Daumier, continued to have moderate success, but was the only paper of its kind, except for the *Petit Journal pour rire*, to reach significant circulation figures (2,600 in 1866) and to survive for any length of time. If there was a significant quantitative development of the press, there was no equivalent extension of its powers.[18]

With the press law of 1868, there was a spectacular change, as if passions pent up for almost two decades suddenly burst out in an explosion of protest and indignation. No less than 140 new titles appeared, almost all in opposition to the regime, whose liberal measures had opened up a Pandora's box of protest, creating an atmosphere in which caricature and satire could thrive again along with the insurrectional spirit that inspired such newspapers as *La Rue* (June 1867–January 1868), in which Vallès spearheaded anti-government attacks and André Gill published his caricatures of prominent figures of the imperial regime, and *La Lanterne* (1868–1869), in which Rochefort brilliantly attacked Badinguet and his family. Other satirical papers sprang up: *La Lune*, which would become *L'Éclipse*; *La Parodie*, which Gill founded with the collaboration of Jules Janin and Victor Hugo; *Les Célébrités populaires*, which, in its seventh number, offered new readers a special deal on a pocket revolver. In 1869–70, still with the exception of *Le Petit Journal*, it was the opposition press that had the huge circulation figures, 120,000–170,000 for *La Lanterne*, 50,000–140,000 for *La Marseillaise*, a paper founded in December 1869, inspired and promoted by Rochefort, persecuted by the government as the most radical of the opposition newspapers, in open war with the imperial regime, and destined to see many of its contributors arrested, fined, and even jailed.[19] Clearly, in the final months of the Second Empire, the climate of vigorous opposition within France, in which caricature and satire could flourish, was in marked contrast to the prevailing situation for most of the duration of the regime, as the differing careers and styles of Daumier and Rochefort, the two most celebrated practitioners of the art of satire, graphically illustrate.

18. See Roger Bellet, *Presse et journalisme sous le Second Empire* (Paris: Armand Colin, 1967), 11–85, and the useful tables at the end of his study, 300–13.
19. See *ibid.*, 276–79.

The range of Honoré Daumier's work as an artist was, of course, much broader than his activities as a political caricaturist. A recent commentator notes that twentieth-century studies of his work have tended to polarize between two views: either they give preeminence to the 4,000 lithographs by which he commented critically in the press on the society of his time or they see this activity as merely ancillary to his achievements in the "higher" art forms for connoisseurs and public patrons.[20] Curiously, in attempting to demonstrate the connection between the two, the same author can afford to make only incidental references to the artist's work as a political satirist. Daumier, however, was a man of profound republican convictions, who, before the Second Empire, had already a considerable reputation as a withering political caricaturist. His cartoons in *La Caricature* and *Le Charivari* ridiculing Louis-Philippe and his ministers in the 1830s, with the famous pear-shaped profiles of the king, earned him both notoriety and a six-month sentence in the Sainte-Pélagie prison in 1833, a spell that is ironically referred to as his "University Period," not unlike his exact contemporary's longer spell at Ham. They clearly took a different course of study, for Daumier's other notorious period as a significant political cartoonist was anti-Bonapartist, during the Second Republic, when he visually lambasted Louis Napoléon's rise to power and created, in sculpture and in his lithographs, the legendary figure of the Bonapartist agitator, Ratapoil, who symbolized the muscular form of Bonapartism in evidence at the time (see figure 16). Unlike many writers and artists during the Second Empire, Daumier did not allow his talents to be appropriated by the regime, though he seemingly did collaborate to the extent of drawing for *Le Charivari* satirical cartoons of Cossacks, of the king of Naples, and the Austrians, which served the emperor's foreign policies. But it has recently been shown how his series of caricatures on China in particular subverted the official discourse of supposedly civilizing colonial adventures of the Empire.[21] In general, his work for *Le Charivari* was, within the limits allowed, critical of the regime and was viewed with suspicion by the au-

20. Bruce Laughton, *Honoré Daumier* (New Haven–London: Yale University Press, 1996), 1–2.

21. See Oliver W. Larkin, *Daumier, Man of His Time* (New York–Toronto–London: McGraw-Hill, 1966), 110, and Monika Bosse and André Stoll "Censure et représentation des barbares: Les stratégies subversives de Daumier sous le Second Empire," in *La Caricature entre République et censure*, ed. Raimund Rütten, Ruth Jung, and Gerhard Schneider (Lyon: Presses universitaires de Lyon, 1996), 299–313.

thorities. His work was frequently subjected to the censor's bans, and in 1860, he was dropped from the staff of the journal, until 1864, as a result of government pressure, it is usually presumed. Now that direct satirical representations of the emperor himself and his entourage were out of the question, with the blunted instruments of his own craft, Daumier was thus compelled to moderate his criticism, proceed more cautiously, and concentrate more on satire of the ideal society that the emperor claimed to be crafting, holding up, in a more realistic and restrained manner, a humorously distorting and disenchanting mirror to the age. His bemused spectators of the demolitions of Paris, his cowering, craggy workers, bent under the burdens of their work, his "petit peuple" packed into the third-class railway carriages, his Prudhommesque bourgeois, his Molièresque doctors, his arrogant lawyers, his venal art dealers, his fashionable ladies causing devastation with their sweeping crinolines were a comic deflation of the pretensions of the regime and a constant reminder that there were harsh realities behind the glossy facades, cruel injustices and hardships dissembled by the pompous official discourse of progress and grandiloquence, dross beneath the gloss. All the cracks and imperfections in the smooth and seamless edifice of the emperor's society, as its glib proponents would have it, seem to sprout forth on the grotesquely gnarled faces and contorted gestures of his subjects as Daumier represented them.

Only in the more permissive climate of the last years of the Second Empire did Daumier return to more overtly political caricature and even then, though a number of his drawings were rejected for political reasons, in the prudent mode of allegory. A picture of a grotesquely fat female with gigantic breasts and a label "Prussia" on her belly was turned down for publication. As Larkin notes, "Daumier in his older and wiser years preferred to attack policies, not personalities. In his best drawings the 'portrait-charge' gives place to the symbol: Peace is a buxom and benevolent female with an overflowing cornucopia and Diplomacy an emaciated hag in the dress of the eighteenth century," with no offense presumed to the empress. But with the fall of the regime, his works become more explicit, summing up the twenty-year rule, for instance, in *History of a Reign,* with a figure representing France bound hand-and-foot between two cannons, one marked "Paris, 1851," the other "Sedan, 1870," or, in another work, France now become Prometheus on the rock, devoured by a Napoleonic eagle. There is much that is Hugolian in this phase, and his "A Page of History," published in 16 November 1870, is a homage of the artist to the poet, a compliment that the author of *Châtiments* returned with a late dedication.[22] Even Daumier, though with dignified restraint, joined in the baiting of the fallen emperor.

Rochefort's satire, by comparison, was virulent, aggressive, personal, in his direct attacks on the emperor, his family, his government, and even his dog. Daumier fully exploited the potential of the visual medium, capturing, with the practiced skill of the caricaturist, both the visual likeness and the essential individual and abstract qualities, the defining characteristics of his subjects, overloaded—as the source of the term suggests (*caricare,* "to load" in Italian)—with usually comic exaggeration, in varying degrees according to whether realistic representation was the primary aim or satirical efficacy. Such is the art of the caricaturist, or what Max Beerbohm called his "gift for dispraise." Rochefort, with a gift for vituperation, worked in a verbal medium—though not exclusively, for he fought a number of notorious duels—relying more on an aggressive rhetoric, on discursive irony, either in his own discourse or in manipulating with devastating raillery the discourse of others. His one-man weekly journal, more pamphlet than newspaper, *La Lanterne,* which his former employer, Villemessant, founded for him because he was too dangerous to keep on at *Le Figaro,* was an enormous success, selling more than 100,000 copies, due to the mordant wit of its sole contributor, as the celebrated first sentence of the first number (31 May 1868) shows: "According to the *Almanach impérial,* France contains 36 million subjects; without counting the subjects of discontent."[23] Many of his readers were convinced Bonapartists. Even the emperor was seen with his copy. "Rochefort brought the exaggerated burlesque of vaudeville into print," as Williams writes, "a technique likened by one historian [Pierre de la Gorce] to 'the daring naughty boys who write on walls.' " The second number was forbidden to be sold in the streets. For an article in the eighth number, on Caesar and Cassius, he was accused of inciting the assassination of the emperor. By the time he produced the eleventh, he was compelled to escape to Brussels, where the Hugos, father and sons, welcomed him, and to smuggle his publication across the border, like the great poet's own attacks on the Empire several

---

22. Larkin, *Daumier, Man of His Time,* 169, 166, 182.

23. For the rest of the provocative article, with which Rochefort threw down his glove to the Empire, see Éric Vatré, *Henri Rochefort ou La comédie politique au XIXᵉ siècle* (Paris: Lattès, 1984), 73–75.

years previously and like many other subversive works since, by similar means, famously in plaster busts of the emperor! "It can no longer be said that he has nothing in his head!" Rochefort is said to have remarked on the ruse. But unlike Hugo, he did not stay in exile, returning secretly to France to contest a by-election and allowed by the authorities to remain because he won. But it was still as a journalist that he continued to make his mark. The former vaudevillian—Morny warned against him just before he died—and former contributor to *Le Charivari*, who had made his reputation as a witty and combative journalist with *Le Figaro*, had become increasingly militant until, as editor-in-chief of *La Marseillaise*, he was eventually arrested, in February 1870, and sent to take his turn in Sainte-Pélagie, where he remained until the fall of the Empire.[24]

The effectiveness of Rochefort, and the danger for the imperial regime, was a devastating combination of caustic wit and uncompromising aggression. He employed the former to excellent effect in an article in *La Lanterne* in 1868 on the Bonapartes:

> As a Bonapartist, I prefer Napoleon II; it is my right. I shall even add that he represents, to my mind, the ideal sovereign. No one will deny that he occupied the throne, since his successor calls himself Napoleon III. What a reign, my friends, what a reign! Not a single tax, no useless wars, . . . no consuming civil list, no pluralistic ministers at one hundred thousand francs for five or six functions. There, indeed, is a monarch such as I can understand. Ah! yes, Napoleon II, I like you and I admire you without reservation. Who, therefore, will dare to insist that I am not a Bonapartist?[25]

In a more hostile and serious vein—to give an example of his virulent polemical aggressiveness—there is the famous article that he published in *La Marseillaise* on 11 January 1870, in which he or his collaborator, Ernest Lavigne, had famously written: "Scratch a Bonaparte, find a ferocious animal." The emperor's cousin, Prince Pierre Bonaparte, a reckless and hot-tempered man, had challenged Rochefort to a duel in response to an article, in the same publication, attacking the imperial family. In an altercation

24. Roger L. Williams, *Henri Rochefort, Prince of the Gutter Press* (New York: Charles Scribner's Sons, 1966), 27, 33; Vatré, *Henri Rochefort*, 87, 53.

25. Quoted in Burchell, *Imperial Masquerade*, 151, and in Williams, *Henri Rochefort*, 27–28.

at the prince's residence on 10 January, when a young "journalist," Yvan Salmon, or Victor Noir, as he called himself, and another journalist appeared as seconds (in fact, in relation to another challenge in which the prince was involved in response to a previous article!), Pierre Bonaparte shot Noir, who died in the street below.[26] The next day, Rochefort wrote in *La Marseillaise:*

> I was weak-minded enough to believe that a Bonaparte could be other than a murderer!
>
> I dared to imagine that a straight-forward duel was possible in that family in which murder and ambushes are a tradition and a common practice.
>
> . . . Today we weep for our poor and dear friend, Victor Noir, murdered by the bandit Pierre-Napoléon Bonaparte.
>
> For eighteen years France has been in the bloody hands of these cut-throats, who, not satisfied with shooting down Republicans in the streets, lure them into treacherous traps to slit their throats in their homes.
>
> People of France, don't you think that we've had enough!

The government certainly had had enough of Rochefort and, denying him parliamentary immunity, sent him to jail for inciting revolt and contempt of the emperor. The irony of Rochefort's subsequent career, not that it would be any consolation to Napoleon III, was that he went on to denounce the Third Republic, supported Boulanger, and discredited his reputation with virulent anti-Semitic rhetoric at the time of the Dreyfus affair!

AT A SAFE DISTANCE

There was, quite naturally, a considerable body of caricature and satire in the foreign press directed against the imperial regime and its leaders, in continuation of the tradition mentioned above and encapsulating international rivalries, providing a popular and comic dimension to diplomacy, carnivalesque interludes in the serious business of the pursuit of national interests.[27] But more significant for our purpose are the attacks on the em-

---

26. For a full account, see Williams, *Manners and Murders,* 131–50.

27. For a notable example, see James M. Haswell, *Napoleon III. from Popular Caricatures of the Last Thirty Years with the Story of His Life* (London: J. C. Hotten, 1876?).

peror and the Empire from writers who had escaped from France, usually to Brussels or London, either at the time of the coup d'état or subsequently, when they were no longer made welcome by the censorship laws and practices. There was, for instance, a *Charivari belge,* amongst several Belgian satirical newspapers opposed to Bonapartism. But there was not total freedom, particularly in Belgium, where, under pressure from the government of France, the Belgian minister of justice, Charles Faider, introduced already in December 1852 a law allowing the prosecution of authors of works offensive to a foreign government.[28] Nevertheless, émigré opponents of the Second Empire were not, once abroad, subjected to the rigorous external constraints that plagued those who stayed behind. Yet this relative freedom, at least from the point of view of less partial readers, subjected their works to no less rigorous internal constraints, laws of credibility and appropriateness. The grounds and evidence on which the charges are based and the degree of wrath and indignation needs to be proportionate to the offenses that are denounced. The second point is crucial, for, if the criticism is too mild, as was frequently the case within the country under surveillance, there is complicity; if it is extreme, the intended pragmatic effect is not realized and the ridicule is turned back upon the ridiculer. Numerous satirical works attacking Napoleon III and his regime from abroad indulged in excesses that seem no less discreditable than those that they denounced. We could even call it the "Hugo syndrome," since much of the satire of this kind that appeared, usually with Belgian or English imprints, was inspired by the exiled poet, or even published in his name. The poet Albert Glatigny even wrote a volume of *Nouveaux Châtiments* in the wake of the military defeat of 1870.[29]

One such work, conveniently short, is a twelve-page treatise entitled *L'Organographie physiogno-phrénologique de Badinguet, d'après Gall et Spurzheim,* whose author's name appears as Victor Hugo in the book, most probably a pseudonym of the virulent political satirist Antoine

28. See Jacques Hellemans, "Napoléon le Petit et la presse belge, du coup d'État à la proclamation de l'Empire," in *La Caricature entre République et censure,* ed. Raimund Rütten, Ruth Jung, and Gerhard Schneider (Lyon: Presses universitaires de Lyon, 1996), 285–87. The law required a preliminary complaint from the offended government, but in March 1858, even this proviso was dropped.

29. Albert Glatigny, *Le Fer rouge: Nouveaux Châtiments* (France et Belgique: 1871), twenty-one poems composed between 5 September and 12 October 1870, glorifying the Republic and Hugo.

Rocher. As the title makes abundantly clear, the work is a blatant example of the use of (pseudo-)scientific authority for political ends, for the author attempts to explain all the vices of the emperor by the evidence of his physiognomy on the strength of his own observations of Louis Napoléon and the supposedly hands-on experience of a phrenologist who has "palpated the Imperial cranium." It was presumably seriously intended, but becomes a comic text in retrospect, reading like a parody of a satire by its excesses. The whole work is a catalog of disobliging judgments, phrased in an extraordinary jargon. Even in the age of the primacy of physiological models of interpretation and explanation when the method was likely to command credibility, as we saw earlier in the portrait of the emperor in the Larousse encyclopedia, it is difficult to believe that its application in this work would convince any but the most naive or partisan of its readers. Thus, the emperor's "bilious" complexion is said to show a propensity for the most heinous crimes; his chin reveals signs of "ruse"; and his mouth gives evidence of "base and nasty duplicitousness." His cheeks reveal "envy" and his nose "a character of animal ferocity," whilst his little eyes, as Adelon and Buffon would have noted had they had a chance to observe them, betray "the phlegmatic ruse, the profound dissembling, the sinister agitations of a criminal soul." Even the movement of his eyebrows has significance: the more rapid ones expressing "the wildest and cruelest passions," the slower ones exhibiting the signs of a latent "satyriasis" *("satyrianisme")*. There is "fanaticism, stubbornness, a veiled irritability, and a heart of stone" evident in the forehead. The whole effect of the emperor's physiognomy reminds the author of a certain Benoît, *"whose organ was very active"* and who killed his mother and friend to rob them to pay for his lust for women: "Benoît's temperament was, like that of the emperor of the French, neuroto-lymphatic." At the risk of doing violence to the author's method, a cumulative mass of evidence deduced from "the illustrious cranium of the son of Hortense," a brief schematic listing of the principal remaining *"penchants"* that are revealed must suffice: *"alimentativité"* near the ears (i.e., "mindlessness brought about by good food and wine"), a lack of *"philogéniture"* and *"affectionnivité"* (i.e., a lack of a tender heart, as in the case of Bouteillier, who killed his mother), *"destructivité"* above the ears (a feature of the marquis de Sade, Caligula, Nero, and Charles IX), *"secrétivité"* (i.e., hypocrisy, lying, subterfuge, duplicity), *"acquisivité"* and *"estime de soi"* on the top of the head, *"approbativité"* (i.e., a taste for titles, approval, decorations, and monomania), a lack of *"conscienciosité"* and of *"idéalité,"* but a highly developed *"destructivité"* and *"acquisi-vité,"* along with a penchant for imitation. The case study concludes with a survey of affective traits, notably carnal desires, lust, debauchery, apathy, inconstancy, for, in Napoleon III, to sum it all up, *"matter* is victorious over *mind."* In conclusion, we are invited, firstly, to accept both that his case proves the validity of the science of Gall and Spurzheim and that their science is born out by his case, then to meditate upon a page of quotations on the ravages brought about by the emperor's sexual activities, leading to the scientific assertion that the exhaustion of "the generative organ" (*"l'organe générateur"*) sometimes destroys the brain and eats away "the spinal marrow." With this prospect in mind, as if there were some link, the author ends on a flourish to denounce the censorship of the felonious emperor's government, predicting that Truth will emerge and the People will fulfill their mission to avenge his crimes.[30]

Another equally colorful example of such attacks is *Les Deux Cours et les nuits de St.-Cloud,* a work which appeared in several editions (1852, 1860, 1862, 1865, 1870) either anonymously or under the signature (with variations in spelling) of Hippolyte Magen, a pseudonym of L. Stelli. This text is one of several denunciations of the emperor from the same source, variously printed in London, Guernsey, and Brussels, which uses history rather than science as an authenticating grounding for its attacks and specializes in the supposed moral turpitude of the Bonapartes rather than their political skulduggery. The true author of this book is presented as a collective entity, called LEGION, for it is a kind of composite testimony of the disaffected associates of the emperor and its aim is to "be truthful, only obey justice, fight tyranny, love the People, and hate vice." The emphasis is on vice, as, in Part 1, the author surveys the depravities of the Bonaparte family and, in Part 2, the profligacy of its latest scion. Thus, reportedly, Laetitia ran a brothel with harlot daughters Pauline and Élise, her son, Napoleon I, poisoned his mistress, committed incest with his sisters Élise and Caroline—curiously Pauline is omitted—ran a girls' seminary for his pleasures, raped two girls, assassinated Fouché, stole from the public coffers, and so forth. Joseph led an immoral life in Spain. Lucien committed rape and incest. Jérôme indulged in depraved tastes, along with

30. Viscount Victor Marie Hugo [Antoine Rocher?], *L'Organographie physiogno-phrénologique de Badinguet, d'après Gall et Spurzheim par Victor Hugo 1853* (London: Librairie Universelle, 1871), 3–5, 6–9, 11–12.

rape and murder. Joachim Murat was guilty of theft and treason. Hortense, to whom a whole section is devoted, was the emperor's mistress, had so many lovers that she did not know who were the fathers of her children, stole the tune of "Partant pour la Syrie" from a musician at her salon, picked up a student for her pleasure in the Tuileries gardens amongst the prostitutes, was foisted by the emperor, who had made her pregnant, onto poor Louis, somewhat mysteriously presented as "the only man in the family who was honest and good," no doubt as an added torment for Louis Napoléon, who was not the son of Louis but the bastard product of an incestuous liaison, as an equally mysterious "authentic document," in the hands of an "editor of the *Bulletin français*" supposedly proves. It is hardly surprising, therefore, that Louis Napoléon should follow in the traditions of this family, with its "dissolute ways," and that he should even sum up "all the vices of his race." It is hardly surprising also that he should proceed to "sully, oppress, steal from, torture, tear apart, and deplete" his country.[31]

The style of this work, with its characteristic vigorous accumulation of rampaging denunciations as all the energy of its author's malice is poured out onto the page, is exuberantly charged, with, in parts, a quaint and precious vocabulary that is presumably intended for clever effect.[32] According to the contorted logic of the satire, the vices of Louis Verhuell-Bonaparte are proof in themselves that he belongs to the depraved family: *"Bon sang ne peut mentir."* There is a section on the prostitute-courtesan "miss Howard," her crooked *"entreteneur"* "Jack-young-fitz-roi," their rides in "Hyde-Parck," her deal with Louis Bonaparte "in exchange for the paradise to which the siren transported him," the pact between "the prostitute of London and the bastard of Holland." But what is most remarkable about the portrait that emerges of Prince Louis Napoléon—yet to become emperor at the time of publication of the first edition at least—is that already in 1852 the satirists were projecting the image of a man jaded and worn by his debaucheries. Here the president of the Republic is pilloried less for his political actions than for the sexual proclivities in which his po-

---

31. Hyppolite Magen [L. Stelli], *Les Deux Cours et les nuits de St.-Cloud* (London: Bridges, 1871), 8, 79, 90, 86, 87.

32. It also defies translation, as in the following example: *"Cette race prolifique a merveilleusement provigné; il en est sorti une foule de princellons, filous et mauvais drôles, dont la vie, qui a longtemps couru la pretantine, s'écoule dans la propination et le maquerélage."* Magen, *Les Deux Cours,* 89–90.

litical power allowed him to indulge, like a degenerate and degenerating Lothario: "facile pleasures," sadism, sex every night with prostitutes who "confront the cadaverous odors that he spreads," "overcome the disgust that his papulous skin exhales."[33] To a limited degree—more limited than has usually been supposed, as we have previously noted—the emperor would go on to live up to the satirical image forged by the enemies of the president, or at least do little to dissipate it.

At the end of his pasquinade, amid appeals for vengeance and retribution, the author invites the reader to leave "this Elysian pandemonium," with its infectious filth, to depart from "this brothel in which the Napoleonic scum, which never sobers up, will continue its perpetual sacrifices to the infamous COTYTTO, the goddess of debauchery."[34] But not for long, for, with the marriage of the emperor, another chapter needed to be covered, another target for the satirist's venom appeared on the scene. In *Histoire satyrique et véritable du Mariage de César avec la belle Eugénie de Gusman, ou la France de César-1853,* supposedly by the same author,[35] a work which he immodestly situates in the noble tradition of Tacitus and Juvenal, much of this new and shorter "work of flagellation" is directed against Eugénie, the "modern Lavallière," whose presumed lack of culture and love of bullfighting are held against her, but whose family history is reviewed, as in the previous work, with disobliging revelations about her mother: daughter of "Kirpatrick," a butter, sugar, and sardine merchant— wine merchant would be too noble a profession, no doubt, for a satire— who wished to "*desardinize* herself," married a "cripple" for his title, had two daughters of unidentifiable paternity, "so great was the number of men made happy by the dissolute marquise," though the charge is repeated that, in any case, Eugénie was probably sired by Lord Clarendon. At least, the author adds, "the two mothers of Louis and Eugénie are similar as far as their morals are concerned." But as for Eugénie herself, apart from an affair with the duc d'Osuna, the author has little (yet) to reproach her. He quotes a couple of popular ditties about her and notes her new name with the workers of Paris: Countess de Bréda, y Carotas, y Bastringo,

33. *Ibid.,* 95, 96, 97, 113.
34. *Ibid.,* 120, 124.
35. Ridley, in his bibliography (*Napoleon III and Eugénie,* 655), questions the attribution of this work to Magen, who, he points out, was imprisoned in Cayenne when it was first published in 1853.

y Cravacho, y Mabillo, y Badingo, or, more simply for some, the second Lola Montès. The heavy artillery is directed once again at Napoleon III, for whose "cadaverous and devastated face" Lola II can only feel pity and revulsion. He condemns the arrests and deportations of those guilty of *"lèze-Montijo,"* claims that Miss Howard has born three children by him, conveniently so, since, as *"la Montijo"* has a particular infirmity and may be sterile, there are some imperial bastards available to carry on the traditions. A later edition includes a farcical anecdote, in which the redhead Eugénie finds Caesar in bed with *la belle comtesse* de Cast——, and the news that Miss Howard is pregnant again! The pamphlet closes on a rousing denunciation and a threat addressed to the emperor as Caïn, a name inspired, no doubt, by Hugo's use of the biblical name for his "father of crime" in *Châtiments:* "Beyond the thousands of bayonets which cross to protect you from your fears, can you not see the millions of arms coming together to avenge our martyrs?" The vengeance was a long time coming, but when it did with the collapse of the imperial regime, it was, as we shall see, all the more acerbic.[36]

CHÂTIMENTS

It was reported in the government newspapers on 23 August 1852, as we have noted, that the emperor, on being presented with a copy of *Napoléon-le-Petit* at Saint-Cloud, quipped: "Look, gentlemen, here's Napoleon-the-Little, by Victor Hugo-the-Great." Whether the emperor's touch of humor was instrumental in deciding Hugo to produce a separate volume of poems castigating his enemy, instead of integrating them into *Les Contemplations,* is not known, but he wrote to his publisher, Hetzel, the following month, announcing his new plan and, in November, was working on what he then called *Les Vengeresses,* a "natural and necessary counterpart of *Napoléon-le-Petit.*"[37] Hugo certainly did take offense at the emperor's irony, for, in one of the poems of *Châtiments,* entitled

36. Hyppolite Magen [L. Stelli], *Histoire satyrique et véritable du mariage de César avec la belle Eugénie de Gusman, ou la Femme de César—1853* (London: Jeffs, 1871), 17, 25, 29–30, 31.

37. See P. J. Yarrow, introduction to *Châtiments,* by Victor Hugo, ed. P. J. Yarrow (London: Athlone Press, 1975), 19. The poems referred to in this section are from this edition; their locations are given in the text by "book" and poem number.

"L'Homme a ri" ("The Man Has Laughed"), he reproduces the anecdote and replies emphatically, promising to make his enemy's flesh sizzle with the red-hot iron of his verse: *"Ton rire sur mon nom gaîment vient écumer; / Mais je tiens le fer rouge et vois ta chair fumer"* (III, 2). This response gives an indication of the ardor with which the poet pursued the task and, most significantly, of the performative function of the poems. As Hugo insists in a number of his poems, he considered the *Châtiments* themselves to be the emperor's chastisement. With God as his witness, so he claims, he promises in another poem, "A l'Obéissance passive," to go "to this Corsican," with "justice in his soul and a whip in his hand" (II, 7), then to hunt down his prey, "this wolf on whom I set a pack of stanzas" (II, 7) ("Le Parti du Crime," VI, 11). To the emperor's ironic observation, his only known comment on Hugo's work, the poet follows up the earlier lambasting with almost 7,000 lines of satirical poetry, a masterpiece of sustained invective, which would be a source of inspiration and of constant reference to the enemies of the emperor and the Empire capable of appreciating its dazzlingly versatile effects.

He had already moved to Jersey, where, as he purportedly told Plon-Plon, the ocean would be a source of consolation and inspiration and where he would compose all but a half dozen previously written poems of the collection. *Châtiments* was completed in October 1853 and published in Brussels the following month, in two formats: an official, expurgated edition with whole passages replaced by lines of dots for the sake of the Faider law, and an unexpurgated edition, supposedly published in Geneva and New York, which came out in a reduced format and copies of which were duly smuggled into France. For the poet, with his blithe disregard for generic distinctions, "the muse is history" ("Joyeuse Vie," III, 9); the collection is an elaborate attempt to reverse history with poetry, as the passage from the two poems that frame the collection indicates, also inverting symbolically the initials of the perpetrator of the present abominable condition: from *"Nox"* to *"Lux."* We have already seen that Victor did not gracefully accept defeat. The themes of *Châtiments* are familiar from the other two anti-Bonapartist volumes: the infamy and barbarism of the coup d'état; the rapacity of the Bonapartists and the cowardice of those who allowed the infamy to occur; the martyrdom of the innocents of the massacre of 4 December; the contrast between the glorious exploits of the uncle and the crimes of the nephew; the contrast between, on the one hand, the orgies of the court and the sufferings of the victims of repres-

sion; the crassness of the emperor's supporters, the politicians, the courtiers, the senior army officers, the judges, and, particularly, the dignitaries
of the Church, set against the integrity, courage, and hardships of those
who had opposed the regime, himself included, of course; the luxuries of
those in power contrasted with the squalor of the poor; the shame of the
harlots of the Tuileries opposed to the redemptive role of women in preparing the glorious, *universal* Republic of the future, foretold notably in
"Lux," when France would be free, when all peoples would be "out of
the abyss," when the whole world would be but "a single family," when
all would be "peace and light," a "sublime vision," which, in this text also,
Hugo has no doubt, will manifest itself. But the poet has also a more immediate purpose than indulging in such prophetic divination. His work
has a double purpose and is directed at two main "addressees": France and
its new emperor. It is no longer a question of waking up a France caught
napping by the wily tyrant, but of shaking the country, or the People, out
of their crass acceptance of the regime and shaming them for their subservience:

> *Réveillez-vous, assez de honte!*
> *Bravez les boulets et biscayens.*
> *Il est temps qu'enfin le flot monte,*
> *Assez de honte, citoyens!* ("A ceux qui dorment," VI, 6).[38]

Addressing again the "great nation" that is France, he chides her: "You
prostituted yourself to that miserable man!" ("Applaudissement," VI,
16). If he excoriates by his verse the "vile rogues," the "saber carriers,"
and the "miter wearers" who support their Caesar—"I hold them in my
verse as in a vise" (I, 11)—the real force of his contempt, that the poet
pours forth with all the venom he can muster, belongs to the "wretched
man" himself, whom he addresses directly at the most intense moments
of outrage and on whom he enacts the chastisement, scourging him with
the verbal lashings of his satire, diminishing him with his scorn, stretching
him on the rack of his invective, willing him a more capital punishment
than execution: "Shame, and not death" ("Nox"). In the earlier poems
of the collection, Louis Napoléon is given a voice to bark out his orders
and to hatch his plot. Thereafter he is subjected to the retribution. The

---

38. "Awake, enough shame! / Brave the bullets and the muskets. / It is finally time for
the tide to rise, / Enough shame, citizens."

voice of the poet is both one and many, in all its aspects (personal, political, prophetic), directed in disdain to the prince and his minions, in pity to their victims, in exhortation to France and the People, in complicity with the Revolution, the Ocean, the Muse Indignation, Juvenal, and in supplication to God, whilst Napoleon III is stigmatized under a multiplicity of names, names of thieves, brigands, tyrants, and murderers, "cursed names," for he is of the race of Cain: "Mandrin," "Cartouche," "Louvel," "Lacenaire," "Robert Macaire with his worn-down boots" (III, 1), "the Corsican," the "false prince," the "brigand Bonaparte," *"Bonaparte apocryphe"* (VI, 11), with irony, *"Monsieur Napoléon," "César,"* "this bandit Caesar," "this bat Caesar" *("César chauve-souris")* (VI, 8), "this sated Nero" (I, 8), the *"président Bobêche"* (II, 6), the *"cockney d'Eglington et d'Epsom"* (VI, 5), *"Guet-apens"* ("Ambush") (II, 7), "Napoleon the Dwarf," the "disgusting dwarf," "the highwayman" ("La Fin"), "wretch" (VI, 1), "scoundrel," *"l'homme sépulchre"* (VI, 11), "Boustrapa" (from *Bou*logne, *Stras*bourg, *Pa*ris), the "monkey" of the first emperor, who is, of course, by comparison, *"petit, petit"* (VII, 6).

In this collection, all types of metric forms are represented, lines and stanzas of varying length, rhymes of all kind, given an original force. Henri Meschonnic has shown, in his study of this work, whose enunciation is at least as inventive as its denunciation, how Hugo institutes what he calls a "political poetics" in this clash of language and politics. Hugo mobilizes the full battery of the rhetoric of irony and contestation: antithesis, diminution, accumulation, dialogism, personification, bestialization—the eagle becomes vulture, of course, but there is also the whole imperial menagerie, "all the sharks, all the swine" (III, 13); "hyenas, wolves, jackals, not anticipated by Buffon" (VI, 5). But *Châtiments* is particularly remarkable for the immense variety of genres and modes that it employs. Hugo saw this as the essence of his book, "the very character of my book, sarcasm in all its forms, from the bitterest sarcasm to invective. The book must have everything in it, the reader must see in it epic, lamentation, satire, and even punning."[39] With the title of each "book" ironically parodying Bonapartist slogans—"Society Is Saved" (I), "Order Is Re-established" (II), and so on—the poet has recourse to the full gamut of his considerable versatility, within the general frame of what we would call satire and what he calls

39. Quoted by Yarrow, introduction to *Châtiments,* 24–25, from Adèle Hugo's *Journal intime.*

"epic," in view, no doubt, of its scope: "Enough stocks [*pilori*] to make an epic." There are notably ironic "idylls" (II, 1), lyrical outbursts, caricatural portraits, a fable—not surprisingly, about a monkey in a tiger's skin (III, 2)—allegorical dialogs (III, 15; V, 4), a biblical tale (VII, 207), descriptions, stirring narratives, none more so than the famous and truly epic account of Napoleon I's "Expiation" (V, 13). There are also several songs, including one to the tune of Malbrouck (V, 1) that we now know as "For He's a Jolly Good Fellow," which, no doubt, Hugo would have found either scandalously inappropriate or ironically apposite. In general, though there are laments and bitter ballads, it is the People who naturally sing, "as the lion roars" ("L'Art et le Peuple," I, 9), whilst, throughout the collection, the oppressors dance their saraband in the Tuileries. Perhaps Hugo expected the People to sing his songs as they rose up against the tyrant.

For all the nobility of his cause and the brilliance with which Hugo seeks to fulfill his aims, *Châtiments* raises certain questions about its motivations and effects. Is the medium too lofty for the message? Do the verbal pyrotechnics not distract from the purpose and detract from the efficacy of the volume? The fact that the Second Empire survived for seventeen years the publication of *Châtiments* does not, of course, mean that Hugo failed, but one can safely speculate that, whoever the intended or implied readers of the volume were supposed to be, only a select few poetic souls are likely to have been stirred by its elevated polemics. Furthermore, though the poet speaks in the name of the republican opposition to Louis Napoléon and his regime, that is for the exiles, the People, Justice, and, ultimately, God, *Châtiments* is not an entirely disinterested text. Hugo's correspondence with his publisher, Hetzel, at the time of the completion of the volume, reveals, for example, a strange concern that Napoleon III might fall before his collection appeared, as if the publication of the book were more important than the outcome that it was supposed to bring about, or, more precisely, as if it were vital that the outcome should be brought about by his book.[40] There is a strong element of self-affirmation in the work, as is suggested by the famous last poem of the collection (before "Nox"), "Ultima Verba," a poem that, it seems, was originally entitled "Moi." Here, Hugo accepts his status as an exile, since "human conscience is dead," expresses his resolution to remain so as long as "Caesar reigns," even if he is

40. See Sheila Gaudon, "Prophétisme et utopie: le problème du destinataire dans *Les Châtiments*," *Saggi e ricerche di letteratura francesa* n.s. 16 (1977): 409–11.

the last to do so: "And if there is only one remaining, I shall be that one."
As Gaudon points out, even if we do not see in this poem, as certain critics
have done, signs of an inflated ego, Hugo clearly sees himself as *Vox cla-
mantis in deserto,* the desert that he evokes in the same poem, "where God
protests against man."[41] Will the voice be heeded? Does it really matter, as
long as the man behind the voice can enjoy the pleasure of being right?
Hugo's last word runs counter to the pragmatic purpose of the book, as
the publication history of the volume suggests, for, unlike *Napoléon-le-
Petit,* it did not sell well and left the publisher with a considerable deficit.[42]
Nevertheless, this did not prevent the triumphant enemies of the emperor
from rushing into print a new edition of Hugo's decorous invective. The
first French edition appeared on 20 October 1870, less than six weeks after
the battle of Sedan.

SHADES OF HUGO

Like the *Châtiments,* the Magen texts presented above were republished
in France after the fall of the Second Empire, along with many others of
the same kind, as is indicated in the list of political pamphlets advertised at
the back of the 1871 edition of the *Histoire satyrique et véritable du mariage de César,* works "forbidden and condemned in France under the government of Badinguet, whose entry is now free." Satirical and polemical
attacks on the emperor had been virulent enough in the last months of the
regime, but, after Sedan, there was an even more intense assault on the
fallen leader and his defeated government by republican journalists and
writers. The impulse to defile the reputation of Napoleon III is, of course,
attributable in some degree to the blame attached for the humiliating military defeat and to a natural triumphalism at the fall of a reviled enemy. But
the fervor of the campaign, the pitiless pillorying of the emperor and the
Empire, the insistent dwelling upon past misdemeanors and misconduct,
whether imaginary or real, the old chestnuts, the hoary tales trotted out,
many with very little relevance to current political issues, suggests that
more deep-seated motives were at work, a kind of collective bloodletting

41. See *ibid.,* 421, 425–26. Gaudon writes: "this unpragmatic attitude will have for the
book consequences that Hugo did not seem to foresee: this book, which he wanted to be
effective, will not sell. The voice crying in the wilderness can in no way be heard" (426).
42. See *ibid.,* 426.

or settling of accounts. As Matthew Hodgart suggests: "If the occasions for satire are infinite and inherent in the human condition, the impulses behind satire are basic to human nature. Indeed, they probably go back beyond human nature, to the psychology of our animal forebears."[43]

Zola is the writer who most successfully depicted the manifestations of the instinctive in human behavior. In fact, he was himself very much involved in the process of baiting Napoleon III after his defeat. He had, of course, cause for complaint, having sought to make his way as a young republican journalist under the strictures of the last years of the Empire. Paradoxically, it was the emperor's press law of 11 May 1868 that allowed Zola to launch into a career of political journalism. Between June 1868 and August 1870 Zola wrote political articles for republican newspapers, denouncing the extravagances and injustices of the imperial regime, notably in *La Tribune,* where, as Mitterand puts it, "he juvenalizes and he flagellates the government in fine fashion," in *Le Rappel,* shoulder to shoulder with the sons of Hugo and Henri Rochefort, and in *La Cloche,* a paper modeled after *La Lanterne.* "In the manner of Hugo, he conceived an epic interpretation of the birth, the history and the decadence of the regime, whose collapse in the near future he foretells, in shame and bloodshed."[44] These articles are daring, full of insolent irony. They are directed more against the regime, which Zola views as a huge orgy, than against its leader, for here, as in his *Rougon-Macquart* novels, the emperor remains a shadowy presence. But the novelist and the journalist are clearly working in tandem, as we see from the following brief extract of an article in *La Cloche* (13 February 1870), entitled "La Fin de l'Orgie" ("The End of the Orgy"): "Ah! what a rush for the spoils [*curée*] the Second Empire is! From the day after the coup d'état, the orchestra beat time for the first waltzes, and quickly the languid tune became a diabolical gallop. They got their hands on the dishes, right into the sauce, eating greedily, tearing morsels from each other's mouth. They rushed into the satisfaction of their appetites, with animal rage, and, when they had gorged themselves, they went on eating. They are still eating."[45] As we saw earlier, Zola took part also in the republican campaign to recall the bloody foundations of

43. Matthew Hodgart, *Satire* (New York–Toronto: McGraw-Hill, 1969), 10.

44. Henri Mitterand, *Zola journaliste, de l'affaire Manet à l'affaire Dreyfus* (Paris: Armand Colin, 1962), 92, 97.

45. Zola, *Oeuvres complètes,* 13:260.

the imperial regime, attacking Louis Napoléon's coup d'état and the systematic veil cast over the compromising political deeds of the regime in the recent past. For another of his articles for *La Cloche,* on 5 August 1870, an attack on the army ("Vive la France!"), he was summoned to appear before the magistrates four days later, but the disastrous turn of events in the Franco-Prussian War saved him from being charged and perhaps from finding himself also on the way to Sainte-Pélagie.

After the war in 1871 and 1872, again for *La Cloche,* the novelist was still a part of the opposition press under the conservative Republic, censuring reactionary government policies as he had done under the Empire. His attack on the duke de Broglie, leader of the conservative coalition, in *Le Corsaire* on 22 December 1872, for example, even caused the paper to be suspended and prompted calls for Zola to be brought to trial. Amongst his "Lettres parisiennes," as his column for *La Cloche* was called, Zola included a number of anti-Bonaparte pieces, including a remarkable satirical scene, published on 25 May 1872, that is set in Chislehurst and in which LUI, planning his return to power after the defeat of Sedan, receives regular reports of a speech in progress in the French Assembly by his stalwart supporter and former minister (in several capacities), Eugène Rouher, to gain concessions from the Republican government. As the telegrams come in and as he meditates upon his fate, smoking cigarette after cigarette, all that is left of his virility, for the cigar or cigarette is coded by the satirists as a symbol of his self-indulgence:[46] "This tobacco is exquisite. Ah! I can see my poor Tuileries in the smoke." All the time he hears the *"croââ, croââ, croââ"* of the crows circling around the house: "It's strange that there are crows in this country. In the Tuileries I had warblers in the greenery." When news of Rouher's failure arrives, the incorrigible voluptary sinks resignedly back into his cosy *"dormeuse":* "I never had one as soft as this in France. Marguerite's skin was not as smooth as this satin. If I were to put my feet higher, on the fireplace. There! too bad, now I'm not going to budge again! . . . I'll smoke a cigarette." Another text (29 May 1872) evokes the major stages of LUI's crimes: Strasbourg, Boulogne, Paris, 2 December, Sedan, and deplores the fact that he still remains free. Elsewhere (10 July 1872), Zola, the Naturalist writer, reflects on a theme that he will take up again much later in *La Débâcle:* the destiny of France hav-

---

46. See Steve Murphy, *Rimbaud et la ménagerie impériale* (Paris-Lyon: Éditions du CNRS–Presses Universitaires de Lyon, 1991), 107.

ing been determined by "the more or less healthy bladder of a man. A physiologist historian would derive a whole system from the fact, a whole scientific explanation." In another article (1 July 1872), he warns against the endless ambitions of the Bonapartes: "A strange family that never dies, which goes on, with its pale and moribund children. They have their ups and downs like adventurers, their pockets empty one day, then safes full of money the next day. They live in palaces, they die on rocks. They mint coins with our blood. And they are still there, at our throats, or at the bottom of some ditch, watching us and ready to jump on our shoulders."[47]

Zola's shafts are relatively mild compared to the caricatures of the satirical press immediately before and after the fall of the regime or to satirical texts by other writers, even by the poets Verlaine and Rimbaud, better known for their more ethereal and esoteric productions, and, even more surprisingly, by Gautier, known for his adhesion to the regime. The association of journalistic satire and poetry is not as surprising as it may at first seem, as we learn, for example, from Steve Murphy's fine book on Rimbaud's early verse, which explores the links between the themes of the young poet's texts and the virulent anti-Bonapartist caricature of the period 1870–1872. Poets, with their veiled and subtle allusions, and journalists, with their more crude and blatant references, combined forces in the vilification of the Bonapartes. Before his stormy liaison with Rimbaud, Verlaine collaborated with the composer Emmanuel Chabrier on two uncompleted comic operas, *Vaucochard et fils 1er* and *Fisch-ton-kan,* both satires of Napoleon III and his dynasty. In the first, a clownish sovereign, *"roi bobêchard,"* pacifies his rebellious subjects by associating them with his prosperous candle-ring factory—a play on words linking *"bobêche"* with Bobêche, a famous comic actor of the First Empire. In the second, a sequel set in China, Napoleon III–Vaucochard–Bobêche provides an opportunity to lampoon the emperor's grotesque appearance. Verlaine also wrote some anti-Bonapartist poems, but this vein was more thoroughly tapped by his "companion," Rimbaud, whose "Recueil Demeny," collected together at the end of 1870, and whose contributions to the *Album zutique,* which belong to the period September 1871 to (roughly) the end of 1872, reveal a republicanism nourished by both a familiarity with and an interest in the spirit and the techniques of the anti-imperial caricature of the time—he did sketches himself—and by a reading of Hugo and Rochefort, trans-

47. Zola, *Oeuvres complètes,* 14: 57–61, 116, 106.

posed into his own characteristic poetic practices. Parodic poems on the birth of the imperial prince, the "son of Mars," combine mockery of the imperial family with political allusions to the reactionary beginnings of the Third Republic. There is a sonnet condemning Bonapartist militarism framed parodicly in the rhetoric of republican propaganda, poems mocking the involvement of the prince imperial in the delusory victory at the battle of Saarbrücken, with familiar sexual connotations for cannonballs and with a parodic spoof on heroic images of the same action, which involved the imperial father and son, and a sonnet evoking the "evil" that prevailed in the subsequent defeats. Amongst other poems, yielding unexpected associations with anti-Bonapartist satirical themes, there is a remarkable sonnet, "Rages de Césars," which recalls Zola's mocking sketch presented above and shows the defeated emperor, a prisoner at Wilhelmshöhe, smoking a cigar, his dull eyes lighting up at the thought of past pleasures, before he lapses into his customary stupor.[48]

Rimbaud's satire, though visual in its effects and trenchant in its charges, represents an oblique form of raillery, requiring a sophisticated process of deciphering to tease out its meanings. The manner of the main anti-Bonapartist caricaturists, such as André Gill, Alfred Le Petit, Faustin, were far less subtle, bringing about a cruel, uncompromising, and systematic abasement of the emperor and his family. The elaborator of the Napoleonic ideal is shown in humiliating circumstances: crushed by Hugo's volume, or playing the joker or the clown, or as a plaything of his mistresses, or limping off the battlefield, or even reduced to his painful bodily operations: holding a syringe and having it inserted into his backside, receiving a symbolic colonic irrigation at the hands of Kaiser Wilhelm, failing in his attempts to urinate. The pious Eugénie is depicted as a war-monger, or as a nymphomaniac in lascivious postures, or shown naked but retaining her devout look to the heavens, or in the company of her lover, Leboeuf, or (supposedly) subject to flatulence, or represented as a camel or a cow. The shy young prince imperial, otherwise known by the republicans as

---

48. See Murphy, *Rimbaud et la ménagerie impériale,* 115, 60, 39–40, 57, 121–23, 105–25. The *Album zutique,* which remained unpublished until 1943, is a collection of irreverent poems and sketches by a group of some twenty rebellious poets and artists who were sympathetic to the Commune and opponents of the Parnassian movement. It consists of 120 pieces—of which Rimbaud contributed 24 and Verlaine 12—usually accompanied by obscene caricatures and drawings and signed in the name of the Parnassian poets that were being parodied, such as Leconte de Lisle, François Coppée, Albert Mérat.

284 / Napoleon III and His Regime

"Charognard," "Scrofuleux IV," *"le Foetus impérial," "le petit Badin-guet," "le petit Loulou,"* is mocked for his premature participation in the war, as a little boy playing with cannonballs, for example, always shown with big ears, depicted receiving his sexual as well as his military initiation.

One of the most striking and systematic examples of such anti-Bona-partist caricature, which uses the timeless satirical method of animalizing its human targets, not only to debase them but also to capture essentially the particularities of their baser human characteristics, is Hadol's *La Ménagerie impériale, composée des ruminants, amphibies, carnivores et autres budgétivores qui ont dévoré la France pendant 20 ans,* which presents a full gallery of satirical portraits of the principal imperial personages, including mistresses and ministers, notably, Marguerite Bellanger as a cat, toying with a rat with Napoleonic moustache and hat; Cassagnac as a porcupine; Ollivier as a snake; Haussmann, of course, as a beaver, trowel in hand; Dr. Conneau as a leech; Joachim Piétri, the prefect of police, as a fly; Persigny as a monkey; Prince Napoleon as a hare (suggesting his cowardice); Mathilde as a sow (for her greed); Pierre Bonaparte as a wild boar, fully armed; the prince imperial, the new Eaglet, as a canary (i.e., *"serin,"* a ninny) riding a bike; Eugénie as a crane (playing on the French word *grue* for a prostitute); and the emperor, not as an eagle, far from it, but as a vulture clutching in its bloody claws the body of a naked woman representing France (see figures 17–19).[49]

The intensity of satirical attacks in the early months of the Republic matched the ferocity with which the opposition press attacked the emperor and his regime during the last months of the Second Empire. Such aggression was clearly a function of the previous repression. The liberalization of the regime and especially its fall in the humiliation of the military defeat, the deprivations of the siege of Paris, and the bloody crushing of the Commune released deep wells of resentment, held in check for so long, gushing forth in an almost carnivalesque spirit of defiance, vilification, reversal, degradation of the fallen tyrant, made vulnerable to all imaginable humiliations. Like the dogs of Compiègne, ravenous and subjugated, the satirists leapt on their quarry, re-enacting their own *"curée."* In the symbolic modes of texts and images it was a violent and ritualistic execution, like the mob hanging Mussolini upside down.

49. For other examples, see the illustrations in Murphy, *Rimbaud et la ménagerie impériale.*

BITTER AFTERMATH

Satire and caricature are themselves unrestrained modes that feed upon excess. By virtue of his origins, his appearance, his bungling failures and his calculated and calculating successes, his political methods, and, above all, his pretensions, Napoleon III provided the satirists of his day with an abundance of material for them to practice their art. It is highly unlikely that the caricaturists and satirists of the Second Empire, whether working circumspectly from within, railing loudly from without, or pouring their vitriol on the fallen sovereign, had much effect on the course of events. But their own excesses did much to counterbalance the extravagances of the regime and its leader, and their images did even more to tarnish the historical image that they had desperately sought to project.

In fact, there is considerable evidence that the satirical baiting of the ex-emperor was prolonged well into the Republic and well after his death. But as the Second Empire began to recede into the past, with its leader dead and buried in England, it became no doubt less a question of settling scores and more a matter of setting the historical record straight, even through the whimsy of satire and caricature. Thus the publication of Hugo's *Histoire d'un crime,* despite the long delay since its composition, was still of topical interest. Hippolyte Magen produced an illustrated *Histoire du Second Empire* (1878), a heavily documented work, written in far more measured tones than his earlier satires, but showing a firm purpose in attempting to undermine the Napoleonic legend and to correct the lies foisted by the regime of Napoleon III on a credulous public. In a much more humorous vein, Touchatout, that is Léon-Charles Bienvenu, produced two volumes of a *Histoire tintamarresque de Napoléon III,* which appeared in 1874 and 1878, having been previously issued in installments. The author had been a typesetter who had become a regular contributor to the satirical journal *Le Tintamarre* in 1865, then co-owner in 1868, and had written a vaudeville, *L'Homme qui veut se faire un nom,* produced at the Déjazet theater in 1866. He had then made a name for himself with the publication of the first volumes of his *Histoire de France tintamarresque revue et mise en désordre,* confirming his reputation as a witty satirist. His entertaining illustrated biography of Napoleon III is clearly to be interpreted as a parody of the illustrated histories and biographies issued during the Second Empire, which showed the emperor in a heroic light. Touchatout's work is a voluminous debunking, but, as the first volume shows, even anti-Bonapartist satire was subject to censorship during the early years of the Third Republic, when *l'Ordre moral* prevailed. The author claims that the real life of the "hero of Sedan," "who put back the national clock by fifty years," is not well known. His history, amply illustrated "to enlighten the masses by a lack of respect for idols," will put this right, subject to the good will of the censors of the Republic.[50]

At the start, the newborn prince is represented as a goose emerging from its shell wearing a crown. His mother sends a telegram *(sic)* to his father, announcing the birth—"Your son, born this morning, healthy, very ugly, legs too short"—to which the king of Holland replies: "If you only knew how little I care" *("Si vous saviez comment cela m'est égal")*. His mother takes care of his education: "You are stupid, my son. Oh well! don't say much; people will take that for profundity." Louis Napoléon presents himself as a republican in theory, since the Republic divides its subjects least, but a monarchy brings in the most money. He teams up with Persigny, Vaudrey, and Mme. Gordon: "Fialin engaged on propaganda in the day and Madame Gordon at night." The Strasbourg coup attempt is presented as a Ubuesque farce, with the prince dressed in an infantry surgeon's pants, a Swiss hat, a Turkish saber, "municipal" boots, and a chain made out of a pair of Mme. Gordon's garters and a Cross of the Commander of the Legion of Honor cut out of a can of sardines by Persigny (see figure 20). He addresses the garrison in his German accent: *"Soltats! . . . che ne fus barlerai pas te moi peaucup; mais fus affez tus gonnu mon ongle! . . . Eh bien! . . . je fiens fers fus pur gontinuer sa clorieuse dratition!"* After another farce, in Boulogne, where he is shown shooting his own grenadier, we see him in Ham receiving the attentions of his mistress, then living it up in London. The wit becomes of necessity less flippant and more acerbic as the story reaches the coup d'état, with biting portraits of the prince's co-conspirators. Thus Saint-Arnaud: "irascible, mocking, brutal, a professional knacker, it was impossible for Louis Napoléon to find a more appropriate man to force the lock of a Constitution." But the tone lightens up again on the topic of the emperor's marriage and his advertisement for a suitable wife: "A MATURE MAN deformed and ugly, but of bad habits, would like to marry a noble, beautiful, virtuous, and distinguished young girl, who could play the piano for him whilst his hairdresser tints his hair, and, every morning, gently squeeze out with her nails the little white pimples that grow around his nostrils." The comedy of his courtship of Eugénie is narrated and the marriage takes place: "The mass was held at the high altar; the chapel of the Virgin being under repair." As the "history" becomes a year-by-year chronicle of events of the Empire's domestic and foreign policies up to 1866, the illustrations suddenly disappear from the volume; evidently Touchatout and his illustrators had strayed into forbidden territory. Nevertheless, Haussmann's "philanthropic" demolitions are mocked, along with the press laws of 1858, and there is a long, satirical development on literary censorship, which clearly had some topical relevance, for it was not unusual for satire of the Second Empire to be used as an indirect comment on the restrictions imposed by the conservative Third Republic in its early years. In fact, the years 1861–1866 are glossed over in twenty pages and the volume ends with a declaration to its readers, announcing that the next volume, *La Dégringolade,* will have to wait to be published because of the restrictions of censorship that have rained down on the author after the publication of installment 60 of the present work.[51]

By 1878, in a more tolerant atmosphere, the second volume appeared, covering the years 1866 to 1872. There are amusing comments on the "tawdry" Universal Exposition, when, Touchatout claims, there were so many foreign dignitaries in Paris that they lined the streets to watch the Parisians go by. There are some wry observations on the Mexican adventure, which ended with two or three dozen cruel executions, "one in Mexico and the rest on the Paris stock exchange." The emperor's amorous escapades are ridiculed, with even the empress's ladies-in-waiting having to tie bits of broken bottles around their garters in case they met him on the stairs. The "liberal Empire" is denounced as a contradiction in terms and the plebiscite as a hoax. Touchatout refuses to describe the battles and the defeats of the war, but satirizes members of the imperial family, such as Mathilde, who, whilst Guillaume was marching on Paris with five hundred cannons, was running away with sixty-two parcels. After the emperor has rendered up to God his last cigarette, there is a clever and prolonged parody of the emperor's will, addressed to his son—"it is indispensable that you never neglect a single opportunity to save France"—with a codicil leaving to Touchatout himself his remaining moustache cosmetics and half a million francs of Mexican shares on condition that he recognize all his

51. *Ibid.,* 19, 36, 83, 109, 136, 303, 430, 439, 799.

illegitimate children, buy a copy of his *Vie de César* and have it illustrated by Hadol, and write the *"tintamarresque"* history of his reign.[52] But the second volume does not have the impact of the first, inevitably so, no doubt, for satire, which needs to be short and incisive, suffers its own *"dégringolade"* when too prolonged. Even more than the previous volume, it lacks the bite and intensity of immediacy. Like many of his contemporaries, Touchatout was already, as it were, flogging a dead horseman.

52. Touchatout [Léon Bienvenu], *La Dégringolade impériale: Seconde Partie de l'Histoire tintamarresque de Napoléon III,* dessins de [drawings by] G. Lafosse (Paris: 1878), 103, 504.

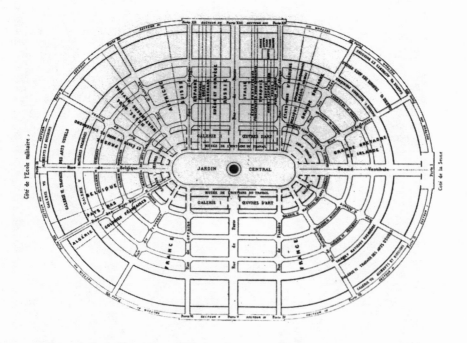

14. Plan of the building for the Universal Exhibition of 1867
Doe Library, University of California at Berkeley

15. *The Empress Eugénie,* portrait by Franz Xavier Winterhalter
Courtesy Metropolitan Museum of Art

16. Ratapoil at a Bonapartist military review, drawing by Daumier
Courtesy Bibliothèque Nationale de France, Paris

17. Napoleon III, "The Vulture," from Hadol's *La Ménagerie impériale*

18. Prince Napoléon, "The Hare,"
from Hadol's *La Ménagerie impériale*

19. Princess Mathilde. "The Sow,"
from Hadol's *La Ménagerie impériale*

20. Louis Napoléon leading his troops in the streets of Strasbourg, from Touchatout's *Histoire tintamarresque de Napoléon III*

21. *La danse,* by Jean-Baptiste Carpeaux

22. A contemporary cartoon: Hugo, author of *Les Châtiments*, striking down
Napoleon III

23. The cover of the anti-Bonapartist publication *Histoire des amours, scandales et libertinages des Bonaparte* shows the emperor and Marguerite Bellanger.

24. Photograph of Napoleon III by Nadar

Courtesy Bibliothèque Nationale de France, Paris

chapter 11

Vaudeville

PALACE OF VARIETIES

"For many Americans today," writes John D. Jump, burlesque is "a kind of variety show with a heavy emphasis upon sex, featuring broad comedians and strip-tease dancers."[1] Much the same could be said to define the Second Empire, at least as far as the leisure activities were concerned among the more privileged circles of the court, of the "*monde*," and of what came to be called the "*demi-monde*." This latter term gained currency from the title of a play by Alexandre Dumas *fils*, *Le Demi-monde*, *comédie en 5 actes en prose*, which opened at the Gymnase-Dramatique on 20 March 1855. The term came to refer in general to the gas-lit boulevard world of highly dubious respectability in Paris, where gentlemen of the higher social orders would rub shoulders, and much more, with women of equally dubious respectability who were not welcome in the "*monde*" proper. In fact, there was much overlap between these social spheres, and they had much in common. They shared, for instance, a passion for show,

1. John D. Jump, *Burlesque* (London: Methuen, 1972), 1.

for dressing up, for titivation and titillation, for transforming serious matters into comic turns, and for offering alluring displays of female flesh.

Entertainment at the court was by all accounts, as we have noted, irretrievably dull for most of the time. There was, however, some dancing, with the emperor deigning awkwardly to turn the handle of the mechanical piano. There was some singing too, but nothing too serious. Gounod sang some Spanish songs which brought tears to the empress's eyes. In a similar vein, Lilly Moulton gave a rendering of some native American airs, resourcefully improvising on "Nelly Bly" when she forgot the words: "Nelly Bly wipes her eye / On her little frock. / Nelly Bly, Nelly Bly / Dick a dick a dock." But the high points of the court entertainment were undoubtedly the costume balls, when the ladies especially could indulge in the prevailing taste for elaborate disguise. At a fancy-dress ball in the Tuileries on 9 February 1863, for example, four women dressed as bees emerged from four huge beehives to dance a tribute to the emperor. On another occasion, early in 1866, the empress appeared (predictably) as Marie-Antoinette, the marquise de Gallifet (bizarrely) as the Archangel Gabriel, and Nieuwerkerke (appropriately in the view of some) as Pontius Pilate. Then there were the charades and, more elaborately, the *tableaux vivants*. On one occasion, Marie-Anne Walewska dressed up as "The Dream of Herculaneum," whilst, on another, the marquise de La Masismas represented Ophelia and was accompanied by a piano medley from the composer Ambroise Thomas, of a new opera called *Hamlet*. Louise de Mercy-Argenteau took to several parts: Queen Philippa of Hainaut asking for the life of the seven citizens of Calais, Mary Stuart leaving France, Joan of Arc at Chinon finding Charles VII amongst his courtiers, and, in a three-tableaux set, Judith made prisoner by the soldiers of Holofernes, meeting him at a banquet, and slaying him amid all the sleeping guests. Clearly history was an inexhaustible source of entertainment, particularly when protection was assured from its rigors. Amateur theatrics also helped to pass the long evenings. "At Compiègne, Fontainebleau, or St.-Cloud," Louise de Mercy-Argenteau writes, "theatricals were indeed the favourite pastime." The empress herself enjoyed dressing up in a variety of costumes and even, once, took part in a play, a work written by the highly successful society novelist and author of light comedies Octave Feuillet, who was a welcome guest at receptions not only at the court but at Morny's and at the salon of Mathilde.[2] This fad for theatrical performances, for costumes

2. Christiansen, *Tales of the New Babylon*, 29–30, 35; Richardson, *La Vie parisienne*, 65–66; Mercy-Argenteau, *The Last Love of an Emperor*, 47, 51.

and disguises may be interpreted in various ways: symbolically perhaps, as a sign of an uncertain identity, economically, as a stimulus to the garment industry, politically, in imitation of the Court of Louis XIV, or merely as pure *divertissement,* purposeful distraction from more political activities.

But even matters of some importance were turned into theater at the court, as on the occasion of the production at Compiègne, in the fall of 1865, of an impromptu show by the marquis de Massa, called *Les Commentaires de César,* in honor, of course, as we have already noted, of the emperor's historical researches and achievements. It was a revue, interestingly, in imitation of the popular theater. The star of the show was the princess de Metternich, with her husband at the piano and Viollet-le-Duc as the prompter. After Julius Caesar had failed to put in an appearance in the prologue, the performance, as planned, turned into a variety show dealing with events of the year. For comic relief, there was a mock circus mule, in imitation of the main attraction of the Champs-Élysées circus and with accessories lent by the director of the Variétés theater. Princess de Metternich sang songs in praise of the empress. There was also a re-enactment of a cordial encounter between French and English squadrons at Plymouth, which gave the prince imperial a role as "The Future." The entertainment was so successful that the emperor granted the author's request to be posted to Mexico "where the war was then raging"! Viel-Castel grumpily and scornfully alludes to the court amusements of a similar occasion at Compiègne, with their "charades and other such nonsense": "Mme. la duchesse de la Pagerie organizes, as she does every year, her *tableaux vivants,* the whole posse play charades, and that restless little monster, Princess de Metternich, amuses the company with her ballet-dancing."[3] Thus, even in the usually staid atmosphere of the court, the spirit of the vaudeville was in evidence, with songs, dances, shows, costumes, a little fairground and circus hilarity, some mythological travesty in the *tableaux vivants,* anecdotes, and even a touch of farce.

The term *vaudeville,* which, in its diverse applications, conveniently sums up many aspects of the diversions of the Second Empire, was supposedly derived from the Val de Vire in Normandy, where Olivier Basselin gained a reputation for comic and satirical drinking songs in the fifteenth century, songs that came to be known as "*vaux-de-vire.*" It was then asso-

3. Legge, *The Comedy and Tragedy of the Second Empire,* 132–33; Viel-Castel, *Mémoires,* 5 December 1863.

ciated with the theater in the early eighteenth century, when "*comédies en vaudeville*" were put on by strolling players, and was linked to the more satirical and "burlesque" parodies of the serious genres. The two terms became associated with the light entertainment of the music hall, with a tendency towards obscene humor and striptease. Satire, risqué comedy, songs, dances, striptease, and minimal plot coherence, remained the recurrent components of these associated popular genres, to which must be added the revue, the plotless, irreverent vignettes and songs about current affairs, the cabaret, and, of particular relevance to the Second Empire, the opérette or opéra bouffe. All were manifestations of the enduring spirit of the carnivalesque and the *esprit gaulois,* in which the denizens of the Second Empire, at least amongst the leisured classes of the capital, found boundless opportunities to indulge.

GAY PARIS

If at times the theater came to the court, more frequently the court, or certain members of the court, went out into the theater and, more generally, to the characteristic diversions that the "*vie de ville*" offered: music and assignations at the Café de Paris or the Café de Bade, performances at the Théâtre Italien, the Bouffes-Parisiens, or the Variétés, a spin at a dance hall like the lavish Bal Mabille, the "Temple of the Cancan," with its gilded mirrors and five thousand gaslights, where admission was three and a half francs and the girls were at different prices. Paris was alive with theaters and addicted to enjoyment. "It was not to every taste, but it was a glorious world of show, tinsel and veneer." The end of the year reviews in particular became a popular tradition, with skits on recent events and parodies of recent plays, with inventive decors and costumes. The Goncourt brothers were less fortunate perhaps in their choice, or lacking the *joie de vivre* necessary to enjoy such a spectacle, as they describe their disappointment at a visit to the Variétés on New Year's Eve in 1860 to see *Oh! là là! qu'c'est bête, tout ça!,* a revue in 3 acts and 22 tableaux by Théodore Coignard and Clairville, which contained a striking "*tableau*" set in a photographer's studio, affording opportunities for scenes of nudity. "The play," they complained in their *Journal,*

> is nothing but a pretext for showing, in each act, the drawing-room
> of a brothel. Nothing but the false modesty of actresses undressed

with a few scissor cuts, short skirts and flimsy bodices. The censors have allowed them to display in *tableaux vivants* all the little obscenities that you find in photographs. Right down to photographs of laundresses, whose breasts you can see, as they iron and bend over, as if you held them in your hands. The director of this exhibition has been decorated. As far as we are concerned, between him and the man who keeps le *Gros 9,* there is not the slightest difference."[4]

The dominant genres in the popular theaters were the melodrama and the vaudeville. The latter consisted of songs and dialogues strung along a loosely woven plot, leading to a rousing chorus as a finale. The audience would heartily join in, for, as the popular saying of the time required, "everything finishes with songs" (*"tout finit par des chansons"*). There were anecdotal vaudevilles, turning on an intriguing event of the past or the present, and more farcical productions, in which parody and satire provided much of the humor. The spirit of the boulevard theater filtered up the generic scale to the opéra bouffe or opérette, which incorporated the songs and irreverent tenor of the café-concert and the vaudeville. Morny, in his varied activities, exemplifies this mobility. The president of the Legislative Assembly moved freely between the corridors of power and the wings of the theater, even dashing off a number of lighthearted plays himself under the pseudonym of M. de Saint-Rémy.[5] It was never at all clear

---

4. Burchell, *Imperial Masquerade*, 10; Goncourt, *Journal,* 31 December 1860.

5. Usually light comedies performed at his own home, at Princesse Mathilde's, or at an official theater, they were brief and witty scenes dealing with rather anodyne sentimental complications in high society, such as *Pas de fumée sans un peu de feu (comédie en un acte),* which turns on a stray love letter causing suspicion and confusion. This play was first put on in Princess Mathilde's salon on 10 April 1864. In general, Morny's plays were works with some sparkle, but little fire, though *M. Choufleuri restera chez lui le . . . ,* which premiered to the public at the Bouffes-Parisiens on 14 September 1861, having been produced for the first time in the salons of the Présidence du Corps Législatif on 31 May of the same year, was a much livelier and wittier work, with revisions to the script by Ludovic Halévy and music by Offenbach. Morny, in fact, was one of Offenbach's most ardent supporters, obtaining for him French citizenship and the Légion d'Honneur. The work is an updated version of Molière's *Le Bourgeois gentilhomme.* Of note is the ballad sung by the *ingénue,* Ernestine, whose father wants her to marry an aristocrat, but who loves a young musician, Babylas Chrysodule, about Pedro's bizarre guitar: *"La guitare enchantée du muletier Pedro"*— *"Qui jusques au fond des familles / S'en va troubler les jeunes filles! / Ding! ding! ding!"* See Williams, *The World of Napoleon III,* 66–68, who notes that this play was produced as recently as 1951 in Paris and quotes Rochefort's ironic review of earlier performances: "How fortunate is this

if the "*demi-monde*" was imitating the court or vice versa, or if the license of the latter was reflected in the licentiousness of the former. Burchell suggests that the world of the "*demi-monde*" was "very much on the model of the imperial court, with an elaborate hierarchy, a loose code of conduct and a frantic interest in clothes and ostentation." Its favorite locales were at the heart of the emperor's utopia, "for the most part near the boulevard des Italiens and including theaters like the Variétés and restaurants like the Maison Doré and the Café Anglais—an area described by Lord Hertford as "*le clitoris de Paris.*" This domain was presided over by the women whose rank was exhibited in the degree of ostentatiousness of their costumes, the expensiveness of the gifts that they received, the status of their protectors, and the extravagance of their *hôtels.* There was some picturesque new vocabulary (or some recycled old vocabulary) applied to them and to the distinctions amongst them, notably, *cocodettes, lionnes, grandes cocottes, grandes horizontales, filles de marbre, amazones, comédiennes, biches, lorettes,* with the term *wagons* (of first and third class), introduced in the early sixties, reflecting the innovations in public "transport" and the joys of travel. As Count Albert de Maugny explains, under the pseudonym Zed, the so-called fashionables, very rich and high-living gentlemen or officers in the Imperial Guard, came to be known as *cocodès* and the beauties that they courted, by association, as *cocodettes,* not to be confused with the more common *cocottes.* As for the last-mentioned term, in his dictionary definition, Pierre Larousse, who, as we have noted, was an opponent of the imperial regime, records that it refers to women kept by "rich idiots bent of destroying themselves," and, on a high moral tone—the dictionary was still at the letter *C* under the Empire—that "this is the age of corruption, and the example comes from on high." By contrast, some years later, Zola, more moralistic and conservative by then than he is often supposed to have been, showed somewhat ambivalently in *Nana* that the corruption ravaging the upper classes came from the streets. Clearly, views on this matter, as on so many other matters, were determined by political convictions. But on the basis of outward appearances, it was not easy to differentiate, as Louise de Mercy-Argenteau affirms, between "the Society *cocodettes* and the *demi-mondaines cocottes,*" for "the former showed a morbid curiosity in all things relating to the latter. They were dressed by

---

author whose participation in a fruitful coup d'état has saved him from the necessity of living by the pen!"

the same dressmakers, their carriages rivaled one another in elegance and style, they patronized the same places of amusement, their jewels were very often paid for by the same generous hand." Even the aristocratic lady herself confesses to venturing out, with two other gentlewomen of the court, to attend a masked ball given by Cora Pearl, anxious to learn "by what contrivances" those "dreadful and fascinating persons" could so easily win over their fathers, brothers, and husbands, but found them "repulsive, silly, and [having inspected the *cabinet de toilette*] dirty."6

Like the buildings created by the regime, the dazzling looks of the most successful courtesans of the age were not always what they seemed, more theater than reality, for, indeed, it was in the theater that they made their entrance into this society, though their talent for the dramatic art, rather than their physical attractions, left much to be desired. Cora Pearl was a case in point. She made a disastrous debut as Cupid in Offenbach's *Orphée aux enfers* in January 1867, despite going on stage almost naked in a costume of blue feathers and diamonds. "After twelve unappreciated appearances," writes Cyril Pearl—no relation!—"she returned to the boudoir where her talents were less in doubt." Her protector, for some seven years in fact, was none other than Plon-Plon, who "often liked a touch of vulgarity in his mistresses" and became her lover in 1866. She was really Emma Crouch, born in Plymouth, and had decided to stay in Paris, with an appropriate change of name, at the age of seventeen, abandoning her lover, William Buckle, who ran a dancing establishment in Covent Garden. She spoke French, it is reported, with a Cockney accent, but neither this nor her lack of refinement were impediments to her rapid rise, which was due to her alluring body, her outrageous stunts, and a string of lovers, including Morny, the Murats *père et fils* and the young prince of Orange, otherwise known as Citron to the boulevardiers. She was not much of an actress, but she could put on a good show. Her memorable performances included dancing a cancan on a carpet of orchids, bathing before her

---

6. Burchell, *Imperial Masquerade,* 74–75; Zed [le comte Albert de Maugny], *Le Demimonde sous le Second Empire: Souvenirs d'un sybarite* (Paris: Ernest Kolb, [1892]), 130; Mercy-Argenteau, *The Last Love of an Emperor,* 23–24. Burchell argues earlier that, "during the years of Louis Napoleon's masquerade," when women were "painted and gilded," and were, first of all, like the furniture and buildings and the palace itself, "objects of decoration and then objects of pleasure," when lust was confused with love and surface beauty was regarded as the ultimate value, "the example was set by the imperial court with its emphasis on outward splendor and its array of beautiful women." Burchell, *Imperial Masquerade,* 62.

guests in champagne in a silver bathtub, and offering herself as the "*plat du jour*," naked, on a silver platter in a large pie. Her mansion, provided by Plon-Plon, was commonly known as Les Petites Tuileries. She survived the fall of the Empire, but was expelled from France in 1872 when she ruined her new lover, Alexandre Duval, who shot himself in her drawing room, evoking her celebrated response: "*Sale cochon, il a foutu mon beau tapis*" ("The filthy pig, he's ruined my lovely carpet"). Thereafter she trailed around Europe before dying of cancer in poverty in a garret in the rue de Bassano.[7]

Cora Pearl's extravagances were only surpassed by those of the legendary La Païva. By birth a Russian Jewess, Thérèse Latchman, she had been briefly married to a Portuguese nobleman, Albino-Francesco de Païva-Araujo, whose name she kept, at least in a simplified version. She was kept in fabulous luxury by a Prussian count, eleven years younger than herself, a man with the rather unromantic name of Guido Henckel von Donnersmarck, a future prince, who had made lots of money in the mining industry. The Hôtel de Païva was a showcase of sumptuousness, the most luxurious private residence of its kind in Paris, famed for its onyx staircase, for its elaborate ceiling created by the academic painter Paul Baudry—who would later decorate the new Opera—with its motif of naked nymphs, including the lady of the household, and her bed which was supposed to have cost 100,000 francs. When she was eventually able to marry Henckel, after the fall of the Empire—he, of course, was conveniently on the opposing side—her wedding present from her triumphant groom, who had watched the Prussians march past from the Hôtel Païva, was, ironically, Eugénie's necklace with three rows of diamonds, which the ex-empress had been obliged to sell.[8]

La Païva seems to have managed rather well without a preliminary stint in the theater, but the stage was the usual launching pad for a career in "*galanterie*." Bernard Briais writes, with considerable enthusiastic overstatement but a fair measure of truth, at least as far as the society of the capital was concerned—though there were certainly fewer high-class courtesans than has often been imagined—that "the whole of France seemed to have become a stage on which a gigantic opéra bouffe was being

7. Cyril Pearl, *The Girl with the Swansdown Seat* (London: Frederick Muller, 1955), 150, 146–47.

8. Burchell, *Imperial Masquerade*, 78; Richardson, *La Vie parisienne*, 71–72.

played." Dancers made less headway than actresses, with a few exceptions, such as Rigolboche, that is, Marguerite Bédel, at the Casino-Cadet and the Prado, and Mogador, that is Céleste Vénard, at the Bal Mabille, who both had lucrative alternative careers. But the household names amongst the *lionnes* were usually actresses, in the tradition of Alice Ozy, whom Victor Hugo had propositioned in verse, but to whom she preferred his son, Charles, even though he was a less expert poet. There was Blanche d'Antigny, who rose through the ranks to star at the Palais-Royal and the Folies-Bouffes theaters, seeking to supplant Hortense Schneider as queen of the opéra bouffe, but fêted as much for her revealing costumes, her sumptuous toilettes, and her lavish lifestyle. Léonide Leblanc, who lit cigarettes with banknotes, counted amongst her admirers the indefatigable Plon-Plon and the duc d'Aumule, Henri d'Orléans, the son of Louis-Philippe. Caroline Letessier, who played in comedies at the Palais-Royal theater in 1855–1858, won the heart of both a nephew of the czar of Russia and the son of the prince of Monaco. Anna Deslions, a sort of working-class empress of the *lionnes,* given her remarkable resemblance, according to some, to Marie-Antoinette, had clients from both the highest ranks and the literary world, as a famous anecdote illustrates, worthy of the vaudeville, when, in a case of double booking, Plon-Plon (at it again) met the vaudevillian Lambert-Thiboust in her staircase and exchanged witticisms.[9] Jane de Tourbey, that is Marie-Jeanne Detourbay, yet another of Plon-Plon's conquests, rose from the ranks of the Théâtre de la Porte-Saint-Martin and earned the affection of the son of the minister of justice, Ernest Baroche, and his fortune in 1870 when he was killed in Le Bourget.

But the grand duchess of them all was, of course, Offenbach's star, Hortense Schneider, whose career was in its zenith with that of the Empire, as her greatest triumph, in *La Grande Duchesse de Gérolstein* at the Variétés, was planned to coincide with the Universal Exposition of 1867. Such was the status of the actress and the confusion of ranks that she is said to have gained admittance to the Exposition through the Porte d'Iéna, which was reserved for royalty. Indeed, royalty flocked to see her performances, though Bismarck seems to have outdone them in the vigor

---

9. Bernard Briais, *Grandes Courtisanes du Second Empire* (Paris: Tallandier, 1981), 10, 203. Briais quotes the staircase exchange: "—To be deceived by a man of wit, said the prince, is nevertheless good fortune. —Dishonored by a prince [*une Altesse*], replied the vaudevillian, is nevertheless an honor" (113).

of his applause. But Hortense received so many crowned heads, or yet-to-be-crowned heads, like the Prince of Wales, into her crowded dressing room and more private quarters that a spiteful rival, Léa Silly, famously dubbed her "*le passage des Princes.*" She was invited along with Offenbach and the Variétés cast by the emperor and the empress to perform at the Tuileries and at Compiègne, for, as Dufresne remarks, "at the time when the liberal Empire replaced the authoritarian empire, many barriers fell, many taboos disappeared. There was a kind of intermixing of the social classes." Indeed, the theater became a melting pot of all ranks and stations and nationalities, a place of adulterated permissiveness, pleasure, and displays, where all distinctions and signs of distinction were effaced, where upright citizens and dignitaries fraternized with glorified *horizontales,* to form a parodic society given over to the great leveler: sex. As the Goncourt brothers wrote in their diary after a visit to the theater: "From the stage to the auditorium, from the wings to the stage, dancers' legs, smiles from actresses, opera-glasses scanning the scene, all this comes together, designating on all sides Pleasure, Orgy, Intrigue. It would be impossible to collect together in less space any more stimulation of appetites, any more invitations to coition. It is the night Stock Exchange of women."[10]

The Goncourts' association of sex and the stock exchange is more than a rhetorical flourish, for the overheated libidos of the "protectors" of the *lionnes* of the Second Empire and their less prestigious sisters went with an overheated economy. Hortense Schneider's dressing room was indeed a microcosm of a society in which titles, in both senses of the term, freely circulated like the women from investor to investor, and speculation went along with the spectacles of wealth and pleasure that they denoted. Zola's "man-eater," Nana, was also a voracious consumer of fortunes in this new hyper-consumerist society. The "note of the flesh" and the "note of gold," as the same author imaginatively summarized the dominant themes of *La Curée* (*The Kill*), the other novel in which he laid bare the extravagances of the Empire, were inextricably linked. There were no social or national boundaries for the patrons of the *demi-mondaines.* Bankers and financiers were as good as government officials and aristocrats, old and new, as long as they could pay. Foreign business was particularly welcome, as clients, ennobled by their birth or by their industry, came to spend their fortunes in Paris: Russian princes, Oriental potentates, South American

10. *Ibid.*, 203, 180; Goncourt, *Journal,* 1 March 1862.

speculators, Hanoverians, Prussians, Dutch flocked to Paris. The rousing chorus at the end of Act I of *La Vie parisienne* sums it up, as a bevy of foreign travelers arrives at a Paris station:

> Here we are, here we come,
> From every country in the world, . . .
> Italians, Brazilians,
> Japanese and Dutchmen,
> Spaniards and Romanians,
> Egyptians and Prussians . . .
> Everyone is running, everyone is rushing,
> To come and taste, O Paris,
> To come and taste the raptures
> Of your days and of your nights.

No doubt because of rhyming difficulties, Americans and English are absent from the list, but they were well represented, big spenders usually from the southern states and the less welcome "sons of Albion," moneyed, titled, and led by Lord Henry Seymour and the reprobate prince of Wales. English fashions was very much *à la mode* in Paris, as were English nannies, like the prince imperial's Miss Shaw, along with English-style clubs such as the Jockey Club, horse races, and more innocent pastimes such as cricket at the Paris Cricket Club in the Bois de Boulogne. A more exotic visitor, Khalil-Bey, an Oriental millionaire with racehorses and English manners, lovingly declared that the whole of Paris was his mistress,[11] no doubt before he lost his fortune, like Daudet's Nabab. Others, more cynically, referred to the city simply as "the brothel of Europe."

The notion that Parisian life under the Second Empire was a continual round of pleasures, as the preceding survey suggests, is largely based upon anecdotal evidence. The anecdote—from *anekdota*, "unpublished things"—which is the staple of the vaudeville, of the revue, indeed of the gossipy and joking genres with which the view of Paris as a den of vice and dissipation is associated, has the distinct disadvantage for the sociologist and the historian of passing off the particular incident as a general trend. The brief account of some piquant event, which supposedly exposes a hidden truth, is easily taken to reveal, not the exceptional and the incidental, but the whole matter. The degree to which the escapades of the *cocottes*

11. See Briais, *Grandes Courtisanes du Second Empire,* 97.

and their keepers reflect a general state of affairs is open to question. In the seventeen years that the Empire lasted, there were undoubtedly infinitely more long spells of dull routine than there were glittering social occasions, more mediocre lives than daring adventures, more drab bourgeois existences and desperate struggles against poverty and destitution—the stuff of Naturalist novels—than displays of finery, even within the confines of Haussmann's new city of light. Yet at its high points, which moralists would consider its low points, the Empire never failed to put on an entertaining show, for all its hollow pretense, for all its fanfaronade and flummery. As one of the pillars of the regime, Count Fleury, famously remarked: "It was not exactly a proper empire, but we had a devil of a good time."[12]

CRINOLINES AND CANCAN

The phenomenon of the crinoline was, and still is, taken to be a token of the Second Empire, not only for its particular style, but as a sign of the intense preoccupation with fashion at that time. In the so-called Age of the Crinoline, Paris supposedly became the fashion center of the world. Magazines and journals duly fed the craze, and as is the natural dynamic of the fashion industry, there was a constant desire for novelty and elaboration. New fabrics and designs regularly emerged, with inventive names redolent not only of the spirit of the age, but of its military achievements, with zouave jackets, garibaldi shirts, the malakoff skirt, dresses in magenta and solferino colors, crimean green. There was even a Bismarck brown, at least before 1870! Elaborateness and bright colors were the order of the day. Gowns were made in rich and heavy fabrics, with a plethora of adornments: flowers, feathers, ribbons, fringes, trimmings of all sorts. Women of all levels of society who had the means to indulge the vogue were affected by the passion for fashion. In *Au Bonheur des Dames,* Zola's novel set in a women's department store, the novelist, typically capturing the obsessive nature of women's relation to fashion in imperial society, describes the compulsively commercial aspect of the new industry, the new merchandising ploys that earned Aristide Boucicaut, among others, a fabulous fortune with their exclusive lines in ladies' fashion wear. The preoccupa-

12. See Burchell, *Imperial Masquerade,* 64.

tion with dress was, like much else at the time, in the mode of excess. Fashionable women changed their outfits several times a day. As Therese Dolan notes, "if aristocratic distinction once belonged to bloodlines and court privilege, it now rested on more overt symbols of wealth." The crinoline itself was traditionally a mode of dress that was essentially aristocratic and became a requirement for those who aspired to that status. Costly, extravagant dress was such a marker of social distinction and success. The ostentation of the crinoline dress, in particular, required large quantities of fine textiles, some seventeen yards for a simple taffeta dress, twice as much for a more elaborate garment. So much material was used for the bottom half of the outfit, as the wits remarked to explain the décolleté, that there was not enough left for the top. The fashion "furnished a feminine code of economic and social rivalry in an industrial society based on male competition and success."[13]

Men's fashions, by contrast, were staid, conventional and functional, only at all elaborate in the colorful waistcoats that they wore. The impractical stovepipe hat was replaced for social occasions by the gibus (or *chapeau claque*), and the man-about-town tended to wear the more racy bowler. Shoes replaced boots, and the more elegant gentleman ordered them from a supplier, named, appropriately, Schumacher. But if men's clothing tended towards the standardization and uniformity of the active gentleman, women's attire, as was usually the case in early capitalist societies, required a greater degree of social differentiation afforded by their decorous social appendages. "Clothes become organized," writes Philippe Perrot, "as significative differences within a code and as status symbols within a hierarchy." But such codes, even in their diversity, can also blur social distinctions, when wealth and beauty are the only requirements and a woman endowed with the latter can gain access, through the right connections, to the former, as in the permissive society of the Second Empire. Thus Maxime du Camp remarked pointedly to the effect: "One does not know nowadays if it's honest women who are dressed like whores or whores who are dressed like honest women."[14]

13. *Ibid.*, 66; Dolan, "The Empress's New Clothes," 27.

14. Allem, *La Vie quotidienne sous le Second Empire,* 136; Philippe Perrot, *Fashioning the Bourgeoisie: A History of Clothing in the Nineteenth Century,* trans. Richard Bienvenu (Princeton: Princeton University Press, 1994), 9; Maxime du Camp quoted in Christiansen, *Tales of the New Babylon,* 83.

Though she had little control over some of the consequences outside court circles, it was usually the empress who set the trends and the styles. She has been credited with introducing the crinoline fashion around 1853, supposedly favoring the voluminous skirt to hide her pregnancy and the accompanying décolleté to show off her bosom to the best advantage. Her influence was not by any means limited to this particular garment. As well as the eighteenth-century styles that she promoted, as we have already seen, she also set trends in hats, both broad-brimmed varieties and a more coquettish plumed creation, known as the Eugénie hat. But she was most widely associated with the fashion for copious skirts draped over hooped petticoats beneath a tightly fitted bodice. *Punch* referred to her as Queen of Fashion, Comtesse de la Crinoline, Goddess of the Bustles, and Impératrice de la Mode.[15] The name *crinoline* derived from the French *crin* ("hair") and the Latin *linum* ("thread"), in reference to the rigid material such as horsehair woven with linen used to support the petticoats. As the skirts became ever larger, steel or whalebone hoops were used to provide the support. By 1856, the steel cage, which had to be lowered down over the woman's body, had been introduced; it gave the characteristic bell-shape to the outline of the outfit.

If it was the empress who was the guiding spirit of the trend, the House of Worth, 7 rue de la Paix, with its Salon de Lumière and its staircase "like Jacob's ladder with an angel on every step," became the temple of the crinoline cult, where Charles Frederick Worth, the high priest of ladies fashion reigned, aided by his acolytes, Miss Mary and Miss Esther, with undisputed authority. He dressed most of the ladies of the court and, of course, always in a different creation. Significantly, he also dressed some of the more affluent courtesans of the era. As one visitor observed: "At Worth's the faubourg Saint-Germain sits between two kept women, and the world of officialdom meets the faubourg Saint-Germain. . . . He is reconciling all political parties, and mingling all social classes. An artistically rumpled bit of fabric has achieved what wit has been unable to contrive." A short, nervous man, Worth would receive his more fortunate clients in his floppy red beret, smoking a cigar, speaking sparingly in halting French with a thick English accent. He was reputedly opposed to crinolines and

15. See Sandra Shannon's article in *Pre-Impressionism, 1860–1861: A Formative Decade in French Art and Culture,* ed. Joseph Armstrong Baird (Davis: University of California at Davis, 1969), 73–74; and Dolan, "The Empress's New Clothes," 23.

sought to undermine the fashion, but this did not prevent him from making a fortune out of designing them. Son of a poor solicitor in Lincolnshire, he had been a draper's apprentice for Swan and Edgar in Piccadilly, London. He became the appointed dressmaker to her highness, having risen to prominence with the help of the patronage of Princess Metternich, a more outspoken opponent of the crinoline, who recommended him to the empress. As his fame increased, so, of course, did his prices, exponentially, to such a degree, in fact, that even the princess complained: "He is expensive, horribly expensive, monstrously expensive."[16]

The crinoline fashion, as fashions go, was remarkably durable, constantly defying reports that it could not endure its inconveniences, and impervious to the scorn that was heaped upon it by caricaturists and wits, who found the hypertrophied form of the skirt a ready-made source of humor. One joker narrated that customs officers at Saint-Lazare station had found fifty partridges in a lady's cage during the off-season. Other wits complained about having to widen the boulevards even further, but roadsweepers, it was claimed, were happy to leave it up to the fashionable ladies to sweep the streets with their skirts. In 1856 Charles Vernier published a whole series of caricatures by such masters of the art as Cham (Amédée de Noé), Félix Nadar, and Daumier called *Crinolinomanie.*[17] *Punch* in England and Daumier in France reveled in comparisons between the crinoline and balloons, with ladies floating in the air, whilst Daumier demonstrated the effects of the craze on the men who had to negotiate the ballooning dresses. Offenbach's librettists were, of course, in on the act. In *La Vie parisienne,* a lady sits next to a gentleman on the canapé and loses sight of him in her skirts. At Compiègne it was maintained that the theater, which had been made to accommodate eight hundred spectators, could only seat five hundred because of the crinolines in the audience. On a more serious note, no doubt, Mérimée warned against the dangers of the skirt catching fire, claiming to have seen a young woman perish in that way. Bac saw in the crinoline, in the masses of muslin, velvet, and taffeta, in which, as a boy, he was condemned to move and vainly seek a comforting hand, a broad significance: "The whole of the Second Empire is

16. On Worth, see Burchell, *Imperial Masquerade,* 67–68. The visitor in question was Joseph Primoli, a nephew of Princess Mathilde; quoted in Richardson, *La Vie parisienne,* 240–41.

17. Dolan, "The Empress's New Clothes," 23, 25.

summed up in that sensation: a series of illusions, a beautiful theater that will go up in flames in a few hours to bury under its ashes all of its plumed frivolity."[18]

But the durability of the fashion, despite such mockery and dangers, suggests that the crinoline had more than a decorative purpose and was related more profoundly to fundamental socio-political factors. Thus, indulging in some imaginative semiotics but not without a ring of truth, Briais suggests that there was a direct relation between the fortunes of the Empire and the size of women's skirts: "As the Empire blossomed, the crinoline also took on a distinct fullness, reaching the height of extravagance when the regime was at the summit of its glory, as if the wind that filled the sails of the good ship prosperity, at the same time inflated the huge skirts, to such good effect that the crinoline has remained one of the symbols of the age." An attractive analogy, but the measure of the cloth was not only equal to the measure of the wealth of the clients or of their husbands and protectors. On the fortunes of the Empire, Louise de Mercy-Argenteau, who was happy to wear the crinoline, held a different view, attributing a political significance to the style, claiming that "the ample, even ridiculously ample skirt has always coincided with the greatest power of woman. In periods of history where woman was all-powerful you find the crinoline." Similarly, Therese Dolan has recently argued that, beneath the "comic veneer" of the lampooning of the impracticalities of the crinoline, "ran a subtext on woman's power and her domination of men. . . . Mastery of space, generally a male prerogative, was visually and psychologically arrogated to the female." But the opposite, and presumably more traditionally feminist view would surely be more compelling. The total impracticality of the dress was surely a form of bondage. One half of the woman was literarily locked in a cage. Sitting, getting into a carriage, traveling, and other normally simple everyday actions became an elaborate operation. Moving in the crinoline was often compared to steering a boat, and much more difficult to maneuver. The woman was reduced to a state of virtual immobility and powerlessness, becoming a creature of mere elegant display, condemned to endeavor at every moment to maintain her composure and to devote the leisure that her role afforded her to doing little else but move about with grace. As a lady of the court later ruefully

18. Dolan, "The Empress's New Clothes," 23, 25; Ferdinand Bac, *Intimités du Second Empire* (Paris: Hachette, 1931–32), 2:1.

and interestingly observed: "To walk with so immense a paraphernalia around one was not very easy; and the narrow bust, placed in the centre of this volume of material, appeared to be detached from the rest of the body altogether."[19]

As Perrot observes, "clothing is ambivalent. It reveals as it veils, and showcases the sexually charged body parts it conceals." Where the crinoline skirt was overly veiled, the décolleté was overly revealing. Bac remarks that the body of the woman became an object split into "two independent versions": "It was the done thing to offer up 'the whole of the first floor' but to hide away 'the ground floor.' "[20] This discreet encasement and this immodest exposure both reduced the woman to an essentially passive, paralyzed, decorous state, as an overblown mannequin, quintessentially feminine in both shape and movement, grotesquely accentuated by the huge swaying skirts and overdetermined female silhouette. Graphically and emphatically, the point is made by the famous Winterhalter composition, *L'Impératrice Eugénie entourée de ses dames du Palais* (1855) (see figure 3), which was placed in the entrance to the Chinese salon at Fontainebleau and was disrespectfully called *Au rendez-vous des grisettes*. Attempts have been made to identify the individual *"dames d'honneur"*[21] in the profusion of elegant colorful costumes and the studied arrangement in the idyllic eighteenth-century landscape setting. But individual identities are a matter of indifference, as the petrified, marbled torsos statuesquely protrude from a sea of undifferentiated fabric.

The crinoline fashion supposedly faded out in 1867, after a vigorous campaign against it,[22] yielding to a flattening of the hoops at the front and a narrowing of the circumference of skirts, which became only ankle-length, hanging straight down at the front, though the back remained bulky with the introduction of the bustle. The empress, by 1867, had turned against the crinoline, either, as has been suggested, because she be-

19. Briais, *Grandes Courtisanes du Second Empire*, 137; Mercy-Argenteau, *The Last Love of an Emperor*, 37; Dolan, "Guise and Dolls: Dis/covering Power, Re/covering Nana," *Nineteenth-Century French Studies* 25 (1998): 377–78; Carette, *My Mistress, the Empress Eugénie*, 173–74.

20. Perrot, *Fashioning the Bourgeoisie*, 12; Bac, *Intimités du Second Empire*, 2:102, 1:198.

21. For a key, see Martinoir, *Mathilde et Eugénie*, 122–23, Kurtz, *The Empress Eugénie*, 62–63.

22. Allem, *La Vie quotidienne sous le Second Empire*, 146–47.

came tired of the extravagances that it involved and evoked or because she was eventually persuaded to set a different trend by Princess Metternich. Or was it that, as she became more actively, more aggressively, more virilely, involved in the affairs of state at this time, with the emperor's powers diminishing, throwing off the crinoline as she stepped into the political breaches, she turned against the most evident symbol of subjugation of her gender?

The crinoline and the cancan, though both characteristic of the Second Empire, are not normally associated, for obvious reasons, but their very incompatibility as both emblems of the era may well be significant. The origins of the cancan have variously been attributed to the *chahut,* a dance observed by soldiers serving in Algeria under the July Monarchy, to traditional fertility gambols in several societies involving high kicking or to a variation of the polka. It had been banned as indecent in Louis-Philippe's time, as it would be in Britain in 1874, by order of the lord chamberlain. It was usually confined to lowly dance halls during the Second Empire, but, in a characteristic promotion of popular cultural forms, found its way onto the stage, particularly when it was incorporated into Offenbach's *Orphée aux enfers.* It was then given prominence as a public performance, conferring on Offenbach and the dance itself, in Cyril Pearl's words, "a joint immortality," for the tune from that play is the one by which the dance is still instantly recognizable and always exemplified. But more generally, the dance itself did not consist, as it has come to be experienced, of lines of leggy chorus girls on the stage, titillating tourists in Paris-by-night locales, but was rather a frantic individual performance, by both men and women, considerably less choreographed than the stage version. It was significantly coded at the time as akin to fiendish possession, drunkenness, and lunacy: "everybody following their own demon," "nothing more than a drunkard's lurching." Mark Twain famously described the scene at the Jardin Mabille:

> The idea of it is to dance as wildly, as noisily, as furiously as you can; expose yourself as much as possible if you are a woman; and kick as high as you can, no matter which sex you belong to. There is no word of exaggeration in this. . . .
>
> . . . Shouts, laughter, furious music, a bewildering chaos of darting and intermingling forms, stormy jerking and snatching of gay dresses, bobbing heads, flying arms, lightening flashes of white

stockinged calves and dainty slippers in the air, and then a grand final rush, riot, a terrific hubbub and a wild stampede! Heavens! Nothing like it has been seen on earth since trembling Tam O'Shanter saw the devil and the witches at their orgies that stormy night in "Alloway's auld haunted kirk."[23]

The cancan may be interpreted, like many more modern dances from, socially and chronologically, the charleston to break dancing, as an anarchical boot in the face of social restraints and conventions of decorum, a liberating release of pent-up libidinal energy. It may be construed also, in a more significant relation to the times, as the converse of the crinoline, substituting uninhibited movement for paralyzing grace, exposing those very parts of the female body that the crinoline veiled and immobilized under layers of fabric and a cage, diverting the voyeuristic gaze from the elegantly sensuous shoulders and breasts to the more carnal private parts, replacing fantasies of seduction with phantasms of copulation. Appropriately ritualized into dance, the cancan was no doubt as close as the Second Empire came to being the frenzied orgy that it was reputed to be.

LE STYLE EMPIRE

The cancan was not the only dance that caused raised eyebrows and mutterings to the effect that it betokened the decadence of the Empire. As the new Opera was constructed, Garnier commissioned a number of sculptors to decorate the facade: Guillaume for *La musique,* Jouffroy for *La poésie lyrique,* Perraud for *Le drame lyrique.* The task of portraying *La danse* (see figure 21) was entrusted to Jean-Baptiste Carpeaux, a young, uneducated but talented artist from a lowly, working-class background in Valenciennes, who had worked his way up by winning the Prix de Rome in 1854, by sculpting a bust of Princess Mathilde in 1862, and by carving a statue of the prince imperial in 1865. When the work was unveiled on 27 July 1869 and showed a group of naked women dancing in gracious ecstasy around the figure of Bacchus, a storm of controversy broke out. According to a modern commentator, who praises the creation, "no previous sculp-

23. Williams, *The World of Napoleon III,* 101; Pearl, *The Girl with the Swansdown Seat,* 220–21; Christiansen, *Tales of the New Babylon,* 61; Mark Twain, *The Innocents Abroad* (London: Century, 1988), 94.

tor had charged inanimate matter with such a paroxysm of joy, such a passion for life. *La danse* remains a perfect symbol of those feverish years, that rush to the abyss which posterity calls *la fête impériale*." But many contemporary observers were less than enthusiastic about the composition, finding it either morally or aesthetically offensive, even resolving to ruin it, as indeed someone attempted to do on the night of 26–27 August by hurling a bottle of black ink at the figures. Art students rallied around to defend the statue from further abuse, chanting anti-bourgeois slogans. The press weighed in, divided on the issue and, a few days after the incident, a warning note was left at the foot of the statue, threatening to smash it up if it were not removed.[24]

There was clearly more to the furor that *La danse* provoked than the offense to bourgeois morality of a public display of nude figures. Naked mythological figures, whatever prurient pleasures they might have secretly stimulated, were, of course, accepted conventions of high art, and the citizenry of Paris did not make a habit of shying away from unclad statues in public places. As Leppert explains: "It is a commonplace that during the Victorian age painting provided a principal and socially sanctioned outlet for representing the otherwise unrepresentable in a society obsessed with the human sexuality it worked so hard to control." Nudes were commonplace in much official art that won honors and approval from the regime with no hint of scandal from the general public. Despite his highly limited interest in painting, the emperor was very fond of Cabanel's art and bought his *Birth of Venus* and *Nymph Abducted by a Faun,* and awarded him the Légion d'Honneur. *The Source* (1856), a standing female nude, a version of the classical Venus Pudica, was another public favorite and was painted by Ingres, who was president of the École des Beaux-Arts. A naked Venus by the same painter was on display in the Ingres installation at the 1855 Universal Exposition, between his *Jeanne d'Arc* and his *Apotheosis of Napoleon I.* Indeed, there is a striking similarity between *La danse* and a later painting by another academic artist, William Bouguereau, *Nymphs and Satyr* (1873), showing four naked nymphs dancing around an unusually submissive satyr and urging him into the water. This well-known painting, which was sold to an American, John Wolfe, in 1873 and which would be reproduced widely in America on ceramic tiles, porcelain plates,

24. Richardson, *La Vie parisienne,* 200; Pinkney, *Napoleon III and the Rebuilding of Paris,* 87; Christiansen, *Tales of the New Babylon,* 58–60.

and cigar boxes, also had an interesting and controversial history. It was praised and defended against adverse criticism, significantly by Garnier himself when it was a question of borrowing it back for display at the 1878 Universal Exposition. It was installed in the Hoffmann House Hotel in New York, to the admiration of such patrons as Joe "Gin" Rickey and Buffalo Bill Cody, and began the vogue in America for the "bar-room nude." A copy of the painting was the object of a publicity stunt in 1960 by Salvador Dali, who offered to produce an alternative and better painting on the same theme to replace it in the Barberry Room in the Berkshire Hotel in New York City. The trade in naked nymphs was both a rewarding and a risky business. The objection at the time to *Nymphs and Satyr* was that the female figures represented were not sufficiently mythological, but were more like high-class courtesans on a romp. One suspects that the boundaries between artistic and realistic representation were similarly perceived to have been breached in the objections against *La danse,* particularly as the context required a certain gravitas. It has been suggested that the sculpture made explicit what many suspected to be during the Second Empire the opera house's unofficial and unadvertised function "as the smartest brothel in Paris." Bac reports the outrage of the empress when she was finally informed, on the basis of police reports, that the theater had been invaded by women of notorious "dissoluteness": "It is a congress of prostitutes." Dancing girls on the facade of the new Opera suggested that the institution functioning in the rue Le Peletier, the old opera house, had become more a place of entertainment than of edification, as did its offerings: love duets, jolly tunes, some flashing sword-play, scenic tableaux, interludes of dance music for the girls to show their paces: "In other words, a bit of this should be followed by a bit of that—and not too much of anything. It was a policy which brought the proceedings closer to the popular tourist vaudeville of 1869, *Paris-Revue*."[25]

In an article entitled "Une Allégorie" published in *La Cloche* on 22 April 1870 and prompted by an official report that the sculpture would be removed, Zola, not surprisingly, gives a more politically motivated interpretation of *La danse*. The opposition journalist impudently explains the

25. Richard Leppert, *Art and the Committed Eye: The Cultural Functions of Imagery* (Boulder, Colo.: Westview Press, 1996), 240–43; Mainardi, *Art and Politics of the Second Empire,* 50–51; *William Bouguereau,* 182–86; Bac, *Intimités du Second Empire,* 1:125; Christiansen, *Tales of the New Babylon,* 66–67.

government decision, not as a gesture to public morality—otherwise the ladies' breasts in the Tuileries would be covered up—nor as a result of pressure from the "pious folk of Paris"—who, in any case, sneak out by moonlight to have a peep at "the lovely merry women"—but simply because, as the title of his article suggests, the statue represents the Empire itself, a violent satire of the imperial dance, with women up for sale and men up for bribery: "On this ridiculous and pretentious facade of the new Opera, in the middle of this hybrid architecture, with its shamefully vulgar Napoléon III style, the true symbol of the regime bursts forth." Suddenly, amongst the dull, cold, chaste, and stiff columns of the monument, by which, "to deceive history," the Empire hides "its hot nights under its cheap and crude daubs," there appears this revelation, as if a senator stripped off to reveal his scars or a minister danced the cancan at an official reception. "Sometimes art," Zola sententiously adds, "has its unconscious cries of truth." He is amazed that M. Carpeaux is on such good terms with the Empire, particularly in view of the significance of this work, for, in Zola's interpretation, the gentleman who has taken off his shirt in the sculpture is none other than the poetical personification of Napoleon III himself, celebrating at a ball in the Tuileries his victory of 2 December, whilst the "goddesses," he claims, are "the deified images of certain highborn ladies whom respect prevents me from naming."[26]

The statue, then, is an invitation to dance issued by "the god of pleasures," now that the blood has been washed off the streets, and the women, casting off their clothes and their shame, have responded to the call "like drunken bacchantes." For eighteen years now, Zola goes on, the tambourine (*"tambour de basque"*) has been leading the merry dance. Then just as the dance is slowing down, as the god grows old and tired, along comes M. Carpeaux, naively, with this "hostile allegory that posterity will name without any doubt the 'pleasures of the Second Empire.' " The government, of course, immediately appreciated the revolutionary meaning of the composition, but did not wish to show indecent haste in removing it in case its message became clear. But M. Ollivier (the government leader spearheading the reforms of the "Liberal Empire") has not only caught on to the seditious message of *La danse*, but, acquiring the novelist's own sensitivity to the significance of stains, sees the ink stain as a reminder of the "bloodstain of the Empire" of 4 December. Zola ends

26. Zola, *Oeuvres complètes*, 13: 278–79.

by suggesting that Monsieur Carpeaux has just enough time to catch the next train to Brussels![27]

Zola's article reveals that he had clearly been reading at this time a little too much Victor Hugo, as he was later to acknowledge. But it is also interesting for the incidental comments of Zola, the art critic, defender of Manet and opponent of *pompier* art, on what he calls "this Napoleon III style," exemplified by the Opera, with its "false brilliance," its "pompous banality," its "grotesque eclecticism." The Opera itself is a remarkable example of the Imperial manner and its passion for elaborateness and excesses. "What style is that?" Eugénie is said to have remarked impatiently on seeing Garnier's plans. "That's no style—not Greek, not Louis XVI, not even Louis XV." "Madame, those styles were for those times," he replied. "This is the style for the time of Napoleon III."[28] It was, indeed, appropriate for the times, grandiose in its conception: a grand foyer staircase, with marble steps and handrails of onyx, an enormous stage, ceilings decorated with mythological scenes, a legacy of the Empire to the new regime, when it opened in 1875.

The official doctrine of the regime in artistic matters, as in its political and social policies, was eclecticism, happily accommodating a variety of styles as long as they had the desired effect of creating a dazzling display. Like the political philosophy of Bonapartism born out of the need to reconcile elements of the ancien regime, the First Empire, and certain democratic ideals inspired by the Revolution, an equivalent attempt was made in the artistic field, as Adolphe Thiers explained, to combine "the qualities of different schools into a harmonious ensemble," inspired by the belief of Victor Cousin, the philosopher of eclecticism, that "every one of the Schools represents, in some manner, some aspect of the Beautiful."[29] By appropriating the best of a variety of trends and combining them into a single style, universal beauty and artistic supremacy, it was believed, could be attained, as was appropriate to the new age.

In less utopian terms, we might suggest that the fundamental characteristic of the Imperial style was the lack of any characteristic style. We have already observed the degree to which the architects reworked antique

27. *Ibid.*, 13:280–81.
28. *Ibid.*, 281; Eugénie quoted in Christiansen, *Tales of the New Babylon*, 394.
29. Quoted by Mainardi, *Art and Politics of the Second Empire*, 69, from *La Grande Encyclopédie* and from Victor Cousin, *Du Vrai, du beau et du bien* (Paris: Didier, 1854), 206.

styles for the monuments of the era, adding their characteristic panache. The owners and designers of the *hôtels privés* similarly valued style itself, rather than any particular manner. They proudly flaunted their ornate ironwork, their caryatids, their statuary, and their marble interiors. Some of the more sophisticated dwellings, in deference to Eugénie, adopted aspects of the Louis XVI–Impératrice style in furniture, effectively designed by Georges Grohé. But usually, more variety was sought. Here there might be a pseudo-Gothic hallway, over there an imitation Louis XIV salon; up there a Louis XV bedroom, through there a Henry II dining room; there was also likely to be a rococo salon or bedroom.[30] Such a composite of several styles was abetted by improved manufacturing technology, which could reproduce an assortment of furniture and household decorations, if not yet on a mass scale, at least in quantities and variety sufficient to adorn the homes of a large section of the better-off members of society, just as the crafts of the goldsmith and the silversmith had become more mechanized, with plated metals, pseudo-silver, gilt moldings allowing the upper middle classes, with not too much of an investment, to dine in not quite real style. "The bewildering eclecticism of the time was accepted without question by the rich bourgeois, since it corresponded entirely with his own views on art and decoration." Interiors would bulge with paintings in Classical styles, pseudo-Gobelin tapestries, neo-Greek friezes, imitation period furniture, from several periods, furniture decorated with silver, bronze, mother-of-pearl, creating, particularly with the familiar heavy upholstery, the overly stuffed effect. Oriental designs were much sought after. Excessively sumptuous patterns went with decorations that, above all, emphasized all that glistens and shines: marble, onyx, crystal, with gold leaf adorning ceilings, walls, and mirrors. The total effect was one of unwieldy sumptuousness. Thus the furniture of the Second Empire, as Richardson notes, "ended, as it had begun, in pastiche and copy, and this was a confession of failure," pleasing a "*nouveau riche* society which was enamoured of luxury and comfort, and anxious, above all, to create effect."[31]

30. According to Richardson, "the rococo is the real furnishing style of the Second Empire. It reached its peak in about 1860; it still existed in the first years of the Third Republic. It was a homogeneous style, and perfectly adapted to everyday life." Richardson, *La Vie parisienne*, 231.

31. Burchell, *Imperial Masquerade*, 193–94; Richardson, *Le Vie parisienne*, 231.

If there was no prevailing style, there were certainly common tendencies, even a shared dynamic of imitation, profusion, and ostentation, with little concern for authenticity. "Imitation was a normal feature of Second Empire life," as Burchell writes. "Little was real, and little was what it appeared to be on the surface." This process, like any form of sensationalism created to impress, needed to be taken to excess to maintain its theatrical effect. The art which thrives on such theatricality, on creating illusion and perpetual novelty, on constantly inventing new combinations, ever forcing its effects, privileging multiplicity, the monumental, the erotic, the grandiose, is the baroque, whose primary characteristic, whose "genius," as Genette notes, is "syncretism": "its essential nature is openness, its distinctive attribute is to have nothing distinctive about it and to push to their extreme characteristics which are, indiscriminately, from all places and all times."[32] Less as a conscious borrowing than as an irresistible development, the dominant mode or manner of Second Empire art, at least in its extreme manifestations, emerges as a kind of second-degree, low baroque, as a burlesque, parodic, strident, strutting version of that delicate but no less ostentatious art which bears in its distinction the traces of its own extinction.

The ultimate expression of this voluptuous, extravagant art in its decadent manifestations was found in the courtesan's boudoir and in her "pièce de (non)résistance," the bed, like Nana's final "caprice," her "sanctuary," described towards the end of Zola's novel, with its own borrowings from "authentic" sources.

The new bedroom was glittering with an opulence that was truly royal. The velvet drapes, flesh-coloured like the tea-rose pink sky on fine evenings when Venus is gleaming against the soft glow of the setting sun on the horizon, were dotted with the bright stars of silver buttons, while the barley-sugar gilt mouldings descending from each corner and the gold lace round the central panels seemed like darting flames, tresses of red hair floating loose, half-veiling the stark simplicity of the room and emphasizing its voluptuous cool tints. Opposite stood the gold and silver bed with its glittering new carvings, a throne fit to display the royal beauty of her naked limbs, an altar Byzantine in its luxury, a worthy setting for the irresistible

32. Burchell, *Imperial Masquerade,* 196; Gérard Genette, *Figures II: Essais* (Paris: Seuil, 1969), 222.

power of the curved slit of her sex, which she was flaunting shamelessly with the divine arrogance of some awe-inspiring idol.

This baroque creation, in which silver, gold, and draperies become stars,
flames, and flesh, and where the lusty and the wealthy come to join in *la
danse*—slang for lovemaking—is a fleeting monument to the excesses of
an age which sought fulfillment in shows, thrills, illusions. It is a reminder,
too, like one of La Païva's beds, on which it is based, which was in the
shape of a huge shell pulled by four swans, with a siren at the head, that
the Second Empire invented, before the word was coined to describe
it—in fact, in the year of the regime's demise (1870)—kitsch. Little wonder that Bismarck could observe of it, whilst plotting the disappearance of
this age of gaudy surfaces, of dazzling splendor, of restless indulgence, of
deceptive appearances, of theatrical illusions and fugitive visions: "From a
distance it's stunning. When you get closer, however, there's nothing
there at all."[33]

LA VIE PARISIENNE

There is a certain appropriateness in the fact that only the outer shell of
the new Opera house was completed during the Second Empire, during a
reign, as we have seen, with such a taste for shiny facades. Much the same
could be said of the genre of the opéra bouffe, which Offenbach perfected.

Jacob Offenbachen (1819–1880), whose father, Isaac Eberst, alias Offenbacher, had changed the family name to Offenbach when moving from
Offenbach am Main to Cologne in 1802, was taken to Paris with his
brother, Julius, to pursue a musical career in 1833. Now called Jacques,
the talented cellist studied briefly at the Conservatory, played in the orchestra at the Opéra-Comique, composed waltzes there for a while before
launching out as an independent performer on the salon circuit and in the
boulevard theaters, with ambitions to write light comedy of his own, but
struggling for several years (figuratively) to make a name for himself. In
1850 he was engaged by Arsène Houssaye as musical director and conduc-
tor at the Théâtre Français. But as if needing to wait for the right climate

33. Émile Zola, *Nana*, trans. Douglas Parmée (Oxford–New York: Oxford University
Press, 1992), 400; Briais, *Grandes Courtisanes du Second Empire*, 146; Burchell, *Imperial
Masquerade*, 21.

to appear in which his art could fully flourish, during a five-year period he nevertheless drew inspiration from the success of Florimond Ronger, otherwise known as Hervé, his counterpart at the Palais-Royal theater, to whom is attributed the honor of having created the genre of the operetta, a genre that, in Zed's words, "is superlatively light, spicy, and rebellious, born of an ultra-refined civilization, marvelously adapted to Parisian society of the time" and to Offenbach's genius.[34] On the strength of the success of his one-act comic operas at the Palais-Royal theater, he acquired his own stage, the Bouffes-Parisiens, in 1855, the year of the International Exhibition. With Ludovic Halévy as his librettist and Hortense Schneider as his star, three careers were launched at the Bouffes-Parisiens. *Ba-ta-clan, chinoiserie musicale,* which opened on 29 December 1855 in larger premises with a libretto written entirely by Halévy, was an instant success, parodying the grand opera style of Meyerbeer, who good-humoredly attended, as did Morny on frequent occasions. In June 1856, Offenbach performed *Les Dragées de baptême* in honor of the christening of the prince imperial and was invited to present *Les Deux Aveugles* at the Tuileries later that year.

But despite his prodigious industry and growing reputation, Offenbach was an infinitely better musician than businessman. Plagued by debts, he needed a major success and a major work to survive. *Orphée aux enfers* (*Orpheus in Hades*), which opened on 21 October 1858, conveniently provided it, but only when a leading critic, none other than the so-called Prince of Critics, Jules Janin, even more conveniently six weeks later, did him the inestimable favor of thoroughly denouncing the work's profanation of antiquity in the *Journal des Débats,* thereby ensuring its box-office triumph (even without Hortense Schneider) and a run of 228 performances. In 1860, Offenbach collaborated with Halévy and Hector Crémieux on Morny's *M. Choufleuri restera chez lui le . . .* and had a ballet performed at the Opera, *Le Papillon,* which ran to 42 performances and thoroughly pleased the emperor. In 1862 he wrote a hymn "God Save the Emperor," which would haunt him after the fall of the Empire. With the addition of an old school friend of Halévy, Henri Meilhac, to work on the libretto—and a little help from Morny—the tried formula of an operetta on a mythological theme was repeated, bringing about a further resounding success in the shape of *La Belle Hélène*. With Hortense

34. Zed, *Le Demi-monde sous le Second Empire,* 175.

Schneider as the star, the new work opened at the Variétés on 17 December 1864. It was the first of three stunning successes which brought Offenbach international fame (or notoriety). *La Vie parisienne* (libretto by Meilhac and Halévy), with its contemporary setting, was no less a success than the mythological works, to its creator's surprise. It opened at the Palais-Royal on 24 June 1866 and had a run of almost 200 performances. Seizing an opportunity for even more publicity, Offenbach and his collaborators put on at the Variétés, from 12 April 1867, *La Grande Duchesse de Gérolstein* to coincide with the next Paris Exposition. For the crowned heads and lesser mortals who flocked to see this lighthearted satire of an absurd German principality, it was more of an attraction than the exhibits. For a figure whose career of remarkable productivity seemed to adumbrate the rise and fall of the Second Empire and whose spirit of levity seemed to epitomize the frivolity of *"la vie parisienne"* during the period, a military farce was a fitting climax. The Prussian victory at Sadowa had already occurred. Bismarck had taken time off from plotting the Empire's downfall to enjoy the farce and, as François Mauriac would later remark, the mad laughter of Charlotte of Mexico could be heard behind *La Grande Duchesse de Gérolstein*.[35] Though he was still to produce his masterpiece of fantasy opera, *Les Contes d'Hoffmann,* which he would never see performed—he died on 5 October 1880, four months before it opened at the Opéra Comique on 10 February 1881—the upheavals of the war and the Commune, the ferocious rejection of the Empire and all that it represented at the beginning of the Third Republic, the regime of *l'Ordre moral* were not conducive to light opera. He was, furthermore, doubly suspect for his German origins and his Bonapartist affiliations. Despite some moderate successes, particularly in America, overcome by illness and debts, his dazzling performance was virtually over.

Offenbach's opéra bouffe does present a problem of interpretation, and it has often been construed as a satirical commentary on the Second Empire under the veil of light humor. To view it as at all subversive in intention, however, requires as much ingenuity as Zola showed in interpreting *La danse* in such a light. The adulterous escapades of the gods of Mount Olympus in *Orphée aux enfers* could be said by a stretch of the imagination to reflect such goings-on in the emperor's court. But the revolt of the gods against Jupiter—*"Aux armes, dieux et demi-dieux! / Abattons cette tyran-*

---

35. Burchell, *Imperial Masquerade,* 278.

nie" ("To arms, gods and demigods! / Let us bring down this tyranny")—which is about boredom and their diet of nectar and ambrosia and is easily assuaged by the prospect of an entertaining trip to hell, hardly constitutes a revolutionary appeal to the enemies of the French emperor! Unless depicting adultery amongst the ancient Greeks is considered a questioning of the status quo, the critic would be even more tested to find a seditious message in *La Belle Hélène*, which tells in light tones the old story of the abduction by Paris of the far-from-unwilling Helen of Troy. These works direct their humorous effects far more at other musical, artistic, and literary works in a spirit of travesty and parody of grand opera, grand art, and grand literature than at contemporary realities. Like the Swedish Baron de Gondremarck in *La Vie parisienne*, the audience came to be entertained, not enlightened, and certainly not to be confronted with disturbing political issues:

> I should like to go to some theaters,
> Not those where you get bored to death,
> But those where skittish actresses
> Display countless perfections to your gaze. (Act I)

Though more than a little impertinent, Offenbach's operettas were not perceived as being subversive by the regime. They were subject to the scrutiny of the censor and met the standards of permissiveness that were applied to such works. Their composer enjoyed Morny's protection and access to imperial favor. Like Morny, Offenbach acted as a conduit between the court, the "*monde*," and the "*demi-monde*." With his eccentric appearance and manners, with his displays of wit, he fulfilled a role, as has often been said, equivalent to the court jester, whose impertinences were tolerated. If anything, he also fulfilled for the regime the useful purpose of distracting the public from more serious political matters and of creating a euphoria that was conducive to a cheerful acceptance of the prevailing order. The apolitical themes, the distancing effect from contemporary realities of the mythology and the music, the formalized permissiveness that the theater allowed, all created a conscience-numbing impact that far outweighed the force of any critical components of the mockery. Scruples would be spirited away in the infectious gaiety of the show.

This is not to say that Offenbach's works are without a far-reaching implicit political relevance. Far from fostering political awareness, they do the opposite, promoting a debonair insouciance with regard to social and economic realities. The opéra bouffe, as *La Vie parisienne* in particular shows, condones and confirms the self-congratulatory, fantasized ideology of the regime. It fuels its delusions of inviolability. It idealizes an economy of reckless spending and validates the irresponsible ethos of the fortunate few free-spending men and free-loving women who keep the dizzy round of pleasures "turning, turning, turning." It places a premium on vanity and capricious sexuality, presenting society as no more than an arena for an endless bout of flirtation and sentimental escapades, like a vaudeville farce. It valorizes levity as a universal attitude and wit as an appropriate response to all situations. It exalts the pursuit of pleasure as the source of happiness; "Yes, such is Parisian life," exclaims Métella at the end of the work, with great insistence. "Endless pleasure and enjoyment! / Yes, such is Parisian life, / There it is, there it is, there is happiness." It presents technological progress as merely a means to facilitate pleasurable indulgence. Just as there is sex without any of the encumbering realities, its jaunty military airs promote a militarism that is mere spectacle, divorced from an awareness of the slaughter of war. The droves of funny foreigners, arriving en masse to spend their fortunes in "the sovereign city," confirm the nationalist conviction that Paris, posturing as France, is the very hub of civilized values. Most significantly too, there is the extraordinary belief in the unaccountability of hedonism. But above all, Offenbach's world fosters the illusion that life itself is a theater and that *la vie parisienne* is the reality of Parisian life.

The opposition press did not hesitate to blame the emperor for the more disreputable activities of this "*vie parisienne.*" Louis Veuillot, for example, the Catholic editor of the clerical *L'Univers,* in an article on 11 November 1870, even blamed him for causing the downfall of the country by saturating it with pomp and lasciviousness and by teaching it to enjoy "the vaudeville, the café-chantant, obscene dancing." For Hugo and company, of course, he personally directed the orgies in the Tuileries and at Compiègne, transforming Paris into a modern Sodom and Gomorrah. But there is, in fact, little evidence that he participated in the more animated excesses of the regime. Viel-Castel claimed that the emperor was the only "decent man" ("*homme comme il faut*") at the court, the only man with true dignity.[36] Startling as the suggestion may seem, he should largely be excluded from *la fête impériale.* By the time he became emperor, he had

36. According to Bac, *Intimités du Second Empire,* 1:236.

lost most of the debonair spirit of his youth and, in a posture similar to his role in the coup d'état, seemed to leave it to his half-brother and his ilk to orchestrate and participate in the more vigorous intemperate diversions of his reign. His hedonism was, as we have seen, much more discreet. In any case, the watchword of the regime for both the emperor and those he ruled, in their different ways, was neatly and simply summed up by Jupin in *Orphée aux enfers:* "Let's keep up appearances, at least, let's keep up appearances, that's all that matters" (Act II).

chapter 12

Fictions

Napoleon III in literature

We have dealt so far at some considerable length with what literary critics call the literariness of historical texts as they relate to Napoleon III, attempting to demonstrate that the bounds between purportedly objective accounts and literary creations are not as clear as they are often taken to be. Thus, to reverse the process and look at overtly literary evocations of Louis Napoléon is not entirely a matter of idle curiosity, for literary texts do create or more usually perpetuate representations of historical figures, images which determine our understanding just as much as those found in conventional historical works.

The Second Empire was not conducive to the free flowering of French literature nor to the establishment of harmonious relations between writers and the government. There was a climate of both moral and political censorship and control which not only banned overt political criticism, but inhibited free expression. A number of major writers fell foul of the authorities. Famously Flaubert and the Goncourt brothers had to defend their works before the courts. Baudelaire had to pay a 350-franc fine and expunge some of the more daring of his *Fleurs du mal.* To obtain official favor, literature had to be apolitical or political in the right direction, whilst opposition had to remain heavily disguised or express itself in an unpublished form, for example, in discussion in the republican cafés such as the Café de Madrid, in songs in more popular meeting places, or in lectures in educational institutions.[1] It was not a time for the representation of anything less than flattering portraits of the emperor. As was the case with historical works or light opera, literary texts had to maintain a respectful distance of exotic indirection to gain acceptance. Some official patronage also helped to avoid friction with the sensibilities of the authorities. The novelist Arsène Houssaye, who seemed to enjoy a certain amount of latitude, was a case in point. He was a celebrated man-about-town, a successful director of the Comédie-Française, an associate of Morny, an indefatigable author of popular fiction and of trendy novels that chronicled the intersections between the *"monde"* and the *"demi-monde,"* presenting a whole compendium of adulterous relations and dalliances between fashionable courtesans and wealthy playboys in the *"beau monde."* This boulevard Balzac managed to escape official censure by larding his descriptions of vice with moralistic discourse on virtue, thereby making gestures of acquiescence to official morality, which the aesthetically more scrupulous writers were not prepared to make. However, he did produce, as Maurois demonstrates, a rather daring allegory on the imperial marriage in the manner of a Chinese fable, in which the son of Heaven, who is "fond of women," is torn between "an ancient mistress" (like Miss Howard) and "an extremely beautiful creature who had come from a northern country" (like Eugénie from the opposite direction), reputedly an adventuress like her mother, and whose marriage plans are abetted by an Academician (like Mérimée).[2] But as we have noted, the court had a tolerant attitude to situational satire, as long as it was suitably veiled or masqueraded as something else.

But the fact that there are no significant realistic portrayals of Napoleon III by the major writers of the Second Empire, or indeed thereafter, can-

---

1. See Anne Roche, "L'opposition au Second Empire dans quelques-unes de ses expressions et représentations littéraires," *Revue d'Histoire littéraire de la France* 74 (1974):33–35, who notes that there was a body of officially sanctioned literature, notably plays by Sardou and Augier and stories by the comtesse de Ségur, which presented republican and legitimist opponents in an unfavorable light.

2. Maurois, *Miss Howard and the Emperor,* 74–76.

not be solely attributed to the efficacy of the imperial censorship. It is as if the leading novelists of the age sensed that, whereas the society of the Second Empire was a mine of fictional themes, the emperor himself was too elusive a figure to portray at all convincingly without lapsing into polemics or propaganda, like Hugo. Napoleon III was, in a sense, for the scrupulous realist, at the confines of the unrepresentable. Certain unwritten novels seem to confirm this suggestion. Between 1875 and the time of his death in 1880, there was Flaubert's, for example. Despite the shock of the official reception of *Madame Bovary* and his natural political skepticism, he was on the whole favorably disposed towards the Second Empire, which decorated him, saw him invited to the Tuileries, and had him as a regular guest to Princess Mathilde's salon. He later planned to write, and produced extensive preparatory notes for, a novel which he proposed to call *Sous Napoléon III*, for he regretted having completed *L'Éducation sentimentale* too soon and would have liked to produce a sequel. One episode, which he saw as the logical denouement of the work, would have depicted the defeated emperor at Sedan with his soldiers hurling insults at him—a scene that Zola would take up when he came to write *La Débâcle*. But it is clear from the preparatory notes that the future novel would have focused far more on the society of the Second Empire than on its politics, and very little on its leader.[3]

Even Zola, as he later acknowledged, did not do justice to the character, partly because of his lack of direct experience of the emperor, though that was never a deterrent for the documentary practices of a supposed "experimental novelist" in other areas. The emperor does, of course, figure in a number of the *Rougon-Macquart* novels, but significantly only in three of the twenty novels of the series does he appear directly: in *La Curée* (*The Kill*—1872), *Son Excellence Eugène Rougon* (1876), and *La Débâcle* (1892). Even there he is presented almost invariably "focalized" as other characters see him, either at a distance or in some distancing perspective. In *La Curée*, as we saw, he is not very imperial, merely the man with the lecherous look at the reception in the Tuileries (Chapter 3) and later in a brief appearance in the Bois de Boulogne at the end of the novel (Chapter

---

3. See, on Flaubert's plans for this work, Durry, *Flaubert et ses projets inédits*, 254–55. On Flaubert's attitudes to the Second Empire, which exercised Sartre, see also Hazel E. Barnes, *Sartre and Flaubert* (Chicago and London: University of Chicago Press, 1981), 297–300.

7) as an "apparition" to the distraught heroine of the work, Renée. In *La Débâcle* he appears eight times, but, as we shall later see, he is little more than a shadowy, pathetic figure, more symbolically inactive than alive as a real character, as he contemplates the ruins of his army and his regime. In Zola's most political novel, *Son Excellence Eugène Rougon,* the emperor does play a more prominent part. But he only appears as a remote figure in the public spectacle of the baptism of the prince imperial (Chapter 4) and at the reception at Compiègne (Chapter 7). Even when he is shown presiding over a meeting of the Conseil des Ministres (Chapter 11), he appears detached from the proceedings, with his "vague looks" and his "dull expression," barely saying a word, lost in thought. He is a little more animated in his discussion with Rougon at the end of the same chapter, revealing his love of political intrigues, but, in the lunch that follows, at which he does nothing but ogle Clorinde—who is based on la Castiglione—he is returned to the lecherous image of himself. Rather than a character, then, with any degree of human presence, depth, or complexity, Zola's emperor is a mere spectacle, a walking monument, impenetrable, silent, elusive. In other texts he is simply alluded to in a character's discourse, usually in disobliging terms as a womanizer and sometimes even then, at a secondary degree of indirectness, by reference to some article or a book.[4]

Thus, in *L'Assommoir,* the workers pass around an illustrated pamphlet, *Les Amours de Napoléon III,* in which the emperor is said to have seduced a thirteen-year-old kitchen wench and is shown with bare legs and his "Legion of Honor sash." In the second chapter of *Le Ventre de Paris,* Gavard, who has turned against the emperor after supporting the coup d'état, evokes the nightly orgies in the Tuileries. Only Nana, who is a great supporter of the Empire, which is good for her business, seems to have a good word to say for the emperor: "Weren't people all happy, hadn't the Emperor done everything possible for the lower classes? What scum they were! It'd be a disaster for everybody, that Republic of theirs! May God preserve our Emperor as long as possible!" Indeed, as Descotes remarks, "in the *Rougon-Macquart,* there is only one area in which the authority of the Emperor is without limits: the world of debauchery, of pleasure, the

4. See Philippe Hamon, *Le Personnel du roman: Le système des personnages dans les "Rougon-Macquart" d'Émile Zola* (Geneva: Droz, 1983), 61–62.

empire of womanizing and of the brothel—the realm of Nana."[5] When Zola was planning *Son Excellence Eugène Rougon,* he decided to divide his study of political life under the Second Empire into two novels, the first, that is *Son Excellence Eugène Rougon* itself, dealing with the period of the authoritarian Empire, from 1852 to 1860, the second covering the period from the liberal reforms of 1860 to Ollivier's ministry in 1870, a novel which would certainly have necessitated giving the emperor a greater presence and more visibility. But, as Zola's plans and priorities changed over the years, he failed to write this second political novel, not for any lack of familiarity with the issues involved, many of which he had dealt with as an opposition journalist. He wrote instead his military novel, *La Débâcle,* in which Napoleon III could more easily be assigned a symbolic role.

Certain writers belonging to later periods and to different cultures have understandably been less reluctant to attempt to represent Napoleon III more fully in their works, as the sample of texts presented below will show. Others, as we shall also see, merely perpetuate the inherited stereotypes, but in interesting ways. The claim is not, by any means, that this variegated corpus is at all comprehensive, for, as is quite natural, these largely minor works, mostly written by less celebrated writers, tend only to resurface to the reader's attention, after the period of their publication or performance, by a process of chance encounters. A more thorough, systematic, and lengthy trawling of the literary archives would no doubt bring several others to light. But this sampling of literary representations of Napoleon III, ranging from the rhapsodic to the sardonic, does offer valuable insights into the ways in which the historical figure has been perceived, in addition to the historians' interpretations. If it adds nothing to our factual knowledge of the historical figure's career, for in these works the facts are often distorted, it does add considerably and vividly to our understanding of the images of the emperor that were fabricated out of the materials of the past and conveyed down to posterity. Even on the basis of such a few texts, we are confronted with, in a variety of genres, an extraordinarily multi-faceted picture of the emperor, which goes a long way to demonstrating why his historical image is yet to be fixed.

5. Émile Zola, *L'Assommoir,* in *Oeuvres complètes,* ed. Henri Mitterand (Paris: Cercle du Livre Précieux, 1967–70), 2: 605; Zola, *Nana,* 298, 45; Maurice Descotes, *Le Personnage de Napoléon III dans les "Rougon-Macquart"* (Paris: Archives des Lettres Modernes [V], no. 114[392–396], 1970), 45.

But first, an aside on the emperor's own fruitless attempt at literary creation, which must be counted as his least-consequential failing.

NAPOLEON III THE NOVELIST

There was no more minor a novelist than the emperor himself, though he does rank with Flaubert and Zola in one respect, in having planned to write a novel about himself, or more precisely about his accomplishments, and having failed to do so. His brief literary ambitions were not without precedent in the family. A number of the Bonapartes fancied themselves as writers. Napoleon I was, after some youthful attempts, far too preoccupied with ruling the world to turn his hand to literary pursuits, but he was very fond of plays, built his own theater on Elba, was particularly partial to tragedy, and supposedly knew much of Corneille by heart. His brother Jérôme also, as king of Westphalia, built a splendid private theater, where its director, a certain Blangini, even though there was no shortage of funds for costumes, put on an operetta with naked performers. Lucien also created his own theater, in Rome, though the repertoire was far more staid and classical than his younger brother's. "The Bonapartes," as Stackton remarks, "were nothing if not theatrical, and they were never off stage for any longer than they could help." The emperor's sisters Pauline and Caroline enjoyed acting in comedies, whilst Élisa favored tragedy. Louis, the future emperor's father, was an energetic author, writing plays, poetry, and, most interestingly, a novel, called *Marie, ou les peines d'amour* (1812), in which, not surprisingly, the figure representing Hortense has a less than admirable role. He even helped his brother Joseph with his novel, *Moïna* (1814), a tale about a young soldier and a shepherdess suffering the rigors of war and brief domestic bliss in an Alpine peasant's hut. Lucien, for his part, wrote, as well as epic poems, a novel about a beautiful huntress in Ceylon, *La Tribu indienne* (*an* VII).[6]

A taste for literature was clearly in the blood of the Bonapartes, as well as in the air of the times. Plon-Plon, as we have seen, inherited his father's passion for the theater—as well as his taste for actresses—in which he indulged with pompous performances in his Pompeian house. Morny, of course, though he was not of the blood line, acquired the family's pen-

6. Stacton, *The Bonapartes*, 35, 13–15, 41–42, 104.

chant for the stage. Napoleon III, however, though he could boast of being a practicing historian and journalist at various points in his career, did not follow the literary traditions of the family, for he was not in the least bit fond of literature, though this indifference has yet to be cited as further proof of his dubious lineage. In the leisure hours at the court, poetry readings would make him even more somnambulistic than he normally seemed to be, and he would mercilessly mock the unlikely situations and sentiments depicted in the popular novels of the time that engrossed and enthused the ladies of the imperial entourage.[7]

Nevertheless, towards the end of his reign, he did write an outline of a novel which he never seems to have begun to write, dealing with a grocer who returns to France from America to see for himself if the rumors spread by refugees that France was a destitute land ruled over by a tyrant are true, only to find all manner of wonders instead.[8] This projected work was possibly a reply to Hippolyte Taine's *Notes sur Paris* (1867), in which the author wryly pretends to be the editor of the observations of a remarkably erudite pork merchant, Frédéric Thomas Graindorge, who had died in 1865 at the age of fifty-five. Taine's imaginary character, who is the vehicle of his criticism of contemporary Parisian life, had supposedly left Paris at the age of twelve, made his fortune in America and returned home to find and condemn in his writings, at least in part, the frivolity and immorality

---

7. See Fleischmann, *Napoléon III et les femmes,* 19. Louis Napoléon's journalistic activities were not limited to his days at Ham. As Kulstein notes (*Napoleon III and the Working Class,* 92), he actively collaborated on propaganda pamphlets and articles for the official press, wrote anonymous or pseudonymous letters and articles himself and even contributed anonymous pieces to the *Times* of London. See *Papiers et correspondance de la famille impériale* (Paris: Imprimarie Nationale, 1870), 1:385–88: "Projets d'articles (tracés de la main de l'Empereur)." Among the works spuriously attributed to Louis Napoléon is an interesting spoof collection of eighteen satirical poems in English, *Poems by Louis Napoleon* (London: 1852), including a clever parody of Poe's "The Raven," entitled, of course, "The Eagle."

8. The authorship of this outline, which appears in the *Papiers et correspondance* (1:218–19 in the 1870 edition and 1:202–303 in the 1871 edition) and which the editors claim to be in the emperor's handwriting, has been a matter of discussion. See H. N. Boon, *Rêve et réalité dans l'oeuvre économique et sociale de Napoléon III* (The Hague: Martinus Nijhoff, 1934), 154, and Kulstein, *Napoleon III and the Working Class,* 93, who notes that "Napoleon III and his office more than once prepared propaganda novels. A report on the press in 1869 stated that *Le Petit Journal* was planning to publish a propaganda novel on the First Empire from 'the Emperor's office.' " The emperor's outline is also reproduced in part in Séguin, *Louis Napoléon le Grand,* 331–32.

of Second Empire society.[9] Taine, who was a highly influential historian, philosopher, and literary critic of the time, even though he had accepted the right of the new regime to rule after the coup d'état and the plebiscite, frequented Princess Mathilde's salon, and held a prestigious position as professor of the history of art at the École des Beaux-Arts since 1864, was an independent, liberal thinker and very much a part of the intellectual opposition to the regime. The emperor's character, as can be seen from the text of his plan below, has the opposite experience.

PLAN OF A NOVEL IN THE EMPEROR'S HAND

M. Benoît, an upright grocer of the rue de la Lune, had left for America in 1847. After having traveled in the lands that stretch from the Hudson to the Mississippi, he came back to France in April 1868, having spent almost nineteen years away from his country. He had picked up distant echoes of all that had happened in France since 1848, without realizing what changes had occurred. Some French refugees had told him that France was groaning under despotism and that he would find the country that he had left so prosperous in the time of Louis-Philippe thoroughly debased and impoverished. Our friend Benoît arrives then in Brest in the transatlantic steamer. He arrives in the harbor full of prejudices, regrets, and apprehension: "Now then, what are those black vessels, so ugly compared to the beautiful sailing ships that I left behind?" he asks the first sailor that he meets. "Ah! those are battleships, the emperor's invention. They're iron-plated and protected from cannonballs, and this transformation has destroyed to a certain degree the supremacy of England at sea.—That's possible, but I still miss our old vessels with their poetic mast and sails. [in the margin: "Passports eliminated"]

Near the town hall, he sees a crowd coming to vote. Astonishment at universal suffrage.

Astonishment at the railways that crisscross France; and at the electric telegraph system.

9. The full title of Taine's work: *Notes sur Paris. Vie et opinions de M. Frédéric Thomas Graindorge, docteur en philosophie de l'Université d'Iéna, principal associé commanditaire de la maison Graindorge and C° (huiles et porc salé, à Cincinnati, États-Unis d'Amérique), recueillies et publiées par H. Taine, son exécuteur testamentaire* (Paris: Hachette, 1867).

Arrival in Paris; improvements. The octroi out at the fortifications.

He wishes to buy certain objects, which are less expensive, thanks to the trade agreement. Iron half as cheap, etc. He thinks that there are a lot of writers in prison. Error.

No riots; no political prisoners; no exiles.

No prisoners in custody at all.

Acceleration of progress.

The stamp eliminated.

Civil death eliminated.

The old-age fund.

The convalescent home in Vincennes.

Coalitions.

Haulage policing abolished.

Controls abolished.

Military service reduced, pay increased, medal instituted, retirement increased.

Reserves increasing the strength of the army.

Funds for disabled priests.

Civil imprisonment.

Brokers: a tradesman who sent an assistant to sell or buy merchandise was arrested.

General Councils.

Clearly the emperor's fiction would have been even more patently propagandist than his history, with added complacency at such a (utopian) catalog of his achievements. As literature, however, at least on the strength of this outline, even the most ardent Bonapartist might be led to suggest that Napoleon III's main contributions to the history of the novel are twofold: to have confounded the view that we all have a novel in us and to have confirmed the view that there are very many novels that are better for never having been written.

P R E T E N D E R

The best-known but not by any means the most convincing appearance of Louis Napoléon in a literary work, to which a number of historians have referred, is the role that he plays in another guise in a novel written by another historical figure, less eminent politically but infinitely more successful than the emperor at the novelist's art. Louis Napoléon met Benjamin Disraeli during his first prolonged stay in England after his arrival from Switzerland in 1838, when he was welcomed even into the Tory circles of British high society. They had Count d'Orsay and Lady Blessington as common friends. They met again during the prince's second stay in London, after his escape from Ham, and Disraeli, who was chancellor of the exchequer at the time, was in the party that accompanied Queen Victoria on her state visit to Cherbourg in August 1858 when the new Paris-Cherbourg railway was inaugurated. He had a particular dislike of the empress, which dated from the imperial couple's visit to England in April 1855 and was later confirmed, when, as prime minister, he tried to prevent the prince imperial from going to Zululand only to be met with stubborn opposition from both the queen and the young man's mother.[10]

Endymion (1880) is the last of Disraeli's dozen novels, which, along with his plays, poems, and short stories, represent a considerable literary achievement, considering the author's other activities, even though his works are largely unread today except as a commentary on the social mores and politics of much of nineteenth-century Britain. The novel was written and published after he had left office, that is when, at the age of seventy-five, as the first earl of Beaconsfield and prime minister, his Conservative government had been defeated in 1880, the year before his death. The plot of the novel, which is fictitious, though several of the characters are based on known public figures, begins in 1829–30 and follows the rise to political prominence of Endymion Ferrars after the tragic death of his mother and suicide of his father, a failed politician. Endymion's twin sister, Myra, devotes her life to her brother's career to the extent of marrying a prominent politician, Lord Roehampton, who is based on Lord Palmerston. But of more interest to us is a colorful, episodic character of the novel, Prince Florestan, son of the beautiful Queen Agrippina, exiled from an unspecified kingdom, who leaves the boy in the care of Mr. Sidney Wilton, a cabinet minister. The docile boy does well at Eaton but blots his copybook soon after by leading an unsuccessful invading force on his homeland. The taciturn young man is shipped off to America, but returns to make a second attempt to take over his country and is imprisoned for

10. See Ridley, *Napoleon III and Eugénie*, 380, 598.

life "in the strongest fortress of the country." He escapes, of course, ever convinced that some day he will rule. In the meantime he lives in a mansion in Carlton Terrace and is received in London society, though reluctantly by some, who accuse him of being an intriguer. He is accompanied by a short and swarthy gentleman, known as the duke of St. Angelo, who is clearly based upon Persigny and who plays a similar role in relation to the dispossessed Prince Florestan, ever ready to promote his interests. Florestan has an unbending belief in his destiny to rule his kingdom, an "over-confidence in his star."[11]

One of the more interesting scenes of the book is the mock medieval tournament, based on the Eglington Tournament, organized by the earl of Eglington on his estates in Ayreshire in August 1839, which Louis Napoléon attended as the Visiting Knight with Persigny as his squire, and received much hostile criticism for doing so in France.[12] In the novel the prince appears at Montfort Castle, where the transposed event takes place, as the Knight of the White Rose and speaks frankly to Lady Roehampton about his life and ambitions. "Life is a masquerade," he remarks, in his fancy dress, "at least mine has been." He talks warmly of his mother, Queen Agrippina, and, confidently, of the kingdom that is destined to be his, just as earlier in a conversation with his ward he speaks grandly on the same theme: "I am the child of destiny. That destiny will again place me on the throne of my fathers. That is certain as I am now speaking to you. But destiny for its fulfilment ordains action. Its decrees are inexorable, but they are obscure, and the being whose career it directs is as a man travelling in a dark night; he reaches his goal even without the aid of stars or moon."[13]

The novel is in general about ambition, about the restoration of lost political power and, more particularly, about the influence of women on the careers of men, their passionate and energetic ambitiousness in political life, a favorite Disraeli theme. Thus Myra, obsessed by her brother's advancement, reflects: "I have brought myself, by long meditation, to the

11. The Earl of Beaconsfield [Benjamin Disraeli], *Endymion* (London: Longmans, 1900), 177, 250.

12. See Ridley, *Napoleon III and Eugénie,* 122–23. Louis Napoléon was dressed in "a polished steel cuirass, trimmed with crimson satin, and a visored helmet with a high plume of white feathers." As noted above, amongst the many insults that Hugo uses to refer to Louis Napoléon in *Châtiments* is "*le cockney d'Eglington et d'Epsom.*"

13. [Disraeli], *Endymion,* 258–59, 180.

conviction that a human being with a settled purpose must accomplish it, and that nothing can resist a will that will stake even existence for its fulfilment." It has been suggested that Prince Florestan represents a "more Romantic younger self that Disraeli never completely suppresses." Certainly, whatever the resemblances between the fictional character and his model or his maker, the outcome of the prince's ambitions departs on one essential point from historical precedent. As the political novel veers into romance, Prince Florestan does indeed become king of his land, in a noticeably bloodless takeover, just as Endymion married to the widowed Lady Montfort—he had been her protégé—becomes prime minister. The new king is also in want of a wife and marries into the English aristocracy, taking as his queen to share his "resplendent throne" the lovely widowed Lady Roehampton, Myra herself, Endymion's sister.[14] There are triumphal scenes as, to much acclaim from his people, the prince ascends the throne, establishes a "liberal" but "conciliatory, firm" government and welcomes his queen with much fanfare. And all ends even better as the still-unnamed kingdom of King Florestan proves to be a trusted ally to Britain in the years that follow. Disraeli is seemingly indulging in some fictional wishful thinking—or wishful regretting—not only on political matters, for the moral is clear: a noble, self-sacrificing, radiant, accomplished, English widow would have been a much better match for the real prince than that simpering Spaniard. He may well have been right!

LIBERATOR

Another eminent Victorian found literary inspiration in the deeds of the pretender, but in a different genre and in a far different spirit. As she viewed the troop movements each day from her Champs-Élysées apartment window in the fall of 1851, the invalid poetess Elizabeth Barrett Browning wrote enthusiastically to her friend Mary Russell Mitford: "Vive Napoléon III! What a fourth act of a play we are in just now!" But it was as a poet rather than as a dramatist that she wrote even more admiringly about the prince, convinced that the role of poetry was to engage with the burning issues of her age. She welcomed the coup d'état, describing it as

14. *Ibid.*, 118, 451. On Florestan's links to Disraeli himself, see Daniel R. Schwarz, *Disraeli's Fiction* (London: Macmillan, 1979), 148.

"a grand thing, dramatically and poetically speaking." She even saw Louis Napoléon himself on the day of the coup d'état and defended his action in animated arguments with her husband, the poet Robert Browning, and her brother, George, on grounds that would have endeared her to the prince-president himself: "There's a higher right than a legal right"; the people had chosen him and he was therefore justified in his action. He was for her in many ways a kindred spirit, as well as a distantly heroic figure on horseback, of course, to be admired from her window, or even, as has been suggested, rather curiously, an object of her "subconscious search for a father-substitute." Be that as it may, politically, as a convinced republican, she shared with Louis Napoléon a theoretical belief in the primacy of the will of the people and in the necessity of manhood suffrage. She was also convinced romantically that political salvation always came from the deeds of the inspired individual, the leader of genius, and not from the institution of a socialist state stifling individual merit. Fourier was her *bête noire*. For her, the particular form of government was unimportant, as long as it was sanctioned by popular consent. But above all, she lionized Louis Napoléon as a valiant campaigner for the cause of the emancipation and unification of her adoptive and beloved homeland, Italy. Her admiration for him dated from his early Italian campaign of 1849. Ten years later, her hero-worship knew no bounds. Her dream of a united Italy was revitalized, as were her spirits, when she learned of the formal alliance between France and Sardinia. "When, in April, it was reported that French troops were pouring into Piedmont she thought Napoleon 'sublime.' " The French intervention in Italy was for her a holy crusade, and the victories at Magenta and Solferino exhausted her with joy. Her disappointment at the Villafranca agreement (11 July 1859), which merely ceded Lombardy to Piedmont, gave the Central States back to their rulers, and left Venetia under Austrian rule, saw her bedridden for three weeks, such were her identification with the cause and the delicacy of her health. But her faith in Napoleon III had only been dented, for she tended to blame England in league with Prussia for preventing "the perfecting of the greatest Deed given to men to do in these latter years."[15]

Her *Poems before Congress*, written in 1859 and published in March 1860, express her disillusionment at the diplomatic outcome of the war,

15. See Margaret Forster, *Elizabeth Barrett Browning: A Biography* (London: Chatto and Windus, 1988), 263–65, 336–39; Alethea Hayter, *Mrs Browning: A Poet's Work and Its Setting* (London: Faber and Faber, 1962), 128, 238, 120, 123.

as in "An August Voice," which condemns the re-establishment of the Italian dukedoms, and "Christmas Gifts," which attacks the pope's attachment to his secular power in Italy. But her most controversial poem in this slim volume, "the most provocative and execrated of all her political poems,"[16] is her nineteen-stanza ode, "Napoleon III. in Italy." It begins by asserting that Louis Napoléon is the elect of eight million people, "by their manhood's right divine":

> With a universal shout
> They took the old regalia out
> From an open grave that day;
> From a grave that would not close,
> Where the first Napoleon lay
> > Expectant in repose,
> As still as Merlin, with his conquering face
> Turned up in its unquenchable appeal
> To men and heroes of the advancing race,
> > prepare to set the seal
> Of what has been on what shall be
> > Emperor
> > Evermore.

The poet notes that on the day she did not give "voice and verse" to "acclaim and sing / Conviction, exaltation, aspiration," but now that Napoleon has left far behind "the purple throng / Of vulgar monarchs" to "help in the hour of wrong / The broken hearts of nations to be strong," the poets of the people can praise him, "Sublime Deliverer!" Is it a dream? she asks, or will Italy be "loosed at length / from the tyrant's thrall." We are urged to "shout for France and Savoy," "shout for the helper and doer":

> For this he fought in his youth,
> Of this he dreamed in the past;
> The lines of the resolute mouth
> Tremble a little at last.
> Cry, he has done it all!
> > "Emperor
> > Evermore."

16. Hayter, *Mrs. Browning*, 130.

The "people's instinct" found this man, elected him and crowned him. The "people's blood" runs through him, "creates him absolute," this "wonder," who, compared to all leaders before is "Larger so much by the heart / larger so much by the head." As if such praise were not enough, the encomium concludes in stirring fashion:

> Courage, courage! happy is he,
> Of whom (himself among the dead
> And silent), this word shall be said;
> —That he might have had the world with him,
> But he chose to side with suffering men,
> And had the world against him when
> He came to deliver Italy.
> > Emperor
> > Evermore.[17]

The quality of the poem does not, perhaps, match the intensity of the feelings and convictions that inspired it, nor does the adulation, as the author was frequently reminded, jibe with the manifest motives of Napoleon III's Italian policy, which was far from disinterested. Poignantly, the poet in "A Tale of Villafranca," which appears in the same collection as "Napoleon III. in Italy," tells her child: "In this low world, where great Deeds die, / What matters if we live?"[18] She was indeed to die soon after, on 29 June 1861, buoyed by the proclamation of the Kingdom of Italy (on 17 March 1861), in despair at Cavour's recent death (6 June 1861), and still clinging to the dream, yet at least spared the revelation that her hero would pursue his policy, not for Italian unity, but for an Italian confederation and that before long he would be an emperor nevermore.

PRISONER

Louis Napoléon's imprisonment in the castle of Ham from 7 October 1840 to 25 May 1846 provided the inspiration for a novel by Roger Régis, *La Belle Sabotière et le prisonnier de Ham* (1937), which won the "Prix du

17. Elizabeth Barrett Browning, *Napoleon III in Italy and Other Poems* (New York: Francis, 1860), 9–13, 16, 19, 22–23, 25, 28.
18. *Ibid.*, 38.

Récit Historique" in 1936. The author, Roger Régis-Lamotte, was also a popular short-story writer, a poet, and a playwright, who published most of his work in the interwar years.

His novel is a skillfully crafted, very readable romance, with, as one might anticipate, a happy ending for the prince, who escapes "towards his destiny," and a cozy bourgeois arrangement for the pauper girl. The action begins the night of the prince's arrival at Ham, which is presented from the point of view and the consciousness of Éléonore Vergeot, "la belle Sabotière" herself, who happens to be out at a late-night rendezvous with her swain, Jacques, in the shadow of the fortress, when a platoon of horsemen go clattering across the lowered drawbridge. The "sudden flash of a cigarette" belonging to "you-know-who" alerts the attentive reader to the identity of one of the company, particularly as the girl has just furnished her ardent companion (and the reader) with a brief lesson on the recent unreasonable treatment of "the nephew of the Great Man," "the poor prince," at the very time when a boat is triumphantly bringing back the body of the uncle. Jacques is more interested in seducing Éléonore than in politics, or in marriage. Her anguished hesitations over Jacques and her sympathy for the prince supply the necessary psychological motivation for what follows. Allusions to the "Sleeping Beauty's castle" provide the appropriate code of romance in which to present the proceedings.[19]

The novel is systematically constructed out of a series of "scenes." Thus, after some nervous troop inspections, the next morning, the commanding officer of the fort, Demarle, already terrified at the prospect of being another Hudson Lowe, visits his dignified prisoner, observing his "thin and pale face," his "blue eyes," his "heavy moustache"—with a "*mouche*" under his bottom lip, as, we are told, was the fashion for officers at the time—dressed, rather incongruously though suggestively in view of the six years of domesticity ahead, in a blue military tunic, grey hussard pants, and carpet slippers! Two months later, we encounter Éléonore in the daylight: a tall strapping wench of twenty, with a "nicely shaped bust," "muscular arms," "long legs," in short "a fine-looking girl," as the local lads would put it, with her light-brown hair, her limpid blue eyes, her straight nose, her mouth "a little full but [reassuringly] healthy" and

19. Roger Régis, *La Belle Sabotière et le prisonnier de Ham* (Paris: Les Éditions de France, 1937), 240, 9, 6, 7, 10.

"above all, that freshness of complexion, that dazzling pink and satin skin which is, perhaps, the most desirable of beauties." Just what the doctor (Conneau) would have ordered, no doubt, for Louis! for the days are long in the prison, playing cards with General Montholon and Dr. Henri Conneau, who have both nobly agreed to share his captivity along with the prince's devoted servant, Charles Thélin, who, at least, is free to live outside the fort and to do the shopping.[20]

Fate, which is the law of romance, takes a hand in the events. Éléonore is busy ironing for some rich clients when their niece, Gabrielle, a spirited girl from Paris, arrives, rhapsodizing about the handsome prince in the castle. The two girls go out to catch a glimpse of his silhouette walking on the ramparts. Then Éléonore learns that she has been appointed as linen maid at the fort. But it is Gabrielle who first gains access to the prince's quarters by pretending to be a handkerchief seller. She is rewarded with the sale of a dozen handkerchiefs and a kiss on the hand. But as the narrative switches to the present tense to mark the dramatic importance of the events, on a cold Christmas Eve night of 1840, the prisoner is meditating in despair and alone in front of a crackling fire on the trials of his past: 1815, the emperor's departure from Malmaison to Waterloo; 1829, life at Arenenberg and Augsberg and a kiss for Mathilde, who has now abandoned him; 1831, the instant death of his brother at Forli—as Régis would have it—from a gunshot wound; 1836, Strasbourg, America, England; 1840, Boulogne, his sentence and present plight: "He will never be emperor." But consolation is at hand. A blushing Éléonore brings in his dinner, which he gallantly shares with her. He kisses her hand: "on her working-girl's fingers on which her labors have left their mark, she feels the touch of the mouth of the prince, of Caesar's heir." Their lips meet. As the chapter ends, "after a long kiss, he leads Éléonore, her head on his shoulder, towards the open door of the bedroom, over there, in the shadows."[21] Not such a bad Christmas after all! Meanwhile, Gabrielle is having to make do with Thélin!

Returning to the past tense, the next day, Éléonore receives permission

20. *Ibid.*, 16, 23. Montholon, as we have already noted, was at Saint-Helena and has even been suspected of poisoning the emperor. He could well have been a double agent, but there is no hint of this in the novel, except that, when he does plan to escape, Louis Napoléon is careful not to tell his gouty companion.

21. *Ibid.*, 60, 67.

to stay. The weeks go by in domestic contentment. Éléonore sews, as be-
fits the stereotype, for throughout the novel she will have an inexhaustible
supply of embroidery to do. The prince reads, somewhat improbably,
Rousseau's *Julie, ou La Nouvelle Héloïse* (1761), a novel of the impossible
marriage between a tutor and his pupil—thus a possible, though remote,
intertext—as well as works by more contemporary writers and, with special
interest, works by economists and theoreticians such as Fourier, Saint-
Simon, and Proudhon. Then there are Éléonore's spelling and mathematics lessons. Louis Napoléon is peculiarly attached to a collection of caricatures from *Le Charivari* on the wall, reminding him of his past adventures,
even the one that shows him with a huge nose and a huge Mme. Gordon
at his side in Strasbourg. For the time being, he is happy just to plan the
extinction of pauperism. Little Eugène is born, away from Ham, of course.
The prince writes his pamphlets and articles and cultivates his flower garden—just as his uncle had done in similar circumstances, the commander
worriedly observes.

Indeed the commander had cause for concern, for politics and romance
always work at cross-purposes. Despite his comfortable domestic arrangements, the prince's ambitions are rekindled when soldiers at the fort discreetly reveal their allegiance. Amongst the astonishing mixture of
probable and improbable visitors who make the trip to see him—Louis
Blanc, Le Bas, Vieillard, Chateaubriand, Alexandre Dumas, Mme. Gordon, Lady Hamilton, Lord Malmesbury, even Sir Robert Peel, who was
British prime minister at the time—Miss Howard, already in full bloom,
makes an appearance. The temptation to include this colorful character in
his novel, particularly as she provides a pretext for some anti-English clichés on "Puritanical conformity," was clearly too great for the author,
who even has her financing the prince's Boulogne adventure with her millions, even though in reality, in 1836, Elizabeth Ann Haryett was only seventeen years old, a very minor actress, living still with her jockey lover, Jem
Mason, in London. In the extensive scene between "Loulou" and
"Lizzy," which takes place during Éléonore's absence, this most admired
woman and richest courtesan in England, Miss Henriette Howard (in fact
Elizabeth), who is introduced and described as the daughter of a "brewer"
(in fact a bootmaker) from Dover (in fact Brighton) called Herriott (in fact
Haryett), urges him to escape and offers to provide passports through the
good services of Sir Robert Peel![22]

22. *Ibid.*, 137, 142.

At the news of his father's death—which, in point of fact, occurred two months after Louis Napoléon's evasion—and with Éléonore conveniently away again, giving birth to a second child, the prince makes his escape. The episode is narrated with suitable suspense and tension. By the well-documented ploy of disguising himself as one of the workmen, here Bertrand rather than Bertou, and despite his feelings of guilt at leaving Éléonore, he makes his way with Thélin and the spaniel that Miss Howard has left behind and that he has somewhat unimaginatively called "Ham," whilst Dr. Conneau plays for time by pretending that he is ill in bed. With a nice novelistic touch, when the prince and Thélin reach Valenciennes station, they ask for information about the Brussels train from a railway employee who turns out to be "la belle Sabotière's" unfortunate lover, Jacques: "He had no idea. He had a unique opportunity to take revenge."[23] When they finally arrive in Brussels, Régis has them dining at the best restaurant in the Belgian capital, which was highly unlikely, since King Leopold, whose wife was Louis-Philippe's daughter, was on the best of terms with the French government and had an extradition treaty covering political offenses. But it was the natural thing for a character in a novel to do.

But the historical novelist's most imaginative invention is the scene of the final chapter of the novel, which forms an epilogue to the main plot and occurs seven years after the events that have been described, when Louis Napoléon had indeed become the emperor. Pierre Bure, Louis Napoléon's foster brother, now Treasurer of the Household under the Second Empire and living in Saint-Cloud, takes his wife and two sons, Eugène and Louis, to see the "good" emperor and the lovely empress go by in their carriage in the park. The empress stops the carriage to admire the children. "All my congratulations, madame!" she enthuses to Mme. Bure, totally oblivious to the irony of her words, "you have beautiful children, there; I would love to have children like them one day!" The former prisoner of Ham and "la belle Sabotière" exchange a last look, hers intense,

---

23. *Ibid.*, 219. This episode may have been inspired by either of two incidents that occurred during Louis Napoléon's escape to Brussels: he was waiting at Saint-Quentin for a post chaise to travel to Valenciennes when he made an inquiry of a man who, he later discovered, was the public prosecutor of Saint-Quentin; at the Valenciennes railway station, a gendarme from Ham recognized Thélin and came over to chat to him, inquiring of the prince's health, whereupon Thélin claimed that he was no longer in the prince's service and was working for the railway company. Ridley, *Napoleon III and Eugénie,* 191.

his characteristically "lost in vagary, indifferent," with not so much as a twitch of his *impériale* to betray the truth![24]

THE CHASTISED

Despite the numerous inaccuracies of detail, Régis's novel is an engaging work, weaving a substantial basis of fact with some imaginative fabrication inspired by the traditions of romance into a largely fictional construction that is far neater in its arrangement than the illusive truth, but no less so than many purportedly factual histories. Despite the implicit claim of its title, the same cannot be said of *Napoléon III: Pièce historique en cinq actes, dont un prologue, et huit tableaux* (1908), whose action extends from Ham to Sedan, for it is a work that, with the barest of historical outlines as a base, mixes two parts travesty and one part melodrama into an extraordinarily fizzy cocktail of derivative propaganda, which it is difficult to imagine any but the most naive of spectators taking at all seriously. The authors, Julien and Marcel Priollet, wrote vaudevilles and comedies in the early part of the twentieth century, Marcel being also an extraordinarily prolific popular novelist whose works alone occupy ten double-column pages of the Bibliothèque Nationale catalog. Their play was first put on in Paris at the Comédie de l'Époque on 27 December 1907, "amidst the bravos of the public," as Legge reports.[25]

In the first tableau, Pompinel, a worker at Ham, who enthusiastically sings Béranger songs but has scant respect for the prisoner, proposes to the commander's daughter, Hélène Dupré. But she loves the prince, who

---

24. Régis, *La Belle Sabotière,* 238–39.

25. Legge, *The Comedy and Tragedy of the Second Empire,* 393. Legge records details of other stage representations of the emperor at the turn of the century: a play entitled *La Savelli* by Max Maurey, produced in December 1906; an "old French féerie" put on in a Berlin theater, in which Napoleon III, sporting his "grand cordon of the Légion d'honneur," is caricatured by a "low comedian" and dances a cancan. Before that, he notes, there was a play produced at the theater of Kreuznach in Germany, within a month of the death of the prince imperial, which shows the young man in love with a gamekeeper's daughter, Miss Mary, whom the empress tries to buy off, then narrowly escaping a shooting attempt by a rival in love with the same girl, then being slain by the Zulus. The last scene of the play takes place in the crypt of the Catholic Church in Chislehurst, where the empress gives her dead son's last letter to Miss Mary and discovers that he had been secretly married to her! Legge, *The Comedy and Tragedy of the Second Empire,* 392–94.

seems strangely to be alone in the prison, and offers to help him escape even though this would mean punishment for her father, a supporter of Louis-Philippe, and disgrace for her brother, Georges, who is at Saint-Cyr. "I only think of you, you are everything to me. Go, go," she exhorts him. After an emotional struggle between his love and scruples, on the one hand, and the call of destiny, on the other—"Mine is the destiny of a man born on the steps of a throne"—he departs with tender vows and a promise not to reveal how he escaped, dressed in the clothes that Pompinel had left for Hélène to sew![26]

The next three tableaux cover three crucial days of the coup d'état, 2, 3, and 6 December 1851. In the first Louis Napoléon is shown in the Élysée, fulfilling his destiny—"I must yield to the invincible force which pushes me towards the throne"—giving his instructions to Morny and Maupas, then to Saint-Arnaud, as they come in to report the events of the day. He gives a special order to arrest Victor Hugo: "I mistrust poets who get involved in politics." The prince's companion since childhood, the faithful military commander Bernard, warns him that his actions are a crime, but pledges his loyalty "up to the final fall." As day breaks, the prince addresses a soliloquy in the manner of Rastignac to the waking Paris that he is about to conquer, declaring with a decided lack of originality: "*Paris! à nous deux!*"[27] The next day in the humble Dupré home in the rue de Picpus, where misfortune and coincidence are in evidence since Louis Napoléon's escape and Dupré's suicide in prison in disgrace, Mme. Dupré advises Hélène, who is sewing, of course, to accept the same Bernard's marriage proposal. Georges has vowed revenge against the prince and his unknown accomplice. Pompinel also appears, coincidentally, as does Victor Hugo himself, hiding from the police. Coincidentally too, Bernard also puts in an appearance to prevent a search of the house, unwittingly saving Hugo's skin. Pompinel goes off to tear down government posters. Hugo goes off after a fine speech about the People sowing the glorious and bloody seeds of Progress and Liberty to institute the ideals of 1789 and 1830—without mentioning 1848! Georges has a plan to kidnap Louis Napoléon at a forthcoming rendezvous with a dancer, which, we learn in the beginning of the next tableau, fails because Morny went instead!

26. Julien Priollet and Marcel Priollet, *Napoléon III: Pièce historique en cinq actes, dont un prologue, et huit tableaux* (Paris: Librairie Théâtrale, 1908) 18, 14.

27. *Ibid.*, 31, 35, 31, 39.

The return to the Élysée on 6 December marks the high point of the (melo)drama, as Victor Hugo gives himself up to save Georges from execution and to confront his sworn enemy. Louis Napoléon's Hugolian remark "this man is everywhere" and Morny's no less Hugolian reply "Yes . . . and you cannot find him anywhere" are the poet's cues to enter! This episode appears nowhere in *Histoire d'un crime,* of course, but Hugo the character, in reply to his adversary's claim to have saved society, taunts him at great length with a flood of rhetoric and invective reminiscent of, and at times verbatim from, *Châtiments:* "But what can force do against Ideas"; "How can one not hate you, Louis Bonaparte, sad little dwarf ready to rig yourself out in the old castoffs of the greatest of emperors"; "And if, tired of the struggle, your adversaries of today gradually line up under your banner, there will still be one left, and that one will be me."[28] As if this pièce de résistance is not enough, Hélène also appears after the poet's departure, successfully pleading for the pardon of her brother and, in the process, transforming the tyrant into a noble and generous spirit. Georges is even promoted to the rank of captain and seems to have no scruples in accepting the honor of serving the dictator!

In this play history is reduced to a set of grandiloquent gestures and immoderate emotions, rather in the Hugolian manner, but with infinitely less art. Historical issues and actions become a play between the forces of good and evil, in conformity with the conventions of melodrama. The historical situation, with a few convenient twists and turns of a plot ruled by coincidence, becomes merely a pretext for the display of the powers of sentiment and of the primacy of love and honor. As the last four tableaux of the play transport us to the last days of the Empire, in a huge elision familiar to the readers of Hugo's own works on the same topic, similarly motivated by an overriding scheme of crime and punishment rather than by any attempt to portray the complexities of the historical process, a new force for evil emerges.

In tableau 5, set at Saint-Cloud on 12 July 1870, the destiny of France is in the balance. Hélène is now a countess at the court and "*dame d'honneur*" of the empress, who suspects that she is the emperor's mistress, as does her brother Georges, now Colonel Dupré, as a result of yet another misunderstanding, but Hélène remains unsoiled being "in a sense the morganatic wife of Napoleon III." In this capacity she has a more impor-

28. *Ibid.*, 69, 76, 78, 79.

tant function as the force for good countervailing Her Highness's evil appetite for war. Despite the news of the withdrawal of the candidacy of Prince Hohenzollern, Bazaine, the empress and the prime minister (*sic*) press for military action, whilst Hélène pleads with the emperor for peace. Two days later (in tableau 6), the empress has her way: she persuades the prime minister of the validity of the *casus belli;* she reveals in a soliloquy addressed to God that her jealousy of Hélène as much as her concern for the destiny of her son is a primary motive for her actions; and, denouncing Rochefort, "the vile *Lanterne,*" and "the tireless fighting spirit of the exile of Jersey,"[29] convinces the emperor to go to war, to do his duty, to save the Empire or die with his army. Georges too, still refusing to believe in his sister's innocence—though she is only guilty of her love for the emperor—goes off to do his duty.

The two final tableaux, headed with a decided lack of originality "Napoléon-le-Grand et Napoléon-le-Petit" and "La Débâcle," echoes of Hugo's lasting influence and Zola's novel, take place on the day of the battle of Sedan (1 September 1870). Through yet another coincidence, Pompinel's house just happens to be on the road from Sedan to Bazeilles, in which the emperor seeks respite from the battle, and provides the setting for the play's second great *coup de théâtre.* Napoleon III calls upon the manes of his uncle, whose ghost appears in a "terrible apparition" to bring not help but "chastisement" for his crime, "*le Deux Décembre.*" "Victor Hugo's prediction!" the trembling nephew cries, cowering before the mighty specter, "and it is you, my last hope, who come to administer it." The ghost tells him that his only hope of expiation is to die in the midst of his troops. All go off to fight bravely, Georges and Napoleon III in the hope of dying, one for honor, the other for "forgiveness." Later that day, in tableau 8, in the office of the sub-prefect of Sedan, the failed hero gives his order to surrender, mortified by the horrors of the battle and the deafening sound of cannon fire. Hélène puts in an unexpected appearance, though, by now, unexpected appearances are quite expected. She learns from Bernard that Georges has duly died bravely, forgiving her with his last words. Bernard seems to think this an opportune moment to repeat his marriage proposal. A Prussian envoy arrives, with the unlikely name of Bronsart de Schellendorf, which, we must assume, is not a vaudeville joke. He pays homage to the "admirable valor" of the French army,

29. *Ibid.*, 98, 121.

claiming (quite improbably, but clearly for the benefit of the audience's sensibilities) that the king of Prussia wept at the sight of their bravery. Napoleon III gives him the surrender note, but has to face one more defeat: Hélène tells him that she loves him no more, adding, in an impassioned outburst of republican zeal, her prediction that soon France "will rush at the invader, . . . will restore the last vestiges of our dying greatness, and out of the ruins of the Empire will spring, like an apotheosis, the proud and serene image of the Republic!"[30] Since, as the fallen emperor observes, before he literally and literarily falls "crushed" at her feet, *she is* France, she has chosen Bernard with whom, echoing the ending of Zola's *La Débâcle*, to regenerate the country.

To the bitter end the play associates history with sentiment and, fully consistent with Hugo's own rhetoric, the destruction of the corrupt Bonapartist empire with the emergence of an ideal Republic, exalting, like the author of *Châtiments*, the salutary mission of the People and the regenerative role of Woman. It is as if Hugo's own anti-Bonapartist texts had been adapted for the theater with the techniques of the same writer's historical melodramas, but without his genius. The play is not without interest for its unrefined and thereby all the more revealing demonstration of the persistence of public attitudes to the Second Empire even forty years on, as well as of the durability of republican idealism and myths. There is a certain wry irony in reading such an expression of faith in the military recovery of France in a play written almost on the eve of the First World War. But from a critical point of view and from the posthumous view of our two legendary foes, though Napoleon III is well and truly chastised on the stage in this work, his expiation can surely be no less warranted than Victor Hugo's for having inspired such a dreadful play.

Her Majesty

If, as the Priollets' play suggests, Eugénie's stock was not very high in Republican France even in her gracious old age—she died on 11 July 1920 at the age of ninety-four—she was much better appreciated in the Anglo-Saxon world, judging by *The Empress Eugenie: A Three-Act Play* (1938). The author, Mrs. Belloc Lowndes, sister of Hilaire Belloc, was in fact

30. *Ibid.*, 141, 144, 160.

French by birth on her father's side and spent her early years in France. After her father's death she and her brother lived between France and England with their English mother, the poet Bessie Parkes Belloc, who was a friend of several writers, including notably George Eliot and Elizabeth Barrett Browning. Marie Belloc was married to the journalist Frederic Lowndes, whose specialty was obituaries, reputedly very good ones, for *The Times.* She was a prolific writer, publishing almost fifty novels, of which her crime stories were the most popular, as well as collections of short stories, memoirs, an edition and translation (with M. Shedlock) of two volumes of letters and pages from the *Journal* of the Goncourt brothers, and five plays, of which *The Empress Eugenie* was the last.

Though not overtly a feminist text either by traditional or modern criteria, this play is a complicitously feminine text, a sympathetic view of the triumphs and disasters in the life of one gracious lady written by another, presenting a view of the empress totally opposed to the myth of the harpy of the Tuileries and very much at odds with historians' views of the part that she played in the life and politics of the Second Empire. Stereotypes apart, it is a somewhat gossipy text in parts and thoroughly anecdotal, consisting of a dozen scenes, each one carefully dated and each one presenting a single illustrative incident from the noble woman's life. Drawing no doubt upon her rather selective readings, the author slips further anecdotes into the anecdotal scenes—for instance the "By way of the chapel" incident or the "After tonight no one will dare insult you" incident—such that the play becomes a series of vignettes, a sort of theatricalized (re)version of extracts from Viel-Castel's memoirs, as they relate to the empress, that are every bit as sympathetic to the subject as he was hostile.

The action begins in the autumn of 1845, in the drawing room at the duke of Alba's palace in Madrid, where the duke of Sesto reveals that he loves Eugenie's sister, the duchess of Alba, and where a nun, Sister Margaret, predicts that Eugenie will be a queen and live a life of brilliance and splendor, a life in which the kindness of her heart, her generosity, her fine intellect will enable her "to do great things for thousands of unhappy human beings." This she proceeds to do, at least in this play. In the drawing room in Princess Mathilde's house on 31 December 1852, she is already on good terms with the emperor, enough to snub Plon-Plon, to praise most enthusiastically Alexandre Dumas and *The Three Musketeers,* which the emperor pretends that he has read and admires to please her, and to prompt Mathilde to try to persuade her cousin to look elsewhere for a better match. However, despite disparaging court gossip about her past, despite Mme. de Fortoul's slights and the objections of Mathilde, Persigny, Plon-Plon, and Fleury, the emperor, showing rare resolution in this play, declares his love for Eugenie, takes her in his arms and offers her his throne. As Mathilde remarks to the cynical Morny: "How long d'you give this crazy passion, Morny? He has never been faithful to any woman for longer than six months. Not even Miss Howard, and she—she knew all the tricks."[31]

Mathilde's calculations prove to be both right and wrong, for the emperor is indeed unfaithful, but the love survives the five scenes of Act 2, thanks to the stoical forbearance of the empress. In August 1855, in the reception room of the Palace of Saint-Cloud, the imperial couple receives Queen Victoria, Prince Albert, the princess royal and the prince of Wales for the briefest of discussions on the Crimean War. The emperor proudly shows off his Garter; Prince Albert says not a word. Then, when this illustrious company has departed without him, Bismarck arrives (late), speaking scornfully of the foolishness of the court, for, as he puts it: "It's a musical comedy Court"—though he does makes an exception for Eugenie—and menacingly vowing to teach France a lesson. In the next scene, Eugenie, as if to prove the point, visits a cholera hospital in Amiens in July 1866, reveals her noble heart and courage, disproving rumors of her frivolity, though a week later she is presented firstly surrounded by her ladies-in-waiting in a recreation of a sitting for Winterhalter and his famous painting, then discussing crinolines with Worth in a scene which extraordinarily ends with her doing a Highland fling with the duke of Atholl! To demonstrate her rectitude and to rectify such excesses, she next reveals to the Prussian ambassador, Count von der Goltz, in the summer of 1868 in her sitting room at Saint-Cloud, that she has known all along that he was in love with her—"After all, I'm a woman first, and an Empress a long way afterwards"—but has been content to be discreetly grateful for his love.[32] He, in turn, reveals that Bismarck is her enemy and confirms that Marguerite Bellanger is her rival, whereupon, in a significant departure from the

31. Mrs. Belloc Lowndes, *The Empress Eugenie: A Three-Act Play* (New York–Toronto: Longmans, Green, 1938), 52.

32. An authentic detail, for, as Ridley notes on the Baron von der Goltz's love: "She enjoyed his admiration, referring to him as 'poor Goltz.'" Ridley, *Napoleon III and Eugénie,* 478.

legendary visit to see Margot-la-Rigoleuse—would a lady of her rank demean herself to go to visit such a woman!—she persuades Goltz in this play to bring the emperor's mistress to Saint-Cloud a few hours later. Unfortunately this insight into the famous confrontation turns out to be most disappointing, and hardly convincing at all, though inevitably prepared to the advantage of the wronged wife. In awe of the empress, Margot simply falls to her knees and weeps, readily consenting to obey the request of the "Empress of the French" to leave "Tou-Tou" (as the emperor likes her to call him) alone and agreeing, no doubt too, with her wise observation that "men are fickle and he more fickle than most." Nevertheless, six weeks later, Act 2 ends in the same place on a tender domestic scene with the emperor, now looking "dejected and ill," showering affection on his "darling" wife, as she sits sewing (!) and gently chiding him for his infidelities. Their peace is shattered by the arrival of the empress of Mexico, who rants on at the "King of Babylon" for abandoning her "treasure," Maximilian, demands that he send a million men to Mexico, and accuses Eugenie of trying to poison her with a glass of lemonade![33]

More expeditiously Act 3 presents the action at the Tuileries on 2 and 4 September 1870, where Eugenie, very much in charge, confronts General Trochu and refuses his request to allow the emperor to return to Paris from the theater of war, then reluctantly agrees to escape in the nick of time with Prince Metternich and Count Nigra as the mob invades the palace. By way of compensation General Trochu pays her a parting compliment: "I've no reason to love the Empress. But I never met any man half as brave as she has shown herself to be in the last few days." In the next scene she has become a white-haired widow, "but still a beautiful woman," in her exile in Chislehurst on a "splendid June day in 1879," where she bravely receives the shattering news of the death of the prince imperial in Zululand. Despite her grievous loss, a few days later, she magnanimously begs indulgence from Queen Victoria for Captain Carey, whose supposed cowardice had led to her son's death.[34] Finally, as unlikely

33. Belloc Lowndes, *The Empress Eugenie,* 61, 77, 82, 90, 99.

34. The author simplifies, no doubt for the sake of concision and dramatic effect, a complex set of circumstances and views, for the attitude of both Eugénie and Queen Victoria changed as proceedings against Lieutenant J. B. Carey dragged on into August. The court-martial sentence against Carey was quashed, but he was blamed for abandoning the prince imperial. Interestingly, Mrs. Belloc Lowndes has Eugénie read a letter from Carey to his wife about the incident, a letter which, in reality, was communicated to Eugénie in mysterious circumstances and which Eugénie sent to Queen Victoria. The letter in the play is a simplified version of the real letter, which is reproduced in Ridley, *Napoleon III and Eugénie,* 645–46.

as it may seem, the last scene of the play, set at the Hôtel Continental in Paris on Armistice Day, 1918, in a room overlooking the Tuileries Gardens, brings together Eugenie and Georges Clemenceau, head of the government at the time, who had been imprisoned by her husband.[35] They rejoice together at the return to France of Alsace and Lorraine. The author misses a chance to acknowledge the part that the empress played in the restoration of the two provinces when she produced and passed on to Clemenceau a letter that King William of Prussia had sent her just after the Franco-Prussian War, in which he justified the annexation on strategic grounds alone.[36] But it is enough, in this scene, to show the courage of the empress in not dwelling upon the past and in seeking henceforth "peace, tranquillity, forgetfulness," as the crowd acclaims a great victory and its leader, Clemenceau.[37]

This play, which in some respects is a well-documented account of certain episodes drawn from the history of the Second Empire, is clearly in the main a systematic vindication of the empress, no doubt directed against the opprobrium that was still attached to her name and reputation long after the fall of the regime. Historical events are a mere backdrop for the displays of Eugénie's unshakable virtues. As for the emperor himself, he cuts a rather pathetic figure in this play, though a jolly good chap, really, despite his fickleness in love. He is shown to be out of touch with reality, ignorant of what others are doing in his name, capable of the silliest of remarks—as, for instance, when he boasts that Eugenie is descended from Don Quixote—"good-natured" to a fault, "so good, so kind, so generous," overindulgent with his son, with "far too much heart," a kind of domesticated softy, an inept but doting husband, whose only real act of courage, it seems, was to marry Eugenie.[38] As the real force behind the throne, Eugenie's virtues suggest also, by association, that the play is a vindication of the Second Empire itself, a regime that, for all its failings—which, for Heaven's sake, she did her very best to correct!—and for all its failures—which, by God, she did all she could to avoid!—has prepared a glorious future for France. The law of this play seems to be that, in front of every strong woman, there's an unsuccessful man!

35. It is in fact true that Eugénie rallied to the cause of Republican France during the Great War. See Ridley, *Napoleon III and Eugénie,* 638.

36. See Kurtz, *The Empress Eugénie,* 257–58, 361.

37. Belloc Lowndes, *The Empress Eugenie,* 114, 115, 129.

38. *Ibid.,* 31, 48, 61, 89, 70, 94.

COLONIALIST (AND LECHER)

What is, almost certainly, the most recent appearance of Napoleon III of any significance in the world of fiction occurs in the late Brian Moore's last novel *The Magician's Wife* (1997). The author, Irish-born (in Belfast, in 1921), a Canadian citizen after emigrating in 1948 and a resident in the United States after 1959, won numerous literary awards, was the author of twenty well-crafted, intriguing novels, and was shortlisted three times for the Booker Prize. He has been admired for his limpid and economical style, which succeeds remarkably in suggesting and exploring the "moments of crisis" in his characters' lives. Displacement and failure are common themes, as is a preoccupation with superstition, miracles, the supernatural or, at least, with the doubts and dilemmas of his characters situated at the margins of faith. He has been particularly praised for his success in depicting female characters, their problems of identity and self-expression, their sexuality, as in his first and best-known novel, *Judith Hearn* (1955).

The Magician's Wife, a typical work for a writer who has confessed to deriving pleasure from lulling his readers into believing that they are reading one kind of novel and then, halfway through, discovering that it is a different kind of book, has two distinct settings: provincial France and the court at Compiègne in Part 1, Algeria at the end of the same year in Part 2. The novel narrates, from the point of view of his wife, Emmeline, the story of how Henri Lambert, a magician, illusionist, and inventor, is recruited by Napoleon III's Bureau Arabe to trick the restless Berber leaders into believing that France's "holy man" has powers superior to those of the marabouts of the tribes of Kabylia, thereby gaining precious time for the emperor's army to recover from the exertions of the Crimean War and be ready to complete the conquest of Algeria the following year. Since the capture of Algiers in 1830, settlers from France, Italy, and Spain had been progressively occupying the more fertile Algerian lands around the coastal areas, driving the Muslims into the less fruitful territories inland. A bloody and protracted war between the French forces led by General Thomas Bugeaud against the Muslim resistance of Abd al Qadir had lasted for most of the July Monarchy. The Second Republic had declared the occupied territories an integral part of France, though the "mixed" and "Arab" territories had remained under the rule of military commanders, administered directly through the *"bureaux arabes"* and the local chiefs. Napoleon III returned Algeria to military rule under the governor-generalship of General Randon, who oversaw a program of renewed colonization which had the effect of driving the tribes away from the newly colonized areas. But yielding to the demands of the settlers, he created a separate ministry and put an end to military rule. Plon-Plon became minister for Algeria and the colonies in June 1858 and followed a policy of assimilation extended to the Muslim population, though he never bothered to visit the country himself. Moore's novel deals with the period immediately preceding this initiative and is set during the year before French armies under the command of General Randon and General MacMahon subdued the restless tribes of Kabylia.

However important the political and colonial setting, the novel is mainly a study of a woman's less than satisfactory relationship with her eccentric husband, of her need to come to terms with his fame and with her own sense of unfulfillment and with the inadequacies of her marriage. She is tempted to engage upon an affair with Colonel Deniau, who stage-manages the whole operation of her husband's performances in Algeria. Emmeline, as she is called, comes from Rouen and is in certain ways yet another version of her fictional contemporary, Emma Bovary, though less gullible than Flaubert's character, less emotive and endowed with a very modern and somewhat anachronistic system of values, which leads her, for example, to be repelled by the cruelty to the animals in *la curée* in Compiègne, to her growing ideological objections to France's colonial conquests, and to her revulsion before the evidence of slavery practiced in Algeria. As the novel begins, her husband is thoroughly engrossed in his experiments with automatons in their manor house nears Tours, when the invitation to the last "*série*" at Compiègne, from 22 to 28 November, sets the plot in motion. Emmeline must reluctantly buy outfits from Monsieur West, who is presumably based on Worth[39]—and who is faithfully represented with his English accent and "his loose silk smock, black velvet trousers and a huge velvet beret." She equally reluctantly catches the imperial train at the Gare du Nord, and, with her sense of alienation from this social scene, has to put up with a series of trials: the inconveniences and rigorous protocol of Compiègne, the repulsive massacre of hundreds of animals and birds at the shoot and the even more enervating sight of the brutality of *la*

39. Curiously, however, she does put on what is called "an elegant Worth crinoline" for her last evening at Compiègne.

curée, and, to cap it all, the emperor's unwelcome attentions. When she sees Napoleon III for the first time, at the opening reception, she is struck by how he "differed from his photographs and paintings, seeming to be shorter, stouter, his waxed moustaches longer, his eyelids drooping languidly as though he had just wakened from sleep." The empress, of course, is wearing a Monsieur West dress. There follow: a performance of an unidentified play at the court theater, where she, like her Flaubertian counterpart, is moved by the vividness of the acting, here the "great" Coquelin and Madeleine Brohan; a visit to Pierrefonds with the suspiciously attentive Deniau; a poetry reading by Gautier, which almost puts the emperor to sleep, and a performance of magic tricks by her husband, which wakes him up, "his sleepy lizard eyes lit with approval." In their audience with the emperor, His Majesty, with his "long thin waxed moustaches and goat-like pointed beard, [which] made him resemble a satyr in a Rubens painting," seems more interested in her than in her husband's tricks. He has her sit next to him at lunch, invites her to the discussion of her husband's vital Algerian mission in his study. He appears ill—"she realized, with shock, that his cheeks were rouged"—but he is still sprightly enough, as she discovers when she finds herself next to him watching *la curée* in the long gallery overlooking the Cour d'Honneur of the château. At the crucial moment, in this culminating scene, "a hand touched her back, pushing askew the hoop of her crinoline and sliding down to fondle her buttocks. She turned to face the Emperor's sly concern. 'Are you cold, Madame? Do you need another wrap?' "[40] With the problem of the inhibitions in her marriage still unsolved, with doubts about her husband's love, with the sad memories of her miscarriage and her still-born child, and still reeling from her experiences at Compiègne, she is shipped off to Algiers with her husband.

The second part of the book relates the Algerian adventure still from the point of view of Emmeline's impressions and her excited discovery of the exotic Arab world. She duly meets the governor-general, visits the Kasbah, is almost unfaithful to her husband with Deniau. Her husband is far too preoccupied to pay much attention to her, busy bamboozling the natives, presenting himself as a French sorcerer. There are some dangerous adventures and ugly encounters in the desert, as the French meet hostility

40. Brian Moore, *The Magician's Wife* (Toronto: Alfred A. Knopf, 1997), 12, 18–19, 48, 51, 57, 65.

in the local tribes. There is for her the agonizingly painful loss of their servant, Jules, from cholera and her growing sense of disquiet at the immorality of the mission, indeed of the whole colonialist venture. She even reveals the truth of her husband's purpose and tricks to the old and wise marabout, Bou-Aziz, and his daughter, Taalith. Though she confesses this act of betrayal to her husband, it does not influence the outcome of their adventure, and the illusionists are themselves deceived in the belief that their mission has been accomplished. Obviously no Isabelle Eberhardt, no reckless Romantic Emma Bovary, she. As the novel ends, she returns home resignedly with her husband, from this land of fierce passions and of a deep-rooted faith in the will of God, back to Second Empire France, where all this is lacking, back to a world in which the emperor wears rouge, in which the mass in the private chapel of Compiègne has "no more meaning than a military parade,"[41] in which she will live out the pretense of her marriage. Back to the real world of illusions.

Caesar

The works that we have looked at so far all deal with a particular aspect of the life of Louis Napoléon or imprison him within the reductive confines of a stereotyped persona, seemingly confirming the view that this inscrutable figure is beyond representation within any degree of depth or complexity. Alfred Neumann's two-volume fictionalized biography is a notable exception, constituting a remarkable achievement of sustained applied scholarship and imaginative writing. Neumann (1895–1952) was a novelist, poet, and playwright, credited with contributing to the popularity of the historical novel in his time. Throughout his career, he had an abiding interest in powerful European leaders, notably in his early story *Der Patriot* (1925), which deals with the murder of Emperor Paul of Russia and was staged in London in 1928 under the title *Such Men Are Dangerous*, whilst, in the novel for which he won the Kleist Prize, *Der Teufel* (*The Devil*) (1926), he studies power struggles during the reign of Louis XI. The second volume of his novel on Louis Napoléon is dedicated to his "dear friend" Thomas Mann, "in heartfelt admiration," including an epigraph borrowed from the master's works—though not, one would think,

41. *Ibid.*, 69.

one of his profoundest thoughts: "History is what has happened and what goes on happening in time." Volume 1, *Another Caesar* (1934), covers the time period from Hortense's pregnancy to the coup d'état; volume 2, *The Gaudy Empire* (1936), takes up the plot from the first years of the Empire down to the funeral of Victor Noir, with a brief double epilogue set on the day of Sedan, then on the day of the fallen emperor's death.

Apart from its impressive scope and detail, Neumann's massive work is remarkable for its use of the technique of "point of view," in the old (pre-Genette) and rather ambiguous sense of the term, namely, as it applies both to the filtering of narrated events through the vision of a character and to the presentation of the character's own inner thoughts or discourse. Indeed, a more appropriate epigraph to the work might have been: "History is what is perceived to have happened and what is perceived to go on happening in time." The widespread use of these techniques is a reminder that this work belongs to the age of the introspective or phenomenological novel, of which Thomas Mann's fiction represents, of course, a supreme example. Thus Neumann fills in the gaps of the series of known events with elaborate probing into the character's motives, self-questioning, speculation, even, at times, dreams and hallucinations. Exceptionally, Louis Napoléon is here endowed with a rich inner life, which is shown in stark contrast to his legendary stumbling, formalized, lethargic, outer actions. All of this is set within a panoramic depiction of the times in which the new Caesar lived and the momentous historical events that he occasioned, or that were occasioned in his name.

The imaginary recreation of the inner discourse and focalized experience is not by any means limited in this "novel" to Louis Napoléon. Indeed, the first volume opens from the "point of view" of King Louis, his father, as he awaits Hortense's arrival at Toulouse on 12 August 1807, ruminating on his anguish at his physical deformities, his sexual desires, his mistrust of his wife, and his resentment against the War Lord, that is, Napoleon I—Neumann has a fondness for inventing associative nicknames for his characters. Hortense, to his surprise and suspiciously, tempts him to have intercourse, like a "moth to the flame"—Neumann also has a fondness for portentous chapter headings, many of which derive from mythology or recondite adages. We see Louis talking to Admiral Verhuell at the Dutch embassy in Paris, "a man in his prime, with a big nose, and shrewd, weary eyes"—Neumann clearly subscribed to the Verhuell theory. The whole "comedy" of the marriage is acted out until the birth of the new prince imperial, on 20 April 1808, with Admiral Verhuell acting as the "proxy" for the absent father at the formal signing of the birth certificate. Much of what follows is presented from Hortense's point of view: the abdication, the separation, the birth of the Aiglon, the birth of her son by Flahaut, the fall of Napoleon I, the quiet life at Arenenberg. The focalization shifts to Le Bas, young Louis's tutor, during his early years, with the narrator, in a Freudian mode, dwelling upon the discovery of a drawing of a naked woman, looking remarkably like Hortense, in the boy's algebra book. "Oh, that's only a woman for the Emperor," as his young Oedipus innocently remarks.[42] Louis Napoléon vows to re-establish the Empire himself on the death of his uncle; he does well at artillery school, like the War Lord himself; then, after Le Bas has been fired, he declares himself a republican, much to his mother's dismay; and he embarks upon his Italian adventures with his brother, Napoléon Louis, who agonizingly dies of pneumonia "supervening upon" measles. All of this is recounted with a considerable narrative skill that supplements the psychological insights. The first of the three "books" ends appropriately with news of another young death, that of the duke of Reichstadt, on 22 July 1832. The way is clear for Louis Napoléon, like the author, to rewrite the Napoleonic legend.

Two themes dominate the rest of the volume: the pretender's belief in his destiny and the patience that he requires in order to fulfill it. But there is time enough in history's happenings for his gallantries: mistresses in Baden-Baden, young Englishwomen smelling of lavender water, *cocottes* from Paris (without any olfactory specifications), Mathilde, to whom he becomes engaged (at least in this novel) even as he dallies with a "fair-haired English woman who claimed to be the natural daughter of Sir Hudson Lowe, the gaoler of St. Helena"—there seemed to be no limit to the Bonapartist connections. But as the narrator pompously comments: "No use, no use. Behind every woman, behind every night, stood the devil of patience, martyrising the proscribed spirit with the hellish drops of time." Even allowing for the distortions of translation, Neumann's prose is often turgid, just as his dialogue can be stilted. For example, when the arch-Bonapartist Persigny, nicknamed here the Prophet, comes bursting into Louis Napoléon's life, the young man asks himself awkwardly: "Is the time

42. Alfred Neumann, *Another Caesar,* trans. Eden Paul and Cedar Paul (New York: Alfred A. Knopf, 1935), 19, 23, 66.

ripe for me to join hands with such a roisterer?—Does my shirt of Nessus make my skin ache so fiercely that anything I can scratch myself with will be welcome?" But there is the comic relief of the Strasbourg fiasco, when the formidable Miss Gordon literally sweeps him off his feet, when he persuades her to strike up a duet with Colonel Vaudrey for the cause, when, entering into the spirit of the occasion, our intrepid hero in his mock Napoleonic hat speculates, with remarkable foresight, that "perhaps my Second Republic or my Second Empire will be a comic opera; perchance a good operetta," when the would-be emperor muffs his lines, and when the whole venture collapses into farce.[43] Hortense's death provides a touching interlude and London life a dazzling supporting cast. But as the ragtag invasion force sets sail, with the symbolically crippled osprey (sea-eagle) on board, pecking viciously at Persigny, the comic mode returns in the shambolic confusion of the events at Boulogne-sur-mer, which end up with a Napoleon in the sea.

With some elevated musings from the narrator on the citadel theme— citadels are durability, worse than life and death, only God can turn stone into spirit, life is a struggle against durability, for Neumann was a great admirer of Stendhal's *La Chartreuse de Parme*—the final "book" begins firmly within the perspective of the prisoner, who meditates at length upon his fate, and tells the familiar story of his stay at Ham: the "fresh" laundry girl, with some curious domestic details about his changes of underwear, which are presumably novelistic *effets de réel,* the little garden, Éléonore's pregnancy, his bladder troubles, chills and rheumatism, the visitors, including again Sir Robert Peel with a handy passport for him to use, the workmen at the citadel, the disguise—despite the difficulty of the "big nose," another motif—and the escape. London life again, a visit to the Tower for more modulations on the theme of the citadel, along with further recurrences of the thematic signposts of the book: patience, the pretender's "star," his big nose again (obsessively), the dynamics of self-doubt and will. Miss Howard makes an entrance and due account is taken of her beauty, but Neumann's real passion in the whole biography is politics and political philosophy. No doubt, then, because of the author's passionate interest in the matter, the Revolution of February 1848 and the June Days are narrated in a curiously stylized, semi-poetic style: Red wrath running wild, the quaking earth throwing up barricades, a direct address

43. *Ibid.*, 181, 182, 185, 238.

by the narrator to the common folk of Paris, the chorus of the Greek tragedy (the people) forcing their way onto the center-stage (the Hôtel de
Ville). It is the very opposite of Flaubert's stark narrative of the same
events. "The revolution," the narrator concludes about the June Days,
"lacked vitality, or had only the vitality of a mediocre tragi-comedy." Now
the Name becomes the dominant leitmotif, as Louis Napoléon takes up
his seat in the National Assembly and, despite his inadequacies as an orator, draws support, rises to the top: "the Name exercised a charm, and the
prophet [Persigny] was a master of his trade as magician. To the middle-
aged and the elderly, the Name conveyed memories of the legend; to
young people it spoke of liberalism; to the timid it brought assurance of
order in the State; to the deceived and the oppressed, it conveyed a guarantee of social justice." As events move towards the climax and the denouement of the coup d'état, Eugenia surprisingly makes a premature
appearance, provoking the jealousy of Venus (Miss Howard) and provoking not only Louis Napoléon's unqualified admiration but thoughts of
her as a future empress. Matters certainly come to a head both in fact and
fiction as the day approaches: Miss Gordon threatens to shoot the president, but shoots herself instead; Le Bas lectures his former pupil on his
obligations to the presidential oath and is added to the list of arrestees. But
we see none of the action during the night of the coup d'état, since we are
once again restricted to Louis Napoléon's own point of view. He goes to
bed with Hugo's odes—but, then, Hugo himself had already recounted
the action, in his particular manner. As the volume ends, we see Louis Napoléon at his desk, urging Morny to avoid bloodshed: " 'Monseigneur,'
said his brother, 'you must certainly put on gloves when you are making a
revolution. But the gloves will not prevent your fingers getting stained
with blood, and some of the blood will run under your nails.' "[44]

The second volume, as voluminous as the first, is also divided with a
sense of symmetry into three "books," the emphasis becoming now even
more markedly upon political history, after a somewhat ironic description
of "The New Happiness" (the title of Book 1) in the new Paris that
Haussmann is constructing: "Life is splendid, and waxes more splendid
from day to day. Everyone shares in the Emperor's happiness and good
fortune. Look around you. Life means well by us. Never have women been
so beautiful or played so important a part. No country has ever had a more

44. *Ibid.*, 480, 503, 589.

lovely empress." Nevertheless, there is remarkably little on the emperor's women in this book, dominated as it is by politicians, political commentators, and political commentary. The exception is la Castiglione, nicknamed Judith, who, of course, has a political role to play and occasions an intriguing scene in which the Florentine beauty, in her lilac négligé, lying on a low divan, and the emperor, wreathed in a cloud of tobacco smoke, exchange few words but an abundance of thoughts, mostly on his part, as the world-weary and cynical politician of love reveals his immunity to her wiles: "He knew that the obedient silk would next slip away from the Amazonian thighs and the Praxitelean shoulders. He was familiar with all these sculptural unveilings, and with the appearance of the brilliant Anadyomene which would thereupon be revealed." But the reader is spared the actual performance as the gunshot of the supposed assassination attempt puts paid prematurely to the evening's entertainment.[45] In general, the emperor is still as "inscrutable as ever, veiled in clouds despite the glaring sunshine of his triumph; one whose motives no one could fathom."[46] Even in the penetrating psychological novelist's probings of his thoughts, questions are the most common form of this inner discourse, as either the narrator attempts to recreate the relentless self-questioning of the man or the author passes on his own bafflement at his character's inscrutability even in the act of scrutinizing his mind. But this imaginative inner discourse does serve a useful narrative function in skillfully linking the different strands of the story with retrospective allusions and passages of recollection that convey a certain sense of necessity to the events of some fifteen years, events which are at times somewhat ponderously narrated, represented, summarized, or at some considerable length disquisitioned upon. There is, however, the excitement of the Orsini assassination attempt and execution, the "Galop infernal" of Offenbach's Bouffes-Parisiennes (sic), battle scenes at Magenta and Solferino, seen, of course, from the perspective of Kepi, as the emperor is now called since he embarked upon his military expedition. There is also the drama of Charlotte's visit—and the incident of the (now) orangeade—and the "murder" of Victor Noir.

45. On this incident from a straight biographical perspective, see Ridley, *Napoleon III and Eugénie*, 399.
46. Alfred Neumann, *The Gaudy Empire*, trans. Eden Paul and Cedar Paul (New York: Alfred A. Knopf, 1937), 7, 82, 8.

But the most striking feature of this second volume is the emergence of two alternative and politically conflicting "points of view," Morny's and Rochefort's. The shift is doubtless brought about for the sake of necessary variety in such a lengthy narrative, but also—and mainly—to provide differing political perspectives on events. Morny, of course, establishes a precious link between the worlds of politics and theater, though there is shown to be little fundamental difference between the two. Rochefort, the "tyrannophobe," who is introduced remarkably early in the volume and, after Morny's death, becomes a privileged, and not always convincingly omnipresent observer, representing the perspective of opposition to the regime. Indeed, much of the conflict in the middle of the book concerns the struggle between these two, with the emperor eclipsed from the scene. There is little on the life of the court and much on the Italian and German policies of the regime, reflecting the author's own interests and expertise. Bismarck's visit to Biarritz at the beginning of Book 3 and his cleverly represented walk with the emperor on the sea-swept terrace are clearly a high point for the author, if not for the reader. But there is naturally an appropriateness to the fading presence of the emperor as a character, commanding less and less attention in the novel as his own physical and political powers fade. Yet there is a nicely contrived scene, in which he does play a leading part, in a section entitled "Gog and Magog," at a ministerial council meeting, on 5 July 1866, two days after the Battle of Sadowa. The empress is in full cry on her pro-Austrian hobbyhorse, and the emperor, seemingly half-asleep then simulating complete sleep, nevertheless prevails with his noninterventionist views in the debate through a neatly engineered and opportune intervention on the part of La Valette, the minister of the interior and future foreign minister, much to Eugénie's displeasure. Indeed, much of the point of the last sections of the work is to depict a vigorous, acute and guileful mind at work within a failing body. With articles from *La Lanterne* thundering forth, with Rochefort, the "Chronicler," the "Observer," now at center stage, and with the "Offenbachiade" gaily cavorting in the background, the virtual end of the novel corresponds with the arrival of an even mightier adversary: "The old and terrible thought, dredged from the profound by this young and terrible man with his stark candour, now emerged. Not petty forces, not revolution in masquerade as staged by the counterfeit Second Empire (travesty of the First), would bring about the desired change. This will be the work of the Great

Incendiary, the everlasting prototype of annihilation.—This would be the work of War."[47]

The author shrinks from evoking in any detail the Prussian victory—no doubt a case of tactful reticence on the part of a Prussian-born author. But in any case, his novel is essentially the story of the New Caesar, and Napoleon III's fall from political power marks the end of Neumann's tale. Both parts of the short epilogue are retrospective musings by the defeated man. In the first, set on 2 September 1870, the "unhappy Emperor," the "deflated Emperor," relives in his carriage on the way to captivity the last few weeks of the frenzy of war and the last few hours when, despite his physical sufferings as he had ridden into "the terrible affray," he had been condemned to live on. The second section, dated 9 January 1873, shows the "old man who had once been Emperor" on his deathbed, reflecting pathetically upon his chances of a triumphant return to power and on the prospects of his son, the "child of hope," but succumbing to his ailments, smiling "until the moment when death took him at 10.45; even then the smile remained."[48]

Such is the scope, the vividness, the relentless sweep of this work that, with some complicity (perseverance and indulgence) from the reader, it is a text that, at times, creates the illusion of being not a history but of (re)presenting history itself, which is a tribute to the writer's talents in the complementary arts, both as a novelist and as a historian, and in marked contrast to the simplistic reductiveness with which the emperor is represented elsewhere. There is, of course, a bitter irony in the fact that the most sympathetic, comprehensive, and comprehending recreation of Napoleon III's life should have come from the very country which destroyed his Empire.

47. *Ibid.*, 33, 539.
48. *Ibid.*, 547–48, 551–52.

chapter 13

Tragedy

HUBRIS

The term *tragedy* is used with remarkable frequency to refer to the end of the Second Empire even by commentators who have not shown any particular sense of awe at the Emperor's or his regime's achievements. This suggests that the much-abused term is being applied in such instances, not in the loose and current sense of an unexpected calamity, but with the perception that events did indeed, in their essential aspects, conform to the pattern of the noblest of the classical genres. Thus, to quote one of many such instances, J. P. T. Bury writes: "The last four years of the Second Empire have about them an air of classic tragedy and impending doom." The tragic effect, as classical poetics informs us, derives from the combination of a particular plot structure (*mythos*) and a thematic configuration or total pattern of imagery (*dianoia*): the tightly knit web of circumstance which, by necessity or probability, brings about the peripety of the hero's change of fortune from happiness to misery, deriving from the effects of some human weakness or blindness, arousing in the spectator pity and fear and bringing about, through the suffering that it entails, an uplifting vision of the fateful logic of events. If we can still accept that the verbal artifacts of much literature can and do imitate more or less the eventualities of life and bring into focus their significance, it can be no less the case that the essential aspects of a series of historical events can be shown to conform to and can be explained by the paradigms of certain literary forms, without doing any more violence to the complexity of such events than do any other forms of historical interpretation. This is particularly true when such events betray within themselves a pattern of completion and when they are related to those genres which, like tragedy, bring about a deeper understanding of reality rather than to those which promote evasion from it. At a most obvious level of generality, the fall of the house of Napoleon III has its "literary correlative" in the common motif of tragedy. As Frye notes: "There is a great deal in tragedy about pride or race and birthright, but its general tendency is to isolate a ruling or noble family from the rest of society."[1]

In ancient Greece, to entertain the public, dramatists would usually present after their trilogy of tragic plays a satirical work in which the gods and heroes were mocked in a parodic performance.[2] The Second Empire reversed the trend, acting out its tragic fall after the vaudeville of the *fête impériale*. The pivotal year is usually reckoned to be 1867, when the Empire was at its apogee, displaying its prosperity and economic progress, attracting eleven million visitors to its festivities, to wonder at its accomplishments, at the Universal Exposition, held (ironically) on the Champ de Mars. The regime was riding high on the wheel of fortune, or so it seemed.

During what would later be revealed to be the twilight years of the regime, there was ample evidence of serious problems threatening its very existence, but little willingness to face up to them and to assess realistically their consequences. After the disastrous failure of the Mexican adventure in the area of foreign affairs, the Prussian victory at Sadowa may well have led to some satisfaction at Venetia's liberation and at the humiliation of Austria, but it brought about a fundamental shift in the balance of power in Europe to France's detriment and without any compensatory territorial

1. J. P. T. Bury, *Napoleon III and the Second Empire* (London: English Universities Press, 1964), 140; Northrop Frye, *Anatomy of Criticism* (Princeton: Princeton University Press, 1957), 207, 52, 219.

2. See Clifford Leech, *Tragedy* (London: Methuen, 1969), 13–14.

gains for France's neutrality in the conflict. The emperor singularly failed in his subsequent attempts to wrest compensation in the Rhineland, Belgium, and Luxembourg with the offer of an alliance with Prussia, which led to nothing but the humiliation of diplomatic failure before Bismarck's diplomatic maneuverings and the added setback of a decline in relations with Britain, which supported Belgium's continued autonomy. At home, a recession in 1867–1868 seemed to belie the promises of the Exhibition. The Crédit Mobilier, the investment bank of the Péreires, collapsed, marking the end of the boom, and economic stagnation set in. As the republican Jules Ferry, whose famous attack on Haussmann's "fantastic" finances led to further discomfort for the regime, declared: "The catastrophe of the Crédit Mobilier is the counterpart of the reverses abroad." There were, furthermore, open demonstrations of hostility to the Empire, riots against conscription, arrests of marchers in the streets singing "La Marseillaise," a spate of strikes in 1869 and 1870 leading to clashes with government troops. Attacks from a hostile republican press brought further discredit to the regime and reopened the question of its legitimacy. The elections of 1869 revealed the opposition's strength; only just over a million votes separated the supporters of the Empire (4,438,000) from those who opposed the regime (3,355,000). On 10 January 1870, Pierre Bonaparte shot Victor Noir, and the funeral, on the 12th, turned into a demonstration in which a hundred thousand protesters took part. Many of the pillars of the Empire had either passed away (Fortoul, Billault, Morny, Thouvenel, Fould, Walewski) or passed into disfavor (Persigny, Rouher, Baroche). By the end of the decade, "more than ever before," the now seriously ailing emperor "seemed to be alone, a man of 1848, left in isolation to face increasing difficulties and to confront a new generation."[3]

But there were enough reasons to fuel the delusion that such setbacks and crises could be smoothed over and that the future of the regime was bright and secure. In November 1869 French prestige was given a boost when the empress presided over the opening of the Suez Canal. The year "1870 began under the same happy auspices, and life in Paris was as entertaining and as glamorous as ever." The round of elegant distractions in high society went on largely undisturbed, as if, indeed, it could go on forever. *Tout Paris* was in a heady state of collective *hubris,* as can retrospectively be seen, in the crucial state "from which point the road to what

3. Bury, *Napoleon III and the Second Empire,* 152–53, 156.

might have been and the road to what will be can be simultaneously seen"—by the observer, of course, and not by the deluded participants, at the crucial moment when "the wheel of fortune begins its inevitable cyclical movement downward."[4]

The year 1870 was also that in which the emperor sought to achieve what he called the "crowning of the edifice," the liberal measures, some of which had been cautiously introduced since 1860, but which, in the winter of 1869–1870, brought about radical changes, a new political freedom, and an impression of renewal. The cynical view is that he was forced to make such concessions because of the strength of the opposition pressure or because of his own physical weakness and lack of will to resist it. The more charitable view, substantiated by his early writings, is that he always envisaged such reforms and that the granting of liberties was to be the natural outcome of his grand scheme, inspired by the "Napoleonic Ideas" and by the need to complete the unfinished task of his illustrious uncle, of whom he had written thirty years earlier: "He would have consolidated liberty; to do this, he had only to relax the threads of the network he had formed. The government of Napoleon, better than any other, could endure liberty, for this simple reason,—that liberty would have confirmed his throne, whereas it overthrows thrones which have not a solid basis."[5] He clearly believed, hoped, or gambled that the latter scenario would apply. Indeed, his primary goal, and the empress's obsession at this time, in view of the emperor's failing health, was to secure the future of the Napoleonic dynasty with thoughts of handing over the reins of power to the prince imperial in 1874, when the young man would come of age.

At the emperor's prompting a decree had been issued in November 1860 allowing the Senate and the Legislative Body to debate the speech from the throne and allowing the latter chamber to debate legislation in the presence of ministers. Further reforms followed, leading to the more drastic measures introduced by the *sénatus-consulte* of 12 July 1869 and ratified on 6 September, which allowed the legislature to elect its own officers, increased its powers to initiate and amend government bills, to question ministers, to vote on the budget by sections. Though the emperor retained his prerogatives on ministerial responsibility—still reserving the right to name and convoke ministers, refusing to authorize the cre-

---

4. Burchell, *Imperial Masquerade*, 306; Frye, *Anatomy of Criticism*, 213.
5. *The Political and Historical Works of Louis Napoleon Bonaparte*, 1:340.

ation of the post of prime minister—on the dissolution of the legislature and on plebiscites, Émile Ollivier agreed to form the first government of the Liberal Empire on 27 December 1869 after secret talks which had required him to travel to Compiègne in disguise, without his glasses and wearing a false nose! Ollivier, whose father had been driven into exile by the coup d'état, had been one of the first republicans elected to the assembly in 1857, an eloquent opponent of the regime at first, but gradually rallying to the Empire under Morny's influence and becoming a staunch advocate of liberal reforms. He had famously remarked, after talks with the emperor in 1865: "What great things we will do together if Napoleon III really wishes to establish liberty!" In January 1870, when the new cabinet was formed, such great things indeed seemed possible. The appointments "unleashed a wave of optimism which was immediately registered on the Bourse." Further reforms ensued, with modifications to the Constitution, conferring further privileges on the legislature, devolving constituent powers to the people and transforming the Senate into a true legislative body on an equal footing with the lower house (except in matters of tax legislation). The emperor conserved his plebiscitary prerogative, which was invoked in article 46 of the new constitution, calling for a plebiscite on the newly established Liberal Empire. The plebiscite on 8 May 1870, in which the nation was asked to sanction the liberal reforms, led to an astonishing show of support. As Léon Gambetta remarked, "The Empire is stronger than ever." The emperor, when presented with the result in the Salle des États in the Louvre, spoke grandly of the ambitious plans of his government to increase the greatness and prosperity of the nation and advance the progress of civilization. As Williams notes, "Historians have been inclined to forget that the constitutional reforms of 1870 produced a wave of optimism in France. Only a few suspected the true nature of the Prussian peril, and the government had taken office on January 2nd with a friendly statement on German nationalism. France was on the verge of a new and happier era, and the Emperor, addressing the Corps législatif relative to the results of the plebiscite, concluded, 'More than ever before, we may envision the future without fear.' "[6]

The emperor himself, however, was one of the few to be aware of the full extent of the "Prussian peril." Colonel Stoffel had been sending re-

---

6. Williams, *The World of Napoleon III*, 246, 254, 262; Gambetta quoted in Burchell, *Imperial Masquerade*, 318.

ports on the strength of the Prussian armaments, the steel guns made by Krupp, the massive reserves of the Landwehr, the efficient German system of communications, Prussia's plans for rapid mobilization, and the supply depots near the French border. But his warnings went largely unheeded by the military establishment of France. By contrast, the French army went in for brilliant uniforms, embroidered battle flags, golden eagles and dashing cavalry charges, and for a belief in the traditional bravery and invincibility of the Napoleonic troops. As early as 1867, Napoleon III attempted to introduce a major program of reform to match the Prussian advances in military manpower, to replace the established lottery system of army recruitment, with its provision for buying out of the service, by a form of conscription, and to introduce an army reserve of some 600,000 men, a Garde Mobile, equivalent to the Prussian Landwehr. But the emperor's plan was met with almost total resistance by the press and the Legislative Assembly, whose members feared loss of support in their constituencies from such unpopular measures. For more than a year there were discussions, proposals, counterproposals, modifying and scaling down the emperor's original schemes. As Séguin writes, "What a pitiful debate! A pathetic discussion during the course of which we see the representatives that France has given herself blindly preparing her misfortune."[7] In face of such opposition, the emperor drew back from dissolving the Assembly and allowed the bill to be passed, on 14 January 1868, making no more than token changes to the recruitment law of 1832. It was his first fatal act of inaction. "The final tragedy of this sorry failure," as Bury remarks, "for which ruler and ruled were alike responsible, was that the country as a whole, quite unable to follow the technicalities of the prolonged discussions of 1866–8, fondly believed that it now had a trained army of 1,200,000 men which the Emperor had proclaimed as his objective. It was soon to make the bitter discovery that it had been living in a paradise of fools." "Believe me," the playwright Victorien Sardou confidently declared as the war fever mounted, "we will go through Prussia like a knife through butter." "From Paris to Berlin," claimed Marshal Leboeuf, the war minister, "it will be a mere stroll, walking stick in hand."[8]

7. Séguin, *Louis Napoléon le Grand*, 391. According to Séguin, with a population of 22 millions in 1866, Prussia was able to mobilize an army of 700,000 men, whilst France, with a population of 32 millions, could only call upon 385,000 (*ibid.*, 387). On the arguments used against the emperor's plans, see *ibid.*, 391–93.

8. Bury, *Napoleon III and the Second Empire*, 175; Sardou quoted in Burchell, *Imperial Masquerade*, 329; Leboeuf quoted in Frerejean, *Napoléon IV*, 103.

HAMARTIA

The truly tragic effect arises, whatever its protagonists might claim, not from the crushing consequences of the infernal machinery of some external fate, nor from the free will that unwittingly chooses a disastrous course, but from the "interrelation of character and circumstance," from the character's fatal participation in the encompassing process that leads to catastrophe. It stems from a curiously paradoxical combination: "a fearful sense of rightness (the hero must fall) and a pitying sense of wrongness (it is too bad that he falls)."[9] Fate is at its most ironic in tragedy, not merely exercising its irresistible force, but drawing the victim into complicity with its workings. The often repeated dictum that the country that declares war is not necessarily the cause of the war is frequently applied to the Franco-Prussian conflict, usually to exonerate Napoleon III and to lay the blame on Bismarck. But this is only true to a point. The emperor wanted peace, feared war, argued against mobilization, but did not have the physical or the moral strength to impose his will and had to take not only the ultimate responsibility as the head of state but also the blame for not having more vigorously resisted the call to war. It was not that he had no choice, but that he lacked the will to impose the right choice. The irony of the situation, as Burchell notes, "was that he had come to power on the strength of the Napoleonic Legend and, no matter what his better judgment might be, he could not deny it now."[10] More and more, the emperor's policies were shaped by pressures from the public, leading him to violate the golden rule that he had long ago formulated for the ruler: to lead the nation and not be led by it. He was not only pressured into committing his country to war by responding to France's desire for war, but his very name impelled him to lead his army into an inevitable debacle. Finally, and indeed with an imperious finality, he would pay the price of his earlier successes. In tragedy the past catches up with the present, exacting its vengeance for the latitude that has been given.

The events leading up to the war are well known, as is the decisive part that the empress played in bringing them about. When Queen Isabella of Spain was deposed by an uprising in September 1868, France feared that a republic or a monarchy would be established in Madrid, hostile to French

---

9. Leech, *Tragedy,* 38–39; Frye, *Anatomy of Criticism,* 214.
10. Burchell, *Imperial Masquerade,* 328.

interests and security. The empress, who had recently been excluded from involvement in the affairs of state, mainly by Ollivier's efforts, threw herself passionately into the intrigues brought about by the crisis surrounding the question of the Spanish succession, about which she had a personal sense of involvement. She had Carlist sympathies, but, in an intriguing turn of events, favored Isabella's son, Alfonso, prince of Asturias, who was supported by the duke of Sexto, Eugénie's girlhood paramour, now married to Morny's widow. The candidacy of Leopold, prince of Hohenzollern-Sigmaringen, which Bismarck had secretively been promoting for a year and which came to light in Paris on 2 July 1870, was interpreted, despite the kinship of the young prince with Napoleon III on his mother's side, both as an affront and a threat to France, since the young man, an officer in the Prussian army, was a subject and a distant cousin of the king of Prussia, who was head of the Hohenzollern family. The empress had no doubt that it was a *casus belli*.[11] The emperor saw the situation as an opportunity to embarrass Bismarck. When French protests, threats, and diplomatic representations led to the news of the withdrawal of the Hohenzollern candidacy on 11 July, the crisis seemed to have been resolved to France's honor, to Prussia's discomfort, and to the emperor's relief. But he submitted to pressure from the court, the public, the government, the foreign minister, the duc de Gramont—a fervent anti-Prussian—and, especially, his wife to demand guarantees from the king of Prussia that the latter would not sanction any renewal of the candidacy. Now it was the turn of the king of Prussia, who was at the time at the spa in Ems, to be outraged and for Bismarck to seize the opportunity to avenge an affront and to provoke a war. The famous Ems telegram from the king, Bismarck's "red rag to the Gallic bull," his abridged and more abrasive version of the king's telegram informing his chancellor of the interview with the French ambassador, Benedetti, which Bismarck published in the press, fueled the clamorings for war in both Berlin and Paris.

As matters thus came to a head in the heated discussions of the cabinet at Saint-Cloud on 14 July 1870, the emperor argued for a peaceful settlement, for an international conference, for mediation from Britain. The empress, vigorously supported by Leboeuf, urged war. The marshal claimed that France was ready and that the enemy was not. The emperor was not convinced, but was ill, tired, outnumbered, and, overcome by a

11. Nichols Barker, *Distaff Diplomacy*, 185, 195–96.

dizzy spell, retired to bed according to some accounts, leaving the field free for the empress to argue the case for an offensive. The ministers decided to mobilize the troops. The emperor was woken. He signed the decree. Or as was most likely the case, he simply gave in to the pressure of public opinion. Whatever the circumstances, it was a fatal error, a second act of inaction, the error of judgment that admits disaster in the play, the ultimate extravagance. "Tragically, he was too weak to prevent his country from destroying itself in one final access of unreality." Tragically indeed, for, as Frye points out, tragedy lies not in the moral significance of the decisive act, but in the "inevitability of the consequences of the act." The next day, the government presented a request to the Legislative Assembly for financial backing for war. Leboeuf gave his word of honor that the army was ready for war. "What do you mean by 'ready'?" he was asked. He famously replied: "What I mean by that is that, if the war were to last for a year, we would not need to buy a single gaiter button." There had been crowds in the streets since the previous evening, shouting "Down with Prussia!" "To Berlin!" "*Vive la guerre!*" even "*Vive l'Empereur!*" People sang "La Marseillaise," and the police were ordered not to stop them. They sang "Partant pour la Syrie" as well, and Hortense Schneider's hit song from *La Grande Duchesse de Gérolstein,* "Oh! How I Love Military Men!"[12]

N E M E S I S

Frerejean reports, but without any indication of the source, a (nevertheless likely) conversation between the emperor and his son, which supposedly took place in 1869 during the absence of the empress at the time of the inauguration of the Suez Canal and which reveals Napoleon III's sense of impending disaster. He has just read a page of Bossuet to the boy, declaring: "You see, Louis, you think that I am the master of the world, but I am nothing but the plaything of destiny. God can strike me down or send me back into exile." When the boy laughs at his father's gloomy prediction, he adds:

12. On the emperor at Saint-Cloud, see Frerejean, *Napoléon IV,* 103, and Williams, *The Mortal Napoleon III,* 145; Burchell, *Imperial Masquerade,* 319; Frye, *Anatomy of Criticism,* 38; Ridley, *Napoleon III and Eugénie,* 562.

"Louis, don't laugh. You already know that the whole of my life is a dream. I believe in vain that I am building on firm ground, the ground trembles beneath me. You know that tomorrow belongs to God."

"Papa, why would God strike you down?"

"Because God delights in punishing men's pride. He has struck down lesser and greater men than me. You have read the story of Louis XVI, you know Napoleon's off by heart."

We have already noted the profound fatalism of the man, as attested by his "last love," the Countess de Mercy-Argenteau, who records his belief that his destiny was already mapped out in the stars, that his reign would come to an end with a Prussian victory. "It is written, it is written; nothing can change what is written," he would insist to her. He subsequently wrote to her a simple missive from the theater of war: "*Alea jacta est.*" His fatalism was, no doubt, the source of the stoicism, the "sublime" stoicism, as the empress observed, with which he would face the inevitable crushing defeat in war and, no doubt also, the source of the undeniable heroism with which he sought to confront what he considered to be his destiny.[13]

There can have been few military leaders in the whole of history less fit for battle and less confident of success than Napoleon III at such a decisive juncture in the fortunes of his country when, too ill even to ride a horse in an appropriate ceremonial parade at the head of his troops as they left Paris to face the enemy, he had to take the train to Metz on 28 July 1870, unheralded, from his private railway station in Saint-Cloud. His physical condition had considerably worsened since 1866, at least in spells. His features were now frequently drawn with pain, his eyes become even more dull than before, his figure stouter, his gait more lethargic than ever. To the arthritis, neuralgia, and hemorrhoids that had long plagued him came the urinary problems related to the suspected bladder stone, which was diagnosed in 1865 but which he refused to have attended to until the following year, when the first probings took place, with the patient always keeping a veil of secrecy over the true seriousness of his condition. In a consultation by a team of doctors that took place on 1 July 1870, there was disagreement over the diagnosis, and only one of the doctors signed

13. Frerejean, *Napoléon IV*, 93; Mercy-Argenteau, *The Last Love of an Emperor*, 172–73, 180; the empress on her husband's stoicism, in Bierman, *Napoleon III and His Carnival Empire*, 390.

the report, which was dated 3 July and which, mysteriously, was kept secret from all but either the emperor himself or the empress, or possibly both. Secrecy again prevailed, for the timing was again fatal. As Williams points out, "what had been simply a medical question on July 1, the day of the consultation, had become political as well with the astonishing news of the Hohenzollern candidacy for the Spanish throne on July 2."[14] Did the emperor alone suppress the truth of the seriousness of his condition in the midst of the diplomatic crisis? Did the empress do the same for the same reasons, or, as has been suggested by her detractors, for her own political ends, urging her sick husband to war, to the command of his troops, to his probable collapse or death, which would be, she may have imagined, to her own advantage or to the advantage of their son, who accompanied his father to the front?

Taking command of the so-called Army of the Rhine in Metz, the emperor planned to invade the southern German states. Despite utter chaos in his army, lacking ammunition, supplies, maps, and discipline, the first military action, at Saarbrücken on 2 August, brought about a modest victory, but, racked with terrible pain, the emperor was forced to dismount frequently from his horse. The defeats of Froeschwiller and Forbach forced the army into retreat and supreme command was handed over to Marshal Bazaine, who proceeded to lead his army of 100,000 men into a trap at Metz. The emperor and Marshal MacMahon had retreated to Châlons, where frantic telegrams from Paris thwarted their plan to return to defend the capital and ordered them to relieve Bazaine at Metz. By the end of August MacMahon had succeeded in rallying the Army of Châlons into something of a fighting force and set off towards Metz with Napoleon III and his baggage train pathetically trailing along. "This was the conspirator," as one of Zola's characters observes in *La Débâcle*, with remarkable (and not very convincing) insight into the emperor's precise condition,

> the dreamer lacking the energy when the moment comes for action. He was said to be a very good man, quite capable of a great and generous thought and very tenacious in his silent determination; he was very brave too, a fatalist scorning danger, always prepared to face his destiny. But at times of crisis he seemed all in a daze, as though paralysed when faced with having to do anything and powerless to react

14. Williams, *The Mortal Napoleon III,* 140. See also *ibid.,* 108–109, 118–19.

against fortune if she turned against him. It made Maurice wonder whether there was not some special physiological condition underlying this, aggravated by pain, whether the illness from which the Emperor was obviously suffering was not the cause of the increasing indecision and impotence he had been showing since the outset of the campaign. It might have been the explanation of it all. A stone in a man's flesh, and empires collapse.

Deprived of the leadership and seemingly denied any possibility of playing a heroic role, the emperor appeared to have become an encumbrance, at best an irrelevance, now truly what his enemies had accused him of being from the start, a parody of the Napoleonic leader, reduced to a state of futile impotence, a hollow figure, a travesty of a Bonaparte, a phantom warrior: "And the wretched Emperor, this poor man who no longer had a place in his own empire, was to be carried round like some useless clutter in the baggage of his troops, condemned to drag after him the irony of his imperial establishment, his bodyguards, coaches, horses, cooks, vanloads of silver utensils and champagne, all the pomp of his robe of state, embroidered with imperial bees, trailing the roads of defeat in the blood and mire."[15] But the tragic situation brings its own nobler ironies. Out of this forlorn state, the wretched masquer would rise to take on a nobler part and achieve a majestic status.

MacMahon was outmaneuvered and forced to take refuge in the fortress town of Sedan, close to the Belgian border. The prince imperial was sent to safety. The emperor insisted on remaining, to share the fate of what used to be his army, now placed in an untenable position surrounded by hills and Prussian artillery. On the night of 31 August, another of Zola's characters, having just seen the emperor, seems to hear vague distant sounds: "Was it the terrible order: March on! March on! shouted from Paris, which had hounded this man on from stage to stage, dragging the irony of his imperial escort along the roads of defeat until he was now cornered in the frightful disaster he had foreseen and come deliberately to meet? How many decent, ordinary people were about to die through his fault, and what an utter breakdown of this sick man's whole being, this sentimental dreamer, silent while dully awaiting his doom!"[16] The scene

15. Zola, *The Debacle*, 77–78.
16. *Ibid.*, 176–77.

was set. The actual battle of Sedan began early in the morning on 1 September, as the theater of war was still draped in a curtain of morning mist.

After two weeks of pain, of sleepless nights, unable to eat, the emperor prepared to play his part in the decisive battle in the vast amphitheater of Sedan. He needed to dress up for the occasion, for his last performance. Suffering from what has been called "the curse of the usurpers," from which Henry V of England had died, suffering even more than his uncle at Waterloo, who had been dizzy with pain from hemorrhoids,[17] Napoleon III doubtless knew that his own Waterloo was upon him. He had to be on a horse. Towels were stuffed into his pants to soak up the blood. He was ready now to take the stage, perhaps even wearing makeup for the final act of make-believe. Zola describes him, as ever, in the perspective of one of his characters: "It was indeed Napoleon III, who looked taller now that he was on horseback, and his moustache was so waxed and his cheeks were so rouged that he at once thought he looked much younger, and made up like an actor. Surely he must have had himself made up so as not to go round displaying to the army the horror of his colourless face all twisted with pain, his fleshless nose and muddy eyes [*l'effroi de son masque blême, décomposé par la souffrance, au nez aminci, aux yeux troubles*]." Zola was much criticized by certain of his contemporary readers, who denied the authenticity of the detail of the emperor's makeup. The novelist, as usual, claimed that it was based on reliable sources, eyewitness accounts and military histories, but argued also, significantly for the theme of this book, in an article in *Le Figaro* of 10 October 1892, that "On these small details of history, when the witnesses are divided, when there is doubt, the poet has the right to choose the version that he needs for the greatness of his work." As, indeed, does the historian. For Zola the artist, the emperor's makeup was "superb," "worthy of one of the great heroes of Shakespeare, raising the figure of Napoléon III to a tragic melancholy of infinite grandeur."[18]

As the German artillery relentlessly pounded and decimated the demoralized and confused French army, the wounded MacMahon was removed from the action and General Ducrot took command and ordered a retreat

17. Fraser, *Napoleon III (My Recollections)*, 184; Stacton, *The Bonapartes*, 141.

18. Zola, *The Debacle*, 192. Zola's article is reproduced by Henri Mitterand in the Pléiade edition of the *Rougon-Macquart* series: 5:1454–60. See also Zola's interview of 20 August 1895 in *Entretiens avec Zola*, ed. Dorothy E. Speirs and Dolorès A. Signori (Ottawa: Les Presses de l'Université d'Ottawa, 1990), 156–67. On the question of the rouge, see Legge, *The Comedy and Tragedy of the Second Empire*, 216–18.

westward towards Mézières. But General Wimpffen, overconfident, over-
bearing, reckless, and supplied with a secret letter from the Ministry of War
in Paris with orders to take over command if MacMahon were to fall,
countermanded Ducrot's plan, gave orders to counterattack and break out
of the city. Brave cavalry charges by the French proved ineffective against
the German positions, which relentlessly rained their artillery fire on the
French. Their dispossessed leader, the emperor, rode bravely into this hell-
fire, courting death, seeking death on the field of battle, but being denied
a glorious military end and condemned to witness the destruction of his
army. "It was his fate to see the tragedy through to the end." As Zola's
narrative describes one moment of the scene,

> he advanced all alone amid the bullets and shells, unhurriedly, with
> his usual gloomy, indifferent bearing, going to meet his destiny.
> Perhaps he could hear behind him that implacable voice hounding
> him on, the voice screaming from Paris: "March on! March on! Die
> like a hero on the piled-up corpses of your people, fill the whole
> world with admiration and awe so that your son may reign!" So he
> went on, urging his horse at a gentle trot. For a hundred metres he
> went on. Then he stopped and waited for the end he had come to
> find. Bullets whistled by like a hurricane, and a bursting shell had
> bespattered him with earth. Still he waited. . . . Then after this seem-
> ingly endless wait the Emperor, with his fatalistic resignation, under-
> stood that his hour was not yet.

Indeed, for four to five hours, Napoleon III remained in the thick of the
battle, with shells bursting all around him. Of the staff that accompanied
him, two, General de Courson and Captain de Trécesson, were killed by
shell-fire. "His cross was the saddle and, nailed to it by sheer will, Napoleon rode to and fro all morning across the field of carnage, smoking an
endless chain of cigarettes as bullets and shell fragments sang about his
ears." Convulsed with pain, he would occasionally stop and dismount for
a momentary respite, then move on, seemingly impassive, in his tortuous
extravaganza (etymologically "wandering") across the battlefield,
amongst the "bodies without heads, legs without bodies, heaps of human
entrails attached to red and blue cloth, and disembowelled corpses in uniform, bodies lying about in all attitudes."[19]

    19. Burchell, *Imperial Masquerade,* 334; Zola, *The Debacle,* 193; Bierman, *Napoleon III
and His Carnival Empire,* 358–59, the latter quotation from *The Times* of 6 September
1870.

In the meantime, above the slaughter of the battle, high upon a wooded hill with Sedan and the killing fields in full view, the German military leaders, the king of Prussia, Generals von Roon and von Moltke, Bismarck, their staff, along with sundry observers, contemplated the battle scene and the demolition of the imperial army in the serenity of their exalted perspective. "In the middle, against the dark background of the forest of the Ardennes, draped across the horizon like a curtain of antique verdure, Sedan stood out with the geometrical lines of its fortifications, lapped by the flooded meadows and rivers on the south and west." Theirs was the lofty, privileged view of war as a glorious spectacle, war as theater, aesthetically uplifting, purged of its gory detail. Theirs was the point of view of the powerful and the victorious, marveling at the gallant and futile charges of General Margueritte's cavalry against the invincible German gunners, awed by the destructive power of the "avalanche of iron" that poured from the German artillery, watching the tragedy unfold in its awful inevitability: "The King had been calmly looking on and waiting since first thing. One or two hours more, perhaps three, it was only a matter of time, one cog moved the next and the crushing machine was in action and would finish the job." Theirs was a "divine" perspective, as they watched, in the terminology of the ancient theater, the human action of the *orchestra* from the heights of the *theologeion,* where the Gods in ancient times contemplated the fated unfolding of events: "There were foreign officers there, aides-de-camp, generals, court officials, princes, all provided with field glasses, and since early morning they had been following the death-struggles of the French army like a play. And now the terrible drama was drawing to its close."[20]

"A cruel spectacle," Séguin writes, "Shakespearian. Even Richard III, when he wandered on the field of battle, was able to fight and take his chance." But the French emperor had been powerless even before the battle had begun. Yet driven back into his own headquarters in the sub-prefecture of Sedan, it was Napoleon III himself, affirming his right as the emperor rather than as the commander of the army, who took the initiative to surrender, revolted again by the carnage of the battlefield, as he had been at Solferino, and hoping now that he could save thousands of lives by his personal submission and obtain the best possible terms for his beleaguered troops. As he wrote to the king of Prussia:

20. Zola, *The Debacle,* 196, 234–35, 294.

MY BROTHER, Having been unable to die among my troops, it only remains for me to turn over my sword to Your Majesty. I am Your Majesty's devoted brother.

NAPOLEON.

Was the surrender a purely humanitarian gesture, or did the emperor have in mind a final military ploy? Once again, on such an essential fact of history, the true motives remain obscure. Louise de Mercy-Argenteau reports a conversation with a certain Raimbault according to whom the emperor's plan was that the French should break through the German lines whilst the enemy was off guard celebrating the surrender. "I will be called a man without honour," he is supposed to have said. "Never mind. In cases like this treachery is allowed."[21] Whether or not he had such a plan in mind, he did insist to Bismarck that he and his army had surrendered, but not the French nation. The Republican Government of National Defense would indeed prolong the war for five months, but, by 4 September, when news of the defeat had reached Paris, the Empire had virtually fallen.

On the morning of 2 September, Napoleon III, as he was now in name alone, was waiting to meet the king of Prussia in the latter's headquarters at the château of Bellevue, two miles west of Sedan, where he had been escorted by Bismarck and von Moltke. During the delay caused by the heated discussions of Generals Ducrot and Wimpffen over the surrender, a German precondition of the meeting of the monarchs, Napoleon III passed the time reading from an edition of Montaigne's *Essays* that he found in the library. No more appropriate source of consolation could have been found in his dire circumstances than the work of the stoical philosopher, a fellow sufferer from the agonies of a bladder stone. According to the Bavarian officer who witnessed the scene, the emperor, dispossessed of his earthly kingdom, was meditating upon a passage from Montaigne's commentary on Cicero's views on the immortality of the soul, which, no doubt, gave him cause for some chastening reflections as he considered the implications to his own extreme situation. In Montaigne's view "presumptuous aspirations for greatness" would be judged in the afterlife and the vices hidden from the "the sight and knowledge of human justice" would be exposed to divine judgment. But, at least, we might hope, he was spared by the arrival of the king the irony of reading a later passage by

21. Séguin, *Louis Napoléon le Grand*, 408; Williams, *The Mortal Napoleon III*, 154–55; Mercy-Argenteau, *The Last Love of an Emperor*, 193.

Montaigne on military life: "No occupation is as enjoyable as soldiering—an occupation both noble in its practice (since valour is the mightiest, most magnanimous and proudest of the virtues) and noble in its purpose; there is no service you can render more just nor more complete than protecting the peace and greatness of your country. You enjoy the comradeship of so many men who are noble, young and active, the daily sight of so many tragic spectacles, ..."[22]

ANAGNORISIS

After the battle of Sedan, the history, genre, and portrait painter Olivier Pichat absurdly produced a painting in the old style, showing Napoleon III prancing on his horse at the head of his troops in the thick of the battle.[23] Such an attempt to show the emperor in his former heroic guise was both clearly inappropriate in the circumstances and even, unintentionally no doubt, a parodic gesture, given the crushing defeat of the French army on the day and the role that the emperor played in the action. It would have been no comfort either to the fallen leader or to his image, for the show, the pageantry, and the pretense were decidedly over. In any case, Napoleon III's heroism had been of another kind from that of the glorious warrior, a heroism wrought out of dignity in martyrdom, humiliation, and defeat. It belonged not to epic display but more to the order of tragedy, bringing about depths of suffering that provoke pity and fear in those who contemplate the spectacle and, in the fallen victim himself, a deep sense of the discovery, the recognition, and understanding of the full consequences of his fate and of his responsibility in its cause. Rather like Shakespeare's Lear after his wandering across the heath, he has discovered that he is not "ague-proof" and that, in Edgar's oft-quoted words, with their own echoes of Montaigne: "Men must endure their going hence, even as their coming hither: Ripeness is all" (Act 5, Scene 3). Napoleon III had wandered pathetically across the battlefield and had been left to confront the

22. Quoted from Book 3, Chapter 13, of *The Essays of Michel de Montaigne*, trans. and ed. M. A. Screech (London: Allen Lane, 1987), 1244–45, with the substitution of "tragic spectacles" for "sublime dramas" as a translation of "*spectacles tragiques*." For Montaigne on Cicero's views, see Book 2, Chapter 12. On this incident, see Williams, *The Mortal Napoleon III*, 155–56, and Fraser, *Napoleon III (My Recollections)*, 208–10.

23. See Legge, *The Comedy and Tragedy of the Second Empire*, 216.

full extent of the catastrophe, denied the glorious exit of death in the field, left to meditate upon his fall.

But characteristically, his deeper thoughts on the true significance of the terrible experiences that he had both suffered and witnessed would remain largely a mystery. For example, on the day after the battle, he wrote to the empress straightforwardly, with tragic simplicity, the following letter:

> My dear Eugénie, it is impossible for me to tell you what I have suffered and what I suffer. We undertook a march contrary to all principles and contrary to common sense; it could only lead to a catastrophe. Now it is complete. I would have preferred death to have been witness to such a disastrous capitulation, and yet, in the present circumstances, it was the only way to avoid the butchery of 60,000 people.
>
> And if only all my torments were concentrated here! I think of you, of our son, of our unfortunate country. May God protect it! What will happen in Paris?
>
> I have just seen the King. He had tears in his eyes when speaking to me about the pain that I must have been feeling. He is making available for me one of his châteaux near to Hesse-Cassel. But what does it matter where I go! . . . I am in despair. Goodbye, I kiss you tenderly.
>
> NAPOLEON.[24]

As in the extraordinarily matter-of-fact account of the debacle that, in the early days of his captivity, the emperor supposedly wrote either at Verviers, where he caught the train for Germany, or at the château of Wilhelmshöhe near to Cassel, mentioned in his letter to Eugénie, there is no attempt to interpret the causes or the meaning of the disaster, which is attributed to a military blunder followed by a humanitarian gesture. Who was to blame according to the fallen emperor? Bismarck for his duplicity, the European powers who had failed to support France, public opinion in France for its rashness, his wife's fervent desire for war, the liberal Empire, the insufficiently liberal Empire? Did he ever wonder on that long day and during the even longer days that would follow if, like many an autocratic military leader, he had not sufficiently taken heed of the winds of change which

24. Quoted in Giraudeau, *Napoléon III intime,* 421.

sweep away in the natural course of events truly democratic leaders, but which prepare a more violent, dramatic end to those who cling to their power, who refuse to bring about an adequate transition to another order and who hang on until they are brought down? A ten-year term as president of an authoritarian Republic would have spared him the ignominy of his downfall. But he had chosen the dynastic order, which impelled him to maintain his rule for the sake of his name, his son, his line, beyond its natural expiry date.

By an extraordinary coincidence, another stark confrontation with his destiny would await him at the château of Wilhelmshöhe. The building had once been the residence of his uncle Jérôme when he was king of Westphalia. He had visited the palace in his childhood. So had the Emperor. The château still contained many souvenirs of the first Napoleonic era. In one of the state rooms was a portrait of Queen Hortense, dressed in dark velvet, over a grand piano on which lay, according to Louise de Mercy-Argenteau, who visited Louis Napoléon there, a copy of "Partant pour la Syrie" and a large bunch of hortensias. As he remarked to his visitor, "there are many things one cannot explain, Comtesse, and one thing is certain; my mother was here, waiting for me." The wheel of fortune, at its lowest point in its tragic trajectory, had brought him back to exile, to captivity, to Germany, to the dynastic past before his own fateful attempts to reinstate it, to a final encounter with his mother. When he first saw the picture, he asked to be alone. As Séguin writes: "As if destiny wished to crush him even more, now he discovers in a salon a large portrait of his mother, in front of which he sinks into meditation."[25] What did he read in her eyes—pity or reproach? What would have been his tragic inner monologue in such a moment of prostration? Only a novelist could tell.

PHARMAKOS

Whether or not, or to whatever degree, Napoleon III blamed himself—he seems to have told the king of Prussia that public opinion had impelled him to wage war—blame was unceremoniously and ceremoniously heaped upon him, even before the final outcome of the Franco-Prussian War was

25. Mercy-Argenteau, *The Last Love of an Emperor*, 213–14; Séguin, *Louis Napoléon le Grand*, 414.

known. Hence, no doubt, his request to the king of Prussia to be spared the ignominy of being transported to his prison through French territory. But he could not be protected from the scorn that would be poured upon him. Zola describes the shameful, the "cruel" departure of the emperor from the château of Bellevue, avoiding Sedan "for fear of the anger of the defeated and starving," his "lamentable flight in an open carriage" across the "tragic plateau of Illy, strewn with corpses," his encounters with parties of prisoners along the way, "moving to one side to let the carriage pass, some silent but others beginning to grumble, and again others getting more and more exasperated and bursting into booing, with fists shaking in a gesture of insult and cursing," the night spent at an inn in Bouillon, surrounded by French refugees "amid murmurings and catcalls." Then "the paraphernalia of the imperial household," that had followed him on the campaign, was spirited away in the dark of night, "off into Belgium too, through dark byways, like thieves in the night."[26]

Such was the magnitude of the disaster that the blame had to be concomitant with it. It came from the new government. The National Assembly sitting in Bordeaux passed a resolution expelling the emperor and his dynasty, declaring it responsible for "the ruin, the invasion, and the dismemberment of France." The Council of Inquiry into the capitulation of the army pronounced in May 1872 that "the whole blame for the disasters at Sedan rested with Napoleon III," a charge to which he nobly replied from his exile in Chislehurst in England:

> I am responsible to the country, and I can accept no other judgment but that of the nation regularly consulted. Nor is it for me to pass an opinion on the report of the Commission on the capitulation of Sedan. I shall only remind the principal witnesses of the capitulation of the critical position in which we found ourselves. . . . The honour of the army having been saved by the bravery which had been displayed, I then exercised my Sovereign right, and gave orders to unfurl a flag of truce. I claim the entire responsibility of that act. The immolation of 60,000 men could not have saved France, and the sublime devotion of her chiefs and soldiers would have been uselessly sacrificed. I obeyed a cruel, but inexorable, fate. My heart was broken, but my conscience was easy.[27]

26. Zola, *The Debacle*, 332–33.
27. Legge, *The Comedy and Tragedy of the Second Empire*, 47–48, 265–66.

He was, of course, taking the blame, or at least the responsibility, for the surrender. But, for the war, it was a matter of "fate," a convenient, evasive metaphor for the actions of all those who were to blame, but whom, with typical taciturnity and tact, he thereby refrained from incriminating.

In France, with few exceptions, former enemies united less nobly in a wholesale condemnation of the emperor, who became the scapegoat for the nation's woes. It was no longer just the opposition press and the satirists tearing him apart, calling him Badinguet, the coward, the assassin, the rogue, the traitor, dragging his name in the mud, making of him openly the butt of public obloquy. He refused to refute the calumnies, responding, as the empress later recalled, that "certain catastrophes are so painful for a Nation that it has the right, even unjustly, to shift the blame for it on its Leader."[28] It was as if he instinctively understood that there was something more ritualistic about the defamation heaped upon him. He was, in a sense, like the tragic kings, dying for their people, taking on their sins. Indeed, in such a scheme, with typical tragic ambiguity, the scapegoat, the victim, is both innocent and guilty. The disaster that he is expiating surpasses in its enormity anything that he has done to bring it about. But by his very position, he is guilty of being the *apology* of a guilty society, whose sins he is condemned to propitiate and of which it cannot speak. Yet, in such an anthropological perspective, the very transfer of blame and guilt to the victim confers upon him the dignity of a new innocence. This ritual process is akin, in a secular, historical context, to the symbolic immolation of the divine ruler, the tearing asunder of the sacrificial body. Both, paradoxically, at the historical level—with the fall of the Empire leading to the conflagration of the Commune—and, logically, at the mythical level—with the ritual death of the king bringing about the holocaust—Napoleon III achieved what his numerous successes never obtained for him, a heroic status, even at the very moment of his most terrible defeat.

DISJECTA MEMBRA

On 4 September, the last day of the Empire, as we have already seen, the empress was still in the Tuileries bravely and desperately trying to save the regime, but a crowd of two hundred thousand people was surrounding

28. See Séguin, *Louis Napoléon le Grand*, 422–23.

the palace, singing "La Marseillaise," clamoring for the downfall of the Empire and for a return to a Republic, which was duly proclaimed that day. All Eugénie could do was to flee in a cab with a small case, her jewel box, and her reader, Mme. Lebreton. She was smuggled out of Paris by the court dentist, an American, Dr. Evans, then, eventually, to England on a yacht. That night, there was much rejoicing in the streets of Paris, and "people amused themselves by singing obscene songs about the fallen empire to the tune of 'Partant pour la Syrie.' "[29] No doubt, Flaubert would have enjoyed depicting the irony of the scene in the novel that he never wrote.

But of more significance and relevance to our theme than where the imperial family went or how it got there or what happened to it afterwards is what it left behind. After the fall of the regime, the new government made an inventory of the objects belonging to the imperial apartments in the Tuileries. Amongst the hundreds of heteroclite, familiar objects that were placed under seal in the Pavilion of Flora, which contained the kitchens of the Tuileries and which was not destroyed by the Communards, amongst the vases, the tea and coffee services, the inkstands, the snuffboxes, the porcelain and crystal ornaments, the chairs and tables, the priedieu, the boxes of cigarettes and cigars, were found vestiges of the trials and glories of the imperial past: a bronze eagle, a case containing the emperor's Knight of the Garter costume, a prayer book that had belonged to Madame Mère, a golden lorgnette that had belonged to the duke of Reichstadt, the grey greatcoat worn by the emperor at Waterloo, satin shoes of Empress Joséphine and Queen Hortense, and a portfolio of music containing Hans Guido von Bülow's *Ouverture héroïque et Marche des Impériaux de la tragédie Jules César de Shakespeare pour Grand Orchestre* (1865), dedicated to "His Majesty Napoleon III, Emperor of the French."[30] As Mark Anthony aptly asks, of an earlier Caesar's fall, in Shakespeare's tragedy:

> —O mighty Caesar! Dost thou lie so low?
> Are all thy Conquests, Glories, Triumphs, Spoils,
> Shrunk to this little Measure? (Act 3, Scene 1)

All are reduced to mere Relics of a fallen dynasty, objects that are now charged with irony. Tokens of an age that was already irretrievably past.

29. Burchell, *Imperial Masquerade*, 339.
30. See Legge, *The Comedy and Tragedy of the Second Empire*, 240–44.

Epilogue

The French reverses in the Franco-Prussian War brought about the collapse of the Second Empire. But curiously, defeat, imprisonment, and exile did not put an end to the ambitions and the extravagances that had characterized the regime, nor to the ironies, mysteries, and misfortunes that had surrounded it. Despite the fact that, from his place of detention in Germany, the emperor had written to his wife to tell her that all he wished for in the future was to be able to live quietly with his family in England, "in a little cottage with bow windows and a creeper," others—and, no doubt, his other self—had other ideas. The imperial past was not to be so easily shaken off. Napoleon III was not to be left in peace and would still be impelled to follow his star, however dimly its light now shone. In fact, there is a strange sense of vestigial recurrence in the life of the toppled emperor and his family after the fall of the Empire, as if the show still had to go on, in an empty and distant theater, petering out in forlorn performances that reitered past vainglories.

After her escape from the Tuileries the empress had been reunited with the prince imperial in Hastings and had subsequently set up home and court again in Camden Place in Chislehurst, Kent, in a large Georgian house, which had the inestimable advantage for the empress of being close to a Catholic church and which, by a curious coincidence, was owned by Miss Howard's trustee, a certain Mr. Strode. Even earlier, Louis Napoléon had courted with some success a Miss Emily Rowles, whose father had lived in the same house, that is until she had found out about Miss Howard and put an end to the relationship. By the time the emperor joined his family in March 1871, a sizable court had already assembled, with a whole retinue of servants in attendance. Several houses in the vicinity were occupied by refugees from imperial circles. Surprisingly large crowds greeted the emperor's landing at Dover and cheered him on his arrival at Chislehurst, with his eighteen wagonloads of luggage. By then, there were sixty-two people in Camden Place. The emperor had aides-de-camp and chamberlains in attendance. There were Bonapartes residing nearby in London, such as Prince Louis Lucien Bonaparte and Plon-Plon. The latter was now living with Cora Pearl; he visited frequently, but without Cora. Pilgrims came to Chislehurst from France to pay their respects. Some supporters sent money. There was also a string of distinguished English visitors, including Mr. Gladstone, the prime minister, and Queen Victoria, who returned a visit that the imperial couple had made to Windsor Castle. In quieter moments, the imperial family watched cricket games, much bemused. But all was not ceremony and sports. The emperor could not be idle. He drew up a plan to found an International Council to secure permanent peace in Europe. He worked out an old-age-pension scheme. He invented, had built, and had tested a cylindrical stove to provide a cheap form of central heating for the poor.[1] It was like being back in Ham, but in far more comfortable circumstances.

Yet even after the pounding at Sedan, old political instincts and habits died hard, for the emperor had a long-standing interest and much experience in political intrigue. Though the facts as ever are obscure, some reports suggest that he had no plans at all and preferred to bide his time indefinitely, whereas, according to others, the emperor plotted his return to power with the irrepressible Plon-Plon and three army commanders, even securing Bismarck's assurance that he had no objection to the emperor's reinstatement. One plan was for the emperor to travel in March 1873 to Switzerland, where he would join Prince Napoleon, dress up in his general's uniform, and take over the country whilst two-thirds of the deputies, who lived in Paris and commuted to the parliament in Versailles, were blocked in a tunnel in the government train! Another plan involved landing secretly in a corner of France and proceeding to Châlons to assemble an army of fifty thousand men.[2] More than the promise of a glorious re-

1. See *Oeuvres posthumes et autographes inédits de Napoléon III en exil,* ed. le comte de la Chapelle (Paris: E. Lachaud, 1873), 143–44.
2. See Frerejean, *Napoléon IV,* 194–96; Guest, *Napoleon III in England,* 192; Fraser, *Napoleon III (My Recollections),* 244–45.

turn from Elba of his own, such schemes sound more like formulas for the repeat of the fiascos of Strasbourg and Boulogne, from which he was fortunately spared by his final misfortune.

After a period of reasonable health, there was a recurrence of his condition in the latter part of 1872. The painful operations that he underwent, as it has been claimed, were perhaps largely prompted by his desire to return to France at the head of an army. He had to be on a horse, of course. He had tried to ride on three occasions during his exile, but each time to painful effect. Sir Henry Thompson, a distinguished genito-urinary surgeon, practiced in lithotrity, a method for crushing bladder stones with a lithotrite and a suction device, performed the first operation on 2 January 1873 along with Sir William Gull and Sir James Paget, crushing the stone and removing fragments. There was a second operation four days later, removing more debris. A third operation was scheduled for 9 January, but, before it could be performed, the patient died. His last words, to the faithful Dr. Conneau, were reported to be about Sedan. "Death, which had disdained him there, came quietly to claim him at 10:45."[3] There were huge crowds at the funeral on 15 January, including a deputation of Parisian workers. Behind the hearse, drawn by eight horses, the prince imperial walked alone, followed by Prince Napoleon and other members of the imperial family, representatives of the English royal family, Italian generals representing Victor Emmanuel, French marshals, generals, admirals, former senators and ministers, deputies, and a crowd of several thousand ordinary men and women. He was buried in a general's uniform with his sword at his side, his képi at his feet, the sash and the cross of the Legion of Honor on his chest along with his medals, much as he had been in his official portraits.

Even after the emperor's death, the legend did not rest in peace; the Bonapartist agitprop persisted. The prince imperial was now hailed as Napoleon IV, particularly when he reached the age of majority and when some six thousand Bonapartist supporters attended a rally at Camden Place on 16 March 1874. Coins were struck with his effigy, and pictures

3. Williams, *The Mortal Napoleon III,* 167. For variations on his exact last words, see Guest, *Napoleon III in England,* 195, Giraudeau, *Napoléon III intime,* 422, Frerejean, *Napoléon IV,* 199, Séguin, *Louis Napoléon le Grand,* 424. Adding a dramatic turn to this event, it has even been claimed that the empress was responsible for administering a fatal dose of chloroform; see Mercy-Argenteau, *The Last Love of an Emperor,* 286–87.

394 / Napoleon III and His Regime

circulated in France, showing the young man in a French general's uniform, even though he was by then a cadet in the British army. He needed to gain his spurs. The fateful opportunity came with the British setbacks in the Zulu War and the dispatch of reinforcements to invade Zululand. Such was the opposition to his plan to take part in the expedition that it took the intervention of Queen Victoria in his favor for him to be allowed to join the British forces in South Africa as an observer attached to the general staff. On 1 June 1879, he was caught in an ambush by a band of Zulus whilst on reconnaissance duty with a party led by Lieutenant J.B. Carey, who would later be cashiered for his negligence in abandoning the prince imperial. When the Zulus emerged from the long grass, Carey and the others, losing two men and their guide in the attack, galloped off to safety, but the prince's saddle strap broke as he attempted to mount his horse. Injured in one arm, he was left alone to face the assault of the Zulus, who riddled him with assegais. Was he a victim of the "military complex" of the Bonapartists, of a reckless and extravagant desire to demonstrate his valor, to repeat the military glories of the dynasty? Or did he wish to compensate for the ridicule that had been caused by his presence at the front in 1870 and to avenge defeat by proving his gallantry? Or was he, his father's son, seeking to fulfill, in his turn, the Napoleonic destiny? Whatever may be the case, there was a mighty irony in the last Napoleon dying in such circumstances, in the uniform of the enemy of the first.

It was now the turn of Eugénie to wish to die, a Niobe weeping at the ruin of broken dreams, fainting on the desolate spot where her son had died. A tragic figure in perpetual mourning, she would live out her long life (until 1920) in the Hampshire home of Farnborough Hill, to which she moved in the spring of 1882 and where she had built an abbey and a mausoleum amongst the relics of the dynasty: a museum devoted to the Empire; Winterhalter's portrait; a statue of the prince imperial with his favorite dog by Carpeaux; David's monumental picture of *Napoleon Crossing the Alps;* a bronze statue of Napoleon III by Klésinger. Soon after the prince imperial's death, there was a show in Paris, in which Zulus were exhibited in a booth, re-enacting the slaying. The English poet laureate penned a more fitting tribute, finding consolation in the tragedy, as did Verlaine.[4]

4. See Legge, *The Comedy and Tragedy of the Second Empire,* 394. For Verlaine's poem, see his *Oeuvres poétiques complètes,* ed. Y.-G Le Dantec (Paris: Gallimard, 1962), 253–54.

The death of the prince imperial signified the end of the dynasty's political aspirations, to all intents and purposes.[5] Henceforth, rehabilitation could only come in the symbolic forms of history books, literary works, and visual-media representations. Whilst in captivity in Wilhelmshöhe, reflecting on his policies during the preceding eighteen years in an apologia that is attributed to the marquis de Gricourt but, according to Legge, was written by the emperor himself, he remarks, "We must not judge of things as they are, but as they *might have been.*"[6] The comment rings of special pleading, but it has a new relevance today in view of the contemporary fashion for "virtual history," for "counterfactuals," and for the conviction that there was nothing inevitable in the events of the past, that the historian's tendency to turn supposed causes retrospectively into sufficient reasons is illusory, and that "what if?" speculation on historical events is not an idle pursuit. Thus briefly, rather obviously and somewhat coyly—for she asserts that "speculation is not the province of the historian"—Richardson argues in 1971 that "the history of modern France would have been very different if Napoleon III had made a successful marriage, if the

---

5. Though there would still be an eventful aftermath to it all. Plon-Plon, having become an ardent republican, even made a bid to seize power in 1883, attempting to bring about his own version of a bloodless coup d'état, but ended up in prison for three weeks as a result of his efforts. Reflecting a deep division that had grown in the Bonapartist ranks between the conservative and clerical adherents to the prince imperial's cause and Plon-Plon's radical tendencies, the prince imperial had named in his will Plon-Plon's son, Prince Victor, as his successor, snubbing the father.

The Bonapartists decided in 1891, after the death of Prince Jérôme Napoléon, that Prince Victor, if ever he should reign over France, would be dubbed Napoleon IV, since neither his father nor the prince imperial had ever been proclaimed emperor. After Prince Victor's death in 1926, his son, Louis Bonaparte, who had lived with the empress in Farnborough, fought bravely in the Foreign Legion in North Africa and for the French and Belgian resistance movements, was imprisoned by the Gestapo, was released, thanks to the intervention of the Italian royal family, and fought again in the French resistance movement, surviving a skirmish in which his cousin, Prince Murat, was killed. He was decorated by General de Gaulle, on whose resignation in 1969 he interestingly made known his readiness to take on whatever role his country wished! Holt, *Plon-Plon*, 255–71. Louis Bonaparte died on 3 May 1997, leaving two sons and two daughters, Charles, Catherine, Laure, and, of course, Jérôme—rather than Louis.

6. Legge, *The Comedy and Tragedy of the Second Empire*, 283. The work in question is Raphaël de Gricourt (marquis), *Des Relations de la France avec l'Allemagne sous Napoléon III* (Brussels: J. Rozez, 1870); English translation: *France and Germany, or Imperial Rule under Napoleon III* (London: R. Hardwicke, 1871).

Liberal Empire had survived, if the Franco-Prussian War had not occurred." She further suggests that, even after the fall of the Empire in
1870, the imperial regime might have been restored under Napoleon IV,
but "the death of the Prince Imperial in the Zulu War in 1879 finally
ended the hope of a Third Empire," adding, with a more obvious fondness for the fallen regime than the one that replaced it, "it is easy to see
what France has lost as a republic; it is difficult to see what it has gained."[7]
As has already been made clear, I would argue, quite differently, that the
virtual scenario should begin, not with the imperial marriage, but with the
restoration of the Empire, when Louis Napoléon heeded not the voices
of Le Bas or Proudhon, but, along with other, fathomless impulsions, the
promptings of Hortense, of Morny, of Persigny, and, no doubt, of a host
of future beneficiaries from his act of self-promotion. Had he been able to
curb his dynastic ambitions—and the ambitions of those around him—on
the considerable political and moral strength of his continuing position as
president of the Republic, he would have been better placed to bring
about a smoother transition to a more liberal state. He would have had no
need for a dynastic marriage, and above all, he would have had less need
for the elaborate apparatus of state, with all its excesses, which made him
vulnerable to criticism and to suspicion at home and abroad. He would
likely have developed a more pragmatic foreign policy, avoiding the intemperate ventures to which he was prone or to which he was induced, and
which would lead to his downfall. As his health declined, he would have
been in a position to bring about a smooth transition of power inspired by
the needs of the present rather than by the myths of the past and the fantasies of the future. France, then, could well have had its "*Belle Époque*" earlier than it did and been spared the extravaganza of the "*fête impériale.*"

Be that as it might have been, the historians' verdict on Napoleon III
is still as "far from conclusive and unanimous" as it was shown to be a
quarter of a century ago, in Osgood's anthology of conflicting assessments, entitled, unflatteringly, *Napoleon III: Buffoon, Modern Dictator, or
Sphinx?* However, since then, the modern tendency to debunk the reputa-
tions of the heroes of the past has naturally been accompanied, though less
visibly, by the equivalent tendency to redeem the villains, with the result

7. Richardson, *La Vie parisienne*, 11. For the theory and several examples of virtual history, see Niall Ferguson, ed., *Virtual History: Alternatives and Counterfactuals* (London:
Picador, 1997).

that a more balanced view of Napoleon III's accomplishments prevails, though he must doubtless remain one of history's most elusive and controversial figures, ever resisting final assessment. We can still perhaps do no more than agree, in general terms, with Zola's assertion of more than a century ago (in his interview of August 1895), a view which has often been echoed by later commentators, that Napoleon III was "much better than the legend has represented him so far."[8] But we do need to add that he was undoubtedly also less worthy than the legend that he sought to promote about himself and his regime. Perhaps because our (post)modern times value ambiguities above certainties, what is clear, however, is that there is a growing interest in and even a certain fascination for the figure and his age, as historians, politicians, and writers, or sundry "skillful pen-pushers," as Flaubert would have it, are ready, like Séguin, to seek to rehabilitate him, or, at least, like Minc, to revisit the case of a leader who was responsible for so many achievements and so many failures—some by himself, many by others, but all in his name.

As we have seen, he has frequently been represented in literature, though not yet, to any effect, in the visual media. But there are signs that his time will come, as it has done already for his son. In 1997, for example, in the wake, no doubt, of the publication of the biographies of Frerejean and Lachnitt the same year, a project for the production of a joint Franco-British film, *The Last Napoleon,* was announced, a major movie with a budget of thirty million pounds to be produced by Terry Langman, with Catherine Deneuve expected to play the role of the empress. But such recognition may not all yet be limited to verbal and visual representations. Since 1995 at least, a committee of some two hundred politicians, writers, and historians has been lobbying the French government for the return of Napoleon III's remains to France. We may yet witness, as unlikely as it may seem, a final ironic twist in Louis Napoléon's fate, as he is buried, if not with his uncle in the Invalides, then in the Panthéon, less than a stone's throw away from the remains of his arch-enemy, Hugo, to the eternal discomfort and indignation of the poet.

8. See Zola interview in *Entretiens avec Zola,* 158.

Bibliography

WORKS OF NAPOLEON III

Histoire de Jules César. 2 vols. Paris: Plon, 1865–66.

History of Julius Caesar. 2 vols. New York: Harper and Brothers, 1865–1866.

Oeuvres de Louis-Napoléon Bonaparte publiées par M. Charles-Édouard Temblaire. 4 vols. Paris: Librairie Napoléonienne, 1848.

Oeuvres de Napoléon III. 5 vols. Paris: Plon, 1856–69.

Oeuvres posthumes et autographes inédits de Napoléon III en exil. Ed. le comte [Alfred] de la Chapelle. Paris: E. Lachaud, 1873. Translation: *Posthumous Works and Unpublished Autographs of Napoleon III in Exile.* Ed. Count de la Chapelle. London: Sampson Low, Marston, Low and Searle, 1873.

Papiers et correspondance de la famille impériale. 2 vols. Paris: Imprimerie Nationale, 1870 (vol. 1); Paris: Librairie L. Beauvais, 1872 (vol. 2). Another edition, "collationée sur le texte de l'Imprimerie Nationale." 2 vols. Paris: Garnier Frères, 1871.

The Political and Historical Works of Louis Napoleon Bonaparte, President of the French Republic: With an Original Memoir of His Life Brought Down to the Promulgation of the Constitution of 1852; and Occasional Notes. 2 vols. New York: Howard Fertig, 1972 [1852]. [Volume 1: Political Life of Prince Louis Napoleon Bonaparte, 1–160; Works of Prince Louis N. Bonaparte: Political Reveries. Ideas of a New Constitution, 1832, 161–185; Political and Military Considerations on Switzerland. Exile. 1833, 187–245; Ideas of Napoleonism, 247–389; Historical Fragments: The Revolutions of 1868 and 1830, 391–462. Volume 2: Analysis of the Sugar Question, 1842, 1–91; Extinction of Pauperism. 1844, 93–126; A Few Words Relative to Joseph Bonaparte, 127–156; Opinions on Various Political and Administrative Questions, 157–226; Reply to M. de Lamartine. 1843, 227–239; The Past and Future of Artillery. 1846,

241–256; *L'Idée Napoléonienne,* a Monthly Publication. 1840, 257–288; The Revision of the Constitution. 1851, 289–315; Miscellaneous Papers, Correspondence, etc., 317–330; Papers Relating to the Coup d'État, 1851-2: I. Authentic Account of the Events of December, 1851, by A. Granier de Cassagnac. II. The Last Sitting of the Legislative Assembly, December 2. III. Confiscation of the Property of the Orléans Family. IV. New Electoral Law, 331–439]

GENERAL BIBLIOGRAPHY

Agulhon, Maurice. *Marianne au combat: L'imagerie et la symbolique républicaine de 1789 à 1880.* Paris: Flammarion, 1979.

Allem, Maurice. *La Vie quotidienne sous le Second Empire.* Paris: Hachette, 1948.

Analyses et réflexions sur Flaubert: "L'Éducation sentimentale": l'histoire (ouvrage collectif). Paris: Éditions Marketing, 1989.

Ashley, Maurice. *The Glorious Revolution of 1688.* London: Panther Books, 1968.

Aubailly, Joël. *Les Ancêtres de Napoléon III.* Préface de Jacques Jourquin. Paris: Éditions Christian, 1998.

Bac, Ferdinand. *Intimités du Second Empire.* Vol. 1, *La Cour et la ville;* vol. 2, *Les Femmes et la comédie;* vol. 3, *Poëtes et artistes.* Paris: Hachette, 1931–32.

———. *Napoléon III inconnu.* Paris: Félix Alcan, 1932.

Baird, Joseph Armstrong, ed. *Pre-Impressionism, 1860–1869: A Formative Decade in French Art and Culture.* Davis: University of California at Davis, 1969.

Barbéris, Pierre. "À propos de 'Lux': La vraie force des choses (sur l'idéologie des *Châtiments*)." *Littérature,* no. 1 (1971): 92–105.

Baring-Gould, S. *Family Names and Their Story.* Baltimore: Genealogical Publishing, 1968.

Barthes, Roland. "Le discours de l'histoire." *Poétique,* no. 49 (1982): 13–21.

———. *Roland Barthes par Roland Barthes.* Paris: Seuil, 1975.

Barton Payne, J. *Encyclopedia of Biblical Prophecy: The Complete Guide to Scriptural Predictions and Their Fulfillment.* London-Sydney-Auckland-Toronto: Hodder and Stoughton, 1973.

Baudelaire, Charles. "Le dandy." In *Oeuvres complètes,* ed. Claude Pichois, 2:709–12. Paris: Gallimard, Bibliothèque de la Pléiade, 1976.

[Beauharnais, Hortense de]. *Mémoires de la Reine Hortense,* publiés par le Prince Napoléon. Avec notes par Jean Hanoteau. 3 vols. Paris: Plon, 1927.

———. *The Memoirs of Queen Hortense.* 2 vols. Ed. Prince Napoleon with a foreword and notes by Jean Hanoteau. Trans. Arthur K. Griggs and F. Mabel Robinson. London: Thornton Butterworth, 1928.

Bell, David F. *Models of Power: Politics and Economics in Zola's "Rougon-Macquart."* Lincoln–London: University of Nebraska Press, 1988.

Bellet, Roger. *Presse et journalisme sous le Second Empire.* Paris: Armand Colin, 1967.

Belloc Lowndes, Mrs. [Marie]. *The Empress Eugenie: A Three-Act Play.* New York–Toronto: Longmans, Green, 1938.

Bennett, Tony. "The Exhibitionary Complex." *New Formations,* no. 4 (1988): 73–102.

Berthier, Patrick. *Guillemin, légende et vérité.* Lys: Les Éditions d'Utovie, 1982.

Bierman, John. *Napoleon III and His Carnival Empire.* New York: St. Martin's Press, 1988.

Boon, H. N. *Rêve et réalité dans l'oeuvre économique et sociale de Napoléon III.* The Hague: Martinus Nijhoff, 1936.

Bourachot, Christophe. *Bibliographie critique des mémoires sur le Second Empire, 2 décembre 1852–4 septembre 1870.* Préface de S.A. le Prince Murat. Paris: Éditions La Boutique de l'Histoire, 1994.

Bresler, Fenton. *Napoleon III: A Life.* London, HarperCollins, 1999.

Briais, Bernard. *Grandes Courtisanes du Second Empire.* Paris: Tallandier, 1981.

Brinton, Crane. *French Revolutionary Legislation on Illegitimacy, 1789–1804.* Cambridge, Mass.: Harvard University Press, 1936.

Browning, Elizabeth Barrett. *Napoleon III in Italy, and Other Poems.* New York: Francis, 1860. American edition of *Poems before Congress.*

Burchell, S. C. *Imperial Masquerade: The Paris of Napoleon III.* New York: Atheneum, 1971.

Burke, Peter. *The Fabrication of Louis XIV.* New Haven–London: Yale University Press, 1992.

Bury, J. P. T. *Napoleon III and the Second Empire.* London: English Universities Press, 1964.

Campbell, Stuart L. *The Second Empire Revisited: A Study in French Historiography.* New Brunswick, N.J.: Rutgers University Press, 1978.

Carette (*née* Bouvet), Mme. *My Mistress, the Empress Eugénie; or, Court Life at the Tuileries.* Authorized translation [of *Souvenirs intimes de la cour des Tuileries*]. London: Dean and Son, 1889.

Carpenter, Scott D. "Of False Napoleons and Other Political Prostheses: Writing Oppositionally from the Second Empire." *Nineteenth-Century French Studies* 25 (1997): 302–19.

Carrard, Philippe. *Poetics of the New History: French Historical Discourse from Braudel to Chartier.* Baltimore–London: Johns Hopkins University Press, 1992.

Castelot, André. *Napoléon III: L'Aube des temps modernes.* Paris: Perrin, 1999 [1974].

Charlton, D. G. *Secular Religions in France 1815–1870.* London–New York–Melbourne: Oxford University Press, 1963.

Cholakian, R. "An Uncensored Author of the Second Empire: Arsène Houssaye." *Revue de Littérature comparée* 41 (1967): 416–22.

Christiansen, Rupert. *Tales of the New Babylon: Paris, 1869–1875.* London: Sinclair-Stevenson, 1994.

Cobban, Alfred. *A History of Modern France*. Vol. 2, *From the First Empire to the Second Empire*. Harmondsworth: Penguin, 1961.

Dansette, Adrien. *Les Amours de Napoléon III*. Paris: Arthème Fayard, 1938.

———. *Louis-Napoléon à la conquête du pouvoir: Le Second Empire*. Édition revue, corrigée et augmentée. Paris: Hachette, 1961.

Des Cars, Jean. *La Princesse Mathilde*. Paris: Perrin, 1988.

Descotes, Maurice. *Le Personnage de Napoléon III dans les "Rougon-Macquart."* Paris: Archives des Lettres Modernes (V), no. 114³⁹²⁻³⁹⁶, 1970 (6).

[Disraeli, Benjamin] Beaconsfield, Earl of. *Endymion*. London: Longmans, 1900 [1880].

Dolan, Therese. "The Empress's New Clothes: Fashion and Politics in Second Empire France." *Women's Art Journal* 15 (1994): 22–28.

———. "Guise and Dolls: Dis/covering Power, Re/covering Nana." *Nineteenth-Century French Studies* 25 (1998): 368–86.

Du Camp, Maxime. *Souvenirs d'un demi-siècle*. Vol. 1, *Au temps de Louis-Philippe et de Napoléon III, 1830–1870*. Paris: Hachette, 1949.

Duff, David. *Eugenie and Napoleon III*. London: Collins, 1978.

Dufresne, Claude. *La Divine Scandaleuse: Hortense Schneider*. Paris: Perrin, 1993.

Dumoulié, Camille. *Don Juan, ou l'héroïsme du désir*. Paris: Presses Universitaires de France, 1993.

Durry, Marie-Jeanne. *Flaubert et ses projets inédits*. Paris: Nizet, 1950.

Duveau, Georges. *La Vie ouvrière en France sous le Second Empire*. Paris: Gallimard, 1946.

Echard, William E. *Napoleon III and the Concert of Europe*. Baton Rouge–London: Louisiana State University Press, 1983.

———, ed. *Historical Dictionary of the French Second Empire, 1852–1870*. Westport, Conn.: Greenwood Press, 1985.

Ellis, Geoffrey. *Napoleon*. London–New York: Longman, 1997.

Emerit, Marcel. "Histoire et légende: La naissance de Napoléon III." *Revue de la Méditerranée* 12 (1952): 172–85.

Epton, Nina. *Josephine: The Empress and Her Children*. London: Weidenfeld and Nicolson, 1975.

Faber, G. S. [George Stanley]. *The Revival of the French Emperorship Anticipated from the Necessity of Prophecy*. London: Thomas Bosworth, 1953. First American edition: *Napoleon III. The Man of Prophecy; or, The Revival of the French Emperorship Anticipated from the Necessity of Prophecy*. New York: Appleton, 1859. From the American edition: Toronto: W. C. Chewitt, 1865.

Flaubert, Gustave. *Carnets de lecture*. Ed. Société des Études littéraires françaises. Paris: Club de l'Honnête homme, 1973.

———. *L'Éducation sentimentale*. Ed. Michael Wetherill. Paris: Garnier, 1984.

———. *A Sentimental Education: The Story of a Young Man*. Trans. and ed. Douglas Parmée. Oxford–New York: Oxford University Press, 1989.

Fleischmann, Hector. *Napoléon III et les femmes, d'après les mémoires des contemporains, les pamphlets, les journaux satiriques, des documents nouveaux et inédits.* Paris: Bibliothèque des Curieux, 1913. Translation: *Napoleon III and the Women He Loved.* Trans. Dr. A. S. Rappoport. London: Holden and Hardingham, 1915.

Forster, Margaret. *Elizabeth Barrett Browning: A Biography.* London: Chatto and Windus, 1988.

Fraser, Sir William [Augustus]. *Napoleon III (My Recollections).* 2nd ed. London: Sampson Low, Marston, [1896].

Frerejean, Alain. *Napoléon IV: Un destin brisé.* Paris: Albin Michel, 1997.

Frye, Northrop. *Anatomy of Criticism.* Princeton: Princeton University Press, 1957.

Gaillard, Françoise. "Une inénarrable histoire." In *Flaubert et le comble de l'art: Nouvelles recherches sur "Bouvard et Pécuchet,"* 75–87. Paris: SEDES, 1981.

Gaudon, Sheila. "Prophétisme et utopie: le problème du destinataire dans *Les Châtiments.*" *Saggi e ricerche di letteratura francesa,* n.s., 16 (1977): 403–26.

Genette, Gérard. *Figures II.* Paris: Seuil, 1969.

Gidel, Henry. *Le Vaudeville.* Paris: Presses Universitaires de France, 1986.

Gildea, Robert. *The Past in French History.* New Haven–London: Yale University Press, 1994.

Giraudeau, Fernand. *Napoléon III intime.* Paris: Paul Ollendorff, 1895.

Gleize, Jean-Marie, and Guy Rosa. " 'Celui-là.' Politique du sujet poétique: les *Châtiments* de Hugo." *Littérature,* no. 24 (1976): 83–98.

Goodspeed, D. J. *Bayonets at St Cloud: The Story of the 18th Brumaire.* Toronto: Macmillan, 1965.

Goodwin, Barbara, and Keith Taylor. *The Politics of Utopia: A Study in Theory and Practice.* London: Hutchinson, 1982.

Granier de Cassagnac, Bernard Adolphe. *Récit complet et authentique des événements de Décembre 1851.* Paris: Plon, 1851. Translation: *The Bonaparte Plot.* London: 1851.

Grant, Elliott M. *The Career of Victor Hugo.* Cambridge, Mass.: Harvard University Press, 1946.

———. *Victor Hugo during the Second Republic.* Smith College Studies in Modern Languages, vol. 17. (Northampton, Mass.: Smith College, 1935).

Groupar [research group], eds. *Le Singe à la porte: Vers une théorie de la parodie.* New York–Berne–Frankfurt am Main: Peter Lang, 1984.

Guérard, Albert. *France: A Modern History.* New edition. Ann Arbor: University of Michigan Press, 1969.

Guest, Ivor. *Napoleon III in England.* London: British Technical and General Press, 1952.

Guillemin, Henri. *Le Coup du 2 décembre.* Paris: Gallimard, 1951.

―――. "Louis Napoléon Bonaparte." In *Vérités complémentaires,* 269–324. Paris: Seuil, 1990.

―――. *Napoléon tel quel.* Paris: Éditions de Trévisse, 1969.

―――. *Rappelle-toi, petit.* Illustrations by Bédé. Lys: Éditions d'Utovie, 1978 [1945].

Halstead, John, ed. *December 2, 1851: Contemporary Writings on the Coup d'État of Louis Napoléon.* Garden City, N.Y.: Anchor Books (Doubleday), 1972.

Hamon, Philippe. *Le Personnel du roman. Le système des personnages dans les "Rougon-Macquart" d'Émile Zola.* Geneva: Droz, 1983.

Hayter, Alethea. *Mrs Browning: A Poet's Work and Its Setting.* London: Faber and Faber, 1962.

Histoire populaire contemporaine de la France illustrée. Vols. 2 and 3. Paris: Hachette, 1865–66.

Holt, Edgar. *Plon-Plon: The Life of Prince Napoleon [1822–1891].* London: Michael Joseph, 1973.

Hugo, Victor. *Châtiments.* Ed. P. J. Yarrow. London: Athlone Press, 1975. Also: Ed. Jacques Seebacher. Paris: Garnier-Flammarion, 1979.

―――. *The History of a Crime: The Testimony of an Eye-Witness.* 4 vols. Trans. T. H. Joyce and Arthur Locker. London: Sampson Low, Marston, Searle and Rivington, 1877–78.

―――. *Napoleon the Little.* London: Vizetelly, 1852.

―――. *Oeuvres complètes: Histoire.* Ed. Sheila Gaudon. Paris: Robert Laffont, 1987.

Hugo, Victor Marie, Viscount [Antoine Rocher?]. *L'Organographie physiognophrénologique de Badinguet, d'après Gall et Spurzheim par Victor Hugo 1853.* London: Librairie Universelle, 1871 [1853] [printed in Brussels].

Jiménez, Ramon L. *Caesar against the Celts.* Staplehurst: Spellmount, 1996.

Kerry, The Earl of, ed. *The Secret of the Coup d'Etat: An Unpublished Correspondence of Prince Louis Napoleon, MM. de Morny, de Flahault, and Others, 1848–1852.* With an Introduction by the Earl of Kerry and a Study by Philip Guedalla. London: Constable, 1924.

Kertzer, David I. *Ritual, Politics, and Power.* New Haven–London: Yale University Press, 1988.

Kranzberg, Melvin. "An Emperor Writes History: Napoleon III's *Histoire de Jules César.*" In *Teachers of History: Essays in Honor of Laurence Bradford Packard,* ed. H. Stuart Hughes, 79–104. Ithaca: Cornell University Press, 1954.

Kulstein, David I. *Napoleon III and the Working Class: A Study of Government Propaganda under the Second Empire.* [Sacramento?]: California State Colleges, 1969.

Kurtz, Harold. *The Empress Eugénie, 1826–1920.* Boston: Houghton Mifflin; Cambridge: Riverside Press, 1964.

Labracherie, Pierre. *Napoléon III et son temps*. Geneva: René Julliard, [1967].

Lachnitt, Jean-Claude. *Le Prince Impérial, "Napoléon IV."* Paris: Perrin, 1997.

La Gorce, Pierre de. *Histoire du Second Empire*. Vol. 1. Paris: Plon, 1905.

Laing, Margaret. *Josephine and Napoleon*. London: Sidgwick and Jackson, 1973.

Larkin, Oliver W. *Daumier, Man of His Time*. New York–Toronto–London: Mc-Graw-Hill, 1966.

Larousse, Pierre. *Grand Dictionnaire Universel du XIXᵉ siècle*. Vol. 11. Paris: Administration du Grand Dictionnaire Universel, 1974.

Laughton, Bruce. *Honoré Daumier*. New Haven–London: Yale University Press, 1996.

Lecaillon, Jean-François. *Napoléon III et le Mexique: Les illusions d'un grand dessin*. Préface de Frédéric Mauro. Paris: L'Harmattan, 1994.

Leech, Clifford. *Tragedy*. London: Methuen, 1969.

Legge, Edward. *The Comedy and Tragedy of the Second Empire: Paris Society in the Sixties, Including Letters of Napoleon III., M. Pietri, and Comte de la Chapelle, and Portraits of the Period*. London–New York: Harper and Brothers, 1911.

———. *The Empress Eugénie, 1870–1910: Her Majesty's Life since "The Terrible Year" together with the Statement of Her Case, the Emperor's Own Story of Sedan, an Account of His Exile and Last Days, and Reminiscences of the Prince Imperial, from Authentic Sources*. London–New York: Harper and Brothers, 1910.

Leguèbe, Éric. *Napoléon III le Grand*. Paris: Guy Authier, 1978.

Leppert, Richard. *Art and the Committed Eye: The Cultural Functions of Imagery*. Boulder, Colo.: Westview Press, 1996.

Lettres de Londres. Paris: Levasseur, 1840. [Attributed to Persigny]

Lévi-Strauss, Claude. *The Savage Mind (La Pensée sauvage)*. London: Weidenfeld and Nicolson, 1966 [1962].

Lowndes, Susan, ed. *Diaries and Letters of Marie Belloc Lowndes, 1911–1947*. London: Chatto and Windus, 1971.

Magen, Hippolyte [L. Stelli]. *Histoire du Second Empire, 1848–1870*. Paris: Librairie Illustrée M. Dreyfous, [1878].

Magen, Hyp(p)olite [L. Stelli]. *Les Deux Cours et les nuits de St.-Cloud*. [1860]. Part 1 as: Hipolyte Magen. *Prostitutions, débauches et crimes de la famille Buonaparte depuis Létitia, mère de Napoléon-le-Grand jusqu'à Napoléon-le-Petit*. London: Bridges, 1871. Another ed. of *Les Deux Cours et les nuits de St.-Cloud*. Paris: Association Générale Typographique, [1870].

———. *Histoire satyrique et véritable du mariage de César avec la belle Eugénie de Gusman, ou la Femme de César—1853*. London: Jeffs, 1871 [1853].

Magraw, Roger. *France, 1815–1914: The Bourgeois Century*. New York–Oxford: Oxford University Press, 1986.

Mainardi, Patricia. *Art and Politics of the Second Empire: The Universal Expositions of 1855 and 1867*. New Haven–London: Yale University Press, 1987.

Maringue, Maurice. *Henri Guillemin, le passionné.* With a preface by François Mitterrand. Précy-sous-Thil: Les Éditions de l'Armançon, 1994.

Martinoir, Francine de. *Mathilde et Eugénie: Deux cousines pour un Empereur.* Paris: Criterion, 1992.

Marx, Karl. *The Eighteenth Brumaire of Louis Bonaparte.* New York: International Publishers, 1963 [1852].

Maurois, Simone André. *Miss Howard and the Emperor.* Trans. Humphrey Hare. London: Collins, 1957.

McMillan, James F. *Napoleon III.* London–New York: Longman, 1991.

Mercy-Argenteau, Comtesse Louise de. *The Last Love of an Emperor: Reminiscences of the Comtesse Louise de Mercy-Argenteau, née Princesse de Caraman-Chimay. Describing Her Association with the Emperor Napoleon III. and the Social and Political Part She Played at the Close of the Second Empire.* Ed. La Comtesse de Montrigand. London: William Heinemann, 1926.

Mérimée, Prosper. *Épisode de l'histoire de Russie: Les faux Démétrius.* Paris: Michel Lévy, 1853. Translation: *Demetrius the Impostor: An Episode in Russian History.* Trans. Andrew R. Scoble. London: Richard Bentley, 1853.

Meschonnic, Henri. *Pour la poétique IV: Écrire Hugo.* Paris: Gallimard, 1977.

Minc, Alain. *Louis Napoléon revisité.* Paris: Gallimard, 1997.

Mitterand, Henri. *Zola journaliste, de l'affaire Manet à l'affaire Dreyfus.* Paris: Armand Colin, 1962.

Montandon, Alain, ed. *L'Honnête Homme et le dandy.* Tübingen: Gunter Narr, 1993.

Moore, Brian. *The Magician's Wife.* Toronto: Alfred A. Knopf; London: Bloomsbury, 1997.

Moore, C. H. "Verlaine's *opéra bouffe.*" *PMLA* 83 (1968): 305–11.

Murphy, Steve. *Rimbaud et la ménagerie impériale.* Paris-Lyon: Éditions du CNRS–Presses Universitaires de Lyon, 1991.

Neumann, Alfred. *Another Caesar [Neuer Cäsar].* Trans. Eden Paul and Cedar Paul. New York: Alfred A. Knopf, 1935. [Also as: *The New Caesar.* London: Hutchinson, 1934].

———. *The Gaudy Empire [Kaiserreich].* Trans. Eden Paul and Cedar Paul. New York: Alfred A. Knopf, 1937. Also as *Man of December: A Story of Napoleon III and the Fall of the Second Empire.* London: Hutchinson, 1937.

Nichols Barker, Nancy. *Distaff Diplomacy: The Empress Eugénie and the Foreign Policy of the Second Empire.* Austin-London: University of Texas Press, 1967.

Nicolson, Harold. *Diplomacy.* 3rd ed. New York: Oxford University Press, 1964 [1939].

Normington, Susan. *Napoleon's Children.* Dover, N.H.: Alan Sutton, 1993.

Osgood, Samuel M., ed. *Napoleon III: Buffoon, Modern Dictator, or Sphinx?* Boston: Heath, 1963.

Les Papiers secrets du Second Empire. Brussels: Office de Publicité, 1870–71.

Payne, Howard C. *The Police State of Louis Napoleon Bonaparte, 1851–1860*. Seattle: University of Washington Press, 1966.

Pearl, Cyril. *The Girl with the Swansdown Seat*. London: Frederick Muller, 1955.

Perrot, Philippe. *Fashioning the Bourgeoisie: A History of Clothing in the Nineteenth Century*. Trans. Richard Bienvenu. Princeton: Princeton University Press, 1994. Translation of *Les Dessus et les Dessous de la bourgeoisie: Une histoire du vêtement au XIXᵉ siècle* (1981).

Le Petit Homme Rouge [Ernest Alfred Vizetelly]. *The Court of the Tuileries, 1852–1870: Its Organization, Chief Personages, Splendour, Frivolity, and Downfall*. London: Chatto and Windus, 1907.

Pinkney, David H. *Napoleon III and the Rebuilding of Paris*. Princeton: Princeton University Press, 1958.

Price, Roger. *A Concise History of France*. Cambridge: Cambridge University Press, 1993.

Priollet, Julien, and Marcel Priollet. *Napoléon III: Pièce historique en cinq actes, dont un prologue, et huit tableaux*. Paris: Librairie Théâtrale, 1908.

Proudhon, P. J. *Napoléon III: Manuscrits inédits, publiés par Clément Rochel*. Paris: Société d'Éditions littéraires et artistiques, 1900.

———. *La Révolution sociale démontrée par le coup d'État du 2 décembre*. Paris: Garnier, 1852.

Régis, Roger. *La Belle Sabotière et le prisonnier de Ham*. Paris: Les Éditions de France, 1937.

Reichert, Robert W. "Anti-Bonapartist Elections to the Académie Française during the Second Empire." *Journal of Modern History* 35 (1963): 33–45.

Richardson, Joanna. *Princess Mathilde*. London: Weidenfeld and Nicolson, 1969.

———. *La Vie parisienne*. London: Hamish Hamilton, 1971.

Ridley, Jasper. *Napoleon III and Eugénie*. London: Constable, 1979.

Robb, Graham. *Victor Hugo*. London: Picador, 1997.

Roche, Anne. "L'opposition au Second Empire dans quelques-unes de ses expressions et représentations littéraires." *Revue d'Histoire littéraire de la France* 74 (1974): 33–45.

Rogeard, M. A. *Les Propos de Labienus: La critique historique sous Auguste*. 4th ed. New York: H. de Mareil, 1865.

———. *The Strictures of Labienus: The Historical Critic in the Time of Augustus*. Trans. Dr. W. E. Guthrie. Philadelphia: T. B. Pugh, 1865.

Rouart, Jean-Marie. *Morny: Un voluptueux au pouvoir*. Paris: Gallimard, 1995.

Rubel, Maximilien. *Karl Marx devant le bonapartisme*. Paris–The Hague: Mouton, 1960.

Rütten, Raimund, Ruth Jung, and Gerhard Schneider, eds. *La Caricature entre République et censure*. Introduction by Roger Bellet and Raimund Rütten.

Lyon: Presses universitaires de Lyon, 1996. Revised French edition of *Die Karikatur zwischen Republik und Zensur*. Marburg: Jonas Verlag für Kunst und Literatur, 1991.

Saint-Rémy, M. de [Charles de Morny]. *Les Bons Conseils: Comédie en un acte*. Paris: Michel-Lévy, 1862.

———. *Les Finesses du mari. Comédie*. Paris: Michel-Lévy, 1865.

———. *Pas de fumée sans un peu de feu: Comédie en un acte*. Paris: Michel-Lévy, 1866.

Saint-Rémy et Offenbach, MM. *M. Choufleuri restera chez lui le. . . . Opérette bouffe en un acte*. Paris: Michel-Lévy, 1861.

Salles, Catherine. *Le Second Empire*. Paris: Larousse, 1985. Histoire de France Illustrée.

Schwartzenberg, Roger-Gérard. *L'État spectacle: Essai sur et contre le Star System en politique*. Paris: Flammarion, 1977.

Séguin, Philippe. *Louis Napoléon le Grand*. Paris: Bernard Grasset, 1990.

Speirs, Dorothy E., and Dolorès A. Signori, eds. *Entretiens avec Zola*. Ottawa: Les Presses de l'Université d'Ottawa, 1990.

Spitzer, Alan B. "The Good Napoleon III." *French Historical Studies* 2 (1962): 308–29.

Stacton, David. *The Bonapartes*. New York: Simon and Schuster, 1966.

Stoffel, Baron [Eugène Georges Henri Céleste]. *Histoire de Jules César: Guerre civile*. Paris, Imprimerie Nationale, 1887.

Les Titres de la dynastie napoléonienne. Paris: Imprimerie Impériale, 1868.

Touchatout [Léon Bienvenu]. *Histoire tintamarresque de Napoléon III illustrée de nombreux dessins noirs et coloriés*. Paris: Bureau de L'Éclipse, 1874.

———. *La Dégringolade impériale: Seconde Partie de l'Histoire tintamarresque de Napoléon III*. Dessins de [drawings by] G. Lafosse. Paris: 1878.

Truesdell, Martin. *Spectacular Politics: Louis-Napoleon Bonaparte and the "Fête Impériale," 1849–1870*. New York–Oxford: Oxford University Press, 1997.

Tulard, Jean, ed. *Dictionnaire du Second Empire*. Paris: Arthème Fayard, 1995.

Turnbull, Patrick. *Eugénie of the French*. London: Michael Joseph, 1974.

Vallès, Jules. *Oeuvres I: 1857–1870*. Ed. Roger Bellet. Paris: Gallimard, Bibliothèque de la Pléiade, 1975.

———. *Oeuvres II: 1871–1885*. Ed. Roger Bellet. Paris: Gallimard, Bibliothèque de la Pléiade, 1990.

Vatré, Éric. *Henri Rochefort, ou La comédie politique au XIXe siècle*. Paris: Lattès, 1984.

Viel-Castel, Horace de. *Mémoires du Comte Horace de Viel-Castel sur le règne de Napoléon III, 1851–1864*. Avec un avant-propos et des notes par [with a foreword and notes by] Pierre Josserand. Paris: Guy Le Prat, 1979 [1942].

———. *Mémoires du comte Horace de Viel-Castel sur le règne de Napoléon III, 1851–1864*. 6 vols. Paris: 1883–84.

White, Hayden. *Metahistory: The Historical Imagination in Nineteenth-Century Europe*. Baltimore-London: Johns Hopkins University Press, 1973.

Wikoff, Henry. *Napoleon Louis Bonaparte: First President of France*. New York: George P. Putnam, 1849.

William Bouguereau, 1825–1905. [Catalog]. Paris: Musée du Petit-Palais; Montreal: Montreal Museum of Fine Arts; Hartford, Conn.: Wadsworth Atheneum; 1984.

Williams, Roger L. *Henri Rochefort, Prince of the Gutter Press*. New York: Charles Scribner's Sons, 1966.

————. *Manners and Murders in the World of Louis-Napoléon*. Seattle–London: University of Washington Press, 1975.

————. *The Mortal Napoleon III*. Princeton: Princeton University Press, 1971.

————. "A Tragedy of Good Intentions." *History Today* (April 1954): 219–26.

————. *The World of Napoleon III, 1851–1870*. New York: Free Press; London: Collier Macmillan, 1965. Originally published as *Gaslight and Shadow: The World of Napoleon III, 1851–1870*. New York: Macmillan, 1957.

Wilton, Andrew. *The Swagger Portrait: Grand Manner Portraiture in Britain from Van Dyck to Augustus John, 1630–1930*. London: Tate Gallery, 1992.

Wolf, John B. *France, 1814–1919: The Rise of a Liberal-Democratic Society*. New York–Evanston–London: Harper and Row, 1963 [1940].

Zed [le comte Albert de Maugny]. *Le Demi-monde sous le Second Empire: Souvenirs d'un sybarite*. Paris: Ernest Kolb, [1892].

Zeldin, Théodore. "Biographie et psychologie sous le Second Empire." *Revue d'Histoire moderne et contemporaine* 21 (1974): 58–74.

————. "The Myth of Napoleon III." *History Today* (February 1958): 103–109.

Zola, Émile. *The Debacle [La Débâcle]*. Trans. Leonard Tancock. Harmondsworth: Penguin, 1972.

————. *La Fortune des Rougon*. Ed. Henri Mitterand, preface by Maurice Agulhon. Paris: Gallimard, 1981. Translation: *The Fortune of the Rougons*. Gloucester: Alan Sutton, 1985. Also: *La Fortune des Rougon: Épisode du Coup d'État en Province décembre 1851*. Ed. Gina Gourdin Servenière. Geneva: Strategic Communications, 1990.

————. *The Kill [La Curée]*. Trans. A. Teixeira de Mattos. London: Granada, 1985.

————. *Nana*. Trans. Douglas Parmée. Oxford–New York: Oxford University Press, 1992.

————. *Oeuvres complètes*. Ed. Henri Mitterand. 15 vols. Paris: Cercle du Livre Précieux, 1967–70.

————. *Les Rougon-Macquart: Histoire naturelle et sociale d'une famille sous le Second Empire*. Ed. Henri Mitterand. 5 vols. Paris: Gallimard, Bibliothèque de la Pléiade, 1960–67.

Index

About, Edmond, 98
Adelon, Nicolas Philibert, 270
Agulhon, Maurice, 55*n*10
Alba, duke of, 222*n*23, 223–24, 353
Alba, Francisca, duchess of (Paca), 210,
    215*n*10, 222*n*23, 223–24, 353
Albert, Prince, 196, 218, 354
Album zutique, 282–83, 283*n*48
Alcañices, Pepe, marquis of, 216, 224,
    224*n*26
Alexander I, czar, 112
Alfonso, prince of Asturias, 375
Algeria, 172, 187, 238, 315, 357–60
Allégorie à la gloire de Napoléon III (Cabas-
    son), *figure 5*, 155
Allem, Maurice, 203
Alphand, Mme., 166
America, United States of, 177–78, 187,
    345
Antigna, Alexandre, 157
Antigny, Blanche d', 306
Apothéose de Napoléon 1er (Ingres), 194
Arenenberg, 166, 225–26, 345, 362
Ashley, Maurice, 76*n*10
Auber, Esprit, 214
Augier, Émile, 330*n*1
Augsberg, 225, 345
Augusta of Bavaria, 103

Augustus, 82, 125, 196, 201, 257
Aumule, duke d', 306
Austria, 155–56, 163, 172–74, 176–77,
    180, 369

Bac, Ferdinand, 115*n*34, 125, 127–28,
    131*n*20, 166, 225, 312–13, 318
Bacciochi, Count Félix, 241–42
Bacciochi, Princess, 97
Bade, Marie de, 226
Bal Mabille, 301, 306, 315
Balzac, Honoré de, 53, 200; *Eugénie Gran-
    det*, 228
Baraglini, Countess, 225
Barbier, Auguste: his *Iambes*, 78
Baroche, Ernest, 306, 370
Barthes, Roland, 5, 158, 252
Barthez, Dr., 220*n*19
Basselin, Olivier, 300
Battle of Solferino, The (Janet-Lange), *figure
    9,* 156
Baudelaire, Charles, 133, 200, 261, 329; *Les
    Fleurs du mal*, 261, 330
Baudin, Victor, 15, 39, 43, 52
Bazaine, General Achille, 351, 378
Beauharnais, Alexandre de, 101, 109–10
Beauharnais, Eugène de, 101, 103, 110,
    198

Beauharnais, Hortense de (mother): and
 Flahaut, 23, 24*n*18; influence on son, 69,
 94, 108, 127–28, 166, 226–27, 244,
 286, 362, 396; supposed indiscretions,
 100, 113–17, 272; and Napoleon I, 101,
 104, 110; as queen of Holland, 103*n*10;
 marriage, 107, 109–17, 361; supersti-
 tions, 134; death, 363, portrait, 386.
Beauharnais, Stéphanie de, 103, 218
Beerbohm, Max, 266
Belgium, 173, 269, 275, 370, 387
Bell, David F., 164–65
Bellanger, Marguerite (Justine Marie Le
 Boeuf, Margot-la-Rigoleuse), 87, 235,
 237–38, 238*n*47, 240, 246, 281, 284,
 figure 23, 354–55
Belloc Lowndes, Marie, 352–53; *The Em-
 press Eugénie,* 352–56
Benedetti, Count Vincente, 375
Bienvenu, Léon-Charles (Touchatout), 285;
 Histoire tintamarresque de Napoléon III,
 285–88, *figure 20; L'Homme qui veut se
 faire un nom,* 285
Bierman, John, 93, 217, 229*n*36, 238
Billault, Auguste Adolphe Marie, 370
Bismarck, Count Otto von: diplomacy, 173,
 366, 370, 374–75, 385, 392; at 1867 Ex-
 hibition, 239, 306–307, 325; on the Em-
 pire, 323, 354; at Sedan, 382–83
Blache, Noël, 51–52
Blanc, Louis, 9, 62, 77, 184, 346; *L'Organi-
 sation du travail,* 184*n*5
Blessington, Lady, 134, 228, 231, 338
Bobèche, 282
Boccherini, Luigi, 247
Bois de Boulogne, 201, 211, 308, 331
Bonaparte, Caroline (Murat), 97, 102, 105–
 106, 125, 271, 334; her children, 106
Bonaparte, Charles (Carlo Buonaparte), 101
Bonaparte, Charles Lucien, prince of Canino
 (cousin), 14
Bonaparte, Élisa, 97, 102, 105, 271, 334;
 her children, 105
Bonaparte, Jérôme (uncle): in coup d'état,

14; president of Senate, 79; descendants,
 96–98, 106; youth, 102–104; marriages,
 103, 113; ambitions for son, 219, 221; attitude to Napoleon III, 226; satirized,
 271; theater, 334; king of Westphalia, 386
Bonaparte, Joseph (uncle): at 18 Brumaire,
 66; youth, 101–102; king of Naples and
 Spain, 103*n*10, 107, 209–10, 271; descendants, 104; his novel *Moïna,* 334
Bonaparte, Laetitia (Letizia) (Madame
 Mère), 101–102, 166, 271, 389
Bonaparte, Louis (father): youth, 96, 102;
 king of Holland, 103*n*10, 226; marriage
 and sons, 104, 107, 110, 113, 117; literary works, 110–11, 334; attitude to Napoleon I, 111–12, 361; attitude to son,
 111–12, 114, 244, 272, 286, 361
Bonaparte, Prince Louis Lucien (cousin),
 392
Bonaparte, Louis Napoléon. *See* Napoleon
 III
Bonaparte, Lucien (uncle), 66, 97–98, 102,
 104, 271, 334; literary works, 334
Bonaparte, Napoleon. *See* Napoleon I
Bonaparte, Napoléon Charles (brother),
 107, 111
Bonaparte, Prince Napoléon Eugène Louis
 (prince imperial) (son), 300, 371, 379; in
 Zululand, 94, 338, 348*n*25, 355, 394,
 396 name, 104; baptism, 164, 215, 332;
 birth, 215, 220; satirized, 283–84; exile,
 391–94
Bonaparte, Prince Napoléon Jérôme (Plon-
 Plon) (cousin): political activity, 9, 14,
 46, 94–95, 97–98, 176, 193, 392–93,
 395*n*5; nickname, 97, 103; minister for
 Algeria, 97, 358, 360; and Rachel, 100,
 231 appearance, 114; extravagances, 204,
 254, 334, 304–306, 334; and Eugénie,
 210, 219, 354; satirized, 284, *figure 18*
Bonaparte, Napoléon Louis (brother), 107,
 111, 113; death, 107*n*16, 345, 362
Bonaparte, Pauline, 102, 103*n*10, 271, 334
Bonaparte, Prince Pierre Napoléon, 9, 98,
 106, 267–68, 284, 370

Bonaparte, Prince Victor (and descendants), 395n5

Bonaparte family: 96–100; civil and imperial, 97; naming system, 100–108

Bonapartism, 1, 17, 90, 94–95, 167–70, 183, 320

Boon, H. N., 335n8

Bossuet, Jacques Bénigne, 376

Boucheporn, 116

Boucicaut, Aristide, 309

Bouffes-Parisiens, 301, 302n5, 324, 365

Bouguereau, William, 157, 338; *Nymphs and Satyr*, 317–18

Bourges, Michel de, 41

Briais, Bernard, 305–306, 313

Broadley, A. M., 256n12

Broglie, Achille, duke de, 281

Brohan, Madeleine, 359

Browning, Elizabeth Barrett, 340–41, 343, 353; *Poems before Congress*, 341–43

Browning, Robert, 134, 341

Bruix, Eustache, 66

Buckle, William, 304

Buffon, comte de, 270, 277

Bugeaud, General Thomas, 357

Buisson de Longpré, Irène de, 116

Bülow, Hans Guido von: his *Ouverture héroïque et Marche des Impériaux de la tragédie Jules César de Shakespeare pour Grand Orchestre*, 389

Burchell, S. C., 204, 301, 302n5, 303, 322, 371, 374

Bure, Pierre (and Mme.), 229, 347

Burke, Peter, 150

Bury, J. P. T., 368, 373

Bylandt-Palsterscamp, Charles Adam de, 115, 115n35

Cabanel, Alexandre, 156, 317

Cabasson, 155

Cabet, Étienne, 182, 196

Cabinet noir, 261, 261n17

Caesar, Julius, 13, 55, 77–89, 167, 266, 300; *Commentaries*, 80, 85, 153; *The Civil War*, 87

Cambacérès, duke de, 213

Cambodia, 172

Campanella, Tommaso, 182

Campbell, Stuart L., 52, 77, 184n5

Camus, Albert, 243

Camus, Marie Louise Françoise Éléonore, 229

Cancan, 93, 315–16, 348n25

Candide (Blanquist journal), 78

Canrobert, general, 15

Caraman-Chimay, Prince Alphonse de, 238

Carette, Mme., 210, 212

Carey, Lieutenant J. B., 355, 355n34, 394

Caricature, La, 255, 264

Carini, Colonel, 40–41

Carpeaux, Jean-Baptiste, 316, 394; *La danse, figure 21*, 316–19, 325

Carpenter, Scott E., 258–59

Carrard, Philippe, 109

Castellane, Boniface de, 114–15

Castelvecchio, Count Félix de, 114

Castiglioni, Virginia, countess of (la Castiglione), 234–36, 240, 274, 332, 366

Catherine de Médicis, 252

Catherine of Württemberg, Princess, 97, 103, 106

Caussidière, Marc, 62

Cavaignac, General, 9–10

Cavour, Count Camillo di, 174, 236, 343

Célébrités populaires, Les, 263

Chabrier, Emmanuel, 282

Chadwick, Edwin, 201

Cham (Count Amédée de Noé), 263, 312

Changarnier, General, 11–12

Charivari, Le, 255, 263–64, 267, 346

Charivari belge, Le, 269

Charlemagne, 39, 84, 160, 164, 167

Charles I, king of England, 75–76

Charles II, king of France, 75–76

Charles IX, king of France, 35, 270

Charlotte, Princess (empress of Mexico), 178–79, 325, 355, 365

Chateaubriand, François-René, vicomte de, 6, 346

Chaumont-Quitry (chamberlain), 234–35
Chéri, Rose, 230
Chevalier, Michel, 184*n*5
China, 165, 172, 264
Chislehurst, 281, 348*n*25, 355, 387, 391–93
Cholera outbreaks, 197, 215
Chopin, Frédéric, 238
Christiansen, Rupert, 199–200
Civil list, 91, 97, 162, 252–53
Clairville. *See* Coignard, Théodore
Clarendon, Lord, 218, 221, 273
Clary, Julie, 102–103
Clemenceau, Georges, 356
Cloche, La, 89, 280–81
Cobban, Alfred, 18
Code Civil (and Code Napoléon), 91, 192
Coignard, Théodore, and Clairville: their *Oh! là là! qu'c'est bête, tout ça!*, 301
Collot, Jean-Pierre, 66
Comédie-Française, 254, 330
Commentaires de César, Les (show), 80, 300
Commune (Paris), 44, 284, 325, 388–89
Compiègne château: *séries*, 161–62, 253, 332, 357–60; emperor's escapades, 242, 327; theatricals, 299–300, 307, 312
Comptes fantastiques d'Haussmann (Ferry), 198
Conneau, Dr. Henri, 72, 284, 345, 347, 393
Constitutionnel, Le, 190, 262
Constitutions: Second Republic, 10, 12, 14, 17, 20, 34, 64, 79; Second Empire, 372
Coquelin, Constant, 359
Cornu, Hortense, 81, 114, 166
Corsaire, Le, 281
Coup d'État of 1851, pp. 2–3, 6–7, 13–30, 37, 319, 361, 364; in the provinces, 16–19, 26, 30, 60–61; interpretations, 18–68, 89–95
Coup d'État permanent, Le (Mitterrand), 3
Courson, General de, 381
Cousin, Victor, 320
Coutts, Burdett, 228

Cowley, Lord, 217, 236
Crémieux, Hector, 324
Crimean War, 97, 156, 163, 172–73, 176, 354, 357
Crinoline, 251, 309–16
Crinolinomanie (Vernier), 312
Cromwell, Oliver, 62

Dali, Salvador, 318
Dansette, Adrien, 15*n*9, 73*n*7, 114–15, 117, 226, 227*n*33, 229, 237, 238*n*47, 241, 245
Danton, Georges, 35, 62
Daudet, Alphonse, 99; *Le Nabab*, 99, 308
Daumier, Honoré, 255, 263–66, 312; *History of a Reign*, 265
David, Jacques-Louis, 155, 394; *Napoleon Crossing the Alps*, 394
Debray, R., 248
Decazes, Élie, 115
De Gaulle, General, 3, 395*n*5
Déjazet, Virginie, 230
Delacroix, Eugène, 253
Deleuze, Gilles, 164–65
Demidov, Prince, 227
Demi-monde, 298–99, 302–309, 326, 330
Descotes, Maurice, 332–33
Deslions, Anna, 306
Devienne, Adrien, 238*n*47
Dickens, Charles, 134
Disraeli, Benjamin (earl of Beaconsfield), 131, 338, 340: *Endymion*, 228, 338–40
Doche, Eugénie, 230
Dolan, Therese, 250, 310, 313
Don Juan, 241–46
Drouet, Juliette, 39
Drouyn de Lhuys, Édouard, 218–19
Du Camp, Maxime, 7, 182, 204, 310
Ducarre, M., 203
Ducrot, General Auguste Alexandre, 380, 383
Dufaure, Jules, 79
Duff, David, 229*n*36
Dufresne, Claude, 307

Dumas *fils*, Alexandre, 223; *Le Demi-monde*, 298

Dumas *père*, Alexandre, 33, 41, 259, 346; *The Three Musketeers*, 353

Dupin, Charles, 14

Duplan, Jules, 22

Duroc, General Michel, 110

Duruy, Victor, 81; *Histoire des Romains*, 81

Duval, Alexandre, 305

Duveau, Georges: his *La Vie ouvrière en France sous le Second Empire*, 203n34

Eberhardt, Isabelle, 360

Eberst (Offenbacher), Issac, 323

Echard, William E., 171

Écho du Nord, L', 88

Éclipse, L', 263

Eglington, earl of, 339

Eighteenth Brumaire, 42, 66

Eighteenth Brumaire of Louis Bonaparte, The (Marx), 6, 61–68

Elections: (1848), 9, 10, 28, 38; (1869), 370

Electoral laws, 12–13

Elphinstone, George Keith (Lord Keith), 24n18

Elphinstone, Margaret Mercer, 24n18, 25

Élysée palace, 214–17, 238–39, 350

Emperor at Solferino, The (Meissonier), *figure 8*, 156

Emperor Napoleon III, The (Flandrin), *figure 1*, 152–53, 156

Empress Eugénie, The (Winterhalter), 250, *figure 15*

Empress Eugénie Surrounded by Her Palace Ladies, The (*L'Impératrice Eugénie entourée de ses dames du Palais*) (Winterhalter), *figure 3*, 153, 314, 354

Épinal, images d', *figure 4*, 154–55

Espel, Countess d', 230

Étampes, duchess d', 254

Eugénie (de Montijo), empress: courtship and marriage, 12, 164, 209–20, 230–39, 244–45, 258, 330, 364–65; superstitions, 134; portraits, 153, 155, 158; charity, *figure 13*, 162–63, 191; political views and activities, 176–77, 179, 233, 351, 366, 370–71, 374, 378; fashions, 204, 207, 299, 305, 311, 314–15; early life, 220–24; last years, 247, 388–89, 391–94; cult of Marie-Antoinette, 250–52, 299; satirized, 273, 284, 286; taste, 32–21; and Disraeli, 338, 340; in play of Belloc Lowndes, 352–56; death of son, 348n25, 355n34

Evans, Richard J., 5

Evans, Dr. T. W., 214, 389

Événement, L', 28, 38

Exhibitions: (1851), 194; (1855), 194–95, 317; (1862), 191, 194; (1867), 87, 156, 179, 194–95, 202, 239, 254, 286, *figure 14*, 306, 324–25, 369; (1878), 318

Faber, George Stanley, 135–36

Faider, Charles, 269

Farnborough Hill, 394, 395n5

Faustin, 283

Fenaux, Jean-Paul, 22

Ferguson, Dr. Robert, 245–46

Ferry, Jules, 198, 370

Fête impériale, la, 11, 317, 327, 369, 396

Feuillet, Octave, 299

Figaro, Le, 262, 266–67, 380

Fisch-ton-kan, 282

FitzJames, James Stuart. *See* Alba, duke of

Flahaut de la Billarderie, Charles Auguste, comte de, 14, 16n9, 17, 23–26, 58, 115–16

Flameng, Léopold, 155

Flandrin, Hippolyte, 152–53, 156

Flaubert, Gustave, 7, 21–23, 98, 120, 124, 246, 249, 261, 329, 331, 397; *L'Éducation sentimentale*, 21–23, 249, 364 *Madame Bovary*, 261, 331, 358, 360; projected novel, *Sous Napoléon III*, 331

Fleischmann, Hector, 228–30, 240–41

Fleury, Émile Félix, count de, 15, 58, 157, 309, 354

Fontainebleau palace, 161, 211, 216, 252–53, 299, 314

Forbach, battle of, 378
Fortoul, Hippolyte, 370
Fouché, Joseph, duke d'Otrante, 271
Fould, Achille, 219, 370
Fourier, François, 189, 196, 341, 34
Franco-Prussian War, 2, 166, 172, 174, 356, 367, 374–88, 386, 391, 396
Franz Joseph, emperor of Austria, 177
Fraser, Sir William, 125, 174
Frauenfeld, Stahli von, 226
French Academy, 78–79, 87
Frerejean, Alain, 215, 233, 376, 397
Freud, Sigmund, 362
Froeschwiller, battle of, 378
Frye, Northrop, 369, 374n9, 376
Furet, François, 109

Gall, Franz Joseph, 271
Gallifet, marquise de, 299
Gambetta, Léon, 372
Garnier, Charles, 202, 253, 316, 320
Gaudon, Sheila, 279
Gaulois, Le, 181
Gautier, Théophile, 78, 98, 151, 156, 282, 359
Gazette de France, La, 262
Genette, Gérard, 322
Gildea, Robert, 19
Gill, André, 263, 283
Girardin, Émile de, 254
Giraudeau, Fernand, 29, 90, 192n16
Gladstone, William Ewart, 392
Glatigny, Albert: his Le Fer rouge: Nouveaux Châtiments, 269, 269n29
Glória, Maria da, 226
Goltz, Count von der, 354–55
Goncourt, Edmond and Jules de, 98, 120, 260, 329; Journal, 124, 200, 242, 301–302, 307, 353; Germinie Lacerteux, 205–206
Gordon, Éléonore, 71, 121, 216, 227, 286, 346, 363–64
Gounod, Charles, 299
Gramont, Antoine Agénor, duke of, 375

Grand Dictionnaire Universel du XIXᵉ Siècle (Larousse), 120–21, 270
Granier de Cassagnac, Adolphe, 25–26, 58, 284
Granville, Lord, 220
Grévégnée, Françoise de, 222
Gricourt, marquis de, 395
Grohé, Georges, 321
Gros, Antoine-Jean, 157
Guérard, Albert, 19
Guéronnière, M. de la, 125
Guest, Ivor, 131
Guillaume, Eugène, 316
Guillemin, Henri, 15–16n9, 50, 56–61, 65; Le Coup du 2 décembre and "Louis Napoléon Bonaparte," 58–61, 107–108, 183–84, 203, 243, 331; "Rappelle-toi, petit," 57
Guizot, François, 70, 77; Histoire de la Révolution d'Angleterre, 70n2, 74
Gull, Sir William, 393

Hadol, 288; La Ménagerie impériale, 284, figures 17–19
Halévy, Ludovic, 302n5, 324–25
Hamelin, Mme., 234
Hamilton, Lady, 346
Hamlet (opera), 299
Haussmann, Baron Georges Eugène, 197–99, 202, 206, 284, 286, 309, 364, 370
Hegel, Georg Wilhelm Friedrich, 6, 62
Heine, Heinrich, 63
Henckel von Donnersmarck, Guido, 305
Henry V, king of England, 127, 380
Hertford, Lord, 303
Hervé (Florimond Ronger), 324
Hetzel, Jules, 274, 278
Hidalgo y Esnaurrizar, José Manuel, 178–79
Histoire populaire contemporaine de la France, figure 10, 156
Hodgart, Matthew, 280
Hoffmann, E. T. A., 198n26
Hohenlohe-Langenburg, Princess Adelaide of, 218

Hohenzollern, Prince Clodwig Karl Victor of, 351
Hohenzollern-Sigmaringen, Prince Leopold of, 375, 378
Holt, Edgar, 46, 395n5
Home, Daniel Dunglas, 134–35
Hôtel de Ville (Paris), 164, 364
Hôtel-Dieu (Paris), 201
Houssaye, Arsène, 323, 330; "Ode to Napoleon III," 93
Howard, Miss (Elizabeth Ann Haryett): future emperor's mistress, 132, 217–18, 220, 228–29, 231–32, 330, 346–47, 354, 363–64; raises his children, 229; role in coup d'état, 232; satirized, 272, 274
Hübner, J. A., baron von, 15n9
Huddleston, Ferdinand, 211
Hugenschmidt, Dr. Arthur, 236
Hughes-Wilson, Colonel John, 73
Hugo, Charles, 39, 266, 280, 306
Hugo, François-Victor, 280
Hugo, Victor: attacks, 2, 3, 14–15, 23, 30, 31–49, 78, *figure 22,* 327, 331, 397; supports Louis Napoléon, 10; role in coup d'état, 14–15, 349–50, 364; seances, 45, 135; contrast with Louis Napoléon, 46–49; role in June Days, 46–47; influence, 52–53, 55, 58, 61, 63, 181, 280, 282, 299, 320, 330–31, 351–52; love life, 235, 306; journalism, 263; and Rochefort, 266–67
—"A la colonne de la Place Vendôme," 38
—*Châtiments,* 31–33, 38, 53, 181, 257, 266, 274–79, 339n12, 350, 352
—*Les Contemplations,* 274
—*Histoire d'un crime, L',* 21n14, 28, 32–33, 37–47, 93, 285, 350
—*Napoléon le Petit* , 28, 31–37, 53, 61, 178, 181, 274, 279
—*Notre-Dame de Paris,* 53
—*Les Orientales,* 8

India, 223
Indochina, 172
Ingres, Jean-Auguste-Dominique, 156, 194

Invalides, 215, 397
Ionesco, Eugène, 106
Isabella II, queen of Spain, 223, 374
Italian question: expedition to Rome, 11–12, 122, 341; war against Austria, 155–56, 163, 172, 174–76; policies, 173–74, 236, 251; and Browning, 341–43

James II, 70, 75–76
Janet, Ange-Louis (Janet-Lange), 156–57
Janin, Jules, 263, 324
Joinville, Prince de, 25, 72
Jones, Ernest, 111
Joséphine, Empress, 101, 105, 107, 109–11, 113, 116, 134, 160, 164, 177, 213, 218, 252, 389
Jouberthou, Alexandrine, 104
Jouffroy, François, 316
Journal des Débats, Le, 262, 324
Journal des Villes et Campagnes, 262
Juárez, Benito, 177–79
July Monarchy, 8, 70, 108, 183, 315, 357
Jump, John D., 298
June Days (1848), 9, 16, 38, 46–47, 50, 58–59, 64, 363–64

Kahn, Jean-François, 47
Kerry, earl of, 16n9
Kertzer, David I., 159, 159n6
Khalil-Bey, 308
Kirkpatrick, William, 222
Kissinger, Henry: his *Diplomacy,* 173
Kitsch, 323
Klésinger, 394
Kulstein, David I., 190, 193, 335n7–8
Kurtz, Harold, 216n10

La Bédoyère, Count Charles Huchet de, 240n50
La Bédoyère, countess de, 234–35, 240n50
Labenne, Count Alexandre Louis Ernest de, 229n37, 347
Labienus. *See* Rogeard, Louis-Auguste
Lachnitt, Jean-Claude, 397
La Gorce, Pierre de, 119, 266

Laity, Lieutenant, 71; *Relation historique des événements du 30 octobre 1836*, 71*n*4
Lamartine, Alphonse de, 10, 57
La Masismas, marquise de, 299
Lambert, Bernard, 57
Lambert-Thiboust, 306
Langlade, Favart de, 230
Langman, Terry, 397
Lanterne, La, 51, 263, 266–67, 280, 351, 366
Laprade, Victor de, 78
Larkin, Oliver W., 265
Larousse, Pierre, 120, 270, 303
Lassus, Jean-Baptiste, 214
Last Napoleon, The, 397
Laughton, Bruce, 264
La Valette, marquis de, 366
Lavigne, Ernest, 267
Lazerges, Jean Raymond Hippolyte, 157
Le Bas, Philippe, 94, 182, 346, 362, 364, 396
Leblanc, Léonide, 306
Leboeuf, Marshal Edmond, 283, 373, 375–76
Le Boeuf, Justine Marie. *See* Bellanger, Marguerite
Lebreton, Mme., 389
Lecaillon, Jean-François, 180
Leconte de Lisle, 283*n*48
Ledoux, Claude Nicolas, 194
Ledru-Rollin, Alexandre, 10
Leech, Clifford, 374*n*9
Legge, Edward, 252, 348, 348*n*25, 380*n*18
Leguèbe, Éric, 28, 203*n*34
Lenormand, Mlle., 134
Le Nôtre, André, 254
Léon, Count, 132
Leopold, king of Belgium, 218, 221, 347
Le Petit, Alfred, 283
Leppert, Richard, 317
Lérignan, Paulette de, 242
Lesseps, Ferdinand de, 216
Letessier, Caroline, 306
Lettres de Londres, 72, 72*n*5, 94, 124

Levillain, Henriette, 132*n*23
Lévi-Strauss, Claude, 102, 105
Lévy, Dr. Michel: his *Traité général d'hygiène*, 120
Liberty Guiding the People (Delacroix), 54
Lind, Jenny, 230
Lionnes, 304–307
Liszt, Franz, 238
livret (workers'), 192
Longchamp, 198, 201
Longpré, Laure de, 109
Louis XIV, 150, 164, 252, 254, 300
Louis XVI, 250, 253, 377
Louis XVIII, 112, 114–15, 240*n*50
Louis-Philippe, king of France, 8, 24*n*18, 63, 71–72, 79–80, 252, 264, 347, 349
Lowe, Sir Hudson, 344, 362
Lowndes, Frederic, 353
Lune, La, 263
Luxembourg, 173, 370

Machiavelli, 119
MacMahon, Marshal, 32, 358, 379–81
Magen, Hippolyte (L. Stelli), 17*n*11, 271, 273*n*35; *Les Deux Cours et les nuits de St.-Cloud*, 271–72, 279; *Histoire satyrique et véritable du Mariage de César avec la belle Eugénie de Guzman*, 273–74, 279; *Histoire du Second Empire*, 285
Magenta, battle of, 156, 341, 365
Magnan, General, 12–13, 55
Magraw, Roger, 19
Malmesbury, Lord, 346
Manet, Édouard, 179, 320
Mann, Thomas, 360–61
Marbeuf, count de, 101
Marchand, Count Louis Joseph Narcisse, 80
Margot-la-Rigoleuse. *See* Bellanger, Marguerite
Margueritte, General Jean Auguste, 382
Marie-Antoinette, 250–53, 306
Marie-Louise, Empress, 103, 116, 252
Marius, Gaius, 84
"Marseillaise, La," 54, 370, 376, 389
Marseillaise, La (newspaper), 263, 267–68

Martini, Padre Giovanni Battista, 247

Martinoir, Francine de, 215*n*10

Martyn, Major Mountjoy, 231

Marx, Karl, 6, 38, 50, 178; *Eighteenth Brumaire of Louis Bonaparte*, 61–68

Mason, Jem, 231, 346

Massa, marquis de, 80, 300

Masson, Frédéric, 117

Masuyer, Valérie, 114

Mathilde, Princess (cousin): receptions, 78, 97–98, 211, 215, 215*n*10, 259–60, 299, 302*n*5, 331, 336; and cousin, 129, 226–27, 231–32, 234–35, 345, 362; and Eugénie, 219, 353–54; marriage and lover, 227, 260; satirized, 284, 287, *figure 19*

Maugny, Count Albert de. *See* Zed

Maupas, Charlemagne Émile de, 13, 15, 16*n*9, 58, 349

Maurey, Max: his *La Savelli*, 348*n*25

Mauriac, François, 56, 325

Maurois, André, 61

Maurois, Simone André, 216, 231, 330

Maury, Alfred, 81, 114

Maximilian, Archduke (emperor of Mexico), 177–79, 355

McMillan, James F., 2, 174, 184*n*5

Meilhac, Henri, 324–25

Meissonier, Jean-Louis-Ernest, 156

Mérat, Albert, 283*n*48

Mercy-Argenteau, Count de, 238

Mercy-Argenteau, Countess Louise de: memoirs, 77, 99, 116, 133–34, 204, 249, 377, 383, 393*n*3; and the emperor, 235, 238–39, 241, 246–47, 386; at court 299, 303–304, 313

Mérimée, Prosper: and Eugénie, 211, 216, 220–21, 237, 237*n*46, 258–60, 330; and Napoleon III, 258*n*14; his *Épisode de l'histoire de Russie: Les faux Démétrius*, 258–59

Méry, Joseph, 214

Meschonnic, Henri, 277

Mesnard, Jacques André, 17

Metternich, Prince Clemens Lothar, 175

Metternich, Princess Pauline de, 161, 207, 300, 312, 315

Metternich, Prince Richard von, 1, 300, 355

Mexican expedition, 87, 156, 165, 172, 177–80, 287, 300, 355, 369

Meyerbeer, Giacomo, 324; *Le Prophète*, 214

Michel de Bourges, 41

Millaud, Moïse, 262

Minc, Alain, 3, 27–28, 66, 117, 167, 173–74, 182, 397

Mitford, Mary Russell, 340

Mitterand, Henri, 280

Mitterrand, François, 3, 57

Mocquard, Amédée, 238

Mocquard, Jean-François, 13, 234

Mogador (Céleste Vénard), 306

Moltke, Count Helmuth von, 382–83

Moniteur universel, Le, 163, 190, 212, 262

Monmouth, James Scott, duke of, 76

Montaigne, 384; *Essays*, 383–84

Montandon, Alain, 132

Montès, Lola, 274

Montholon, General, 73, 73*n*7, 345, 345*n*20

Montijo, Don Cipriano, count of (Eugénie's father), 209–10, 221–22, 222*n*23

Montijo, Eugenia de. *See* Eugénie, Empress Montijo, Don Eugenio, count of, 222

Montijo, Maria Manuela, countess of (Eugénie's mother), 12, 210–12, 216–17, 216*n*10, 218, 221–24, 235

Moore, Brian, 357; *The Magician's Wife*, 357–60; *Judith Hearn*, 357

More, Thomas, 182

Morel, A., 121

Morny, Auguste Charles Joseph, count de (M. de Saint-Rémy): Bonapartist, 10; role in coup d'état, 13–17, 24–25, 29, 55, 58–60, 198, 230, 349–50, 364; origins, 23, 99, 116–17; talents and wit, 99–100, 236, 354; pleasures and society, 130, 299, 304, 330; policies, 176, 372; death, 87, 370, 396; and Rochefort, 267, 366; and Offenbach, 324–26; and the theater,

334–35; plays: *La Corde sensible, ou les dadas favoris*, 257; *Pas de fumée sans un peu de feu*, 302*n*5; *M. Choufleuri restera chez lui le . . .* , 302*n*5 324.

Moulton, Lilly, 299

Murat, Anna, 220

Murat, Joachim, king of Naples, 23, 97, 103*n*10, 106, 272, 304

Murat, the princes, 9, 304, 395*n*5

Murphy, Steve, 282, 283*n*48

Mussolini, Benito , 284

Nadar, Félix, 312

Napoleon I, emperor (uncle): myth and glory, 6, 38–39, 165–66; statues and pictures, 9, 68, 68*n*30, 153, 164, 244, 252; coronation, 13, 165; defeat, 24*n*18, 377, 380, 389, 362; compared to nephew, 45, 56, 62–63; death and return of body, 72, 73*n*7, 74, 165; exile on St. Helena 80, 170, 345*n*20, 362; his *Précis des guerres de César*, 80; influence on nephew, 87, 90–91, 93–94, 123, 128, 130, 166; birthday, 91, 160, 164; family relations, 96, 96*n*1, 101–108, 110–12, 116, 236–37; marriage, 109; and Elba, 114, 334, 393; ceremonies and court, 160, 164, 254; domestic policies, 168–69; foreign policy, 169–70, 175; and women, 246, 272; satirized, 256, 256*n*12, 271, 361; and literature, 334; ghost, 351

Napoleon II, king of Rome, duke of Reichstadt: birth and baptism, 101, 103, 164; in Vienna, 105; death, 107, 131, 362; Rochefort's assessment, 267

Napoleon III, emperor: reputation, 1–4, 327–28, 388, 396–97; as president, 8–13, 90–95; abortive *coup* attempts, 12, 42, 71–74, 108, 114–15, 127, 166–67, 210, 227–28, 277, 281, 286, 345–46, 363, 393; role in coup d'état, 13–30, 62–68, 127, 281; satirized, 31–47, 256–88, *figure 17, figure 20, figure 23*, 319; as historian, 69–89; at Ham, 74, 81, 118, 129–30, 184, 196, 209, 227*n*32, 228, 286,

343–47, 363, 392; illnesses, 87, 245–46, 377–79, 381, 393–94; provincial tours, 91–92, 157, 211; family, 96–108; conception and birth, 107, 109–17, 286, 362; character and appearance, 118–33, *figure 24;* in England, 126, 131–34, 228, 230–32, 247, 338, 345, 363, 391–93; and parents, 128–29, 128*n*15; and Napoleon I, 128, 249; superstitions, 133–35, 376–77, 388; public image, 151–58, 161–63, 163; court, 160–62, 254, 299–300, 354, 392; courtship and marriage, 164, 209–20; foreign policy, 171–80, 369–70, 372–76, 396; reformist ideas, 181–88; populist measures, 189–95; rebuilding of Paris, 195–201; assassination attempt, 202, 365; attitudes to urban poverty, 204–208; love affairs, 224–47; in literature, 329–31, 331–33 (Zola), 337–40 (Disraeli), 342–43 (Barrett Browning), 343–48 (Régis), 348–52 (Priollet), 355–56 (Belloc Lowndes), 357–60 (Moore), 360–67 (Neumann); and literature, 335–37, 335*n*8; journalism, 335*n*7; death, 367, 393; fall, 377–86, 393

—"Analysis of the Sugar Question," 99

—*Avenir des idées impériales, L'*, 167

—*Extinction of Pauperism*, 59, 183–88

—*Histoire de Jules César*, 70, 77–89, 81*n*19, 288

—*Historical Fragments: The Revolutions of 1688 and 1830*, 70–71

—*Idée napoléonienne, L'*, 167

—*Idées napoléoniennes, Des*, 1, 72, 90–91, 166–71, 177, 371

Napoleon III (Winterhalter), *figure 2*, 153–54

Napoleon III, the Empress, and the Prince Imperial Surrounded by Their People (Flameng), *figure 6*, 155

Napoléon III distribuant des secours aux inondés de Lyon (Lazerges), 157

Napoléon III visitant les inondés de Tarascon (Bouguereau), *figure 12*, 157

Napoléon III visitant les ouvriers des ardoise-ries d'Angers (Janet-Lange and Antigna), *figure 11,* 157
Narváez, Ramón, 224
Natta, Marie-Christine, 132n23
Neumann, Alfred, 360–61; *Another Caesar,* 361–64; *The Gaudy Empire,* 361, 364–67
Ney, Marshal Michel, 240n50
Ney, Napoléon Henri Edgar, prince of Moskowa, 240n50
Nichols Barker, Nancy, 176–77
Nicolson, Harold, 175
Niel, Adolphe, 157
Nietzsche, Friedrich, 248
Nieuwerkerke, Count de, 227, 260, 299
Nigra, Count Constantine, 355
Noir, Victor (Yvan Salmon), 98–99, 268, 361, 365, 370
Normington, Susan, 113, 115

Offenbach, Jacques, 179, 198n26, 302n5, 307, 323–28, 365; *Ba-ta-clan, chinoiserie musicale,* 324; *La Belle Hélène,* 257, 324–326; *Les Contes d'Hoffmann,* 325; *Les Deux Aveugles,* 324; *Les Dragées de bap-tême,* 324; "God Save the Emperor," 324; *La Grande Duchesse de Gérolstein,* 306, 325, 376; *Orphée aux enfers* (*Or-pheus in Hades*), 304, 315, 324–25, 328; *Le Papillon,* 324; *La Vie parisienne,* 308, 312, 325–26
Offenbach, Julius, 323
Ollivier, Émile, 78, 235, 284, 319, 333, 372
Opéra bouffe (operetta, opérette), 158, 301–302, 305–306, 324–26, 363
Opéra-Comique theater, 323, 325
Opera house, 202, 253, 305, 316–20, 324
Organographie physiogno-phrénologique de Badinguet (Rocher?), 269–70
Orléans, Ferdinand Philippe, duke of, 24n18
Orléans, Henri d', 306
Orsay, Count Alfred d, 132–33, 228, 231, 338

Orsini, Felice, 365
Orx, Alexandre Louis Eugène, count d', 229n37, 347
Osgood, Samuel M., 396
Osuna, duke of, 215, 223, 273
Oudiné, Eugène André, 152
Ozy, Alice, 306

Paca. *See* Alba, Francisca
Padoue, Mlle., 226
Pagerie, duchess de la, 300
Paget, Sir James, 393
Païva, La (Thérèse Latchman), 254, 305, 323
Palais-Royal group, 193
Palmerston, Lord, 338
Panizzi, Antonio, 166
Paris: rebuilding, 195–201; urban poverty, 201–208; population, 202–20
Parkes Belloc, Bessie, 353
Parodie, La, 263
Parody, 248–49, 285, 322, 326
Parquin, Major Denis, 71–72
"Partant pour la Syrie," 92, 212, 212n4, 272, 376, 386, 389
Patrie, La, 190
Patterson, Elizabeth, 98, 104, 106
Patterson, William, 103
Payne, Howard C., 17n11, 261
Pays, Le, 190, 203, 262
Pearl, Cora, 204, 254, 304–305, 393
Pearl, Cyril, 304, 315
Pedro, Don, 226
Peel, Sir Robert, 346, 363
Pereire brothers, 184n5, 370
Perraud, Jean Joseph, 316
Perrot, Philippe, 310, 314
Persigny, Jean Gilbert Victor Fialin, vicomte de: ardent supporter, 10, 71–72, 91, 99, 124, 176, 190, 239, 362–63, 396; role in coup d'état, 14, 17; minister of the interior, 92, 219; and Madame Gordon, 227; satirized, 284, 286; as St. Angelo, 339; and Eugénie, 354; disfavor, 370. See also *Lettres de Londres*

Persigny, Mme. (Églé Napoléone Albine Ney), 240
Pestiférés de Jaffa, Les, 157
Petit Homme Rouge, Le. *See* Vizetelly, Ernest Alfred
Petit Journal, Le, 263, 335*n*8
Petit Journal pour rire, Le, 263
Peuple, Le, 190
Pichat, Olivier, 384
Pierrefonds castle, 161, 359
Piétri, Joachim, 82*n21,* 284
Pinkney, David H., 201
Pius VII, 111, 160
Pius VIII, 112
Plebiscites: (December 1851), 19, 21, 30; (May 1870), 372
Plombières agreement, 174
Plon, Henri, 89
Plon-Plon. *See* Bonaparte, Prince Napoléon Jérôme
Poland, 173, 176
Pompidou, Georges, 57
Porte-Saint-Martin, Théâtre de la, 306
Portrait of the Prince President (Vernet), 152
Press laws, 11, 52, 78, 262–63, 280, 286
Presse, La, 262
Prévost-Paradol, Lucien Anatole, 78–79, 79*n*15; *Les Anciens Partis,* 78; *Essai sur l'histoire universelle,* 79
Price, Roger, 19
Priollet, Julien and Marcel, 348; *Napoléon III: Pièce historique,* 348–52
Progrès du Pas-de-Calais, Le, 262
Proudhon, Joseph, 9, 61, 346, 396; *La Révolution démontrée par le coup d'État du 2 décembre,* 61, 94, 94*n*40
Punch, 251–52, 311–12

Quinet, Edgar, 77

Rachel (Élisa Rachel Félix), 93, 98, 100, 230–32, 240
Raitt, A. W., 258*n*14
Ranc, Arthur, 52
Randon, General Jacques César, 358

Rappel, Le, 206, 280
Rastignac (in Balzac's *Le Père Goriot*), 349
Ratapoil, 264, *figure 16*
Réal, Pierre François, 66
Recruitement law, 373
Régis-Lamotte, Roger (Roger Régis), 343–44; *La Belle Sabotière et le prisonnier de Ham,* 343–48
Reine Crinoline, La, 251
Rémusat, Charles de, 77, 124
Renan, Ernest, 98
Renard, Mme., 229
Revival of the French Emperorship Anticipated from the Necessity of Prophecy (Faber), 135–36
Revolution, Die, 61
Revolutions: (1830), 74; (1848), 249, 363
Richardson, Joanna, 253, 321, 321*n*30, 395
Ridley, Jasper, 73*n*7, 215*n*10, 219*n*19, 221, 224*n*26, 229*n*36, 240, 273*n*35, 347*n*23, 355*n*34
Rigolboche (Marguerite Bédel), 306
Rimbaud, Arthur, 282–83, 283*n*48; "Recueil Demeny," 282
Rive Gauche, La, 257
Robb, Graham, 47
Robespierre, Maximilien, 62, 110
Roche, Anne, 330*n*1
Rochefort, Henri: satire, 262–63, 266–67, 280, 282, 302–303*n*5, 351, 366; and Victor Noir, 267–68; and Boulanger, 268; in Dreyfus affair, 268
Rocher, Antoine, 269–70
Rogeard, Louis-Auguste, 257–58; *The Strictures of Labienus,* 257–58, 258*n*13
Ronger, Florimond. *See* Hervé
Roon, count Albrecht von, 382
Rossini, Gioacchino, 179
Rouher, Eugène, 17, 157, 177, 281, 370
Rousseau, Jean-Jacques, 109; *Julie, ou la Nouvelle Héloïse,* 346
Rowles, Emily, 391
Rowles, Henry, 228, 391
Roy, Claude, 57

Rue, La, 263
Russell, Lord William, 24*n*18

Saarbrücken, battle of, 283, 378
Sadowa, battle of, 87, 180, 325, 366, 369
St. Clothilde Church, 157, 253
Saint-Arnaud, Marshall Leroy de, 13, 16, 29, 58, 219, 286, 349
Saint-Augustin church, 253
Saint-Cloud palace, 161, 211, 250, 253, 274, 299, 350, 354–55, 375, 377
Saint-Rémy, M. de. *See* Morny, Auguste Charles Joseph, count de
Saint-Simon (and Saint-Simonians), 184–85, 187, 196, 346
Sainte-Beuve, Charles Augustin, 88, 98, 120, 184
Sainte-Pélagie prison, 264, 267, 280
Salons, 152–53, 156
Sand, George, 88, 184
Sardou, Victorien, 330*n*1, 373
Sartre, Jean-Paul, 56
Satire, 249, 255–57, 285
Satory, 209, 215, 220
Saunier, Mme., 226
Savoy (Savoie), 172–73, 342
Saxony, duke of, 218
Scheffer (ballet dancer), 230
Schiller, Friedrich von, 226
Schneider, Hortense, 306–307, 324–25, 376
Schoelcher, Victor, 17*n*11
Schwartzenberg, Roger-Gérard, 150–51
Sebastopol, fall of, 172, 178
Second Empire: rituals and ceremonies, 158–66, 254–55; foreign policy, 171–80, 369–70, 374–75; economic growth, 183, 369; public works, 183; educational reforms, 183; populist measures, 189–95; style, 249, 251–55, 317–23; censorship, 261–65, 286, 329–30; journalism, 262–63; liberal Empire, 87, 287, 307, 319, 371–72, 396; theater life, 301–302; fashion, 309–16; strikes, 370; army, 373; downfall, 389–90

Second Republic, 8, 11, 24, 26, 29, 43, 63–64, 67, 91–93, 276, 357
Sedan, battle of, 7, 14, 43–44, 70, 127, 181, 247, 279, 281, 331, 351, 363, 367, 379–88
Séguin, Philippe, 2–3, 28–30, 112, 171–73, 195, 203*n*34, 254–55, 335*n*8, 373, 382, 386, 397
Ségur, comtesse de, 330*n*1
Séréville, Louise Chapelain de, 226
Seymour, Lord Henry, 308
Shakespeare, William, 380; *Hamlet*, 67, 127; *Julius Caesar*, 389; *King Lear*, 384
Shaw, Miss, 308
Shedlock, M., 353
Shelburne, Lady Emily, 24
Siècle, Le, 52, 262
Silly, Léa, 307
Smyth, Ethel, 224
Society of December 10, pp. 64, 67
Solferino, battle of, 156, 175, 341, 365, 382
Souza, Adélaïde de, 116
Spain: uprising, 374; Spanish succession, 375
Spurzheim, Jean Gaspard, 271
Stackelberg, count de, 238
Stacton, David, 96*n*1, 110
Stelli, L. *See* Magen, Hippolyte
Stendhal, 131, 210; *La Chartreuse de Parme*, 210, 363; *Le Rouge et le Noir*, 130–31
Stoffel, Baron Eugène, 82, 82*n*21, 372–73; *Histoire de Jules César: Guerre civile*, 82, 82*n*20
Strode, Mr., 391
Suez Canal, 172, 370, 376

Tacitus, 13, 77, 273
Taine, Hippolyte, 98, 120, 336; *Notes sur Paris*, 335–36
Taisey-Chatenay, marquise de, 242–43
Tales of Hoffmann, The, 198*n*26
Talleyrand, Charles Maurice de, 23, 66, 116, 127

Temps, Le, 198

Ténot, Eugène, 52; *Paris en décembre 1851,*
51–52; *La Province en décembre 1851,* 52

Thélin, Charles, 247, 345, 347, 347*n*23

Thiénon (painter), 116

Thiers, Adolphe, 9–10, 77, 320

Third Republic, 32, 44, 68, 285–86, 389

Thomas, Ambroise, 299

Thompson, Sir Henry, 393

Thorigny, Pierre François Elisabeth Leuillon
de, 14

Thouvenel, Édouard, 370

Times, The, 335*n*7, 353

Tintamarre, Le, 285

Tirso de Molina: his *El Burlador de Sevilla y
convidado de piedra,* 243

Titres de la dynastie napoléonienne, 190–91

Tocqueville, Alexis de, 121–22, 248; *Recollections,* 122–23

Touchatout. *See* Bienvenu, Léon-Charles

Tourbey, Jane de, 306

Tragedy, 368, 374–76, 384

Trécesson, Captain de, 381

Tribune, La, 51, 280

Trinité, La (church), 253

Troplong, Raymond Théodore, 17, 79, 259

Truesdell, Martin, 161–63, 164*n*13, 165,
193–94

Tuileries palace: extravagant entertainment,
160, 162, 207, 214, 233, 241–42, 252,
276, 278, 299, 307, 319, 327, 332;
joined to Louvre, 201; ruin, 281, 388–89

Tunisia, 172

Turnbull, Patrick, 229*n*36

Twain, Mark, 315–16

Univers, L', 327

Vallès, Jules, 50, 51*n*5, 263; *Le Bachelier,* 50

Variétés theater, 300–301, 303, 306–307,
325

Vasa, Princess Carola av, 218

Vaucochard et fils 1er, 282

Vaudeville, 298, 300–302, 308, 318, 326,
369

Vaudrey, Colonel, 71, 228, 286, 363

Vendôme place and column, 166, 211, 244

Venetia, 341, 369

Vergeot, Alexandrine Éléonore (La Belle Sabotière), 228–29, 229*n*36, 230, 232,
240–41, 344–48, 363

Vergeot, Antoine-Joseph, 229

Verhuell, Admiral Charles Henri, 114–17,
115*n*34, 361–62

Verhuell, Christian-Antoine, 114

Verlaine, Paul, 282, 394

Vernet, Horace, 152, 156

Vernier, Charles, 312

Versailles, 220, 392

Veuillot, Louis, 327

Victor Emmanuel II, 393

Victoria, Queen, 6, 123, 125–26, 133, 218,
221, 338, 354–55, 355*n*34, 392, 394

Vieillard, Narcisse, 93, 346

Viel-Castel, Count Horace de, 15*n*9, 26,
60, 250, 260; *Mémoires,* 26–28, 80–81,
119–20, 126, 130, 174–75, 217,
227*n*32, 230, 233–34, 236–37, 251,
259–61, 300, 327, 353

Vigée-Lebrun, Louis Élisabeth, 250

Villa Eugénie (Biarritz), 161, 219*n*19, 253,
366

Villafranca agreement, 341, 343

Villemessant, Henri de, 262, 266

Villeneuve, Count de, 115

Viollet-le-Duc, Eugène-Emmanuel, 214,
253, 300

Vizetelly, Ernest Alfred (Le Petit Homme
Rouge), 135*n*28, 225, 233, 242

Voirol, General, 71

Wales, Prince of, 307–308

Walewska, Countess Marie-Anne, 100,
234–37, 237*n*46, 240, 299

Walewski, Count Alexandre, 99–100, 106,
167, 176, 218, 220, 230, 234, 236, 370

Washington, George, 93, 125

Waterloo, battle of, 24, 345

Weber, Max, 151

Wellington, duke of, 9, 24*n*18

Weydemeyer, Joseph, 61
White, Hayden: 5; *Metahistory*, 4, 49, 67
Wilde, Oscar, 70, 132
Wilhelmshöhe, 239, 247, 283, 385–86, 395
William I (Wilhelm, Guillaume), king of
  Prussia (then emperor of Germany), 239,
  283, 287, 356, 375, 382–83, 385–87
William of Orange, 70, 74–76
Williams, Roger L., 4, 100, 152, 175, 225,
  236–37, 245, 266, 302–303n5, 372, 378
Wilton, Andrew, 153
Wimpffen, General Emmanuel Félix de,
  381, 383
Winterhalter, Franz Xavier, 153–54, 354,
  394
Wolf, John B., 18
Wolfe, John, 317
Worth, Charles Frederick, 311–12, 354, 358

Zappi, marquis, 226
Zed (Count Albert de Maugny), 303, 324

Zeldin, Theodore, 2
Zola, Émile: novelist, 50, 120, 205; opposi-
  tion journalist, 50–52, 88, 280–82, 318–
  20, 325, 333; "J'accuse," 51; reviews of
  Histoire de Jules César, 88–90; on Napo-
  leon III, 181–82, 380n18, 397
—*L'Assommoir*, 332
—*Au Bonheur des Dames*, 309
—*La Curée*, 161, 241–42, 307, 331–32
—*La Débâcle*, 181, 281, 331–33, 351–52,
  378–82, 387
—*La Fortune des Rougon*, 52–56
—*Nana*, 303, 307, 322–23, 332–33
—*Les Rougon-Macquart*, 6–7, 52, 280, 331
—*Son Excellence Eugène Rougon*, 124, 161,
  164–65, 331–33
—*La Terre*, 191
—*Le Ventre de Paris*, 52–53, 332
—"What Poor Young Girls Dream Of,"
  206–207